Roads Through
the Everglades

ALSO BY BRUCE D. EPPERSON

*Bicycles in American Highway Planning:
The Critical Years of Policy-Making,
1969–1991* (McFarland, 2015)

*Peddling Bicycles to America:
The Rise of an Industry* (McFarland, 2010)

Roads Through the Everglades

The Building of the Ingraham Highway, the Tamiami Trail and Conners Highway, 1914–1931

BRUCE D. EPPERSON

McFarland & Company, Inc., Publishers
Jefferson, North Carolina

ISBN (print) 978-1-4766-6479-8
ISBN (ebook) 978-1-4766-2502-7

LIBRARY OF CONGRESS CATALOGUING DATA ARE AVAILABLE

BRITISH LIBRARY CATALOGUING DATA ARE AVAILABLE

© 2016 Bruce D. Epperson. All rights reserved

No part of this book may be reproduced or transmitted in any form or by any means, electronic or mechanical, including photocopying or recording, or by any information storage and retrieval system, without permission in writing from the publisher.

Front cover *inset* Group gathered at the "end of the trail" at the Monroe-Collier county line—Tamiami Trail, Florida; *background* photograph of Florida Everglades © 2016 iStock

Printed in the United States of America

McFarland & Company, Inc., Publishers
Box 611, Jefferson, North Carolina 28640
www.mcfarlandpub.com

For Hans F. "Rags" Bowker,
who has had more than enough roads
to last one man a lifetime

Res ipsa loquitor ("the thing speaks for itself"):
While the phrase is known in Great Britain, it has become so common
in the U.S. as to constitute a colloquialism. It is one of those Latinisms
that has made its way into the legal lexicon to the point where
its usefulness is unquestioned....
The phrase refers to the doctrine that, in some circumstances,
the mere existence of an accident, incident or condition
is so contrary to sound judgment as to immediately raise
an inference of negligence. Thus, there is no need to continually
refer to the elements constituting the tort in presenting a narrative
of facts. A mere recitation of the events suffices.
—*A Dictionary of Modern Legal Usage* (1987)

Table of Contents

Introduction: Other People's Money   1

Part I: The Ingraham Highway

1. "Weariness is no name for the suffering I underwent"   13
2. "Roads should be built so the land can be shown"   28
3. A Habit of Asking Favors, Leniency, etc.   44
4. "This you failed to do"   60
5. "A rather superficial excuse"   74

Part II: The Tamiami Trail

6. Not Such a Terrific Job   87
7. The Only Dry Ground for Twenty Miles   104
8. Careful, There's a Little Shine on That Bottle   120
9. "Innumerable complications"   133
10. "All was sweet and everything was sitting pretty"   148
11. When Do We Cross?   166
12. As for Business, There Hasn't Been Any   182
13. A Pullman Car Named "Convict Labor"   197

Part III: Conners Highway

14. Don't Call Me Fingy   211
15. "Plenty of grease, gumption and gasoline"   223

Chapter Notes   235
Resources and Bibliography   262
Index   269

Introduction:
Other People's Money

On December 17, 1987, a group of Florida state and local officials gathered at a remote highway interchange in Martin County twenty-five miles northwest of West Palm Beach. They were there to cut the ribbon on the last stretch of Interstate 95 to be completed along the highway's 1,250 miles (384 of those miles in Florida) from Holton, Maine, to Coral Gables, Florida.[1] The first segment of I-95 to be opened in Florida in 1959 was an existing expressway in Jacksonville that only required new signs and a few minor modifications. The first all-new portion, a short stretch just north of downtown Miami, opened a year later. All the other Florida work had been finished by 1973. In addition to being the last link in I-95, those 36 miles through Palm Beach, Martin and St. Lucie counties also comprised one of the last segments of the originally mapped Interstate system. Only the incredibly difficult and expensive extension through Glenwood Canyon in western Colorado, finished in 1992 after 17 years of construction, and parts of the Century Freeway in Los Angeles came later.[2]

There was nothing particularly difficult about the by-now notorious I-95 "Missing Link." Most of it was scrubland, cattle pastures and farms. To understand why I-95 needed 28 years to finish in Florida, one must go back to 1953, four years before Congress approved the Interstate system. That year, the Florida road department broke ground on the Sunshine Parkway, a 131-mile limited-access toll road from the Golden Glades interchange in North Miami to Fort Pierce, about half-way to Cape Canaveral. When it was finished, Phase 2 began, a 197-mile extension from Fort Pierce that looped around the southwest edge of Orlando to Wildwood, south of Ocala. After it was done in 1958, the road's name was changed to Florida's Turnpike.[3]

When I-95 was almost complete, down to Fort Pierce from Jacksonville, and up from Miami to the north edge of Palm Beach County, the state road department announced it would be inefficient to build two multi-lane highways almost side-by-side. Instead, the two ends of I-95 would simply feed into the Turnpike's toll plazas at Fort Pierce and Palm Beach Gardens, 34 miles apart. In actuality, former governor C. Farris Bryan had promised the underwriters of the initial Turnpike bonds that he would not permit the Missing Link to be built until all the bonds for the first two phases were paid—an estimated 30 years.[4]

By the time of the ribbon-cutting, I-95 travelers crossing the Missing Link paid a dollar, three cents a mile; the toll for the entire 304-mile length of the Turnpike (after it was extended south from Golden Glades to Homestead in 1964) was less than two cents per mile. Walt and Roy Disney radically changed the game in 1971 when they opened Disney World practically beside the Turnpike near Kissimmee, southwest of Orlando. Fort Pierce was the fork in the road for northbound traffic. Orlando-bound drivers stayed on the Turnpike; those headed to the Space Coast and Jacksonville paid their toll and switched to I-95. Where Orlando traffic had only been about half of that headed up or down the Atlantic Coast at the fork in the early 1960s, by 1987 the two were about equal. The Missing Link was a cash machine.

There was only one problem. The Interstate Highway System had been created expressly to be a *freeway* system. The concept of a national system of toll roads had been considered, and rejected, during Franklin Roosevelt's administration. Eisenhower convinced Congress to approve the interstates in 1956 because they were based on a highway trust fund financed with gasoline, tire, and battery excise taxes and administered through the states. Tolls, except for some select bridges, were outside the rules. Even such staggeringly expensive projects as the Eisenhower Memorial Tunnel in Colorado were free.[5] Florida fought to keep the Missing Link from 1972 on. With the aid of former Governor Bryan's promise, and the support of anti-sprawl activists in the nearby tony seaside village of Stuart, the state was able to put off the day of reckoning for years, but the gap in the freeway system eventually had to be closed. It was probably the grimmest ribbon-cutting in memory. At least the state and local officials had the consolation of knowing that federal money had paid for somewhere between 80 and 90 percent of the $222 million the link had cost.

The Missing Link is an almost perfect metaphor for the history of Florida in the modern era, because the state's history after the Civil War is largely the story of its infrastructure, and infrastructure is, to a large extent, just another name for money. Preferably, someone else's money. There is even a buzzphrase for it: OPM, Other People's Money. Before there was an I-95 there was US-1. And before there was US-1 there was the Dixie Highway, of which some traces still remain. The Dixie Highway was promoted by a former bicycle and automobile dealer named Carl Fisher who was developing a barren, hard-to-access barrier island in Biscayne Bay he optimistically called Miami Beach. He never put a dime of his own money into the Dixie Highway, but by the mid–1920s he got it done. It ended at the foot of the Collins Causeway across the bay to Miami Beach before the county paid to extend it to the farming village of Homestead, 25 miles south of Miami.[6]

The infrastructure triumvirate in Florida has been comprised of the three Rs: railroads, reclamation and roads. The roads came first, but lasted for little more than a historical blink of an eye before fading out of the picture for some 150 years. For most of the period between Juan Ponce de Leon's landing near St. Augustine around 1513 and Florida's entry as a territory into the United States in 1821, water was Florida's primary means of transport. Its three largest settlements were St. Augustine, Key West and Pensacola; each accessible to the other only by ship. There were four enduring roads, only one of which was blazed after the founding of the United States.

The Royal Road (also known as the Old Spanish Trail) ran from St. Augustine to Tallahassee (Fort San Luis) and later the Apalachicola River. It is known that one Enrique Primo de Rivera obtained a contract around 1680 for hauling provisions between St. Augustine and the Spanish colonial settlements in the area between Tallahassee and the Apalachicola River, and to improve the trail. He succeeded in making the Royal Road passable for oxcarts between Tallahassee to Gainesville, but from there to St. Augustine it remained a mere trail, and when Fort San Luis was abandoned in 1704 its church ornaments and other baggage had to be transferred to pack mules at Gainesville. It subsequently fell into disuse as the British assumed control over the area.[7]

The second important early road was the King's Highway, built by the British in 1765 to connect St. Augustine to its Georgia outposts. It was taken over by the Spanish in 1784 when East Florida was ceded by the British at the Treaty of Versailles (beginning the so-called "second Spanish era"). However, its importance diminished greatly after the transfer because Spain no longer had garrisons to the north, Georgia and the Carolinas now being part of the United States. The southern half continued in use as the connection between St. Augustine and Jacksonville, the latter located at the site of a former cow ford on the St. Johns River.[8]

To avoid antagonizing the Spanish, a third road, the Alachua–St. Marys Road, evolved from a trail used by English nationals and Tory sympathizers who had been driven out of the colonies by the American revolution. It ran from Micanopy, near Gainesville, northeast to Roses Bluff, near present-day Fernandia Beach, and was intended to circumvent East Florida. Except for some short segments, the Alachua-St. Marys Road withered away after East Florida was transferred to the United States in 1821 and most Tories either returned to England or moved to one of its island colonies.

A fourth road was built around 1840 by the U.S. Army from Fort Mellon, 20 miles northeast of today's Orlando, to Fort Brooke at Tampa. Fort Mellon sat on the bank of Lake Monroe, the farthest upriver (southwest) point one could reach by boat on the St. Johns River from its mouth at Jacksonville. For decades the Tampa Trail, which the Army used to supply a string of forts, was the recognized way to cross the state south of the Old Spanish Trail, as it was the shortest path between navigable points on the east and west coasts, at least if the St. Johns was running high enough. It also marked the unofficial southern limit of civilization until about 1870, when General Henry S. Sanford bought an old Spanish grant of 20,000 acres on the south rim of Lake Monroe. Six years later Sanford hired a young railroad clerk from St. Louis named James Ingraham to help him build his self-named town and a railroad to follow the old Tampa Trail.[9]

As was true in most of the United States, government subsidies for transportation development were at best sporadic until the canal era. The Erie Canal, built between 1817 and 1825, was owned by the State of New York, with seed money provided by a tax of 12½ cents levied on every bushel of salt carried more than 100 miles on the Hudson River. Pennsylvania went $17 million into debt by 1835 building canals. Ohio built 731 miles of canal for a total cost of $16 million between 1827 and 1846. Yet, despite the fact that these canals paid for themselves, in almost every case except the Erie, they were sold to private firms or transferred to abutting local governments after 1850 in a wave of anti-statehood sentiment.[10]

The canals were quickly overshadowed by the great western and northern trunk rail lines: the Union Pacific; the Southern Pacific; the Great Northern; the Burlington; the Illinois Central; the Santa Fe. Unlike France and England, the United States chose not to build national railroads or even to directly subsidize their construction. Instead, railroads were encouraged to build through huge "checkerboard" land grants of alternative sections (square miles) extending out as far as twelve miles on either side of the rail line—7,680 acres to the linear mile. And often, the hastily built, poorly operated railroads that resulted were simply a pretext to justify the land grants. The railroads rarely kept the land grants they received, transferring them to sister firms that were closely held by a handful of the railroad's promoters. The promoters also typically owned the construction companies that built the new lines, grossly overcharging the railroad for shoddy work, leaving it saddled with debt and bad infrastructure. The publicly held railroads often started life as weakened, debt-ridden, asset-stripped giants doomed to eventual receivership. The promoters made their money from the closely held ancillary firms, leaving the individual share- and bond-holders of the railroad (or the governments that indemnified its securities) holding the bag when the inevitable collapse occurred. The most famous example was the Crédit Mobilier, the finance and construction syndicate that built the Union Pacific's transcontinental line.[11] Florida railroads were typically no different.

Florida was admitted to the union in 1845, and its legislature created the Internal Improvement Fund in 1855 as a central clearinghouse for the sale of lands transferred ("patented") to the state by the federal government. In addition, the Fund could grant land to enterprises—mostly railroads, but some canal companies and reclamation programs, as way of underwriting the costs of their construction. The improvement made the land valuable and the sale of the land helped pay for the cost of developing the infrastructure without any cash outlay by the state. The legislature initially authorized the grant of 3,840 acres of land for every mile of railroad track laid. About 500 miles of railroad were built up to the Civil War using this system.[12]

Unfortunately, the legislature also instructed the Fund to issue up to $10,000 in bonds for every mile of track laid. The railroads would give the Fund $10,000 of their bonds and the Improvement Fund would exchange them for an equal amount of state-backed bonds. The Civil War bankrupted all the railroads. They were sold at receivers' sale for cents on the dollar, almost always to reconstituted groups of their original owners. However, the Improvement Fund was saddled with the payments on the bonds. It went into receivership, and was unable to function until 1881 when Hamilton Disston, scion to the Connecticut saw- and file-making empire, bought four million acres of land for a million dollars in cash, with an option to buy another 12 million acres contingent upon their successful reclamation, almost a third of Florida's total land mass. His drainage efforts were only marginally successful, and he could claim only a small part of the optioned land by the time the panic of 1893 brought his work to a halt. He mortgaged the entire operation for two million dollars and never returned.[13]

But Disston's purchase put the Improvement Fund back in business. The railroads were the biggest beneficiary. By 1904, Henry Flagler's Florida East Coast extended down the east coast to Homestead, and he was contemplating the feasibility of extending his line to Key West.[14]

In 1912, S. Davies Warfield acquired a disparate group of cross-owned southern railroads that extended from North Carolina, Georgia, and Alabama as far south as Tampa. He unified them under the name Seaboard Air Line. By the early 1920s Warfield was weighing the possibilities of breaking Flagler's south Florida monopoly by running an extension from Tampa, around the north shore of Lake Okeechobee, into West Palm Beach and down to Hialeah, just outside Miami.[15]

Henry Plant, Flagler's great competitor in the construction of railroads and luxury hotels, died in 1899. The Atlantic Coast Line was a unified system of small railroads stretching from Richmond, Virginia, to central Florida. It was owned by the brothers Henry and William Walters. The Walters and Henry Plant had worked together to create express trains for passengers and fruit since the 1870s. When Plant died in 1899, everyone expected his will to direct the sale of the Plant System rail holdings to the Atlantic Coast Line system. It is believed that the intercession of one of Plant's sons resulted in a change to his father's will, which prohibited the sale of any asset and directed that the entire estate be placed in a trust.

But as written the will left no provision for the payment of taxes or for the household maintenance of his widow Margaret. She sued the trustees to break it. She was successful

Florida roadbuilding at the turn of the century was a mix of the old and new. Although there was no effective state road department until 1917, after the Civil War the federal government had imposed a constitution that created a weak state government with strong counties. A side effect of this was that it also prevented road supervision from being pushed down to the township or village level, as was true in many Midwest and northeast states. Therefore, in those Florida counties where the citizens pushed for better roads, bond financing could be arranged more easily than in many wealthier northern states. At the start of the Great Depression, Florida counties collectively owed $161 million on road bonds and had to be rescued by the state. Here, the road superintendent in Lee County shows off his new high-tech road grader about 1912. (Photographer unknown. Library of Congress, LC-USZ62-23094.)

and in July 1902 Margaret sold the Plant System railroads for $46.6 million to Henry Walters, William having died the year before.[16] The same year, Henry Walters acquired the Louisville and Nashville railroad. This made the Atlantic Coast Line one of the two largest railroads in the south. In 1915 the ACL ran from Jacksonville across the middle of the state to Tampa and was in the process of extending down the Gulf coast to Charlotte Harbor (Punta Gorda) and Fort Myers, which it reached in 1918.[17]

As noted earlier, the only highway of any importance prior to 1915 was the Dixie Highway, the Tampa Trail long since having been turned into a railroad grade for the Atlantic Coast Line. Carl Fisher, one of the fathers of the Lincoln Highway, the "Main Street of America" running from New York City to San Francisco along the route of today's U.S. Highway 40, was also behind the Dixie Highway. An insatiable booster, Fisher first proposed the Lincoln Highway in September 1912 to promote his obscure hometown, Indianapolis, and his equally obscure motorcar race, the Indianapolis 500.[18] The squabbling over routes between competing towns and counties and the various organizational details bored and irritated him, so he quit the Lincoln Highway Association a year later when he bought 600 acres of land on a barrier island in Biscayne Bay from John Collins, who was building a wood causeway to connect it to Miami on the mainland.[19]

Fisher, a former car dealer, knew that an increasing proportion of tourists would be coming down to Miami each winter by car, and he also knew, having tried it himself, that the route was all but impassible. Hence, the Dixie Highway proposal. However, this time around, Fisher knew enough to hire a front man, William S. Gilbreath, who introduced the idea for a north-south version of the Lincoln Highway—the "Cotton Belt Route"—at a meeting of American Road Congress in November 1914 in Atlanta. There was a lot of arguing about the route, but none about the destination—the foot of the Collins Causeway.[20]

Nobody in any of the southern states seriously discussed the idea of state funding because there was no such thing. In 1915, the Florida road department spent $974. In 1926, thanks to the federal highway trust fund and one of the highest gas taxes in the nation, the State of Florida spent $13.7 million before the economy started to sour.[21] Roads may have been late to the dance and shown up in plain dress, but by the time of the Great Depression Florida roads, fueled by a gas tax largely paid for by tourists and snowbirds, they had become the belle of the ball.

* * * * *

This is the story of three highways built through the Florida Everglades between 1914 and 1930. The Ingraham Highway was a 45-mile road extending southwest from Homestead to Flamingo, a settlement on Florida Bay, through what is today Everglades National Park. It was started in 1914 and construction ended 1922 with the road not fully completed. The last five miles in Monroe County were left unsurfaced and the highway was never a reliable all-weather route until it was incorporated into a fully paved 1956 road built for Everglades National Park.

The Tamiami Trail, constructed between 1915 and 1930, was a 284-mile highway extending west from Miami across to Marco Junction, twenty miles south of Naples, then north along the Gulf of Mexico coastline to Tampa. The 154-mile segment between Miami and Marco Junction, across the Everglades and Corkscrew Swamp, was considered one of the engineering marvels of the era. Although its ribbon-cutting ceremony was held in April 1928, work on low-lying stretches near Naples and the replacement of wooden bridges at Fort Myers and Port Charlotte with permanent cement spans required another eighteen months. The entire route is still in use today, but some replacement segments and new bridges have been introduced over the years.

Conners Highway was a 51-mile toll road that started at what was then called the Twenty-Mile Bend on the bank of the Palm Beach Canal northwest of West Palm Beach, about ten miles from the present Palm Beach International Airport. In 1923 a county highway ran up along the canal bank from West Palm Beach to the Twenty-Mile Bend, then turned due west towards Belle Glade. (This is today's U.S. Highway 441.) Conners Highway split off from this road and continued along the canal northwest to Canal Point on the shore of Lake Okeechobee. From Canal Point, the highway then followed the shoreline north to Okeechobee, thirty-five miles farther, on the northernmost point of the lake. It was started in 1923, finished in 1924, and was acquired by various governments in stages between 1930 and 1934, eventually ending up in the hands of the Florida road department. It is still in use today as a federal highway.

There has not been a systematic study of the development of the surface transportation system in the Everglades and adjacent Big Cypress–Corkscrew Swamp areas. In 1939, J. E.

Dovell prepared a seminal study on the history of Everglades reclamation as a doctoral dissertation.[22] It inspired a generation of academic research that focused not on the Everglades itself but on the history of its reclamation: how the plans were developed; how the construction was financed; what infrastructure was built; how well or how badly it functioned. Most attempted to answer the lingering question of why so often good technical advice was rejected in favor of the bad.[23]

Rail and canal development have received less attention. (That is, canals primarily developed for transportation, not drainage.) The development of Florida's rail network and system of navigable canals have all too often been viewed merely as a vehicles to defraud the state's Internal Improvement Fund and deny affordable homesteads to smallholders. While not without some truth, that portrayal is two-dimensional and oversimplified.[24]

Before 1915, there was no reliable, east-west route across the state south of Orlando, and it could be argued that none existed in the summer wet season south of the old Royal Highway between Tallahassee and Jacksonville. With very few exceptions, roads south of Orlando were little different then they were at the time Florida entered the Union in 1845. The urgent need for better surface transportation in a state that was being suddenly wrenched out of a neo-feudal, antebellum slumber by an invasion of northern tourists, northern money, and northern values was something all these roads had in common. However, it was only one of three factors they shared.

The second was their promoters' faith that they would serve as a way to reach previously inaccessible land holdings, thus increasing their value and promoting their sale, usually to farmers and suburban smallholders. The third factor was that all three roads were built at a time when the political and administrative structure of American highway finance was undergoing momentous change. In 1915 the State of Florida created its road department. A year later, the federal government approved its first federal highway act, providing for

Fifteen years of technological change in road building. An Austin Western road grader and scarifier works the Tamiami Trail in the former Lee County, now Collier County, in 1927. (Photographer unknown. Collier County Museum, Naples, FL, No. 88.42.27.)

$75 million dollars in matching aid to the states. In 1921, the second federal highway act greatly centralized overall control in the federal Bureau of Public Roads and removed authority from city and county officials in favor of state highway departments. As an inducement for each state to cooperate in this two-level federal-state system, federal assistance was increased five-fold to $75 million per year on a 50–50 matching basis.[25]

The importance these three factors played varied considerably between the three roads examined, in terms of their absolute impact, their importance relative to each other and in their timing. However, all three factors did play a part in each of the three roads, and it is this consistency, this repetition, that goes to the heart of this work.

The development of transportation linkages as way to open new land for speculation or development was not a new phenomenon. Only the mode was different. In many, if not most, of the cities of the American northeast and Midwest, the development of streetcar systems was undertaken not by the government, but by private land developers who used streetcar lines as a way to make land they had purchased for new subdivisions accessible to the city center. Unless a potential homeowner in these outlying neighborhoods could quickly and conveniently get to downtown, speculators would stand little chance of selling off blocks of land to developers. The price of developable land closer to town or located along an existing transit line was so much higher than for a distant greenfield site that it was frequently cheaper for the speculator to build a streetcar line than pay for this higher priced land.[26]

These streetcar lines ceased to serve a beneficial purpose from the standpoint of the land speculator once the subdivision achieved build-out. Incapable of being run at a profit, the developer-operator could only hope to reduce costs and provide the minimum level of service demanded under the franchise agreement he had had signed with the local government to gain the use of the street for the transit company's tracks. Most of these streetcar companies were taken over by their respective local governments by 1900. A few were acquired by other private firms, mostly electrical utilities. Even fewer continued to be operated by their original developers until they were converted to bus lines in the 1920s, and almost all were eventually consolidated into municipal operations.

Similarly, beginning about 1895, large corporate landowners in South Florida, most affiliated with railroads, canal companies, or timber producers, began to build roads to promote the value of their land portfolios. These were generally modest gravel farm-to-market roads, sixteen to twenty feet wide. Often the cost was shared between the land companies, abutting farmers, and local governments. But by 1915 the landowners examined in these three stories elected to undertake large-scale ventures to open up large tracts of their holdings.[27]

The funding structure for each road was unique. The Ingraham Highway started as a privately financed road, switched to county bond funding as part of a special road and bridge district when the private money ran out, was finished to a minimal extent with more private money when the bond money was exhausted, and was completely finished only when its designation as state road was extended from the Royal Palm State Park to Flamingo shortly before Everglades National Park took it over.

A native of Buffalo, William J. Conners had been a winter resident of Palm Beach since about 1907. In 1921, he purchased 13,000 acres of land on the east shore of Lake Okeechobee and expanded an existing farm with plans to become a major supplier of winter vegetables to the northeast. Shortly before announcing the road, he bought another 30,000 acres from the Model Land Company, the real estate subsidiary of the Flagler railroad system, along with roughly 3,000 house lots in Okeechobee City, which had been co-founded by that firm. The Conners Highway was completed in mid–1924 after 18 months of construction. It cost approximately $1.8 million to build, all of it provided by Conners. He attempted to float a million dollar bond issue in 1924, but was unsuccessful, as the underwriters wanted him to provide additional collateral from his personal estate, a condition Conners found unacceptable. Although the road reportedly earned over $2,000 a day in tolls during the winter tourist season, business correspondence appears to indicate that the road was not very profitable, and almost certainly did not generate a positive rate of return on its large initial investment. The profits were made from the sale of land by the Conners real estate firm.

Ironically, this sowed the seeds of the toll road's own downfall. The growing numbers of farmers and homeowners living alongside it chafed at having to pay a (relatively steep) toll to reach their land, and insisted that the Conners organization provide relief. Later, they turned their attention to Palm Beach County and the state, requesting that they lease or buy the road. The state attempted to do so in 1927, but the purchase was nullified in the courts because the enabling legislation did not follow proper appropriation formalities. It was then leased, and subsequently purchased, by Palm Beach County and transferred to the state.

The crucial cross–Everglades 156-mile segment of the Tamiami Trail from Miami to Fort Myers was originally funded with the same type of special road and bridge districts that allowed the work on the Ingraham Highway to continue after its initial private funding had been exhausted. Parallel districts were created in Dade and Lee counties. After these funds were spent, work was continued by private companies in Monroe and Collier counties (the latter split off from Lee County in 1923), and finally completed with large infusions of state-federal highway funds.

But while their funding structures were different, the driving force behind each road was the same: the need to access land. The Ingraham Highway was started by the Model Land Company, the real estate division of the Florida East Coast Railroad. It owned 240,000 acres in the Cape Sable district southwest of Homestead granted to the railroad in 1912 in a settlement agreement with the state. Almost immediately, the railroad gave former governor William Jennings (who, as general counsel of the state's Internal Improvement Fund, had negotiated the settlement agreement) 41,600 acres of this land, and the railroad's general counsel William Dewhurst (who had represented the railroad across the table from Jennings) 24,280 acres.[28] Both Jennings and Dewhurst were anxious to attract large-block buyers for their land. They also contributed towards the road, ostensibly to access a new park that governor Jennings's wife, May Mann Jennings, was trying to convince the legislature to acquire at Paradise Key, twelve miles from Homestead. The funds ran out when the road came up a mile short, at Taylor Slough, so with the help of the Dade County Tax Assessor, James Jaudon, they were able to convince the Dade County Commission to create the road and bridge district and float a $100,000 bond issue.

James Jaudon would soon put the skills he learned helping organize the Cape Sable Road and Bridge District to work when he organized the bond issue for Dade County to start work on the Tamiami Trail. Once that was accomplished, he bought a 207,360 acre tract of land on the Gulf Coast—essentially the entire north 12 miles of Monroe County—from A. W. Hopkins of Grenville, Illinois. The Tamiami Trail would cut through the northeast corner of this land. His firm, the Chevelier Corporation, built the "loop road" portion of the Tamiami Trail at a cost of over $300,000. This was dwarfed by Barron Collier, a New York advertising magnate, who purchased a million acres of land in Lee County, split it off to form his own county, and loaned it over a million dollars to keep the construction of the main route of the Tamiami Trail going until the state could come up with staggering amounts of money needed to finish it.

By 1926, William Conners had sold over 2,000 of the house lots and most of the unplatted land in Okeechobee City. Yet, it is unlikely that he was able to generate sufficient sales to recoup both the acquisition price of the land and pay for the $1.8 million it cost to build the road. He died in 1929. Over the protracted acquisition process, which included some seven years of leases and installment payments, his estate received about $660,000 from Palm Beach County and the state to acquire the highway.

And therein lies the great irony. All three of these roads failed as land development tools. William Dewhurst and William Jennings sold their land *en bloc* to speculators for about five dollars an acre. Preparing for condemnation proceedings leading to the creation of Everglades National Park, the Model Land Company assessed their 270,760 acres of Cape Sable land at $5,036,800, but ended up selling 210,057 acres for an average of $1.40 an acre in 1948 and 1949 because nobody else wanted it, and because they had already paid $200,000 in taxes on it since 1912 and didn't want to pay any more.[29]

The heirs of the Chevelier Corporation, the organization that James Jaudon created to develop the A. W. Hopkins tract, fought condemnation, not because of the price, but over mineral rights. They were convinced by the success of the Sunniland oil field, near Immoklee, in 1943 that the Everglades sat atop a huge pool of crude oil, and that south Florida would become the next great oil bonanza. It was not until a series of deep on- and off-shore test wells all came up dry in 1954–55 that "oil fever" subsided among the Everglades landowners. Sunniland itself was closed down about 1961, a victim of salt water infiltration.

Pinecrest, the inland townsite that Jaudon and his associates laid out in the mid–1920s, briefly flourished in the 1960s as a haven for drug dealers, poachers, and a cast of general malcontents that had been driven out of Everglades National Park. It was crushed to death in the early 1970s between the creation of Big Cypress National Preserve, which extended federal jurisdiction up from Everglades National Park, and the Miccosukee Tribe, which had over the years developed a deep affiliation with, and affinity for, the Tamiami Trail. The Miccosukee Tribe incorporated in 1962 and established a headquarters at the fork of the main Tamiami Trail and the loop road ("30-mile junction") near Pinecrest. The tribe, which considers the Trail to be within its jurisdiction, was deeply concerned about the adverse effects that illicit activities were having on its young people and the homes of its members along the isolated loop road. It policed the loop road strenuously and openly. After a few high-visibility confrontations, the malcontents slunk into the farthest corners of the Everglades, or more often, went in search of another frontier.

Conners Highway itself proved to be a problem—it was prone to summertime flooding in wet years. As late as the mid–1950s, when it was a federal highway, it had to be closed at times because water would flow in sheets across the road, threatening to wash away the surface. It wasn't until the Herbert Hoover dike surrounding Lake Okeechobee was completed about 1960 that the problem was finally solved.[30] Far from becoming a major inland city, a rival to Orlando or Lakeland, Okeechobee reverted to becoming a sleepy town whose main businesses are sport fishing, catfish farms, and solid waste disposal.

* * * * *

The origins of this book date to 2007, when I was named a National Parks Scholar by the National Park Foundation and the Eno Transportation Foundation. For seven months I lived and worked in Everglades National Park, my cabin almost overlooking one of the last undisturbed remnants of the original Ingraham Highway. The park was a world apart—a tropical paradise where cell phones didn't work, panthers screamed at night, the mosquitos moved in visible clouds, the alligators were as common as stepping stones (no pets permitted), and you were reminded each and every day that you, puny human, had no business being here.

From the National Park Foundation, I would like to thank Jim Evans, and from the Eno Transportation Foundation, Janet Abrams, former Vice President and Chief Operating Officer. The funding for the National Parks Scholars program was provided by a grant from the Ford Motor Company Fund. From Everglades National Park, I would like to thank my supervisor, senior planner Fred Herling, then-superintendent Dan Kimball, and the numerous park rangers who were willing to go out of their way to show me the back waters, "non-navigable" canals, 1935 hurricane graves, unacknowledged archaeological sites, and other places and things that were way, way off the official register. I also thank the staff of the Archives and Special Collections at the Daniel Beard Center for their help in accessing the Superintendent's Monthly Reports, the close-out report for the construction of Park Road 1 (The 1956 Main Road) and the land acquisition records from the 1940s and early 1950s.

At the Helen Muir Florida Collection of the Miami-Dade Public Library, I would like to thank John Shipley and the staff of the Florida Collection. By my notes, I spent about 160 hours in front of the microform reader, going through the Miami and Fort Myers newspapers day-by-day. The Florida Collection desk is the St. Elsewhere of information services; an island of data floating serenely in an ocean of chaos, or so it seems. Next door, at HistoryMiami (the former South Florida History Museum) I thank Dawn Hughes and Ashley Trujillo, who assisted me with the Jaudon Collection and for a couple of heart-stopping hours, the misfiled J. B. McCrary Papers. Jennifer Guida and her staff at the Collier County Museums found and copied the Florida Road Department construction logs for the Tamiami Trail and digitized several of the images appearing in this book. The staff at the Department of Special Collections of the Richter Library at the University of Miami were helpful in pointing me to the finding aids for the Model Land Company Collection and Mary McDougal Axelson Collection. Although he is now at another institution, former director William Brown should be commended for the quality cataloging used to accession these collections. The Palm Beach County Library was the source of many of the *Palm Beach Post* stories relating to Conners Highway. The Alvin Sherman Library and the Panza-Maurer Law Library at Nova Southeastern University in Fort Lauderdale were the source of most of the digital articles available through JSTOR, EBSCO, ProQuest Genealogy, the *New York Times*, the Library of Congress digitized historical magazine collection, and other electronic databases requiring either a library subscription or a large transmission bandwidth.

Part One:
The Ingraham Highway

••1••

"Weariness is no name for the suffering I underwent"

"My advice is to urge every discontented man to take a trip through the Everglades," wrote Alonzo Church after his three-week slog from Fort Myers to Miami in the spring of 1892. "A day's journey in slimy, decaying vegetable matter which coats and permeates everything it touches, and no water with which to wash it off, will be good for him … it is enough to make a man swear to be content ever afterwards with a board for a bed and a clean shirt once a week."[1]

Church and twenty-one other men made up an expedition organized and led by James E. Ingraham, president of the South Florida Railroad, and later head of the Model Land Company, the real estate division of Henry Flagler's railroad empire. Most of Church's companions were volunteers selected from among the railroad's employees especially for the trip. The South Florida was a short line running between Sanford and Kissimmee in what is now the Orlando metro area. In 1883, three years after it started, it was acquired by Henry Plant. Most people know at least a little about Flagler, the former John D. Rockefeller associate who gradually eased himself out of the Standard Oil Company after 1881 to begin a second career in Florida railroads, land development and luxury hotels. Starting with a ragged assemblage of small, local, and often decrepit railroads he cobbled together between 1885 and 1892, Flagler built the magnificent Florida East Coast system that stretched from Jacksonville to Miami, and eventually overseas to Key West. But Henry Plant had many of the same ideas, had them first, and implemented them more rationally.[2]

Plant was a Connecticut native who made his fortune when his employer, the Adams Express Company, then the nation's largest railway package express firm, panicked in the face of the imminent Civil War. Afraid its southern assets would be impounded once hostilities began, the company ordered Plant, its superintendent for all operations south of the Mason-Dixon line, to immediately sell its entire southern division for whatever price he could get. Instead, Plant bought it himself, forming the Southern Express Company. In 1879, six years before Flagler, he started buying up short lines in Georgia, Florida, and South Carolina, merging them into an integrated system. One of these was the South Florida. It had been started by Henry Sanford and Royal M. Pulsifer, editor of the Boston Herald. Although it was less than fifty miles long, Pulsifer and Sanford planned to push on past Kissimmee to connect the town of Sanford with Tampa Bay and, eventually, Charlotte Harbor. However, Pulsifer ran out of money and the two men sold out to Plant in 1882.[3]

Plant carried out much of their plan, extending the line to Tampa in 1883, then made that port the nucleus of a Florida-based transportation empire that included railroads, the Plant Steamship Company, a fleet of inland steamers, wharfs and warehouses, and luxury hotels, including the two-million dollar Tampa Bay Hotel, completed in 1891. At the time of his death in 1899, the Plant System had the most extensive rail network in Florida, its 1,196 miles of track far outpacing Flagler's 466 miles, which grew to only 609 miles even after its Key West extension.[4]

Ingraham, a 42-year-old career office man, was an unlikely expedition leader. He was born in 1850 in Wisconsin, the son of an Episcopal minister. The family moved around a lot, and as a result James grew up with an outgoing, tolerant disposition. He started his railroad career in St. Louis, apparently clerking for a year or two before Sanford hired him in 1874. Two years later Ingraham moved from Sanford's personal staff to that of his new railroad. As part of his duties, he was attending a conference between Plant and Flagler in Tampa in February 1892. The two men were discussing issues related to land development and rail connections when Plant looked up from a large map everyone was bent over and asked "Mr. Ingraham, could we build a line from here to here?" pointing to Fort Myers, then Miami. "Mr. Plant, that is right across the Everglades," Ingraham replied. "Well," Plant answered, "what of it?" Ingraham told them that as far as anyone knew, only two Europeans had crossed the Everglades east-to-west, during the Seminole Wars. An 1882 party had done it north-to-south, but they had Seminole guides. There was no record of any west-to-east crossing. "But," he added "I would be very glad to run a [survey] line across there."[5]

A boat dropped the party off on the bank of the Caloosahtchee River near where downtown Fort Myers is now located on March 14, perilously close to the start of the summer wet season in May. The men loaded their boats and gear onto ox-carts for the six day hike along the trail to Immokalee (then known as Allen's Place), then to Fort Shackleford, where the perpetual wetlands began.[6] The trail from Fort Myers to Fort Shackleford was along an old road called "Captain Ker's Route" that followed the high ground through the northern reaches of the Big Cypress Swamp, and was mostly pine scrubland. After passing the fort one entered the Everglades proper, which was not a still-water swamp, but a shallow river moving generally southwest.

"Many of our men, unaccustomed to walking, were terribly fatigued," noted compass-man Church. "That night I was awakened by the melancholy cries of 'Oh Lord, Oh God!' repeated in the most supplicating tones." Fearing someone was injured or had taken ill, Church left his tent to investigate, but "discovered it was our President (Mr. Ingraham) trying to find for his blistered and aching limbs a more comfortable position."[7] Keep in mind that at this point the expedition was on dry land, with the gear still being conveyed on carts.

The next day the group arrived at Fort Shackleford, built in February 1855 and burned (when empty) the following December. Dubiously blamed on the Seminoles (it was more likely an accident by a squatter), the alleged arson helped precipitate the Third Seminole War when troops retaliated by vandalizing Billy Bowleg's home.[8] Forty years later the fort was "merely a clump of pine trees on the edge of the prairie bordering the Everglades," located about thirty miles south of today's Clewiston. Church found that "not a vestige or sign of the fort remains." Here, the carts (and one alarmed expeditioneer) turned back, the land to the east being too wet for wheels or oxen. From now on, the expedition variously resorted to backpacking or, more typically, loading packs and gear into the boats, then paddling or hauling them, depending on water depth and the density of vegetation.

By the eleventh day out of Fort Myers, both flour and corn meal had run out. Provisions had been based on the assumption that the group could make five miles a day after leaving Shackleford, but they were, in fact, averaging less than three. On the fifth day after entering the Glades, the group could make only 14,000 feet of progress.⁹ By day 15 (nine days from Shackleford) "our men showed plainly the effects of the hardships they had undergone; their faces were haggard, their eyes bloodshot, and none had their usual energy." Three gave out entirely and had to be carried in boats. "We decided to throw away everything we could possibly do without in order to make room in the boats for the sick men." It was not all horrors, however. "Early next morning, as I lay chilled and stiff, thinking with a sort of horror of the disagreeable business that was before us and wondering if we were to have any breakfast," Church recalled, "Mr. Newman touched me on the shoulder and handed me a cup of warm coffee with sugar and milk in it, which made me feel like a new man."[10]

Later that day, the party came across a Seminole, Billy Harney, who told them Miami was still twenty-five miles away. "Our faces fell several feet because at the rate we had been going it would take us five days to get there," noted Church. However, John Newman, the party's engineer, knew better, because two days earlier he had identified an island he remembered being in the flow of Miami River, 19½ miles upstream from the mouth. (This was near the present-day intersection of Krome Avenue and Okeechobee Road.) Given the two day's progress they had made since then, Newman believed they were about eight to ten miles out. However, by this time even expedition secretary's Wallace Moses's official log, which was invariably upbeat, notes that "the constant wading in water and bog appears to have weakened all to a greater or lesser extent." Church recalled that "we had only enough rations, on half allowance, for two more days."[11]

Harney lived nearby, so the expedition hired him as guide. Harney and Newman took Harney's canoe, with Ingraham and Moses following in one of the expedition's canvas boats. The other 17 men would continue to slowly work their way southeast. The advance party aimed for William Brickell's trading post at the mouth of the Miami River, where they could buy provisions and return. They started at 5 a.m. on the morning of April 5. Proving Newman right, the advance party reached the Miami Falls rapids, four to five miles from Biscayne Bay, about 9 a.m. Billy Harney shot the rapids; the others portaged. They arrived at Brickell's about noon. There was a delay while Ingraham bought supplies at Brickell's store and Newman hired a second canoe and its owner. Leaving Moses and Ingraham behind, Newman started back up the river about 3 p.m. They could not make it all the way back and camped out for the night along the way. Meanwhile, Church's men found a pair of pants that the one of the advance canoe team had tied to a tree. "The sight of those pants was worth a gold mine to us," Church recalled, "because it assured us we were on the right track and the party ahead of us had been delayed in getting to Miami. Therefore we should not expect Mr. Newman back until the following day." Rations were again adjusted to allow for at least a meager breakfast.

The boats and main party met up mid-morning the next day "and as soon as we could find a convenient place we stopped and cooked a fine meal." Meanwhile, Ingraham had arranged for a small fleet of boats to go up the river to bring everyone back to Julia Tuttle's place at the old Fort Dallas, on the north bank of the river across from Brickell's. The expedition concluded there on Thursday, April 7, twenty-one days after leaving Fort Myers, seventeen days after first entering the Everglades at Fort Shackleford.[12] "Weariness is no name for the suffering I underwent and comfort no expression for sensations of pleasure when I threw myself down on the ground by the fire Mr. Newman had made and rested," recalled young Church. He soon left Florida for the more civilized environs of New Orleans, where he eventually made a living as an insurance executive.[13]

* * * * *

Miami Falls, also known as the Miami rapids, was where the freshwater river emerged from the Everglades and fell into the saltwater estuary that extended another four miles southeast to the mouth of the river at Biscayne Bay. The falls were near the northeast corner of the present-day Miami International Airport. They were dynamited about 1912 when the river was converted into a drainage canal extending to Lake Okeechobee. This photograph was taken about 1896, probably by Coconut Grove pioneer Ralph Middleton Munroe, an avid photographer. (Florida Division of Library and Information Services, No. N038907.)

The expedition was proof that the Seminoles had chosen their battlefield wisely a half-century earlier, making the Seminole Wars a drawn-out, morale-sapping, indeterminate quagmire that would end or cripple the careers of seven straight commanding generals. By the time it ended, enlisted men were being rotated through the Everglades combat theatre every three months to preserve them in fighting condition—and keep them from deserting. It would receive intense scrutiny from military scholars during the eerily similar Vietnam

War. The region's reputation was already legendary. So what was Ingraham and his bunch doing there? Ingraham's own story of two railroad magnates idly speculating about a new rail line in a Tampa drawing room during the winter of 1892 makes for a good story, but has some serious credibility gaps.

First, Plant's tracks stopped at Punta Gorda (Charlotte Harbor), fifty miles north of Fort Myers. He never did extend the line farther south during his lifetime. After he died in 1899, his wife Margaret sold the route to the Atlantic Coast Line Railroad, but even they didn't push the line through to Fort Myers until 1904.

Second, at this time, the Flagler System barely existed. In 1892 Flagler had relatively little up-to-date trackage except for the segment between Jacksonville and St. Augustine, almost no equipment to run over it, and certainly no one to manage it, which is why he hired Ingraham and his associate, fellow Plant System executive Joseph Parrott, in October. Flagler's interest in railroads originally extended no farther than addressing the practical problem of affordably moving construction materials into St. Augustine to build his stupendous 1880s hotels, then getting their pampered guests in and out of town in the style to which they were accustomed, given the lack of good roads, railroads, and steamboats around St. Augustine. That's one of the reasons he was in Tampa to talk with Plant: he depended on one of Plant's railroads to connect with his St. Augustine-to-Jacksonville line for service through Georgia and South Carolina.[14]

The mouth of the Miami River, looking south towards Coconut Grove, 1896, four years after the Ingraham Expedition. Brickell's Trading Post stands on the far bank, while Julia Tuttle's place, which would become the site of Flagler's Royal Palm Hotel, is in the foreground. Because of the date and quality of the photo, it is almost certainly another Ralph Middleton Munroe shot. (Florida Division of Library and Information Services, No. RC05722.)

Flagler was almost forced to buy the motley assemblage of small railroads that, once combined, ran from Jacksonville on the north to Daytona on the south. He unified them under the service mark "East Coast Lines." His horizons expanded about the time he hired Ingraham when he bought a railroad called the Florida Coast & Gulf. The price was right because it had no tracks, stations, or equipment. In fact, it had no assets at all—except a charter permitting it to run its lines all the way down the Atlantic coast. Flagler changed its name to the Jacksonville, St. Augustine & Indianville and pulled it under the East Coast Lines umbrella. Hoping to attract northbound winter freight in citrus, pineapples, and pine lumber, he extended his network in February 1893 to Rockledge, just south of Cape Canaveral.[15] By now, he had already decided to press on to Lake Worth, next to West Palm Beach. He began assembling land in late 1892 for his Royal Poinciana Hotel, breaking ground in May 1893 and completing it the following February. The first scheduled-service passenger train pulled up to its special station a month later. But at that point, as far as Henry Flagler was concerned, Lake Worth was the end of the line.[16]

Then why the expedition? Sitting at camp the first night at Ft. Myers before starting out, Ingraham and John Newman debated the chances of making it to Miami. Newman was optimistic, because he believed there had to be a headwater divide somewhere in the middle of the uncharted marsh, splitting the slow-moving river flows into eastward and westward halves. That would mean there was a relatively high, dry plateau somewhere in the middle, useable if only a modest number of drainage canals were built radiating out from the center to the edges. Although the crossing would be difficult, if it could be done, it would benefit the whole country, "for if this land can be rendered fit for cultivation it would be the most productive of any in this state ... it might support an immense population and would doubtless supply the United States with sugar, rice and fruits adapted to the climate." Newman couldn't help tweaking Ingraham's nose about the social benefits of this kind of work as compared to the projects the railroad magnates were more accustomed to: "with the money spent on hotels in the City of St. Augustine to gratify the luxurious tastes of our millionaires, I believe this land could be drained and the promoter of such a scheme would have the right to be considered the greatest philanthropist of his age," he said.[17]

Over the years, Ingraham gave alternative explanations for Plant's decision to organize the expedition. Sometimes he said it was to survey a rail line, but his earlier and more detailed accounts pointed to the prospects of a large-scale reclamation project. In 1911 he told a Congressional committee that "the project of draining the Everglades attracted the attention of Henry B. Plant in the early nineties, but he was by no means sure that the scheme was feasible; so I, acting under his direction, undertook an expedition through the region." In addition, Ingraham almost immediately concluded from his traverse that "the Everglades, along the whole 160 miles of the eastern side, are rimmed by a rock ledge ... there was nothing to prevent the water of the lakes from flowing into the ocean and leaving the land drained, if vents could be made in this long ledge."[18]

Moreover, just three weeks after making it into Miami, James Ingraham walked into a Tallahassee meeting of the trustees of the state's Internal Improvement Fund and announced that he was prepared to drain a million acres of the Everglades. Now.[19]

The Fund was the creature of the Florida Internal Improvement Act of 1855. The Act was the foundation upon which the state planned to build railroads, drain swamps, dredge canals, and provide the infrastructure necessary to pull it out of the wilderness and pull it into the burgeoning industrial revolution that was radically remaking the northern states. The State of Florida did not take possession of the land within its own boundaries at the time it was admitted to the union—the federal government retained ownership, by treaty, and as long as those lands remained unusable because they were flooded, the federal government retained title to them.

It was the task of the Internal Improvement Fund to take possession of those lands delegated ("patented") to the state by the federal government under the Federal Swamp and Overflowed Lands Act of 1850. The Fund then either sold the land outright or awarded it through in-kind grants to private companies to encourage them to construct canals, levees, dykes, wharfs, and other improvements—but especially railroads. The amount that the Fund could award through in-kind land grants was set by formulas within the state Internal Improvement Act of 1855. For reclaimed lands, a company could take half of the drained lands, and the state took the other half, in alternating square miles (called sections), checkerboard-fashion. For railroads and navigable canals, a company typically received an alternating checkerboard extending six miles in either direction of the centerline.[20]

Unfortunately, the Internal Improvement Fund also got itself into the business of issuing state-backed bonds to support railroad construction. The railroads used these bonds as collateral on the notes they used to pay for their construction equipment and material,

The Miami River Canal (right) and the south branch of the Miami River, looking northwest, in the direction James Ingraham's party approached Miami in 1892. The photograph was taken from a viewing tower at a popular tourist attraction of the era located near the confluence of the two branches. The road in the foreground is today's NW 12th Avenue. The cofferdam barely visible in the distance marks the former location of Miami Falls. Photograph 1915. (Detroit Publishing Co. Library of Congress, LC-D4-72404.)

especially iron rails, which they mostly bought from the New York mill of one Francis Vose, described in an official state report as "a little, grasping weazened-faced fellow, with a heart no bigger than a mosquito's gizzard."[21]

By the late 1860s, Vose held over a million dollar's worth of IOUs from several railroads, most of whom went bankrupt and defaulted. The bankrupt roads were then sold for pennies on the dollar (usually to restructured groups of their original investors), while the Fund was stuck with the responsibility to cover the bonds that backed their debts. Land sale revenues came nowhere near covering the bond payments, and Vose refused a lump-sum settlement of 20 cents on the dollar, preferring to force the fund into receivership.

One condition of the receivership was that land could only be sold "for legal tender." The Fund hired salesmen to scour the country in an effort to find homesteaders who would pay cash for small plots, but with interest compounding on the bond debt, the Fund gradually fell farther and farther into arrears on the Vose debt. This rendered it moribund. It held three million acres, but couldn't sell them because they were overflowed lands that everyone considered useless. They could be made salable if they could be granted as in-kind contributions to large consortiums who would agree to drain them in exchange for half the land. But the Vose suit receivers would only allow land to be sold for cash, not granted, and nobody would buy the lands because they were useless—a viscous, self-defeating cycle.[22]

Newly-installed Governor William Bloxham broke the logjam in 1881 by signing a contract with Philadelphia saw-making heir Hamilton Disston for a colossal 12 million acres of option land—a 50-mile-wide, backward "L"-shaped corridor of land that started at the headwaters of the Kissimmee River near present-day Winter Haven, extended south along the river to Lake Okeechobee, then turned west to follow the Caloosahatchee River to the Gulf of Mexico at Fort Myers.[23] However, after signing the contract, the Voce receivers refused to approve it. Bloxham went to Philadelphia and convinced Disston to pay a million dollars in cash for another four million acres of land, enough money to pay off the Vose receivers and lift the receivership.

Disston's new Atlantic and Gulf Coast Canal and Okeechobee Land Company immediately set to work dredging the Kissimmee and Caloosahatchee Rivers. Most of his land sales occurred north of Lake Okeechobee. Kissimmee was essentially a two-horse trading post before Disston made it his corporate headquarters, and Fort Myers tripled in size after becoming the base for his southern dredging operations. Ultimately, he dug eighty miles of canals and received 1.6 million acres of option lands before the panic of 1893 did him in. He mortgaged all his land and equipment for two million dollars, washed his hands of the project, and died of a heart attack three years later.[24]

But the million dollars put the Fund back into business again, and Ingraham stepped up to snatch that opportunity. It's still something of a mystery what he was up to. He claimed to represent no one but himself, but he was apparently still a Plant System employee, as he represented the railroad on an unrelated, relatively routine matter later in the same meeting.[25]

After he made his offer, the Fund's trustees scheduled a meeting the following month and invited representatives of the six railroads that held the largest outstanding claims to Fund lands. The whole idea behind the Improvement Fund was that it was supposed to be the central clearinghouse for the distribution of patented lands in the state. Unless you have only one entity setting the rules for how someone can become eligible to receive Township X, Range Y, Section Z, and is keeping track of who is in the pipeline working toward the purchase or grant of each piece of land, chaos will ensue.

However, since about 1880, the legislature had periodically made it their business to do an end-around the Fund by promising some railroads a land grant in excess of the normal six-mile-to-each-side checkerboard pattern permitted in the Florida Internal Improvement Act. Sometimes these were in the form of per-mile awards; at other times block grants. Neither typically had any relation to the project, such as lying adjacent to the right-of-way of the railroad. They could be anywhere. As a result, by the time Ingraham made his offer, more land was owed by the Fund than had actually been patented from the federal government to the state. In desperation, the Fund had started issuing "certificates," which were basically IOUs for vaguely described lands to be transferred "in conformity with the act of the legislature," promised "whenever the same shall have been patented to the State of Florida." Under the federal Swamp and Overflowed Lands Act, this could not occur until the land had been drained and made usable. At this point, the amount of land already privately owned, granted by the state through the legislature or the Fund, or promised through certificates was getting uncomfortably close to what was believed to be the total land area of the state.[26]

Therefore, Ingraham's proposal seriously threatened to upset the applecart. Because this was a drainage plan, not a railroad line, it did two things at once: first, it made him eligible for the 50–50 checkerboard land grant under the 1855 Florida Internal Improvement Act *and* it simultaneously made this reclaimed land ready to be patented under the 1850 federal Swamp and Overflowed Lands Act. It was unclear who would have the superior legal claim to the newly patented lands: Ingraham, who, as the reclaiming agent, had made the land patentable by draining it, or the railroads that had a first-in-time claim to whatever land was conveyed from the federal government to the Improvement Fund through their certificates. It was no surprise, then that the railroads objected *en bloc* to Ingraham's proposal (including his own South Florida Railroad).[27] The minutes blandly note that:

> it was decided that in view of the fact that there was hardly a sufficient quantity of lands patented or to be patented to the State to satisfy the land grants of Rail Road Companies earned but not yet satisfied, that the Board could not accept any of the propositions to drain or purchase any of the unpatented State lands.[28]

Reviewing the incident several years later, a state investigative report wryly noted that "there seems to have been in the minds of the Trustees … the idea that the Fund belonged to the railroads under these grants."[29]

* * * * *

Six months after the Everglades expedition, Ingraham began work as vice president of Flagler's East Coast Lines, in charge of all its real estate operations. This was still about six months before the extension into Lake Worth was finished. The traditional story says that Julia Tuttle, the plucky widow whose father had acquired the land around the old Fort Dallas at the mouth of the Miami River, convinced Flagler to extend his line another 80 miles to Miami by sending him orange blossoms the day after much of the state was hit by a plant-killing frost in 1894. Not so. The real reason was land. Millions of acres of it. There are really two parallel stories when it comes to Flagler's Florida land empire. The first has to do with his efforts to obtain acreage directly through land grants from the state for railroad construction. In the end, these proved to be only moderately successful. The second concerns the way he was able to gain access to land through joint ventures with other firms that had already succeeded in receiving large grants from the Internal Improvement Fund.[30]

When the Ingraham expedition finally canoed into Miami, they stayed at Tuttle's place, not because they had anything against the Brickells across the river, but because Ingraham and Tuttle were already acquaintances. They had met in Cleveland in 1890, at a dinner party. Tuttle already knew that her father had made her a substantial South Florida landholder, and she mentioned that she was about to move down there and start making some money off her properties, especially one at the old Fort Dallas on the Miami River. She told Ingraham that someday, someone would build a railroad there, and to encourage it, she would be willing to give half her property for town sites. "Perhaps you will be that man," she added mischievously.[31]

But by itself, getting half a townsite hardly justified a hundred miles of new track. In 1893, the legislature, in one of its bursts of land generosity, had approved an Act granting any railroad constructed south of about Daytona a bonus of 8,000 acres per mile of track in addition to the usual 3,850. The problem was that much of the land along the coastal ridge from Cape Canaveral to Miami was already spoken for by a man named Albert P. Sawyer.[32]

In 1882, a former civil war surgeon named Dr. John Westcott formed the Florida Coast Line Canal and Transportation Company to dig an inland waterway paralleling the Atlantic coastline. (Today, after much improvement by the Army Corps of Engineers, it is known as the Intracoastal Waterway.) But by 1885 only 26 miles had been dredged. Additional investors were brought in, including Albert P. Sawyer, president of the Domestic Electrical Manufacturing Company of Boston. Sawyer wasn't all that interested in the canal company itself; it was the land grants it would receive from the state that caught his attention. He and a partner, George Piper, formed a parallel company, the Boston & Florida Atlantic Coast Land Company. It would purchase the lands awarded to the canal company, then develop, improve, subdivide and sell them. Piper and Sawyer started out by buying a hundred thousand dollar's worth of the canal company's current and anticipated land deeds running all the way from St. Augustine to south of Fort Dallas.[33]

In November 1892, Flagler had written to Sam Mattox, the canal company's secretary, implying that his railroad would not extend its route once the work to Rockledge, near Cape Canaveral, was done unless the canal company agreed to share the land they received under their grants:

> Other [rail]roads constructed in Florida have received from 6,000 to 20,000 acres of land for each mile of road constructed. These grants have nearly, if not quite exhausted the lands at the disposal of the state for such purposes. Your own canal has received from the state a grant of alternate sections within the six-mile limit along its route. Our railroad will practically follow the same course, and for this reason we are shut off from any possible subsidy at the hands of the state. We believe therefore that you can well afford to aid us in this undertaking by dividing with us your land grant. If you cannot do this we should receive at the least 1,500 acres for each mile of road which we shall construct south of Rockledge, however not to exceed 104 miles.[34]

In 1895, the canal company's directors authorized the transfer of 103,000 acres to the newly renamed Florida East Coast Railway (FEC) to encourage the railroad's extension from Fort Pierce to West Palm Beach, a distance of only about 80 miles. The extension from West Palm Beach to Miami (70 miles) cost the canal company another 94,000 acres, mostly in what is today Broward and north Dade counties. On the other hand, the FEC never directly received any of the land offered by the State of Florida under the 1893 special land grant of 8,000 acres per mile of track as an inducement to extend south. (It did, however, receive some of the land due it under the standard statutory 6-mile-to-a-side checkerboard grant of 3,850 acres per mile.)[35]

Flagler also agreed to financially bolster the ailing canal company. Starting in early 1893, Flagler made the first of several cash payments to the firm that eventually totaled

$185,000. In return he received debenture bonds and promissory notes, but these were never repaid; instead he accepted 25,000 acres of land. It says a lot about the dynamics of the Florida land business at the turn of the century that a canal company would be so eager to subsidize the construction of what was certain to be, when completed, its biggest competitor. But as George Bradley, the president of the canal company, wrote Albert Sawyer, his counterpart at the Boston & Florida land company, Flagler's involvement would make it easier "to sell our lands," as they could take advantage of the FEC's superior advertising prowess and otherwise "ride their coat-tails." Finishing the canal in order to get all the land grants was the goal—it appears that almost everyone involved assumed that once it was completed, the canal, going head-to-head against both the railroad and coastal steamers, was going to fail.[36]

The canal was completed in January 1896. Three months later, the first scheduled-service FEC passenger train pulled into Miami. The land bounty brought forth by the canal company deal led Flagler's lieutenants to restructure his organization. All the land not used for rail operations were moved into a new corporation, the Model Land Company. There were several exceptions: the short-lived Fort Dallas Land Company sold lots on the high-value land Julia Tuttle had given the firm in what would soon become the City of Miami. The Perrine Land Co. was formed to deal with the "Perrine Grant," a large, very fertile grant held by the descendants of Dr. Perrine. These faced a unique set of legal problems resulting from his sudden death in an ambush during the Second Seminole War. The Chuluota Land Co., formed in 1912, sold land in Central Florida. The Okeechobee Model Land Company held land between Lake Worth and Lake Okeechobee, and, together with the Consolidated Land Company, started the town of Okeechobee on the north side of the big lake. It sold almost all its holdings, mostly farmland along Lake Okeechobee and town lots in Okeechobee, to a single buyer in 1923.[37]

Albert Sawyer had promised to transfer additional lands from both the canal company and, for the first time, from the Boston & Florida, if the FEC would press through to Miami. But canal company general manager George Miles urged Sawyer to deliver the Boston & Florida land in the form an undifferentiated one-half ownership in town lots in the new immigrant communities the Boston & Florida was setting up in what is today Broward and Palm Beach counties. That is, the Boston & Florida should not simply deed over half the land to the Model Land Co. with each firm owning its own plots outright, but should instead share every lot on a 50/50 joint ownership basis. By doing so, Miles advised, it would "prevent our lands from being discriminated against by such a powerful organization as the RR Company would be if they decided to offer advantages to settlers which we are not in a position to parallel." Miles was afraid, probably with some justification, that Model Land Co. agents would push customers towards MLC lots, ignoring Boston & Florida property, even if the lots were in the same neighborhood.[38]

Four towns were created, initially as immigrant colonies for Germans or Scandinavians. These were Linton (today's Delray Beach); Boynton (Boynton Beach); Modelo (named after the Model Land Company; now Dania Beach); and Halland (Hallandale). Platted in July 1895 by Ingraham himself, Modelo appears to have been the first of these new towns. It was located approximately thirty miles north of Miami and five miles south of Frank Stranahan's compound on the New River that would later become Fort Lauderdale. It was later renamed Dania in honor of its original settlers, four hundred Danish families recruited together as a group. The streets originally carried such names as Valhalla and Skandia. It was located by the FEC railroad tracks, about two miles inland from the canal and the ocean. Between the two was low-lying, perpetual marshland, so the Model Land

The reclamation of the Everglades and the dredging of navigation canals were considered such technological marvels that work sites were popular tourist stops, and postcards and other souvenirs of the largest and most powerful dredges were hot sellers. This photograph of a rail-track drag-line shovel is from a stereoscopic view-card made about 1912. (Detroit Publishing Company. Library of Congress, LC-D4-72412.)

Company dug two ditches, throwing the spoil up in between to raise a connecting roadway. This road, built to ease Miles's fear that the FEC was trying to monopolize the freight traffic to the new town, was one of, if not the first Model Land Company road projects. It remains to this day as Dania Beach Boulevard, and was extended over the waterway via a drawbridge to the beach after World War II.[39]

Shortly after he had gotten Modelo up and running, Ingraham visited his brother-in-law, Luther Halland, in New York. Halland, the son of a Swedish minister, was popular within the local Swedish community. "Why don't you go down there and start a Swedish settlement?" Ingraham asked. Halland agreed, and with a friend, Olog Zetterland, laid out Halland on what is today the Dade-Broward line. But relations between the canal company and the Model Land Co. soon began to sour. George Miles questioned Ingraham's choice of location (not enough high, dry ground, he thought). He also complained that settlers preferred the better-located Model Land Co. farm parcels over the town sites. Miles wrote Sawyer privately urging him that the Flagler debt be repaid only through the joint venture colonies, not through outright land grants. In his view, the only real advantages of being involved with the Flagler interests were better advertising and cheaper rail freight rates.[40]

As of February 1897, only about $7,500 in land sales had been made in Modelo and Halland. The 1900 census indicated that only 10 households lived within the town of Halland—everyone else was a farmer. A 1909 Geological Survey map of north Dade County didn't even include it.[41] This worried Sawyer and Miles at the canal company and the Boston & Florida, but not Flagler and Ingraham. It was their intent all along that the Model Land Company "work in sympathy with the plans of the FEC Railway for building up along its line thriving settlements to increase the revenues," Flagler said. Deferred payments; time payments; mortgages—all could be considered. Cash on the barrelhead was not the ultimate measure of success. Flagler estimated that "every new settler is worth $300 a year to me. He has to bring in everything he uses and send out everything he produces over my railroad."[42]

On the other hand, George Miles complained bitterly about the "outrageous freight charges" the settlers at Halland were having to pay, and he was not the only one. Ingraham received a letter from the Reverend Jacobson in New York City, passing on complaints he had received from his former parishioners who had relocated to Halland. He told Ingraham that the owners of furniture that cost $37.00 were being charged $20.00 to ship it from Jacksonville to Halland, while "the same goods could have been sent to Kansas City and back again for less." One area newspaper estimated that a tomato farmer moving into Halland, building a house and shed, then planting, harvesting and marketing his first year's crop paid the FEC $400 in freight.[43]

Ingraham's response was to cut out the Halland Land Company and hire his own Swedish recruitment agent. (Ingraham's brother-in-law, had, by this time, returned to New York and Olof Zetterlund was running the firm on his own.) Frederick Morse, the influential Dade County independent real estate agent who represented both the Model Land Company and the Boston & Florida, cautioned Sawyer that he had better learn to get along with Flagler's people if he expected to make any money out of the joint-venture colonies.[44]

In February 1898, Rufus Rose, who had been the chief drainage engineer for Hamilton Disston during his uncompleted multi-million acre project back in 1881–86, appeared before the trustees of the Internal Improvement Fund on behalf of a new FEC subsidiary, the Florida East Coast Drainage and Sugar Company. The "sugar company," as everybody started calling it, offered to drain everything between the present-day towns of Boca Raton (55 miles north of Miami) and Florida City (25 miles south). In essence, it was a renewal of the offer James Ingraham had put before the trustees back in 1892. The sugar company sought, and was granted, 20,000 acres of land for each 200,000 cubic yards of canal excavated.[45] At least one observer later wrote that he thought it was part of plan to link railroad and canal grants with reclamation grants to take control of all the land in present-day Broward and Dade counties that had not already been deeded by the state.[46]

The subsidiary prepared a stock issue and ran three survey lines out to the west from Miami, Biscayne (today's Miami Shores) and Modelo, but as early as May 1899 Ingraham privately admitted to George Miles that Flagler "was not prepared to go on with the sugar co." Work was never started, and after being granted one two-year extension, a second was denied and the franchise expired in 1902. At the same meeting that Ingraham warned Miles that Flagler would probably not proceed with the sugar co., Miles replied that he was planning to extend the coastal waterway to St. Augustine in the north and to connect it with the St. Johns River to provide a route to Jacksonville. After hearing this, Ingraham warned Joseph Parrott that the waterway would "afford competition enough to effect [our] rates unfavorably." Relations between the two corporations further soured. Miles urged Albert Sawyer's son Hayden not to use the same land agents as the Model Land Company.[47]

Ingraham pressed Sawyer for the lands still due from the canal company and the Boston & Florida. Sawyer continued to waffle. In 1903 Albert Sawyer died after years of poor health. In 1904 the state froze the land grants to the canal company (a settlement was worked out two years later). Finally, in 1910, the FEC sued the canal company, claiming it was owed 75,600 acres of land. In January 1913 they settled for 20,000 acres in today's Dade, Broward and Orange counties and the cancellation of Sawyer's 1893 loan debt. All told, counting both the canal company and its Boston & Florida land subsidiary, the Flagler interests received somewhere around 242,000 to 249,000 acres between 1893 and 1913, about eighty percent of what they were originally promised. On the other hand, they ended up receiving about 250,000 acres from the state, approximately a fifth of what they expected under the terms of the 1893 legislative land bonus for railway extensions south of Daytona.

By 1903, Flagler and Ingraham were claiming that the state owed the FEC Railroad just over 2.2 million acres: 220,000 to fulfill the obligations the Improvement Fund had made to the short line railroads before they had been absorbed into the FEC in the 1880s, and 2,040,000 acres for the track south of Daytona and Rockledge via the 1893 legislative land grant bonus.[48] In 1900, William Jennings, a populist Democrat, was elected governor, and automatically became chairman of the Internal Improvement Fund. In 1897, the Swamp Land Bureau of the Interior Department had originally approved the state's "List Number 87," identifying a total of 2.9 million acres in land patents, only to revoke it a few months later at the request of the federal Indian Bureau amidst concerns that little or no provision had been made by the state to protect Seminole homelands. That took over a year to resolve. Then, in July 1902, came the bombshell. When the land from List No. 87 was released, Jennings began selling it. For cash. Just like the 1855 state act said he was supposed to. "In the judgment of the trustees," Jennings stated, "the drainage, settlement and cultivation of the swamp and overflowed lands remaining undisposed can best be accomplished by a sale of a portion of said lands." Moreover, he recommended that further dispensation of lands not be made until *after* they had been drained.[49] The railroads, of course, claimed that they had first rights to those lands because of the certificates they held from the legislative bonus grants that had been handed out for thirty years.

Jennings left office in 1905, replaced by Napoleon Bonaparte Broward. History has caricatured Broward as the "mad drainer of the Everglades," but as the foremost historian of early Everglades reclamation, J. E. Dovell, points out, this is not necessarily so. The purpose of the Internal Improvement Fund always was to systematically accept patented lands from the federal government and distribute them so they could be made productive. At the same time it was also the intent of the Fund to use sales revenues and the strategic grants of land to build the infrastructure necessary to turn useless acreage into productive farms, fields and towns by either enticing private parties into doing the work or paying for it directly using the cash raised from land sales. Instead, the Fund had been hijacked by the legislature and the railroads, who had been promised millions of acres of land for doing work they were going to do anyway, and who neither improved those lands, nor permitted others to do so.

Governor Jennings cut off the give-away of the only remaining lands left, the southern wetlands, by asserting that the terms of the 1855 state act required the Improvement Fund to grant them only to private parties for reclamation purposes. Alternatively, they could be reclaimed by the government itself, then sold for cash. The problem with this bluff was that the government had no drainage program to back it up. So to put some teeth in Jennings's position, Broward was forced into an aggressive reclamation program, although in all honesty, it is something he did believe in and had advocated for many years.[50]

More centrally to our story, when Jennings's term ended, he was succeeded by Broward as governor. Broward, in turn, appointed Jennings as the Improvement Fund's general counsel, effectively putting him back in charge of it. The railroads and canal companies pressed their certificates on the Fund's trustees, some going back to the late 1870s. Initially, nobody had any idea how many certificates had been issued. After Jennings ordered an audit, the total was found to be a little over 800,000 acres, which the Fund's auditor called "a fruitful source of embarrassment and litigation."[51]

Finally, in November, the trustees released a legal opinion prepared by Jennings. The 1850 Federal Swamp and Overflowed Lands Act provided only for the transfer of newly patented lands *directly* from the federal government to the Fund. Because the land title went directly from the federal government to the Improvement Fund, only the Fund had the power to dispose of these lands. Because it was never given ownership or control of the lands, the legislature did not have the power to make any grants of land patented to the state through the 1850 federal act. This included the legislation that granted Flagler 8,000 acres per mile for the Miami extension.

Likewise, the nefarious certificates had been awarded only for lands granted through special legislative acts, not under the formulas contained in the 1855 state act itself. Therefore, all the certificates were void. The land and railroad companies sued, of course, but throughout 1906 and 1907 most settled out of court. Those that didn't usually lost.[52] The FEC's record was mixed. It claimed that the Fund owed it 67,000 acres indirectly through a grant made to the Palatka and Indian River Railway Company in the 1880s. After investigation, the attorney general agreed and ordered the Fund to make the transfer in 1910. In 1912 the Model Land Company accepted 210,000 acres to settle the FEC's outstanding claim of 2,040,000 acres for the Miami line. About 74 square miles of this was located in Palm Beach County, but the majority, 254 square miles, was in a desolate, far-off, almost mythical place known as "Cape Sable," at very tip of the Florida peninsula.[53]

••2••

"Roads should be built so the land can be shown"

When it comes to the building of the Ingraham Highway, there are two obvious questions: first, why would anyone take so much trouble to build a road simply to go to such a far-off, Godforsaken place as Cape Sable; and second, why did it follow just about the worst possible route to get there?

The first is far easier to answer. While Cape Sable may have been far off and accessible only by boat, it was hardy a wasteland. To the contrary, by the turn of the century it had already caught the eye of homesteaders and botanists alike as a promising locale for tropical agriculture, and it had already been homesteaded by a sizeable number of smallholders. In the early decades of the twentieth century, Cape Sable was quite an attractive piece of real estate, even if that attraction turned out to be, in the end, more a matter of appearance than hard economics.

The second question is a little more complex. The Ingraham Highway, or the Cape Sable road as it was also known, existed from 1914 until much of it was replaced by a new highway built by the National Park Service in 1956. The old highway was built in two stages. The first, constructed in 1914–15, was a fairly typical scarified farm-to-market road, seven miles long, gravel surfaced, with only modest provisions for drainage. It started at the village of Longview, a little west of Detroit (later, Florida City), and followed the current state highway (State Road 9336) to Everglades National Park, at the present main entrance, ending about two miles southwest of there in what is today a service depot for the park.[1]

It followed what had been a pack trail, then a rough, dry-season wagon road to a clearing in a pine hammock that contained a log cabin and a dining shelter. This was "Camp Jackson."[2] It was the remnant of a base camp built during a six-month-long surveyor's expedition led by William Krome for the FEC Railroad in 1902–03. After he finished, it had been regularly used by surveyors and work crews moving through the "Cape Sable District"— roughly the area within today's Everglades National Park between the Homestead entrance and Flamingo. As more homesteaders became interested in the relatively cheap Cape Sable land, real estate firms and land speculators increasingly relied on Krome's old supply trail until it was no longer adequate, so it was improved it to the point where it could reliably— if not comfortably—be used by an automobile all year round. In late 1914 or early 1915 a temporary plank causeway was extended across a broad, shallow river called Taylor Slough to reach Paradise Key, a spectacularly beautiful hammock a mile or so from Camp Jackson that later became Royal Palm State Park, the nucleus of Everglades National Park.

2. "Roads should be built so the land can be shown"

It wasn't until a special road district was created by Dade County and a $100,000 bond issue approved in 1915 that the second phase of the Ingraham Highway began. A new road, following a different route out of Homestead and Florida City, was built. It connected up with the original 1914–15 scarified road about six miles southwest of Florida City.[3] From there it followed the original route for about seven miles to Camp Jackson and Paradise Key. The planking of the causeway was torn up and the pilings buried under rock and gravel fill used to construct a new causeway across Taylor Slough. Shortly before exiting the park, the highway turned southwest for four miles, then due west again for another eight. At this point, the road swung to the south and was planned to run due south for over ten miles but in the end this proved impossible and the route had to be changed in 1918. After going south for about five miles, it turned southwest again, taking a more or less straight line into Flamingo.

It has long been accepted wisdom that access to the state park was the main reason the road was built—or at least the reason it was started. But there are many interesting

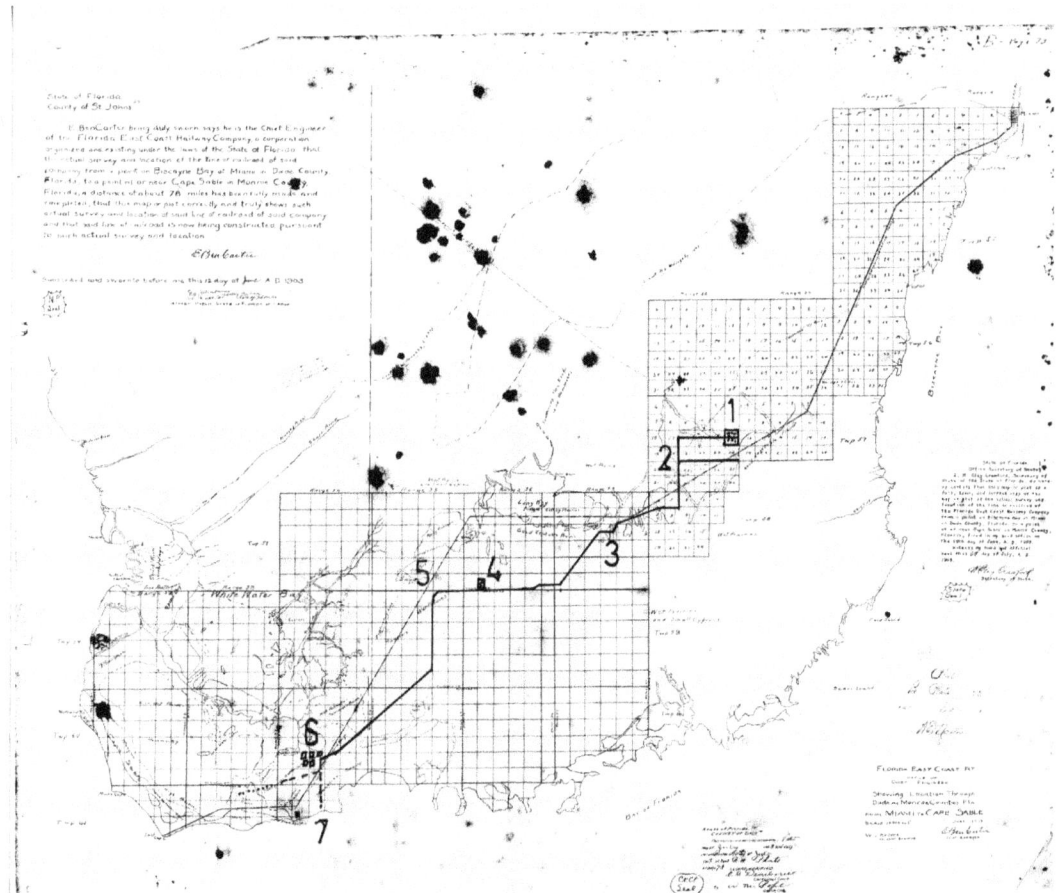

William Krome's 1903 plat for a Cape Sable railroad route to Key West, with a map of the 1915–1922 Ingraham Highway drawn over it. (1) Homestead; (2) Camp Longview; (3) Paradise Key (Royal Palm State Park); (4) Jennings Grove; (5) Cement Bridge; (6) Flamingo Village (Coot Bay); (7) Flamingo Dock (Flamingo Post Office). (Plat Book "B," Page 73, Public Records of Dade County, Florida.)

holes in this explanation. As the Smithsonian's Charles Simpson, a part-time Coconut Grove resident, pointed out in 1916, why was it necessary to run the highway straight through the middle of Paradise Key? And why did former Governor Jennings and his wife May Mann Jennings, president of the Florida Women's Clubs and the driving force behind the creation of the new state park, write an "official" history that said Paradise Key's location was unknown "until the year 1914," although it had been mapped on Bill Krome's 1903–04 plat, and had been visited—and written about—even before that? Finally, wouldn't it have make more sense to run the road about four miles north of where it eventually went so it would ascend Long Key (also known as Long Pine Key), a natural viaduct that would have lifted the road above the water and muck for almost a third of the way to Flamingo? After all, this was the route Krome proposed for the Cape Sable railroad on his plat, and it was the route the National Park Service used for its 1956 road.

Years later, Marjory Stoneman Douglas, in her memoirs, wrote that "The state built the road and so forth, and the Jenningses owned a lot of land nearby. I cast no aspirations, but there is something inevitable in thinking the Jenningses wanted to develop the land and that having the road built with public funds didn't hurt." Mrs. Jennings was lauded as a hero, Douglas's comments dismissed as "catty," and her claims never taken seriously.[4]

* * * * *

Getting to Paradise Key across Taylor Slough before the Cape Sable road was built was a dicey proposition, especially during the summer wet season. This photograph is taken very near to where the plank causeway would be built in 1915, only to be replaced with an earthen causeway a year later. (Photographer: John K. Small. Florida Division of Library and Information Services, No. SMX-0106.)

Cape Sable is a crescent-shaped peninsula running northwest by southeast, 25 miles long by six miles at its widest point. To the north are the freshwater Whitewater and Oyster bays, the receiving basin for the Shark River, the larger of the two slow-moving rivers originating from Lake Okeechobee.[5] To the south are Florida Bay and the Gulf of Mexico. The Cape proper is a barely perceptible bump projecting south from the crescent about midway along the south shore. It marks the division between the Gulf of Mexico and Florida Bay. But when people speak of "Cape Sable" they mean the entire peninsula, not the blunt little projection. By land, Cape Sable could, in 1903, theoretically be entered at its eastern end through a narrow, two mile-wide gap between Coot Bay, a cove extending south from Whitewater Bay, and Florida Bay. A scattered group of homesteads comprising the village of Flamingo was dotted across this gap. However, the land northeast of this gap was deeply inundated and most was heavily overgrown with mangroves. It acted as a moat between Flamingo and the rest of the world. Reaching Flamingo by land before 1904 required an overland expedition of some sixty miles from the nearest supply point, the harbor at Cutler, ten miles south of Coconut Grove, a twenty-mile hike along the established trail to Camp Longwood near the future site of Homestead, then a forty mile uncharted slog across the Everglades from Longwood to Flamingo Post Office.[6]

So getting to the Cape in those days was strictly a marine proposition. And that accounted for much of its allure. From the sea, Cape Sable looks like paradise: Its beaches are beautiful, and at the East Cape the land rises up from the beach into a series of grassy sand dunes, opening to lush hammocks that have grown from the older, established dunes behind them. As one goes west into the Middle Cape, the separation between the beach and the hammocks grows wider, with the dunes dropping down into tidal marshes before rising up into the hammocks. The marshes grow wider and the hammocks less numerous the farther one moves west, with the whole Cape gradually becoming lower and wetter. Geologically, the Cape is actually a second, more inland series of keys in which sand and plant life have filled in the gaps between the coral rock humps.[7]

One of the first to be captivated by it was Dr. Henry Perrine, a physician and botanist who served as United States consul in Mexico, where he became a self-taught botanist. He and Richard Rush, the Secretary of the Treasury, were the men the State Department sent to England to iron out the problems endangering the release of the James Smithson bequeath. Their success enabled the establishment of the Smithsonian Institution. Perrine submitted several Smithsonian-related reports to Congress on the potential value of tropical fruits, spices and other plants, and in 1838 Congress granted him and two associates, James Webb and Charles Howe, a township of land (36 square miles) near Cutler to use as a plant nursery and agricultural research station.[8]

But Perrine and Howe were also interested in the more southerly lands of Cape Sable. Perrine wanted to experiment with a new type of sisal (it now bears his name) and Howe wanted to establish a settlement there. Perrine asked the federal government to survey the Cape, calling it the "sheltered seashore of ever-verdant prairies in a region of ever-blooming flowers in an ever frostless tropical Florida." But before he could press his case, Perrine was killed in April 1840 in a guerrilla attack during the Second Seminole War, as were two of Howe's sons.[9]

William Harney was the army officer tasked with tracking down and taking revenge on Perrine's killers. He detested the whole Seminole War, but as a disciplined officer he did an efficiently barbaric job of it, killing some two dozen Seminoles, including the leader Chakaika, in December 1840. It was the last major act in the Second Seminole War, although neither side admitted it until President Tyler agreed in 1842 to let the last 300 Seminoles live in peace in the Big Cypress Swamp region. Harney, a friend of Perrine's, renewed his request for a federal survey of Cape Sable. In fact, he was so enthusiastic about its commercial prospects that he began planning his own tropical fruit and sugar plantation there. He wrote Florida's Senator David Levy Yulee asking: "can you do me the favor to get an order to have it surveyed at once, so I can employ men to commence in clearing and planting at once?" He did not get his wish, as the federal government did not generally survey overflowed lands until after they had been drained.[10]

The Cape was being homesteaded without surveys, and by 1898 Flamingo had become a fairly substantial town, mostly in two clusters, the larger along the south edge of Coot Bay and the smaller along the shoreline of Florida Bay two miles south and on Joe Kemp Key island just offshore. This southern village was often referred to as Flamingo Dock or Flamingo Post Office. The Everglades National Park Flamingo visitor center now stands on the site of Flamingo Dock, but the north half was abandoned decades ago, although Coot Bay was the location of the south ranger station from 1947, when the park was formed, until 1958 when the Flamingo Visitors' Center and Marina was built.[11]

Among the first settlers were the Irwin family of Missouri and the Roberts clan of Jacksonville, who both arrived about 1895, and the Douthits, who moved from Allapattah to the Cape in 1902. The Irwins had homesteaded Joe Kemp Key, and the mother of the Irwin boys still lived there in a stilt house in 1922. The Douthits were reportedly the largest farmers, with about five acres under the plow, but the Roberts, an extended family of "Uncle Steve" Roberts, his sons and nephews, were the most numerous. They specialized in growing and processing sugar cane and cane syrup. It could be a rough life. The naturalist Leverett Brownell visited in 1893, and said the place was "populated by a rugged group of men who appeared to be refugees from justice." Brownell reported that flea powder "was the staff of life," and he saw an oil lamp flame smothered by mosquitoes. (A century later, a biologist's mosquito trap on nearby Whitewater Bay counted the highest density of that insect ever recorded: a little over 320,000 captured in a 24-hour period.)[12]

The peak years of Flamingo's prosperity were between 1898 and 1904, during which about fifty families lived in the village and scattered along the East Cape. There was a school and a post office, and reportedly a second post office farther out, at least for a little while. However, prosperity was brief. According to one road contractor of the 1920s who knew the area well, it was no coincidence that these were also the peak years of plume hunting. Asked what people did for a living, one of the Irwin women replied farming, of course and "well—mostly this and that." "This and that" was a polite euphemism for the twin illegalities of stealing timber for charcoaling and plume hunting.[13]

To try to control the ravenous destruction of the plume hunters, the Audubon Society hired Guy Bradley, himself a former plume hunter for Guy Chevelier in the Ten Thousand Islands, as a private game warden and posted him to Flamingo. In 1905 he was shot down near Joe Kemp Key by a man named Walter Smith when he tried to arrest Smith's son for poaching. The State of Florida made feeble efforts to bring Smith to justice, but plume hunting was lucrative, Smith was rich, and the state shrugged its shoulders as soon as it realized that the prosecution would not be fast and cheap. Smith walked free. However, Bradley's father was a long-time local and had been postmaster and a storekeeper for several years. The locals burned Smith's house to the ground while he and his family were away. They got the message and left for Key West.[14]

Gradually charcoaling also started to dwindle as the circle of tree stumps widened ever farther out, requiring lumber to be hauled farther back to the kilns. Finally, in 1910, a hurricane inundated most of the plowed fields with saltwater, rendering them useless for anything except sugarcane. Within a few years, a visitor to Flamingo reported

> although we had been told that this was the location of the settlement, we could see but three habitations. One dismal looking house on pilings stood to the westward. Another was on a small point of land to the east. The third, which we later learned belonged to the Irwins, perched on the island directly ahead. A rutted road indicated that there might be other habitations still further to the west.[15]

At the time William Krome made his survey in 1903, there were only nine settlers. In 1912, when the state transferred ownership of most of Cape Sable to the railroad and the Model Land Company, the only remaining homesteaders were the Irwin household and the extended Roberts family, who had built up a substantial business shipping syrup to Miami. The Model Land Co. sold 400 acres of land to the Roberts clan for a mere 25 cents per acre—ten to twelve dollars being the standard price for dry land—to avoid any possible legal troubles or hard feelings that could get in the way of land sales to the cattle ranchers or sissle growers the company hoped to attract to the cape.[16]

The first survey of the area was undertaken by Deputy United States Surveyor John Jackson in 1847. It was Jackson who first established Camp Longwood. Jackson's advance camp was five miles southwest, near the place Bill Krome later named Camp Jackson. While Jackson did stake out some of the township and range lines near his advance camp, he did not penetrate very far in any one direction, probably getting no more than four or five miles south and eight or nine miles west.[17]

In 1874 another deputy federal surveyor, M. A. Williams, apparently re-chained and

The Roberts family home at Flamingo Dock, about 1925. Like most of the structures on the beach side of Flamingo, it was destroyed in the Great Labor Day Hurricane of 1935. (Photographer: John K. Small. Florida Division of Library and Information Services, No. SM-2227.)

verified the work Jackson had done before the Civil War. Like Jackson, he did not penetrate west of the dividing line between ranges 37 and 38, nor go south of township 57 (i.e., three or four miles southwest of Paradise Key).[18] The first survey to go deeply into the Cape Sable area was Bill Krome's 1902–03 expedition. Krome was a 26-year-old surveyor who had just arrived in south Florida after working for railroads in South Carolina and Georgia, then for the port of Jacksonville. After learning that the FEC needed a surveyor he applied and was sent to the as-yet unplatted hamlet twenty-five miles south of Miami the railroad was already calling "Homestead."

There is a lot of speculation about when Flagler decided to build the magnificent, but economically suicidal, overseas extension to Key West. Flagler biographer Edward Akin believes a Florida state senator from Key West named Jefferson B. Browne talked Flagler into it in 1895, a year before the FEC finished its Miami extension. But on the other hand, Flagler's 1901 will specifically forbade the use of his estate to build any additional rail lines south of Miami, even though he himself had authorized two extensions, to Cutler and Homestead, in 1901 and 1904.[19]

It appears that Flagler had largely decided on the Key West extension by April 1904. While taking a yacht trip down the keys with Bill Krome and FEC executives that month, Andrew Anderson, one of Flagler's oldest Florida friends, recalls Flagler telling him "It is perfectly simple. All you have to do is build one concrete arch and then another, and pretty soon you will find yourself in Key West." At a February 1905 public meeting in Key West Flagler announced that he would build the Overseas Railway.[20]

An African American member of the Krome Expedition of 1902–03 at work with a whisk (to bring mosquitos up out of the grass) and a smudge pot (to drive them away), probably just before a meal is served. Headgear of the same design is still routinely used today in the Cape Sable region during the wet season. (Photographer unknown. Florida Division of Library and Information Services, No. RC14007.)

Flagler's change of heart was primarily the result of the American acquisition of the Panama Canal enterprise. In 1889 the French venture collapsed, and with the death of its sponsor, Ferdinand de Lesseps in 1894 all hope for assembling a new syndicate ended. In 1902 its owner, the Compagnie Novelle, offered the entire project to the United States at a 60 percent discount and Congress accepted the French offer in May 1904. Flagler apparently believed that closest seaport to the canal would have an inherent economic advantage for cargo shipments, drawing east-bound ships out of the canal like a magnet. He was wrong. The technologies of that era made transferring cargo more expensive than actually hauling it, especially by sea. Until the shipping container was standardized in the late 1950s, the safe bet was usually to leave a cargo in the bottom of the boat until it arrived at the port closest to its final destination. From 1912, when the overseas railroad to Key West was finished, to 1935, when it was destroyed in the Great Labor Day Hurricane, the volume of freight hauled on the Overseas Railway was never more than a small percentage of its initial projections. It was always primarily a passenger line—and a money loser.[21]

But by late 1902, when Krome was hired, planning for the overseas extension was already underway, even if no decision had yet been reached. The purpose of his survey was to determine if a Cape Sable alternative to a Key Largo route was feasible. The party started in December 1902 and expected to be in the field some six months. Krome moved onto John Jackson's old site and installed significant improvements before setting out on his survey. It was a well-built base; photographs show at least one log cabin and an open-sided cooking and dining shelter made of timber and cut lumber.[22]

Krome writes about the expedition as being an arduous endeavor, but he does not have any of the lurid depictions of suffering that Alonzo Church wrote about. Krome was better prepared and had a semi-permanent base camp. His expedition was not self-contained; members of his team made several runs back into Homestead and Miami for provisions. He had selected his men more carefully, and provisioned them, black and white alike, well. Nevertheless, a decade later, he privately wrote a colleague that "it was the hardest trip that he had made in exploring the 'glades; that the low bushes were so close together with rocks so near the surface that they could not pull their canoes along with them."[23]

The team ran about 300 miles of survey line, starting about two miles northeast of today's Everglades National Park Homestead entrance, then moving due west about fourteen miles, then southwest to Whitewater Bay, running branch lines out as they went. From there they canoed south to Florida Bay, then back east along the shoreline at the southern line of Township 60. They discovered that Long Pine Key, the existence of which had been doubted, was actually a substantial 12,000 acres, and that Whitewater Bay was only about half the size formerly believed. In June 1903, the FEC Railroad filed Krome's survey as a plat in the official records of Dade County.

Interestingly, one thing that Krome never talked about was the widely-rumored island of giant royal palms that was supposed to be somewhere in the area. However, several years later, after visiting Paradise Key with John Small of the New York Botanical Garden, he wrote to Small:

> I cannot say that I enjoyed the trip. I have for so long felt that the hammock and the recesses of the Glades and big mangrove swamp beyond were spots reserved for the pleasure of only those few who were willing and able to surmount the difficulties that encompassed them, that I am selfish enough not to relish their being 'thrown open to the public.[24]

This seems to verify what many who knew Krome hinted at, but never discussed in public: that he had confirmed the existence of Paradise Key in 1902, but kept the information to himself and a small coterie of trusted associates. He did, on the other hand, place it on

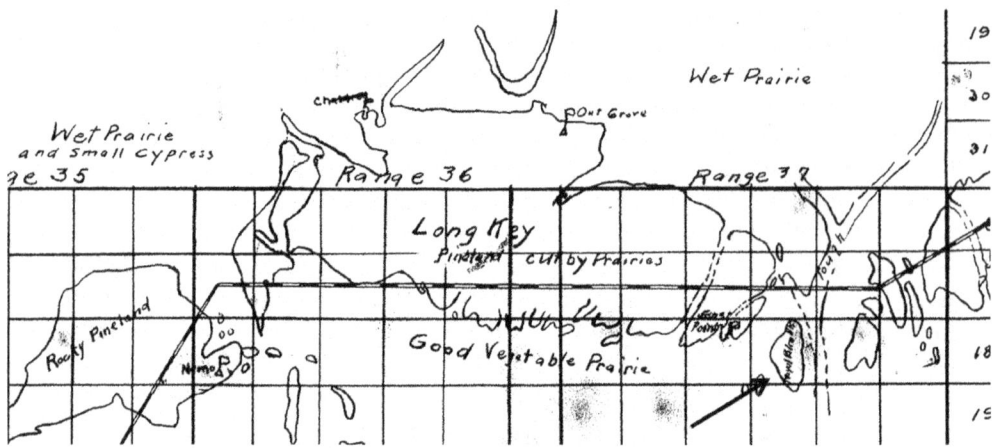

A detail from Krome's 1903 railroad plat. The arrow points to Paradise Key, which is marked "Royal Palms." The hammock immediately to the east of Paradise Key, on the other side of Taylor Slough, is Pine Island, and the group of small hammocks to the northeast of Pine Island is today collectively known as Parachute Key. It is on one of these hammocks that Krome's "Camp Jackson" was probably located. (Source: Plat Book "B," Page 73, Public Records of Dade County, Florida.)

the 1903 plat, marked, rather inconspicuously, with the label "royal palms." Its size, shape and location are quite exact. It had clearly been closely surveyed.[25]

He reported that "[while] the most serious obstacles encountered were heavy muck and dense saw grass of the Everglades, and the jungles and mosquitoes of the Whitewater Bay region, the muck with proper drainage will eventually become fine faming land and the mosquitoes will disappear to a great extent." But in private he was more doubtful: "I have been to see Krome," related a colleague, "who says that Twp 59-37 (a 6-mile by 6-mile square centered seven miles due south of Paradise Key) is the poorest land he knows of ... and that if he had it for sale he would sell it for most any price."[26]

Traditionally, much of the credit (or blame) for the building of the Ingraham Highway has been given to the popularity of Paradise Key and its institutionalization into Royal Palm State Park. In actuality, Krome's Camp Jackson probably deserves more credit. Due to its location and because it had been so well built, it started to be used by surveyors, amateur explorers and land salesmen soon after Krome had finished with it. Certainly by the time the first roadwork was started in 1914, there was already a well-defined, if unimproved, cart trail between Camp Longview and Camp Jackson.

Botanist John Small reported that getting down to Paradise Key over the "Homestead Road" from Cutler to Camp Longwood, then over Krome's trail to Camp Jackson, required a week's round trip before the railroad was extended to Homestead in 1904, three or four days afterwards.[27] Two Model Land Co. real estate agents, Pepper and Goodman, traveled to Camp Jackson in 1912 and reported:

> We left Miami morning of the 24th [of April] by automobile and followed rock road out from Detroit until we came to the old camp Jackson trail where we left the auto and walked to Camp Jackson, a distance of about five miles, arriving there about 6 p.m., where we remained that night with Mr. McRae and his crew [of surveyors].[28]

Seeking soil samples, they fanned on foot the next day to the south and southwest, getting about four miles south of Paradise Key. They reported that "we have heard that several claim to have been on this township ... [and] to have made the trip down and back in one day from Homestead, which we feel certain is a physical impossibility." Pepper and Goodman's description of having to walk "about five miles" from the end of the road suggests that they parked about three or four miles west of Detroit. This is consistent with surveyor Roy Marsh's 1912 road map of the Redland District, which indicates that the county road ended near the old site of Camp Longview.[29]

The county road network was expanding rapidly at this point, all the way from Perrine to Goulds to Detroit. After 1911 the Model Land Company was besieged with requests from farmers asking them help pay for new roads. With the exception of a few major county projects (the Dixie Highway from Homestead up to Goulds, connecting with the Old Cutler Road coming down from Coconut Grove being one example) landowners generally had to arrange the construction of the roads on their own. A county surveyor would stake out the section or half-section line, and the landowners pooled their funds and paid a contractor with a scarifier and roller.[30] J. E. Ingraham, in a letter to his local land agent, Frederick Morse, had to admit that he did not know what a "scarified road" was and asked for an explanation. Morse replied:

> A "scarified road" is one in the Homestead country which is made by running a scarifier over the surface after the trees and stumps are removed, which cuts off the upper part of the rock and the dirt, leaving a reasonably hard and smooth surface underneath. The scarifier used in that section is after the fashion of a plow with chisel cutters adjusted at the proper height from the ground and pulled by a steam or gasoline roller.[31]

Scarifiers were a necessity in the Homestead-Redland area for preparing ever-larger virgin fields for crops that required more than a few of inches of soil (like tomatoes). They were, in essence, a series of finger or chisel plows designed to turn up and break apart soft limestone. Ironically, scarified fields were an accidental by-product of road-making. In early 1914 A. W. ("Al") Lindgren took delivery of a 16-ton steam tractor made to his specifications just for scarifying. A former FEC employee, he was primarily interested in getting road-building contracts from the Model Land Co., other land developers, and individual farmers. A couple of farmers near Homestead, watching him at work, asked if he could do the same thing, only deeper, for their fields. He tried it, and succeeded. Reportedly, he learned to scarify as far down as twenty inches, almost twice as deep as his competitors. A revolution was started.[32]

When preparing a field the scarifier was run in successive 90-degree passes anywhere from a half-dozen to ten times until the stone was broken into small gravel, which mixed with the already existing, but usually thin, layer of overlying soil. But for making a road, the broken gravel thrown up by the plow was shoveled into the low spots and stump hollows, then the steamroller was unhitched from the scarifier and run back-and-forth several times on its own to compact the road. By the early 1920s large caterpillar tractors were becoming the preferred motive power, replacing steam rollers, because they could pull entire racks of chisel plows, not just the one or two used on steam tractors. Lindgren himself invented and built a unique scarifying plow based on a potato digger that threw the broken rock into a hopper that fed a rock crusher. That cut the number of passes needed in half. With a caterpillar, roadmakers usually employed a separate tow-behind compaction roller, often filled with water, which was then emptied for travel between jobs.

In addition to powerful tractors, constructing a scarified road involved the prodigious use of explosives. In 1913 Frederick Morse complained that on one job "the county refuses to furnish the dynamite necessary for this work, as they sometimes do, so it is going to double the cost." "Doubling the cost" meant $200 per centerline mile, which was the norm

A Homestead-area field being scarified with a steam tractor about the time of World War I. (Photographer unknown. Florida Division of Library and Information Services, No. RC14007.)

for a Perrine-Homestead area road at this time. Landowners paid $12.50 for every 40 acres they abutted, a total of $50.00 per mile for each side of the road. The county kicked in the remaining $100.00 per centerline mile.[33]

In some cases the landowners saved the money by doing the work themselves, as F. J. Pepper related to Ingraham:

> We find these farmers are doing most of the work themselves, and they probably have about 1,000 feet rocked; the county allows them to get the rock without charge from a nearby pit, and the county has agreed to roll the road for them free of charge when the rock is laid in place. The farmers interested in this road are a hard-working class.[34]

At other times, things did not go so well. Sidney Harrison, Ingraham's chief clerk, later vice president of the Model Land Company, inspected a new road a couple miles north of Homestead and complained to Morse that "the party who laid it out either could not follow his compass, or else the compass must have been groggy, for he did not follow the center line correctly." He asked "is there not some way in which this matter can be straightened, I know the roads can be, but cannot the man who is running these lines be straightened?"[35]

Up to 1914, the Model Land Co. held many of its sites around Homestead off the market. It was pushing its holdings in the Perrine area, which it owned jointly with the Perrine family. Henry Perrine had been granted the land in 1838 subject to the condition that it be settled. His death in the Seminole Wars made that condition impossible. In spite of this, his widow, Ann, attempted to secure the patent in 1862. She was unsuccessful until the FEC intervened on the behalf of the family, prevailing in court in 1899. Ann Perrine then granted an undivided one-half share to the FEC, an act the railroad's own attorneys confidentially concluded was probably invalid, as she did not exercise sole control over the land. Ingraham was therefore anxious to get the Perrine Grant surveyed, improved and sold as quickly as possible. "If we are going to make any sales this winter [1913–14], and I think we should be able to dispose of some $50,000 worth of property there, at good prices, roads should be built so the land can be shown," he wrote to Frederick Morse. Consequently, the Cape Sable lands took a back seat until 1914 when he was able to turn Perrine matters over to Morse and the Model Land Company's other primary local sales agent, Frank Pepper.[36]

* * * * *

In early April 1914 the FEC asked the Dade County Commission to survey a highway route from Homestead to Cape Sable. It offered to pay the costs if the county would provide the survey crew. The commission agreed. "It is believed that the plan of the railroad is to encourage the preliminary development of this country by means of a wagon road, and then to build a [railroad] line down to the cape" reported a local newspaper. "Little is generally known of the Cape Sable Country and only occasionally do reports of the successes which the pioneers of that section are having." Col. C. H. Zoll, a local engineer, was hired to do the job.[37]

Zoll's survey line was anywhere from a mile to four miles south of Krome's proposed 1903 railroad line. The biggest difference was that it crossed directly across Paradise Key east-west, then immediately angled southwest for three miles before turning due west again. Krome's 1903 rail line passed a mile north of Paradise Key and kept going straight west, over higher, dryer land, not turning southwest until it was almost all the way to Whitewater Bay. The rail line was actually closer to the 1956 main road built by the National Park Service than the 1914–1922 Ingraham Highway.

Construction of the road started almost immediately after Col. Zoll finished his survey. By June, nine miles of new scarified road had been built and a rock crusher disassembled, moved to somewhere near Camp Jackson, and reassembled. The road, according to John K. Small, the botanist from the New York Botanical Garden who had been visiting Paradise Key for many years, followed the route of the old surveyors' trail. It later became State Road 205, then State Road 9336. It is still the main route between Homestead/Florida City and Everglades National Park. Newspaper articles specifically referred to it as "The Model Land Company's road," and a company representative claimed that it was their intention to build it all the way to Cape Sable.[38]

In late 1914 Frederick Morse told Ingraham that another real estate agent who specialized in Cape Sable land, Frank Powers, had started asking him for land swaps on behalf of some of the former clients he, Powers, had sold Model Land Co. acreage to. The farmers had bought parcels south of Long Pine Key (west of Paradise Key) and in many cases had planted row crops, but then grown impatient that "the road to Cape Sable had not been completed," and now wanted to move back in closer to Homestead. From this, it can be inferred that a Cape Sable road had been promised to land buyers for some time already. One farmer, T. A. Feaster, hauled in 11,000 crates of tomatoes from his farm a mile or two west of Paradise Key, using broad-wheeled wagons and teams of oxen, so there was already some significant agricultural activity in the area, and it was being adversely affected by the lack of a road, so it is not surprising that the Model Land Company would make the necessary investment to open up their lands, as they had previously in Perrine.[39]

Work ended in late 1914 or early 1915, extending no farther than Camp Jackson, with a rather precarious plank causeway built over Taylor Slough to Paradise Key. John Small wrote that a "scarified road" was built between Homestead and Camp Jackson, and also notes that a "temporary bridge" was erected over Taylor Slough, which was completed "prior to the beginning of 1915" when he visited there.[40]

Former governor Jennings later wrote that *several* Cape Sable landowners had gone in together to put up somewhere between $22,000 and $27,000, intending to build a road "through the hammock," but he never said exactly how far it was planned to go. Jennings's budget for a road to Paradise Key ($1,900 to $2,350 per mile) is much higher than for a typical Homestead area scarified road. One must question whether this was the amount budgeted or the amount actually spent. If the intent was to build much farther out than Paradise Key, but the project was cut short for some reason, than it is possible that much less was spent. On the other hand, in a letter she wrote two years later May Mann Jennings, specifically said that "the land companies *have spent* from $23,000 to $25,000 on the road and fell short of reaching the inlands," referring to land west of Paradise Key. Thus it appears that $24,000 was the approximate amount actually spent.[41]

This is confirmed by notes in William Jennings's pocket notebook for April 8, 1914. On the same day that the FEC representative appeared before the Dade County Commission with an offer to pay for a survey of the Cape Sable road if the county hired a surveyor to do it, Jennings met in St. Augustine with Ingraham, William Dewhurst and Frank Powers. The four discussed financing the Cape Sable Road. They estimated that it would run about 32 miles and cost about $3,000 per mile; $96,000 total. (Zoll's subsequent survey indicated 45 miles to Flamingo; the final figure was a little over 43.) Hence, even before Col. Zoll's men stretched their chains out from Homestead, his financial backers knew that $24,000 could go no farther than Paradise Key, and may not be enough to even get over Taylor Slough.[42]

The financing plan Jennings outlined in St. Augustine had Dade County contributing $20,000, Monroe $10,000, the Model Land Co. $11,200, Jennings $3,200 and Dewhurst $1,600, for a total of $46,000. The owners would also contribute a total of 500 acres for the road's right-of-way. That left $50,000 in construction costs unaccounted for. Some very sketchy notes suggests the possibility that the four hoped to use the sale of Internal Improvement Fund-owned lands in the area to raise the needed revenue, possibly along with the sale of some of their private lands. It appears that at this point, the Cape Sable landowners had reached a financial impasse. It also suggests that it was the Model Land Company that put up the $24,000 or so to build the 1914–15 road to Paradise Key, as they were the principal beneficiaries.

As noted by John Small, this first road was built more like the typical Homestead-area scarified farm-to-market roads than the later highway. One can inspect one of the few undisturbed, abandoned sections of this first road just a few hundred feet south of the Ernest Coe (Homestead) Visitor Center in Everglades National Park. It shows significant differences from the road work done below Paradise Key. There is no borrow canal alongside. The roadside ditches are rather broad and shallow, and there are a few large limestone boulders thrown up, probably by blasting, by the roadside that were not crushed to make fill material. They were, instead, simply left unused by the roadside. However, the road is raised several inches, the drainage ditches were clearly excavated, the road is compacted and crowned and its surface stone has a consistent size. It looks like a well-built pre–World War I scarified county road. The contract that was subsequently issued by Dade County for the 1916–1920 highway stated that the road above the park was 25 percent complete, indicating that much additional improvement had yet to be done. Thus, it should not be assumed that the segment near the visitor center is in the same condition as the Model Land Co. left it in 1915. However, it is much different in design and construction from those segments south of Paradise Key/Royal Palm State Park.[43]

Crossing Taylor Slough likely exhausted the final resources of this first effort. The

The early Cape Sable road, built for only $24,000 and mostly by hand, was little more than an improved trail. Looking across Paradise Key, probably east-to-west, 1915. (Photographer: John K. Small. Florida Division of Library and Information Services, No. SM-0053a.)

slough is only about three thousand feet wide at the point where the road crossed it, but Surveyor Roy Marsh wrote that the "Hammock Slough" was, during the summer, normally up to four feet deep and at its driest point in winter, about "shoe-top" high. The plank causeway was temporary and rather precarious for an automobile to traverse. Several years later, J. B. McCrary of the J. B. McCrary Company, who built the permanent road to Flamingo, estimated that filling and grading Taylor Slough cost between six and seven thousand dollars, so Ingraham, Jennings and Dewhurst probably had good reason to hold up at Camp Jackson.[44]

But there was another reason for suspending work at that point. Jennings, a lawyer, had discovered some better options for funding what was obviously turning into a major project. The first was to form a drainage sub-district, a state-created entity. The second was to have Dade County create a road and bridge bond district. Eventually, both methods were tried.

Chapter 6458 of the Florida Statutes of 1915 allowed the creation of sub-drainage districts within existing drainage districts. Although intended for drainage and reclamation, chapter 6458 also permitted these sub-districts to levy taxes, loan money, and sell bonds for a wide range of improvements, including road and bridge construction. "The organization and control of the area would be within the hands of the owners of the majority of the acreage in the proposed area," Jennings wrote in a memo to Ingraham. Given "the delay of the request by the Board of County Commissioners of Dade County for assistance in the road construction.... I suggest the formation of a sub-drainage district."[45]

But in February 1915 the Dade County Commission itself began the process of creating a special road and bridge taxing district. (The fact that William Dewhurst promised commission chairman Samuel A. Belcher his choice of 1,000 acres of land out of the Dewhurst Tract probably had something to do with this.) The commission appointed a three-man board that included county tax assessor James Jaudon to investigate the viability of such a district and file a report back to the county commission. The investigatory board reported that the increase in value of the land in the district resulting from a new highway justified a $100,000 bond issue, and by the end of February Dade County established the groundwork for Road and Bridge District No. 1, with only the details of its boundaries, the final amount of the proposed bond, and the election date for the approval of the bonds yet to be determined.[46]

However, the landowners, under the direction of Jennings, continued to pursue a drainage sub-district with the same boundaries as the road and bridge district, for two reasons. One, the Internal Improvement Fund was the largest single landholder within the district (33 percent), and while it would be exempt from the taxes of the county's road and bridge district, it would not be exempt from those of a state-law based drainage sub-district. The taxes raised by the sub-district could thus be used to bolster all or part of the tax obligation of the road bonds issued by the county.

Second, fed up by Monroe County's reluctance to build roads (in 1918 it had 4 miles of paved road, the least of any county in the state) the Cape Sable landowners started pressing the Dade County Commissioners to seek a transfer of Monroe County's mainland area to Dade. The Dade County commissioners had made this request once before in 1914 and been rebuffed. They agreed to try again on a more formal basis, but without much hope. The drainage sub-district could, under Chapter 6458, be extended at a later date to include Cape Sable, regardless of whether it was in Monroe or Dade, so it could, if necessary, act as a substitute for a Monroe County road bond issue. This sub-district was formed and approved by the courts in mid-1916, although it does not appear to have ever floated any bonds.[47]

One point of contention was the route the highway should take out of the Homestead/Detroit area. William Jennings, speaking at an organizational meeting for the road and bridge district, proposed running the highway through both Detroit and Homestead. The northern terminus of the highway would actually be a mile north of downtown Homestead. It would run south through town, then turn west. A second branch would start in downtown Detroit, then also run west. Both roads would extend out four miles to today's SW 217th Avenue (then called the Longview Road), then turn south to join the Model Land Company's road seven miles southwest of Detroit. Surveyor Roy Marsh, on the other hand, suggested that the new road should follow the route the Model Land Company had built the year before. The consensus of the meeting was to follow the Jennings proposal, which added or upgraded four or five more miles of existing county roads than would have been the case had Marsh's suggestion been followed. It virtually guaranteed an overwhelming "yes" vote from Homestead, which comprised about 80 percent of the population in the road and bridge district.[48]

On April 20, the new road district and its $100,000 bond issue was approved by the voters, with Homestead approving 76 to 3, but with the newly renamed Florida City divided at 9 to 9. In June, S. A. Belcher announced that the county was ready to go forward with the sale of bonds and preparation of bid documents for the letting of the construction contract. The Monroe County Commission informed their Dade counterparts that they were indefinitely deferring action on Dade's request to transfer some or all of the Cape Sable region to Dade. The Dade commissioners decided to go ahead anyway on the road in the hopes that something could be worked out by the time the work crews reached the Monroe County line.[49]

The road and bridge district bonds were initially offered at five percent interest. "About the Ingraham Highway, so far, we have not been able to dispose of the $100,000 in the road and bridge district," reported road commissioner Belcher. As it turned out, none of the Eastern merchant banks would accept the bonds at a five percent interest rate, so they had to be reissued at six percent. They sold on November 12, to a partnership of two local banks. At the same time, the road contract itself was let. The construction contract received only two bids: the J. B. McCrary Company of Atlanta bid $93,000 and the F. A. Barbett Company bid $94,200.

Almost immediately, there was controversy. Local contractors complained that there were no plans and specifications upon which they could tender a bid. At first there was suspicion that they had been kept in the dark to favor the McCrary firm. But after investigation, the local newspapers were satisfied that the reason no plans and specifications had been shown is because there weren't any, except for the Zoll survey. McCrary and Barbette had, in essence, bid on the project blind. Later, George Pierce, McCrary's project engineer, admitted that the firm had not done any preliminary engineering or project estimation, and had submitted their bid based solely upon the available funds. In fact, he later admitted that he had never walked Zoll's stakeline, not even the parts accessible by truck on the near side of Paradise Key. A local firm, the A. B. Sanders Company, had also bid on the project, but refused to provide a lump-sum figure, instead tendering one based on mileage and volume of fill moved. It was disallowed. McCrary would come to rue the day they won the contract.[50]

There were some last minute problems getting the bonds validated by the court, but these were cleared up by mid–January, and by early February, R. F. Tatum, Homestead's mayor, was reporting that the construction crews were at work west out of town.[51] They would soon link up with the Model Land Company road, just a year old. A little dressing up, some surface improvements, and the first thirteen miles of highway down to Paradise Key would be behind them. J. B. McCrary, however, was headed for a speed bump by the name of May Mann Jennings.

••3••

A Habit of Asking Favors, Leniency, etc.

A manuscript of the "official" story describing how Royal Palm State Park was created out of Paradise Key was prepared by former governor William Jennings for his wife, May Mann Jennings, in the spring of 1916. It is plainly subtitled "Data for use in writing articles," and she repeated entire paragraphs of it verbatim in magazine stories and the dozen or more daily letters that she sent to friends, women's club colleagues and well-wishers.[1]

Almost everyone agrees with the Jennings script that Mary Barr Munroe, wife of the author, editor, and Coconut Grove pioneer Kirk Munroe, was the first to both recognize the value of Paradise Key and act on it. In 1909 she asked James Ingraham to approach Mary Kenan Flagler, Henry Flagler's wife, about donating the land around it for a park. But it was unclear exactly where Paradise Key was located, and who owned it. According to Krome's 1903 survey, it was in Township 58, Range 37, Section 15. In 1910, the Internal Improvement Fund itself surveyed the Cape Sable lands, and verified this, but shifted the location of all the townships west of range 35—where the Homestead entrance to the national park is located today—three miles south to adjust for curvature error. That was only a mile or two east of the key.[2]

In June 1910, the Fund deeded the east half of section 15 to the Florida East Coast Railroad. This was not part of the gigantic 1912 Cape Sable settlement, but was the result of another litigation agreement involving a company that the FEC had been in partnership with. That firm had gone bankrupt and been taken over by the FEC. Because the bankrupt company had defaulted on back-taxes owed the drainage district, they had forfeited their share of claims on land certificates dating back to the 1880s. Thus, when the FEC Railroad settled with the state they received only half-sections instead of entire square miles.

The June 1910 grant, typically, was "checkerboarded." The FEC received half of every other section, including half of section 15. A township is comprised of 36 square-mile sections. The adjoining section 16, which always sits in the center of each township, was reserved for the state board of education for use by the local school boards.

The large landowners, such as the Model Land Company, hoped to sell land in large blocks to corporate farmers or real estate firms. They preferred contiguous townships of land, not scattered checkerboards, so requests from owners to swap land with the Internal Improvement Fund for "blocking up" purposes had become common. In fact, they had become so frequent that the trustees had authorized the Fund's staff to negotiate such swaps on their own initiative starting in April 1910. The FEC and the Fund agreed to one of these "blocking up" swaps in late 1910, according to Jennings, transferring Paradise Key and the entire township surrounding it back into the hands of the Improvement Fund.[3] Thus, counter to Jennings's contention that the situation was irreconcilable until 1914, there initially appears to have been no reason that the Paradise Key situation could not have been rectified any time after 1910, a year after Mary Barr Monroe called it to the attention of James Ingraham and Mrs. Flagler. But there were three problems.

First, there was indeed an issue with the uncertain location of Paradise Key, but it had nothing to do with either the Improvement Fund or the FEC railroad. Instead, it concerned the ownership of section 16, the school board section. When a highly detailed survey was finally taken in 1916, it showed that Paradise Key extended almost up to the division line between sections 15 and 16. Thus, until a detailed chain-and-transit survey was done, there was no way anyone could know with certainty whether Paradise Key lay in section 15 and the north half of section 22, the next section to the south (as was eventually shown to be the case), or was slightly farther to the west in section 16 and the north half of section 21. William Krome's 1903 survey had plotted it with amazing accuracy, but the best that could be expected under the circumstances was about plus or minus 660 feet.[4] Rather inexplicably, this particular section 16 had been sold by the Dade County School Board sometime between November 1904 and July 1905 to a man named Guy Metcalf. It was the only school board reserve section that Dade County had sold off in the entire Cape Sable district.[5]

Metcalf was an intensely interesting character. He started as a newspaperman in Melbourne in 1887. In 1891 he moved the newspaper he owned to Juno, near Palm Beach, renamed it the *Tropical Sun*, and made a few friends and a lot of enemies. For enough money, he would shamelessly pitch your real estate under the guise of news, while trashing that of your competitors by announcing outbreaks of disease (human and bovine), failed crops or fictitious title challenges. He built the road from Lantana to Lemon City under contract to Dade County, which at this time included all of present Dade, Broward and Palm Beach counties. (Palm Beach County was split off from Dade County in 1907 about five miles north of the New River, then, in 1915, Broward County was carved out of Palm Beach and Dade.) For $24.50 a mile, the "construction" consisted of little more than stump clearing and filling the biggest hollows, but that was satisfactory for the job intended, i.e., to convey the coaches of his new stage line. To manage its half-way camp at the New River crossing, he hired a cousin, Frank Stranahan. Flagler's railroad killed the stage line a few years later, but by then Stranahan's ferry and trading post on the New River had already become the nucleus of the City of Fort Lauderdale.[6]

In 1902 Guy Metcalf's father Will became a judge in West Palm Beach, motivating Guy to run for the north division of the Dade school board. Once elected, he quickly gained a reputation for frequently bending and occasionally breaking the rules. In September 1902 the Internal Improvement Fund approved his application to buy land in the township in which Paradise Key was located, but the only land he apparently ever acquired was the section 16 he bought from the school board. The terms of that sale will never be known, because he later stole the book containing the minutes of the school board meetings for the years 1897–1905.

In 1912, he was forced to resign from the school board. Through the influence of his father, he was appointed postmaster at West Palm Beach, but was dismissed in 1915 for an admittedly minor rule violation. (He took a valid check as payment for stamps. Regulations said he could only accept cash.) It was possibly a political set-up. Two years later, he was elected superintendent of the Palm Beach school district. In February 1918, he was arrested for forgery, accused of writing $833 in fake receipts for science equipment to equip a new school, presumably to pocket the money. Free on bail, he went to his office at three the next morning and shot himself. He left a series of notes to family and colleagues asserting that he had no memory of what he had done. Writing that he believed he was going insane, he preferred to commit suicide. A subsequent audit indicated that only about $400 was actually unaccounted for. His claim of senile mismanagement could not be ruled out.[7]

John Small of the New York Botanical Garden recalled returning from a trip to Paradise Key in early 1909 and meeting "six or eight" men on their way into the hammock to secure it (probably by running a wire fence around it), intending to later clear it and plant a citrus grove. "I suppose, judging from the circumstances, the only obstacle which prevented them from accomplishing their purpose was their inability to get title to the tract."[8]

His speculation was undoubtedly right. This impromptu meeting took place before the Improvement Fund/FEC "blocking up" land swap in 1910, so if the men Small encountered were Metcalf's, there is a good chance that the lack of a final survey would dissuade them from damaging the hammock, especially if Small got word to Krome (who lived in Homestead) or Ingraham about what he saw. If Metcalf had trespassed onto railroad land to clear the hammock and plant a grove, he would be courting a suit or a forced purchase. Boundary lines in much of the Cape Sable district remained a matter of guesswork for many years, and a truly accurate survey grid of the whole area was never created until the federal government prepared one as part of the land acquisition process for Everglades National Park in the 1940s. In some places, township lines had to be moved by another three miles.[9]

A second factor that dramatically changed the situation in 1915 was the construction of the Model Land Company road and the subsequent formation of the Cape Sable Road and Bridge District. The third factor was, of course, the March 1913 conveyance of land from the FEC Railroad to William Jennings (41,600 acres) and William Dewhurst (24,280 acres). The Jennings Tract lay immediately southwest of the township in which Paradise Key sat. At its closest point, the Jennings Tract was slightly more than three miles from the state park. Dewhurst's land was immediately west of the Jennings Tract, about nine miles from the park.[10]

Jennings had a penchant for cheap Everglades land. In 1915 he had been accused by the secretary of the National Indian Rights Association of snapping up 100,000 acres of land in what is now Collier County through a front organization, thus preventing it from being acquired by a philanthropic organization for use as a Seminole Indian reservation. In hearings before a congressional investigatory committee in 1912, he was asked if he had received a gift of 27,000 acres from land speculator R. J. Bolles, but an objection was quickly entered by his attorney before he could answer.[11]

Although May Mann Jennings, had been active with the Florida Federation of Women's Clubs for many years, there is nothing in her voluminous papers and correspondence to indicate that she had taken an interest in Paradise Key, or in the idea of a state park to protect it, before November 1914. The "data for use in writing articles" notes that "during 1914, the land companies were building a road from Homestead through the hammock," and explains that "It became evident that if some steps were not taken at once for the protection of the Royal Palms, orchids and other rare growth to be found on the island, that the opening of the road would expose the beauty to all sort of depredation."[12]

This can be interpreted in one of two ways. The first is cynically: it fails to explain that May Mann Jennings, along with her husband, was the owner of one of those land companies whose road now endangered the hammock, and that the reason they had helped build the thing in the first place was to facilitate the sale of scores, if not hundreds, of small truck farm plots just five miles down the road. The other interpretation is more forgiving. The surveyors' trail to Camp Jackson had existed since Krome's 1903 survey expedition. John Small noted that orchid and palm poaching had already become a problem, even before the causeway across Taylor Slough was built. The record proves that May Mann Jennings did work very hard to create the park and keep it going, mostly by, quite frankly, shamelessly begging for money and keeping creditors at bay. Until the state started to give the park a regular monthly operating allowance in 1918, it always teetered on the edge of insolvency. It is very possible that Mrs. Jennings did not learn of Paradise Key until late 1914, and that her interest was piqued by more perceptive, but less influential, proto-conservationists such as Krome, John Small, John T. Gifford, Charles Simpson, the Munroes and others.

Moreover, keep in mind that by the standards of the era, the idea of a "park" did not encompass our current concept of a "wilderness preserve." A few of Mrs. Jennings's friends, especially Charles T. Simpson, complained of the "insane desire to do SOMETHING, ANYTHING to improve, to make a change, to push in with our supposed desire, to rectify the failings of nature." His plan for Paradise Key was comprised of three words: LET IT ALONE. No road. No lodge. No ponds. No walls. No plantings. No plant nursery. Nothing. Of course, he was considered something of a crank.[13] What he was suggesting was considered akin to taking a beautiful painting and turning it towards the wall. Any park was fundamentally judged on how well it served anthropocentric purposes. A primary purpose may be to

Charles Mosier, hired by the Florida Federation of Women's Clubs to be the first superintendent of the Royal Palm State Park, in front of the tent he and his family lived in from 1916 until the lodge was built in April 1917. (Photographer: John K. Small. Florida Division of Library and Information Services, No. SM-0416.)

preserve and protect a unique attribute of nature, but this was done so it could be displayed and enjoyed by people, not to keep it *from* people.

In December 1914, the state's Internal Improvement Fund reserved the one and a half sections containing the hammock for the women's clubs and authorized Frank Powers and W. J. Tweedell to act as interim wardens to prevent trespassers from damaging the place. On December 28, Mrs. Jennings, along with Mary Barr Munroe and several friends, visited Paradise Key by automobile. According to William Jennings, this is the first time his wife had ever been there.[14]

In June 1915, the legislature approved a bill granting fee simple ownership of the 960 acres to the women's clubs and designating the hammock the Royal Palm State Park, but it failed to appropriate any funds for the park's improvement or maintenance. Mrs. Jennings desperately, but unsuccessfully, sought alternative sources of operating revenues, including the Federal Forest Reserve Act and the state's forestry fund.[15] In the end, Mrs. Jennings was left with just one source of funds, the so-called Flagler land endowment

If the bill granting the land to the women's clubs passed, Mrs. Flagler had promised to give the organization another 960 acres to be used as an endowment to support it, but only if the legislature made the conveyance irrevocable. The intent was to provide land that could be rented for farming, a tropical nursery, or other profit-making purposes. The legislation proved satisfactory to Mrs. Flagler, but none of the Flagler enterprises owned land immediately adjacent to the park. In August, after a land inventory, the Model Land Company offered Mrs. Jennings her choice of three parcels, two of them about three miles southeast of the park, and the third about the same distance to the southwest. "These are the nearest lands the Model Land Co. owns to the Palm Hammock and are good farming lands," explained Frank Powers, "all are good."[16]

However, upon consulting local Homestead engineer Roy Marsh, Mrs. Jennings was advised that the "Zoll [1914 road] survey was made in an exceptionally dry time, so the tracts offered may have shown up as much more desirable there than at any time when I have been on them." Each time Marsh had visited the three sites, the water had been "no less than shoe-top deep." Moreover, the field notes from Jackson's 1847 survey and John William's subsequent 1874 survey of the same general area indicated that this was their more-or-less permanent condition. Although Mrs. Flagler and the Model Land Company had selected them on the logical grounds that they were the best and closest sites available, they were not promising. Therefore Marsh agreed with Mrs. Jennings's suggestion that the Internal Improvement Fund swap the lands donated by Mrs. Flagler with a same-sized parcel owned by the state lying immediately southwest of the new park. "This arrangement I would consider advantageous," concluded Marsh, "because it is likely that the road to Cape Sable will be built through one or both of these sections (20–21)."[17]

So Mrs. Jennings appeared before the trustees of the Internal Improvement Fund and asked them to swap one of the 960 acre parcels belonging to Mrs. Flagler with land adjacent to park. They agreed. Afterwards, Mrs. Jennings wrote a friend that the most notable feature of the new configuration is that "now that the State [has] agreed to exchange the land Mrs. Flagler gave us for a section and a half adjoining the park ... the new road will run rather diagonally, which will give us about two miles and a quarter of the hard surfaced road."[18]

The new parcel allowed the road to take the shortest possible path through the hammock proper (due east-west), then turn southwest immediately upon exiting it without entering Metcalf's land. The road continued southwest for four miles before turning due west again—at which point it ran straight through the northern third of the Jennings Tract for six miles, then entered the Dewhurst Tract. After running west through Dewhurst's land for two miles, it turned south at a corner comprised of two 45-degree bends separated by a couple hundred feet. A few years after the canal was finished, the landowner built a novel cement bridge at the bend, and the turn south became known after about 1922 as the "cement bridge." After running due south through the Dewhurst Tract for four miles it exited to the south, after which it curved southwest at a 45-degree bend towards Flamingo.

Except for the land north of the highway, which lay on the south flank of Long Pine Key, the Jennings Tract was wet every rainy season. Although it looked dead flat, the highway cut across a series of low ridges and shallow draws. The ridges were dry year-round, the draws seasonally inundated, as was the land south of the road. Dewhurst's tract, being almost adjacent to Whitewater Bay was usually wet year-round. The Cape Sable road would have been far easier to build had it not turned south after passing through the new state park, but instead had run atop Long Pine Key, where William Krome had platted the railroad in 1903, near where today's Research Road is located within the national park.

In fact, as Charles Simpson pointed out in 1916, from an engineering point of view, just following the 1903 railroad grade and avoiding Paradise Key altogether would have had a shorter crossing of Taylor Slough and an easier route atop Long Pine Key. Much of this was very close to the route used by the Park Service when they rebuilt the main road in 1956.[19] But of course, this would have circumvented all of the Jennings Tract and most of the Dewhurst land, running the road across land then owned by the Improvement Fund and various smallholders.

To be fair, none of the women's club leadership seriously considered the possibility of evicting the road from the state park. "I am proud of the fact that it is to be such a splendid road," wrote May Mann Jennings, "of course, as the road is finished, we will have more people." On the way back from their excursion to Paradise Key in December 1914, Mary Barr Munroe proposed that the road should be named the "Ingraham Highway." Six months later, after the county commissioners had approved the creation of the Cape Sable Road and Bridge District, they agreed to name the hard-surfaced highway, at least that portion in Dade County, after Ingraham. The road's name north of Homestead became fragmented—only a small stretch of the coastal highway in Coral Gables still retains the name "Ingraham Highway," but it became indelibly affixed to the Cape Sable road—the highway from Homestead to Flamingo.[20]

In March 1916 Mrs. Jennings hired a caretaker for the park, "We do not want to have a caretaker who has kith or kin, or any local interest," Mrs. Jennings wrote Mrs. John Gifford, "as far as I am concerned I am still bent on securing Mr. Mosier." The Federation of Women's Clubs would have preferred to hire a local, such as someone from the Roberts or Irwin clans, who could work for part of the year, then go back to farming or fishing during the off-season, but Mrs. Jennings believed that would just invite more of the same type of abuse that John Small and Charles Simpson had warned of. "If we get tangled up locally as to the caretaker, we might have some very serious complications," she cautioned.[21]

Mrs. Jennings, of course, got her way. Charles Mosier, a botanist by training, had worked at Viscaya, Charles Deering's palatial mansion on Biscayne Bay, and had accompanied John Small and David Fairchild on several of their early reconnaissance trips through the region. After informing Moser that he would be interviewed at "Miss Andre's Music Studio" on March 24th, she added that "you understand that these are formalities to which we have to submit, and I think there is no doubt of your employment, in fact we are all anxious for you to take up the work." By the end of the month Mosier and his family had moved out to the new park and set up housekeeping in a tent.[22]

Two days after Christmas, 1915, McCrary's local project manager asked Mrs. Jennings if his men could camp in the park while they worked their way through that stretch. She had no objection, provided that they used only fallen wood for firewood and did not cut any of the standing timber. In fact, at that point, the women's clubs were having difficulty raising enough money to hire Mr. Moser and erect a permanent lodge building, and Mrs. Jennings preferred to have McCrary's men on-site to watch over the park than leave it unattended.[23]

In February 1916, Homestead mayor R. F. Tatum reported to Mrs. Jennings that McCrary's men had started working their way towards the park. He suggested that the women's clubs take advantage of their availability and hire them to dredge a canal around the key and use the spoil to build a grand circumferential boulevard. "This would not only drain the land, but would furnish a boat course and automobile track and fishing grounds—and give access to all parts of the land." Mrs. Jennings replied that "your suggestion about the canal and boulevard around the park has been one of my dearest dreams, but I hardly dared think of it on account of the expense." It would be easy to dismiss Mrs. Jennings's response as simple politeness, except that she did, in fact, ask the McCrary Company to prepare a bid on work matching Tatum's description.[24]

In April, George Pierce, the McCrary project engineer at the time, hired Col. Zoll to do a detailed survey of the park, probably the first ever done, and prepare an estimate of "what the cost of digging a canal 10 or 20 feet wide around the park will be, leaving 100 feet drive way, and throwing the dirt to the middle of the drive and rolling same." Zoll's detailed map indicated that the circumference of the hammock was 14,520 feet (2.75 miles). The estimated cost of the canal and road was $19,226, assuming the work was done while the equipment was already on-site for the highway work. Mrs. Jennings was very grateful for Mr. Pierce's consideration and for the detailed survey, which she was sure Mr. Moser would find most helpful. And that was as far as the idea went. Keep in mind that at this point the total annual budget for the park, not including the construction of the lodge, was less than $2,000 a year.[25]

The Florida State Federation of Women's Clubs was scheduled to meet in Miami on November 21–22, 1916, so November 23 was scheduled as the official dedication ceremony for Royal Palm State Palm. By extension, this also became the unofficial deadline for the completion of the highway from Homestead to the park. In April, Mrs. Jennings wrote to Mrs. John Gifford that "there were threatened injunctions" over the quality of the road being built, and that the complaints had grown so numerous that William Jennings (The McCrary firm's Florida lawyer) had met with George Pierce in Jacksonville, urging him to go down to Homestead and straighten things out. "I imagine, without knowing it, that they are waiting to finish some contract elsewhere, so that they can put the proper machinery on the road," Mrs. Jennings explained. That was probably true. The McCrary company had won the bid on the Tamiami Trail and had started work on it in September, experimenting briefly with various land-based excavators before switching a floating dredge.[26]

An inspection trip was taken by several of the women's club's luminaries on May 14, 1916. The reporter from the *Miami Metropolis* commented that while it "is a most beautiful spot, those Miamians who visited the park yesterday will forego the pleasures of the place until a better road is built." The reporter quoted one of the invited guests, C. L. Benedict, as saying that "the road from Florida City to the park is without question the roughest over which he has ever traveled."[27]

For months Mrs. Jennings had been bombarding the caretaker, Mr. Mosier, and the McCrary project managers with detailed instructions as to how the road was to wind around the trees in the park; often by splitting it to create a single, one-way lane on each side of a

The newly completed county-built Ingraham Highway in Royal Palm State Park, late 1916 or early 1917. Compare this to the road built a year earlier by the Model Land Company. (Photographer: John K. Small. Florida Division of Library and Information Services, No. SM-0300.)

particularly attractive oak tree, for example. Too often for her satisfaction the field crews ignored her. Mrs. Jennings finally put her foot down and ordered that all roadwork within in the park be suspended on July 16. However, it is possible that the dispute really was over whether McCrary was obligated to prepare a foundation pad for the new lodge as part of its contract. In any event, within a week George Pierce had met with Mosier and agreed to have his crews do all the clearing by hand, avoid the valuable trees, and clear sites for the lodge and support structures. The McCrary crews expected to have the road "rocked to the hammock some time next month [August] but not finished."[28]

McCrary crossed Taylor Slough with an earthen embankment punctuated with two timber bridges to let the water through. (These bridges were replaced with higher, heavier timber spans in 1948.)[29] In 2005, both bridges and most of the embankment within Taylor Slough was removed to help restore its historic water flow. The crews doing the work discovered that under the crushed-stone embankment was a set of pilings. These were apparently the remnants of the plank causeway built for the first road of the Model Land Company in 1914–15. It appears that when the McCrary crews came through, they pulled up the plank surface of the old causeway and used it for fuel in its steam-powered equipment, after which the remainder was simply buried under fill.[30] Satellite photos of Taylor Slough clearly indicate where the embankment was located, and the scour marks left by water flow for almost a century through the bottlenecks where the bridges had been.

As the earlier road crew had found, the Taylor Slough was a daunting obstacle. In mid–July McCrary brought in a second excavator. By mid–November, with the Federation of Women's Clubs convention looming, assistant county engineer A. O. Duncan reported that "every man and every piece of road-making equipment was at work," including "graders, scarifiers, and rollers." County Road Commissioner Tweedell authorized the transfer of

Crossing the recently completed rock causeway across Taylor Slough to the new Royal Palm State Park, 1917. Left to right: Lewis Reed, Mr. Hallum, Mrs. Hallum, Ollie [probably Olivia] Reed, Anna Speyer Reed. (Photographer unknown. Florida Division of Library and Information Services, No. N031670.)

county crews and equipment to help. In the end, McCrary finished the final 2,000 feet in the last ten days. It was a road, sort of. Although it was enough to get the 400 officials and guests down to the dedication of the new state park, "the road to the south of Florida City is in terrible shape," complained May Mann Jennings, a few weeks after the conventioneers had left town. "The road to the park is still in an unfinished condition."[31]

Worse, the McCrary company had run out of time. Technically, the contract with Dade County had expired on November 9, twelve days before the dedication ceremony, and under the terms of the contract the McCrary Firm was subject to a penalty of $10 per day. That was not for the work between Homestead and the park; it was for the entire road down to Monroe County. According to the county engineer's estimate, the contract was only 41 percent complete. That was based on mileage, and given the conditions that lay on the far side of the park, it was a deep underestimation of the situation. Nevertheless, County Commissioner Tweedell recommended to his fellow commissioners that a six-month extension be granted, provided that the J. B. McCrary Company pay the costs of maintaining on-site the county's supervising engineer, about $175 per month. The company agreed, as paying for the engineer amounted to only about half of the penalty schedule. J. B. McCrary received a six-month extension to early June 1917.[32] After a year on the job, McCrary's real work was just beginning.

* * * * *

After the dedication ceremony, progress virtually ground to a halt. Frederick Morse reported to James Ingraham in St. Augustine that:

> McCrary sub-leased to Boyd & Bradshaw and they sub-leased to [E. E.] Collins. Both of these parties have fallen down. McCrary has been waiting for a settlement with Bradshaw's bondsman, but Mr. C. B. Chinn, McCrary's local representative, thinks they will have to complete the road and then sue Bradshaw's bondsman. The County gave 6 month's extension [on] December 9 to McCrary, but this was before McCrary's subcontractors had fallen through. It will probably take from 6 to 10 months longer to complete the work, unless arrangements can be made to put dredges on both ends.[33]

The J. B. McCrary Engineering Company was, in essence, a construction broker. It bid on municipal improvement projects, often participating in their bond financing. It then subcontracted out the actual work. Boyd & Bradshaw was a regional municipal infrastructure contractor out of Columbia, Mississippi. E. E. Collins was a Miami-based paving outfit. It appears that both Boyd & Bradshaw and Collins had been on the job from the start, but for the dredge-based excavation on the far side of the park, Collins had hired its own subcontractor, C. S. Brady. But when Brady started submitting bills, Boyd & Bradshaw refused to pay; they had run out of money.

Boyd & Bradshaw's default was actually a benefit for J. B. McCrary. Contrary to what they told Frederick Morse, records show that Boyd & Bradshaw's bonding house paid McCrary $20,000 for their client's default, money McCrary badly needed.[34] McCrary apparently fired everybody and brought in their own foreman, Harry Freeman, a long-time employee of the firm. George Pierce and Col. Zoll were out.[35]

In February, Pierce's replacement, C. B. Chinn, wrote the county commissioners that McCrary had purchased a large dredge and planned to have it in operation "within the next thirty days." But in June, when the contract extension ran out, the county engineer reported that McCrary had advanced only 3.6 percent towards the completion of the project since the beginning of 1917. The "large dredge" turned out to be a "second hand outfit" that the company took delivery of in crates, requiring the better part of six months to assemble. Frank Pepper wrote William Dewhurst that even after they had figured out how to put it together and get it working they had only gone a total of 1,500 feet, and were making headway at a rate of only about 150 to 300 feet per day. Apparently, the dredge they bought was too big for a road canal, drawing more water than was needed to provide the required volume of fill. In other words, the crew had to dig the canal to a size determined, not by the amount of fill actually needed to build the road, but by the depth of water necessary to float the dredge. A good portion of the spoil thrown to the side of the canal was unnecessary. The McCrary engineers hoped the situation would improve when as they moved into the rainy season.[36]

At this point, William Dewhurst finally had enough. Back in June, he had complained to real estate agent Frederick Morse that he could have sold 12,000 acres of land to a group of "Chicago people" for $150,000 but lost out to a competing tract "which they are likely to find much less salable" because the highway had not yet been run through his property. In August he went before the Dade County Commission to complain about McCrary's dawdling. They asked J. B. McCrary himself to come down from Atlanta and explain the situation at the next commission meeting, not only for the Cape Sable road, but also for the Tamiami Trail project, which was also behind schedule.[37]

The company instead sent J. A. McCrary, the firm's vice-president and Joseph Boyd McCrary's brother. He frankly admitted that nobody from the firm had inspected the survey

The first floating dredge put to work on the Ingraham Highway on the far side of the Royal Palm State Park by the J. B. McCrary Company, 1917. John Boyd McCrary, in white shirt, stands on the right. (Photographer: John K. Small. Florida Division of Library and Information Services, No. SMx-0429.)

line of the Ingraham Highway before they bid on it, that they had prepared their bid based solely upon the available funds, and had spent six to seven times more than the $1,000 in contingency funds allowed in the contract to fill the causeway across Taylor Slough. J. A. McCrary's first response to the Commissioners' concerns was his own complaint that his firm was being skewered in the local press, especially over "inside" reports that the Ingraham Highway and Tamiami Trail would take years to finish. "Did that information come from the County Engineer?" Commissioner Tweedell asked the reporter from the *Miami Metropolis*. "No sir," he replied, "we get very little information from Mr. Crabtree."

"Then where did the information about the Tamiami Trail come from?"

"From a representative of the McCrary Engineering Corporation."[38]

Mr. McCrary started to deflate a little at that point.

However, he gamely stuck to the script his brother sent him down with. He requested that the firm be reimbursed for the full cost of the Taylor Slough cost overrun. Chairman Burr rather brusquely brushed this aside by pointing to Mr. Crabtree's report that the McCrary firm had been billing the county for only $500 to $600 in work during each of the last six months. So when had this $7,000 been expended?

McCrary switched to a counterproposal. There remained about $1,500 to finish out the segment between Homestead and the park. McCrary proposed that the firm complete that work, that the County pay the $1,500, and that the remainder of the contract then be canceled. The county could then re-issue a new contract for the rest of the road. Asked whether his firm would sign such a contract, McCrary refused to answer.

Several Homestead area residents had the chance to throw some stones, complaining that they had provided professional services or labor at the request of George Pierce, then been told by the subcontractor, Boyd & Bradshaw, that they, Boyd & Bradshaw, were not responsible for promises made by J. B. McCrary. When they went directly to McCrary, they were told that all billing went through Boyd & Bradshaw. (Col. Zoll, for example, eventually had to sue McCrary for $3,300, winning $1,500.) The Commissioners ordered McCrary to stick to their existing contract, and to get it done promptly, or they would go to McCrary's bondsman. By now J. A. was completely beaten down.

"Just suspend judgment and give us a chance," McCrary whined at the end of the meeting, "will you do that, Mr. Newpaper man?"

"We'll say what we please," replied the triumphant *Metropolis* reporter.

Two weeks later the county commission, having received its pound of flesh, granted a second contract extension, for one year, and for all practical purposes, waived the penalty clause for late performance. "I am glad to say that we are now in a position definitely advise that this work can be completed within twelve months," wrote J. A. McCrary from Atlanta on September first, thanking the commissioners for their one-year contract extension.[39]

Meanwhile, at the park, May Mann Jennings was having her own problems. Always audacious, she had ordered Mr. Mosier to go ahead and hire a contractor to have the lodge built before the Federation of Women's Clubs actually had the money to pay for it. "I have a letter from Mr. Skill from the Star Lumber Company [of Miami], Mrs. Jennings wrote to Mrs. Loveland of Homestead, Chairwoman of the Park Committee, in March 1917. "He has written me a very sharp letter about what he will proceed to do with us if we do not pay the lumber bill." Mrs. Jennings and several of her wealthier colleagues passed the hat and came up with the money in a week or so. The lodge was finished two months later, but the economizing eventually caught up with them. Within two years the septic tank started acting up and Mrs. Jennings and the park committee had to face the fact that they had simply installed one that was too small to handle the crowds that were using the park. A new one would have to be built. "Of course, even then it will have to be cleaned out occasionally … which costs $120," she rued.[40]

* * * * *

In December, James Ingraham wrote Frank Powers that he wanted to make an overland trip "with a Ford automobile" from Homestead to the East Cape, returning by boat and rail through the Florida Keys. Powers passed on the letter to Frederick Morse, who had just returned from the McCrary work site. Morse warned Ingraham that it "would be a practically impossible trip" because "you would have to walk several miles." The dredging crew was about 2,000 feet from the start of the Jennings Tract, and one could drive to within a mile or so of the dredge "but the last two or three miles of the trip [would be] pretty rough."[41]

This must have been a sobering report. The dredge was only about five miles past the state park, a mile or so ahead of the road-making crew. McCrary had built less than four miles of drivable road in sixteen months. Only nine months remained in its latest contract extension. The dredge was still 22 miles from Flamingo; 16 miles from Monroe County. Morse noted that the work crew was moving at a rate of about three-quarters of a mile a month, roughly 165 feet a day. Interestingly, he reported that a party of hunters had driven cross-country atop Long Pine Key to a point about six miles farther west than the dredge, indicating just how much better that route was then the lower, wetter one across the Jennings and Dewhurst lands five miles farther south. Two months earlier the chairman of the Dade County Commission, E. D. Burr, publicly announced that he regretted his previous decision to give the McCrary Company a contract extension, and asked the County Attorney to contract McCrary's bonding house about the possibility of filing for a contract default.[42]

In fairness to the McCrary firm, they were handicapped by two factors. First, as the European war expanded into World War I, an increasing proportion of the labor force was being pulled away into well-paying defense-related work, including construction projects, and after mid–1918, into the military. Road work through a swamp in the poorly paying deep south was not attractive to skilled laborers, such as heavy equipment operators. The same was true for materials. Beginning September 1918, any road project that could not be completed by November was required to secure a special federal materials permit through its state's highway department, and the start of any new highway project was prohibited.[43]

Second, the estimates drawn up by Hobart Crabtree in 1915 had anticipated that work would start from both the Flamingo and Homestead ends of the road. But Monroe County insisted that they would not help pay for the road. The projected end of highway at the Dade/Monroe border was in the middle of an inaccessible wetland near West Lake, so the south end of the road had to be started at Flamingo, because there was no other way to get men and equipment to the Dade/Monroe line. Thus, the only way the road could be built from both ends was if someone blinked in the three-way staring contest between Dade, Monroe and the Model Land Co. and agreed to pay for the five miles of road between Flamingo and the county line, and nobody backed down. So the dredge creeped west and south, crippled by labor and dynamite shortages, working one shift per day.[44]

In February 1918, the dredge passed the site of "Jennings Grove," a homestead being laid out on a small rise of prairie land on the north side of the highway about eight miles past the state park. The Jennings built it in 1919 as a winter home, and presumably, a showplace for prospective land customers. About 150 acres was eventually planted as a citrus orchard with another 150 acres laid out in row crops.[45] Bargeman Lawrence Will, driving from Homestead to Flamingo in the early 1920s, described it:

> Beyond this key [the state park] spread a wide panorama of open prairie, studded with occasional islands of pine, cabbage palm or dense jungle growth. Here the lime rock was, in places, covered with a thin coating of soil. Old fields ridged for tomatoes showed where crops had been planted in past years. Not a human habitation did we discover until about halfway to our destination. I was surprised to see, in this desert prairie, a large two-story house with wide veranda, surrounded by a small grove of citrus trees, and all bordered and set off by rows of young cocoanut palms. Flower gardens proclaimed the presence of a woman in this dismal place. I was told the grove was owned by W. S. Jennings, ex-governor of Florida. It was an incongruous sight. This large house and well-tended grove dropped here in what appeared to be, without doubt, the most worthless and inconvenient spot in the whole Everglades.[46]

Nothing remains of Jennings Grove today. A photograph taken in 1932 shows what may be the Jennings house in the distance empty and abandoned, but maps of the "hole-in-the-donut" agricultural area, comprised of landowners on and around Long Pine Key who were allowed to continue using their lands until the 1970s, indicates that Jennings Grove is "active agricultural land" in both 1940 and 1952, although by 1952 it is almost the last holdout; virtually all its neighbors are shown as "inactive/abandoned." Monthly reports of the park superintendent make reference to the "Jennings Plantation," but as a landmark; there is no mention of anyone actually living there. Unlike the lodge at the state park, which was moved to Homestead in the 1950s after its temporary service as the first Everglades National Park headquarters ended, the fate of the Jennings home is unknown. (The state park lodge, known for many years as "Jack's Hotel" after the move, was mortally wounded by Hurricane Andrew in 1992.)[47]

Will's comments regarding the general bleakness of the landscape and the abandoned tomato fields generally echo the correspondence between the Model Land Company and its sales agents during the 1915–19 period, which indicates that the firm was having difficulty selling Cape Sable land to smallholders. The abandoned tomato fields Will referred to were those that Frank Powers had commented on in 1916; sales he had closed only to have the buyers demand land swaps for tracts closer to Florida City because the highway hadn't been put through yet. Lawrence Will was not the only one struck with the desolation along the new road. Sidney Harrison, secretary-treasurer of the Model Land Company, writing to Frank Pepper in 1920 to thank him for taking the time to drive a prospective client down past Jennings Grove to the Dewhurst Tract, commented that "It is true that if Mr. Kirtland only saw the Ingraham Highway from Homestead to the Monroe County line then he saw the worst conditions and worst lands in the entire district."[48]

What finally got the McCrary Company moving in earnest starting in 1917 was the intercession of the Model Land Company. In mid–January, Dewhurst, Ingraham, and Jennings met with J. B. McCrary personally at the construction site. "Mr. McCrary, the contractor," reported Ingraham, "asked us to consider a proposition he is making for the continuation of the Highway into Monroe County." The Dade County commissioners had just approved negotiations for a new contract for the McCrary firm, extending the deadline and altering some of its terms. However, the firm and the county attorney's office were still working out terms, and the three landowners hoped to strike their own deal that would work in concert with the county agreement.

James Ingraham telegraphed Frederick Morse in mid–April to ask him to go by County Attorney McCaskell's office and get a copy of the proposed contract modification. Morse replied that the terms had already been settled and that the J. B. McCrary firm had signed it; all that was needed was a county commission vote of approval. Did Ingraham still need a copy in a hurry? If so, Morse would send a secretary to McCaskell's office to transcribe it. Ingraham replied that if the contract had already been settled, that would not be necessary. Ingraham was clearly hoping to use information about the new Dade contract to get the best possible deal in his negotiations with McCrary. Ingraham, acting on behalf of the Model Land Company, Dewhurst and Jennings, went ahead and signed his own agreement with the McCrary Company in May 1918.[49]

This was not an insignificant agreement: two later accounts both state that the Model Land Company contract was for $120,000. Most of this was for roadwork within Monroe County; only $17,810 was paid for work in Dade County.[50] The reason that the Model Land Company was willing to take such a large stake was because Monroe County had finally expressed a willingness to float bonds to build their portion of the road. Unfortunately, its confidence proved to be misplaced.

It is unclear whether the Model Land Company had two contracts with the J. B. McCrary Company, or one contract with two separate parts. The first, apparently a supplement to the Dade County contract of April-May 1918, specified that the Ingraham Highway would be completed to the Dade-Monroe line no later than December 31, 1918. William Dewhurst claimed that it contained a huge fifty percent retainage clause, but in the end the Model Land Company only withheld the traditional ten percent. The second part was a contract to extend the canal and road from the Monroe line to Flamingo, roughly five miles southwest.[51]

In the fall of 1918, the Monroe County Commission did authorize the issuance of $65,000 in bonds, but their sale was repeatedly delayed. When Frederick Morse informally asked a friend, Key West City Auditor E. W. Russell, to check on their status, Russell replied that he had been told by the Monroe county clerk that a tacit agreement had previously been struck with James Ingraham that the bonds would not be put up for sale on the market, but would instead be purchased privately by the big Cape Sable landowners. Moreover, the bonds would not be issued as general obligation bonds, but would be backed only by the taxing power of a limited-area special road district that would be formed by the major landowners served by the highway.[52]

In other words, Monroe County's plan was for the big landowners to essentially loan the county the money to build the road by buying all the bonds. Then, these same landowners (or, presumably, their clients, who would buy the abutting land after the road was done) would provide, though a surtax on their property taxes, the money to retire the bonds. But because these were not general obligation bonds, backed by the total taxing power of the county, but rather special-district bonds, every taxpayer was dependent on the uniform solvency of all other landowners in the road district. Each landowner who defaulted on his taxes shifted the burden of meeting the bond payments to the remaining landowners. Their tax bills would go up. As their bills went up, others, many of whom were just eking out a living, would have to walk away and also default, thereby creating an ever-shrinking pool of taxpayers to support the bonds. Very quickly, a tip-over point would be reached where the debt service on the outstanding bonds would exceed the rational value of anybody's property, creating a dead zone of untouchable land until the state stepped in and either paid off or canceled the bonds.

(In fact, the State of Florida was forced to restructure its gas tax after the Great Crash of 1929 so that half of the six cents per gallon collected for roads went to the counties, not for new construction or road maintenance, but so they could pay off all the outstanding bonds they had issued through their special road and bridge districts since 1915. Reportedly, their total indebtedness came to $160 million, close to ten times the annual disbursement of the state road department in 1928.)[53]

"This is the first time that I have heard or understood that it was agreed that the land owners were to buy these bonds," wrote the Model Land Company's secretary, Sidney

Harrison, in reply to Morse's report. "I do not believe Mr. Ingraham ever had any such understanding. I am sure he had not, I do not believe any other landowners in Monroe County had any such understanding." By fall 1919 the press reported that "the matter had apparently been dropped."[54] However, this left the Model Land Company with a much bigger obligation than it had originally intended. With a $120,000 proposed contract, the Model Land Co. planned to pay half and anticipated that Monroe County would pay the other half with the $65,000 bond issue. Now, because it had rushed to try to get its contract piggybacked on top of the modified Dade County contract, it was on the hook for the whole $120,000.

·· 4 ··

"This you failed to do"

It had taken from November 1916 to February 1918 to go seven miles from the state park to a point just short of Jennings Grove. But by November 1918 the dredge had traversed the remaining four miles across the Jennings's land, gone two miles into the Dewhurst Tract and completed the turn south. In March 1919 Dewhurst succeeded in selling much of the north half of his tract to a consortium of Miami investors called the Paradise Prairie Land Company. Thomas Benson, a Miami lawyer, administered it on behalf of Matthew McBride, a local hotel owner, and E. J. Monahan, an engineer.[1] Shortly thereafter, they built a bridge over the canal to access their land to the north using native limestone crushed into powder and burned in a kiln to make cement. It worked, and the corner became known as the "Cement Bridge."[2] From the future site of Cement Bridge, McCrary's crew had gone another three miles south and was about two miles from exiting the south side of the Dewhurst Tract. That was ten miles in just nine months. On the other hand, the construction of the road itself lagged far behind. While the dredge was now about seventeen miles below the park, Frank Pepper reported that the road was drivable only as far as Jennings Grove, eight miles below the park, in November 1918.[3]

Bargeman Lawrence Will later described the setup that the McCrary crews were now using. The dredge was a type known as an American Steel, or A-Frame, "once very popular in the Glades." Steel hulled, nine feet wide and forty feet long, its steam boiler drove an articulated-arm digging bucket and four "spuds," extension feet that withdrew onboard so the barge could float. ("American Steel" was a brand name; the A-Frame that carried the stress of the bucket arm was actually made of timber.) The dredge was so top-heavy that it would capsize if its crew attempted to swing or extend the bucket arm without lowering the spuds, let alone try to dig with it. Although land-based excavators were rapidly switching over to gas or diesel power, the 'glades barges were still true "steam shovels," which meant they needed wood and a constant supply of fresh water. Lots of it—about 750 gallons a day. That wouldn't appear to be a problem in the Everglades, but the water had to be fresh and clean. If it was contaminated, especially if it was brackish, it would foam up in the boiler pipes and lose its head of steam. Everything would come to a halt until the fireman could get a head back up. Pressing a boiler too hard with bad water could cause it to blow.[4]

The "digger" operated the bucket arm from his stand up front. He lowered the spuds, dug up the marl rock, and swinging the arm to the side, deposited it on whichever bank the road was supposed to run. When a nine-foot wide bite at the front of the canal had been made, the spuds were raised, the operator dropped the bucket straight in front of the dredge, and pulled it back. With the dredge unmoored, it actually pulled the whole rig forward. This was repeated a few times, and with the spuds lowered again, digging resumed.

The crew lived in a houseboat, eight feet wide and thirty feet long. Will described the average crew quarters:

> A wide screened window extended the length of each side. These windows were covered with shutters of tattered canvas, which when raised, served as awnings. A screened vestibule at one end contained a bench for the water bucket and wash bowl. A toilet overhung the other. Inside the only furnishings consisted of sixteen bunks, made of one inch boards supported at the ends so they would have a little "give" in the middle. They were furnished with thin mattresses of cotton which compared unfavorably with the straw filled bed tick with which some of us were acquainted with in the army. This houseboat was erected on a steel barge, which although the top was barely above water when loaded, never sank, and strangely, did not even leak.[5]

A converted school bus or floating cook-house alternated at various times as mobile kitchen and dining hall.

A minor crisis arose as the crew completed the Cement Bridge corners from westward to the south. The canal had been on the north (right-hand) side of the road. On the run south, they were planning to switch over to the left. All reports to date indicated that during the wet season the water flow moved from northeast to southwest into Whitewater Bay as part of the Shark River Slough. A canal on the east side of the road canal would catch that water and carry it south to Florida Bay. But real estate agent Frank Powers insisted that during the dry season, salt water flowed to the east away from Whitewater Bay. Powers convinced William Dewhurst that the canal should go on the west side of the highway. (In actuality, saltwater was starting to infiltrate north, out of Florida Bay, farther and farther each year as the historical press of fresh water from the north was being siphoned off by the new reclamation canals being dug across the upper Everglades.)

McCrary himself, along with Hobart Crabtree, the county engineer, drove down to the dredge and took a small boat about half-way to West Lake. Their joint conclusion was that moving the embankment wouldn't make any difference: everything south of Township 59, starting about five or six miles south of the Cement Bridge, was already permanently brackish. If true, that meant it was useless as farmland. Dewhurst started courting the eastern sporting crowd about the possibility of selling the rest of his holdings for a gigantic game preserve, his dreams of $15.00 an acre slowly starting to slip away.[6]

In September 1918, J. B. McCrary appeared before the Board of County Commissioners again and asked that the retainage on both the Tamiami Trail and Ingraham Highway projects be waived. In other words, he asked that they be paid for 100 percent of the work billed and approved by the county engineer instead of having ten percent held back until the project was completed. McCrary cited labor shortages and higher costs for explosives due to the war. He did not tell the board that his firm now had a separate contract with the Model Land Company, or at least it did not come out at the commission meeting. The commission compromised, agreeing to release the accrued retainage to date (about $6,800 for the Ingraham, $12,800 for the Trail), but not agreeing to any permanent change in the contract terms; retainage would continue to be withheld on future payments.[7]

McCrary immediately ignored the second condition. In December, the Third National Bank of Atlanta sent the Dade commissioners a request for payment in the amount of $7,045, the retainage accrued on the Ingraham Highway project as of December 1. Instead of explaining that only $6,800 had been authorized, the Clerk of the Board brusquely replied that "this money is not yet due the J. B. McCrary Company, and will not be due until the final completion of the contract and it is not known at this time just what will be due, and in view of all the circumstances in connection with the contract, the board does not deem it advisable at this time to comply with the request and agree to pay any part of the money retained."[8]

This appeared to be something of an overreaction. However, on October 1, less than a month after asking for payment of the retainage on both projects, J. B. McCrary ordered that work be shut down on the Tamiami Trail. If they had not secured the Model Land Co. contract on the Ingraham Highway, there is a good chance they would have done the same thing on that project as well.

Unfortunately, the McCrary brothers made the mistake of not getting their retainage payments *before* they shut down their Tamiami Trail construction. They had the two board resolutions approving the payments, but resolutions weren't formal contract amendments. They were out $19,000. Six months later, McCrary went to the Bank of Bay Biscayne in Miami, one of the two banks that had underwritten the highway bonds for the Ingraham Highway, and borrowed $7,500 against the $8,611 in retainage that the county owned on work up to April 1, 1919. That was a steep fifteen percent discount rate, but on the other hand, given the odds of McCrary finishing the job and collecting its retainage, it was fully warranted.[9]

* * * * *

The January 1, 1919, completion date came and went. In March, J. B. McCrary reported that his men were less than four miles from the county line. In May, Frank Pepper informed

The Ingraham Highway at the south end of the Dewhurst Tract, approaching the Ninemile Bend, mid–1919. (Photographer: John K. Small. Florida Division of Library and Information Services, No. SM-1608.)

the Model Land Co. offices in St. Augustine that he had just returned from an inspection trip down to Cape Sable. The dredge was less than two miles from the county line, 22 miles below the park. The completed part of the road was about four miles farther back, near the south boundary of the Dewhurst Tract. The dredge had progressed about four miles in six months.[10]

The McCrary crews were encountering some of the worst conditions yet. The original plans had called for the right-of-way to continue due south after leaving the Dewhurst Tract almost all the way to Florida Bay, passing along the east side of West Lake, then turning west to skirt its south shore for six miles before making the final run into the south shore of Coot Bay. However, a survey of the site by Hobart Crabtree and A. O. Duncan, the McCrarys' consulting engineer, found that West Lake and the adjacent Cuthbert Lake were larger and slightly farther east than indicated by William Krome's 1903 survey. Moreover, the two lakes were connected to each other by a sizable pond, Long Lake.[11] (In fact, Krome called West Lake "Long Lake" on his plat.)

So the road had to pass north and west of West Lake. The decision was made to turn the road 45 degrees to the southwest immediately upon leaving the Dewhurst land, more or less in a straight shot for nine miles to the village at Coot Bay. (The 45-degree corner, which still exists, would henceforth become known as "Ninemile Bend") The road would cross into Monroe County about halfway down this angled stretch at a landmark called "the Humpback Bridge."

"The road for the whole 18 miles over which we rode [from the state park] has been machine worked with a scarifier, plow and rollers and has been finished to a smooth but uneven surface to an estimated width of from 10 to 14 feet," Pepper reported. "While the surface is smooth, as just stated it is uneven with a great many rises and small hollows, making it almost impossible to travel faster than ten miles per hour by automobile, and very uncomfortable at any speed." Sidney Harrison of the Model Land Company, who was paying the McCrarys for a good road, was incensed. "According to the contract of course you know that the road had to be hardsurfaced. It is merely what we would call rough surfaced at present and is a long way from what we would call a good hardsurfaced road."[12]

On the other hand, Frank Pepper was doubtful that the road could be improved by further plowing or scarifying, as the roadway was essentially the top of a canal embankment built up of rocks and boulders, overlaid with a thin veneer of crushed stone. Further plowing the road would simply pull the boulders out of the embankment, leaving more voids in the roadbed than were filled by the new gravel created by the plow. To make a smooth roadbed "it would seem necessary to haul in and spread over the surface to a depth necessary to make it uniform, fine pit rock which would be thoroughly rolled and oiled." That would require either assembling a rock crusher at Flamingo or hauling in finely crushed fill from a rock quarry above the park; neither option was seriously considered. (Both the contractors for the Tamiami Trail and the Conners Highway ultimately resorted to laying down temporary railway spurs to haul in huge amounts of finely crushed rock needed to top off those roads.) Pepper also noted a great deal of surplus rock piled at intervals within the Dewhurst property; this was material stockpiled for building turn-outs and stub-outs for future connecting roads "to get up on the main road from the lower lands."[13]

In November, the dredge was 1,200 feet from the county line. The following March, McCrary declared the road to the county line finished. "Mr. Freeman advises me that he has finished the Ingraham Highway in Dade County," he wrote to the Board of County Commissioners on April 5. "We feel that this now leaves the job in splendid shape and we therefore request an acceptance and payment for the work."[14]

McCrary had earlier asked for an acceptance in February, only to be told by Hobart Crabtree to "work over again with the grading and rolling outfit several miles ... from the Monroe County line back this way up to this side of [Ninemile Bend], a total distance of between five and six miles." This stretch ran near West Lake, and was, along with Taylor Slough, the wettest lands the highway crossed. An engineering report prepared for the National Park Service almost 40 years later noted that "southward from Nine Mile Bend the marl and muck overburden becomes progressively thicker until at Flamingo [Coot Bay] it is 11½ feet from the surface to the top of the oolite ... southward from near Concrete Bridge to Snake Bight Road [the Humpback Bridge] the Old Ingraham Highway had been 'floated' on a layer of mixed marl and muck." In other words, from about two miles north of Ninemile Bend on, there never was a stable roadgrade.[15]

Frank Pepper, for one, was dubious. He took a prospective customer down the highway in June 1920, and reported to Sidney Harrison that he was only able to get "*practically* all the way to the Monroe County line." Although he found the road "in better condition then when you made your last trip down [in May 1919], it is still pretty rough.... I suppose the condition of the road is as good as we will be able to expect to get from now on and until the County takes hold of it and brings it up to a better condition we will have to put up with what we have." Regardless, the commissioners, after hearing out a long litany of McCrary woes, formally approved the acceptance of the roadway in June 1920, and waived the accumulated late penalty of $6,198, largely based on McCrary's argument that his firm had been the driving force in securing financing for the road on the other side of the Dade-Monroe line.[16]

Ingraham took a harder line. Unlike the board of commissioners, he wasn't the least moved when J. B. McCrary appealed for his retainage of $1,781 from the Model Land Company in mid–1920: "it is an enormous amount from our standpoint, whereas with your company it is a very small matter." McCrary apparently believed the Model Land Company was short of cash, as he offered to "discount a short term acceptance from you with our bank," but he misunderstood the situation completely.[17]

In June 1920, after getting Dade County's release of the retainage, McCrary had reassigned their foreman, Harry Freeman, and the construction team that had been working on the Ingraham Highway to reinforce the crew already working on the Tamiami Trail, which was going badly. McCrary then subcontracted out the job of building the remainder of the road into Flamingo. McCrary picked Neil Campbell, a well-known canal dredging contractor out of West Palm Beach. (It was Campbell who later claimed that the Model Land Company paid McCrary $120,000 for the job.)[18] The contract called for McCrary to finish the road by November 1920. In September 1920, J. B. McCrary told a newspaper reporter that the five miles had been completed, and that he was on his way to Key West to try once again to convince the Monroe County Commissioners to put the $65,000 in road bonds up for sale, presumably as general obligation bonds. "Unless arrangements are made," said McCrary, the equipment "which was being used on the highway will be dismantled and shipped to Georgia."[19]

Despite what McCrary told the newspapers, the five-mile extension into Coot Bay was apparently *not* completed. Having failed to convince the Monroe commissioners to come through with the $65,000, J. B. McCrary turned back to the Model Land Company. In March 1921, he wrote Ingraham to ask why he hadn't yet approved his draft contract for the next phase of the work, extending the road from Coot Bay out to the far end of Cape Sable. Ingraham rather bluntly wrote back to inform him that no such contract would be forthcoming:

4. "This you failed to do"

> The reason we have not been able to give you a contract for the completion of the road in Monroe County is as we have explained to you time and time again, we could not issue a contract until you had completed what you had [started] … it was last July, or possibly early August [of 1920], while discussing with you the importance of getting the road finished which you then had under contract, together with the additional one thousand feet to take the road out of the swamp [at West Lake] where you had stopped to bring the road onto high land, we told you if you would get busy and complete the road together with this additional one thousand feet, rock and finish it so we could travel over it onto our lands [beyond Flamingo] by November 1st, 1920, we would give you a bonus of one thousand dollars. This you failed to do and under date of March 17, 1921, nearly five months after this date, you write "I hope to finish this contract soon and finish all contracts to date."
>
> Had you carried out your promises and contract to have the road completed we could have used it to carry prospective customers onto our land, but because of the incompleted condition of the road we have been compelled at great expense to carry prospective purchasers onto our lands by motorboat.… As to your claim for losses from this work, it seems to us you are confusing the losses you are sustaining on the Tamiami Trail with the work on the Ingraham Highway. At the price we are paying if conducted in a businesslike manner you have made money on the Ingraham Highway which would have helped to offset some of your losses of the Tamiami Trail, but it looks to us as if all your efforts had been made to put all your forces, time and attention to the Tamiami Trail and more or less neglecting our work.
>
> As to the February [1922] estimate, our Mr. Livingston [Ingraham's engineer] while in the office a day or so ago stated there had been so little work done on our road as would hardly justify an estimate being made.[20]

McCrary was fired.

Lawrence Will, who began work with the new dredging crew that started in January 1922, found the dredge where McCrary and Campbell left it just south of Coot Bay, but it appears that not much of a road was built south of the county line; indeed, his account states that the road was almost impassable beyond the Humpback Bridge when it was wet.

In May 1922 Campbell announced that he had been awarded the follow-up contract to extend the highway from Coot Bay all the way out to the end of Cape Sable for $175,000.[21] But Lawrence Will gives a very different account. According to Will, the Model Land Company advertised for bids in mid-1921. Finally, after some coaxing, the Holloway brothers of Fort Lauderdale, Scott and Hampton, received the contract. Hampton Holloway, who actually supervised the crew, formerly ran the dredge that dug the naval channels at Pearl Harbor, Hawaii, and supervised much of the dredging of the St. Lucie Canal between Lake Okeechobee and Stuart.

Will spoke to Scott Holloway a few days before contract bids were due and Holloway told him he did not plan to bid. However, there were no other experienced, reliable bidders, and the Model Land Company made the Holloways a lucrative offer.[22] Campbell announced that he had been awarded this contract in May 1921 but Will recounted that Scott Holloway first told him the Model Land Co. had advertised for bids in August, and that his, Will's, first day on the job was January 2, 1922, and that dredging began on January 16. This is verified by a letter written by his father, Thomas, who lived in Fort Lauderdale. Thomas Will wrote to his daughter Marion on January 12:

> Lawrence has gone to the Cape Sable country again. Not expected back for some time. Has been here quite a bit since he went onto that job. Running back and forth between here and the Palm Beach Canal bend. Now has taken a boat from there to Cape Sable neighborhood to use in the dredging job. He is to run it and a motor truck. Thinks he will like that kind of work.[23]

Neil Campbell apparently was McCrary's subcontractor in Cape Sable, and his announcement was premature. While he knew there was a second Model Land Co. contract waiting in the wings, he wasn't going to be a part of it, as Ingraham fired McCrary in March 1921, and Campbell went with him.[24] The original plan had been to build a road as well as a canal, but this was removed from the contract early on. The only requirement was that the Holloways had to do some work on the road grade between the county line and Flamingo. They hired a minimal amount of equipment for this: "a tractor, a road grader, and a stripped down Model T," and worked for only a couple of weeks before the wet season of 1922 set in. According to Will, the marl road grade was so poor when wet that it didn't really make much difference if it was smoothed out or not. Without a crushed rock surface it was all but useless except in the dry season.[25]

The Holloways used the dredge left over from McCrary's work, which Will described as a "dilapidated spectacle" that needed constant repair. After digging about a mile west to finish the canal into Flamingo, the dredging crew turned left and headed due south to Flamingo Dock on Florida Bay, leaving only a small cofferdam near the beach to keep the canal water from draining out and stranding the dredge. They then backed up the two-mile canal they had just dug (later the Buttonwood Canal), turned west, and continued on their way west to Lake Ingraham.

Monroe County never did pay for hard-surfacing the road. The attitude of the Monroe County Commissioners was that the Ingraham Highway was essentially a private road for the benefit the Model Land Company and its customers. In 1948, Carl Hawkins, vice president of the Model Land Co., admitted to an attorney for the Interior Department that this was true: "He said that the Model Land Company had never conveyed the Ingraham to the State or Monroe County." On the other hand, "He felt, however, that the Highway has been used by the public so long that the Company probably has lost title to it."[26]

Will said that in 1922 that the road south of the Humpback Bridge "was composed of a grade or fill of light grey, clay-like marl. When dry it made a fairly good road surface, but when wet—oh, boy!—greased glass could not be made any slicker." Marjory Stoneman Douglas had the same memory: "driving on it was like sledding across a plowed field."[27]

The Holloways finished the Cape Sable canal in November 1922. Will does not say how much the Holloways were paid, but based on his description, it appears each three-shift crew was paid a total of $1,000 a month for ten months, that is, $30,000. Adding Hampton Holloway's salary, costs, and profit, it appears the contract must have run to about $75,000. (It also appears that they got to keep the dredge.) The canal was never useful for anything, except for the two-mile north-south stretch between Flamingo and Flamingo Dock. Several sections near Bear Lake and Gator Lake silted back in almost immediately. Elsewhere, its banks have, over the years, eroded to over a hundred feet wide. It has became an environmental disaster, pumping brackish saltwater into the freshwater wetlands south of Whitewater Bay, killing native species and promoting their replacement by non-native invasives. The canal itself is in such bad shape that you can't even canoe down it, and it can't be fixed because most of it goes through terrain that has the approximate consistency of a fresh milk shake.

Two Pennsylvania road contractors, S. F. Guy and Edward Riffle, traveled down the highway in December to Flamingo. They reported the Dade County portion was in "good shape," but in Monroe found "evidences that some machines had previously been badly stuck in this part of the highway and had gotten out only after the occupants had dug the earth from their wheels and had substituted quantities of grass, wood, bark, etc." They met no other cars any farther south than Jennings Grove. A. R. Livingstone, the Model Land Company's engineer, announced a year later in November 1923 that the highway was finally complete and would open on the 15th. However, he cautioned that "while the road will be open for traffic on the date mentioned, visitors to the Cape Sable territory should not expect to find a finished road, such as the old parts of Dade County boast of."[28]

* * * * *

In late 1922 May Mann Jennings sold the remainder of the original 43,000-acre Jennings Tract, including all the land south of the highway, to Hugh Annat. Annat was a developer and merchant from Bellefontataine, Ohio, who had started spending his winters in Miami in the early 1920s. A native of Kirriemuir, Scotland, he returned in the summer of 1925 for a fishing trip. Caught in a sleet storm, he blindly stumbled into the kitchen of a local hotel where he was revived by the kitchen maid, Elizabeth Dunlop. Annat extended his vacation a few weeks, and they were married in September. Annat was 59, Dunlop 23. It wasn't until they returned to Ohio that Elizabeth discovered that she was the wife of a millionaire.[29]

In 1927, Frank Pepper (Frederick Morse, the Model Land Company's original land agent in Dade County, had died in July 1920) reported to the St. Augustine headquarters that his office had received three inquiries in rapid succession for Cape Sable tracts even farther west than Paradise Prairie, some all the way into Whitewater Bay. The first came from Thomas Benson of the Paradise Prairie Company, the second from a recently arrived real estate agent named James Cross, and the third from an established local agent, J. B. Dill. Incredulous, Frank Pepper was finally able to get his friend Dill to tip him off as to what was going on.[30]

In April 1927 the Seaboard Air Line Railroad had, through a combination of purchase, government regulation and litigation, managed to extend its route south from its Hialeah shops to Homestead, to the great annoyance of the Florida East Coast, which considered Homestead "its" town. At the same time, acting through strawmen, it purchased the land needed on the Gulf coast to push as far south as Naples. Florida's third major railroad, the Atlantic Coast Line, already had a right-of-way that extended to Everglades City by virtue of its purchase of Barron Collier's narrow-gage Deep Lake Railroad, which it rebuilt in 1928. There were persistent rumors that the Atlantic Coast Line and the Seaboard planned to merge.[31]

As Cross explained to Pepper, the Seaboard wanted to run a spur line down from Homestead using part of the embankment of the Cape Sable highway until the road turned south at the Cement Bridge. "From which point they would take a generally Westerly course along the North side of White Water Bay to the West Coast, thence North to connect to their line where it comes down the West Coast from Ft. Myers." He added that "the Seaboard has recently had their Engineering force in the Cape Sable District surveying, and this was verified by Mr. Benson." This did not sit well in St. Augustine, and the Model Land Company advised its local agents that "if spur tracks are to be built in that territory the [FEC Railroad] will build them ... [but] you must realize that under the present conditions [we] are unable to construct a spur track at this time. Therefore, in view of all the circumstances I would suggest you advise Mr. Cross that you cannot quote him a price on any of this property." Frank Pepper wrote back two days later to acknowledge that they were informing inquirers that "this land was not on the market for sale." The cost of building the type of spur line Pepper described would have been massive, and given that the Seaboard made a profit of only $31,000 in 1927 (the same year that its dynamic chairman, S. Davies Warfield, died) the plan was dubious at best. But had the Model Land Company been successful in selling off the northern half of Whitewater Bay it could have done a lot to improve its financial position with minimal risk. Seven years later J. W. Hoffman of the Model Land Co. wrote a confidential letter to another area landowner admitting that he would be willing to accept five dollars an acre for these same lands for the proposed new national park.[32]

In early 1929, Ernest Coe of the Tropic Everglades Park Association, which was leading the drive to create a greatly expanded national park out of the Royal Palm State Park, responded to an inquiry from a local newspaper reporter about the condition of the road to Flamingo with a warning that "It is possible to reach Cape Sable by auto, but the trip is strenuous. There are miles of rough roads, with hub-deep ruts, protruding sharp broken rocks and tree growth almost meeting for long stretches of road." At one point it was necessary to ford a ditch 25 feet wide that was armpit deep, and at another place just east of Flamingo it was necessary to divert from the road and drive along the beach. The road from Homestead to the state park was very good, and it was passable from the state park to West Lake. However, the road more or less ended at the county line, and it was often necessary to hire a launch to take one through West Lake and Long Lake, out Alligator Bight into Florida Bay, and around ten miles or so to Flamingo Dock, then up the Model Land Company canal to Coot Bay. "He [Coe] said an attempt to go beyond West Lake by auto at present is not advisable."[33]

In May 1930, a Cape Sable resident, L. W. Loudon, wrote the Model Land Company's headquarters in St. Augustine warning that a bridge about a mile south of the Humpback Bridge was close to collapsing. The Pepper & Potter land company agents investigated and confirmed that this was true, but the Monroe County commissioners told Model Land Company vice-president Hoffman that they could find no contractor who would provide an estimate for the repairs.[34]

J. D. Redd, the Dade County Commissioner for the Homestead area, recommended Frank Irwin, of the Flamingo Irwins, who was now a building contractor in Homestead, for the job. Irwin and Redd walked the highway from the county line to Flamingo, where there was a second bridge. "Mr. Redd spoke as if you could cross both of these bridges with a light car but that they did not seem to be safe for a truck," reported Milo Coffrin of the Pepper & Potter firm to J. W. Hoffman. Irwin agreed to repair both bridges for $500, and to re-surface and remove brush from the road for another $500 per mile. As if to prove their point, while out on their reconnaissance trip, Redd and Irwin came across an old couple stuck in the mud near one of the bridges. "If he [Redd] and Mr. Irwin had not happened along he doubted if the old man would have gotten his car out of there for two or three days," Coffrin wrote. "He said the road was absolutely impassable for a car, and a sign should be posted at the Dade-Monroe County Line, warning that the road is impassible until the same is repaired."[35]

Monroe County did nothing. Two months later the Humpback Bridge collapsed when a farmer tried to drive a truck of fertilizer across it (they did manage to save the truck). In December, the Model Land Company offered to advance the county the money it needed to bid out the repair work. The county was noncommittal. "Apparently they desire the Model Land Company to take on the responsibility of the contract," vice president Hoffman reported, "but this I refuse to do, it being a County road and under the supervision of the County Commissioners it is my thought that the Contract should be let by the Commissioners rather than the Model Land Company." The county rather unhelpfully suggested that the Model Land Co. and local residents petition the state to take over the road, although Dade Commissioner Redd pointed out that state designation "merely gives the highway a state number and does not provide any appropriation for improvements or new construction."[36]

The road stayed closed for another two months, until the winter dry season of 1931, when Irwin was finally hired to fix the bridges, but little else. "It was pointed out," reported the *Homestead Leader*, "that without a top dressing of oil, the road would soon be in a state of disrepair again, and that the re-working necessary would be more expensive than the oil surface would be." The road never was paved. Frank Pepper attended a Rotary lunch just before Christmas, 1934 and happened to sit next to Ernest Coe, chairman of Florida's Everglades National Park Commission. Pepper, who had been trying to sell land on Cape Sable for twenty-five years (and by now had largely given up) asked Coe if he had any knowledge about the condition of the lower Cape Sable Road. Coe replied that he had not been down the road himself for quite some time, but he knew that the Department of Agriculture had a wild cotton eradication program going on in near the Dade-Monroe line that entailed digging up and trucking out the plants. The laborers and equipment were being trucked in, so the road had to be passable for at least a mile or two beyond the Humpback Bridge.[37]

Lawrence Will saw only three houses in Flamingo when he was there with his Cape Sable dredging crew in 1921, but the *WPA Guide to Florida* says that by 1930 the village had re-grown back to "25 houses and shacks," most built by fisherman. "Food and water should be carried," warned the *WPA Guide* for those venturing below the state park, "for the only drinking water is rainwater from the roofs of shacks, and is not always plentiful." Marjory Stoneman Douglas recalled seeing the "remains of an old hotel" when she visited in the late 1920s. It was owned by the Roberts family, and may have been part or all of the elevated clubhouse built in 1917 by New York financier Samuel Untermyer, New York Judge Francis Baker, and William Bowen of the Miami law firm of Shutts & Bowen. The three had bought nine miles of Cape Sable beach adjacent to Flamingo, which they hoped to develop as a winter getaway and game preserve for the wealthy. The clubhouse was a single large screen-porch that could be subdivided into sleeping rooms with canvas curtains. It was damaged by storms and was apparently rebuilt at least once and run by the Roberts family as a "hotel," although guest hostel may be more accurate. Other descriptions refer to it as a restaurant, and at least one calls it a rum speakeasy.[38]

Flamingo was badly battered by the hurricane of 1926, but rebuilt. However, the Great Labor Day Hurricane of 1935 was a direct hit. It passed over Upper and Lower Matacumbe Keys, 25 miles south, moving northwest. An 18-foot storm surge washed over Lower Matacumbe Key, including two WPA work camps with 200 men helping to build a highway from the mainland to Key West. An empty rescue train at Islamorada (it had just arrived from Homestead) was, except for the engine, swept off the tracks. The eye missed Flamingo by 15 miles, but the eyewall passed directly over at 2:00 a.m. on September 3, 1935, with winds of at least 160 miles per hour. Exactly how high, nobody knows for sure, because every anemometer in the storm's path was destroyed. Some were designed to measure gusts up to 200 mph.

The storm wiped out Flamingo and most everything else on Cape Sable. Almost everybody left before the storm struck. The last to leave were Joe Douthit and a recently arrived fisherman and his two small boys. Just before dusk, it became apparent that this was no ordinary storm. By then, it was too late to escape by boat. The only way out was to try the road. Each man took one of the boys. Douthit tore up a sheet and literally tied his boy to him.

Searchers from Homestead could only go a mile or so south of the Humpback Bridge, as West Lake had washed over the road. It took three days to cut through the debris to get that far. They found the two men there, not far apart. Douthit said that it had taken them two days to battle their way to Coot Lake, four miles, and another day to traverse the three and a half miles to West Lake. The boy tied to Joe was unconscious. The boy who had been with his father was never found. All three required hospitalization. Lawrence Will tried to get Joe Douthit to describe it in the early 1960s, but "although Joe by nature was quite loquacious, he'd never discuss this ordeal."

As the storm passed over Islamorada, a 15-year-old girl who had tried to ride out the storm on her parents' yacht panicked and attempted to take its launch to shore. No trace of her or the gas launch could be seen. Her father offered a thousand-dollar reward for her safe return, $750 for the recovery of her body. A couple of the Irwins and Douthits returned to Flamingo Dock, where they had deliberately sunk a sail-powered workboat in the canal to keep it safe, and set out along the Cape Sable beach in search of her.

About six miles from Flamingo they spotted the launch in the mangroves about eight feet above the high tide line. The beach, which was now muddy instead of sandy, was covered with footprints. Following them, they found the girl's body farther west at the shoreline. Irwin later estimated that she had wandered, back-and-forth, lost, along the shore for at least 48 hours before succumbing to exhaustion, dehydration, exposure, "oh, yeah, and the mosquitos."[39]

For days afterward bodies washed ashore, having been blown across Florida Bay from the middle keys. In May 1936, eight months after the storm, fishermen out on Middle Cape found eleven skeletons on the backside of the dunes. The sheriff noted that this was by now a regular occurrence. It brought the confirmed death count to 524, and reduced the missing to a little over 75, even though the sheriff doubted whether more than two or three of the remains would be identified. The clothing and shoes would give some idea of age, gender and maybe, occupation. Park rangers found graves uncovered by Hurricane Donna in 1960, and some intact 1935 gravesites are known of today.[40]

In 1938 Flamingo Dock contained only six buildings, most related to the House Fish Company. "Florida's no man's land is finally going to get help at last," announced the *Miami Daily News* in late 1944. The State Highway Department had been calling the Ingraham Highway State Road 209, but only as far as the state park. After all these years, it was still the case that no real road existed past the Monroe County line, although the House Fish Company was running two twice-weekly shuttles to service the village's only surviving industry, commercial fishing. One ran from Miami, the other from Naples. They delivered ice, gasoline, groceries, and hardware; they returned with iced barrels of fish, mostly mullet. The trucks, military-style Studebaker and Dodge "power wagons," had A-frame derricks welded to their front bumpers and carried winches, planks, and traction mats to get them out of potholes and ruts.

"Several factors have conspired to prevent the strip [from the county line to Flamingo] from being repaired or surfaced," explained the *Daily News* reporter. "The principal reason is that the stretch runs through wasteland, waterlogged even in dry weather, and incapable of supporting even the hardiest family." The second problem was the continued intransigence of Monroe County officials:

> Although Monroe officials know the conditions at Flamingo and the fact that the lack of a good road imperils the entire community during the hurricane months, they hesitate to spend county monies on repairing a road to serve such a small settlement. The Monroe County officials also argue that the huge fish crop, the community's single reason for existence, does not benefit the county, as it is hauled through Monroe County and distributed through Dade and Collier Counties.[41]

The *Daily News*' prediction that help was on the way was premature. The state highway department offered only to send their men and machinery down to rock the road if Monroe County would put up an $8,000 matching share. "We'll do what we can," was the tepid response of Monroe commission chairman Frank Roberts, "but we haven't got any too much money in our road fund. We need most of it right now for repairs to Roosevelt Boulevard [in Key West] and in other more heavily traveled parts of the county road system." The work was never done.

The National Park Service proved to be the purchaser of last resort for most of the big speculative Everglades owners. The Park has been portrayed as a dramatic rescuer of a besieged natural environment from land speculators, developers, corporate agricultural interests, and the Army Corps of Engineers. However, as a reading of the correspondence of the era makes clear, it was also viewed, at least initially, as an economic lifeboat for those large-tract landowners who had purchased—or been given—wide swaths of south Florida wetlands, who struggled under even minimal per-acre property taxes because of the sheer size of their holdings, and after 1929 had little hope of seeing their property either sold or drained.

In late 1934, J. W. Hoffman wrote to Milo Coffrin of Pepper & Potter that "of course, if the National Park Service have decided that that they will include all of the area originally proposed for the park, I hardly think there is anything for us to do, other than to accept the matter and try to get the best out of the property we can." This is not to say they were eager to see the coming of the park, but after ten or twenty years of low-ball bids, partnership offers in flaky ventures, foreclosed mortgages—everything except a decent price, cash on the barrelhead—the potential promise of a government check didn't sound so bad anymore.[42]

At least until 1943. In October 1943 the Humble Oil Company struck oil at 10,600 feet at their Sunniland field near Immoklee. Suddenly, everyone who owned Everglades land thought they were a millionaire again. For example, Judge Daniel McDougal of Oklahoma, who had acquired some 23,000 acres of land in Monroe County as a result of his investment in James Jaudon's Chevelier Corporation before World War I, had originally told his son-in-law Ivar Axelson in early 1943 that "I would rather have $2.50 now, than to have the hope of getting $5.00 at some time in the dim, distant future." But after Sunniland wells, he told the government's acquisition coordinator that he would take no less than $10 per acre.[43]

According to Park Superintendent Daniel Beard, "oil fever" did not quiet until late 1955 when the two 1947 test wells drilled adjacent to the park "that had triggered the stock speculation, public hearings and wild excitement," were capped because they could not produce enough to justify their $6,000 monthly cost. Meanwhile, a Gulf Oil Co. floating rig working just outside the park boundary in Florida Bay drilled to 12,600 feet and came up dry. Other wells that initially drew oil sputtered out in a few weeks, overpowered by salt water intrusion. Humble, Gulf and Marathon let their lease options lapse. At this point many small holders who had been refusing voluntary sales came to the table. Violet McDougal, Judge McDougal's widow, sold 5,660 acres to the park for $21,000.[44] The Sunniland oil field itself was shut down by 1962, a victim of salt water infiltration.

In 1948 the State of Florida, acting as the land agent for the national park, paid the Model Land Company $115,000 for 134,880 acres of land, 83 cents an acre. A few months later, they bought another 75,177 acres for $180,000. The second purchase bought out all of the Model Land Company's holdings inside the new park, including all its shoreline properties. That land, plus the Royal Palm State Park, now grown to 4,000 acres, another 140,000 acres or so that still belonged to the Internal Improvement Fund, and 30,000 acres donated by Miles Collier, Barron Collier's son, made up the core of the new Everglades National Park that President Truman dedicated in Everglades City in December 1947. The two million dollars that the state's Everglades National Park Commission needed to buy land was still caught up in litigation that would not be fully resolved until 1949. After this was resolved, the park's designated boundaries were expanded by about another 170 square miles in February 1950.[45]

However, the purchase of the Model Land Co. acreage had a significant impact on the Ingraham Highway. In his first monthly report in 1945 as the park's first superintendent, Daniel Beard, noted that "The House Fish Company of Flamingo, several sports fishermen, and the National Audubon Society complained about the condition of the Cape Sable Road." However, at this point Beard could only apologize because "the government does not yet own the roadway so public funds cannot be expended." The Model Land Company, who owned about 60 percent of the land under the road, had never conveyed the Ingraham Highway to the government. The state Internal Improvement Fund, the Paradise Prairie Land Company, and William Dewhurst's daughter, Dorothy Dewhurst Parker, owned another 35 percent. The acquisition office was negotiating with all these owners. But about five percent of the land under the highway was in the hands of smallholders, mostly the old 1915 Flamingo Dock and Coot Bay homesteaders or their successors.[46]

Research by the acquisition office indicated that the Model Land Co. had made less than half of the original sales to these smallholders between 1915 and 1922 with easements or dedications in place to accommodate the highway. Fortunately, there were not many such smallholders; perhaps thirty. The state purchased their rights-of-way separate from their land titles, in a manner similar to mineral rights. However, the right-of-way maps ended two miles east of the Cement Bridge, because the 1947 park boundary stopped there. The area within the old Jennings Tract, and some land north of it, were not included in the park boundaries. This became known as "The-Hole-in-the-Donut."[47]

Hugh Annat had bought everything in the Jennings Tract that lay south of the highway in 1922 from May Mann Jennings and her son Bryan. But most of the best land, from one mile south of the highway to three miles north of it, had already been sold to various smallholders. Elizabeth Annat received $131,000 for the remaining 39,000 acres from the State of Florida in early 1951. (May Mann Jennings herself died in April 1963 at age 63.)[48]

But the landowners in an area along either side of the Ingraham Highway and Long Pine Key Road, and from two miles east of the Cement Bridge to the old state park—roughly 30 square miles—refused to sell. Eventually the park was forced into a court settlement that permitted the Hole-in-the-Donut farmers to continue using their land for another 40 years. Many left before then and sold to the park, but some continued to farm the there until the late 1960s, or early 1970s. Only one private owner, a Boy Scout camp of 250 acres, remains.

Most of the farms were located along Long Pine Key Road, and tended to be close to the old state park. Long Pine Key Road, parallel to, and four miles north of the Ingraham, was built in 1919 as a simple scarified road by the United States Sisal Trust. The company had started with 75,000 seedlings in a 40-acre nursery a few miles west of Hallandale. But mature sisal plants require eight feet of space, so the Sisal Trust bought 22,000 acres just north of the Jennings Tract, where they hoped to establish a new alternative to hemp for the making of twine and rope. James Jaudon, former county tax assessor and promoter of the Tamiami Trail, was hired to run the plantation. His first task was to build a four-and-a-half mile road. As you exited the state park, you turned right instead of left, went north a mile, then turned left, going due west. The U. S. Sisal Trust went under in 1921. It sold the land to the South Florida Fruit and Vegetable Company, which in turn sold land in small parcels to farmers on both sides of the road.[49]

The Hole-in-the-Donut was a longstanding jurisdictional problem for the park. The Royal Palm ranger station was literally within shouting distance, but the rangers had no legal authority there, and many of the residents did not want to recognize their authority, no matter how dire the circumstances, even though the nearest local law enforcement, the Florida City police station, was over ten miles away.

In addition, the park had the responsibility for maintaining its roads, but because they were not within the park, Long Pine Key Road and the Ingraham Highway between the old state park and Cement Bridge were the responsibility of the county and state, respectively, even though crews had to travel through six or seven miles of the park to get there. The Hole-in-the-Doughnut farmers considered themselves neglected by the county and the state, and they probably were. They were an expensive and time consuming headache and everyone, not just the federal Department of the Interior, was relieved to see the agricultural area closed in the 1970s.

••5••

"A rather superficial excuse"

"The State Highway Department mowed road shoulders through Paradise Key and filled holes in the road there caused by inundation [but] from the Monroe County line to Flamingo it was impassable all month and Coot Bay could be reached only by boat," park superintendent Daniel Beard reported in October 1947. Two years later he included with his report a photograph taken near the Coot Bay ranger station of his jeep, impossibly mired in a rut, probably one made by a fish company truck. Only a winch was going to get him out. "The Coot Bay temporary concessions structure was bogged down (literally) most of the month because roads were impassable and the Humpback Bridge went out," Beard lamented. "Some gravel was hauled for the [Coot Bay] parking area extension but had to be discontinued because of broken axles, trucks getting bogged down, sprung frames, and attendant 'inconveniences.'"[1] The nadir was reached a year later, in September 1950:

> The Ingraham Highway from Humpback Bridge to Coot Bay and Flamingo was in worse condition during September than ever before since the park was started [in 1945], except for a brief time after the 1948 hurricane. Ruts were knee-deep and only the largest of the fish company trucks could get through (providing they had winches). Attempts to move Service vehicles back and forth soon failed and it became necessary to operate only by skiff down the canal to the ranger station. Stocks of gasoline at the ranger station became low with no way of replenishing them. This seriously affected protection work.[2]

Despite occasional efforts of the Dade and state road departments to haul loads of gravel down to fill in the worst places, the road was really in no better condition than it had been in 1930. "Ingraham Highway was in bad shape," reported the park superintendent in February 1955, "where it went through the Hole-in-the Doughnut. With last year's rains and this winter's dust, topping material along the highway had either washed or blown thin. Many complaints were made and concessionaires [at Flamingo] felt it had hurt business."[3]

Things were a little better above Paradise Key, where the road was an official state highway. In the summer of 1948 the two timber bridges that the J. B. McCrary Co. had installed on the embankment between Royal Palm Park and the Pine Island (now fast becoming the Pine Island Service area), were replaced, "with heavier structures (wood)." The state also graded and rolled the road between the old state park and the Humpback Bridge at the Monroe County line. "Prison labor is being used," Beard noted.[4]

The biggest problem at Royal Palm was the amount of agricultural and commercial traffic that was forced to funnel through the old state park, which had become a chokepoint. Back in 1922 May Mann Jennings had allowed the U.S. Sisal Trust to build the Long Pine Key Road off the Ingraham Highway as it exited the west side of the park. Now, thirty years later, all the market traffic from the Hole-in-Doughnut, including the farms along both the

Ingraham Highway and the Long Pine Key Road, had to funnel through the state park and across the Taylor Slough crossing to get to Homestead and Miami. The farmers didn't like it, the tourists didn't like it, and Daniel Beard didn't like it.

The supervising engineer for the new main park road later explained:

> Actual planning for the park road system was begun with a meeting on the ground in November, 1953 between Superintendent Daniel B. Beard, Assistant Regional Director Edward S. Zimmer, landscape architect Dean Stout, all of the National Park Service, and district engineer George B. Thompson of the Bureau of Public Roads.
>
> The general outline of the road system was agreed upon at this meeting. The principal location decision made at this time was that the new main park road should leave the Ingraham Highway about one mile inside the east [Homestead] park boundary and swing west and north around the large in-holding of private land, returning to the Ingraham Highway below the Concrete Bridge.
>
> This route had the advantages of avoiding the right-of-way problems presented by the private lands and making available for interpretative purposes fine views over the open Everglades. It also made it possible to remove the busy through-highway from Paradise Key, one of the primary wildlife and interpretative areas of the park.[5]

Although the engineer's report suggests that planning did not start until 1953, Daniel Beard and his assistants had been making reconnaissance trips by swamp buggy and airboat, charting possible routes, as early as the winter of 1949–50, especially in critical locations such as the junction of the new road and the access drive to Paradise Key; the access road for Long Pine Key Road; and the location where the new main road should re-join the old Ingraham Highway in the vicinity of the curve at the Cement Bridge.[6]

The most notable feature of the new road was that it swung gently northwest after entering the park, where the old road turned southwest at a 45-degree angle. The old road was rehabilitated for use as a service road between the new park headquarters, just inside the Homestead entrance, and the Pine Island Service Center. The service center was located on the east bank of the Taylor Slough, where the old road had started across the causeway to Paradise Key. Before being bought out, the Pine Island had been the site of several small farms and seasonal vacation cabins.[7]

Proceeding down the new main road, about three miles after the Pine Island road turnoff, a second turn to the left provided access to the Royal Palm ranger station, located about three hundred feet east of where the old lodge had stood. This road, entering from the north, now provided the only way for vehicles to get in or out of the venerable Paradise Key, as the old highway in both directions would be blocked off. It was also decided to use this spur road as the access drive for Long Pine Key Road through the Hole-in-the-Doughnut agricultural area. About half-way between the main road and the Royal Palm Visitor Center another road branched off the spur road to the right. After about a quarter-mile it connected to the old Long Pine Key Road. At this junction a second turn-off headed due south. This provided access to the old Ingraham Highway. Thus, all traffic from both the Ingraham and Long Pine Key roads would be funneled onto this short spur road, then onto the Royal Palm access road, then out to the main road to the park entrance and the state road to Homestead.

The new road main swung a good distance to the north and west of the Hole-in-the-Donut in order to run along the top of what was called the Rock Reef, a relatively high (three feet) outcropping. After curving in a gentle "C" shape, it connected to the Ingraham Highway at the Cement Bridge, then followed the old road grade due south, turning at Ninemile Bend, and going on to Coot Bay. However, where the old road turned west along the canal at what is today the Rowdy Bend trailhead, the new road continued on, curving slightly to the south to head straight to Flamingo Dock by going over a new bridge spanning the Buttonwood Canal about half-way between Coot Bay and Flamingo Dock.

Wild cotton eradication camp in Everglades National Park near West Lake, early 1950s. The removal of invasive plants introduced both intentionally and accidentally through agricultural activities on Cape Sable continues to the present day. While feral crops such as wild cotton have been successfully eradicated, invasive species, including Brazilian Pepper, the poisonwoods, and melaleuca, which take advantage of disturbed soils like abandoned fields, have been especially pernicious. The seeds of several species are so resilient that they can be stopped only by stripping the soil down to the bedrock and encapsulating it in giant entombment pyramids. (Photographer unknown. Florida Division of Library and Information Services, No. C018414.)

The ranger station and concession services would be moved from Coot Bay to Flamingo Dock. Plans had already been prepared for a new visitor center with ranger station, museum, gift shop and restaurant. A new motel, gas station, cabins, marina, and campgrounds were also planned. By installing a salinity gate at the mouth of the canal and a boat hoist at the marina, boaters would be able to access either the saltwater Florida Bay or the freshwater Coot Bay. To the east of the visitor center, across the canal, a maintenance center with dry- and wetdocks, a motor pool garage, warehouse and staff housing would go up. The budget for the new road, 39.2 miles long, was $2,335,100, or $59,569 per mile. The venerable Coot Bay village would be abandoned, its buildings burnt or removed.[8]

The staking was completed by December 1954. The fill material used to raise the road grade below Ninemile Bend was dredged from Florida Bay as a by-product of building the marina and creating navigable approaches to it from the shallow bay floor. Eventually about 860,000 cubic yards were dredged; most of it was used just to get the 8.6 miles from Flamingo to Ninemile Bend. In some places the contractor had to lay down almost eleven feet of fill to reach the limestone bed.[9]

The four miles from Ninemile Bend to the Cement Bridge was the most controversial part of the work. "This section of road was never recommended by the Superintendent and is being constructed without his signature on the plans," Beard noted tersely in March 1956. He did not elaborate on the reasons for his opposition, but his comments about the progress of this section suggest either that he did not think the upgrade was worth the environment costs required in terms of the number and size of borrow pits needed to create fill, or he objected to the placement of the pits so near the road. Although well disguised by the Park Service's landscape architect and the contractors, the truth is that most of the water bodies now identified on the park's map as "ponds" adjacent to the south half of the main road are, in fact, borrow pits. For example, Sweet Bay Pond, at the former site of the Cement Bridge, was originally the more prosaic Borrow Pit Number 1; Paurotis Pond a few miles south was once Pit No. 3, Nine Mile Pond was Pit No. 4, and so on.[10]

The old station at Coot Bay, a recycled and relocated farm house formerly owned by one of the Irwins, lay in the path of the new road. "The old service station at Coot Bay was torn down by park crews to make way for the road construction," Beard reported in late 1955. "This disproves the oft-repeated saying that temporary structures in national parks last forever." The timing of the road work was done in coordination with the construction of the Flamingo service area. Both opened to the public on the same day, apparently without ceremony or fanfare, on December 20, 1957, although a ribbon cutting for the visitor center was held a few months later.[11]

One part of the job that was given less mention was later described by the supervising engineer:

> Another extra job handled under this contract was the obliteration of the Old Ingraham highway from the Concrete Bridge east to the park boundary. This was accomplished by a dragline and bulldozer and paid for on force account basis. [i.e., cost-plus; not flat-fee] The dragline reached across the old canal which paralleled the highway and raked into the canal the windrow of oolite boulders spilled there 40 years ago, and along with it a fringe of hammock vegetation that had grown up on the windrow. At the same time the dozer pushed the oolite road embankment into the canal so that upon the completion of the work both the canal and the road would be largely obliterated.[12]

Based on a comment in the superintendent's monthly report, the work was apparently done around January 1959. By "park boundary," the report means the division line between the old Dewhurst and Jennings tracts, 13,200 feet east of the junction of the old and new highways. At this time the Dewhurst Tract had been fully acquired, but the land within the former Jennings Tract was still part of the Hole-in-the-Donut agricultural area. Including the curve, about 15,000 feet was removed.[13]

Some recent reports have stated that the road was removed in order to facilitate the movement of surface water, but this is not indicated anywhere in the 1959 engineer's report. On the other hand, it does clearly state that it was done to eliminate the Ingraham as a through highway and limit its function to a local-access, farm-to-market road. As a giant cul-de-sac, it would meet the obligation of the park and the state highway department to provide access to the Hole-in-the-Doughnut farms, but at the lowest possible cost. With the two miles removed, it could not be used as a "back door" between the old state park and Flamingo. The only traffic the Ingraham Highway and the Long Pine Key road could subsequently carry was that from the abutting farms and the Boy Scout camp. Its maintenance costs would be minimal, and could be provided by either the state or county. No longer would highway department crews have to traverse some seven or eight miles of park road to reach an isolated six-mile stretch of public highway.

Was it a "grudge strip," intended to isolate the Hole-in the-Doughnut and to coerce the farmers to sell out? There is no indication of this. The farmers along the Ingraham Highway had little reason to go south to Flamingo. Most of them were clustered just west of the former state park. The new configuration was certainly a faster and safer way of getting to Homestead than going through the old state park and across the Taylor Slough on the McCrary causeway, especially during tourist season. It also was better for security. In January 1959, robbers attempted to hold up an automobile transporting the weekly payroll of the Iori Farms, the largest agricultural operation in the Hole-in-the-Doughnut, located near the end of the Long Pine Key Road where the Daniel Beard Center is now. Rangers and the sheriff's office foiled the attempt because they had received advance warning. The Rangers threw a barricade across the road after the robbers had gone past and they were trapped.[14] In summary, it is almost certain that the west end of the road was taken up for traffic reasons—it was no longer safe for through traffic, and was isolated and expensive to patrol and repair—and not for anything having to do with surface water, and certainly not to coerce the Hole-in the-Doughnut farmers into moving out.

The tragedy was that the Cement Bridge, one of the few enduring cultural landmarks located within park, was destroyed without a trace. It, the highway, and Monroe Station up on the Tamiami Trail (1928) were probably the oldest remaining cultural artifacts from Florida's modern "railroad era" within the park. (The Royal Palm Lodge was purchased and moved to Homestead about 1957 when it was made redundant by the first visitors center at Parachute Key.) "Wilma [the hurricane, in 2005] exposed a long-running problem," noted writer James Hammond, "While skilled at preserving nature, park officials have proven less capable of caring for History." A staff member at Everglades National Park admits that "cultural preservation and cultural interpretation issues appear to be less important here than in most other parks where I have worked. This seems to be a generally shared consensus."[15]

The irony is that the Cold War had more to do with the fate of the Hole-in-the-Doughnut than farm prices or environmental politics. The Cuban Missile Crisis of 1962 created the fear that the Soviet Union would again try to surreptitiously place ballistic missiles on the island. The Army was ordered to install mobile Nike nuclear-tipped interceptor missiles in the southern United States. A Nike unit, HM-69, consisting of four dispersed sites under the direction of a single fire control center, was dispatched to south Dade County. The fire control center and one of the four missile storage and launch sites were located in the Hole-in-the-Doughnut. (A second launch site was located nearby, about five miles east of the park, at the present site of the South Dade Correctional Facility.) The Army purchased the Iori Farms and took it over in June 1963. At first, everything was temporary—trailers and tents. Both men and equipment suffered terribly from the harsh climate.

But the Army initiated a crash building program. The fire control center, a one-story, blocky, cement building about twice the size of a ranch house, was located just off Long Pine Key Road. Two miles south, the missiles were stored in massive cement barns intended to resist a nuclear near-miss. By January 1966, the Army and the state had paved Long Pine Key Road and extended it to connect the fire control center and the missile barns.[16] The fire control center building is today the Daniel Beard Center and houses the park's archives and records center, and other administrative offices. The missile barns also stand, and are used to store equipment during hurricanes. The Long Pine Key Road is now named Research Road.

HM-69 was deactivated in the 1970s, but the loss of Iori Farms spelled the end of the Hole-in-the-Doughnut. The Ioris were the largest employer of itinerant farm labor in the area. Many farmers who didn't have places big enough to employ a planting or harvesting crew for a solid week could call the Ioris and get them hired there for a day or two. Without the Ioris, it simply wasn't cost effective for farm laborers to travel all the way across the park to take jobs in the Hole-in-the-Doughnut. The odds were too great that you would end up sitting out a day or two while part of a field dried or some piece of equipment was getting fixed. If you were going to work small farms, it was better to just stick closer to Homestead and Florida City. Thus, the HM-69 missile base helped accelerate what was already a growing trend towards surrendering the agricultural area to park control.

Some parts of the Ingraham Highway do continue to exist in largely original condition. A short stretch of road within the Pine Island Service Area, used to access an improvised boat ramp into Taylor Slough, is almost pristine. About eight miles of the old highway southwest of the Royal Palm Visitor is in good shape. It varies between almost original conditional and moderately altered. It is used as a recreational hiking and biking trail and has two primitive campgrounds. The trailhead is off Research Road, near the Royal Palm Visitor Center.

As recently as 1987, it was generally assumed by the park staff that the remaining portion of the Ingraham Highway between the old state park and the Cement Bridge not taken out in 1959 would be removed when the road was no longer needed for the park's invasive plant eradication program. The road was believed to lay within lands designated as "future wilderness area" in 1979. However, a 2007 review of the original 1979 wilderness designation maps undertaken as part of an update to the park's bicycle plan raised questions about whether the highway actually was intended to be in a designated wilderness zone, or instead was planned to have the same status as multi-use trails in other national parks recycled from railroad grades, logging roads, and other abandoned uses.[17]

After most of the roadbed in Taylor Slough was removed in 2005 (the two bridges having been removed years before), Park Service staff prepared a proposal in 2006 to grant protection to the remaining portions of the road as a cultural resource. It was criticized by some staff members who expressed concern that such designation would make it more difficult to secure approval to remove all remaining traces of the highway. The proposal was shelved. However, in 2008 an experimental installation of a relatively small number of culverts (approximately 12 to 16) under the highway near Jennings Grove was tried as an alternative to removing the road. Preliminary field ecological surveys appear to indicate that culvert installation is a viable alternative to removal.

The old highway has become an increasingly popular trail facility for hikers and cyclists. Although the old highway contains two primitive campgrounds, park management has been undecided about the extent to which it wants to make further investment in maintaining and preserving the road. The invasive plant eradication program for the former farmlands along the Ingraham Highway was finished in 2014. However, it appears that with the success of the culvert project, a new appreciation for road's cultural value, and an increased openness of the park service towards encouraging nonmotorized uses, the Ingraham Highway may be allowed to remain and will be preserved.

Those with an interest in the Ingraham Highway are fortunate; one of the oldest and best preserved portions of the road can be easily seen and walked to from the park's Coe Visitor Center at the Homestead entrance. If one stands in the parking lot, or better yet, looks out from the terrace of the museum, and looks south, across the main road, one will see, about four hundred feet south and running parallel to the main road, a substantial brushline with a few large limestone boulders peeking out every so often. It's easy to overlook except that the brushline runs in a dead-straight line beside the main road, but branches off a little to the south. This is the old Ingraham Highway. The bushes are growing in the abandoned road's ditches. The road itself is basically unchanged from the configuration it was in when built in 1914–15, then worked over by the J. B. McCrary crews a year later, except for the return of plant life, which is surprising sparse in the middle of the former roadway itself, but often quite thick in the ditches.

* * * * *

Another, little known chapter in the history of Cape Sable roadbuilding is the road that never was: the Great Coastal Highway. If it had been built, travelers heading south out of Florida City on the Card Sound Road to Key Largo would have turned right about six miles south of town and followed the coastline past Flamingo out to the end of Cape Sable. The road would have then doubled back on itself, following the north shore of Cape Sable, then back west again to the Gulf coast, where it would meet the new Tamiami Trail at Everglades City. It was so fantastical that it had to be the work of a crazy-man or a scammer. It was.

First, some background.[18] The Tatum brothers, like the Jennings, the Model Land Company and R. J. Bolles, were mega-landowners in south Florida. They founded Florida City, and owned a large tract of land to its east. One brother, R. B. Tatum, was mayor of Homestead for several years. They also owned and developed much of today's North Miami and North Miami Beach, and the areas north of Carl Fisher's Miami Beach that became Surfside and Sunny Isles. But the Tatum Brothers' biggest tract was a hundred square miles of Everglades northwest of Hialeah flanking the Miami Canal, along today's U.S. Highway 27.

In 1919, one of the brothers, B. B. Tatum, sold the Pennsylvania Sugar Company on the idea of coming down and trying their hand at raising sugar cane. Penn Sugar was a major international company, with a daily output of some 7,000 barrels of white and brown sugar at its Philadelphia mill, mostly using sugarcane shipped in from Cuba. The Tatums offered Penn Sugar a good deal: they could rent as much as they wanted at $1.85 to $3.50 and acre, and decide later if they wanted to buy the land for $12.00 an acre, less the rent already paid. One of the world's leading sugar cane cultivators, General Jose Gomez of Cuba, warned that the soil was insufficient to support annual cane crops, but in 1920 Penn Sugar went ahead with a modest 360 acre test plot. It was hit by a frost and killed. They pressed on, dispatching Ernest R. "Cap" Graham to take over operations.

Graham solved the fertility problem by dumping 500 to 2,000 pounds of phosphate-potash fertilizer per acre on his fields every year. He solved the freezing problem by flooding the fields with pumps just before the freeze, then drawing the water off immediately afterwards—along with massive quantities of phosphates and nitrates. In 1922, the sugar company spent a million and a half dollars on a sugar cane processing mill some ten miles northeast of Hialeah. They incorporated their own company town, calling it Pensuco. However, there was so little sugar cane to feed it that it ran for only thirty days during the 1923 season. The 1923, '24 and '25 seasons were flooded out. Graham decided to cover his bets. By 1925, he switched almost 1,000 acres to vegetables.

In 1923 Graham placed two low dams in the Miami Canal in an attempt to dry out his vegetable fields. Penn Sugar was promptly sued by a neighboring landowner who claimed that the dams inundated his formerly dry lands.[19] The suit was in litigation for several years before the Pennsylvania Sugar Co. won. However, it had the effect of inhibiting both Penn Sugar and the Everglades Drainage Board from more aggressively constructing infrastructure to divert water from north central Dade County. In 1927, Penn Sugar sold the Pensuco mill to the Southern Sugar Company, who dismantled it and moved it to Clewiston, on the southern rim of Lake Okeechobee. Vegetables had proven to be a safer, more reliable investment, but by 1930 the price of almost all agricultural products had collapsed. The company quit planting and withdrew from south Florida entirely in 1931.

Against this backdrop, a man from Philadelphia named J. R. Deane appeared in Miami in August 1923 and made the acquaintance of James Jaudon, the former Dade County Tax Assessor who had become deeply involved in the construction of the Tamiami Trail.[20] Jaudon was already down in the Cape Sable area regularly on one of his jobs as superintendent of the U.S. Sisal Trust's plantation northwest of the Royal Palm Park. He proposed that Deane buy Cape Sable lands, form a drainage district to dig the canals needed to reclaim the land, and sell the parcels by mail-order, as R. J. Bolles had done more than a decade before. "I think that in proceeding along the above lines you should have no trouble in selling this land at $75.00 dollars per acre in the present condition," he wrote Deane. Keep in mind that the going rate for cash sales of Cape Sable lands in small parcels, not fronting on the highway, was about fifteen dollars per acre.[21]

At first, Deane and Jaudon targeted the Dewhurst Tract, but when Dewhurst, a shrewd lawyer, heard that Deane planned to set up a special taxing district to pay for reclamation, he demanded a full cash sale: one hundred percent payment up front. The last thing Dewhurst wanted was to see the return of his land in a foreclosure action, but with the entire acreage burdened by hundreds of thousands of dollars in drainage district bond payments. Deane and Jaudon turned their attention to the land owned by the Model Land Company.[22]

In August, Jaudon proposed the incorporation of an entity called the Royal Palm Sugar Cane & Planting Company to organize the improvement and cultivation of whatever land Deane chose to purchase. Deane agreed, and Jaudon formed it with local officers. After the Dewhurst rejection, Jaudon and Deane looked over a Model Land Company tract about five miles south of Royal Palm State Park. As Frank Pepper informed Sidney Harrison of the Model Land Co. in early November 1923:

> From what you told us in the office of the proposed contract and from what we get from the conversation we had with him last night the [Model Land] Company is considering selling him the land at a stipulated price without any payment of actual money.... From certain remarks made by Mr. Livingston and Mr. Deane on the subject I am of the opinion that Mr. Deane's plan of drainage is to form immediately a Drainage District which on the face of the proposition and without positive guarantee of some time that he will carry out his purchase contract, would seem to be a dangerous proposition for the Company on account of the liability of all the land back into your hands in case of failure on his part.[23]

Sidney Harrison's only response to this warning was a request to have the Pepper & Potter realty firm prepare an abstract of title for two entire townships—72 square miles—in preparation of a sale. Twelve years earlier, Frederick Morse had related to James Ingraham how Bill Krome had told him that one of these, "Twp. 59–37 is the poorest land that he knows of ... and that if he had it for sale he would sell it for any price." "Any price" is just about what Sidney Harrison got.[24]

A few days latter, the Model Land Company's agents in Homestead wrote to Harrison. They had received a telegram from Jaudon "asking us not to reply to any communications regarding his purchase proposition until we had received a full report from him," and they wanted to know what was going on. Harrison replied that he was as mystified as they were. The problem was an evaluation of Township 59–37 by Dr. E. W. Brandon of the U.S. Department of Agriculture that said about the same thing Krome did back in 1911: that the site was not suitable for most agricultural purposes, even sugar cane.[25]

On January 14, the Model Land Co. executed a contract for slightly more than 34,000 acres at ten dollars per acre. The purchaser was not the Royal Palm Sugar Cane & Planting Company, the firm that James Jaudon had set up a few months earlier, but a new, Pennsylvania corporation, one named the Pennsylvania Sugar Land Company, a name striking similar to that of the international firm with the mill in Pensuco. "At the very start I did not like the fact that the title of this company is so much like that of the Pennsylvania Sugar Company, as it is a means of mis-leading prospective investors," complained James Ingraham, "so far he has reported several sales, and sent notes to the First National Bank [of Homestead], but no cash, and, as far we have been able to learn, no cash has been placed in the bank at Homestead for developmental purposes."[26]

The scam worked like this: a Pennsylvania farmer who wanted a second farm, or who had run out of luck in Pennsylvania, paid $75.00 an acre to Deane's Pennsylvania Land Sugar Co. (PLSC) for land that Deane had bought for ten dollars an acre, and fully on credit. The smallholder then had to agree to let Jaudon's Royal Palm Sugar Cane & Planting Company use 90 percent of this land to grow vegetables or sugar cane. Moreover, the owner had to pay all of Royal Palm Sugar Cane's costs of farming, as well as any costs necessary to get the site in shape for its initial planting. In turn, the owner received two-thirds of the net profits from these crops ("net" to be determined by Deane and Jaudon). The owner got to use ten percent of his land for a homestead or planting, assuming he could reach it with anything other than a canoe.[27]

Soon after, Frank Pepper reported to Ingraham:

> I drove down to Coconut Grove and had a nice visit with Dr. David Fairchild [the famous botanist] this morning and asked him to tell me what he knew about Mr. Deane and his proposition.... One of the main impressions that I gained from Dr. Fairchild's conversation was that he does not think Mr. Deane is making an honest and correct representation to prospective purchasers in inducing them to purchase this property, and he expressed a prediction, if handled along the lines as indicated in the literature shown him by Mr. Deane, that later on some purchaser will become disgruntled and the matter will be brought to the attention of some Pennsylvania Congressman, who in the usual political manner, would not hesitate to get up on the floor of Congress and openly denounce the proposition as another Florida swindling land game and might go so far as to state that the property was sold by the Florida East Coast Railroad.[28]

That got everyone's attention. Frank Pepper wrote Ingraham asking if they should twist Deane or Jaudon's arm to get them to tone down their advertising. Ingraham advised against it. "Our attorney thought it best to eliminate all chance of our revising his advertising matter or approving or disapproving of same, in order to avoid complicating the Model Land Co., or making it responsible for any language that he might use," Ingraham replied. Besides, "we have signed the contract, and they have signed the trust agreement, and I don't see what we can do until we have evidence of fraud."[29]

But there was another reason Ingraham wanted to take a hands-off attitude. The maps that Deane and Jaudon had prepared showed both a railroad branch line penetrating deep into the Cape Sable District, and a coast road looping from Florida City out to Lake Ingraham on the far west end of the Cape, as related by James Ingraham:

> We ourselves, have heard some talk of this proposed coastal highway from the cocoanut plantations to Miami ... this may or may not end in talk, but we think there is a reliable possibility of it coming from Miami to Jacksonville, and there is a possibility of it going from Miami to Cape Sable ... we do not desire to be connected with the project in any way that may implicate us, though we have every reason to believe that Mr. Deane is honest and that he will use his utmost efforts to carry out his project to successful issue, and we concur in your opinion that if he gets 50% of what he contemplates doing, that it will be one of the most successful undertakings for the development of Florida that has ever been tried.[30]

The "cocoanut plantations" Ingraham refers to was the Waddell plantation on the far end of Cape Sable, planted by E. A. Waddell in the 1890s. In the 1920s it was inactive, but still being tended to. Two years earlier Lawrence Will had visited it when he was working on the dredge digging the canal between Flamingo and Lake Ingraham and found it in good shape, with caretakers living on-site.[31]

Ingraham's comment about a Miami-Jacksonville road is a reference to the Dixie Highway, first undertaken in 1916 as a private, multi-state voluntary effort to connect Chicago and Miami similar to the earlier transcontinental Lincoln Highway. The Dixie Highway's eastern division entered the state at Jacksonville and followed the FEC tracks to Miami. Flagler, Ingraham, and some of St. Augustine's other leading citizens had formed the East Coast Good Roads Association as early as 1903 to promote it or something like it.[32]

Alas, it was all a pipe dream—or fraud. On June 29, six months after signing a purchase contract for $262,000, Deane reported that he could not make the first installment of $50,000, having made exactly one cash sale for a hundred dollars. A month later, Jaudon learned that he was the president of a non-existent corporation, as Deane had neglected to perfect the charter of the Royal Palm Sugar Cane & Planting Co. Knowing trouble when he saw it, Jaudon generously offered to resign his position with Royal Palm Sugar Cane and cancel his contract with Deane, even going so far as waive any fees and commissions due him. "I regret very much that I cannot actively join you in your planting company plans but my duties have multiplied so fast in the matter of my land on the Tamiami Trail," he explained.

Capt. Jaudon may have been the consummate Florida land wheeler-dealer, but he was no con man, and he was canny enough to know when an overoptimistic, underfinanced land venture had staggered over the line into land fraud. The Royal Palm Sugar Cane & Planting Co. and the Pennsylvania Land Sugar Co. both evaporated into the warm, summer nights of 1924. Jaudon carried on with his Tamiami Trail plans. J. R. Deane seemingly disappeared from the face of the earth, and took with him the dream of a Florida Bay coast road.[33]

But somehow the Whitewater Bay-Cape Sable Loop Road started to appear on the base map of Dade County Road and Bridge District No. 1, and stayed there for decades even after District No. 1 was taken over by the county. When Ernest Coe prepared his first plan for the proposed Everglades National Park in 1930 on behalf of the Everglades National Park Association, he used one of these base maps.[34] In his doctoral dissertation on the history of Coe and the creation of Everglades National Park, Chris Wilhelm points out that the Cape Sable Loop Road was not just a passive background feature that happened appear on a base map. Within the text of the plan itself Coe identified proposed locations, keyed to the map, for marinas, boat docks, and piers jutting out into Florida Bay from the Loop Road. However, when challenged about the idea of a highway between Flamingo and the west coast by Henry Ward of the Izaak Walton League, Coe replied that the road was just "the suggestion of an outside party and not of any significance," a statement that Ward later told another League member was "a rather superficial excuse."[35]

Unaware of the pre-existing history of the Cape Sable Loop Road and poor condition of the lower Ingraham Highway at that time, Wilhelm expresses some confusion over why Coe would draw up plans for an environmentally devastating new coastal highway to the west coast, scattering recreational amenities along it, while at the same time emphasizing the uniqueness of his proposed Tropical Everglades National Park as the nation's first wilderness-based facility. The answer is that the road was there already, at least on paper, and as Wilhelm himself acknowledges, part of the problem Coe faced was justifying the cost of acquiring a massively large piece of real estate expressly for the purpose of keeping almost everybody out of it. Outside of a few, well-contained recreational areas, Coe really had no plans to install infrastructure just to enhance the tourist value of the park. The three zones he did identify, the Homestead/state park area, Flamingo and Chokoloskee, in the Thousand Islands, were already well established areas of human activity.

But the coastal loop road made the early drafts of the park proposal look more "normal," more Yellowstone-like. Coe was a landscape architect, was familiar with roadside architecture, and if necessary, knew how to create renderings of scenic vistas out of what the average congressman (or taxpayer) considered wasteland.

His caution proved unnecessary, however. By the mid- to late-1930s when the plans for the new park started to became more concrete, there was less need to sell it as "something for everyone," and the proposals started to look more like what was actually developed.[36] With the addition of the Shark Valley and Pinecrest visitor centers along the Tamiami Trail to the north, the three activity nodes Coe identified did become the basic configuration of the park. All were more or less along the fringes of the park; only the drive to Flamingo required traversing its interior.

But yet the old Cape Sable Loop Road kept cropping up on the maps. Monroe County's first attempt to build an overseas highway alongside Flagler's railroad grade had ended in 1928 with "a nightmarish jumble of crooked, oil-marl trails and dangerous bridges," and three missing links that required a 40-mile ferry connection that only ran twice a day each direction. Its road department went four million dollars into debt.

In 1932 the county sold the highway to a public corporation, the Overseas Highway Bridge Corporation, that was intended to raise money through private bank loans. Its engineers returned a report estimating that completion would cost $10.7 million. Needless to say, the loans were not forthcoming. The county soon replaced the Highway Bridge Corporation with the Monroe County Toll Bridge Commission. The Public Works Administration, one of President's Roosevelt's New Deal "alphabet soup" programs, agreed to a loan $3.6 million if Florida would provide the rest. The state was not eager to provide over six million dollars. The project looked like a non-starter until the Labor Day hurricane of 1935 blew away the Florida East Coast's overseas railroad. The FEC, in receivership since 1931, had no money to repair the line. They agreed to sell it for $640,000. Suddenly, the project was feasible given the PWA loan. It was completed in March 1938.[37]

In the boom years after World War II, Key West and Monroe County apparently forgot how close they had come to disaster twenty years earlier. In 1959 the Key West Chamber of Commerce lobbied the county commission to allocate money to study a causeway from Key West to Flamingo. In 1961 the county commissioners approached the state to ask for $50,000 to study the feasibility of erecting a causeway from Big Pine Key (about 20 miles above Key West) to Cape Sable, and from there up the west coast to Everglades City. The park superintendent's monthly reports from 1960 to 1963 report regular, if infrequent, bouts of activity at the Key West City Commission, the Monroe County Commission, or most often, the Key West Chamber of Commerce, on various trans-bay causeway proposals.[38]

The logic behind any of the Keys-to-Cape Sable alternatives is questionable. The distance from Key West to Flamingo is 65 miles, mostly because Key West is almost 50 miles west of Flamingo. The distance from Big Pine Key to Flamingo is 40 miles. The distance from Islamorada, the mid-point in the keys and the traditional jumping-off spot for motor launches headed to Flamingo and Cape Sable in the days before there was a road, is 22 miles.

After 1962, mention of a Keys-to-Cape Sable road appears in the superintendent's monthly reports only once more, when park superintendent Stanley Joseph met with John Monahan, state road commissioner, in the summer of 1963 to discuss the status of a proposed Key West to Cape Sable causeway. Superintendent Joseph's report implies that Monahan did not believe the causeway was a priority with the state. That is understandable, given that the highway department was preparing to rehabilitate both the Overseas Highway, and its predecessor, the old Dixie Highway, which follows a separate route between Homestead and Key Largo over its own bridge at Card Sound, joining the Overseas Highway at Key Largo. The new Card Sound High Bridge, plus replacing the old railroad bridges down to Key West, had a much higher priority than building a new trans-bay causeway. After this 1963 discussion between superintendent Joseph and commissioner Monahan, there is no further record of discussions regarding a road or bridge across Florida Bay.

But the Florida City-to-Everglades City coast road is alternatively astonishing and appalling to those who stumble across it in all its sheer audacity and stupidity on the old 1920s and '30s base maps: a 90-mile road across solid mangrove wetlands running anywhere from two miles back of the shoreline to right on the beach. It was an era when anything was thought possible and everything was considered progress. If it is any relief or consolation, it wouldn't have had a prayer. It would have swallowed up all of the crushed rock in the State of Florida without needing even a polite burp.

PART II:
THE TAMIAMI TRAIL

••6••

Not Such a Terrific Job

The first to publicly promote the idea of a coast-to-coast highway across south Florida, was, ironically, the Miami-based conservationist John Gifford. In the July 1914 issue of *Tropic Magazine*, Gifford urged that:

> We should lose no time in building a road due west from Miami across this region to the west coast. According to many reports, Cocoloskee [sic] Bay on the west coast has a great future.... It will be a great tourist route—the first Ocean-to-Gulf highway. If all our organizations get together and work for this one thing and stick to it, it will come sooner or later, and bring with it more than we at present realize. Think of bathing in the Atlantic Ocean in the morning, and in the Gulf of Mexico in the afternoon of the same day.... A road straight across would not prove such a terrific job and would do lots more good than the proposed road to Cape Sable.[1]

The key phrase is that last sentence. Gifford was an early supporter of the Royal Palm State Park at Paradise Key, along with Coconut Grove writer Kirk Munroe, his wife, Mary Barr Munroe, the railroad engineer William Krome, Krome's colleague at the Florida East Coast Railroad, James Ingraham, and New York botanist John K. Small. At this time, the Model Land Company had already started constructing their Cape Sable road, and thus far only the Munroes, Krome, Ingraham and Gifford were taking the idea of saving Paradise Key seriously.

When Gifford wrote his article, it looked like it was going to be a close race to see if Paradise Key could be acquired by some philanthropic organization and saved before the road arrived. Fortunately, the road bogged down in Taylor Slough and May Mann Jennings and her husband, the former governor, put their considerable political clout behind the creation of the state park, which even then was a state facility in name only, as it was paid for entirely with private funds for several years.[2] It is likely that Gifford's cross-state "Orange Glade Highway" (as he called it) was as much a way to draw attention away from proposals to use public money to finance the Cape Sable road (which did happen in late 1915) as it was a serious proposal to build a highway from Miami to Fort Myers.[3]

The real impetus behind the Tamiami Trail was the establishment of the Dixie Highway Association. Indianapolis native Carl Fisher first proposed the creation of a "Dixie Highway" from Chicago to Miami at the fourth annual meeting of the American Road Congress in Atlanta in November 1914.[4] Fisher was a former bicycle and automobile salesman who had made a fortune from the Prest-O-Lite compressed-gas headlight system. He then built the Indianapolis Motor Speedway in 1909. He had been heavily involved in forming the Lincoln Highway Association in 1912 to promote a transcontinental highway from New York to San Francisco. The Lincoln Highway Association originally planned to use donations raised from local booster organizations and governments along the route to finance its construction. This fragmented structure was never completely successful. For example, only $265 was raised in Nevada, although it was one of the hardest stretches to travel, and one of the most expensive to build.[5]

In its 14-year life between 1913 and 1927, the Lincoln Road Association collected and spent about one and a quarter million dollars. But of this, only half actually went to road building. The remainder was used for office overhead, travel, and above all—marketing. The Association had to spend one dollar for every two it solicited from towns, counties, corporations and individuals. That was indicative of the limits of private road finance. It was simply not possible to keep people interested and enthused about a project that lasted 14 years and extended for three thousand miles. Donors could not be expected to reach for their wallets time and time again for a road they could not see and did not know when would come.[6]

But the groundwork laid by the Lincoln Highway Association was enough to get the project started and established, thereby making it impossible for the federal Bureau of Public Roads and the various state highway departments to ignore after the first federal-aid highway acts were enacted in 1916 and 1921. Although the Lincoln Highway was not fully finished until about 1928, after 1921 the remaining work was more technical and financial than organizational and political, and was primarily in the hands of state and federal authorities. The Lincoln Highway eventually became U.S. Highway 40, roughly following the route of today's Interstate 80. Fisher did not enjoy the push and shove of competing local politics, and after 1913 his focus turned to another project he had initiated in 1910: developing Miami Beach.[7]

The American Road Congress, a national assembly jointly sponsored by the American Highway Association and the American Automobile Association, met in Atlanta November 7–12, 1914. Some preliminary organization for the Dixie Highway was done there, but the most important decision was to schedule a dedicated planning conference in Chattanooga the following April.[8] Fisher, irritated by the squabbles that had plagued the Lincoln Highway, tried a different strategy this time. First, he appointed a front man to manage the new association and negotiate the route, Indianapolis seed manufacturer William S. Gilbreath. Second, he circumvented local booster groups and government officials and went straight to the state governors to do the decision-making.[9]

The Chattanooga convention on April 5, 1915, was a disaster. Some 5,000 delegates from ten states and 200 localities met to lobby for locating the highway in their jurisdiction. The meeting degenerated into chaos, mostly because the governors decided to take Fisher at his word and announced that they would select the route themselves without input from the Dixie Highway Association. The Association's "founders" (i.e., board of directors) told the governors that they would not provide financial support if they were not included in the route planning. The governors agreed, only to be shouted down by an audience largely comprised of men, like Fisher, with a vested financial interest in some particular route. William Gilbreath was unable to deliver his address because of the raucous crowd.[10]

The governors and the founders reached a compromise. They would try again at a second meeting on May 20. The governors would select two highway commissioners from each state. In many cases the governors picked businessmen with at least some interest in a given route, but usually balanced this bias by selecting individuals from different parts of their state. This was true in Florida as well. Samuel A. Belcher, a Miami real estate broker and county commissioner, and G. W. Saxon of Tallahassee were selected. The second assembly, also in Chattanooga, was, unlike the earlier convention, calm and businesslike. The agreed-upon compromise that made this possible was that the Dixie Highway would not be a single line on the map like the Lincoln Highway, but instead a network of routes, divided generally into a western and an eastern division with connecting crossovers, looking something like a wavy ladder running from Michigan to Florida.[11]

Within Florida, the eastern division was never in doubt. Entering the state at Jacksonville, it followed the Florida East Coast Railroad down the Atlantic coast to the doorstep of Fisher's new Billion Dollar Sandbar at Miami Beach. The western division was more problematic. There were two options submitted for consideration in May 1915. The first entered the state just north of Tallahassee, which lay on the Old Spanish Trail, the original east-west colonial road between Pensacola and St. Augustine. Over the years, the Atlantic end of Old Spanish Trail had shifted north to Jacksonville to avoid crossing the St. Johns River, but the road was still largely unimproved. The first option followed the Old Spanish Trail from Tallahassee to Jacksonville, where it joined the eastern division. The second option kept the Tallahassee-Jacksonville connection, but added a spur down to Tampa via Lake City, Gainesville, and Ocala.[12]

But both these options reflected little more than the unpleasant reality that the state representatives lacked both the information and the consensus needed to make a firm

James Jaudon (right with unknown others) farming tomatoes on the Allapattah Prairie, about five miles northwest of central Miami, 1903. (Photographer unknown. HistoryMiami, No. X-055-104.)

recommendation to William Gilbreath and his staff at the Dixie Highway Association. Thus, the period between May 1915, when the second Chattanooga conference was held, and January 1917, when the Association published its first official route map, became something of a political free-for-all in central and south Florida for good roads advocates.

Many doubted whether anyone could reasonably expect a cross-state road to be built south of the Old Spanish Trail in the foreseeable future. The safe bet was simply to end the western division at Tampa.

Those who thought otherwise offered three alternatives:

1. From Tallahassee, go southeast to Orlando, then cut east to Melbourne on the Atlantic coast to meet the Eastern Division. This is the route S. A. Belcher initially favored, as he believed that it was simply not feasible to cross the state any farther south.[13]
2. From Tallahassee, go southeast to Orlando. But instead of turning east, continue south through Bartow and Arcadia, *then* turn east to pass through Okeechobee City on the north shore of Lake Okeechobee, continuing on to Jupiter, 30 miles north of West Palm Beach.[14]
3. From Tallahassee, go southeast to Gainesville, then south to Ocala. Bypass Orlando by turning southwest to Tampa. From Tampa follow the Gulf coast south to Fort Myers, then turn east along the levee of the Caloossahatchee River canal to the south rim of Lake Okeechobee, then southeast on the levee of the (as yet unfinished) Miami River Canal into Miami.[15]

Before he left for the May 20 Chattanooga meeting, Belcher expressed skepticism about sending the western division any farther south than Orlando. "There is no show of getting a road down the Miami canal bank for many years," he told a reporter, "and the show is no better working west from the lake," he said, referring to Lake Okeechobee. He preferred a central route that entered the state east of Tallahassee, near Lake City then south to Orlando, turning east to Melbourne, but acknowledged that due to the influence of his fellow commissioner, G. W. Saxon, the most likely route would be Tallahassee-Jacksonville. He was definitely opposed to the "stopgap" solution of creating a spur into Tampa until a final routing recommendation could be made: "If the highway was built to Tampa it would be to the interests of the Tampa people to put off the building of the road across the Everglades as long as possible that the stream of tourists not be turned down the east coast to Miami. Such a move would be fatal to Miami's interests."[16]

Belcher's statements clearly indicate that he had been approached by someone between the April 5 and May 20 Dixie Highway Association meetings about the idea of a south Florida highway. This agrees with a later account of James Jaudon of Miami, who recalled that a small group of businessmen from both coasts met in Tallahassee in late April 1915 while Florida's biennial legislature was still in session to discuss the feasibility of a far south "Miami-to-Marco" cross-state highway.[17]

Capt. James Franklin Jaudon was the Dade County tax assessor, but also a businessman. In fact, he was one of those unique specimens of Florida life before the Great Depression: the obsessively driven, middle-class, self-financed real estate speculator. At the time of his death in 1938 he may have owned as much as 350,000 acres of land in three states, every square foot of it co-owned or mortgaged to the hilt. Born in Waco, Texas, on October 19, 1873, his family brought him to Orlando when he was eight. He worked for one of the contractors building the bridges and culverts on the Florida East Coast's Miami extension for a couple of years. After the FEC reached Miami in 1895 he ran a cartage business until volunteering for the Spanish-American war. Its swift conclusion meant he got no farther than the docks at Tampa before being demobilized, so he returned to Miami.[18]

Mrs. Emma B. Mallon of Philadelphia wrote Jaudon in late 1898 to ask if he would like to partner with her and her son Darrah on a five-acre citrus grove they wished to start somewhere around Homestead. Jaudon wrote back that "I really can't say that that I am favorably impressed with South Dade County as a citrus-fruit country and prefer not to attempt to make a grove here," but the Mallons already had bought land, and the reply was to ask him to go ahead and give it a try. He picked the most promising land out of the tract they owned, and to everyone's surprise guavas did wonderfully and were wildly popular with jelly-makers. Bananas, which most people had never seen before, followed and with the profits, Jaudon, his brother Paul, and young Mallon could prepare the land properly for lemons and grapefruits. Mallon & Jaudon moved from truck farming into being one of the largest fruit and vegetable wholesalers in south Florida. He was elected City of Miami tax assessor in 1906, then moved to the same position at Dade County in 1909, where he remained until 1917.[19]

The official history of the Tamiami Trail Commission, written at the time of the Trail's grand opening in 1928, asserts that the name "Tamiami Trail" was coined at a convention of the Central Florida Highway Association in Orlando on June 10, 1915. Some 276 delegates

Jaudon Brothers Mercantile Company, wholesalers of fruits and vegetables, downtown Miami, about 1910. (Photographer unknown. HistoryMiami No. X-055-116.)

attended this meeting, called to organize the association in reaction to the failure of the Dixie Highway Association to designate a Western Division route in Florida and to lobby for one that would pass through the general area between Gainesville on the north to Arcadia on the south. Newspaper accounts note that "when mention was made of the Tampa-Miami Trail which was proposed recently by president Collins Gillett, of the board of trade, there was spontaneous applause. This route goes straight south through Manatee [Bradenton] to Arcadia, Punta Gorda, to Marco, thence straight east to Miami."[20]

The newspaper story clearly indicates that the *concept* of a Miami-to-Marco highway already existed, and other accounts establish that the name had also been previously developed. Within a week of Belcher's return from the May 20 Chattanooga meeting, Gillett, president of the Tampa Board of Trade, visited Miami on business connected with his Tampa Bay-area citrus groves. While in town, he met with some of the directors of the Miami Chamber of Conference. Vance Helm, the director of the Miami Chamber's Everglades Bureau, later recounted that "prior to that time, there had been some talk about the importance and necessity of building a road across the state, but it had never gotten past the talk stage ... while Mr. Gillett was here we discussed the advisability of converting the talk into action ... he suggested that when we got the thing in motion we should use the name 'Tamiam Trail.'"[21]

Helm recalled that a night or two after Gillett's visit, the board of directors of the Miami Chamber of Commerce had one of their regular meetings, and he, Helm, introduced a resolution providing for the appointment of a three-man Chamber of Commerce committee to evaluate route and funding alternatives. The resolution was approved and banker Locke Highleyman, county commissioner Eugene Stahl, and W. T. Carter were appointed. Before the end of May, Stahl had traveled to Fort Lauderdale in order to meet with the Broward Chamber of Commerce to feel them out about the favored Miami Canal route, which would pass through the southwest portion of their county. The Dade County Chamber of Commerce also contacted its counterpart in Lee County, and in early June the Lee County Chamber of Commerce had contacted S. A. Belcher to assure him that if a far south cross-state highway was chosen for the Dixie Highway, they would be behind it. In referring to the road, the Lee County Chamber of Commerce used the name "Tamiami Trail."[22]

There are other versions of this story. In 1928, William Stewart Hill, an editor for the *Miami Herald*, said that *he* gave Jaudon the idea of the cross-state highway, around May 1915. While Hill did write several articles just before and after the May 20 Chattanooga conference, many of these had to do with the eastern division, parallel to the Florida East Coast Railroad, and the ones that did discuss the western division did so in a general way. L. P. Dickie, Secretary of the Tampa Board of Trade, later claimed that he first coined the name "Tamiami Trail" at the June 10 conference in Orlando, but this is not credible, as the name was already being widely used in the newspapers as early as June 4.[23] The most credible claimant to the name "Tamiam Trail" or "Tamiami Trail" is probably Collins Gillett of Tampa, and the earliest use appears to be around May 27, 1915.

There is a final version of this story. In 1936, only a few years before his death, Jaudon responded to an interview question from the WPA's Federal Writer's Project by writing that he had traveled to Naples immediately before going to Tallahassee in April 1915 at the invitation of Judge E. G. Wilkinson, who Jaudon described as "quiet, retiring, powerful in his influence," and it was at *this* conference that Wilkinson first impressed upon him the need to lobby for a southern cross-state highway with Belcher. Jaudon said that "It was he [Wilkinson] in 1915 who saw that the future of Naples, Fort Myers and the West Coast depended largely on Miami." Prior to this, most local commercial interests believed that isolation from both Tampa and Miami was a financial advantage for the lower Gulf coast, one they should hold on to for as long as possible. Jaudon admitted that Wilkinson was "the real daddy of the Tamiami Trail." Given the timeline of both Jaudon's and Wilkinson's subsequent involvement in the project, this account rings true, but Jaudon does not assert that either he or Wilkinson used the name "Tamiami Trail" at this time.[24]

* * * * *

After the two Florida Dixie Highway delegates returned from Chattanooga with the western division essentially a blank space on the map, two simultaneous issues were in play: (1) could Saxon and Belcher, from whom the Dixie Highway Association was expecting a formal routing report, be convinced to recommend a cross-state highway somewhere through the middle of the state; and (2) if so, along which route?

Saxon preferred a mid-state route, and wanted it to go south from Tallahassee to Orlando to Arcadia, then east to Okeechobee City and Jupiter. Belcher wanted it to stay farther north, Lake City to Orlando, then east to Melbourne:

> There is being advocated a road to be known as the Tamiami Trail which crosses the 'Glades at Fort Lauderdale or Miami that has nothing to do with the Dixie Highway proposition. I again state that I favor a direct central route to be named and dedicated as the Western Dixie Highway, and as many tributaries as possible, but I do not favor the highway branching to the west from Gainesville to Tallahassee, or from Jupiter to Arcadia, as both routes are indirect.[25]

Saxon, of course was livid, as was most of central and north Florida. There was little they could do to retaliate by threatening the interests of the eastern division; that was Carl Fisher's road, and Fisher was the power behind the throne at the Dixie Highway Association. All they could do was to try to put as many roadblocks up as possible for any southern "tributaries." But Belcher's admission that the Tamiami Trail "had nothing to do" with the Dixie Highway indicated the direction the battle of roads was going. Increasingly, the various groups were coming to see the Tamiami Trail and the western division of the Dixie Highway as two separate undertakings that may or may not be related. The Central Florida Highway Association endorsed the Tamiami Trail because they wanted the western division of the Dixie Highway to end in Tampa, and the Trail would provide a connection from Tampa to Miami. On the other hand, S. A. Belcher, while supporting the Tamiami Trail, did not change his opinion that it was a bad idea to send the Dixie Highway to Tampa.[26]

Meanwhile, various interests were battling over the alignment of the Tamiami Trail. Initially, the assumption was that the road would have to skirt north of the Everglades; in other words, that it could not run straight west out of Miami. The first alignment proposed was the middle route, or, as it was later called, the "Seminole Trail." Going from Fort Myers to Miami, it ran southeast out of Fort Myers for about 25 miles along the old wagon route to Immokalee. After Immokalee, it then stretched eastward 30 miles to a mostly mythical place known as "Sam Jones Old Town," near the (very real) site of Brown's Landing (Brown's Store). It was about 35 miles due south of today's Clewiston, near the ruins of Fort Shackelford. This closely followed the route that James Ingraham had taken with his survey party in 1892 up to where they left their oxcarts behind. Ingraham and his men headed southeast to Miami from that point, but the proposed route of the Tamiami Trail continued east for another ten or twelve miles to intersect with the Miami Canal, then southeast along the canal bank into Miami.[27]

The Chamber of Commerce in Fort Myers lobbied for this route over the previous southern option, the Caloosahatchee River route that followed the river east from Olga (ten miles east of Fort Myers) to Sand Point (now Clewiston) on the south shore of Lake

Okeechobee, then along the shoreline to South Point, where the Miami Canal flowed out of the lake, then southeast on top of the canal bank to Miami. At Olga, a new steel bridge had been completed in early 1915 over the Caloosahatchee. An unimproved county road already existed from Olga north to Arcadia, and from Arcadia, the Tamiami Trail could be extended into either central Florida via Orlando, or to the Gulf coast via Bradenton and Tampa. However, under this plan, Fort Myers would be bypassed, although a finished and graded road did connect Olga and Fort Myers along the south bank of the river.[28]

Belcher himself preferred a Cape Sable route, which would extend the Ingraham Highway that the Model Land Company was building to Flamingo on to the west and northwest to Everglade and Marco. This was a highly improbable plan, and likely existed only because Belcher owned a thousand acres of land along the Ingraham Highway at a place known as the Cement Bridge, about twelve miles west-southwest of the Royal Palm State Park.[29] Belcher quickly killed this idea: "It has been stated that I favor a route via way of Cape Sable on up the west coast to Kissimmee. I do favor a route that way at a later period, but not now."[30]

In mid–June 1915, L. P. Dickie first proposed a new, more audacious alternative to the Seminole Trail: the cross-state highway should not turn east at Fort Myers. Instead, it should continue down the Gulf coast through Bonita Springs and Naples to Marco, then head due east all the way to Miami. "The Tampa idea is to have the trail include as many gulf coast towns as possible instead of running directly through the Everglades," summarized one account. Therefore, while Gillett's claim to the name "Tamiami Trail" may be stronger than Dickie's, he does appear to have originated the idea of the Tamiami Trail in its ultimate form, not just as a way of getting from one coast of Florida to the other, but as a way of creating a "Grand Concourse" for the Gulf coast, a coastal highway to match the eastern division of the Dixie Highway, and connecting with the shortest, most direct route into Miami.[31]

In fact, the advantages of this highway to Lee County became obvious in early June, when its voters approved the creation of Special Road and Bridge District No. 1, with $177,000 in bond financing, to construct a road along the coast from Fort Myers south to Marco Island.[32] Since Lee was going to build a coast road all the way down to Marco, why not take advantage of it and use it as the jumping-off point for the cross-state highway? The only drawback was getting over the Caloossahatchee River in downtown Fort Myers where it was five thousand feet wide. Anyone following the coast road had to divert inland to Olga, and the traveler headed north to Tampa had two choices after crossing the bridge: come right back into north Fort Myers and catch the coast road again, or continue north on the county road to Arcadia, and stay inland to Manatee (Bradenton), which had the added advantage of avoiding another inland diversion at Punta Gorda, where the Peace River had yet to be crossed at Charlotte Harbor.[33]

But even in the short run, Tampa-Marco-Miami had a decided political advantage: while the inland cities such as Orlando, Bartow, and Arcadia would get the prestige of the Dixie Highway, the Gulf coast cities between Tampa and Fort Myers would get the Tamiami Trail, even if it was a somewhat illusory line on the map until the mile-long bridges at downtown Fort Myers (Caloossahatchee River), Charlotte Harbor (Peace River) and Bradenton (Manatee River) could be built.

In Miami, James Jaudon was the first to suggest that the Tamiami Trail in Dade County match up to Dickie's plan by having it exit Miami due west along 20th Street (now Southwest 8th Street). But a week later Locke Highleyman told the Dade County Commissioners that he believed that the Sam Jones Old Town route was still the most popular with the people of Lee County. The commissioners sent Highleyman to Tallahassee to secure the permission of the trustees of the Internal Improvement Fund to use the canal bank for the roadway, which they quickly agreed to. In July, the Sam Jones Old Town route was declared "a definite conclusion" and Jaudon was instructed to prepare the necessary paperwork for the creation of a special road and bridge district, the prerequisite for a bond election.[34]

Then, suddenly, in early August, the Dade County Commission announced that Sam Jones Old Town was out, and that the straight-away Twentieth Street route was in. On August 13, the Tamiami Trail commission that had been established by the Chamber of Commerce in May, comprised of Locke Highleyman, Eugene Stahl, and W. T. Carter was disbanded, and replaced with a County Commissioners' Tamiami Trail Commission made up of Locke Highleyman, James Jaudon and R. E. McDonald. The County Engineer, Hobart Crabtree, was instructed to immediately make a survey of the straight-away route.[35]

Crabtree organized a survey party that left Miami on August 5. It included Jaudon and Highleyman, Crabtree's assistant Audley Frederick, and, according to Crabtree's notes, two chainmen, two laborers, and one African American, probably a cook. "Our equipment was two flat bottom Glade boats, two Indian canoes, provisions, and nerves," Jaudon later recalled. They started several miles beyond the end of the county road, on what is now the main campus of Florida International University, and worked their way west 34 miles to near the Dade-Lee County line. They took measurements of water surface elevation, water depth, and muck depth to rock every hundred feet. They averaged about three miles a day, requiring 17 days. Jaudon and Higleyman had to return to town after eight days to keep an appointment, but ventured out again, with two Seminole guides, to re-join the party on August 18, four days before the end, having brought additional canoes and badly needed supplies all the way across the Everglades from Miami.[36]

Jaudon later recalled that one of these Seminole guides was Jack Tiger Tail, who would often be a part of the early survey and rescue crews. Tiger Tail, a member of the Wind Clan, was a popular and influential Seminole; literate, visible, and involved in local affairs. He and his family spent each winter at Coppinger's Tropical Gardens on the Miami River, a popular tourist destination.[37]

Why the sudden change of heart? First, Broward County got cold feet. Broward had only recently been formed, and many of its leaders were understandably leery of taking on a large chunk of debt within a few months of starting operations. "Under a state law, should a bond election fail, a similar election cannot be held in the district until one year has passed," reported the *Miami Metropolis*. "Slight opposition has developed to the bonds in Broward county, and it is feared that that the issue might fail. In that event, the road could not be built for another year providing Dade County voted bonds to build the trail ... therefore to 'play safe,' the trail commissioners have decided hold back the Dade county petition until the Broward bonds are voted." Some large Broward landowners, who owned large tracts of real estate in Palm Beach County, wanted as the price for their support for the Trail to run along the Miami Canal all the way to the south rim of Lake Okeechobee. They did not get this and actively worked to undermine the creation of a Broward road and bridge district.[38]

Ralph Horton, secretary of the Everglades Drainage and Development League, actively lobbied in Broward County to kill the idea of issuing bonds to run the Tamiami Trail up the Miami Canal. "We have crossed the Rubicon," he wrote Thomas Will, the promoter of Okeelanta, near the south rim of Lake Okeechobee, "Tamiami Trail petition was duly and properly killed by counter-petition." Will and Horton not only wanted to see a cross-state highway from Fort Myers running along the south rim of Lake Okeechobee, but they also wanted to see it continue east to West Palm Beach, not veer southeast to Broward and Dade. As Thomas Will noted, they already had a boat connection into Fort Lauderdale via the completed portion of the Miami Canal and its connection to the New River Canal—what they needed was a road that would access West Palm Beach.[39]

Second, the giant Southern States Land & Timber Company, the owners of about a million acres of land in Lee County, informed Locke Highleyman that it would come out in opposition to the road if it were routed through central or north Lee County instead of the Corkscrew Swap area in the south third of the county, where their vast holdings of cypress timber were located. On the other hand, Ralph Horton had warned Thomas Will that the Southern States company might be against any road across their land, including the Fort Myers-to-West Palm Beach road that Will was trying to sell to the Palm Beach County commissioners.[40]

Third, the Miami Canal alignment would have proven a windfall to the Tatum Brothers land empire. The Tatums were second only to the Model Land Company in the amount of land they held in Dade, and were the largest landowner in Broward County, mostly in the southwest part of the county. They held a strip of land that ran five miles on either side of the Miami Canal for practically its entire length in Broward County. The sale of virgin lands in the Everglades along any new highway would soon become a highly contentious issue. If the Sam Jones Old Town alignment was selected, the Tatum Brothers would control

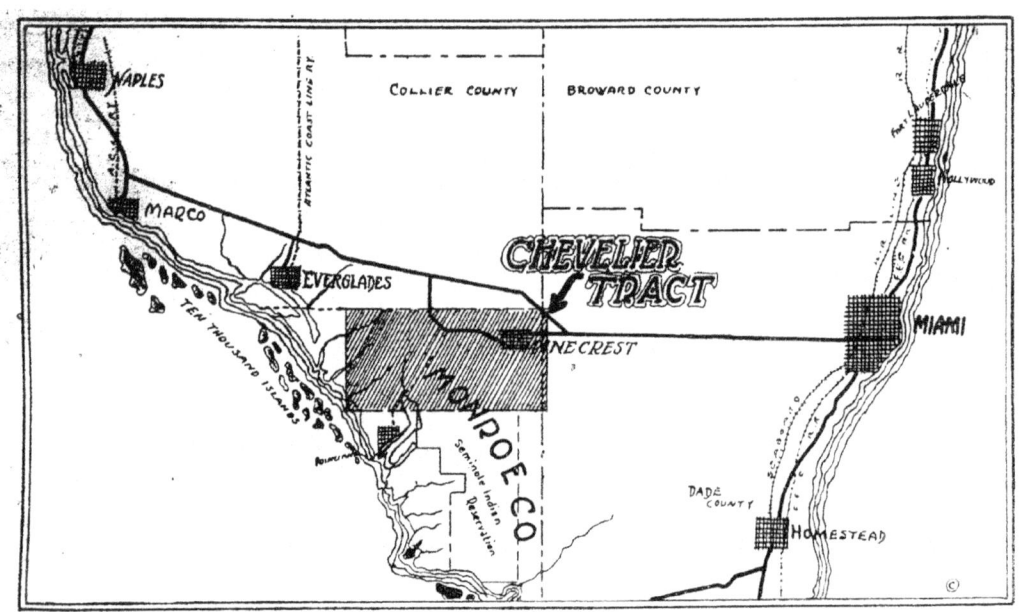

Chevelier Tract on the Tamiami Trail in Monroe County. 207,000 acres, of which a large percentage is fine, loose marl prairie; virgin land ready for immediate development. 30,000 acres in this tract have been sold to the biggest tomato grower in south Florida. Many small tracts have already been sold; plans are under way for extensive cropping this year.

A map of the Tamiami Trail, with James Jaudon's 320 square-mile land holding, Chevelier, also known as the A. W. Hopkins Tract. The map shows the two routes that would be bitterly contested, the north alignment, also known as the "original" or "Jenkins" route, and the south or "Chevelier" alignment, also known as the "loop road." The Seminole reservation was later established at a different location. (Source: *Miami News and Metropolis*, April 22, 1928.)

most of the land adjacent to the road in Broward and several thousand acres in Dade as well.[41]

The advantage of the Twentieth Street alignment was that it involved the fewest number of counties: Dade, Lee, Charlotte, Sarasota, Manatee and Hillsborough. The biggest problem was that Lee County (which at this time included today's Collier and Hendry counties) would be responsible for about 120 miles of the Trail, at the same time that its inland citizens were clamoring for highways from Fort Myers southeast to Immokalee; east to LaBelle and Sand Point, and northeast to meet Charlotte County's proposed road south from Arcadia. By one estimate, about 900 citizens lived along the 120-mile long Miami-to-Marco route in Lee County.[42] Also, nobody was sure if you could build a road across the Everglades.

The reason that Highleyman and Jaudon returned from Crabtree's survey expedition early was because they had to attend a special meeting of the County Commission called to organize a subsequent conference in Tallahassee with the state's Internal Improvement Fund. They wanted to present a plan to finance the road using state reclamation funds. They justified the legality of this move by arguing that most of its cost would actually come from blasting and dredging the borrow canal. The state legislature had just approved a $3 million bond issue and had created a special Everglades Drainage District to manage it, and the Tamiami Trail commissioners hoped to tap into $250,000 of this for the Trail.

"Our idea now is that Lee and Dade Counties [will] pay the cost of constructing the road which will result in the digging of a canal," Jaudon admitted to Judge Wilkinson in Naples. "It is going to be absolutely necessary for us to secure from the Trustees of the Internal Improvement Fund and the Commissioners of the Everglades Drainage District an assurance that they will spend either from their bond issue for this purpose or from the [sale of] lands which we asked them to set aside for this purpose." Jaudon and Highleyman met with the trustees and laid out their request for bond funding, or alternatively, to have the Fund give them land adjacent to the road that they could sell to raise the needed funds. The trustees, citing a lack of information, passed the request on to their chief drainage engineer for evaluation and scheduled a follow-up meeting on October 11.[43]

Meanwhile, during a September 4 meeting of the Dade County Commission, Jaudon and Highleyman asked that the Commission schedule an election to approve $275,000 in county bonds, of which $250,000 would be used for the Miami-to-Marco highway. J. H. Tatum, Mayor of Homestead, objected to the bond issue and asked that the matter be postponed. The newspapers claimed there had been an agreement that both the Twentieth Street alignment and the Sam Jones Old Town route would be financed, but when it became apparent that Broward County would not help build a road along the Miami Canal, the Tatum Brothers withdrew their support for the Twentieth Street alignment. But they also denied that they had ever agreed to the straight-ahead alignment. It was dangerous; it would act as a dam and flood everything in northwest Dade and southwest Broward; it wasn't feasible.[44]

But then Jaudon took the podium. The Tatums may have a dozen reasons against holding a bond election on the straight-ahead alignment, or they may have a hundred, he said. He had exactly 1,428 reasons in favor, and they were legally irrefutable. The Tamiami Trail commissioners, having secured 1,428 signatures on their petition for the creation of a special road and bridge district, made the approval and scheduling of a bond election by the county commission mandatory. There was no dispute over "approving" the election; it was simply a question of determining when it would be held. S. A. Belcher who was running the meeting, agreed that "this discussion can be of no effect," but he did accede to the

Tatums' request to continue the meeting to the following day so that more time could be devoted to debate. While this was occurring a telegram was received notifying the board that the Lee County Commissioners had scheduled an election for October 19 to approve a $125,000 bond issue for a new road district to build the road from Marco Junction to the Lee-Dade county line. After that, the next day's meeting was an anticlimax and the Dade commissioners quickly voted to schedule their bond election on the same day as Lee County's.[45]

Two weeks later, Belcher announced that he "has definitely decided on his recommendations for the central or western route for the Dixie Highway." They varied only in a few details from the report his Tallahassee counterpart, G. W. Saxon, tuned in. The western division of the Dixie Highway should follow the final route hammered out by the Central Florida Highway Association at its conference in Lakeland in September: Tallahassee-Gainesville-Orlando-Arcadia-Okeechobee City-Jupiter. The map should also include an "auxiliary route" that branched away at Arcadia to follow the Gulf coast from Punta Gorda to Marco Junction, then turn east to cross the Everglades to Miami.[46]

On October 12, Gilbreath telegraphed W. T. Carter that the Dixie Highway Association directors "authorized the Florida commissioners, G. A. Saxon of Tallahassee and S. A. Belcher of Miami to designate a loop from Miami along the Tamiami Trail through to Tampa to connect with the recently designated western division" as officially part of the Dixie Highway. This is how it appeared when the first map was published in *Dixie Highway* magazine in January 1917.[47]

The following month saw a viscous slanging duel in the newspapers between Jaudon and the Tatums. The Tatums continued to claim the new highway would flood the county, and that Lee County would never be able to afford the sixty-plus mile stretch of the highway that ran between Marco Junction and the Dade line. A week before the Dade County bond election, Jaudon and the other Tamiami Trail commissioners followed up their previous meeting with the trustees of the Internal Improvement Fund. The trustees first heard the report of their chief engineer. The road and canal were feasible. However, the drainage impacts were uncertain and insufficiently evaluated. He recommended the project be delayed pending further study.[48]

Jaudon and Highleyman followed. Undaunted, they now asked for an outright grant of land valued at $250,000. The trustees countered with an offer to sell 20,000 acres of land in two rectangular parcels on the western edge of Dade County that would straddle the new road. Out of the sale of this land, five dollars per acre would be reserved for the project—if Dade and Lee would promise to spend at least $375,000 on the canal and the cross-state highway, and would put the construction of the canal under the direction of the Fund's chief drainage engineer. The county officials present at the meeting flatly turned down the offer. Jaudon, Highleyman and McDonald went home with empty pockets. However, this did not stop the three from announcing upon their return to Miami that a deal had been struck for 20,000 acres. (The reservation that the appropriation "has practically been decided upon" was buried deep in their report.)[49]

The Lee County election was held on Saturday, October 9. A $375,000 bond issue was approved, of which $125,000 went to the Marco-to-Dade road. In what must have felt like a bit of vindication for Jaudon and Highleyman, on November 20 the voters in a proposed Lee County special district to finance a Fort Myers-to-Sand Point road along the south bank of the Caloosahatchee River—the western half of the cross-state highway along the south rim of Lake Okeechobee—turned down the bond initiative. This had been widely predicted after the Broward County commissioners announced that they would not participate in the funding of any cross-state highway, but would instead focus on running roads along the North and South New River canals.[50]

As a result of the June and October elections, the Tamiami Trail in Lee County was located in two separate road and bridge districts. District No. 1, which floated $177,000 in bonds in June, was created to purchase right-of-way and construct the coast road from Fort Myers to Marco Island. District No. 3 financed the construction of the Marco Junction-to-Dade segment. This came from the $125,000 in bonds approved on October 9.[51]

Hobart Crabtree, the Dade county engineer, released his bid specifications for the Tamiami Trail work in early January. The canal was not to be over 24 feet wide. The road was to be no less than two feet above the designated high water line, with a 24-foot sub-base and a 16-foot finished surface of crushed limestone compacted to seven tons.[52]

The Dade bonds were first offered on January 1, 1916, and unlike the Ingraham Highway bonds, were sold in a single block to a consortium of the Fifth Third Bank of Cincinnati and the Bank of Bay Biscayne of Miami in early February. They bid in at $249,562 (a 9.25 percent discount). With its financial existence secure, Dade Special Road and Bridge District No. 2 was immediately created to manage and disperse the funds. (District No. 1 was for the Ingraham Highway.) The commissioners met a few days later to award the construction bids. As the deadline passed, the submittal box contained only one entry, from the J. B. McCrary Construction Company of Atlanta, and it was contained in an envelope marked "not to be opened unless other unqualified bids are also received." McCrary's south Florida representative, George Pierce, explained that they had not had time to go over the route and specifications, and thus had little confidence in the accuracy of their bid. McCrary had sent one of their engineers, T. L. Wolfe, out to survey the stakeline of the road, but in eight days he was only able to travel out about 20 miles, a little more than half-way to the county line. (He noted, however, that contrary to Crabtree's experience during his August 1915 survey, his men had little trouble finding dry land to pitch their tents each night.) Pierce estimated that McCrary would need at least another thirty days to prepare a reliable proposal. For all intents and purposes, nobody had bid on the project, and it was entirely possible that nobody would.[53] The Tamiami Trail had just reached its first major crisis.

* * * * *

The county's response was to send Hobart Crabtree back out in February 1916 with a larger mapping party to retrace the August 1915 survey. The Lee County commissioners sent their own party of surveyors out a few days later. The two groups hoped to meet at the Dade-Lee line, but were unable to link up. Crabtree's party returned 26 days later, having measured the distance to the Lee County line at more precise 37.5 miles from the zero stake.[54]

The county clerk was instructed to re-advertise for bids. The commissioners were even more pessimistic this time around. Crabtree's new information reinforced the belief of most contractors that the job was too risky to bid as a fixed-price contract. Moreover, the European War was looming, and the federal government was ratcheting up its preparedness, creating a seller's market for construction materials and services. Why bid on an unpleasant, risky, out-of-the-way fixed-priced local road contract when the federal government was offering lucrative cost-plus contracts on things like munitions factories and drydocks? The J. B. McCrary Co. of Atlanta, by then six months into constructing the Ingraham Highway, finally threw their hat into the ring and was awarded the job at $241,500 in May 1916. Hobart Crabtree, the county's engineer, bid $8,500 to act as the supervising engineer. The bids covered the entire amount of the $250,000 bond issue. "If a ten-cent bill comes in comes in outside of these two contracts, there won't be anything to pay it with," commented a clearly worried deputy clerk of the board.[55] McCrary's local representative, George Pierce, "made a veiled suggestion that the McCrary Company was specifically interested in this work because it has hope of securing other work from other parties in this section that will help safeguard them against future loss," noted one local newspaper.[56]

In December, Lee County announced that the McCrary Company was also the low bidder, at $111,800, for the work on the Marco Junction-to-Dade segment. McCrary's representatives told the Lee commissioners that they planned to transport a dredge overland from Miami and put it to work at Marco, but this was a patently absurd idea. There was really no way to get men and heavy equipment to the starting point at the Dade-Lee line until after the Dade County portion of the roadway was finished. Instead, McCrary bought a Monighan steamshovel with a dragline arm and a one-yard bucket, had it shipped to Fort Myers, then barged to Marco Island. The route was almost all sugar sand, utterly incapable of compaction, and the McCrary crew progressed less than half a mile a month. Due to labor shortages caused by the war, work became intermittent by 1917 and Lee County cancelled the contract in 1918. McCrary either sold the Monighan shovel to Lee County, or gave it to them in lieu of defaulting on their bond. Their work was completely wiped out in 1921 by the storm surge from a hurricane.[57]

On the Dade County contract, McCrary subcontracted the work to the J. F. Morgan Paving Company. Morgan ordered a caterpillar excavator and a floating dredge comparable to the one being used on the Ingraham Highway southwest of Royal Palm State Park. Work started on June 26, 1916, at a point near the present day interchange of SW 8th Street and the Palmetto Expressway (Highway 826). From the zero stake to the county line was about 41 miles. This was longer than the straight-line distance of 37.5 miles, because the road was to turn to the northwest about six miles from the county line so as to enter Lee County about three miles north of its boundary with Monroe County. If the road was extended straight west, it would actually enter Monroe, not Lee, about two miles south of the border of those two jurisdictions.[58]

The caterpillar excavator was assembled and started work in mid–August. The boom for the floating dredge arrived in Coconut Grove in mid–September, and its assembly required almost two months. It began work on November 4. The caterpillar excavator was put to work removing the muck that covered the underlying limestone. The original plan was that this shallow ditch would then be filled with crushed rock to form the roadbed. But the peat turned out to be five feet deep in places. A road bed had to be built all the way from the limestone bedrock up to a point about two feet higher than the wet-season water table. That meant either trucking in massive amounts of gravel to fill the ditch left after the overlying muck had been removed, or blasting a borrow canal parallel to the roadway, then dredging the broken stone out the canal, putting it on the roadbed, then rolling it down—coarsely for the under-layer; finely for the finish coat.

In essence, the job required digging two canals. First, a caterpillar steamshovel or a light floating dredge stripped off the overlying muck from the base of limestone over a double-wide canal that was the width of both the new road and its borrow canal. A floating drill barge was moved into place on the side where the borrow canal would go and holes were drilled for the dynamite. For much of the job McCrary and its subcontractors used rod-like star drills driven by sledgehammers. In the early days, it was not uncommon for a star drill to be punched through into a solution hole and disappear from sight. They were expensive and had to be fished out again, if possible.

Later they (and subsequent contractors) used pneumatically-driven rotary impact drills modified from mining equipment. In the end, the final solution proved to be banks of these mining drills mounted vertically on platforms that could be rotated and shifted right and left. The drill platforms were in turn mounted on one end of barges or (for dryer land) self-propelled, elevated, shed-like swamp buggies. These purpose-built drill barges or buggies would drill between three and six holes at a time, six feet apart and twelve feet deep. Drilling would start in the center of the canal. A column of holes would be drilled down the centerline of the canal at six-foot intervals. Two columns would be drilled three feet on each side of this centerline. The drill table would shift the gang of drills back-and-forth to create perpendicular rows based on these three longitudinal lines of center holes.

Using high pressure water jets made out of fourteen-foot steel tubes, one and one-half inches in diameter, narrowed down to one-quarter inch at the tip, mud and rock chips were cleaned out of each hole. The dynamite was inserted using loading tubes. Depending on the density and type of rock, each hole would get 10 to 40 sticks. Twelve sticks, with 20 sticks in the three center holes of each row, was average. Typically, about 30 or 35 holes (five or six rows, thirty to forty linear feet, 1,500 or so sticks of dynamite, each one pound) would be blasted at a time. Considering that three million pounds of dynamite were used, it is a miracle that no men were killed while blasting.[59]

After the explosion, the floating dredge with its scoop bucket then moved in, removing the broken rock from the borrow canal side and piling it on the road side to create the roadbed. "The average life of a bucket was about two weeks," recalled one old hand. "When one of these dredges would break down everything was done to make repairs, and no railway wreck ever received more prompt attention than was given to get them running again."[60]

If a boulder was found to have survived the blasting too big for the dredge's bucket, it had to blown apart directly in front of the dredge in what was called a "front shot," a particularly tricky operation. (It could not be left where it was, because it would hang up the bottom of barges passing overhead.) For this reason, drilling and blasting foremen who could consistently break down a rock layer into one-yard or smaller chunks were especially valued. After drying for a few days, a roller and road grader rough-finished the roadbed to the point where it could be used as an access road by construction crews, although it was still too rough to be used by regular automobiles at highway speeds. If there was excess material it was thrown to the side as an embankment for the road. "The burning question of the hour with the dredge men was: 'Have I got enough material?'" recalled a veteran. "Grade stakes were set by the engineers and a large surplus of material was not permitted. Enough must be dredged, but not too much."[61]

Meanwhile, Lee County's contractors were working their way south from Fort Myers to Marco in Lee District No. 1. J. B. McCrary had been awarded the contract for the Marco Junction to Dade segment in December 1916, but by this time, Captain K. H. Harvey was already at work with his men on another stretch north of this, from Naples to Marco, which he had won with a bid of $44 per acre. Captain Harvey described the job to a reporter:

> We began cutting through the swamp, dumping the mass of marl and sand to one side. This dump is leveled down to grade and surfaced by hand with big heavy hoes and rakes. [It] is truly jungle in every sense of the word, a mass of trees of all kinds, thousands of switches, poles, brush and ferns all woven together with bamboo, rattan, and vine. Perhaps several hundreds would be chopped off at the ground before the mass would fall, so that it could be chipped apart with brush axes.[62]

Harvey and his crew were using land-based equipment, not the floating barge-mounted dredges and excavators McCrary were using. Digging canals and using barges was slower and more expensive, but Harvey's description of hazards they encountered with their heavier caterpillar-treaded equipment explains McCrary's choice of technology:

> It was scrub and mangrove and grass muck. Think of leaves on the trees shaking and trembling, and the whole mass of muck and sand for hundreds of feet in each direction quivering and shaking like a mass of jelly with each vibration of the dredge engine. Then think of putting a 40,000-pound engine across it, with muck and marl twelve feet deep and chancing that the slightest mistake or error of judgment would make a buried and tangled wreck.... We tried planks and log cribbing, but this was too uncertain and treacherous. Finally brush mats piled four feet high, with track laid on top of them, proved the most practical for the dredge to travel over.[63]

At $44 per acre, one steamshovel and a steam engine for the roller were the only pieces of equipment he could afford. Anything thrown up by the steamshovel that was too big to be crushed down by a steamroller had to be reduced the same way the Romans did it—with pick and shovel.

* * * * *

In March 1917, all of Miami was electrified by the story of the lost expedition of surveyor John King. King had set out on February 10 on a surveying mission for Capt. Jaudon. In addition to King and his son, the party included W. R. Catlow, a reporter for the Miami *Metropolis*. They were supposed to be away two weeks. On March 1, Jaudon wired a colleague: "No news King party. Much alarmed. Have Indians, trappers, hunters searching for him. Starting flying machines to locate him tomorrow. Never so worried in my life."[64]

Several search parties were sent out, including one headed by Jack Tiger Tail, who had helped Jaudon locate Hobart Crabtree when Crabtree was doing his initial reconnaissance for the straight-ahead route in 1915. Phil Rader of the Curtiss aviation school also made two flights over the Everglades to try to find them. "For the life of me I can't see how the men could have perished," Jaudon to a reporter. "Before the men left Miami I cautioned them to stick to their boat, every one of them, under any circumstances." On March 11, Jack Tiger Tail and his party returned for more supplies, reporting that they had seen no trace.[65]

The mystery was solved on March 14, when a telegram was received from Key West. King and his men had been found by a sportsman named Richmond Talbot on the Gulf coast, well south of Everglades City. The story that King gave to the press was that he and his men had gone out to survey the "Tamiami Trail Lands" that the Internal Improvement Fund was considering transferring to the Tamiami Trail Commission. However, the canal that had been dug beside the Trail had so dried the central Everglades that they had to portage their canoes for close to two weeks, so they decided not to return to the east, but instead proceeded west, to the Thousand Islands. They ran out of supplies, but survived on game for about a week before finally reaching the Shark River. Fortunately, they came across Talbot, who was fishing and exploring on the Shark River.

Talbot was renting the houseboat *Kennesaw*, owned by Capt. A. N. Whittle of Fort Myers. Talbot and some of his friends had been out fishing in the *Kennesaw*'s motor launch when they came across the King party. They took the men to the *Kennesaw*, where the men could eat and clean up. Meanwhile, Capt. Whittle took the *Kennesaw* down to the mouth of the Shark River to a factory owned by the Manetto Company. (They made tannic acid from mangrove roots.) The Manetto factory had a speedboat that could take King to Key West, were he telegraphed Miami. Talbot and Capt. Whittle, with the rest of the party, went at a more leisurely pace to Key West, where they could catch the train back home. "I find upon my return that there has been a great fervor created over our disappearance, which I do not think altogether warranted," King wrote Talbot a few days later. "No sheriff ever had as many guns or such material, such personnel as hunted us, and how we escaped capture, is more than I can imagine."[66]

By 1928, King had moved to Brooklyn. He may have been chagrined by his reception upon returning to Miami, but Jack Tiger Tail used his new-found fame as leader of the Seminole "rescue" expedition to bolster his standing as a representative and spokesman for the Seminoles who resided part of the year at the Coppinger's Garden and Musa Isle tourist resorts. By 1920 a fifty-foot high billboard featuring his likeness guided visitors from around the state to the then-new suburb of Hialeah, being developed by aviation pioneer Glenn Curtiss and his associates. Tiger Tail continued as a community leader and an Everglades guide until he was shot on the night of March 8–9, 1922, at the Miami River dock at Coppinger's Gardens.

Several hundred attended his funeral. A white plume hunter and petty thief, Charles Veber, was arrested for the murder. Veber, drunk, had allegedly argued with Tiger Tail about the purchase price of some pelts, had gone back to his cabin cruiser, retrieved a rifle, and shot him. A skiff tied to Veber's boat was identified as having been recently stolen from a boat yard near Coppinger's. A rifle in the bottom of the skiff had been purchased by Veber from a Seminole at Coppinger's about two weeks before the shooting.[67]

Veber was convicted of the murder. However, two weeks later, one of Henry Coppinger's sons dropped a bag of baby alligators being moved in the garden's alligator farm. In the subsequent scramble to round them up, Coppinger's other son, Henry, Jr., found a rifle stashed under a large bush. It was identical to the one found in Veber's boat. Henry Jr., told the police that the bush was located on a the path from the dock to the Coppinger house that Charlie Billie, the primary eyewitness to the Tiger Tail shooting, had used on the night of the killing to rouse the Coppingers and summon help. In subsequent interviews with witnesses, white and Seminole alike, the case against Veber started to crumble. An employee at the boat yard where the skiff was stolen admitted letting Veber use it, although he did not have the authority to do so. The medical examiner could not be certain if Tiger Tail had been shot from the water or the dock. The jury in the second trial found Veber not guilty in November 1922.[68] The families living at Coppinger's had already withdrawn into the Everglades. According to Patsy West, former director of the Seminole/Miccousukee Photographic Archive, a tribal inquest determined that Tiger Tail was shot by Charlie Billie as retribution for adultery, and that the killing was an act of justifiable homicide.[69]

* * * * *

CHATTANOOGA, Aug. 22, 1923 (AP) Samuel A. Belcher of Miami, Fla., who was injured in an automobile wreck on the Dixie Highway near Summerville, Ga. Tuesday died later in the hospital at Rome, Ga. The car turned over when Belcher attempted to pass another car. His wife, daughter-in-law and her three children who were also in the car at the time of the accident escaped with minor cuts and bruises. Belcher was Dixie Highway Commissioner from Florida and a former Dade County Commissioner.[70]

..7..

The Only Dry Ground for Twenty Miles

In all the confusion over John King's lost expedition of April 1917, apparently nobody bothered to ask the why he would risk traveling all the way across the Everglades to the Gulf coast, and why James Jaudon was paying him $1,400 to do so.

In the fall of 1916, Jaudon decided to move up from his position as county tax assessor and run for county clerk. Jaudon's primary competition was a man named Ben Shepard. The primary election was held in June, and because Miami was still a part of the deep south, this meant it was really the general election, since the Republican Party was a non-factor. It was an unusually bitter campaign, proof that negative elections are not a recent phenomenon. Shepard won by a handful of votes. Jaudon challenged his place on the fall election, claiming that the vote count was erroneous and that Shepard had failed to file the necessary financial disclosure forms. Things turned ugly when one of the local papers revealed that an independent challenging Shepard in the November general election, I. G. Norton, was actually Jaudon's office clerk. If Jaudon's challenge was upheld, only Norton and the Republican candidate would be left on the ballot. The county's election board certified Shepard's primary win and placed him on the general election ballot. Jaudon filed a writ of mandamus with the Florida Supreme Court to force Shepard off the ballot. On October 23, the court rejected Jaudon's suit. Shepard won easily.[1]

His political career finished, Jaudon redoubled his efforts as a land speculator. Undaunted by the refusal of the Dade and Lee county commissions to accept the conditions placed by the Internal Improvement Fund on the land grant to benefit the construction of the Tamiami Trail, Jaudon and his two fellow "Tamiami Trail Commissioners" went right ahead and closed the deal as a purely private venture. Jaudon, Locke T. Highleyman and R. E. McDonald purchased two blocks of land totaling 20,000 acres (about 31 square miles) straddling the stakeline of the Tamiami Trail in far west Dade County for $100,000. Ten thousand was due in thirty days, with the remainder to be paid in four equal installments every six months. At the one-year anniversary, if they were current on their payments, the Improvement Fund would release up to $100,000 to excavate the Snapper Creek Canal. The sales were not immediately sufficient to meet the Fund's payment schedule, so in March 1917 the three men mortgaged the property so the Fund received timely payment. By August 1917 they had paid off about $37,000 of the mortgage.[2]

The purpose of King's February 11 trip was to survey these lands for the mortgage. They were located roughly 23 and 29 miles west of the Miami city limits and 11 and 18 miles

7. The Only Dry Ground for Twenty Miles

James Jaudon, Dade County tax assessor, in his office in the county courthouse with his two assistants, Addy Hurd and Antonette Harden, 1916. (Photographer unknown. HistoryMiami, No. X-055-39.)

east of Lee County. The story he gave to the press about a "dried up" Everglades notwithstanding, the many photographs King took of the sites indicate that they were almost completely inundated, and King's 500-page report noted that they would be "problematical" for future development, even if a way could be found to drain them, although he concluded that:

> The lands of the Tamiami Trail are at the present moment literally valueless, but with an adequate provision for transportation, coupled with a proper system for the relief of water, all but a minute fraction occupied by the canals and necessary laterals could be made available for agricultural purposes.[3]

King's concern was that if drainage was not done with "engineering intelligence, sound judgment, common sense, persistence, and funds," it would result in the surface muck being washed away, with only the unproductive, impermeable marl underneath left. While not precisely correct from a technical standpoint, King's warning was amazingly prescient for 1917.

After finishing work on the Tamiami Trail Lands parcels, he and his men then spent close to a month "in the headwaters of the Shark River," that is, the watersheds of the rivers that flowed into the Ten Thousand Islands of the lower Gulf Coast. King may have been in a spot of trouble at the end of his trip, but the bulk of his extended disappearance was more a matter of secrecy than crisis.[4] King's aim was to survey the eastern half of was called the A. W. Hopkins tract, a massive 208,000-acre parcel of land 25 miles wide and 12 miles high that was essentially the entire top two rows of townships in Monroe County. A man named Charles Scott and his wife had originally bought it from the state's Internal Improvement Fund in 1901. They sold it six months later to the National Timber Company. National Timber also wanted the twelve school board sections scattered within it (the dead center section, number 16, of each township), so they had Scott, acting as a straw-man, buy them, then immediately flip them to the company. National Timber had a man named E. J. Lucas do a timber survey (a "timber cruise") in early 1908. Lucas reportedly used 14 assistants and took three months to do the job. They found lots of timber, but it was all remote, far from roads and rail lines. There was also lots of shoreline on the Gulf of Mexico, but it was all bayou-like shallows—miles of dredging would be required to open it up to deepwater shipping. In June 1908 they sold the tract to Archibold W. Hopkins of Granville, Illinois, for $62,208, which was less than the $65,800 that Charles Scott had originally paid for it, including the school board acreage. No doubt National Timber had paid Scott more than that, but how much is not recorded.[5]

Hopkins was described rather uncharitably by one of Jaudon's associates as "an old man, 72-years old, married to a young woman." His purchase was heavily mortgaged to the nearby Citizens National Bank of Spencer, Iowa, owned by Franklin Floete (pronounced "floaty") and J. H. McCord. Hopkins had apparently been able to interest Floete in the property because of its vast timber stands; Floete had made his fortune owning a chain of lumberyards and sawmills in Iowa and Illinois. But Floete and McCord became decidedly less than enthusiastic about the land when, in the summer of 1914, the two men, apparently without the knowledge of Hopkins, went down to Florida to look over their client's collateral. The rainy season of 1914 was unusually wet. They found water. A lot of it. A sort of slow-motion panic ensued. They became very anxious for Hopkins to sell it, for whatever price he could get, and pay off his mortgage.[6]

The Jaudon realty office during the heyday of his empire, 1916–22. (Photograph by Mooney. HistoryMiami, No. X-055-180.)

It appears that Jaudon first heard about the property through a farmer and banker from Milford, Iowa, named Carl Torstenson. Milford was only a short distance from Spencer, and Torstenson did business with Floete and McCord fairly often. Carl's son Nansen had started at the University of Iowa a year or two before, and with an empty nest, Carl had started spending his winters in Miami, where he met Jaudon.[7]

Jaudon first wrote Hopkins in September 1916 asking about the land. McCord, in Spencer, wrote Jaudon back to say that "I have parties at work on the proposition now, and would not care to quote prices or terms.... If you will write me about Dec. 1st, I can perhaps give you better information." Jaudon must have suspected that McCord was bluffing, because he scrawled in the corner of the telegram a note: "Is that sort of land moving to any extent nowadays?"[8]

The purpose of King's trip was to find out just the type of information Lucas had already discovered for the National Timber back in 1908. It was actually the second of two trips. Between December 13, 1916, and January 7, 1917, King had surveyed the western half of the tract by boat, sailing, then canoeing, up the Turner, Chatham, Lossman and other estuary rivers. This second trip, From February 11 to March 15, 1917, was intended to survey both the Tamiami Trail Lands and the west half of the Hopkins Tract.[9]

Jaudon took out an option on the property on March 3, about the time King was due back in Miami, for $2,100. Hopkins, Floete and McCord wanted $10,000 to hold the option, but Jaudon replied that he "absolutely will not deposit ten thousand dollars at this time." Jaudon closed the deal a few days later by paying another $7,900. The total sales price was $331,776. The terms of the sale specified that Jaudon was to make a payment of $47,900 on April 2, and $50,000 each year thereafter, with a final payment of $31,776 in 1923. The first $47,000 was clearly intended to be a $50,000 down payment, less the $2,100 option fee. However, these terms were never implemented. Instead, Hopkins and the Citizens National Bank of Spencer extended Jaudon a $300,000 mortgage with a $10,000 initial payment and $10,000 semi-annual payments. The $2,100 paid on March 1 and the $7,900 sent on April 12 constituted the initial $10,000. Jaudon sent a second payment of $10,000 on May 1.[10]

This exhausted his financial resources. His solution was to set up a new corporation, the Chevelier Corporation, to take over the mortgage debt and convert it into equity (i.e., stock) that would be issued to himself, Hopkins, McCord, and Floete. He could also sell minority shares of the firm to outsiders and borrow money to generate the working capital needed to keep going. By the end of 1917 he had sold $28,000 in stock. Twenty thousand of this came from two investors: Carl Torstenson and Daniel A. McDougal each subscribed to $10,000. Judge McDougal was an attorney and Justice of the Peace from Sepula, Oklahoma, just outside Tulsa. He had made a modest fortune working for oil companies preparing oil leases and, as a sideline, speculating in them. Louis Freeman, an Ohio shoe manufacturer, signed up for $5,000. Locals accounted for the rest. It was an adroit maneuver. Jaudon in essence made the Chevelier Corporation, not himself, responsible for the $300,000 mortgage to Hopkins. On the other hand, to raise the money the corporation needed to pay the $10,000 mortgage payments and raise working capital, he was forced to sell stock cheap. McDougal, for example, got a ten percent share of the corporation for only ten thousand dollars. At the time the corporation was formed in the spring of 1918, Jaudon only owned 42 percent of its stock; McCord and Floete's bank owned 25 percent; Hopkins none, only the mortgage.[11]

Another $5,000 in stock went to George F. Cook of Miami for "in-kind services." Cook would soon become the corporation's secretary/treasurer and would, along with Judge McDougal, become the only original partner to remain active in the firm until the very end in the 1940s when much of the land was sold off to the federal government for Everglades National Park. Cook came to Miami in 1903, when he was about 45. Born in Toronto, he worked in construction for the Canadian Pacific Railroad, then as a building contractor in Canada, the Dakotas, Montana, and Minnesota. From there he moved to New York and went into real estate and manufacturing. His son Erben talked him into coming to Miami, and the two started a business building jetties and seawalls. In 1909 he started a steamship line, and this brought him into the circle occupied by I. E. Schilling, who would later become chairman of the Florida road department. After selling the Cook Steamship Company in 1914 he was looking for something new to become involved in, and that is how he found his way to Jaudon. He, and later Erben, would serve as Chevelier's *de facto* director of construction.[12]

There was not a lot of love lost between Jaudon and his Midwest partners, and even less trust. Jaudon's real estate agent in Jacksonville wrote to complain that "I have had this property sold five times, each time McCord would write that it was under option; before the option would expire I would have lost my client.... I would like to have you send me an outline of just what you expect to do with this property so that I can send it to our people."[13]

Hopkins and his Iowa backers thought they had unloaded a troubled asset off onto a hugely ambitious buyer with deep pockets willing to pony over big money to overcome the site's access problems and make it a major timber producer. Failing that, they just wanted to be rid of the place. Whatever scheme paid off the mortgage in cash first was the scheme they most favored. Jaudon, in turn, was only truly interested in the grand picture: he wanted to build his own Miami, Tampa or Fort Myers from the ground up. Lacking any money of his own, he could, if he had to, sell off undifferentiated ownership shares of the land for working cash. But his preferred strategy was to fold the whole tract into a corporation and then sell shares of stock and corporate bonds to pay off the mortgage and install the needed infrastructure. In fact, he told one real estate broker that "I would much prefer to sell your client a part equity in the proposition [i.e., the new Chevelier Corporation] *than to sell them the entire tract.*"[14]

There is some question about whether Jaudon had been taken by Hopkins, McCord, and their associates. He didn't even do an abstract of title on the land until June 1917, more than a month after he had sent the Citizens National Bank of Spencer the down payment. If he had, he would have discovered that Hopkins had paid the National Timber Company thirty cents an acre back in 1908. Jaudon paid Hopkins $1.60 an acre, a 533 percent markup. On the other hand, Carl Torstenson thought that Jaudon got a good deal. Describing Floete and McCord's 1914 trip to Florida to look over the site, he wrote Jaudon that "At that time they must have found the whole Hopkins tract under water, and that trip is still on their minds, and for this reason you got the land for the price you did." As one of the three "Tamiami Trail Commissioners," Jaudon had just bought 20,000 acres of land for $5.00 an acre that had even less potential because it was farther inland and had no timber. Thus, assuming Jaudon had known that Hopkins paid less than $65,000 for the Hopkins Tract, he may have still been willing to pay $332,000, because that appears to have been the going price for that kind of land, at that location and under those circumstances. It was worth a small fortune for its timber, but at the time it was inaccessible.[15]

The real trouble lay elsewhere. Buried in the contract was a provision that prohibited timbering the land until $155,000 of the purchase price was paid. The only exception was if the buyer gave Hopkins two dollars per thousand feet of lumber harvested. An acre of viable timberland contained between 1,200 and 1,500 feet. Really top-notch land yielded about 2,500 feet. Thus, under the purchase agreement, Hopkins would get around $2.50 to $3.00 an acre for most of the forest lands and $5.00 for the old-growth cypress acreage. What this meant was that almost any timber lease would make money for Hopkins, but not Jaudon, because the most Jaudon could expect to get for timber leases under the going rates for that era was $2.50 to $4.00 an acre. Moreover, these payments were not credited towards Jaudon's purchase price.[16]

In addition, the contract was unclear as to whether Jaudon could subdivide and sell off pieces of the land before it was fully paid off. It clearly stated that title would pass to Jaudon after the first fifty thousand dollars was paid, but the title would, of course be encumbered by the notes and mortgages guaranteeing the payment of the full $332,000. It did not say whether the land had to be kept together to insure the value of the collateral, or whether those portions sold off by Jaudon would still be burdened by the mortgage to the Iowa bankers. To a large extent, this is a moot question, because Jaudon was never able to pay off more than $50,000 of the purchase price, so throughout 1917 and early 1918 he was not offering pieces of the Hopkins Tract, only the entire tract or undivided (i.e., partnership) shares of ownership.[17]

There was a final problem, one that Jaudon would not realize for close to a year. As part of the purchase contract, Hopkins required Jaudon to pay the 1916 taxes on the land (about $11,000, five cents an acre). That should have been a tip-off. Unknown to Jaudon, Hopkins hadn't paid his taxes on the land for 1913, 1914 or 1915. The clerk had issued tax certificates against these unpaid taxes. Under the system in place during that era, anyone who went to the clerk's office, bought the certificates and paid the back taxes would have been entitled to receive title to the land. Fairly strong proof that Jaudon was the first serious buyer to ask about the land is indicated by the fact that the day after he sent his first telegram to McCord, someone walked into the Monroe County Clerk's office and paid the back taxes and cancelled the tax certificates. *But they forgot to record the cancellation with the clerk's office and receive an official book and page number entry.* That didn't invalidate the payment, but it left the tax lien on the record books as an encumbrance against the property's title. The burden of proof would still be on the property owner, or more importantly, any subsequent buyer, to show that the delinquent taxes had been paid. In other words, the title was still clouded.

Hopkins, Floete and McCord had sold the land to Jaudon through a warranty deed, meaning they guaranteed good, clean title. Once he discovered that the title was clouded, Jaudon could have sued to invalidate the sale and have his money returned.[18] Instead, he paid his nephew, attorney Paul Taylor, to clear up the title in 1920. "I really believe that had this flaw in the title not been present, that in 1917 or in 1918 the property [as a whole] could have been disposed of at a profit," asserted Jaudon many years later.[19] It is a measure of how invested he had become in his Chevelier dreams that in the face of recalcitrance, disingenuousness and even open hostility from his Iowa partners that he continued to plunge in deeper and deeper, even when he found a risk-free way to exit. It is very likely that by 1920 Hopkins and McCord could not, or would not, find the necessary proof that the back taxes had been paid in 1916. Jaudon's plans were dealt an additional setback in May 1917 when Carl Torstensen, who had been playing the role of Jaudon's on-site spokesman in Iowa, died.

After verifying that the Atlantic Coast Line Railroad had no plans to run any farther down the Gulf coast side of the state than Immokalee in the foreseeable future, he announced that a new corporation, the Tamiami Trail Corporation, would run a railroad along the Tamiami Trail canal embankment from Miami to the west coast. He did not

Jaudon on one of his many surveys of the Hopkins/Chevelier Tract, about 1922–23, at the chickee hut on the Chevelier Canal off Alligator Bay. Standing (L-R): unknown; James Jaudon; Dan House; Ralph Ranson, unknown. Neither of the Seminole guides kneeling in front are identified. (Photographer unknown. HistoryMiami, X-0155-146.)

actually *have* a corporation, a franchise from the county or city to use their rights-of-way, or any place on the embankment to run the tracks, but that did not slow him down. "It is the plan to make the new railroad parallel to the Tamiami Trail to about the county line where the Trail bends northwestward," he told a reporter. "From that point the railroad will continue straight west to the proposed site of Chevelier City." In his written prospectus to the county commission, Jaudon promised the that he would have ten miles ready in two years, and 90 percent of the railroad complete in five years.[20]

Jaudon originally considered making the Tamiami Railway the holding corporation for the Hopkins Tract. "The thought occurred to me," Jaudon wrote McCord," that as I own every share of stock in the Tamiami Railway, that we could agree on a plan for the Tamiami Railway to take over the Hopkins Tract." He wanted to issue $500,000 in stock, of which $400,000 would go to the existing partners and $100,000 would be sold to the public. "We would also be in a better position to offer bonds," he noted, "I am of the opinion that we can immediately bond the Tamiami railway for from $600,000 to one million dollars. We could retire the present mortgage of $300,000 and have ample capital to make such improvements and developments as may be necessary." He did note one technical reservation: under this plan, he was proposing to give the owners of the Hopkins Tract $400,000 in unrestricted stock for their land, then sell bonds to raise $330,000 that would be used to buy the mortgage on those same lands. In effect, he was proposing to buy the same piece of land twice over by issuing $730,000 in securities against a parcel that was only worth $330,000. Even by the minimal standards of that era, this was perilously close to securities fraud. "It might be a better policy to issue only $100,000 worth of stock to the present owners," he added later in his letter. Indeed.[21]

The railroad project was dealt a serious blow in May when the Dade County Commission denied Jaudon's request to use 40 feet of the 100-foot Tamiami Trail right-of-way. In early April, the board had actually passed a resolution approving the railroad, but rescinded it a month later when it realized that between the canal, the road, easements for telephone and telegraph lines, and landscaping, there wasn't any room left.[22]

Jaudon and his associates decided to proceed anyway, using a separate right-of-way running parallel to the Trail in Dade County. The only regulatory hurdle was the need to secure a franchise from the City of Miami to run across its streets. In exchange for the franchise and access to the Miami city docks (which were on land the city had secured from the Model Land Company), the Tamiami Railroad had to agree to provide switching operations at the city dock, free of charge. The Florida East Coast Railway did not use the city docks (they had their own private dock nearby), and it was widely believed that this was because they did not want to install trackage, rolling stock, and a switch engine for the city dock, which served all comers willing to pay a modest dock fee. Instead, it wanted to shift the burden to some other railroad. After all, most of the freight headed into and out of the city dock would probably end up going through Jacksonville or down to Key West anyway, so who cared if another railroad ran a line into the Port of Miami?[23]

The franchise was passed by the City Council on January 28, 1918. The referendum vote was scheduled for April 9. Although it was approved by an overwhelming vote of 220 to 3 (largely because Jaudon and his associates agreed to let streetcars use a large portion of the rail line), the Tamiami Railroad was never heard from again, and in April 1920, when two years lapsed without completion of the railroad or a request for an extension, the franchise expired.[24]

* * * * *

But even before the election was set, the new Chevelier Corporation had started work surveying the site and planning improvements. Jaudon cruised the tract for about ten days in mid–July, then returned with his engineer, F. K. Ashworth, and Ashworth's assistant, Harley Stout, for a second expedition that lasted from September 14 through 25. Both trips used Chokoloskee Island as their jumping-off point, and on both trips D. R. ("Dan") House was hired as a guide. In the second trip, his brother W. W. ("Bill") House accompanied them. Bill House would become a life-long friend of Jaudon's, and in the 1930s, after Jaudon had lost almost everything, he and House would end up where he had started—growing fruits and vegetables together, in Ochopee, just as Jaudon and Darrah Mallon had in Homestead back in 1899. Although Jaudon did not mention visiting the Watson Place during his July 1917 visit, he discussed it fairly extensively in his account of the September trip.[25]

The Watson Place, and the House family, have become famous through Peter Matthieson's novels *Killing Mister Watson* and *Shadow World*. In actuality, most of the few hard facts concerning the notorious incident comes from the historical work undertaken by D. Graham Copeland, head of the diversified Collier development companies, who interviewed many of the original settler families in the Ten Thousand Islands, and by Dr. Charleton W. Tebeau of the South Florida Historical Museum, who followed up on Copeland's work with his own research and wrote a series of books in the 1960s and early '70s, several of which were supported by research grants from the Copeland family. The account given below relies mostly on Copeland's 1946 research notes and Tebeau's books. It is much sketchier than the account in Matthieson's books, which, you must remember, is fiction based on a few kernels of fact and legend.[26]

On October 10, 1910, while making their way by boat down the Chatham River out to the Gulf about twelve miles south of Everglade, a man named Cannon and a boy who

The Watson "murder farm." According to legend, Edgar Watson made himself rich in cane syrup by killing off his farmhands after each harvest. While that is untrue, what did happen will likely never be fully known. Three of Watson's farm hands were killed in 1910, probably by the plantation manager in a drunken argument while Watson was away. But Watson was an arrogant, aggressive man who was feared and hated by many. When he claimed to have killed the murderous manager, but couldn't provide a body, and wouldn't surrender to authorities to help search for it, he was shot by his neighbors, who believed he was responsible. The Chevelier Company used the Watson Place as a test farm, field office and guest house until it was damaged in a 1926 hurricane and allowed to fall into disrepair. By that time construction had moved to the east side of the county, adjacent to Dade. This photograph was taken in 1924, at the peak of Chevelier's activity there. (Photograph by Mary McDougal Axelson. HistoryMiami, No. X-2178-1.)

lived with him at the original homestead of Guy Chevelier, for whom Chevelier Bay was named, saw a foot sticking up out of the water at a place known as Chatham Bend, about two miles from the mouth of the river. The bend wrapped around the farm of a man named Edgar J. Watson. Watson had a checkered reputation, it was late in the day, and Cannon did not want to face potential trouble alone. He continued out into the Gulf to find help and came across a group of clammers, spending the night with them.

The next morning, the group went back in and found Hanna Smith and Green Waller. They had been tied together, gutted in an attempt to keep their bodies from bloating, and weighted down with scrap iron. Smith was a cook and housekeeper at the Watson farm, and Waller was a farmhand there. The men were just as scared of Watson as Cannon was, so they took Smith and Waller back downstream a ways to bury them on the other side of the river. There, in the mangroves, they found a third body, that of Dutchy Melville, a small-time Key West hoodlum. Watson had hired him a few years before as foreman. After working for a year or so, Melville had gotten into a dispute with Watson and left. After a couple of years, Melville re-appeared and asked for his old job back. Watson took him back, but just as a farmhand, because he had hired a new foreman, one Leslie Cox (or Coxe).

Watson had settled on the Chatham Bend property about 1896 or 1897. It was an ancient shell mound, and according to James Jaudon, it was the only elevated area of land on the whole Hopkins Tract, almost twenty miles.[27] By 1905 Watson had built one of the best houses and most substantial farms in the Ten Thousand Islands, rivaled only by George Storter's place in Everglade (Everglades City), Smallwood's store in Chokoloskee, R. M. Collier's store and hotel at Marco, and Mr. and Mrs. Barfield's hotel and canning operation in Caxambas, on the other side of Marco Island. Watson was smart, ambitious and successful, but he was also a drinker, and had a deep mean streak. He almost killed a former Chokoloskee resident named Santini in Key West over a petty insult, and had shot and wounded a man named Bass in Arcadia a couple of years before he moved to Chatham Bend. It was said that he had killed Belle Starr in Oklahoma (almost certainly untrue). Rumors persisted that the secret to his prosperity was that he killed off his hired hands at the end of harvest instead of paying them, although the only known deaths were that of a white carpenter who had a heart attack and a black farmhand who got his arm caught in a cane press.

On October 14, four days after Cannon and the boy first spied the bodies in the river, a black man named Roberts (or Reed, or simply "little Jim") rowed exhausted into Chokoloskee, four miles south of Everglade. He gave Claude Storter, Ted Smallwood and the others confused, conflicting stories. At one point he said that Leslie Cox had killed Smith, Waller and Melville on the orders of Edgar Watson and would have killed him too, but he had agreed to help Cox dispose of Waller and Green in the river, then slipped away. But then he said Cox had killed the others in a drunken quarrel of some sort and that Watson wasn't even there. Someone took Roberts up to Fort Myers in a boat to report the crime to Sheriff Frank Tippins, even though both the Watson Place and Chokoloskee are in Monroe County, which has its county seat at Key West. Once in Fort Myers, Roberts gave Tippins this account:

Shortly before the murders, the Storter brothers and a third man, Henry Short, had come across a young Seminole woman who had been abandoned by her clan for consorting with whites. They took her to the Watson Place for Hannah Smith to take care of. Leslie Cox may or may not have had sex with her. He may or may not have raped her. She may or may not have already been pregnant. She did hang herself in the boatshed. Smith, Waller and Cox argued because Cox would not cut down her body and bury her. Cox shot Waller and Smith. Cox then forced Roberts to dispose of the bodies in the river. Later, Melville showed up and Cox shot him. Roberts slipped away while Cox was ambushing Melville.

On October 16, Watson appeared in Chokoloskee. When he found out what happened, he hired R. B. Storter to take him to Fort Myers an attempt to get there before Roberts. Storter would take him no farther than Marco (roughly half-way) because of the threat of bad weather. Watson continued overland and was caught in a hurricane that struck the lower Gulf Coast on October 18. He did, however, manage to get to Fort Myers, only to discover that Roberts was already there, in custody, and had been questioned by Tippins. He asked Tippins to deputize him so he could legally arrest or kill Cox. Tippins refused. On the other hand, Tippins did not arrest him, according to Bill House, because Watson's daughter was married to Walter Langford, a prominent banker and businessman in Fort Myers.

Watson returned to Everglade and picked up his motor launch where it was stored at Storter's store. He stopped at Chokoloskee and bought shotgun shells at Smallwood's store, despite Ted Smallwood's warning that they had been soaked in the hurricane and were probably bad. Watson proceeded south to Chatham Bend. He told Smallwood and others that he was on his way to get Cox. The House family patriarch, D. D. House, told him he had better bring back either Cox or his body.

On the 23rd Watson returned. He was met at the hurricane-ruined dock by a small group of men led by D. D. House and his sons Bill and Dan. Watson produced a hat with a hole in it, claiming he had killed Cox, but was unable to bring the body. D. D. House told him that they would all need to go to Chatham Bend and find Cox's body and that Watson would need to hand over his shotgun. Instead, Watson pulled it up and fired at the three Houses. It misfired with a slight puff of smoke. Smallwood was right—the shells were bad. D. D. House had anticipated that Watson would do this and fired at him at almost the same instant. *His* shotgun misfired as well. However, Henry Short and the House brothers had rifles with brass cartridges, and they did not miss.

It was later claimed that a party then traveled to the Watson Place and found "skulls and bones littering the place," and that for years afterwards multiple mass graves were uncovered, but none of this has been verified. According to the National Park Service, other than the single grave dug by Cannon and the clammers for Smith, Waller and Melville (which eroded into the river in the 1950s), no gravesites have been identified.

Jaudon found the Watson Place in active use as a farm, mostly growing sugar cane and tomatoes, and to his great surprise discovered that the occupant, one W. F. Brown, wasn't a squatter, but a legitimate tenant, with a multi-year lease from A. W. Hopkins. Jaudon then decided to help Brown use his place as an experimental farm to test various types of tomatoes, onions, peppers, potatoes, and other truck crops, "not on any extensive scale, but sufficient to demonstrate what can be done." However, the Watson "murder place" was so notorious that seemingly every prospect that Jaudon showed around the Hopkins Tract wanted the thrill of spending the night at the infamous farm. In 1918, Jaudon bought out Brown's lease for $4,000 and thereafter used it to house foremen, engineers and corporate tourists, although Brown was allowed to continue farming through at least 1920.[28]

* * * * *

In mid–1917 a new scandal broke when the Miami newspapers reported that the "Tamiami Trail Lands," supposedly provided by the state to the Tamiami Trail Commission to benefit the road construction, had actually been sold to the three commissioners as a private business speculation. Although newspaper ads offering platted home lots for sale within the two tracts stated that they were being sold by the Tamiami Trail Commission, allegedly none of the money actually went to the road project. The charges were leveled by Frank Baker, president of the North Miami Improvement Association. "The so-called Tamiami Trail lands are wholly and solely a private speculation in which three men, as private citizens, have agreed to buy 20,000 acres of undrained Everglades lands adjacent to the Trail at $5.00 an acre and are engaged in selling these lands at as much a higher price as they can get," complained Baker.[29]

The three commissioners admitted that this was true, but countered that the project was more than the road itself. Reminding the assembled reporters that the Tatum brothers had wanted the road stopped because they feared it would act as a dam, flooding their land holdings to the northeast of Miami, Locke Highleyman said that project being financed through the Tamiami Trail land sales was a cutoff canal to the southeast to connect the Tamiami Canal to the Snapper Creek Canal at a point about 25 miles west of Miami. "I have made probably ten trips to Tallahassee," Highleyman said. "Our first visit was to ask the Internal Improvement board to build the Snapper Creek canal out of the [highway] bond money, which they refused to do." The Tamiami Trail commissioners then proposed the current plan, which was the private sale of 20,000 acres of land for $100,000, with the Internal Improvement Fund paying for the Snapper Creek Canal extension after the second payment was made at the end of one year. "It was a very risky thing for me to put my name down back of this $100,000 for lands 22 to 30 miles west of Miami, but wishing to make my word good, I took the risk."[30]

The controversy soon died out when it was discovered that Frank Baker, the man who leveled the charges against the three commissioners, was originally slated to be a commissioner of the drainage sub-district created to dig and maintain the Snapper Creek Canal extension. But the new sub-district was to include a large amount of land belonging to the Internal Improvement Fund, and the Fund's trustees did not accede to its creation because they did not want to pay the taxes. Baker, Jaudon, and Dr. J. L. Homburg, a landowner, were to be the commissioners under this first plan.[31]

Later, the legislature passed the Napoleon Broward District Act, making the formation of sub-drainage districts containing state lands easier, and the Southern Drainage District, as it was now called, was formed. Jaudon and Highleyman were selected by the petitioners to be supervisors and State Representative John Watson picked J. T. Conrad to be the third supervisor. Baker was left out and resented it. Any vestige of controversy died out soon thereafter when it was discovered that the three Tamiami Trail commissioners had, by taking out a mortgage, paid the full $100,000 to the Improvement Fund ahead of schedule, thus triggering the Fund's obligation to finance the drainage improvements. By the fall of 1918, the state engineer determined that the money would be better used to widen and deepen the existing Tamiami Canal and to build a short cut-off canal to the northeast to connect the Tamiami Canal to the Miami River Canal, rather than dig the much longer connector to the southeast to the Snapper Creek canal.[32]

However, Jaudon was forced to admit that the "Tamiami Trail Lands" venture was a purely private speculation and that the three men expected to net between ten and twenty thousand dollars from their purchase. In actuality, the Tamiami Trail Lands were far from a bonanza. During the first year the lands were offered for sale 5,280 acres were sold, a little over a quarter of the total. The purchase price from the Internal Improvement Fund was five dollars an acre, $24,400. The three commissioners repaid $36,630 of the $100,000 mortgage, and this appears to be about what the 5,280 acres sold for. Thus, it appears that they gave nearly everything they made to the mortgage company. However, the last land sale was made in August 1917, the same month the last payment on the mortgage principal was made, suggesting that the commissioners were having trouble selling land that didn't directly front on the future roadway.[33]

In addition, $4,682 in interest had been paid, and was still accruing at the rate of about $400 per month. In short, the three men were in danger of losing their shirts. But to keep the County Commissioners mollified, the ads for the Tamiami Trail Lands dropped any reference to the "Tamiami Trail Commissioners," listing only the Jaudon Realty Company, and later, the Realty Securities Company, a separate firm only loosely associated with both Jaudon and Highleyman.[34]

* * * * *

Starting in the summer of 1917, wildly varying reports on the progress of the Trail started to emerge. In August, the McCrary Company estimated that finishing the Dade County portion of the work would require another two years. The dredge was at the 14-mile point, and the road was drivable for eight miles (two miles shy of today's Krome Avenue), but only as a rough construction road. Two dredges were now in use, a small floating dredge having replaced the caterpillar excavator for use in stripping the overlying muck ahead of the drill barge. A reporter found that the fears of the Tatums had been realized: the road and its embankment were damming the south-flowing water. The land to the south of the road was rapidly drying out, while that to the north was becoming inundated year-round.[35]

At Marco, McCrary had put a one-cubic yard Monighan shovel to work throwing up a low, narrow sand road grade in 1916, but their work was far from vigorous. One report stated that their entire work crew was comprised of only sixteen men. They may have been trying to put off as much of the work as possible until the Dade end was completed, and then tackle the majority of the work by going east-to-west. That made sense, because by starting from Marco, they had to ship in all their supplies to Everglade by boat, then from Everglade City to the work camp by skiff and ox cart.

Hobart Crabtree vehemently denied McCrary's claim that the road would require another two years, but would not provide his own estimate. Asked for clarification as to the situation in Lee County, Jaudon said it was his belief that the stretch from Marco Junction to the Dade line could be broken into two segments: a 25-mile seasonally dry leg from Marco to Turner's River, and a second, continually inundated segment from Turner's River to the county line. A walking dredge, which he believed was actually being operated by a subcontractor of McCrary's, was at work at Marco, but that no work had been done other than surveys east of Turner's river. Overall, he was forced to admit that "progress has not been so good." In October 1918 the McCrary firm (depending on whose version you believed) either quit or was fired, and Lee County gave the job to their own engineer, Ralph Ranson.[36] In January 1918, the McCrary Company asked for a one-year extension of their Dade contract. The county commissioners acceded to this, provided that McCrary paid Hobart Crabtree's additional expenses. This was agreed to.[37]

Increasingly, Jaudon and his associates grew worried about the ability and desire of Lee County to finish the job. Despite having two special districts and over $300,000 in funding, it was clear from the start that its resources were inadequate to improve the entire coast road from the Fort Myers to Marco Island, let alone build the segment between Marco Junction to the county line, roughly 48 miles east. Also, no provision had been made for the proposed new downtown Fort Myers bridge to eliminate the ten-mile diversion to Olga, or to build the nine-mile road link from the north bank of the river to the Charlotte County line. The best guess was that District No. 3 alone was $100,000 short of what would ultimately be needed.[38]

Lee County District No. 1 had been crippled from the start by the refusal of the City of Fort Myers to participate. In-town property owners were not contributing towards the repayment of the bonds. In spite of this, by May 1918, the chief road engineer of Lee County was reporting that the highway from Fort Myers was "already graded and bridged and hard surfaced as far as Naples," about two thirds of the way to Marco. However, by "hard surfaced" he meant "crushed shell," and as schoolteacher Mary Lindstrom recalled when she arrived soon after to start her new job at Marco Island, "bridged" was just as flexible term as "hard surfaced":

> It did not take us long to drive [south] out of Ft. Myers.... The sand shell roadway, worn to a washboard surface, was not bad for that time, but the many "bridges" over swampland and inlets were unbelievable. They were constructed of planks simply nailed to pilings with the cross-planks laid loose. At one so-called bridge two men were working, for there was a hole large enough for a wheel of the bus to fall through. We waited until the men threw a pair of planks across the opening.[39]

Meanwhile, as to the wetlands stretch between Marco Junction and the county line, the Lee County engineering staff could assure Jaudon only that "a little over twelve miles of this road are now graded" and that "the prospects are that the construction will go ahead much more rapidly from now on due to some changes which have been made by the contractor." What these were went unspecified. Privately, Jaudon despaired to a colleague that "it seems to be almost a certainty that Lee County cannot nor will not complete its part of the work for over two years as they have not nor will not call an election to provide sufficient funds to complete it, and they only have 125,000 dollars to build 54 miles of road."[40]

To attempt to inject some life back into a project that was rapidly slipping out of the public's consciousness, Jaudon temporarily joined forces with Fort Myers newspaperman F. E. Harrison, Lee County Sheriff Frank Tippins and county game warden Sam Thompson to resurrect an idea he had fought just three years earlier: the "Seminole Trail," or Sam Jones Old Town route, the one that cut southeast from Fort Myers to Immokalee, then east to the tri-corner of Dade, Broward and Lee. However, where the original Sam Jones Old Town proposal had continued east to the Miami Canal, this new plan turned due south at the Old Town to intersect with the Tamiami Trail right-of-way at the Dade-Lee line.

Jaudon set out on another of his cross-state expeditions. His companion this time was Ross Clark, a former Texas cattle rancher turned New York financial speculator. Clark was attempting to put together a partnership to provide financing for Jaudon's Tamiami Railway, mostly based around the idea of selling future timber harvesting rights to investors. Clark and Jaudon started out, improbably, from May Mann Jennings's Royal Palm State Park near Homestead, northeast along Long Pine Key in an attempt to find a way across the Shark River from southeast to northwest.

This unlikely course was probably resulted from a desire to survey a thousand or so acres of land on the north flank of Long Pine Key, about three mile northeast of the state park. Jaudon was involved with a firm called the U.S. Sisal Trust. It had just planted several thousand sisal seedlings at a nursery west of Hallandale on the Dade-Broward county line. Mature plants need about eight to ten feet between plants and hard, rocky soil, so the Hallandale nursery was only a temporary measure. U.S. Sisal was scouting a site for its permanent grove, out of which it hoped to produce rope and twine. (It did purchase the Long Pine Key tract. Jaudon was hired to manage the sisal plantation as a part-time job, but the trust failed in 1920.)[41]

Unable to get much beyond Long Pine Key, the two men returned to the Homestead area, turned north and tried again on a route about ten miles south of the Tamiami Trail. Jack Tiger Tail spotted them while he was on his way in to Miami. "The Everglades are mighty dry," he told a reporter. "Think maybe [they'll] make it." They didn't. They had to turn back about eight miles short of the Monroe County line. They then took the established auto route across state from Melbourne to Tampa and tried following as much of the route of the Tamiami Trail as they could from west to east, getting almost as far as Turner's River, somewhere northeast of Everglade, and walked several miles farther. The trip apparently did not end well. A boat from the Chevelier Corporation had to come up Turner's River from Chokoloskee to pick up Jaudon and take him to company headquarters at the Watson place on April 18. On April 20 he underwent surgery at Miami City Hospital. "That's what you get for taking a vacation," his friend, newspaperman F. E. Harrison chided him, "or at least for telling me that you were on a pleasure trip."[42]

But the real purpose of the trip was to impress Ross Clark, who was meeting with several New York investors. "I told them we would want $750,000 for the building of the [rail]road to Chevelier and we would also need at least $100,000 for the Chevelier corporation to use in getting out timber," Jaudon wrote a partner. McCord, in Iowa, disdainfully told Jaudon not to get his hopes up: "[A]fter several years of correspondence with gentlemen in New York and other cities, many of whom had a deal 'just in sight,' we cannot put much confidence in your New York prospects." McCord's prediction was borne out. Three months after his expedition Jaudon wrote to Ross Clark: "Your letter of July 27th before me. In substance, you say that it is impossible and impractical to construct the railroad or provide for the finances in the manner suggested in your letter of July 24 and previous correspondence, which of course, is more than a serious disappointment." The decision had been made: there would be no Wall Street financing for the Chevelier Corporation.[43]

F. E. Harrison continued to beat the tub for the Seminole Trail with Jaudon's moral and (modest) financial support, mostly as a scenic and historic route, but the idea went nowhere. The county was already set on building three roads out of Fort Myers: the coast road south to Naples and Marco Island; the east road along the bank of the Caloosahatchee River to Olga, LaBelle and Lake Okeechobee, and the downtown Fort Myers bridge north across the Caloosahatchee. It was a constant tug-of-war between Lee County businesses and residents as to which project should receive priority.[44]

As the rainy season hit in June 1918, Jaudon had nothing to show for his work except bills and demands from the Citizens National Bank of Spencer, Iowa, for money. "I am sorry to find you took too much of a gambler's chance, depending on one season's efforts," McCord wrote. "The two prospects you mention in your letter are more or less like a trunk full of such correspondence which we accumulated during the several years which we tried to sell the property." Jaudon blamed his inability to attract investors or developers squarely on the lack of progress of the Tamiami Trail: "they will not actually produce any definitive sum of money by reason of the delay of the progress on the Tamiami Trail," he wrote McCord. But McCord had, without intending to, let slip just how weak his hand was with his "trunkfull of correspondence" comment: there was nobody except Jaudon and his associates—followers would be a more accurate term—willing to put any time and money into the Hopkins Tract. The Iowa trio hadn't even been willing to spend the money on taxes, preferring instead the risk losing the property to a tax sale rather than pay $8,500 a year, at least until Jaudon came along.[45] (And what must Jaudon have thought when he found out he could have had the property for $35,000 in back taxes if he had only checked with the county clerk's office first!) The trio from Spencer could either continue letting their money ride on the sparkplug from Miami, or give the Hopkins Tract back to the mosquitoes and the alligators. It wasn't really much of a choice.[46]

The overhead of the Chevelier Corporation was running about a thousand a month. The Miami office, with lawyer Paul Taylor and engineer George Cook, who both had their own offices elsewhere in town, cost $500. Three workmen and foreman Boysen at the Watson place cost $400. The corporation had bought a yacht, the Macushla ($10,000), and its captain and crew cost $85 a month. It also owed everybody for just about everything. "We need immediately $49,200; $10,800 on September 1, 1918, and $50,000 plus interest and taxes on each April 1," Jaudon wrote in July 1918, "In other words, the total liabilities of the Corporation today are $425,300." Technically, as of September 1, 1918, the corporation was insolvent, but that didn't slow Jaudon. He had spent $23,000 to dredge out Lossman's River so a boat could be run into and out of Chevelier Bay at either high or low tide—never mind that there was nothing in Chevelier Bay to go to. In fact, there was nothing in the entire 207,000 acres of the Hopkins Tract except for the 40-acre Watson place.[47]

In April 1918 the first American troops landed in Europe and entered combat three weeks later. In August, the state defense council issued its list of "essential" occupations for which employees would be exempt from conscription. Roadbuilding wasn't on the list. J. B. McCrary reported "a general exodus of laborers employed on the two contracts (Tamiami Trail and Ingraham Highway) who became panic stricken ... and hurried to the city to find

7. The Only Dry Ground for Twenty Miles

out where they could get into essential lines of industry," and thus avoid the draft, if one should occur. On September 21, the United States Highway Council instructed state highway commissions to require all new road construction projects to secure a construction permit. However, road construction projects already underway were exempt from the rule. Dynamite became expensive and hard to find.[48]

McCrary asked the Dade County Commission to release the ten percent "retainage," the percentage usually held back to ensure completion of the work and addressing of any final deficiencies identified by county inspectors. The commissioners approved the release of the retainage. They probably should have been more skeptical, especially after Chairman E. D. V. Burr asked J. B. McCrary if the release of the $12,654 in retainage would be applied to securing labor. McCray merely smiled and said "it would come in mighty handy right now and that it was doing the county no good in the bank." The resolution approving the release of the retainage was signed on September 4. Three weeks later J. B. McCrary came and shut down his Tamiami Trail worksite. He did not appear before the board, but sent an employee of his subcontractor, the J. F. Morgan Company of Birmingham, to ask permission to suspend work. When asked, the employee admitted that work had already been suspended and all but a few manual laborers had already left. When asked how long before McCrary planned to return, he replied that he did not know if McCrary had any plans to return.[49]

••8••

Careful, There's a Little Shine on That Bottle

The winter of 1918–19 should have been a bleak one for James Jaudon. He had spent most of October in the hospital, never having fully recovered from his April surgery. His brother died the same month. His financial partners in Iowa were demanding an immediate $50,000 payment in cash for interest and taxes, threatening foreclosure, and refusing to even hear about spending money for improvements. J. B. McCrary had convinced the County Commission to release the Tamiami Trail contract's $12,600 retainage, only to take off on the first train back to Atlanta with his staff afterwards, sending notice to his subcontractor to shut down work. Later, the county found out that nobody had paid DuPont's dynamite bill for $5,047. DuPont sent a demand letter to J. F. Morgan. But the Birmingham company didn't have the money; McCrary hadn't paid them, either. John James, one of the partners in the James & Green construction company, the subcontractor doing the dredging on the Marco-to-Dade segment in Lee County, died of influenza in the summer of 1918. James & Green called it quits in October. Jaudon wrote that "it seems almost a certainty that Lee County cannot nor will not complete its part of the work for over two years," and that they "can see no way, nor have they made plans to complete ... their part of the work." On November 11 the war ended, only to be followed by the depression of 1919–20, the sharpest between the panic of 1907 and the great depression of 1929–38. The whole project had the odor of dead fish about it—a 17 mile-long pile of rubble and stagnant water.[1]

But Jaudon had the skills of a high-wire artist. The Lee County Commissioners knew that the $125,000 received from the sale of Special Road and Bridge District No. 3 bonds was inadequate to build the entire mileage to the Dade County line. If things went well, they were hoping James & Green would have made it from Marco Junction to Turner's River, 34 miles short of the county line, eight miles east of where the narrow-gage Deep Lake short line railroad crossed the road's stakeline at the future site of Carnestown. When they threw in the towel, James & Green was still ten miles short of Turner's River, one or two miles west of Carnestown.[2]

James's death was no doubt the precipitating factor leading to the shutdown, but in an open letter to Lee County Commissioners, Jaudon accused the county of refusing to spend money they had sitting in the bank. The truth is probably in the middle: the county commissioners, who knew that the work could not be completed with the money raised from the October 1915 bond issue, and who were aware that their constituents, unlike the citizens of Dade County, were not likely to approve any more bonded indebtedness, were not willing to spend the bank account of District No. 3 down to zero just to build a road to nowhere. Lee County was simply not willing to risk putting multiple contractors to work in a crash program to finish the road all the way from Fort Myers to the Dade line in the two years that Jaudon and others had promised the Dade portion of the work would require. They had promised two years back in 1915 and now, in 1919, they were still promising two years.[3]

With McCord and Floete breathing down his neck for taxes and interest payments on the Hopkins Tract, and no buyers in sight until there was a way to get in and out of the place, Jaudon approached Lee County in January 1919 with an audacious plan: the Chevelier Corporation would build the road if Lee and Dade counties would agree to reroute it to the south so it passed through the Hopkins Tract in Monroe County. "I believe that you have something like $90,000 unexpended of Special Road and Bridge District No. 3 bond issue," Jaudon told the Lee County commissioners on January 19. "If this is a fact, it seems to me that you have sufficient money on hand to construct a hard-finished road," provided that the Chevelier Corporation paid for the Monroe roadwork. "You would be actually completing and finishing the construction of about 33 miles of hardsurfaced road ... whereas your present plan is to build a grade for a distance of about 51 miles." Lee's current financing plans made no provision for finishing out the roadway, just excavating it; by reducing the road mileage down to 33 miles they would have enough to build a finished hard-surfaced road, Jaudon claimed.[4]

Jaudon's plan would have J. B. McCrary extend Dade's roadbed straight to the county line instead of turning it 45 degrees to the northwest about five miles before the Dade-Lee line along the current survey, the so-called "Jenkins route."[5] By continuing straight west, the Tamiami Trail would enter Monroe about three miles south of the Lee-Monroe line. The original alignment had put the bend in the road expressly to avoid Monroe County, which did not want to bear any of its cost, and to avoid a series of wetlands that ran along the Monroe-Lee boundary. Under the new plan, the road would continue west in Monroe County for eighteen miles, then turn northeast to enter Lee County about twenty miles west of the Dade County line. From there it would continue northwest in Lee County to connect to the original Jenkins route about eight miles west of Carnestown. At this point it was uncertain how far the James & Green crew had managed to get. They claimed to have come up a mile short of Carnestown, but Otto Neal, the superintendent of the dredge that eventually did complete the work, said it was two and a half miles.[6]

The Lee County Commissioners approved Jaudon's plan in February 1919, but allocated no funding. The contract explicitly stated that the road would be built at the expense of the Chevelier Corporation, and Jaudon explained to both Lee and Monroe commissioners that his firm would pay for it by issuing bonds. The contract also stated that Dade had to finish their end of the road first, and if the McCrary company defaulted on the contract and their bondsman was forced to step in and provide for the completion of the work (or pay the surety amount to the county), then the Chevelier contract was voided.[7]

The Dade commissioners also expressed general agreement with the new arrangement, but issued no formal instructions to Hobart Crabtree to change the routing of the roadway, preferring to wait and see how things developed in Lee County. On February 11, Lee County re-let the bids on the remaining work from Marco Junction to Turner's River, near where the road would turn south and head towards Monroe County under Jaudon's new plan. No one bid on a flat-fee basis; Green Construction, the surviving half of the former James & Green firm, won the contract with a bid of 18.5 cents per cubic yard excavated. A new condition was added to the contract, one similar to what Dade already had in place, requiring the contractor to have a supervising engineer on site at its expense.[8]

In spite of the contract language that permitted him to wait until the McCrary company finished its Dade County work, Jaudon went ahead and leased a dredge in Miami and paid to have it towed around Cape Sable to the Ten Thousand Islands. "It will be put to work within 10 days on the building of a roadway through the Chevelier tract," he announced. He apparently wanted to build along the right-of-way originally set out for the Tamiami Railroad, which was to run due east out of Chevelier Bay parallel to, and south of, the Lee-Monroe line.

Three months later, George Cook, the firm's secretary/treasurer, wrote to Jaudon about the "fiasco" of the dredging operations. The dredgemaster brought in with the new dredge, one Ivey, and his wife, rather than getting to work "in ten days" apparently spent close to $1,200 at Roberts's boatyard in Key West getting his vessel in shape. After this, Mr. and Mrs. Ivey sailed to Chevelier Bay and got a crew together in late July or early August, only to run into a nationwide strike by the American Federation of Labor. The Iveys threw their hands in the air and returned to Chokoloskee. Jaudon, in Jacksonville, wired Cook, in Miami, to order Boysen, in Chokoloskee, not to pay the striking laborers. He was too late, the Macushla got to Chokoloskee ahead of Cook's wire, and Boysen had already paid off the workers, told them never to come back, and shipped them off to Fort Myers. To add insult to injury the Macushla blew out her exhaust pipe on the trip and was laid up for repairs in Fort Myers. The labor bill alone was $962, not counting wages for the Iveys.[9]

By the end of the month even the Iveys were gone, the dredge was up for sale, and as Cook wrote Jaudon, "the only funds on hand, so far as I can see, is a balance of $125 in the Chevelier construction account at the Miami Bank and Trust…. My estimate is that it will take something over $1,000 to take care of the Ivey matter and the payroll without taking into consideration the grocery and gas bills."[10] The abandoned canal, the product of two year's effort and some $30,000, is still there. It starts in what is now called Alligator Bay

The earliest version of the Chevelier (loop) Road in Monroe County, between the Dade line and Pinecrest, sometime between 1922 and 1924. (Photographer unknown. HistoryMiami, No. X-1464–5).

and runs three miles east-northeast, ending in the middle of nowhere. By January 1920 Miami newspapers were reporting that "nothing has been done by the Chevelier Corporation."[11]

The corporation's financial situation was precarious. As of fall 1919, it had burned through more than $70,000 in development costs without much to show for it. In addition to the $300,000 mortgage to A. W. Hopkins, it was in debt another $125,000 on various loans, notes, and IOUs. Jaudon, Judge McDougal and George Cook met with McCord, Floete, and Mr. and Mrs. Hopkins and the Citizens National Bank of Spencer in late 1919 and were told that they had two options: one, accept foreclosure on the Hopkins note, or two, sign an agreement prepared by McCord and Hopkins's attorney.[12]

This agreement, which completely restructured the financing of the Hopkins Tract, came to be known as the "Spencer Agreement." It was fairly complex. In essence, it converted the stock equity to bonded debt, gave control to the Iowa owners as bond trustees, squeezed out the small stockholders that Jaudon had recruited back in 1917, and carved out the best land and gave it to a separate corporation. It worked like this:

The Chevelier Corporation would issue $600,000 in bonds. Of this, $400,000 would retire the mortgage and other debt and $200,000 would be sold to raise money to build the Tamiami Trail. The bonds were issued in denominations of $5,000. The holder of each bond would receive 160 acres of land. This meant that Hopkins, for example, would get back title to 9,600 acres (15 square miles) of his land, along with $300,000 in bonds. In addition, 14,000 acres (22 square miles) of land along the Gulf coast would be transferred at no cost to a new corporation called the Chatham Bend Corporation, of which McCord, Floete, McDougal, Cook, Jaudon and Hopkins would each own one-sixth of the stock. This new corporation would have no responsibility for repaying the bonds and would not be controlled by the bond trustees. A one thousand-acre townsite would be laid out.[13]

As Jaudon recounted, because the assets of the Chevelier Corporation became the collateral for the new bonds, which were supervised by a board of trustees, "the actual management of the land passed out of the hands of the [corporate] owners" and once again reverted to the group in Iowa, as they owned two-thirds of the bonds, where previously they had owned 35 percent of the stock and a $300,000 mortgage. As to the town site, "I will say this was not my idea as I would much rather have delayed this sale for future developments, but Judge [McDougal] thought it would raise money immediately—and I believe it will." But the two biggest impacts were the $200,000 in open-purchase bonds that were created to pay for roadwork, and the end of the Chevelier Corporation as a profit-seeking entity. Its only purpose was now to repay its bonded indebtedness—the profits from land sales, if any, were to be made by the Chatham Bend Corporation.[14]

Jaudon later claimed that the Spencer trio had subscribed to the $200,000 in road bonds, but did not pay for them. Actually, the Spencer trio agreed to take half and Judge McDougal agreed to take half. In 1923, they sold an oil lease to the Roland Oil Company for $50,000 of this obligation. At this point, the Spencer trio was responsible for $75,000; Judge McDougal was responsible for $75,000 and Roland Oil for $50,000. Based on the amendment the Spencer Agreement occasioned by this sale, dated February 1923, no road bond payments had yet been made by the Spencer trio or by Judge McDougal. Because of the oil lease, payments were scheduled to start in March 1923 and average about $7,000 a month (with some pauses) until May 1925. Contrary to what Jaudon stated in 1928, it appears, from the Chevelier Corporation's last annual report in 1937, that most, if not all, of the road bond payments were made by 1928.[15]

But it is clear that none of this money was available earlier than April 1923. Meanwhile,

Jaudon fell back on the same argument that the McCrary company had made two years earlier: it was necessary for the road to be finished from Miami out to the Dade County line so he could get his men and equipment into place to start working their way west.[16]

* * * * *

If the McCrary brothers had thought they pulled the wool over the eyes of the Dade commission back in April by getting them to pay the retainage as an incentive to keep going, then pulling out, they were due for a rude shock. G. E. McCaskell, the county attorney, wrote the McCrary's bank in Atlanta, calming informing them that a board resolution did not, without a parallel amendment to the county's budget, create a valid authorization to expend funds, so the retainage could not, after all, be paid "until the work was complete." The most that could be done would be for the county to pay the money into an escrow fund in a private bank; the McCrary firm could then, at its option, borrow against the fund if it was sufficiently confident that the road could be finished on-time and on-budget. All this, of course, assumed that the McCrarys returned and finished the work at all. The McCrarys were apparently hard-up for working cash. They did return to work; the county did put the funds into escrow, and the McCrarys almost immediately borrowed against the escrow at close to a twenty percent discount.[17]

The McCrary brothers really had no choice but to return to the job. Their other crew, at work on the Ingraham Highway, was still four miles from the Monroe County line. The McCrary Co. had just gotten a contract from the Model Land Company to extend the work past the county line to Flamingo, and was hopelessly mired in some of the worst conditions it had encountered so far in the wetlands near West Lake. Immediately after getting the green light to proceed on the Tamiami Trail, The McCrary brothers characteristically announced that they could not go forward. At first they claimed that the hull of the existing dredge was worn out and had to be rebuilt. Then the foremen changed the story to assert that a whole new dredge had to be hauled overland atop the embankment from Miami and assembled, which would take several months. Meanwhile, a caterpillar excavator could remove the overlying muck. By the end of November, McCrary had billed for only $7,172 in work: 23,100 feet of muck stripping and 1,700 feet of drilling and blasting.[18]

J. B. McCrary's singular lack of public relations acumen showed itself once again in the summer of 1919. The proceeds from the sale of the once-controversial Tamiami Trail Lands had gone to the gigantic Everglades Drainage District, which transferred them to a new sub-district called the Southern Drainage District that Jaudon helped create in 1917. The Southern Drainage District was wildly unpopular with the large corporate landowners who lived south of the Tamiami Trail in the Cape Sable District. Frank Pepper, although a friend and neighbor of Jaudon's, was in favor of going before the legislature to have those lands lying south of Perrine removed; W. W. Dewhurst, retired general counsel for the Model Land Company, suggested instead that they simply refuse to pay the tax and fight its existence in court as unconstitutional. James Ingraham sided with Pepper, urging moderation. However, the Southern Drainage District was popular with the smallholders north of the Trail who started seeing a dramatic reduction in wet-season surface ponding, including many owners who had bought land from the Tatum brothers. Jaudon had cannily brought around to his side the men who had once been his staunchest opponents.[19]

Once the dredge preparing the canal and embankment for the Tamiami Trail was about ten miles out, the Southern Drainage District put its own dredge to work digging a cut-off canal to connect the Tamiami and Miami River canals. The mouth of the Tamiami Trail canal was kept plugged to maintain the water level needed to float the dredges and barges of the road building crews. Once the cut-off canal was finished, the Tamiami Canal would flow east down the cut-off and into the Miami River Canal unless it too was plugged. Area landowners wanted the McCrary Company to move their Tamiami Canal dam seven or eight miles west, well upstream of the new cut-off canal. That way, groundwater would start flowing east down the Tamiami Canal, into the cut-off canal, and out the Miami River to tide. The McCrary Company, while it didn't admit it publicly, wanted the Tamiami Canal to stay completely plugged, because they wanted the Miami River to drain down the cut-off canal and *west* into the Tamiami Canal to help keep their dredges afloat during the dry season. In other words, they wanted the Tamiami Canal to function as a lake, not a canal, until they were done, and they wanted the new cut-off canal to act as the connector between that lake and the Miami River. The Southern Drainage District offered J. B. McCrary $600 to offset any inconvenience in relocating their cofferdam; McCrary demanded $3,600. The board at the drainage district said they couldn't afford that kind of money and appealed to the county commissioners, who exploded.[20]

Just before the cofferdam incident, J. B. McCrary had his own experience with a version of John King's 1917 "lost expedition" incident. McCrary, one of his surveyors, James Jaudon, and a Seminole guide, Charlie Tommy, left the Tamiami Trail work camp on March 9 to run a stakeline on the modified "straight line" route that would be used if the Dade County Commission went with the Chevalier Corporation's road. McCrary and his surveyor then planned to return to the McCrary firm's work camp; Jaudon and Charlie Tommy were to go on through to the Hopkins Tract, ending up at either Everglade or the Watson place. On March 15 they were declared missing. J. F. Morgan believed that they found the stakeline too hard a trek to risk returning the same way, so probably decided to continue west to the coast. An airplane was dispatched, but did not spot them.

On the 16th, they appeared in Marathon, in the middle keys. Morgan was correct. It was 14 miles from the end of the unfinished highway to the Monroe line, and all but one mile had been intractable wetlands. Jaudon convinced McCrary that if he turned around, finding the work camp would be like "hitting the sharp point of a needle with a rifle shot," so he should continue on with him, although that meant they would have to go a day or two without rations. They found someone with a boat in Turner's River they could use to get to the Watson place, where the Chevalier Corporation had the Macushla take them to the keys and Miami. "We had no idea people would get so worried about us," McCrary said. Three people who were not particularly worried about the fate of John Boyd McCrary were the Dade County commissioners.[21]

Delayed by McCrary's adventure, the commission soon met and instructed Southern Drainage District commissioner Locke Highleyman to proceed with removing the plug between the Tamiami Canal and the cut-off canal. "How are you going to do it?" He was asked by a commissioner. "Use dynamite, if necessary," he replied." That proved unnecessary. Two weeks later, during the night, the impounded water was released. "Just how this was accomplished, no one seems able to explain," noted a reporter. "It might have been a beaver, or rats, or just ordinary human beings, was the jesting conclusion reached on the street yesterday." The fact that J. F. Morgan's men had already trucked in two thousand dollar's worth of lumber and started work on a cofferdam well upstream of the cut-off canal hints that the likely culprit was Morgan. Facing the inevitable, he and his men took matters into their own hands. The Tamiami Canal was reportedly two feet below its prior level, meaning that the plug had not been cut all the way down to the canal bottom; the drainage district's engineer estimated that if it had been completely removed, the water level in the Tamiami Canal would drop four feet. Morgan's solution appeared to be a compromise everyone could

A 3½ cubic-yard Bay City floating dredge, with outriggers extended and boom and bucket in operation. This is a good example of the type of high-capacity equipment in place on the Trail after the state road department took over operations in 1926. (Photographer unknown. Collier County Museum, Naples, FL, No. 81.17.3.)

live with. It didn't hurt that the lowered water level created some of the best bass fishing to be found in South Florida over the winter.

After the dredge finished digging the cut-off canal, it was turned and floated back to the Tamiami Canal, where it started the job of widening and deepening it. The dredge crew was able to improve about three miles before the $100,000 raised through the sale of the Tamiami Trail lands ran out. But by the spring of 1921 sufficient money had been added through property taxes that the drainage district could contract with the Megathlin & Clark Company to continue the dredging. From that time forward the process of expanding the Tamiami Canal and installing cross-flow culverts continued almost non-stop until the road was finished in 1928.[22]

In April 1920, the J. F. Morgan firm finally floated their new dredge to the 18-mile post and put it to work digging rock, some eighteen months after work was halted in the fall of 1918. In September, Harry Freeman, who had been supervising the construction of the Ingraham Highway since 1916, took over command of the Trail's work crew. J. B. McCrary had made one last appeal to the Monroe County Commissioners, requesting that they allocate money or create a road and bridge district for a bond issue to provide funds to match the money the Model Land Company was spending to extend the Ingraham Highway to Flamingo and, hopefully, out to the far end of Cape Sable. The commissioners held to their long-standing position that the development of Cape Sable was a private venture and that the landowners—the Model Land Co. in particular—were responsible for installing and maintaining the infrastructure needed to develop it. The Model Land Company did hire another firm to dig a canal out to Lake Ingraham, but the road was never built.[23]

The same month the Monroe commissioners turned down the idea of participating in the Ingraham Highway, J. B. McCrary told the Dade County Commissioners that his firm was already $60,000 in the hole on the Trail project (they had lost $58,000 on the Dade County portion of the Ingraham), and that the contract had to be renegotiated. This was viewed somewhat skeptically when the county staff determined that $60,000 was almost exactly the balance remaining from the 1915 bond issue. In other words, McCrary wanted to find a way to empty out the bank account and go home. As he had done when the Ingraham Highway ran into trouble back in 1916, J. B. McCrary suggested that the commission agree to pay some small close-out items and then let him to cancel the contract. This time, he did not even bother to suggest that the county re-bid the rest of the project, but instead urged the county to lease his equipment and do the job itself. That idea did not go very far after County Attorney McCaskill did some research and reported that the McCrary firm did not actually own most of the heavy equipment it was offering to lease to the county. Instead, the county agreed to take over the auditing and financial oversight of the project, and to approve a new $50,000 bond issue, bringing the total budget up to $300,000.[24]

Meanwhile, out in Lee County, nobody seemed to have a firm grasp on the status of the project. In July 1920 Green Construction reported that they had four miles yet to go before the Deep Lake Railroad at Carnestown, which put them a mile and half farther away than James & Green had reported two years earlier. Based on what later construction crews found, this may have been a more accurate assessment of the work than the earlier reports.[25]

The road from Naples to Marco Junction was not yet fully hard surfaced. Of the 36 miles from Marco Junction to the Chevelier Road fork, only 12 miles of grade had been built, very little of it suitable for passenger cars. Clark Taylor, of the *Ft. Meyers News*, told a reporter for the *Miami Daily News-Metropolis* that "under the present methods of construction, only two or three miles of grade a month can be accomplished … if the work takes this longer period of time, the grade and completed road through the A. W. Hopkins Tract and the hard surfaced road through Dade County from Miami will be complete, and Lee County would still be in the course of construction, and the traffic on the trail will be held up."[26]

In January 1921 the Lee County engineer reported that a dredge was at the Deep Lake Railway at Carnestown. This was a Monighan drag-line excavator and not a floating dredge. Unlike the situation in Dade, where the borrow canal had to be blasted through rock lying under two to five feet of muck, the Lee County crews found that the muck simply covered bottomless sand. To build a stable roadbed, they were having to truck in crushed rock and gravel from the coast, and every mile they moved from Marco increased the cost of transporting fill. When he visited the Dade County worksite, the Lee County superintendent was most impressed, not by the road itself, but by the huge embankments of rock piled by the dredges to the side of the canal. It was more than was needed for the road, but had to be excavated to keep the big dredge floated. "In comparing the two counties, Mr. McCaskell stated that what most impressed the Lee County men was the natural rock available for road building, which makes the undertaking at this end easier than at the other end of the trail." J. B. McCrary may have been right—it might have been better to finish the Dade County segment first. Had it been completed all the way to the county line, all that surplus rock could have been trucked across and used to build the roadbed. On the other hand, it should be noted that the Collier Corporation, which took over work southeast of Naples after Collier County was split off Lee County in 1923, was successfully able to excavate the right-of-way from Marco Junction to past Turner's River only after putting floating dredges to work, just as J. B. McCrary had previously in Dade.[27]

* * * * *

Two new factors entered the equation about this time, in the early 1920s. The first had its genesis in January 1916 when Congress passed the Bankhead-Shackleford Federal Highway Aid Act, and President Wilson signed it into law in July. It provided a modest $75 million in construction funds over five years. Its most durable features were matching federal-state funding and the requirement that states create a highway department to administrate and monitor the federal funds they received. The bill was a compromise, passed in the face of vociferous opposition from states-rights advocates who had torpedoed two earlier acts. The Bankhead-Shackleford bill left very little role for federal decision-making, putting the power of the purse squarely in each state's highway department. The problem was that only about half the states even had a highway department, and most of these were merely advisory: the counties still raised all the road money, so they got to decide how it was spent.

Florida had a road department, but it too was advisory. That would change by 1917. To ensure that the money was well spent, the Bankhead-Shackleford funding would be split 50/50. The assumption was that while a state may have no hesitation about turning Washington's largesse into pork, it would have second thoughts about wasting its own money.[28]

But it didn't work as planned. When Thomas McDonald, the head of the Iowa Highway Commission arrived in Washington to start his new job as chief of the Bureau of Public Roads, he found a discouraged agency and an angry Congress. Only $500,000 of the $75 million had been spent. The Bureau didn't trust the states and wanted proof of sound engineering and accounting practices. The states accused the Bureau of only funding costly high-speed interstate highways, not the farm-to-market roads their constituents wanted. The Bureau wanted proof that the states had their local matching funds in the bank before they would release the federal share. The states wanted to match the federal funds with in-kind contributions, such as land or convict labor, not cash. McDonald moved with rapid, some would say rude, swiftness. The political appointees in the agency were replaced with

Shops and warehouses of Alexander, Ramsey & Kerr at Carnestown, five miles north of Everglades City, 1927. (Photographer unknown. Collier County Museum, Naples, FL, No. 88.42.17.)

engineers, many recruited from state highway departments. He transferred $130 million worth of war surplus trucks and other equipment to the states. He issued clear standards that state-aid roads had to meet. Above all, he founded the Highway Research Board and converted a backwater professional group, the American Association of State Highway Officials (AASHO) into a quasi-official organization where highway planners and engineers could meet and hash out their differences outside the prying eyes and ears of politicians and the public.[29]

The effects of the 1916 Highway Act in Florida would be slow, but irreversible: control shifted from the counties to the state road department. Counties that allocated funds to roads that were part of cross-state highways started to receive priority for state funding, which, in turn made them eligible for matching federal funds. In July 1920 the Florida road commission designated six state roads, and in 1923 these were formalized by the legislature into the "State Road System of Florida (first system)": State Road 1 (Jacksonville to Pensacola); State Road 2 (Lake City to Fort Myers via Gainesville, Orlando, Bartow and Arcadia); State Road 3 (Jacksonville to Orlando); State Road 4 (Jacksonville to Miami, the east division of the Dixie Highway); State Road 5 (High Springs, just outside Gainesville, to Sarasota, via Tampa, extended to Fort Myers by the time the 1923 legislation passed). State Road 9 (Apalachicola River, at the start of the panhandle) was soon eliminated as unfeasible and replaced with State Road 8 (Haines City to Okeechobee City to Fort Pierce, north of Jupiter).[30] An additional fourteen roads were designated "state aid" roads, including the Tamiami Trail, but as Jaudon explained,

> it does not spell anything at this stage of the game, because the State Highway Department has not sufficient funds available with which they could aid this road—in fact a 'state aid' road means that the State will aid in the up-keep and maintenance of roads already constructed but not in initiating or constructing a highway. Were the Tamiami Trail designated as a State Highway and if the funds were available in the treasury of the State Highway Board, there is hardly a question but that Hon. I. E. Schilling, who is a member of the State Highway Board, could induce his associates to give a large appropriation to the project.[31]

The situation would change dramatically when Chief McDonald and AASHO convinced Congress to approve the Highway Act of 1921. Instead of financing the Bureau of Public Roads out of general revenues, road building started to be paid from fuel taxes, with a two-cent per gallon tax available to each state. The two-cent state gas tax was optional, but if a state was willing to put up a larger amount of matching funds, it became eligible for more federal money. In essence, levying a two-cent state gas tax was the equivalent of charging a four-cent per gallon tax, because every two cents the state raised was matched by the Bureau of Public Roads. There were ceilings for each state, but some states chose not to claim their full allocation. These unclaimed funds were essentially auctioned off to those states that had already received their full allocation at the 50/50 level by having them bid for the extra money through overmatching. The 1916 Act had authorized $75 million over five years. The 1921 Act authorized $75 million *per year*. The system was so successful that the two-cent state option was later raised to four cents.[32]

In 1924, thirteen states did not charge a gas tax, but by 1926 only four did not. Florida began imposing a gas tax in 1923.[33] Because such a large percentage of the state's motor fuel sales were made to tourists and seasonal residents, Florida very early became quite aggressive in its use of the gas tax. In 1925, it started charging three cents per gallon. Only six states in 1925 were charging a higher gas tax, and only twelve were imposing the same three cents. In 1926, Florida increased its gas tax to four cents, and was raising $10.5 million in revenue, of which $7.9 million was allocated to the state road department. Between 1917 and 1925, annual expenditures from the state road department increased from $24,200 to

$8.5 million. Just at the time that the counties along the route of the Tamiami Trail were embarking on their great venture, the State of Florida was undergoing a transportation revolution. Without that revolution, the Trail would have died in the cradle.[34]

The federal-state funding structure approved by Congress in 1921 was based on the idea of a pay-as-you go motor fuels tax. This was highly compatible with Florida's tradition of making tourists and seasonal residents carry a disproportionate burden of infrastructure development and operating costs. Moreover, the rigid, top-down, technocentric structure imposed by Chief McDonald at the Bureau of Public Roads and AASHO insured that Florida's ingrained "pork chop" patronage culture was locked out of the project-selection and contracting processes. As a result, Florida did not approach roadway development from its usual traditional, conservative Deep South perspective. Instead, it far more resembled the progressive state governments of the Midwest and West. In other words, starting about 1921–22, and continuing until the financial collapse of 1928, road building in Florida was a preview of the "New South" of the 1970s.

The second tectonic shift was the purchase of the Deep Lake Railroad by Barron Collier of New York. At the time, the Deep Lake was certainly nothing to get excited about. In 1900, Walter Langford (Edgar Watson's son-in-law) and John Roach bought a half-section of pineland 18 miles north of Everglades City. The farms and packinghouses along the Turner River had flooded each of the last two years, leading to their wholesale abandonment. Langford, a Fort Myers banker, and Roach, president of the Chicago Street Railway Company, hoped to establish a grapefruit grove and packing house on the higher land farther away from the coast.[35]

There was only one problem. The plantation proved to be a dry-land island surrounded by almost impenetrable wetlands. Initially, the only way in or out was over a narrow corduroy road. When the grapefruit trees started to produce between 1906 and 1908, most of the fruit rotted on the ground for lack of swift transport to the Gulf. (Grapefruit is notorious for its swift deterioration once picked.) So Langford and Roach built a narrow-gage railroad on top of the plank road, using streetcar tracks and a flatcar powered by a Model T engine. Finished in 1913, it was continually, if slowly, expanded and improved over the years. By 1920, some 40 employees were working at Deep Lake, most living in tents and chickee huts. Florida was not strictly a business proposition for John Roach, however. In 1910 he had purchased Useppa Island, a barrier island near Fort Myers next to Boca Grande and Captiva Island, where he built a home and small hotel. The following year, he invited down his friend Barron Collier for a winter visit.

Barron Gift Collier was born in Memphis on March 23, 1873. It was long believed that he had graduated from Oglethorpe College, but recent research suggests that he dropped out of school at 16 to start work.[36] After various entry-level jobs, he signed on with the Illinois Central Railroad as a salesman. He quit when he won a bid to install a gasoline streetlight system in his hometown. From the proceeds he bought a half-interest in a print shop. One of the shop's customers was the local horsecar company, which sold interior advertising space on 9-by-12 inch cards. Collier gradually moved from merely printing the ads to taking over sales to eventually buying out the operation, paying the transit system a flat rate and pocketing everything over that. As horsecar systems converted to cable or electricity, he started to assemble the Consolidated Street Railway Advertising Company as a franchise system.

Most streetcar lines had been laid by real estate companies to get commuters out to their subdivisions. Once the land was sold, they had no reason to do anything but run them as cheaply as possible, or unload them off to the city. Thus, cars ran infrequently, had few seats to maximize capacity, and were invariably crowded. The unfortunate straphangers often didn't even have enough room to read a newspaper or magazine. Collier realized that advertising in the interior of streetcars would often have a captive audience. Collier's men moved into a city and greased the necessary palms to get an exclusive agreement to display quickly-changing advertising cards in every streetcar. They installed frames for the cards just above the windows at eye level to make them highly visible and facilitate swapping out cards quickly and easily. They then bought out or set up a local print shop to churn out the cards, and most importantly, organized an aggressive sales force to sell the advertising. He then sold the whole thing as a turnkey operation to a local operator for cash and a percentage of gross sales. He was a millionaire by age 26.[37]

Collier loved Useppa so much that he soon bought it. (Collier and his brother C. M. Collier are frequently confused with R. M. "Capt. Bill" Collier of Marco Island. R. M. Collier, one of the original pioneers in the Ten Thousand Islands, was not related to either brother.) In 1921, Barron Collier bought the Deep Lake grove and the railroad from Langford and Roach. Acting mostly through a strawman, Walter Fuller, co-owner of the Tampa streetcar system, Collier started buying up the south half of Lee County. In November 1921 he purchased the store and trading post of George W. Storter and his son, George, Jr., and the land around it, which encompassed most of the town of Everglade, which he renamed "Everglades City." Collier started a new town, Port Dupont, a half-mile inland of Everglade on Allen's River as a dock, warehouse and machine shop area (and housing area for black workers). Carnestown, another of his creations, was initially just a warehouse and a couple of sheds located where the stakeline for the future Tamiami Trail crossed the tracks of the Deep Lake Railroad, three or four miles north of Port Dupont and Everglades City.

Meanwhile, McCrary's men soldiered on, averaging, according to supervisor Freeman, about 3,200 feet a month. Several miles behind them, Megathlin & Clark's big dredge was deepening and widening the Tamiami canal so it could effectively drain the 60 square miles of the Southern Drainage District. Jaudon, as was his wont when news had slowed to a crawl, decided that it was a good time to take another one of his cross-state hikes.

This time his companions were George W. Storter and a Seminole guide. Captain Storter was from another one of the pioneering families in the Ten Thousand Islands, his father having settled there in the 1880s to open a store and trading post. It was from Storter's store that surveyor S. J. E. Lucas and 14 assistants spent three months in June 1908 assaying the timber on what would become the A. W. Hopkins Tract on behalf of its then-owner, the National Timber Company.[38]

Jaudon told a reporter that they left from Deep Lake, about ten miles north of Everglades City and six miles north of the stakeline for the Trail. Jaudon was a vice president of the Deep Lake Company, probably in the capacity of superintendent, a job he also filled at other plantations in Fort Myers and Miami. However, Storter later wrote that they had started from his store in Everglades City, four miles south of the stakeline, and had taken a boat up a branch of Turner's River to the proposed route. Storter's route was about twelve miles shorter than Jaudon's. Storter believed the trip would take three days.[39]

Storter's account indicates that they did not travel very far that first day after leaving the boat, mostly because they did not land until after one o'clock. Jaudon's story, having placed the start of their hike over ten miles farther back in Deep Lake, describes the first day as a strenuous, but not exceptionally arduous, hike through mostly pinelands and scrub prairie. This is inconsistent with other descriptions of the area around Deep Lake and Carnestown, which depict deep wetlands and wet, loose sand. Even assuming that Storter and Jaudon walked south down the railroad tracks from Deep Lake to Carnestown, it is doubtful whether they could have gone more than another five or six miles in the same day. It is likely that Jaudon was exaggerating when he gave his account to the press, and that Storter was telling the truth when he wrote his manuscript six years later.

From this point, both accounts generally agree. The second day they hiked about twenty-five miles and camped at a point they estimated to be near the southeast corner of Lee County. The next day, Jaudon claims that through overconfidence, they decided to leave the stakeline in the morning to visit the compound of Captain Tony, a prosperous Seminole farmer and orchard keeper. Storter, on the other hand, says they did this because they had underestimated their provisions and were running out of food.

Captain Tony wasn't home, but his family sold Jaudon and Storter food, which was especially valued by their guide, as the tinned rations his employers fed him were making him nauseous. The family also pointed them in the right direction to the stakeline. But they overshot it, and got lost to the south of the line. (Jaudon says that this was because the stakeline had been recently moved when the decision was made to shift the route from Lee to Monroe counties; Storter believed the stakes had been burned in a prairie fire.)

By now the prairies and pinelands had given way to ankle-deep water over jagged limestone rock, the water hiding thigh-deep pockets of muck. Jaudon says they relocated the stakeline late that day; Storter says they found it early the next morning. In any event, they stopped for the night at a spot they guessed to be about five or six miles southwest of the McCrary work camp. Here, Jaudon discovered that his boots had fallen out of his pack, leaving him with only the wading sneakers he had on his feet. Thoroughly exhausted, they got up the next morning and followed the stakeline in to the work camp and dredge at station 1476, exactly 27.9 miles from the zero stake, seven miles from the county line. The only person in camp was the watchman. He told Jaudon and Storter that everybody else had been sent home. All the work had been shut down. He also told the two men that he couldn't feed them—he hadn't gotten his supply shipment from Miami, and the McCrary firm hadn't left him with a car or truck to get back into town! He sent Storter and Jaudon to the home of a nearby native guide, whom the two men hired to take them to the home of a trapper Jaudon knew a few miles away.

The trapper set out two bottles of Poland Water in front of the men and Storter, thirsty, was about to gulp his down, when the old trapper warned him to be careful: "there is a little shine to that bottle." It was filled with straight moonshine. While they sipped the liquor, he fixed them a "splendid supper." The next morning, Storter was up early, before Jaudon. He couldn't help noticing that Jaudon's "trapper friend" had no spare traps, pelts, or curing frames. His hoes and rakes still had the store labels on them. "He couldn't stand it any longer," Storter recalled, "and stated very emphatically, 'Hell, no; no Indian didn't make that shine.' By past experience, I knew then that I was being entertained by a moonshiner; but being his guest, I did not think it would be courteous to inquire any further."

After breakfast, he ran them down the Tamiami Canal in a powerboat for twelve miles to the McCrary cofferdam. "He told us we would not have to wait very long, as many people came out on the canal to fish, and that we could send a message in to Miami to come out and take us in." Instead, a fisherman in a Model T converted into a pickup gave them a lift into the west suburbs, where they could call Maude Jaudon. They arrived at Jaudon's office four and a half days after leaving. The first thing Jaudon wanted to know is what the hell happened to the J. B. McCrary Company.

··9··

"Innumerable complications"

"Some time ago I wrote the J. B. McCrary Company for you, stating that payment of their actual expenses in the building of the Tamiami Trail would not be paid any at this time and that they would only be paid for 90 percent," reported Dade County attorney McCaskell to his commissioners in August 1921. "I did not tell them to suspend operations." The county had agreed to pay the McCrary Company the $12,654 dollars in retainage back in June 1919, placing it in an escrow fund in a Miami bank instead of withholding it until the project was complete, as was the usual practice, so McCrary could use it as collateral for a line of credit. The commissioners modified the contract again in December 1920, extending it by one year, thus giving the McCrary firm until December 8, 1921, to finish the road. On the same day, the voters approved a new bond issue of $50,000 to supplement the original $241,000 in Tamiami Trail funds passed in 1917.

In July 1921, the money set aside from the initial bond issue was exhausted and J. B. McCrary ordered work to be stopped. It was his position that when the county waived the retainage and agreed to switch to a direct reimbursement system in June 1919 it also agreed to compensate the firm for the actual costs of the construction, no matter how high they went. It was the county's position that they were still operating under the terms of the original 1916 contract: the McCrary firm would build a roughly 40-mile highway for a flat fee of $241,000, and if the job ended up costing more and they lost money, too bad. However, the county now, in September 1921, offered to increase the stipulated amount by $50,000 to reflect the availability of the new funds approved in December 1920; a total of $291,000. However, it insisted that that the contract remain on a flat-fee basis.[1]

"They owe some labor and materialmen's bills for work up to the time they stopped and they desire to get the County to pay" McCaskill's report continued, "in view of the slow progress they were making and the large amount of their expenses which they were eating up the funds very rapidly without any results, I would not think the Board would pay these expenses."[2]

After meeting with both the McCrary brothers, McCaskell felt that "I have an idea that they would let it go at the payment of the labor bills without the payment of the materialmen's bills." In other words, if Dade County covered McCrary's delinquent paychecks, McCaskell feared that the brothers would return to Atlanta, leaving Dade County on the hook for unpaid bills to suppliers. McCaskell recommended that the board take measures that would allow the County to put a lien on McCrary's heavy equipment. The McCrary brothers claimed that they were not the sole owners of the equipment "but I do not know whether they are or not." There was not a lot of trust left between the J. B. McCrary Company and the county.

The abandonment of the worksite, and the Trail's vast isolation, resulted in the first of the mysterious, bizarre, and ghoulish traffic deaths that was to make it famous over the years. On the morning of Thursday, August 11, 1921. Edward White, 31, married, father of two young children, head of the ice cream department of the Southern Utilities Company, stumbled at dawn into the headquarters of the Curtiss flying field, at the southwest corner of what is today the Miami International Airport. He reported that he had been in an accident out on the Tamiami Trail near Glademoor, a barely started subdivision along the Trail about three miles southwest of Curtiss field.[3] His Essex had gone into the canal. Was anyone hurt? Yes, he thought so. Who? The girl who was driving the car may have been trapped inside. Whose car was it? His. When did it happen? A little after sundown last night. That was ten hours ago. Where had he been? Looking for her, then trying to find a farmhouse.[4]

A derrick truck pulled the Essex out of the water. No one was inside, but in the back seat was a complete set of women's underwear. Was this the girl's? White didn't know. Who was the girl? Maude Gilbert. How did White know her? Oh, he picked her up a couple of hours before the crash. She looked like she needed a lift. An officer was dispatched to the address listed for Miss Gilbert. The landlady, Mrs. Dustinberry, reported that Miss Gilbert had left last evening about 7:30 to meet a Mr. White for a date. They both worked at Southern Utilities. He taught her to drive and they became friends after that. Mrs. Dustinberry was unaware that Mr. White had a family. She did not think Miss Gilbert knew this. Edward White was placed under arrest.

Divers recovered Maude Gilbert's body that evening. The coroner reported that she was clothed only in her outerwear. She had drowned. A bruise over her left eye matched the shape of the steering wheel. There were no other "complicating factors," presumably meaning that she had not been raped and was not pregnant. Asked again at the coroner's inquest how Gilbert's underwear ended up in the back seat, White again said that he did not know. The inquest concluded that Maude Gilbert was probably driving, and that she drove off the road into the canal at a moderately high rate of speed while "distracted." White was released. His wife and children had already left town to return to her parent's home in North Carolina. Gilbert's family came to retrieve her body for burial in Connecticut. White disappeared from both public view and the Miami city directory. As early as 1937, the *Ft. Myers Daily News* ran headlines announcing "Trail Deaths Mount: State Aroused."[5]

* * * * *

Throughout fall 1921, the Dade County Commissioners and the McCrary brothers negotiated their contract extension. They agreed relatively quickly to a flat fee augmented by the new $50,000. The sticking point was that the county attorney insisted on maintaining a higher than normal 25 percent retainage; the McCrarys said they would not work under a retainage. In fact, their preference was still to sell their equipment to the county and have the county complete the work. Attorney McCaskell argued that this was impossible because McCrary's equipment was mortgaged, and the county would not buy it unless it could be acquired free and clear. McCrary insisted on no firm deadline and no retainage. McCaskell finally recommended that the board simply wait another eight weeks until December 8 when the current contract ran out and then file for a default with McCrary's bondsman. At present, the county had only $50,000 available from the second, October 1920 bond election. McCrary had posted a bond of $120,750 in 1916. By filing a default with the bonding company, the county would be over $70,000 ahead. Let the bonding company find a replacement contractor, or pay the county to finish the job themselves. The McCrarys capitulated, agreeing to a ten percent retainage, the traditional amount. A new deadline of August 1, 1923, was set. Harry Freeman, the McCrarys' on-site superintendent ordered a new Marion steamshovel to replace the floating dredge. It arrived in November 1921.[6]

If anything, the situation on the Gulf coast was in even more of disarray. There were three issues: the never-ending controversy over which route should be followed for a cross-state highway; if the Marco-to-Miami was route chosen, who should build it and how should it be paid, and how should Lee County's potentially crushing financial burden be managed?

Jaudon had railed almost continuously at the Lee County commissioners for their failure to release funds needed to build the Marco-to-Dade portion of the Trail fast enough to link the new coast road to either the Jenkins or Chevelier routes, so that construction crews and equipment could be sent overland to start working east-to-west. But there was deep suspicion that Dade's portion of the work would never be completed. In addition, there were still the three different routes out of Fort Myers vying for attention: north, due east to Lake Okeechobee, and the Trail. Further complicating matters was that there were no county-wide bonds, just district specific bonds. The $177,000 in bonds for Special Road and Bridge District No. 1, for example, could only be spent on the Fort Myers to Marco road, while the $125,000 approved for District No. 3 could be spent only for a Marco Junction to Dade County road.

Everglades City, 1928. The view is from south to north, with Allen's River (later known as Barron's River) on the left. Port Dupont is off the top of the picture. (Photographer unknown. Collier County Museum, Naples, FL, No. 88.42.81.)

In early 1922 Jaudon tried to convince his old friend Judge Wilkinson of Naples, a Lee County Commissioner, to organize a $660,000 county-wide bond issue, part of which would be used to retire the old district-specific bonds. The old districts would then be wiped out, leaving just one county-wide highway department. The judge demurred, believing that the district bonds could only be retired through a cash purchase, not by exchanging them for county-wide bonds. The Lee County attorney agreed with Judge Wilkinson, and the proposal for the county-wide bond issue was tabled in February.[7] At the same time, the Palm Beach commissioners renewed their efforts to have Lee County prioritize the road east past LaBelle to Lake Okeechobee's Sand Point, which the Atlantic Coast Line Railroad had just renamed Clewiston. The Lee commissioners traveled to Palm Beach in February 1922 and were told by Palm Beach County Commission Chairman Harris that $400,000 had been spent on the cross-state road, but that with current financing, work could extend no farther than Belle Glade, 19 miles from Clewiston. The south Lake Okeechobee route, soon to be State Road 25, was once again shoved to the back burner.[8]

On the same day the Lee commissioners decided not to put a county-wide bond issue before the voters, Jaudon signed a new contract with the county to build fourteen miles of the Marco-to-Dade stretch. This was essentially the same agreement that he had struck on behalf of his Chevelier Corporation back in February 1919. However, no real work had been performed under that contract except for the canal from Alligator Bay that went nowhere. Under the 1920 Spencer Agreement between the Chevelier Corporation partners, Jaudon had been promised $200,000 by Judge McDougal and the Iowa trio. However, as of the end of 1922, only a little less than $3,600 had been paid into the road account. Out of $53,000 in revenue accrued by the Chevelier Corporation in 1921 and 1922 (including the sale of bonds), about two-thirds went to taxes, interest, and to retire past due notes, mostly to banks. Only about $9,500 was spent on labor, equipment and material to install and maintain improvements, and to take surveys and prepare plans. As noted earlier, it wasn't until after the Spencer Agreement was amended a year later, and revenues from the Roland Oil Company and W. J. Willingham (who bought the exclusive rights to develop Pinecrest) started to come in that the road fund started to see any real money.[9]

Jaudon had been weighing two options at this point. He could wait for the J. B. McCrary Company to finish the Dade County work and then extend their road towards the Gulf. This was a more promising alternative now that Dade appeared committed to the straight-to-Monroe alignment. Or, he could wait for Lee County to complete its road the last two miles to the Deep Lake short line at Carnestown, go another six miles to Turner's River, then make the turn south for the last six miles to the Lee-Monroe boundary. At that point responsibility would shift to the Chevelier Corporation. Dade's work was slow; Lee's was stopped altogether. Therefore, if Jaudon wanted to get going, the better bet was to sign a contract with Lee County and build the work through Turner's River himself rather then wait for Lee County to get its act together, even if that meant getting paid in time warrants.[10]

In an odd coincidence, Jaudon actually worked briefly for Barron Collier as vice-president of the Deep Lake Company from mid–November 1921 to late February 1922. One newspaper account says that it was the Deep Lake Company that was supposed to do the Lee County roadwork under the February 1922 contract, but this is unlikely.[11] In March 1922 Jaudon prepared a lengthy list of the personal property that he had loaned or rented to the Deep Lake Company, including a houseboat and covered barge, cots, tents and camp equipment, and office furniture. Some of it was located at Carnestown, some at Everglades City, and the rest at Deep Lake grove. The equipment was sufficient to support about 30–

35 men. If it were being used to build the road it would have been concentrated at one site, Carnestown, or at most divided between Carnestown and Port Dupont. It appears more likely that it was being used for the general repair and upgrade of the Deep Lake properties, especially to build the new facilities at Port Dupont. It is possible that Jaudon was using his time at Deep Lake as a way to get the road project organized, but it is clear from the equipment list that the focus was more on Port Dupont, the railroad, and the Deep Lake groves.[12]

The road contract required Jaudon to build 14 miles of road at 22 cents per cubic yard of roadbed and $2.75 per cubic yard of hard surfacing (i.e., gravel). Lee County had a Monighan steamshovel, and the agreement permitted Jaudon's organization to use it. Jaudon planned to purchase an Orton & Steinbrunner steamshovel for $8,200. The contract called for him to be paid an initial working fund of $3,000, then $1,500 on July 1, $3,000 on August 1 and $5,000 on September 1. Payments would then increase by $2,000 per month until January 1, 1923, when he would receive $12,000, for a total of $45,500. His planned expenses were $46,000: $8,200 for the Orton and Steinbrunner, $3,000 to pay Lee County for its used Monighan, and $34,800 for payroll. In March, Jaudon wrote Lee County engineer R. P. Ranson that "I am trying to arrange my affairs to take up inspection of several steam shovels which have been offered, and am awaiting the Monighan people sending a man down to go over [your] machine #281 so we can proceed with the work as quickly as possible.[13]

The contract stated that "Lee County has over forty thousand dollars in cash and fifty thousand dollars worth of district bonds worth about .95 [on the dollar]," but didn't specify how Jaudon would be paid; in cash or time warrants. In May, McDougal wrote that "I presume that you will have to take county warrants for your pay, as I understood last spring that there was but little money available at that time, considering the large amount of work to be done…. If it is true that you have to take your pay in county warrants, it may be difficult to cash out the warrants."[14]

"Time warrants" were essentially I.O.U.s written against future bonds when a county (or a road district) had issued the maximum amount of bonds permitted under statute. Theoretically, the new road would stimulate additional real estate development, which would raise the appraised value of property within the county (or district), which would lift the cap on bonds that could be issued. A new election would release bonds, and the county would then exchange bonds for the outstanding time warrants. This assumed, of course, that the road did lead to an expanded tax base. It also assumed that the expansion of the tax base was sufficient to give the county commissioners enough confidence to approve a bond issue. And it assumed that if a bond election were called, that the voters would approve it, and the bonds would sell to underwriters, and so on. In the meantime, the contractor had to carry the costs of the construction job, holding I.O.U.'s that had, as McDougal pointed out, a low market value.

It is little wonder that the McCrary brothers, who had undertaken hundreds of construction projects throughout the south, where infrastructure finance was strictly a local matter, could often seem callous and cynical. They had been offered "a bag full 'o nuthin" too many times. So Jaudon took his new contract, and as he had done so many times before, went looking for someone to give him a loan. At this point, there was not even a survey of the Monroe County route, as Hobart Crabtree's June 1921 expedition had been abruptly called off when the McCrary brothers walked off the job a few days later.[15]

On March 1, Barron Collier overturned the table by announced that he had acquired all of the Lee County holdings of the once-mighty Southern States Land & Timber Company.

Port Dupont, 1926. Docks, machine shops, saw mill, blacksmith's shop and boatyard. (Photographer unknown. Collier County Museum, Naples, FL, 88.42.24.)

Southern States, along with the Empire Land Company and the Consolidated Land Company, had once owned over four million acres of land in south Florida and still held huge tracts of virgin land in Lee County. Barron Collier bought all of Southern State's land in Lee County, 603,000 acres, for $1.1 million in cash.[16]

Meanwhile, Jaudon's partners at the Chevelier Corporation were having misgivings about his road-building venture. Judge McDougal was very concerned that Jaudon hadn't yet finished a survey of the A. W. Hopkins Tract:

> If we hire surveyors and send them in there to survey and establish lines for our tract of land, and they find what they think to be the line between Lee and Monroe Counties, starting from that line as a basis, they proceed to survey and stake off lands for thirteen miles south of that line into townships, ranges and sections and quarter-sections without a county line having been first officially located and established by the proper authorities; then suppose five or ten years hence, Lee and Monroe Counties proceed to establish and locate the county line between said counties and they locate it a mile north or a mile south of where our surveyors suppose it to be, it upsets our entire survey and brings on innumerable complications affecting the title of lands and lots conveyed by the corporation to the purchasers of different parts of the tract. Perhaps we will have sold land in Lee County that does not belong to us; or perhaps we will have sold land that that is south of the southern line of our tract and that never belonged to us; and the numbers of the sections will all be mixed up until no one will understand where his land is or should be.[17]

This was not idle hand-wringing. The Cape Sable lands in farthest southwest Dade County belonging to William Jennings, William W. Dewhurst and the Model Land Company went through exactly this type of wrenching realignment in the 1940s, with every property description having to be changed. At one point, several major landowners had their holdings downsized. They sued the government to have the boundaries of their land returned to where they had been located on the ground, not where they were described on paper. In the case of one owner, Elizabeth Annat, successor to most of the huge Jennings Tract, the State of Florida reduced the size of her holdings by almost a quarter by arguing that many of the sections that had been originally conveyed to the Florida East Coast Railroad in 1912 had mistakenly been 800 acres in size instead of the correct 640 due to survey errors.[18]

9. "Innumerable complications"

The Chevelier Corporation had been spending money on surveys for over half a decade and the job wasn't finished yet. Jaudon had paid John King $2,000 to undertake his two expeditions in 1917, and the Chevelier Corporation had sent Hobart Crabtree and B. M. Duncan to go over the Hopkins Tract in June 1921 to find the stakes that Lucas had placed in 1908 for the National Timber Company, and to replace the missing ones, paying him $3,271. They then sent surveyor W. A. Roberts to go search for other stakes placed by Lucas, who in turn was re-surveying baselines laid by a government surveyor named Mickler back in 1885.[19]

Dade County sent Crabtree out in early 1923 to see if he could pin down for once and for all the location of the dividing line between Dade and Lee counties. Crabtree, in agreement with Robert's findings, reported that nothing remained of the monuments set in the government surveys of 1885 or 1873 and everything would have to be re-chained from the nearest permanent reference monument, somewhere in the west Dade suburbs. The best available estimate of the boundary line was exactly 48 miles west of the cornerstone of the courthouse, but it was still an extrapolation. Instead of running survey crews, the two counties agreed to a legal solution: they would stipulate to the 48-mile line. If there were discrepancies, they could be worked out later. In agreeing to a stipulated line, they also set the finish line for the McCrary crews: station 2,333.0, 44.2 straight-line miles from the original zero stake.[20]

In addition, George Cook, the Chevelier Corporation's secretary and head of construction, decided to undertake his own survey of the route. To cross over to the Gulf Coast, Cook and his son Erben commissioned the "Gadget," a six-wheeled half-car, half-tractor based on a Model T. The rear driving axles were connected to chains that drove giant balloon wheels in the middle. The four regular wheels then became idler wheels upon which the machine rocked fore-and-aft. It steered like a caterpillar tractor: by making

The Chevelier Company at work on the west end of the Tamiami Trail, about 1920. One Marion steamshovel, one drilling derrick. (Photographer unknown. HistoryMiami, No. X-625-3.)

one side's driving wheel go forward while the other side's was stopped, or even put into reverse it could turn on its own center. It had pontoons so it could float.

They started on May 3, 1922, with four assistants, and were joined by two hunters, including Thomas Junkin, son of a Chevelier partner. On the eleventh day they discovered a large, high hammock that would eventually become the townsite of Pinecrest, five miles west and one mile south of where the McCrary grade would end at the Dade-Monroe line. They ended up near the headwaters of Lossman's River on Alligator Bay, only about three miles as the crow flies from the Watson place, but about double that by boat. It was near this spot that the Chevelier Corporation had dug their access canal. They built a thatch hut for overnight stays at the head of the canal. Both the hut and the three-mile long canal were abandoned in 1923 when it became easier to access the Chevelier work camp near Pinecrest from the Dade County side.[21]

Based on this trip and another he made in May with Judge McDougal and two prospective investors, George Cook prepared an assessment of the costs of building the Tamiami Trail across the company's land late that year and come up with figures significantly higher than Jaudon had estimated for Lee County. Cooke assumed that Monroe County would provide one steamshovel and that the McCrary company, once their Dade County work was finished, would either sell or lease the one they were using:

> The cost of operating a shovel will average about $40 per day, more rather than less, when accidents and repairs are considered, and this will not include any explosives, and at least $4,000 should be figured for that item, giving an approximate cost of $20,000 for dyke and ditch work for the year of 1923. It will cost around $11,000 to put each of the shovels on the job as one will be installed on a barge ... the road shovel will cost about $5,000 per month to operate and should give us five miles of road at a minimum in seven months at a cost not to exceed $35,000. We should have a surveyor constantly with two men from now on getting road lines, setting corner stakes, and getting levels. It will cost $500 per month to keep them, or about $4,500 for the balance of the year, or an aggregate of $91,000 without any townsite work:

PLAN #1

Dyke & Ditch	$20,000
Steam Shovel	$22,000
Surveying and Expenses	$4,500
Overhead	$10,000
Road Building	$35,000
TOTAL	$91,500[22]

This was about $4,100 per mile. The contract that Jaudon had signed with Lee County for 14 miles of road was based on $3,250 per mile. The amended Spencer Agreement stipulated that the major partners, plus the Roland Oil Company and the Pinecrest developer, W. J. Willingham, would contribute $72,000 towards the Chevelier road fund, but that income stream would not start until March 1923, more than a year after the contract with Lee County commenced. In short, Jaudon had both underpriced the Lee County work and he lacked any way of financing it. The final straw came when Judge McDougal, who was scheduled to be the largest single contributor to the road fund under the Spencer Agreement amendments, warned Jaudon that "I am completely without cash and overdrawn at the bank," and as a result he would be selling some of his stock. (It was to keep this from happening that the partners agreed to sell off the development rights in Pinecrest to speculator W. J. Willingham.)[23]

In May 1922 Jaudon first approached Barron Collier and asked if he go in with him on a new organization to be called the Lee County Construction Company, and provide $3,000 in up-front funding. He hoped that Collier would then loan the firm $43,000 to finance its operating costs from July 1922 to January 1923, and accept $45,500 in Lee County time warrants in repayment. Collier was noncommittal, but made his counteroffer a few weeks later: rather than help finance Jaudon's efforts he would prefer to simply take over the contract and do the job himself, using a Fort Myers construction company he had formed called Alexander, Ramsey & Kerr (AR&K). In early July Jaudon notified the Lee County Commissioners that he had cancelled his contract. As part of the assignment of the contract, he understood that he would be reimbursed for the costs he had incurred so far."[24]

The first inkling Jaudon got that things would now be different was when he submitted his bill for expenses for the four months he had worked on the road project. Most of the bill was for surveys and the rehabilitation of Lee County's Monighan steamshovel. The total came to $1,130.71. He sent the bill to AR&K. The superintendent of Jaudon's Gulf coast farm, O. Z. Bozeman (one of the foremen on the road job), wrote Jaudon that "I gave the letter to C. M. Collier [Barron's brother] and he said that he could not see that they could be expected to pay that bill as there was no contract between you and them, that is, the Alexander-Ramsey-Kerr Co. for them to pay you for what you had paid out." A few days later, Bozeman reported that C. M. Collier "is telling it around town ...that he did not see how you could expect them to pay it and he did not think that they would pay it, so I wanted you to know how he was treating the matter and how he was going and talking to outsiders, I always thought that Mr. Collier always tried to keep the outside world from knowing his business but it looks like that Mr. C. M. Collier is trying to advertise you as a poor business man and it sure do not set well with me."[25]

Jaudon replied that "I am not at all surprised by the delay in the payment of Tamiami Trail account, but it is surprising how many excuses a rich man can make, but never mind, they must pay and it will not put them in an enviable attitude if they delay, for it WAS UNDERSTOOD on July 5th with Mr. Collier, and the County Commissioners that in surrendering my contract that I was to be re-imbursed ... they both had the itemized bill before them, but they thought I had lost the copy ... I hope they will not get out of patience with them and this most unbusiness-like method."[26]

But the Colliers hung tough. They and their lawyers stuck to the line that any reimbursement due Jaudon was the responsibility of Lee County. On the other hand, Walter Sheppard, the attorney for the Lee County commissioners, told Jaudon that "I do not believe that you can get anywhere with the Board of County Commissioners in regard to the full payment of your claim. In other words, there is only a small part of your claim that the Board feels that there is any obligation to pay. It is very clear to me and likewise with the other members of the Board that at the time you surrendered this contract Mr. Barron G. Collier was present and your transaction for its surrender was made with him. In other words, it was our distinct and definite understanding that he was the one to protect you in the consideration of your surrender of the contract." On the other hand, Jaudon had rented a Monighan shovel from the county, and had paid for its repair, and Sheppard wrote that the county would be willing to reimburse Jaudon for those expenses ($181 of the $1130).[27]

Barron Collier held an iron grip over Lee County. O. Z. Bozemen reported in late January that:

> I went to the First National Bank and saw Mr. Pursley about borrowing some money on a note and he said that he could not loan money ... and would not take your endorsement or land as a security and said he was sorry that he could not. Then I went to the Bank of Ft. Myers and saw Mr. J. E. Foxworthy who is cashier of that bank and asked him, and he said he could not take your endorsement ... and could not take your land as security.... Then I went to the Lee County Bank, Title and Trust Co. and asked Mr. Blanding, who is cashier there, and he said that they had all the money out on truck farms that they could carry and did not want to lend any out anyway. I guess there is only one thing for us to do and that is to do business with the Miami banks.[28]

Even Jaudon's old friend and ally, Judge Wilkinson of Naples, counseled him to give up.[29] Jaudon never did get his money out of either AR&K or Lee County. As attorney Sheppard explained to him, his error was that "I remember quite distinctly that there was some bill or claim that you would have made against Alexander, Ramsey & Kerr for expenditures made ... but I never knew anything whatever about the amount until many months afterward and if you had a bill or statement of the account at the time of the conference at which Mr. Collier was present you did not present it so that I could see it, neither the Clerk [of the Board] ... or I did not dream for a moment that you would have a bill for any such amount." Jaudon had presented an itemized bill, but only to C. M. Collier, probably because he thought the Board would blanch at its amount. But by not presenting it to the board, it was not made an attachment to the resolution approving the transfer of the contract to AR&K, so the non-payment was a purely private matter between Jaudon and Collier. That partially explains why Barron Collier was a nationally famous multi-millionaire and Jaudon was a locally affluent Miami land developer, banging on the door of the big time with one hand while staving off creditors with the other.[30]

Shortly after the contract had originally been re-assigned to AR&K, Jaudon wrote to Judge McDougal in Oklahoma that "Lee County has authorized, or rather the legislature has authorized, an issue of fifty thousand dollars worth of bonds to build the road from Turner's River to the north line of Monroe County to connect with us and this money (of course once the bonds are sold) cannot be used for any other purpose." Collier's next move would be to change that.[31]

In mid–October, the Dade County commissioners received a letter from Walter Sheppard, asking them to delay J. B. McCrary's completion of the final four miles of the work. The Lee commissioners "had been unable to reach an agreement with certain land companies in the north portion of Monroe County, and therefore, would, in all probability, follow the original route." This would also mean, the letter stated, "that Dade County would be obliged to swing back to the route first selected," the Jenkins route. At a meeting the next day, Dade County attorney George McCaskell reported to his board that in 1921 the state legislature had authorized Lee County to use $50,000 in time warrants to build the Chevelier Route. McCaskell told the board that he had advised Harry Freeman, the McCrary superintendent, that he should proceed with the straight-to-Monroe route, and counseled the board to do the same. They agreed, and voted to instruct Freeman "to proceed westward."[32]

On December 20, 1922, the Lee County commissioners convened a special meeting at the request of Barron Collier. In light of the fact that the his organization was now building the Tamiami Trail in Lee County, Collier asked for a resolution returning the alignment of the road to the original Jenkins alignment, and to ask Dade County to instruct the J. B. McCrary Company crews to do the same. It was a tricky request: at this point, the McCrary dredge was already a little past the point where it was, according to the Jenkins map, supposed to start curving off northwest to Lee County.[33]

* * * * *

Starting in December, the Pennsylvania Sugar Company started cutting across the completed portions of the Tamiami Trail to install culverts and cross-ditches.[34] Between the Miami city limits and the west boundary of the Southern Drainage District, provision had been made for only four culverts. Approximately eighteen miles west of the Miami city limits, Hobart Crabtree and Harry Freeman had been approached by a group of Seminole men back in 1918. The Seminoles often came around, asking to have farm tools fixed, or selling homemade goods. This was different. This was clearly not to be trifled with. At the head of the group was Jack Tiger Tail and his wife. All the other members of the party were young, single men who lived out in the Everglades and made their living hunting game. Except for Jack Tiger Tail's wife, they all had rifles. They didn't waive them around or make a big show of it, but on the other hand, they weren't family men from the Dania reservation or Coppinger's.

Tiger Tail told them that the dredge was about to cross the Shark River Slough, an ancient, and vital, canoe trail for the Seminole people. Even Captain Wright of the U.S. Army had identified this place on his 1855 military map of Florida as "Harney's Boat Landing." The watercourse had to be preserved at all costs. At all costs. Crabtree and Freeman consulted with each other. Would a bridge over the slough work? Yes. From here to here? Yes. Freeman said it would be built. He promised. Jack Tiger Tail handed his rifle to his wife and raised his hand. The young men quietly turned and slipped away. When they were all gone Tiger Tail politely nodded his head and walked away with his wife. Crabtree asked Freeman if he actually intended to build the bridge. Freeman answered, "Hell, yes. I'm sending a man in to Star Lumber right now to order the wood."[35] In 1927 a permanent cement bridge was built at the location, even though by this time reclamation efforts had lowered the ambient water levels to the point so as to render its original purpose moot most of the year.

In 1920, the Pennsylvania Sugar Company had bought several hundred acres of land from the Tatum Brothers along the Miami River Canal northwest of Hialeah (and they would soon buy several thousand more). Ernest "Cap" Graham was transferred by Penn Sugar to the Hialeah operation in 1921 specifically to diversify it into other areas, such a dairy products, row crops, and beef cattle. Penn Sugar battled high water and poor soils for a decade before throwing in the towel. Their giant mill outside of Hialeah, in what is still called the City of Pennsuco, was sold to another firm and moved to Clewiston, and Graham himself bought much of the best land to start a dairy that his heirs, in the 1970s, developed into the City of Miami Lakes. But in the 1920s the irascible Cap Graham blamed the Southern Drainage District and the Tamiami Trail for his woes.

In late 1922, Graham and the Pennsylvania Sugar Company brought in a contractor to begin cutting openings in the bank of the Tamiami canal. "It is the intention of the sugar company to begin construction of culverts and ditches through the Tamiami canal to allow the clearing of the water standing north of the bank," reported a local newspaper. But at a meeting of the county commission a few days later, Graham announced that he not only intended to cut through the canal bank, but across the road as well. This was rejected by the county. R. A. Coachman (Jaudon's brother-in-law) explained that "Our attorney has advised us that if we put openings in the road we would be jeopardizing our contract and we have not authorized openings because of that." There was much disagreement about whether the county's contract with the J. B. McCrary Company required the road builder to install culverts and if so, how many.[36]

In June 1923, Graham demanded that Fred Elliott, the state drainage engineer, remove the dam in the Tamiami Canal and cut the openings across the Tamiami Trail. Graham hired a civil engineer who calculated that the Tamiami Trail needed a hundred openings 30 feet wide and three feet deep between Miami and the Dade County line. Jaudon, President of the Southern Drainage District, responded that the Tamiami Canal was doing exactly what it was supposed to do: collecting water and sending it east to the cut-off canal, thence northeast to the Miami River Canal and out to the bay. Cutting culverts would just reduce this eastward flow. Elliott replied to Graham that the Dade commissioners objected to the cuts in the road, and the state (in the guise of the Everglades Drainage District) lacked the authority to alter a county facility without their permission. Graham wrote Elliott that "It is now July and no actual work has yet been done towards opening the Tamaimi Trail.... I understand the commissioners contend that culverts are not necessary. Of course we believe otherwise and also believe we have actual facts to back us up, but as I see it, the big point is, that it must be settled once and who controls the drainage of the Everglades." For Graham, showdown time was rapidly approaching.[37]

Jaudon's headaches were coming came from both ends of the line. In January 1923 a new Tamiami Trail Association had been formed in Fort Myers. The occasion was the start of the eight-mile stretch from the north bank of the Caloosahatchee River opposite downtown Fort Myers to the Lee-Charlotte county line. Back in March 1922 a temporary organization called the Tamiami Trail Builder's Committee had organized a motorcade from Fort Myers to Tampa and St. Petersburg in conjunction with a meeting of the state road department to press for an extension of State Road 5 from Sarasota to Marco Junction. They had been partially successful; the terminus of the State Road had been extended to Fort Myers. Now, its spirit, although nothing of the organization itself, was being resurrected to "aid in synchronizing the work of the United States, the state of Florida, and the counties in Florida served by the served by the Tamiami Trail in connection with the construction and maintenance of the Trail."[38]

In actuality, the Tamiami Trail Association was an organization assembled by Barron Collier, paid for by Barron Collier, and largely under the direction of Barron Collier. Mostly a public relations and lobbying group, it served his ends. These were primarily solidifying support on the west coast for moving the route back to the Jenkins alignment, reinvigorating the flagging interest of the west coast in the road, extending the designation "Tamiami Trail" beyond Tampa to High Springs, so that the Trail would become contiguous with State Road 5 (important for state funding), and deflecting attention from the poor progress of the road on the lower west coast by stirring up an "us vs. them" mindset by creating the impression among west coasters that Dade had been responsible for holding up progress on the road thus far.

Towards this end, Barron Collier was voted president of the Association and I. E. Schilling of the state road department was elected a vice-president. Many notables who lived along the route of the highway were on its board: Charles Ringling (who had relocated the winter home of the Ringling Brothers Circus to Sarasota); Guy Livingston, long-time secretary of the Miami Chamber of Commerce, and the mayors of St. Petersburg, Bradenton, and Tampa. Jaudon, of course, was completely excluded.[39]

Down in the Ten Thousand Islands, Collier began organizing his forces. "Sometime in February," recalled dredge master Otto Neal, "Mr. Barron Collier spoke to me in Fort Myers about an old Marion one-yard dredge that I had operated on the East Coast and that I thought could be bought. He said buy it." Neal was under the impression that he had been hired merely to go find the dredge, buy it, move it to Everglade, get it fixed, teach Collier's men how to use it, then collect his pay and go home to Fort Myers.[40]

Neal bought it in Palm Beach and floated it through half-way through the Palm Beach Canal, where it sank and blocked all traffic. It took him twenty days to raise it. He continued to Lake Okeechobee, across it, down the Caloosahatchee River, past Fort Myers, out into the Gulf, and down to Everglades City. It was dismantled at Collier's new workshops at Port Dupont. The rebuilding took a month. One day out of the drydock it sank again. They refloated and repaired it, taking another two weeks.

The first part of the job was to dig a canal from Everglades City to Carnestown. The

9. "Innumerable complications" 145

afternoon of the first day, the bucket struck the underlying rock and tore its lip off. Neal again towed the dredge back to Port Dupont for repairs. Barron Collier was there. He told Neal he now wanted him to stay with the dredge all the way to Carnestown. He also asked Neal how to get a dredge to dig through rock. Neal told him:

> Dynamite was the thing and hand drills made from 1½ in. hexagon steel to penetrate the rock, with the aid of sledgehammers and the good right arms of men. We used this method only for a short time, however, as we discovered that the rock strata was not solid but filled with holes some of them a foot across and with the help of "jetters," a strong stream of water could be forced into these holes cleaning out the dirt enabling us to set the charge of dynamite. This system is still being used around the town of Everglades very successfully.

The dig from Everglades City to Carnestown, where the work of roadbuilding would begin, took from May to November of 1923. Compared to later efforts, this was a small-scale endeavor. In addition to the dredge, "we used a 5-ton Caterpillar, one 3-gang disc plow, one 2-disc plow, one 12-inch turning plow and one very small grader. All the boulders were lifted off the road by hand, sometimes taking the whole crew to move one. At this time there were but fifteen men camped at Carnestown."[41]

Suddenly, the quality of work started to become a matter of controversy. George Hosmer of Miami, writing in the *Ft. Myers Press*, reported in February that the Trail was passable for 15 miles to the south and east of Marco Junction:

> In many places, particularly in the first ten miles [south of Fort Myers] the road is rough and needs some work.... However, good time can be made over the road as far as Marco Junction which is fifty miles from

Otto Neal, who Barron Collier hired in 1923 as his first dredgemaster, with Stephanie Senghaas, daughter of Claus "Snooky" Senghaas, Collier Company engineer. In the background are the portable bunkhouses that D. Graham Copeland, Collier's chief engineer, invented for the Trail job. (Photographer unknown [probably Claus Senghaas]. Collier County Museum, Naples, FL, No. 78.14.38.)

Ft. Myers. From there on the work of placing marl on the road has been going on for some time, and we believe a better job could have been done.... We went sixty-five miles from Ft. Myers, and to within about five miles of the end of the grade. On the other five miles, we understand that there are one or two bad washouts.... This will leave about 22 or 23 miles to the Lee County line that has to be graded and surfaced.... The work of grading the rest of the way will soon be started with a large dredge.[42]

The editor of the newspaper at Estero, fifteen miles south of Fort Myers, claimed that one of the original District No. 3 (Marco Junction to Dade) bond commissioners had provided testimony stating:

Three miles of road grade [had been] constructed in three years on the Tamiami Trail in Lee County, and the bond money reduced from $70,000 to approximately $31,000. Thirteen thousand dollars per mile for poorly constructed, unsurfaced, sand grade... .Situated as was the dredge so far from human habitation, and rarely ever seen except by some chance hunter or the men on the job, many months were frittered away without progress, but the payroll continued, and rumors afloat, later verified, that the dredge gang put in much of their time hunting ... a young man named Nash had been hired some time previously to keep tally on three truck drivers who were depositing marl on a portion of the road in the district. The truck drivers shortly came to him and offered to donate a dollar a day each to his daily wages if he would credit them with three loads for every two that he hauled. He refused and his discharge was shortly secured.[43]

The *Estero Eagle* and several other newspapers around the state called for Judge Wilkinson of Naples to convene a grand jury to investigate whether Lee County had the competence to manage so many large road projects all at one time. Nothing came of it. A reporter asked Barron Collier in March if he planned to split off his land to form a new county. Collier had no comment. Jaudon wrote Judge McDougal in Oklahoma that "of one thing you can be certain: a new county will be created."[44]

In April, when the legislature met in session, both Jaudon and Collier set up war room in hotels across town. Collier was pushing for his new county. Jaudon was trying to attract money to get the Monroe route built. In public, he told the capital press corps that "his purpose in Tallahassee is to assist in every possible way with the creation of the proposed Collier County [because] to Jaudon the creation of Collier means the earlier completion of the Tamiami Trail." At first it was. But within a few weeks, it became apparent that one of the reasons Collier wanted his own county was so he could cancel out the existing Lee County road contracts and re-award them to his own firms, building them the way he thought they should be built, where he thought they should go.[45]

From that point on, Jaudon started fighting "Collier County" with every argument he could muster. "He has not in the past two years demonstrated his ability nor intentions to do a single thing that he now claims," he wrote in a memo intended for the Storters, Judge Wilkinson, and his other friends on the Gulf coast, "No, he is not going to do anything but build a few more stopping places [like Useppa] along the coastline of a wonderful game and fish preserve.... Instead of trying to get people to settle on his optioned land and purchase it, he is and has been buying from actual settlers and developers their holdings as fast as he can." In short, Jaudon accused Collier of trying to create a vast, depopulated, private fish and game preserve of over 600,000 acres and with fewer than 200 residents.[46]

In fact, Collier *was* trying to establish a series of rod and gun clubs and hotels in Useppa, Caxambas (north Marco Island), Deep Lake and Everglades City. But that did not mean he was lacking plans for the rest of the area. Jaudon's real concern was that Collier also planned to include within Collier County either all of mainland Monroe County (an echo of Dade's move in 1915), or just the northern one-third: *his* land.

It seems that Collier may by be trying to have our land in Northern Monroe County added to a new county he is getting created out of southern Lee—"Collier County"—and while I do not know how serious

Pulling a cart of dynamite up to the drilling rig using an improvised log railway near Turner's River, four miles east of Carnestown, about 1924. (Photographer unknown. Collier County Museum, Naples, FL, No. 88.42.59.)

> he may be, he has Senator Malone [of Key West] with him ... if he gets us into his county and controls us he will have the new county bonded and WILL TAX US TO DEATH and build the Tamiami Trail through his land in southern Lee.[47]

Moreover, Collier wanted the county seat of the new Collier County to be located in Everglades City, which was actually a remote village, not in the logical place, Naples, where shops, professional services and banks were already located. Barron Collier, of course, wanted to develop his own city from scratch. That was the problem. Jaudon really didn't care much about Pinecrest; that's why he was willing to sell the development rights as one big block to W. J. Willingham. His dream was the port city of Chevelier, planned for the Gulf coast, twelve miles from Everglades City, ten from Chokoloskee Island. Not only that, but Chevelier City would be the county seat of Chevelier County. Jaudon believed that's why Collier wanted Everglades City as his county seat: to knock the underpinnings out from under both Chevelier City and Chevelier County.

> [I]t will be fatal to us to have Everglade, his town, named as the county seat, for we would then have hard going to have a county created later with Chevelier as the county seat, so it looks as if our best bet is to have Naples named as the county seat—seat of the new county of "Collier" and then try to outgrow Everglade and at the session of 1925 or '27 [the legislature only met in odd-numbered years] get our town declared the county seat of another new county.[48]

Jaudon's back-up plan was to go to Dade County and try to restart their efforts to seek legislative approval to transfer the mainland portion of Monroe—or at least the northern third—to Dade. Jaudon's wife Maude wrote him: "I know you are very busy and have your hands awfully full. Still, I realize how much you enjoy all the many difficulties. In fact, I believe you get more down-right pleasure than any other man alive, which accounts for your sunny disposition."[49]

At least that was until the Tamiami Trailblazers came along.

··10··

"All was sweet and everything was sitting pretty"

As near as Jaudon could recall, he had taken at least five trips across the Everglades. In 1915, he had started out with Hobart Crabtree's first Dade County survey, the one he had to break off in order to meet with the county commission and the state about that land grant business, then had gone back out again with Locke Highleyman and a couple of canoes of supplies to help Crabtree finish the job. In June 1918 he had tried going both directions by auto with Ross Clark, the former Texas cattleman. That same year, he accompanied J. B. McCrary on foot when McCrary wanted to survey the straight-to-Monroe route. In 1921, he and George Storter made their west-to-east trip, the one where they found McCrary's work camp shut down. He had also accompanied Ralph Ranson, the Lee County engineer, several times on surveys of the Jenkins stakeline and over the Chevelier Tract, often with the House brothers, as far back as 1917.[1]

In February 1922 George and Erben Cook drove across from Miami to the Watson Place in 21 days in the "gadget," the first purpose-built swamp buggy ever successfully used in the Everglades. The following June, the Chevelier Corporation experimented with an 8,000-pound Topp-Stewart 4-wheel drive tractor pulling a trailer containing a cookhouse and various extraction gear for the tractor and other vehicles. Judge McDougal and his daughter, Mary made it all the way to the west coast in six days, where they exchanged the swamp yacht for a boat and spent the night at the Watson place. The Topp-Stewart setup was considered promising, but not yet practical enough for its intended purpose of ferrying around prospective investors on the Chevelier Tract.[2]

Jaudon was, therefore, beside himself to learn on March 27, 1923, that Collier's Tamiami Trail Association was planning a ten-car motorcade across the state. It was being billed as the "first attempt to cross the Everglades." Not only did they ignore the crossings that he, John King, the Cooks, George Storter, J. B. McCrary, and others had made, in most accounts, the spokesman for the Tamiami Trail association, Ora Chapin, didn't even bother to mention James Ingraham's expedition of 1892 or Michler's crossing of 1857!

They started on April 4, exactly the same day that the Collier County legislation was scheduled to be introduced in committee in Tallahassee. "The Collier outfit planned a 'coup' by putting a motor-cade through southern Lee County," wrote Jaudon at the time, "I had this news in advance and wrote Erben to have his crew cut a road as far west of

The Tamiami Trailblazers' April 1923 expedition was intensively covered by the press, including *The Florida Grower*, a Tampa-based magazine with a nationwide circulation. It is still in publication. (Photograph by Burgert Bros. Florida Division of Library and Information Services, No. RC04681.)

Roberts Lake and meet them on the Lee-Monroe County line, and I guess we are set to see that the motorcade comes through us." "Erben" was, of course, Erben Cook, son of George Cook, Chevelier's secretary-treasurer and now Chevelier's superintendent of construction. His assistant was Nansen Torstensen, the son of Carl Torstensen, the Iowa banker who had initially put Jaudon in touch with Hopkins, McCord and Floete back in 1915. After finishing out a year or two at the University of Wisconsin, he enlisted in the army, becoming an aviator. This led to his stationing in south Florida, where he renewed his father's contacts with Jaudon. He resigned about 1922 and became an associate at Jaudon Realty and a part of the Chevelier team.[3]

The "Tamiami Trailblazers" were 23 men, in ten cars. Most were rugged Ford Model T's along with a smattering of Overlands, Buicks and a 3,200-pound Elcar limousine. They were led by Chapin, manager of the trust department of the Title and Trust Company of Fort Myers.[4] On Day 4, the Trail Blazers had reached the end of Tamiami Trail roadbed at the Royal Hammock Park, a few miles past Marco Junction. Soon, one car after another became stuck and a messenger had to be sent asking for a help from Barron Collier's work camp at Carnestown, fifteen miles away, to pull cars out of the muck. They sent a small, versatile caterpillar tractor called a "Celetrac" that would travel with the Trailblazers for the rest of the trip.

All the cars were rescued by Day 6 (April 9), except for the two-ton Elcar, which had to be temporarily left behind. So far, the group hadn't even made it to the Deep Lake Railroad line, where the serious wetlands began. By this time Torstensen, a pilot, had returned to Fort Myers to catch a train to Miami where, if needed, he would charter an airplane. Jaudon told George Cook to have his son stay at either Roberts Lake or the Pine Island work camp. "Don't let them PASS WITHOUT GOING THRO MONROE COUNTY," he emphasized, "get the press to stress this part of the trip."[5]

By Day 7, nothing had been heard from them for four days. The *Miami Metropolis* and the *Miami Herald* teamed up to send a car, driver and mechanic from the Miami Motor Club out to the far end of the McCrary work area. They were able to penetrate beyond the McCrary dredge, eventually making it to a point two miles west of the Dade County line and four miles south of the Lee-Monroe boundary. They were trying to make it to Pine Ridge, a work camp for the Chevelier Corporation located not far from where Pinecrest would be located.

Two miles before getting there, they encountered a Chevelier survey crew, who said they had traveled northwest the day before and had seen no sign of them. The Chevelier men also advised the reporter that a car could never get through from Marco Junction to the McCrary work camp by following the original Jenkins stakeline—it went through the heart of the Big Cypress Swamp. Their only hope was to go well north of Carnestown— even north of Deep Lake—after leaving the Lee County roadgrade, thus skirting the Turner's River estuary, and make it to the Lee County Pine Ridge, then follow it south into Monroe County and hope that there was some "land bridge" near Robert's Lake between the Big Pine Ridge in Lee County and its counterpart in Monroe on which the Chevelier Corporation's work camp was located. However, nobody knew of one.[6]

As the Chevelier field man predicted, the Trailblazers had attempted to circumvent Turner Slough by going north of Carnestown, near Deep Lake grove. However, Collier's men rounded up the Trailblazers by going up and down the Deep Lake railway to find them and they all spent the night of Day 5 at the Rod and Gun Club in Everglades City. Two tractors eventually got the Elcar out; after a few more days its owner had to give up; it was eventually shipped back to Fort Myers. An Overland had a wheel smashed getting pulled out; it was sent to Carnestown for repairs.

By Day 9 (April 12) most of the cars were running out of provisions. Years later, Frank Lewis recalled:

> We ran out of provisions after a week of rain. We had been tramping through the swamps for hours, we were hungry and it devolved on Alfred [Christensen] and me to do something, so we finally found a sack of wet flour in one of the cars, caked all over the outside of the sack, scooped out some in a big enameled pitcher, dipped up some muddy water with an empty tomato can tied on a stick from a water hole, and mixed up a batter. Alfred found a paper package containing some white powder which he sprinkled in that made the mess foam fine. We poured some in a skillet and soon had a flapjack nearly an inch thick frying in bacon grease. I cupped my hands and hollered "humbuckseee!" which is Seminole for "dinner is ready," and we were soon surrounded by hungry men who ate our flapjacks with relish. There were sixteen of us and it kept me busy flipping flapjacks and making more batter until all were satisfied. They said they were the best flapjacks they ever had.[7]

After leaving the Turner River, the group entered the Lee County Big Pinelands, and worked their way southeast. They found the Jenkins stakeline and kept going southeast, crossing the Lee-Monroe line a day or so later. The group came upon the crude road that Cook and Torstensen had prepared for them about the same time that Cook and his men found them with their special truck fixed out with dual wheels on both the front and rear. Cook guided them down the rough-hewn road. They had successfully accomplished what

10. "All was sweet and everything was sitting pretty"

the Chevelier field engineer thought was probably impossible: finding a "land bridge" between the Lee and Monroe pine ridges, a narrow gap of high, dry land between Alligator Slough and Roberts Lake. The group set off for Chevelier's work camp, about six or seven miles from where the McCrary dredge was at work. After finding the Cook-Torstensen road, one of the drivers, not realizing that it been quickly hacked out of the pine barrens for tractors and trucks, not cars, went too fast and broke an axle on a stump.[8]

On Day 10, pilots L. B. Carr and Nansen Torstensen located them. Six cars and the Celetrac were at a place called "Billy Robert's Camp," four miles from the Dade County line. Two miles farther away, at Chevelier's camp, was a second, larger group. A third, smaller group, mistakenly identified as traveling in the Elcar, was spotted 15 miles still farther west, near the Lee-Monroe Line. Carr landed at Billy Robert's camp to deliver food. He reported that the five-and-a-half miles between it and the McCrary work camp was "pretty poor." "We don't know how we are going to get them over that marsh ground," he said."[9]

The aircraft supply flights started to become a regular part of the expedition. (Jaudon later claimed they were paid for by the Chevelier Corporation.[10]) A second flight on Day 11 (April 14) brought mostly repair parts, gas, oil and support equipment such as rope and block and tackle. By Day 16 the seven surviving cars hadn't moved for the better part of four days. Four miles from the McCrary camp, many of the men had started shuttling back-and-forth into town every three or four nights so they could spend a night at the Roberts Hotel. Harry Freeman of the McCrary Company headed out from the work camp with a bunch of rope and spare wheels, looking to lash them to the wheels of the cars to allow them to "float" over the muck. Six of the men staying at the Roberts Hotel returned to Fort Myers. Roughly twelve of the originals were left, either out in the field or at the hotel.

The Tamiami Trailblazers stop for lunch, probably during the first few days of their cross-state expedition, April 1923. (Photographer unknown. Florida Division of Library and Information Services, No. RC01599).

Essentially, it was Freemen and his men who got the cars out. They moved them a quarter of a mile at a time, often using a winch or block and tackle. Sometimes the Celetrac would pull; sometimes it would anchor the winch; once in a while it would have to be winched. The job took two days. The cars (or what was left of them) were heaved up on the Tamiami Trail road grade on Day 18, only to discover that they couldn't drive into town because the Southern Drainage District had cut across the embankment to install some of the culverts demanded by Cap Graham's Pennsylvania Sugar Company, and they wouldn't interrupt their work to help them across. Freeman and Erben Cook loaned them the lumber the next morning to make a temporary bridge. By the time Miami could have the official welcoming for the last of the stragglers in the Royal Palm Hotel park downtown, there were only ten of the original 25 left; the others had either caught the train home or already started driving to Fort Myers by way of the northern loop.[11]

When the Trail Blazers returned to Fort Myers, they presented a bill to the Chamber of Commerce for $1,118.16, less the $330.05 that had been donated by various Miami civic societies. This included 156 meals at 75 cents per meal, cigars, gas, car parts and other items. The chamber agreed to pay a bill of $81 for groceries they had ordered from a Miami store to have sent out to the McCrary work camp during the week when the men were stranded four miles from the dredge. The reporter did not relay the chamber's exact language, other than to note that the request appeared "to get their goats." Later, Jaudon would inform a Chevelier stockholder that "[T]he real result of this famous motorcade trip was to establish, I believe, permanently, the routing of the Tamiami Trail through the property of the Chevelier Corporation in Monroe County. The circumstances attendant thereto were, no doubt, quite expensive to the corporation, but I believe well worth all expense incurred."[12]

Before returning to Fort Myers, the men who had been staying at the Roberts Hotel were hosted at a lunch thrown by the Miami Advertising Club. Ora Chapin announced that Collier's first dredge had started work the day before (i.e., Otto Neal's dredge). He explained that if Collier County were created at the ongoing legislative session up in Tallahassee, Collier had promised that all the bonds necessary to build the road would be underwritten by New York firms. The Club adopted a resolution advocating the creation of the proposed Collier County.[13]

On the other hand, two different members of the Trailblazers told reporters that they did not think the original Jenkins alignment was feasible, and that the best route would be to run the road from Marco Junction to about 10 or 12 miles past Turner's River, then turn it south into Monroe County. Another said "all [of us] believe the most feasible route is via Lee County to a point 12 to 15 miles east of the Turner River, thence southeast into Monroe County." While not running through as much of the Chevelier tract as he originally wanted, this was more than good enough for Jaudon. The Dade County commissioners decided to take no position in the routing controversy, which was starting to engulf Lee and Monroe counties as well as the Chevelier firm, Alexander, Ramsey & Kerr and the J. B. McCrary Company. The McCrary dredge was now just a little over a mile from the Monroe line on the "straight-line" route, and when the dredge reached that line, and the roadway work atop the embankment behind it was finished, McCrary's job would be complete. Dade had received no request from Lee County to build a road in its jurisdiction along the Jenkins alignment, and would consider the matter if it came up, but would not abandon two to eight miles of road it had paid McCrary's men to dig.[14]

In Tallahassee, the battle over the creation of Collier County was becoming the event of the legislative season. Jaudon's belief that the Tamiami Trailblazers had been organized solely to lobby for the Jenkins alignment was probably unfounded. While it is true that

10. "All was sweet and everything was sitting pretty"

Collier did organize, support and publicize the trip, the Trailblazers themselves had no political route-making agenda, other than possibly a shared belief that the southern alignment was preferable to the LaBelle–Clewiston–Palm Beach route. It appears that Barron Collier wasn't interested in using them as a way to drive a wedge between the Chevelier and Lee County interests; instead, it is more likely that he wanted them to gobble up headlines so as to keep his efforts to create a new county out of the newspapers. And he succeeded: between April 10 and April 19, (Day 7 and Day 16) when most of the legislative work was going on in Tallahassee, the Trailblazers had a least one major story a day in the Miami and Fort Myers newspapers, and on at least three days, they took up at least half of page one. Several participants, probably relying on data provided by Barron Collier's New York advertising company, stated that the motorcade pulled in 35,000 column-inches of front-page publicity in American and European newspapers. Collier was a man who always had his eye on the long-term.[15]

The Trail Blazers would end up serving as a kind of Swiss Army Knife for Barron Collier's publicity machine. It did revitalize interest in the Tamiami Trail at a time when many thought the project was dead and most had forgotten about it. It was also a way of deflecting criticism in Dade County that it had spent hundreds of thousands of dollars on a road that went nowhere because the Gulf coast counties appeared to be so disorganized. It was probably not a means to overtly sabotage Jaudon and his associates at the Chevelier Corporation. However, Collier very much wanted to get the Jenkins alignment built, and he was willing to put a lot of his money behind that objective. If he could succeed without destroying Chevelier's plans, fine. If he had to torpedo them, that was okay too.

On one side of the Collier County succession battle were the Collier brothers, Barron and C.M., and Walter Coachman of Jacksonville, president of the Consolidated Land Company, and state Senator William H. Malone of Key West. Ironically, Coachman was a cousin of Jaudon's wife, Maude Coachman Jaudon. On the other side were the Lee County commissioners and the city of Fort Myers.

In late March, a week or so before the Trail Blazers left Fort Myers and a couple of weeks before the Collier and Hendry County bills were introduced in committee, Senator Malone wrote W. O. Sheppard, the Lee County attorney, asking about the status of the county's contract with the Chevelier Corporation. Sheppard replied on March 28 that the board had approved a resolution agreeing to the Chevelier alignment with four conditions: (1) that all affected landowners agree to the change; (2) that Jaudon post a $10,000 surety bond; (3) that by the time the Lee County contractor reached the turnoff, Chevelier would have substantially completed their work; (4) that the road be toll-free and maintained as a public road. Sheppard wrote Malone that no agreement had been secured from the landowners and no bond had been posted. Therefore, in January 1923 the Lee County Commission had approved a resolution reverting the road back to the Jenkins alignment. Sheppard then passed on a copy of this letter to the Monroe County Board of Commissioners.[16]

A day later, based on this information, Otto Kirchheimer, the clerk of the Monroe county commissioners, wrote George Cook, informing him that the county was canceling its request for bids on the steamshovel that it had planned to buy and share with the Chevelier Corporation. "Our understanding was that if your project was to be a part of a cross-state highway, we were interested," the clerk wrote, "but if Mr. Sheppard's statements are correct, our interest ceases."[17]

Actually, Sheppard's letter to Senator Malone was slightly in error. On December 20, 1922, Barron Collier appeared before the Lee County commission and asked them to approve a resolution returning the alignment of the Tamiami Trail east of Marco Junction to the original Jenkins alignment. They agreed to this, and approved the resolution. A few days later R. A. Coachman, a Dade County commissioner met with Collier and the Lee County commissioners and was told of Lee County's decision, and was asked to re-align the road in Dade County. On December 30, the Dade County Commission voted not to change the "straight-ahead" alignment.[18]

There was the obvious problem that McCrary's dredge was already past the six-miles-to-go point where, under the original alignment, they were supposed to start turning to the northwest—as much as four miles past. The county's relationship with the McCrary firm was already strained. There was no way that McCrary would complete both the straight-ahead alignment and the Jenkins route without a change order, and by one estimate, McCrary was going to lose as much as $200,000 on the Tamiami Trail contract. If the County asked for a change order, it was a certainty that McCrary would attempt to regain some of those losses through the supplemental contract. Everyone at the county, from Hobart Crabtree to the commissioners, just wanted J. B. McCrary to get the contract completed in the most straightforward manner possible and go away.

But there were also some very sticky legal questions involved in switching back to the Jenkins alignment. One was Sheppard's assertion that the Chevelier Corporation had defaulted on their contract to Lee County by not acquiring a bond. In fact, the Chevelier Corporation *had* posted a bond, in March 1922, but had posted it in favor of Dade County, not Lee County. On the other hand, Lee County Commission apparently knew of this and approved it, as a simpler and more straightforward procedure, at the time.[19]

Another, and bigger, problem was Chapter 8730 of the State Statutes (1921), which appeared to authorize Lee County (their Road and Bridge District No. 3, to be precise) to issue $50,000 in time warrants, but only for the purpose of building the Chevelier alignment. "Lee County may be forced to build its portion of the Tamiami Trail into Monroe County, irrespective of a decision to revert back to the original plan," reported the *Miami Herald*. "Whatever Lee County's ultimate decision, it became known yesterday that George E. McCaskell, [Dade] county attorney, had advised Harry Freeman, superintendent in charge of construction for Dade County, to proceed westward to the Monroe County line as the plans provide." For the time being, the Jenkins alignment was on hold, and the Chevelier route was still approved, but by now, nobody had any illusion about how much longer the entire Marco-to-Dade segment would remain a part of Lee County[20]

Initially, Barron Collier's new county was believed to be a foregone conclusion. But by the time the Trail Blazers were finally rescued by Harry Freeman and his men at the McCrary dredge, the Fort Myers newspapers were cautioning that "Collier May be Defeated." However, a week later, Collier himself came down from New York City to fight the battle. He recruited Mr. and Mrs. J. M. Barfield of Caxambas, on Marco Island. They ran the Caxambas Hotel and a large fruit and jelly canning operation. Mrs. Barfield, an unassuming, plain spoken woman was particularly influential in getting across to the legislators the problems the southern Gulf coast towns such as Naples, Marco, Caxambas, and Everglades City were having getting elected officials up in Fort Myers to pay attention to their concerns. There was a perception at the county courthouse in Fort Myers, according to the Barfields, that the longer Lee County remained isolated from Tampa and Miami, the more the city would prosper from its monopoly over the Ten Thousand Islands.

On April 22, the House Committee of County Organization, which had earlier declined to vote out a bill, scheduled a rehearing so Collier himself could testify. A day later, unnamed senators told a reporter that the only thing holding up matters was that the proponents of the new Collier and Hendry counties could not agree among themselves how to carve up

Lee County. On May 10, the House and Senate approved the bill creating both new counties, and it was signed by Governor Hardee the next day. Collier County came into existence on July 8, 1923.[21]

A month later, Jaudon and Ben Sheppard settled on Jaudon's year-old claim for the expenses he incurred in mobilizing the forces he handed off to Alexander, Ramsey & Kerr. Out of $1,130, Jaudon received $181 for parts for the Monighan steam shovel and a month's care and feeding of a team of oxen. "At the time of the cancellation of your contract, all was sweet and everything was sitting pretty with you and the Collier interests, and you were to have been protected by the Collier interests, as all the commissioners together with myself distinctly remember, and the subsequent change in conditions in regards to your relations with the Collier interests should not operate to the injury of Lee County," Sheppard wrote. Jaudon, at least initially, had supported Collier's efforts to form a new county as a way to get Collier to partner with him on the Lee County road building contract. He had soon been in for a rude awaking: you didn't partner *with* Barron Collier, you only worked *for* him.

Nevertheless, that initial support stuck in the craw of the Lee commissioners. "Yes, I was a factor in the creation of Collier County, but its creation at the last Legislative Session was simply an inevitability," Jaudon replied, "I am still convinced that had a small part of the efforts been devoted to a sensible area, county seat, and a proper bill, that we would have faired better."[22]

* * * * *

At 10:15 a.m. on Monday, January, 23, 1923, a dragline steam shovel broke the earth on the north bank of Caloosahatchee River, commencing work on the short stretch of the Trail between the river, opposite downtown Fort Myers, and the Charlotte County line. While it was far from the most spectacular segment of the Trail, these eight miles were special, for two reasons. Out on the river, past the steamshovel, could be seen the barges of the Caloosahatchee River Bridge Company, which had already been at work for over a year building the piers for the five-thousand-foot causeway. The road north of the bridge would link the Trail from Tampa to one of the last major hurdles to be overcome. When the Caloosahatchee Bridge was finished, only the Peace River Bridge at Punta Gorda (Charlotte Harbor), 21 miles north of the Caloosahatchee, and the Manatee River bridge at Bradenton, 35 miles south of Tampa, would be left to finish a true Gulf coast highway from Tampa to Marco, one that needed no inland diversions around bays or estuaries. Second, the steamshovel was not just breaking ground on a highway, it was inaugurating State Road 5, the first section of the Tamiami Trail to receive funding as part of Florida's federal-aid highway system.[23]

The Federal Highway Act of 1921 required state highway departments to designate seven percent of their highway mileage as "federal-aid highways." These were eligible for federal matching funds. As Florida road commissioner E. P. Green explained when Florida's reorganized federal-aid system was announced in 1922, this didn't mean a lot: the state had a road budget of only three and a half million dollars. Hillsborough County alone planned to spend three million on new roads in 1923. However, by consolidating the state's 1,000 convicts from their present 27 or 28 work camps into four or five; by acquiring additional heavy equipment; and by increasing state spending somewhat (thereby making the state eligible for an equally larger amount of federal funds), Green hoped to significantly accelerate the state's work program. However, he cautioned that experience had shown that a highway built to the federal Bureau of Public Roads standards could rarely be done for much less than $30,000 per mile.

Largely due to these constraints, at the time it was designated, State Road 5 only went from High Springs (near Gainesville) on the north to Sarasota on the south. This was extended to Fort Myers in 1922. At this time, the state-aid highway system was still very limited. It was not until 1925, when the state raised its gasoline tax to three cents a gallon and collected $5.4 million, making it eligible for an equal amount of matching federal funds, that Florida had a statewide highway program worthy of the name. When the extension of State Road 5 was announced the press wanted to know if the Tamiami Trail south of Fort Myers would be included once the segment north of town was finished? Probably, at least some of it. Did the federal-aid designation include the bridge being built over the Caloosahatchee? No. State Road 5 did extend all the way to the city limits, including the bridge, but private toll roads and bridges were not normally eligible for federal-state funds.[24]

Lee County took over the Caloosahatchee River Bridge Company in November 1923. It was a combination of both push and pull factors: the private company was in money trouble, a result of higher than expected construction costs, and the state and the county both wanted the project to be taken over by Lee County to make it eligible for federal-state funds. The county informed the bridge company in October that it was exercising the option in its contract to take over the company, and both parties agreed to let arbitrators set the price of the transfer. They ruled a month later that the bridge company was entitled to roughly $66,000. In return, the bridge company was required to turn over all the work completed to date and all building materials and equipment.

Lee County finished the job and the span opened on March 12, 1924. No longer was it necessary for traffic headed north to Sarasota and Tampa to have to drive some ten miles inland, cross the river at the bridge at Olga, then drive back again. The bridge at Olga was also the junction to Arcadia. Many travelers to Tampa skipped Punta Gorda and Sarasota, going due north to Arcadia, then cutting over to Bradenton on the State Road. While Miamians saw the Trail as a way of getting to Fort Myers, many west coasters saw it as a way of uniting the coastal communities and overcoming the obstacles posed by bays and estuaries such as Charlotte Harbor and the Caloosahatchee and Manatee rivers.[25]

In September 1923 the McCrary work crews finally reached the Monroe County line. After some cursory smoothing and finishing, Harry Freeman ordered his men to dismantle the equipment and move it back to Miami for shipment to Atlanta. On October 11, the Dade County Commissioners went on a formal inspection trip to review the entire length of the highway. The clerk sent a telegram to J. B. McCrary, inviting him to participate in the inspection. He declined to attend. The commissioners found the road "exceedingly rough in spots," and instructed the county engineer to ask McCrary to complete the job. McCrary replied that according to the specifications provided, the work was finished. A neutral estimate said that the work the commission sought would cost between thirty and thirty-five thousand dollars. McCrary claimed it would cost $100,000. The parties could not reach an agreement, and litigation loomed. On January 15 this was averted when the parties agreed to arbitrate the dispute. The McCrary firm selected Georgia governor Clifford Walker and Georgia collector of internal revenue Josiah Walker to the panel. Dade County selected *Miami Herald* editor Frank Stoneman and *Miami News-Metropolis* editor Arthur Keene. The four panelists selected E. B. Douglas of the E. B. Douglas Company of Miami as the fifth member.[26]

A month later Otto Neal and his dredging crew reached Carnestown from Everglades City. "We arrived with the Marion at Carnestown about November 1923 and there we were asked to start the fill connecting Carnestown with the "old Lee County grade" which was to the westward about two and a half miles," Neal later recalled. "The methods we used

10. "All was sweet and everything was sitting pretty" 157

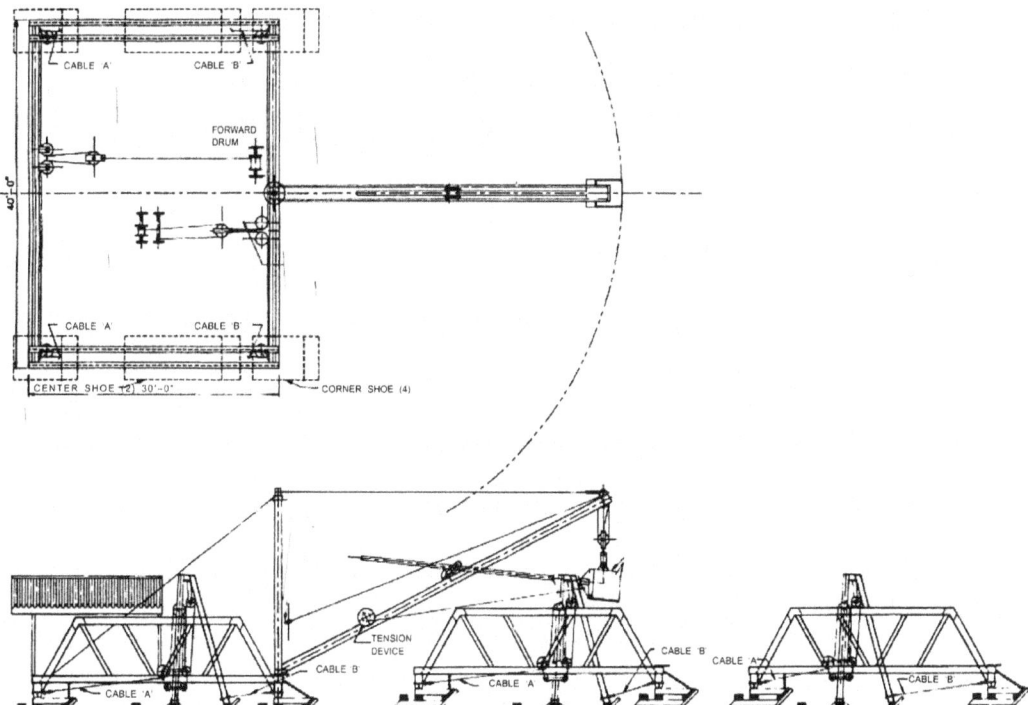

How a Bay City walking dredge walks. The frame has four fixed feet on each corner of the frame and two longer walking feet, one on each side. When dredging, the walking feet are stowed up. When ready to move, they are pulled to their forward position by cables attached to winches. The feet are lowered, raising the entire frame up off the ground. The winches then pull the walking feet to their aft position, moving the dredge forward. The feet are then raised up, moved forward, and the cycle repeated. To turn the dredge, only one of the walking feet is used. The walking dredge was originally designed to straddle a canal, with one set of feet on each canal bank. Bay City made about 265 walking dredges. They also came in a crawler version, with caterpillar treads on each corner and no walking gear. (Drawing courtesy Collier-Seminole State Park, Florida.)

going into Carnestown were found to be successful [going] westward and we arrived at the Lee County grade on the 20th of December 1923." At that point, the Marion was towed back to Carnestown, where it was put to work dredging the canal it had just dug, this time going back south to Everglades City. This was done to improve the temporary roadway alongside the canal by throwing up material from the bottom of the canal. Everglades City, the adjacent town of Port Dupont, and Carnestown formed the heart of the Collier empire, and it was vital that men and material be able to moved easily between the three. Work began on a bridge across Allen's River to connect Everglades City and Port Dupont.

In February 1924, George Storter, who was now chair of the board of commissioners of Collier County, wrote Jaudon to report that Neal's crew had taken delivery of a Bay City walking dredge, had barged it into Port Dupont and were assembling it at Carnestown. They started west towards Turner's River about March. The Bay City walking dredge was the salvation of the Gulf coast construction teams. Developed about 1918 by the Bay City Shovel and Equipment Company, the walking dredge was a square steel frame, 40 feet wide and thirty feet front-to-back. Four wooden "shoes" projected down from each corner, each about four feet long and eighteen inches wide. The derrick for the shovel, the shed for the boiler and a control cab sat on cross-beams atop the frame. The customer usually planked over the frame to create a deck. In the center, along each side beam, was a walking shoe, ten feet long and two feet wide.

To walk the dredge forward, the derrick was locked in the straight forward position. The walking legs moved in a circular motion, as if they were attached to the paddlewheel of a steamboat. While in the stowed (up) position, a winch and cables moved them to the forward-most position. They dropped down, picking up the dredge so the four fixed feet were off the ground. Cable winches then pulled the dredge forward about five feet. The legs were now in the full-back position relative to the dredge frame. The legs were raised, lowering the dredge back down to the ground. The process was repeated as needed. To turn it, only one walking leg was engaged. They were extremely good in unstable conditions, and were originally designed to straddle a canal, with the streambed running underneath the frame.

Bay City supplied retrofit kits to convert their walking dredge into a crawler dredge with caterpillar treads on each corner of the frame. It is not known if Collier's operation converted any of their walking dredges but they did use both walking and crawler versions on the east end of the Trail. It appears that only walking dredges were used between Naples and Turner's River.[27]

However, in February 1924, Collier's operation was still relatively small, according to Otto Neal: "there was just three of us started on this job, an operator and oiler on the dredge and a gasoline boatman who kept us in supplies, as the only transportation we had in those days was by water, he recalled. "The dredge at this time was operated only by single shifts and we made about a half-mile per month," he noted. The real assault on the Jenkins survey line would take the better part of year to gear up for, requiring a lot more men, equipment, preparation, and above all, money. In July, the Collier Company crew was two and a half miles east of Carnestown.[28]

On January 10, the Chevelier Corporation's crew started west from the abandoned McCrary work camp on the Dade-Monroe line. Jaudon later claimed that his crew was ready to go in November, but had to wait for the Southern Drainage District to complete the installation of the last of the 22 culverts and cross-canals required by state drainage engineer F. C. Elliott.[29]

For the first time, Jaudon was prepared, organized, and adequately financed. Erben Cook's secret weapon was a pneumatic drill wagon. Looking for all the work like a large garden shed bolted atop a giant swap buggy, its diesel motor powered both an electrical generator and a huge Ingersoll-Rand air compressor. The air compressor, in turn, drove a set of downward-pointed rotary mine drills attached to a rotating table about nine feet across. Starting with a single drill, improved versions of the drill rig later held four drills in a row. The table could be raised, lowered, and spun to provide whatever drill pattern was necessary for the dynamite that would be dropped down the holes. Instead of a floating dredge, Erben's crew would use land-based steamshovels. According to former Lee County and Chevelier engineer Ralph Ranson, in July 1924, Cook's men were five and a half miles west of the Dade-Monroe line, although this probably reflects the position of the farthest advance crew, either the clearing team or the drilling team, both of which were at least a couple of miles ahead of the dredging and grading crew.[30]

On February 15, the clerk of the Dade County Commissioners received a letter from W. D. Lanier, the Collier County Clerk, "asking for information as to what progress had been made on the Tamiami Trail by Dade County, and at what point it would meet the portion of the trail being built by the Collier interests." The commission instructed the county engineer to prepare a reply, and the general feeling of the board was that the request

10. *"All was sweet and everything was sitting pretty"*

A Bay City walking dredge in action on the Jenkins alignment in Collier County, about 1927. The man standing in the foreground with a camera is Tom Stephens of the state road department. (Photographer unknown. Collier County Museum, Naples, FL, No. 88.42.24.)

indicated "a lack of knowledge on the part of West Coast interests ... [as] Dade county has built 42 miles straight west into the Everglades a road of solid rock. Reaching the Monroe county line, the work is being carried forward by the Chevelier Corporation, working in the direction of Collier County. It is expected that the Collier county link in the trail and the Chevelier will join somewhere on the Collier-Monroe line."[31]

Having fought the McCrary Company for seven years just to get the straight-line road grade built to Monroe County, the Dade commissioners were not pleased by the insinuation that they now had a duty to go back and pay for another six or seven miles of road to build a diagonal segment up to Collier County to complete the Jenkins route. Some idea of general reaction of the Dade commissioners to the letter can be judged by their reply to the rest of the letter. Invited to Fort Myers for the grand two-day gala to celebrate the opening of the new Caloosahatchee River Bridge, it "was taken by several of the commissioners as a premature jubilee, insamutch the 33 miles of the trail remaining to be built are perhaps the hardest to be supplied. Moreover, the Dade commissioners feel they have been pioneers from this side and have been waiting for several years for the West Coast interests to meet them."

This turned out to be a major strategic blunder. The bridge opening jubilee was a two-day paean to Barron Collier, who arrived in town with Coleman DuPont to give the keynote address. None of the original promoters from either coast—Judge Wilkinson, Captain Jaudon, George Storter, nor any of the Dade commissioners, gave a speech. Francis Perry, formerly of the Tampa Camber of Commerce, was the only pioneer from the days of the 1915 Dixie Highway conference invited to speak, and even then only briefly. Barron Collier's biography was run in two successive issues of the Fort Myers *Daily Press*. Although he had thus far played a relatively minor role in either its funding or construction, he was clearly the man of the hour.[32]

Moreover, the bridge dedication itself was spit into two rather brief morning and afternoon events, with the middle given over to the "first annual convention" of the Tamiami Trail Association. Although formed only shortly before the Trail Blazers' expedition, the Association was now portrayed as the organizer and sponsor of that trip, and at the bridge-dedication convention Collier trotted out the members of the expedition and one of their beat-up Fords on stage like so many show ponies. Collier was setting up the Tamiami Trail Association to act as the official policy-making organ of the Tamiami Trail, a single-state version of the Dixie Highway Association or the Lincoln Highway Association.[33]

It was predictable that the Tamiami Trail Association would attempt to sway official policy and public opinion in the choice between the Jenkins and Chevelier routes. Barron Collier wanted the road returned to the original survey line and Jaudon, who had just started working from the Dade County end, wanted to retain the Chevelier alignment. A month after the bridge dedication, Ora Chapin, vice-president of the Tamiami Trail association, wrote a letter to A. W. Corbett, president of the Everglades Development Corporation in Miami. Complaining that nobody from Miami had shown up at the Tamiami Trail Association conference or the ribbon-cutting, Chapin stated that "we are confronted, apparently, with a condition and not a theory, in the matter of the apparent absence of co-operative effort." This "absence of cooperative effort" was, apparently, the stubborn refusal of the Dade county commission and civic leaders to recognize that Collier County would have a highway "all the way through Collier County" by the time that Dade got its road completely finished. Without exactly saying so, Chapin implied that the Collier interests were going to build the Jenkins alignment whether Dade liked it or not, and if there was no road to meet it on the east side of the Collier county line, then they were just going to continue building along the survey line until they got to the McCrary road grade, jurisdictional issues be damned.[34]

Although a little more tactful, Barron Collier was even more explicit when he wrote to E. G. Sewell, president of the Miami Chamber of Commerce. The agreement that Captain Jaudon and his Chevelier Corporation had struck with Lee County several years ago was "for only a temporary period," and that "the Chevelier Corporation had failed to carry out this agreement." This agreement included the deflection of the Tamiami Trail into Monroe County. But now it was "ancient history," and "our engineers have long since restored the original plans of building the trail to the Dade County line." There was no longer any doubt of where the Collier Companies stood: they were building the road all the way to Dade. From that point forward, it became a race between the two crews: Otto Neal's men, headed eastward; and Erben Cook and his crew, headed towards the Gulf coast, eight miles south of them. It would have been a great comedy if there hadn't been so much money going to waste.[35]

* * * * *

But what was more surprising, because it was far more subtle, was the use of the Association to redefine the Tamiami Trail itself. Within a few weeks, Ora Chapin would almost casually slip in a reference to "the north end of the Tamiami Trail which now extends to High Springs."[36] High Springs? High Springs was in Alachua County, near Gainesville. It had no particular geographic or economic significance, other than being the north terminus of State Road 5. Chapin's shift added another 126 miles to the Trail, for a total of 432 miles.[37]

The idea that the Tamiami Trail Association would now try to redefine a road whose very name reflected its Tampa-to-Miami function was not lost on the press, at least on the Atlantic coast. What is this "Tamiami Trail Association?" harrumphed the *Miami Post* in fall, 1925. "Who is behind it and who elected Mr. Chapin?" Most of all "We would like to know by what authority Mr. Chapin and his association has for adding six counties and more than a hundred miles to the length of the Trail.... The Tamiami Trail by its very name designates its location and sets an absolute limit on its length."[38]

The success of the Association was proven by the swiftness and vociferousness by which the Gulf coast papers—the Fort Myers *Press* and the pugnacious Estero *Eagle* came to the defense of the Association. Chapin's "High Springs-to-Miami" refocus had already united the Gulf coast counties from Collier on the south to Levy, on the bank of the Suwanee River, on the north. (Monroe, as always focused on the keys, was typically ambivalent about anything occurring on the mainland.) Only short stretches of State Road 5 in Marion County (near Ocala) and Alachua County (where High Springs itself was located) did not front on the Gulf of Mexico—and of course, the segment in Dade. High Springs-to-Miami would be the Gulf coast's version of the eastern division of the Dixie Highway. By 1926, Chapin stretched his red line another thirty miles or so to the north, to Lake City, on the Old Spanish Trail. Belatedly, in 1926 some prominent Miami realtors did attempt to get a "Tamiami Trail Completion Association" off the ground, but none of the traditional booster organizations (the chamber of commerce; board of trade; motor club) climbed on board, and it swiftly passed into oblivion.[39]

Not only did it make political sense, it made fiscal sense in the new era of federal-aid highway finding. State Road 5 had been one of the original five state-aid highways designated in 1921. The 1921 federal Highway Act had called for each state to designate seven percent of its road system as "federal aid highways" to prevent it from dissipating its federal funds through "logrolling"—making every county happy by designating at least a few farm-to-market roads as federally eligible. Florida had complied with both the spirit and the letter of the law. Moreover, in the so-called "Miller Bill," passed by the Florida legislature in 1923, no new work on federal-aid highways could commence until state roads 1–5 and 8 were completed. The Miller Bill was an anti-pork act, intended to further concentrate highway funds on a few priority projects, and keep them focused until the work was finished instead of trying to tackle the entire seven-percent system all at once during a period when Florida did not have enough money to meet this seemingly lofty goal.[40]

Everyone involved with the Tamiami Trail agreed that it was critical that the designation of State Road 5 be extended from Fort Myers to Marco and across to Miami. From the state's point of view, it was relatively unimportant anymore what did or didn't comprise the "Tamiami Trail"; what mattered was what was or wasn't "State Road 5." Except for major projects such as the Peace River bridge in Punta Gorda and the Manatee River bridge near Bradenton, most of State Road 5 from High Springs to Fort Myers had been completed by 1924, even if it hadn't been built to federal (i.e., AASHO) standards. Thus, it helped shift the equation when detractors in Dade County complained that they had already spent so much on their portion of the road in the face of uncertainly about whether Lee and Collier counties would ever come through with their commitments. "Why look," the west coast counties could now say, "here's a 432-mile highway, of which 357 miles are finished and in daily use. Of the impassible sections, 36 miles are in Dade County! Now, who's the slacker?" This was, in fact, an argument that Ora Chapin of the Tamiami Trail Association used more

Tamiami Trail, 1924. Note the culverts being prepared for installation by the Southern Drainage District after landowners in north Dade and south Broward counties threatened to sue over flooding caused by the road damming up the east Everglades' historic flow of water from Lake Okeechobee to Florida Bay. Also note the massive amount of excess spoil created to accommodate the too-deep-draft dredging barge brought in by the McCrary firm in 1919. (Photographer unknown. HistoryMiami, No. X-055-150.)

than once to defend Lee and Collier counties against accusations in the Miami press that they been slow and inadequate in their support.[41]

However, it did little to endear him to the Miami newspapers. "A detailed report on what is being done to push the Tamiami Trail to completion from the west side is given in a letter from Ora E. Chapin," reported the *Miami Daily News-Metropolis*. "From Mr. Chapin's letter it would appear that the Collier county interests are not cooperating in joining with the Chevelier corporation over the shortest possible route through Monroe county, but are determined to build to the Dade county line straight eastward, reaching a point from which a jog will have to be built connecting with the Tamiami Trail in Dade county." George Hosmer, general manager of the *Fort Myers Press*, tried to pour oil on the roiling waters: "Mr. Collier is determined to build straight east to improve his property, but I believe he is too good a business man not to connect with the short cut being built through upper Monroe county by the Chevelier corporation." Chapin, on the other hand, had no intention of backing off: "One of the great difficulties in this whole thing is the lack of direct information and the unbelief which seems exist in Dade County as to what Lee and Collier counties are doing." Chapin's comments were particularly incendiary given that they came less than three months before a Dade County election to approve $125,000 in bonds to finish the work left undone by the McCrary Company.[42]

Partially because of what it perceived as the attitude of Collier County in pressing for the Jenkins alignment, regardless of how much extra it cost the people of Dade, while on the other hand acknowledging that the cheapest, straight-ahead route would realize a windfall for the Chevelier Corporation, the *Miami Daily News-Metropolis* did the unthinkable: it endorsed a "no" vote on the July election. Just kill the whole project, at least for the time being.[43]

10. "All was sweet and everything was sitting pretty" 163

But even if it was poorly communicated to the people of Dade County, it was logical to redefine the Tamiami Trail to encompass the full length of State Road 5. It united the Gulf coast counties at a time when many other parts of the state were demanding that the state road commission expand state and federal highway aid beyond the five Miller Bill roads. Getting State Road 5 extended to Miami would not only relieve the Collier companies and Collier County (and maybe the Chevelier Corporation as well) of some of their crushing road building burden, it would help with the reconstruction of some of the early parts of the road, such as the Trail inside the cites of Miami and Coral Gables that had been built before the advent of AASHO standards. Finally, the McCrary Company had left some parts of the Trail work in very poor shape, and the installation of culverts and cross-flow canals had badly degraded the quality of others. The Trail in Dade County was far from finished, and getting more money out of the local citizenry was far a sure bet. Dade would probably need federal-state highway money as well.

In March, the board of arbitrators in the McCrary dispute finally issued its findings. Dade County was entitled to a reimbursement of $18,000. The McCrary Company elected not to turn to its bondman, but to make the payments itself. McCrary never again bid on

When the J. B. McCrary Company declared their work on the Dade portion of Trail "completed" and pulled out, the west ten miles of the road was barely drivable, as this photo, taken near the Dade-Monroe line in 1926, attests. A board of arbitration later ordered McCrary to reimburse Dade County $18,000 for the poor quality of the work. (Photographer unknown. Florida Division of Library and Information Services, No. RC02976.)

another job in south Florida. Nor did McCrary ever send a final accounting of its payments and expenses to the county commission. "There is really no telling how much McCrary lost on that contract," remarked one county commissioner. Paid $293,000, McCrary had to subcontract to county engineer Hobart Crabtree $12,000 for engineering services and return $18,000 to Dade County, for a final net total of $273,000, or $6,205 per mile. McCrary probably lost somewhere around $90,000.[44]

Along with the $18,000 refund, there was still about $7,000 unspent in the Trail's construction fund. The road was thought to need about another $130,000 to complete. Dade County scheduled a $2.3 million bond election, mostly for roads, with $120,000 allocated just for the Tamiami Trail.[45] Opposing the Trail bond issue was the Pennsylvania Sugar Company and its local manager, Ernest "Cap" Graham. Because of his complaints, during 1923 and 1924, the Southern Drainage District had installed 22 culverts in the already completed portion of the Tamiami Trail. On the other hand, he asserted that the original 1915 agreement with the Internal Improvement Fund required that culverts be installed every one-eighth mile, a total of approximately 240.[46]

Graham countered that because the boundaries of the Southern Drainage District ended twelve miles before the county line, they would not be able to provide the needed culverts all the way west. "It is almost inconceivable that there should be an attempt to complete the trail" wrote one of his consulting engineers. "It will require 100 openings 30 feet wide," calculated another.[47]

But by the time of the 1924 bond issue, Graham's relations with his neighbors was pretty bad. He had created his own drainage subdistrict, the Dade Drainage District, built his own dykes and canals, and solved his problems largely by draining and pumping water onto other people's land. When summer flooding became a problem in 1924 he simply dammed the Miami Canal at the Dade-Broward line, flooding the farms of the Griffin family and other large Broward County landowners. One of them, Brown, sued Pennsylvania Sugar, Graham, and State Engineer Fred Elliott. Graham knew that if he could defeat the $125,000 bond issue, he had a good chance to kill the Tamiami Trail forever. With his own drainage sub-district and Elliott largely on his side, if the bond issue went down in defeat, he could tear up the Trail, just as he had torn up some of the dykes of his neighbors in 1924 to drain Penn Sugar's land.[48]

It was a badly kept secret that the McCrary Company had left a Tamiami Trail that existed in name only. "The road today in Dade County could not be called fit for travel," reported a *Miami Herald* investigator. "At least half of the trail is a positive nightmare of jolts, dips, swayings, and quivering jars that shake the traveler to the foundation.... The last 20 miles of the Dade County road is only wide enough for one motor car to pass ... at two or three points it was difficult to discern the dividing line between the road and the bank of the canal ... for the last 20 miles [the canal] is little more than a rude ditch or creek."[49]

For once, both the Chevelier and Collier interests had a common cause: without the Dade bonds, both their efforts could be for naught. The *Ft. Myers Press*, which had provocatively taken to calling the highway the "Tamyami Trail," suddenly reverted to the traditional spelling. Barron Collier came over to the Atlantic Coast to walk over the new road that George and Erben Cook had built for the Chevelier Corporation with Capt. Jaudon. "This has certainly been no child's work and it is work that should not be wasted," he told the assembled reporters. Bill House, an old friend of Capt. Jaudon and now a part-time Collier employee (as was almost everyone in Chokoloskee) came across the state, catching a lift from an Alexander, Ramsey & Kerr truck to the end of the Collier County road work, then hiking overland to the Chevelier base camp near Pinecrest. After a night's sleep and a couple of meals, a supply truck took him into Miami where the press was ecstatic to talk to one of the men who had dispatched the terror of Chatham Bend, Edgar Watson.[50]

Meetings between businessmen and newspaper editors were arranged in Miami and Fort Myers in the weeks leading up to the bond election. "The original plan of the Gulf Coast Association which contemplated boosting the West Coast and was considered by some a spasmodic campaign which would develop sectionalism was completely eliminated and the plans finally developed were those of cooperation and coordination of the Chambers of Commerce and Boards of Trade," explained the *Ft. Myers Press*. The *Miami News-Metropolis* still held out against the approval of the bond issue, but even its position grew half-hearted and its explanatory editorial came out over a month before the election. The turnout, as would be expected for a south Florida election in August, was small, and the Tamiami Trail bond issue (one of eight on the ballot) carried easily. Up in Broward, Brown mounted a vigorous suit (probably with the aid of his neighbors) against Pennsylvania Sugar and Cap Graham's son later wrote that it so handcuffed any further actions by him and Elliott that the sugar company started thinking about selling their Pennsuco mill and pulling out of Florida. The mill was sold and moved in 1927 and the Penn Sugar withdrew from Florida entirely in 1931.[51]

Its last big political job completed, The Tamiami Trail Association quietly began to disappear from the front pages. Barron Collier would not completely dispose of them as a public relations tool, but never again would they assume the role of high visibility pot-stirrer they had played during the spring and summer of 1924. Instead, they became what they had always held themselves out to the public to be, an alumni association for the veterans of the famous cross-state expedition.[52]

••11••

When Do We Cross?

In June 1924, Otto Neal's men were about two and a half miles east of Carnestown. They had added a Bay City dredge in January 1924, and now had two crews at work. "With two dredges working single shifts we went thirteen miles in twenty months," Neal later recalled:

> The rock all the way over this thirteen miles was terrible and the dredges would sometimes be able to dig a fifteen foot canal in depth and then again but four and all the time growing harder as we struggled eastward. It was difficult to determine the amount of dynamite necessary for each "shot" and ofttimes we were compelled to reblow the holes and this was done by dropping "bundles" of tied sticks of dynamite in front of the machines and try it over. It was miraculous that no one was seriously hurt during these operations.[1]

Neal was still using the same dynamiting method he had developed during the dredging from Everglades City to Carnestown: scrape off the overlying marl and use a high-pressure hose to find natural holes in the limestone. However, the holes varied in depth and size, and so did the pattern and degree of fracturing. Sometimes, when his men tried to lift a boulder out with an excavator, they discovered that it was too big or still partially attached to the rock strata. When this happened they had to "reblow the holes," that is, with the excavation equipment in place. "When this condition arose there was only one thing to do—that was to reshoot in front of the dredges. This operation consisted of taking about 40 sticks of dynamite, making them into a bundle with an electric blasting cap in the center, placing two of these bundles in the canal in front of the machine, and blowing them." While exceeding dangerous, there was only one accident, with minor injuries. The only fatality that occurred during the five years the Collier interests worked on the job was a death from typhoid fever, apparently contracted in Miami a day or two before the worker reported to the work site.[2]

Down in Monroe County, Erben Cook's secret weapon was his mobile pneumatic drilling rig. Cook estimated that it could drill as fast as thirty men with sledgehammer-powered star drills. It could drill 250 nine-foot deep holes in one day in any pattern desired. Because the holes were placed in a regular pattern, they fractured the limestone into uniform rubble. The rig had its own bunks and galley, which was a good thing, because by the summer of 1924, it was pulling away from the road building crew. By early 1926, it was over two-and-a-half miles in front of the steamshovel crew.[3] Alexander, Ramsey & Kerr had adopted the same type of technology, building their own three-drill mobile rig that ran on streetcar tracks, which were taken up and put down in sections as the unit advanced.

In September 1924 Collier County approved a $350,000 bond issue dedicated to the construction of the Tamiami Trail. Up to this point, Barron Collier appears to have been paying for most, if not all, of the work himself. As the owner of about half of the assessed value of the land in Collier County, he still would have been paying for much of the road even without a road district, but at least the bonds gave him twenty years to pay, and the Barron was betting that during this time the value of his holdings would increase to the point that the repayment would be virtually cost-free. Once the bonds were sold, the pace of work out beyond Carnestown started to pick up measurably.[4]

Three months earlier, Lee County had approved a $1.250 million road bond issue, out of which $534,000 was reserved for the Tamiami Trail. Since the succession of Collier County, there was only about 35 miles or so of the Trail left in Lee, but they were expensive miles: eight miles from Charlotte County to the north bank of the Caloosahatchee River bridge, a mile over the bridge, through Fort Myers, then about 25 miles past Estero and on to Bonita Springs at the Collier line. Monroe, to everyone's surprise, also approved a $200,000 bond issue, but it was now uncertain whether they wanted to actually put them up for sale.[5]

In March 1925, the Dade County commissioners turned over the management of the Tamiami Trail construction project to the state road department, along with the $125,000 that had been collected from the August 1924 bond election. At the meeting of the state road commissioners, Dade County had hoped that their funds would be matched by state and federal highway funds. Only a few weeks before, the road department had released its annual report indicating that $8.18 million in construction and maintenance funds were available for 1925, including $2.70 million in state gas tax revenues, $1.75 million in auto tax fees and $2.83 million in federal aid. However, the Dade commissioners had to go away empty-handed, due to the still-applicable Miller Bill restrictions. But the state road commissioners anticipated the availability funds relatively soon, probably at the next legislative session. The commissioners also agreed with the estimate offered by the County's road department that fixing McCrary's unfinished work out west and bringing the entire road, from Coral Gables to the County line, to state highway standards would cost between $250,000 and $300,000. This proved to be a vast underestimate.[6]

In March 1925, *Miami Herald* reporter Guy Cunliffe and a staff photographer ventured out to the far reaches of the Tamiami Trail, five and a half miles past the Dade County line where Erben Cook's drill wagon was at work. It had been about eighteen months since the McCrary firm had packed up and returned to Atlanta. What Cunliffe and his companion found was sobering. "The road today in Dade County could not be called fit for comfortable travel," Cunliffe reported. In fact, they returned with photos showing places where there was no road—just mounds of crushed rock piled beside the canal, through which zigzagged a sort of goat path improvised by Chevelier truck drivers.[7]

The first eight miles out of Coral Gables were asphalt. The following six miles were good, rolled rock surface. (This would be about where Krome Avenue is located today.) The following twelve miles were a gradually deteriorating unpaved road. At about the 26-mile point the Trail became two shallow wheel ruts. In many places a car had to pull aside to let an approaching truck pass, at other places, not even this was possible and one had to back up until a turn-off could be found. The *Herald* team found the five-and-a-half mile stretch built by the Chevelier Corp. in Monroe County "is a good highway ...when compared with the 20-mile stretch in Dade County" that preceded it, "but riding upon it is no joyride, by any means."

The *Miami Herald* team also drove south out of Tampa to find out how the west side was doing. They found that "the 30 miles from Marco Junction to ... [Carnestown] is now one of the best portions of the highway south of Fort Myers." The nine miles of road east of Carnestown "is rock surfaced, although it is somewhat rough at present ...[but] is being pounded into excellent shape." It is interesting to note that Cunliffe predicted that the road would take at least three years to complete, based on the rate of progress he had seen. This was probably the first accurate projection to appear in print.

Nineteen twenty-five was an odd-numbered year, which meant the legislature convened in May. Within a few days of the opening gavel, bills adding at least half a dozen roads to the "Miller Bill" list of preferential state-aid highways had been tossed into the clerk's basket. State Road 27, from Fort Myers to Miami, was one of these. With burgeoning state gas tax revenues (Florida was one of only 16 states to charge 3 cents or more per gallon of fuel) and matching federal aid (the more you put up, the more the Bureau of Public Roads would give you), as well as the approaching completion of the original six Miller Bill roads, the highway commission and the legislature were willing to take an expansive approach, and on May 28, State Road 27 was added to the list of preferential highways.[8]

Governor John Martin was dissatisfied with the fiscally conservative chairman of the state road commission, Judge Hendry Phillips. After getting the Miller Bill restrictions lifted and an increase in the fuel tax from 3 to 4 cents per gallon approved, Martin fired Phillips in July 1925 and replaced him with Dr. Fons Hathaway.

Alexander, Ramsey & Kerr developed their own version of a multi-bore drill rig by 1926. The main difference between theirs and the one developed by the Chevelier Company was that AR&K's ran on railroad tracks, which were put taken up and put down as the rig moved forward. (Photograph by William Fishbaugh. Florida Division of Library and Information Services, No. RC03410.)

Hathaway was an early example of the type of professional that would remain rare in the South until the New Deal: the politician-technocrat. Hathaway received the equivalent of an associate's degree from Florida State and a bachelor's degree from the University of Florida in 1904. He was the principal of a high school in Orlando, then moved to Jacksonville to become a high school principal there. He worked his way up through the ranks to become the head of instruction, then superintendent of the Jacksonville schools. In that position, he oversaw a massive $58 million construction program that replaced almost every school in the system. He received an honorary doctorate from the University of Florida in 1916. At the time Martin named him to the chairmanship of the road department, Hathaway was Martin's secretary, what would today be considered his chief of staff.[9]

Three weeks after Hathaway took over, the state road department issued its first contract on State Road 27 to the M. C. Winterburn Co. of Jacksonville. It called for the reconstruction of 10.3 miles the old McCrary road base, starting from a point eight miles west of Coral Cables. It was given the identifier "Project 669-B." (Project number 669-A had been assigned to Dade County's asphalting of the first eight miles for the Trail in Coral Gables and the City of Miami.) The price was based mostly on the amount of material excavated and moved, but specified a total compensation of between $240,000 and $300,000. Henceforth, Project 669 would be assigned to all contracts along State Road 27 between Miami and Fort Myers.[10]

It is difficult to tell where the money the Chevelier Corporation was using to build their road was coming from. It does appear that it was from the "road construction fund" created at the time of the Spencer Agreement, but was not spent in 1920. In October 1922 Franklin Floete died, and J. H. McCord took over the Citizens National Bank of Spencer, Iowa.[11] The following February the officers of the Chevelier Corporation executed what became known as the "Spencer Agreement Amendment." The original Spencer Agreement of August 1920 created $600,000 in corporate bonds. The liabilities of the Chevelier Corporation, including its stock and the original mortgage debt owed to A. W. Hopkins, were turned into $400,000 worth of bonds. The other $200,000 were to be sold to pay for the construction of the Tamiami Trail. McCord, Hopkins and Judge McDougal became bond trustees, essentially giving them control of the corporation. This was also the agreement that transferred 87,000 acres of coastland into a separate corporation, the Chatham Bend Corporation, owned separately by Hopkins, Jaudon, McDougal, Cook, the Floete estate, and McCord. The intent was to cut out the small investors that Jaudon had recruited in the early days.[12]

The amendment was drawn up because two oil speculators, C. L. Freedland and W. W. Groom, of the Roland Oil Company wanted to explore for oil on the Chevelier Tract. Freedland and Groom personally took out an oil lease over the entire site and then leased smaller blocks to Roland for exploration and, hopefully, production. Under the terms of the amended amendment, Judge McDougal would buy $75,000 in road bonds, McCord, Hopkins and the Floete estate together would buy an equal amount, and the oil interests would buy $50,000. These funds would be provided in installments between March 1923 and May 1925, averaging around $3,000 per month from each of the three parties. In this way, the $200,000 road fund, which had been left dry in the original August 1920 Spencer Agreement, would at last be funded. In addition, as land sales were made, half the money would go to reimburse McDougal, McCord, Hopkins the Floete estate for their contributions to the road fund by buying back the bonds they had purchased, and one half would go to retire the larger $400,000 block of bonds, thereby making a profit for the bondholders.

But by the fall of 1924, the Roland Oil Company had pulled out of the arrangement.

Freeland continued as a director of the Chevelier Corporation, but never succeeded in securing a sublease covering the entire tract. In early 1925 the firm sold 50 square miles of land to Thomas J. Peters, a Miami businessman, for lumbering. He never paid a cent after his initial down payment. George Cook foreclosed and reclaimed the land in the early 1930s. Almost all the burden of carrying the company during the time the road was being built was borne by Judge McDougal.[13] In 1925, as the Chevelier road was working its way across Monroe County, he wrote a colleague that:

> While I have done well and made big profits on my investments in Florida, all that I have is in land and paper. I have never received one cent out of the profits of the sale of the lands of our big tract. We have sold about three and one-half million dollar's worth of land out of the big tract, but most of it was sold for 25% cash payment, and some of it was for much less cash, and out of the payment we paid a commission of 5% and had nearly a million dollars' of obligation in the way of road building expenses, floating indebtedness, and bonded indebtedness. So it will be several months yet before we can realize on our first deferred payments. We still have five million dollars of unsold land in the big tract. I never had more property, nor less cash nor more pressing obligations than I have right now.[14]

The biggest beneficiaries of the new arrangement were George and Erben Cook. George had provided James Jaudon with the valuable financial and organizational advice he needed back in the early days when the A. W. Hopkins tract had become the Chevelier Corporation, and had been the corporation's secretary from the start, in addition to running his own construction company (Cook Construction, for example, built the Collins Causeway in Biscayne Bay.[15]) But now, he was reaping his reward: while he had only a small holding in the Chevelier Corporation itself, he and Erben were getting paid to build the Chevelier road, and by all estimates, it would cost more than the $200,000 in bonds that were allotted to it. And unlike the McCrary brothers' fixed price contract, the Cooks had a cost-plus contract. Whatever it cost to get the job done, they would get paid. They might not get much of a mark-up, but they had the comfort of knowing that their costs would be covered.[16]

In October 1925 Alexander, Ramsey & Kerr hired D. Graham Copeland as their chief engineer, replacing E. P. Lott, who had been on the job only a few months. In fact, other than Otto Neal, who had been dredging foreman since February 1923, the Barron hadn't been able to find anyone to coordinate all his various engineering projects. Besides the Trail, he was building a road and bridge to link Everglades City and Dupont; docks at Dupont; shops and warehouses at Carnestown; and starting in 1925, a road from Everglades City, north alongside the Deep Lake railway, to Immokalee. Basil Scott, who had managed the Deep Lake fruit groves, had acted as superintendent for a short time, followed by Lott, and now Copeland. Copeland graduated at the top of his class at the South Carolina Military Academy in 1899, and he received his bachelor's degree in engineering at Rensselaer Polytechnic Institute in 1903. In 1906 he joined the Navy, serving for 14 years before retiring at the rank of Lieutenant Commander.

He ran the Collier construction projects like a military theatre of operation. Everything was coordinated with steam whistles at Everglades City, Port Dupont and Carnestown. The normal shift was nine hours a day, six days a week, not counting a half-hour for lunch and fifteen-minute breaks in the morning and afternoon. Workers got a half-day off for Thanksgiving and a full day off for Christmas. What had been the village of Everglade was rebuilt as Everglades City, laid out on the straight, right-angle lines of a military base with the Collier County Courthouse in the center. "Mr. Copeland took charge," Otto Neal recalled. [He] saw immediately what our difficulties were ... we began to proceed with what seemed incredible speed.... If it hadn't been for D. Graham Copeland I don't see how we would have been half-way across by this time [1928] instead of finishing the hardest road job that has ever been attempted in a long time." The Tamiami Trail work was divided into two crews. The western division was now up to three shovels (probably one steam shovel, one dragline and a walking dredge), a drilling rig mounted on railroad tracks, and rolling bunkhouses and kitchens for its 25 men. The eastern division, which was under the direction of the county engineer, used Otto Neal's old Marion floating dredge and the new Bay City dredge. It required less blasting, as the depth of sand covering the underlying limestone varied between ten and forty feet. Its 24 men commuted in each day by launch from Carnestown.[17]

About the time that Copeland took over, Otto Neal's men crossed a definite, but invisible, point of no return in the center of Section 11, Township 52, Range 31. At this spot, roughly eleven miles past Carnestown, the Collier work crews had to turn from their easterly course to the southeast if they were to link up with the Chevelier road at the prearranged meeting point on the Collier-Monroe line agreed to back in the summer of 1924. The meeting point was six and a half miles from the turn, on a heading nearly due southeast. At this time, the Chevelier crew was at the future town site of Pinecrest, about nine miles from the meeting point, and was still headed west, not yet having reached the spot where they needed to make their turn to the northwest. Neal's men, following Copeland's orders, ignored the turn and continued east down the original Jenkins stakeline.[18]

By January 1926 Neal was four or five miles past the turn. That month, Monroe County petitioned Fons Hathaway to have the state take over the work. In exchange, Monroe County would turn over $150,000 of the two hundred thousand raised in its 1925 bond issue, in the same way that Dade County had earlier done with the $125,000 it raised in its 1924 election. This had to be a crushing blow for the Chevelier Corporation, as they had been counting on the Monroe County bond money as a way of mitigating its costs, which by now were approaching the $200,000 allocated in the Spencer Agreement Amendment.

The Dade County Commission was now utterly confused about what its legal responsibilities were. It had agreements with Monroe County, Lee County and the Chevelier Corporation dating from 1919 and 1922 pledging the straight-line roadway, and was holding a $200,000 bond from the Chevelier Corporation promising its full performance on the Monroe County roadway. The state road department realized that the situation was in such disarray that it sent its own surveyors into Monroe and Collier counties in the fall of 1925 to ascertain the progress each road was making and the feasibility of their respective survey lines.[19]

In response, at the road department's quarterly meeting in January 1926, the state commissioners instructed Dr. Hathaway, along with state road commissioners I. E. Schilling of Miami and E. P. Green of Bradenton, to select a definitive route for State Road 27 between Miami and Marco Junction. Hathaway, for one, had never personally inspected the Trail from the Dade end, so in late January and early February Hathaway, Green, Schilling, and various local officials visited both work sites and looked over several alternative survey lines staked out by state engineers and others. Wisely realizing that the decision was too politically charged make through a small technical committee, Hathaway announced that the routing decision would be made by the full highway commission, and only after all the parties had a chance to make their case at its next regularly scheduled quarterly meeting in Tampa on April 19.[20]

After hearing everyone out, Dr. Hathaway and the state road department issued their decision in a letter sent to the Dade, Monroe and Collier commissioners the day after the Tampa meeting. The state would take over the financing, construction and maintenance of State Road 27 if the three counties agreed to the following plan:

1. Collier County would continue building along the Jenkins survey line, with one modification. Instead of turning southeast at the Dade-Collier line, it would make this turn three miles earlier. Thus, the road would pass through the tri-corner of Dade, Monroe and Collier, and would intersect with the old McCrary road grade roughly four miles east of the Dade-Monroe line instead of eight miles, as indicated on the Jenkins survey.
2. The Chevelier dredge in Monroe County would continue northwest for only two more miles and then turn due north for the Collier county line. This would leave Collier's men with four miles of road to build straight south, starting from where its dredge was then located at Section 10, Township 52, Range 32. The meeting point would be the southwest corner of Section 35, Township 52, Range 32. This moved the connection between the Collier and Chevelier crews at the Collier-Monroe line about a mile east of the original plan, but it shortened the connector considerably, because it took the shortest path—due north/south—between the two roads. In all, Chevelier's dredge had about five more miles to dig, Collier's men four.
3. Monroe would use the balance of the $200,000 it offered to the state to help build the Chevelier road and the connector. The state would then take over its maintenance.
4. The state would build the connection between the east end of the Collier road and the McCrary road grade in Dade County, and would also oversee the complete reconstruction of the McCrary road grade. In other words, the state would take over responsibility for all work in Dade County, except for some short portions within the cities of Miami and Coral Gables.[21]

Probably the most controversial statement was one Dr. Hathaway made after the formal meeting, when he told the assembled reporters that he believed it would take another three and a half years to complete the Trail "even if all conditions are favorable." Barron Collier replied that he would have his portion of the road completed in eight months. The Chevelier Corporation responded that they would be finished to the junction point on the Monroe-Collier line a month or two before that. "Many and wild have been the statements on this feature of the situation," responded the state road department in its magazine, *Florida Highways*:

> Some enthusiasts have even declared that travel might be made over the Trail in three months, or varying longer intervals, if such and such route were adopted. In fact, this sort of "propaganda," as the chairman [Dr. Hathaway] terms it, has hampered the members in their efforts to properly deal with the question. The Department recognizes the construction of this road is a gigantic task. It will insist that the job be done right. It will not be party to any farce, and in order that no one may be misled through enthusiasm or other cause to expect a sooner completion, the chairman has stated his belief as to the time that should be required "because," said the chairman, "the public should known the truth."[22]

In the end, Hathaway had the last laugh: the ribbon-cutting wasn't held until April 1928, two years after he made his prediction, and work on some parts of the road weren't fully complete for another eighteen months after that.[23]

The "propaganda" that Hathaway referred to largely came from Jaudon. The Miami newspapers initially condemned the routing decision. The *News-Metropolis* called it "an evil day for the Tamiami Trail when the Dade County Commission turned over the uncompleted road and a credit of $125,000 to the state road department," and showed a map indicating twelve miles of road—mostly the Chevelier route—that had been "declared useless"

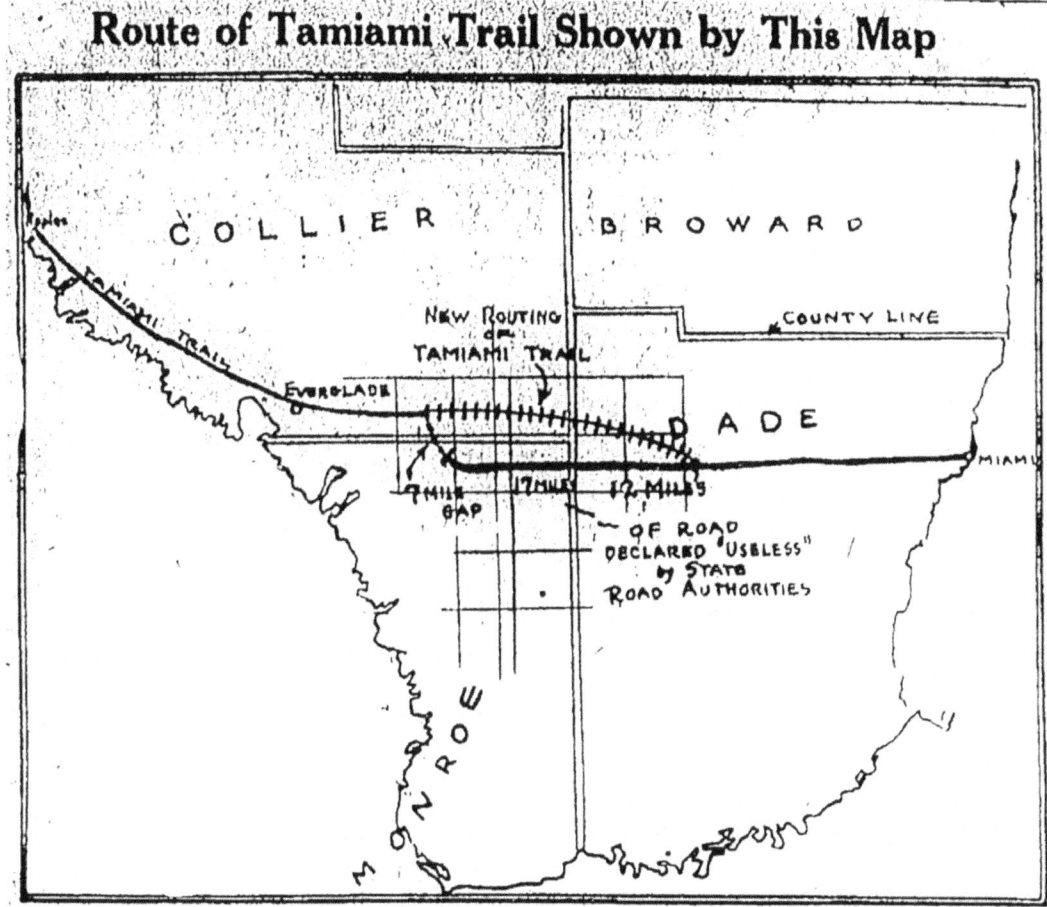

When the state road commission announced that it would take over the building of the Tamiami Trail in April 1926, James Jaudon tried to convince the Chamber of Commerce and the County Commission that the state had abandoned the twelve miles of the road that ran through his land. In the end, he was mostly right. (Source: *Miami News and Metropolis*, April 20, 1926.)

by the state. W. Cecil Watson, Dade county commissioner, said that Hathaway's action "probably will mean that Dade County will give the [road] department no further rights of way through this county, but will take care of its own problems." Watson thought that because of the County's obligation under the 1919 and 1922 resolutions, it probably would have to refuse to sign the state's new agreement and would end up in court over the matter.[24]

However, Watson's counterpart across the street at the City of Miami, C. D. Leffler, told a reporter that "I am so anxious for a Tamiami Trail of any sort that I do not care what route is taken. I do not think any route will vary over 10 miles, and 10 miles is not worth the public quarrelling over." A clearly irritated I. E. Schilling, Miami's representative on the governing board of the state road department, told several newspapers that "It is not the purpose of the department to abandon a single mile of road that has built or begun along the trail." As the specifics of the interlocal agreement drafted by the state road department and sent to three counties became known, the press and most civic organizations initially opposed to Hathaway's plan backed off. Some still pointed out that it was inefficient and wasteful to wait until both the Collier and Chevelier roads were complete before building

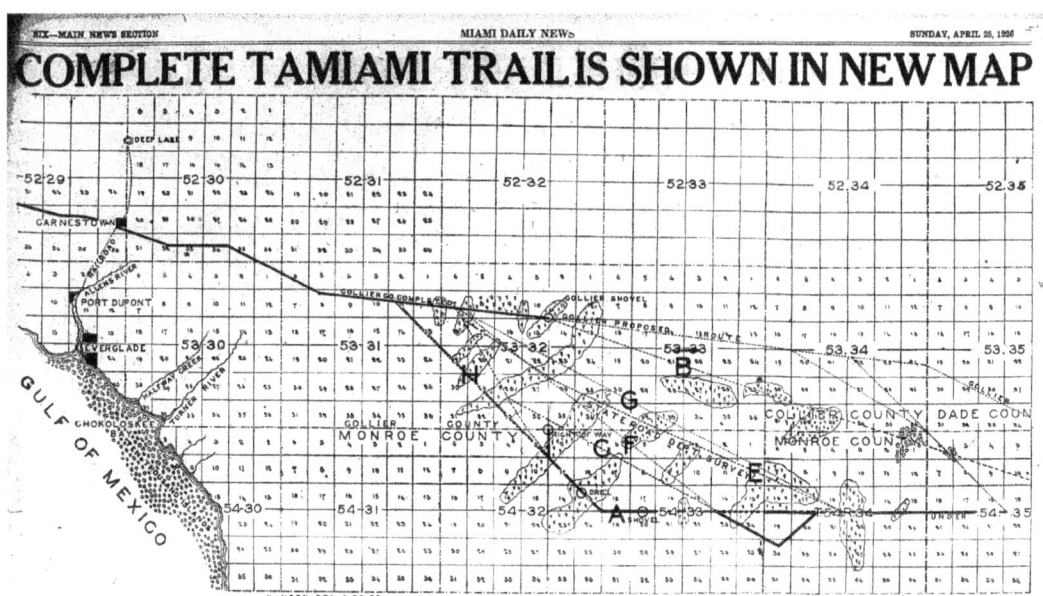

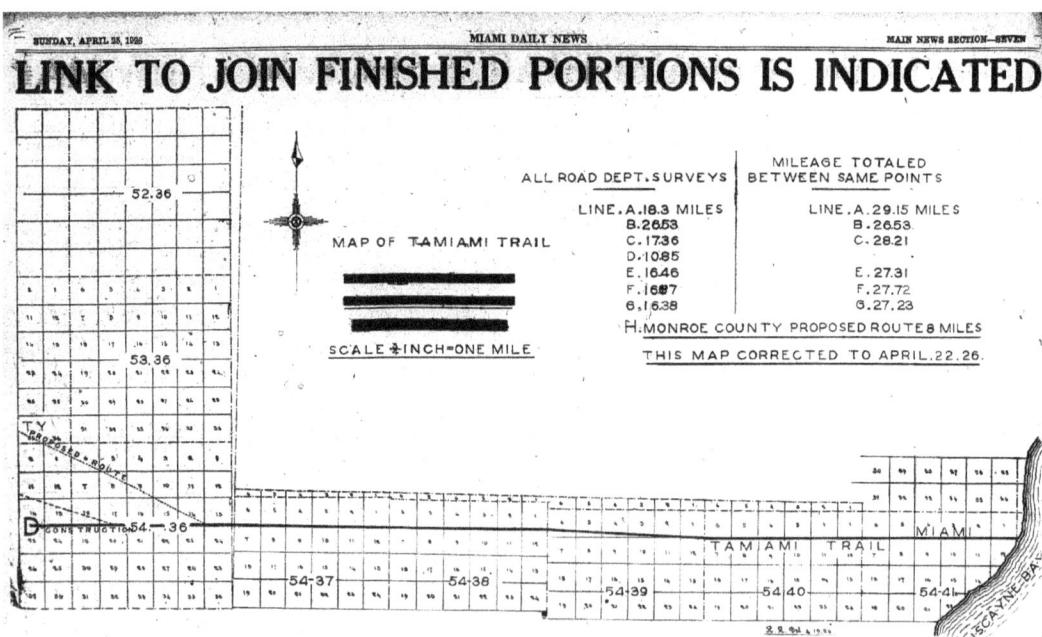

11. When Do We Cross?

both the east and west connectors, instead of pushing through the construction of the shortest connector—probably the one in Monroe. This would permit cross-state travel to begin by using half of one route, then crossing over on the connector and using half of the other. Afterwards, the remaining portions could be sequentially brought up to state standards.[25]

This seemed to be a point on which almost everyone could agree on. In Fort Myers, the Tamiami Trail Blazers held a meeting to discuss Hathaway's letter to the three counties. Generally, they were pleased with the two-route decision, "but the consensus of opinion of those present was that something should be done to make the connection between the Collier county grade and the and the road being built a few miles south in Monroe county." The Monroe County Commission stated that it was in general agreement with the document it had been presented by Dr. Hathaway for endorsement. However, it left the deadline for the completion of the Chevelier-Collier connector "indefinite," and this issue concerned them and would require some negotiation.[26]

In Miami, C. E. Riddell, president of the Chamber of Commerce and Theodore Gessler, president of the Tamiami Trail Businessmen's Association scheduled an open forum at the Central High School for Monday evening, April 26. It was a pep rally organized by Riddell, Jaudon and Gessler. Jaudon, however, claimed he was "too ill to attend." A representative did read a long letter from him containing several *ad hominum* attacks against Barron Collier, Fons Hathaway, and even Governor Martin. Jaudon called on the boards of commissioners of the three counties to reject the draft interlocal agreement sent them by the state, and pledged to put 500 men to work on the trail. But in a blatantly self-contradictory (and patently absurd) statement, he also asserted that only about $50,000 was needed to finish the work in Dade County and the western connector in Collier County, and that state money was not needed, as the necessary funds could be raised through public donation. His representative handed a check for a $1,000 to A. W. Burwell, the chamber of commerce director running the meeting, suggesting that if only a few like-minded Dade citizens did the same, the problem would be solved in a few months.[27]

In Fort Meyers, R. A. Henderson, Jr., made only a few more attempts at credulity. "When Dr. Hathaway says it will take three and one-half years to complete the highway," Henderson explained to the city's Civitan Club, "he means that by the time Trail is entirely finished from Tampa to Miami, every concrete bridge and culvert is built, and every other detail complete, three and one-half years may have elapsed ... it will not take three and one half years to make it travelable. The Collier forces are predicting the completion of its portion of the work by January 1, 1927. By that date, I confidently believe, you may ride at a speed of forty miles an hour from the northern line of Collier County to the Dade County line." He wished he could say "all the way to Miami," but "Dade County has made more noise and done less than any other county."[28]

In terms of his public credibility and civic standing, his letter to the Chamber of Commerce meeting and subsequent press comments, Jaudon's actions were a public relations disaster from which he never fully recovered. Schilling, the Miami-based state road commissioner, commented only that "The proceedings at the Chamber of Commerce forum Monday night seem to have been governed by a lack of information," and released

Opposite: Map of various proposed Tamiami Trail routes considered by the Florida Road Commission, April 1926. The Jenkins alignment is marked "Collier Proposed Route." The Chevelier route is marked "A." The selected route is the dashed line running from "53–34" in the northwest to "54–35" in the southeast. (Source" *Miami News and Metropolis*, April 26, 1926.)

a summary of the proposed agreement that Hathaway had sent to the three counties. Even worse, George Cook, who was actually out building Chevelier's road, sided with Hathaway. After Hathaway announced his plan, Cook told a Miami reporter that "These roads will make a loop through Collier and Monroe counties and give a good road for each, well constructed.... Dr. Hathaway's suggestion furnishes a practical working plan whereby two state roads will be built through the Everglades instead of one, and will make the entire territory a tributary to Miami." Under the Hathaway plan "there will be just as good a reason for the public to use the road through Monroe county as the one through Collier." A few days after the Central High School meeting, at a regular monthly meeting of the Chamber of Commerce, George Cook told the Chamber's board that he "thought the open forum meeting held in the Central school last Monday was not in accordance with the general principals of the chamber of commerce." Chamber president Worth Crow added that "The chamber of commerce as a whole or individually was not responsible the meeting, nor did it influence it in any way."[29]

Crow's comments were motivated by a group of twelve representatives, supposedly from the chamber of commerce, more likely self-appointed, who volunteered to inspect the two roads. Among the twelve were Ivar Axelson, Judge McDougal's son-in-law, and Nansen Torstenson, Jaudon's young associate at the Jaudon Realty Company. Graham Copeland showed them over the Collier County road and told them that Alexander, Ramsey & Kerr planned to complete Dr. Hathaway's modified Jenkins alignment to the Dade County line before starting on the mid-Collier connector south to Monroe County because he did not believe that the Chevelier Corporation could have their portion of the road complete to the Collier County line until mid-1927. Axelson and Torstenson countered that the Chevelier Road would be complete as early as September 1926. Copeland answered that he did not believe this was possible, as the Chevelier equipment still had almost to six miles to go, and his own crews had only been making a mile a month with three dredges working two shifts. Both sides chose to ignore the inconvenient fact that even if they could meet their impossible schedules, both roads ended up at the same place: the McCrary roadgrade in Dade, which was virtually impassable. The Collier and Chevelier crews were in a race to nowhere.[30]

Whether intentional or not, the chamber of commerce's inspection trip descended into farce when Barron Collier lent them one of his launches, the 60-foot, relatively deep-draft Vailima, based in Everglades City, for the trip home to Miami. Collier did not provide a pilot and they ran the boat aground in the Florida Bay shallows off Cape Sable. They remained stuck for 22 hours until a passing boat took Ivar Axelson to Key West. Unable to hire a tow boat, he hired a launch to take him to Marathon, where he could telegraph for a boat to be sent from Florida City. Predictably, their report recommended that Hathaway's plan for parallel roads be dropped, and suggested that all construction be discontinued in Collier except for the north-south connector and "slight repairs" to the Trail in west Dade County, after which a cross-state road could be opened in four months, a schedule the state road department dismissed as "wild" and "propaganda"[31]

For all practical purposes, the Chevelier Corporation had fallen apart. Unbeknownst to most of his partners, in the summer of 1924, Jaudon had purchased 20,000 acres (31 square miles) land in Collier County from a group of owners in West Union, Iowa. About 2,500 acres lay either beside, or very close to, the Trail near Carnestown. Jaudon was still interested in getting the Chevelier road built, but not because it would help develop Pinecrest (that land had been optioned to W. J. Willingham) or his other Chevelier lands. The proceeds of *those* sales would, after the Spencer Agreement and its 1923 amendment, benefit primarily the bondholders, that is, the Iowa crowd, Judge McDougal and the oilmen. No, he wanted the Chevelier road built because it would be the fastest way to help sell his new Collier County holdings, which he was selling in 5-, 8- and 10-acre parcels for $110 per acre.[32]

One of those he talked into buying a parcel was Marjorie Stoneman Douglas, daughter of Judge Frank B. Stoneman, editor of the *Miami Herald*. Educated at Wellesley, Stoneman Douglas ditched her alcoholic husband in Massachusetts and came back to Miami in the 1920s to work as a reporter for her father's paper and to make $100 a week from George Merrick copywriting ads for his new development, Coral Gables. As was the case almost everywhere, the $880 investment in an eight acre tract of Jaudon's land, five miles east of Carnestown, that looked so good in 1924, lost its shine after two hurricanes and the stock market crash. Stoneman Douglas quitclaimed it back to Jaudon in the 1930s, losing the $440 she and Marion Manley had already paid on it.[33]

A few years after the Tamiami Trail opened, Judge McDougal complained to his daughter Mary and her husband Ivar Axelson (who by the mid–1930s had taken over the management of the McDougal family interests in Florida):

> I have always contended everyone in a business or a property should work for the benefit of all, and that nothing affecting the business should be kept from any of those interested. In the Chevelier Corp. I protected the shares of Cook and Jaudon and paid the taxes and carried the entire corporate expense for years; but every time Jaudon or Cook or McCord got a chance to grab off something they never failed to do it. I don't feel like working for those wolves any longer.[34]

To reach a consensus among the three counties and the state road commission, Hathaway applied two strategies that have since become textbook chess gambits in the political game of state-local highway funding. They are as relevant today as they were in 1926. The first is the thinly veiled threat to take your money elsewhere: the state highway department announces that if an agreement is not immediately reached with the locals, outside forces beyond its control will compel it to transfer the money now allocated for the job to another project located far away, in another jurisdiction. This instantly frames the debate. The alternatives are no longer the state's preferred project *here* versus the locals' preferred project *here*. It is the state's preferred project for *here* versus the state's preferred project for way over *there*. How to justify this move as something more than a naked power play is the function of the second strategy.

The second strategy is to appeal to technical purity and the evils of politics: in the face of entreaties for negotiation, assert, hand over heart and eyes rolled to heaven, that the highway department is not, never has been, and cannot, no never can be, a political agency, and so must never allow itself to be involved in the unseemly and irrational business of making deals. Even if it wanted to, it is staffed by engineers and accountants, not administrators or politicians, and wouldn't know how to trade a horse to save its collective life. Of course, there is another name for a "horse trade" or a "deal." It's called "compromise." Of course, when the door is closed and the shades are drawn, that's a different story. And Fons Hathaway, unlike his predecessors, had one foot in both worlds: he was a passably good engineer, and a superlative public administrator.

The Dade and Monroe county commissions had a joint session in May to discuss Hathaway's proposed agreement. Some specific language worried the respective county attorneys. For example, the Monroe road was to be built "according to specifications of the state," while the Collier road was required to be built "as per present specifications." There was no phasing for the various segments, and both commissions wanted a specific date set for the north-south connector and the reconstruction of the old McCrary roadbed in Dade

County. Publicly, Hathaway was unmoved. He announced that while "We have no supplemental agreement to submit. We have gone as far as we can on this proposal."[35]

Governor Martin played his part when he wrote to Dr. Hathaway expressing his concern about the amount of unspent highway funds building up in the state treasury. In calendar year 1926, the road department expected to receive about $6.5 million from auto registration and $8.0 million from the state's 4-cent gas tax. As of July 1, 1926, the road department had an unallocated balance of $7.2 million. "I would suggest to you gentlemen the wisdom of letting more contracts for the spending of these," Governor Martin wrote, "as this is entirely too much to be kept as a balance in your department." If the department could not utilize the money efficiently, Martin would recommend to the legislature that its revenues be reduced. This was a gun pointed at the heads of the three counties: if they did not quickly approve the interlocal agreement, Hathaway should take his money elsewhere or *he* would risk losing it.[36]

Dade was under the most time pressure. The first contract to rehabilitate the old J. B. McCrary roadgrade, contract 669-B, had already been let to M. C. Winterburn and Company of Jacksonville, and the state department had advertised for contract 669-C, but that was now delayed pending the signing of the agreement. The Dade County Commission simply didn't trust Barron Collier, and believed that he would have Alexander, Ramsey & Kerr build their portion of the road, and then either stall on the north-south connector in Collier and Monroe or simply walk off the job without finishing it. They wanted language that specified that the two portions of the road had to be finished at the same time. Hathaway said he couldn't spend any more time negotiating. The Dade County Commission approved the agreement "in principal" with the resolution stating that it was their understanding that completion of the entire plan simultaneously was integral to the concept behind the agreement. Hathaway said that he didn't have a problem with any of the Dade commission's actions and he would take immediate steps to advertise 669-C, which it did on June 17.[37]

Monroe, which had asked the state over a year earlier to take over their part of the Trail, was the next to execute and return their agreement, in late July. On August 1st, the R. C. Huffman Construction Company was awarded 669-C, for 12 more miles of the old McCrary roadgrade in Dade. On August 6th, Alexander, Ramsey and Kerr was awarded contract 669-V for the last 31.8 miles remaining in Collier County and four days later they were awarded contract 669-X from Royal Palm Hammock to Marco Junction. All together, these contracts ended up paying almost $2.5 million, and were only the first three of six contracts let for the Miami-to-Fort Myers segment.[38]

* * * * *

One of the first forms of state aid marshaled by Dr. Hathaway and the road department to speed the construction of the Tamiami Trail were units of convict forces. As early as April 1926—a month before he had issued his two-route decree, Hathaway announced that until the counties acceded to his agreement and contracts could be let, "we will use convicts west of the Deep Lake railroad to do the surfacing [of the road]. An order has been placed for the necessary lumber to build stockades to house these convicts and as soon as these buildings can be erected a transfer of labor will be made."[39]

The use of convict labor by state highway departments was common throughout the southern states and was actually considered a progressive reform. Prior to the 1920s, it was more common for southern states to lease their prisoners to private interests. This both reduced the need for penal facilities and earned revenue for the state. The earliest customers for this "convict leasing" system were cotton plantations, but they came to be seen as undesirable clients because they needed laborers for only a few months out of the year, then wanted to return them to the government. Mines and railroads were more lucrative, but also more lethal, with mortality rates up to 20 percent per year. It was also typical for clients to return an equal proportion of their convicts so ill or broken that they could not earn a living after being released from incarceration, which promoted recidivism.[40]

In Florida, the most notorious customers for the convict leasing system were "naval stores" firms: makers of rope, oakum calking, and especially turpentine. Turpentine harvesting, as practiced in Florida in the late 18th and early 19th century, slowly killed the Longleaf pines upon which it depended. The trees were slashed with chevrons that slowly ascended the tree. If done right, a tree could live for seven or eight years before dying—but it would die. Ironically, that was just about the median life expectancy of a leased convict in most of the turpentine camps. The vast majority were blacks arrested for vagrancy or other misdemeanor crimes, then retained for years in the penal system through a series of trumped-up demerits. Other, segregated camps were comprised of whites who had similarly committed relatively minor offenses, but had attempted to escape from their initial assignment to a county prison farm, were mentally ill, combative or classified as some other type of "problem."

In 1919, Florida eliminated convict leasing in the state prison system, but it continued at the county level. It was abolished completely in 1923 after a white prisoner, Martin Tabert, was allegedly whipped to death at a private convict camp at Clara, Florida.[41] A Senate investigation revealed that many county sheriffs were taking bribes from the naval stores industry to simply continue the same practices that the state had attempted to prohibit in 1919, only using a different source of manpower. Another factor was the federal Highway Act of 1921, which offered states greatly augmented levels of federal matching funds, but at the same time required them to implement greater centralization of control over the management of those funds. The 1921 Act did not prohibit the use of convict labor as a match for federal funds, but it did require that such labor be under the direct management and control of the state highway department. Thus, from 1924 on, all Florida convict gangs (now referred to as "state forces" in official State of Florida documents) had to be under the supervision of the road department whenever they were in the field doing work.[42]

Even after the conversion to state forces, the dispersion of convicts into work camps was controversial. Security at the work camps was principally done by convict-trustees, prisoners who were given guns and the right to shoot their escaping fellows. (Shooting an escaping fellow prisoner was one of the main means by which a convict could earn a pardon; until the 1950s, Florida, like many southern states, had no parole.) On the other hand, trustees could be bribed. A report prepared in mid–1926 by the bureau of prisons found that Florida had 778 prisoners in work camps and 894 at the state farm at Raiford. So far that year, 20 prisoners had escaped from Raiford, with 10 recaptured. A total of 68 had run away from the work camps; 43 were returned. The report recommended that part of Raiford be converted from a prison farm to a full penitentiary. The work camps were a disaster waiting to happen.[43]

The Tamiami Trail convict camp was built in May 1926 a few miles south of Deep Lake grove, near Carnestown. State forces were used for three projects: 669-Z, a bridge and abutments at Carnestown for a north-south highway that would later be designated State Road 164; 669-W, the reconstruction and surfacing of the original 16-mile Lee County roadbed east of Carnestown; and for part of the work out at the east end of Collier County. The SR 164 bridge was valued at $9,924 for federal aid purposes, and the Marco-to-Carnestown reconstruction was valued at $345,600, mostly for resurfacing.[44]

A convict crew works a state highway in central Florida, about 1930. (Photograph by the Farm Security Administration. Library of Congress, No. DIG-8a35438u.)

D. Graham Copeland appeared to treat his convicts decently, probably out of enlightened self-interest. Unlike the old days, he could not send back sick, injured and broken men at will and expect to trade them in for fresh bodies. He had to make due with the forces he was given. When the reconstruction of the road from Carnestown to Royal Palm Hammock was completed on schedule and on budget in May 1927 he gave all 69 prisoners the day off and trucked them into Everglades City for a parade and picnic, followed by games and concerts.[45]

But the wolf finally came to the door after one of the hottest, wettest summers in southwest Florida history. On Monday, October 25, 1927, five convicts escaped, including Will Brown, the "Tampa Kid," serving a sentence for murder, George Coker, another lifer, and Sam Maxwell, serving 20 years. The crew was working near the Royal Palm Hammock, south of Naples. Brown, Coker and Maxwell jumped their guard, took his revolver, and using the other two convicts, both comparative short-timers, as human shields, commandeered a dump truck. It ran out of gas only a couple of miles up the road, but the dump truck driver had two other guns that they took. They used the white, civilian dump truck driver to get the driver of a car to stop, then forced the motorist to take them to Fort Myers. That car ran out of gas just short of town, and they used the same procedure to commandeer a third car and driver, who was able to get them across the Caloosahatchee River bridge. Once north of the river, the five abandoned the car, and ran into the woods, apparently in the direction of the Atlantic Coast Line Railroad bridge across the river.[46]

So many law enforcement and corrections department staff were drawn into the pursuit of the Tampa Kid and his gang that the work crews sent out the next day were badly undermanned. Eight convicts working out at the end of the grade in eastern Collier County unarmed the single guard assigned to them, and ordered the civilian dump truck driver to take them to the end of the road, where they took off overland towards Miami. There were now thirteen convicts on the lam.

However, Capt. J. H. Hansford of the corrections department, after taking roll and figuring out who comprised the new escapees, realized that they were not long-timers, nor violent criminals. He figured that after a long night in the Everglades, with every nervous survey camp and homesteader's farm ready to let loose with a shotgun anytime the dog barked, they wouldn't get far, nor would they have much starch left by morning. He simply drove into Fort Myers and took the north road to Miami, then drove out to the Huffman Company work camp at 30-mile junction where the Chevelier and Collier roads split. Sure enough, a tired, dispirited group of eight convicts, one with superficial birdshot wounds in his back, had already straggled into the Huffman camp to gave themselves up and been told that Hansford would soon be there. All they wanted to know is if they could lay down in some shade and sleep until he got there. By noon the group was back at the Carnestown stockade and Capt. Hansford was on his way back north again to Fort Myers to attend to the real problem—the smart and dangerous Tampa Kid.

Early Wednesday morning, the Tampa Kid's crew came out of their hiding place. They walked along the tracks to Tucker's Corner, 13 miles north of Fort Myers, until a gas-powered maintenance cart of the Atlantic Coast Line with two employees, Hahn and Thorne, came up from the south. The escapees forced the two railroad men to take them on north. They soon encountered a southbound "speeder" piloted by G. D. Widden, a section foreman. (A speeder was a retired interurban car fitted with a gas engine and cut away in back for tools and track material.) The five transferred to the speeder, and forced Widden to take them another twenty-five miles north to near Arcadia, where they again melted into the woods. That was the Tampa Kid's big mistake: it allowed Hahn and Thorne to return south, go over the railroad bridge and straight into downtown Fort Myers. By the time the five convicts left the speeder and entered the woods, Capt. Hansford had already fetched his car and was heading north. The DeSoto County sheriff had a bloodhound who picked up the scent at the spot where the group left the speeder. Surrounded, the three armed convicts started shooting and the sheriff's men and Hansford returned fire, killing the Tampa Kid, Coker, and Maxwell. The two misdemeanor prisoners, unarmed, hit the deck when the shooting started and were not injured.

It is commonly believed that the stockade near Carnestown evolved into the Copeland Road State Prison, but this is not true. The Tamiami Trail stockade was dismantled when construction ended in 1928 or early 1929. One of Barron Collier's businesses, the Collier County Canning Company, was located a few miles north of it, across the tracks from the Deep Lake groves. The canning company was abandoned in 1939 after the death of the Barron, and the land, about 50 acres, was donated to the state. The Copeland Road Prison was built by the Florida Department of Corrections on this site in 1951, first as a transit station for prisoners being shuttled between the east and west coasts, then as a facility for level-two (medium security) prisoners. Once again, it became a base for work crews sent out during the day to remove litter and maintain landscaping on state and county roads. It held an average population of 68 prisoners. It was closed due to high costs in 2002. It fell into disrepair and in 2012 it was acquired by a private firm and rebuilt. It is now used to provide specialized training for law enforcement agencies, industrial security departments, and protection service contractors.[47]

••12••

As for Business, There Hasn't Been Any

The 1925–26 tourist season was unexpectedly slow in Miami. By March, several of the prestigious Miami Beach resorts, and all of the middle-class hotels, had rooms available, something unheard of in previous years. In January 1926 the *Prince Valdemar*, a 240-foot retired Danish naval sailing ship that was being towed to Miami for remodeling as a floating hotel, snagged on a sandbar at the entrance to the port channel. It would have been a minor incident, except its ballast had already been removed and the tide started to run out at the same time the afternoon's usual seabreeze started to kick up towards shore, catching the ship's rigging. Together, they caused the snagged, top-heavy ship to heel over until its masts touched the water. It sank in an hour, blocking the only way in or out of the port for a month. Port Jacksonville was already overloaded, and in September 1925 the Florida East Coast reported its inadequate Miami yards and sidings (the money had all gone into building and maintaining the overseas railway to Key West) were stuffed with 2,200 rail cars waiting to be unloaded, many holding building supplies and construction equipment. Midyear building permits in both the City of Miami and Miami Beach were only running at half the previous year's rate.[1]

In July 1926 Miami's Bank of Little River failed, a victim of bad real estate loans, mostly to insiders. The bank was part of the "Manley-Anthony System," actually a consortium of two bank holding companies, the Bankers Financing Company of Jacksonville, owned by J. R. Anthony, and the Bankers Trust Company of Atlanta, owned by W. D. Manley. The two owned a dozen or so banks, but controlled nearly 200 others by acting as a regional check clearinghouse and deposit insurance company that allowed locally-owned banks to maintain cash reserves smaller than would be needed if they were acting independently, and was cheaper than joining the federal reserve.[2]

In February 1926 Addison and Wilson Mizner, the developers of Boca Raton in Palm Beach County, bought the Palm Beach National Bank from Howard Smith and D. Lester Williams, who in turn were partners with J. R. Anthony in another local bank, the Palm Beach Bank and Trust Company. Palm Beach Bank and Trust should have been in good shape. As of February 1926, its deposits had increased two-and-a-half-times since September 1925. But the Mizner Development Corporation was functionally insolvent, in spite of pre-selling over 1,100 home lots. The Mizner brothers' main partner, Coleman DuPont, had pulled out, and Wilson Mizner, a compulsive gambler, was skimming funds. The Mizners started to rapidly withdraw money from their new acquisition in the form of loans collateralized with promissory notes from the valueless Development Corporation. Within two months they had received loans worth 200 percent of the bank's net worth. When Palm Beach Bank and Trust ran out of lending capacity, the Mizners used it as a straw borrower to loan almost $400,000 from at least six other Palm Beach County banks, all controlled or influenced by Manley and Anthony. The money was passed through to the Mizner Development Corporation.

On June 21, in court testimony in Palm Beach related to a dispute over the ownership of some Mizner Development Corporation stock, a disgruntled stockholder asserted that the firm had long been insolvent and was being run as a Ponzi scheme, propped up through the sales of building lots the firm had no way of developing and with bank loans it could not possibly repay. On Monday, June 28, the Commercial Bank and Trust Company, one of the big lenders to the Mizners' bank, did not open for business. The next day, Palm Beach Bank and Trust itself failed. A bank run ensued on every Manley-Anthony bank in Georgia, and within two weeks, 83 banks—twenty percent of the Georgia banking system—was shuttered. Twenty-seven Florida banks, 25 in the Bankers Trust System, also closed.[3]

Farther south, in Broward County, Joseph Young's "Hollywood-by-the-Sea" had become the fastest growing city in Florida by 1925. Suffering from high property taxes and low budgets, both of James Ingraham's original settler communities, Hallandale, to the south, and Dania, to the north, saw the rapidly growing city as the solution to their problems, and both agreed to be into annexed into Hollywood in December 1925 (Dania) and January 1926 (Hallandale). But by the summer of 1926, Young was forced to close most of his sales offices up north due to poor sales. His associates advised him to temporarily abandon his latest project, Hollywood Hills, a two square mile addition to the city, located inland of the original two sections. Young refused; the Hollywood Hills Inn was already completed, and the first few homes had already been built, so he claimed it made no sense to stop laying streets and sidewalks. (The Hollywood Hills Inn never opened; it later became the Riverside Military Academy.)[4]

On July 27, a tropical storm (probably a Category 1 hurricane by today's Saffir-Simpson Scale) hit Palm Beach County. Moving in from the southeast, the storm only brushed Miami and Ft. Lauderdale, but caused extensive damage between Pompano and Jupiter. Forty boats moored in Lake Worth were sunk, and the causeway over the lake was washed away. The roofs of many homes were lost. The great Flagler Hotels, the Royal Poinciana and the Breakers, both of wood frame construction (the Royal Poinciana was reportedly the largest wood-frame building in the world) suffered damage, but their managers announced that they would be able to open as scheduled in December.[5]

Fort Myers reported only stiff breezes and thunderstorms, but the squally weather claimed two victims from the Tamiami Trail work crews when lightning struck a metal shed holding half a ton of dynamite at a storage depot near Naples. The two men, truck driver Claude Hare and assistant Robert Shaver, were employees of the Prichard Hauling Company. They had pulled their truck into a car barn at a camp maintained by the Harty Construction Company. The garage was the closest building to the explosives shed, about a hundred feet away. It was destroyed along with several other buildings, including the mess hall and superintendent's home, both about 250 feet from ground zero, but Hare and Shaver were the only fatalities. Keep in mind that a thousand pounds of dynamite was the average used on a single sizeable roadway shot—50 holes, eighteen feet wide and sixty feet long. Moving around and storing the thousands and thousands of pounds of dynamite (by one estimate, 3.5 million sticks total) was a logistical nightmare. There were two to three shots a day on both sides of the Trail, but in an accident, the dynamite used in just one shot could do catastrophic damage, so no more than a half-ton could be kept or carried in one place at one time.[6]

On September 15, 1926, the Miami newspapers reported that three tropical storms lurked offshore. Storm warnings were issued at 11:00 a.m. on the 17th. The hurricane hit twelve hours later. The eye passed over downtown Miami at approximately 6:45 a.m. The anemometer atop the Alison Hospital on Miami Beach peaked out at 132 mph at about 7:15 a.m. (Today, this would be considered a Category 4 hurricane.) Damage was especially heavy between downtown Miami and Dania, thirty miles north.[7]

By the 21st, there were 114 confirmed dead in the Miami-Miami Beach area, 56 in Hollywood-Dania and 26 in Fort Lauderdale. It took a week to learn that another 300 died—mostly black agricultural workers from the Bahamas and Jamaica—in the towns along the south rim of Lake Okeechobee when the pitiful marl dyke gave way and water rose from ankle-deep to head-high in a minute or so.

About a third of Everglades City and most of the lower-lying Port Dupont, a mile further up the river, were flooded. Several of the oldest buildings in Everglades City—little more than sheds—were ruined, but the Rod and Gun Club and the new bank building survived intact. Everything, however, was covered in a coat of grayish marl mud. Irving Holmes of the Collier Company reported only minimal damage to the Tamiami Trail. "I drove out over the Trail," he reported the next day, "and no damage has been done to the grade, and none to the newly constructed bridges. Some of the bridges on the older part of the grade had their side rails blown down, but are now repaired." Everglades City, Carnestown and Deep Lake looked terrible "but actual damage is comparatively light."[8]

The Flamingo Hotel, pride of Miami Beach, was rebuilt in time for the winter 1926-27 season, but manager Charles Krom wrote developer Carl Fisher in January that "It will be two weeks tomorrow since the Flamingo opened and as far as business is concerned, there just hasn't been any."[9] The effects rippled all the way to Spencer, Iowa. On Sunday, November 7, J. H. McCord (Franklin Floete died in 1922) put his head cashier on the train to ask the Federal Reserve Bank of Chicago for a $50,000 loan for the Citizen's National Bank. McCord gave the cashier an envelope and instructed him to turn in the letter if the loan was denied.[10]

The day before, on Saturday, McCord had telephoned his counterpart at the First National Bank of Spencer. His bank was short was cash to open on Monday, McCord said, but was expecting a shipment from its clearinghouse, the Chicago Mercantile National Bank on Monday. Could he borrow $4,000? It was a common enough request, and the president of the First National readily agreed, but explained they had already closed the time-locked vault. It couldn't be opened until 9:00 a.m. Monday. He should call back then if he still needed the currency.

McCord did call back on Monday, and an assistant cashier from the Citizens National Bank came and collected the $4,000, leaving off a check in the same amount from the Chicago Mercantile Bank. At about this time, McCord's head cashier was meeting with the Chicago Federal Reserve. McCord's bank was already below its reserve requirement—the amount of cash or gold required to be on deposit at the fed, between five and ten percent of customer deposits. The loan was denied. The head cashier handed the fed's representative the letter McCord had given him. It said that the Citizens National Bank of Spencer was now insolvent and that the fed should send a receiver to accompany the head cashier on his return trip to Spencer to reorganize the bank.

The Citizens National Bank did not open on the morning of Tuesday, November 10. It had only $4,400 on hand. The check given to the First National Bank bounced. Believing they had been defrauded, they sued and tried to have the bank liquidated, not reorganized. But because Spencer had only two banks, the Citizens National Bank was, relatively speaking, too big to fail, so it was reorganized and sold, and McCord escaped criminal prosecution. He did, however lose his Chevelier Corporation bonds. "The Hopkins estate still have $200,000 of the bonds and McCord had $100,000," Judge McDougal told his daughter in 1934, "but most of them I think were scattered out among his creditors, at a time when they were still supposed to have some value."[11]

That didn't keep Judge McDougal from trying to use the bonds to secure a "large" loan at the Security State Bank of Ponca City, Oklahoma, a month after the Iowa bank collapsed. The Oklahoma bank cabled the Southern Bank in Miami to ask about the solvency of the Chevelier Corporation. The Southern Bank passed the buck by claiming that it was a Gulf coast venture over about which they had no real knowledge. They forwarded the cable on to Jaudon. "I would certainly consider these bonds gilt edge security," replied Jaudon. At this point, the corporation had not had a directors' meeting in six months and nobody really knew what it was worth.[12]

The period between July 1926, when McCord's bank failed, and January 1927, when Jaudon submitted a one-page letter in lieu of an annual report, marks the time when the Chevelier Corporation fell apart. Each of the directors started to pursue their own interests. McCord wanted to stay out of jail; McDougal and his daughter and son-in-law started to make their own deals for the Hopkins land; the Cooks were looking to milk as much construction money out of the firm as they could on the Chevelier road, and, Jaudon started over again with his Collier County real estate venture.[13]

The land speculation that had driven the south Florida economy for over a decade ended. The great market bubble that jazzed the nation during 1927–29 passed right over south Florida. For all practical purposes, the Great Depression started in Florida two years early, in October 1926, and with a slow deflation, not a great crash. While Carl Fisher's hotels were back to profitability by 1928, this was made possible only by raising rates on the least profitable meal plans and cutting costs. Between 1925 and 1929, regional bank deposits fell 75 percent; building permits declined 90 percent.

By mid–1927, both Dania and Hallandale had de-annexed themselves from Joseph Young's Hollywood. Young himself simply disappeared one day in 1928, leaving behind a large home on Hollywood Boulevard and a five-acre beachfront lot upon which he had planned to build a retirement estate. (It became, after much wrangling, a city park.) He also left behind an unpaid bill for almost a million dollars to the Cleveland company, the Highway Construction Company, that had built all the streets and sidewalks in Hollywood Hills. The Highway Construction Company sued to foreclose on 25,000 building lots, only to discover they were all mortgaged to the Mercantile Investment Company of New York. In an inspired move, the two firms merged and formed a new company, Hollywood, Inc., that took over the Young holdings. It developed these properties into the 1990s, but only after the Hollywood Hills subdivision sat ignored, a vast expanse of silent streets and empty foundation slabs, until after World War II.[14]

F. Irving Holmes, a Lee County banker involved with the construction of the Trail from its earliest days, later recalled that the Gulf coast road project was probably the most *unaffected* project in the state:

> The trail organization was the least disturbed of any of our organizations by the hysteria that sent the whole state clean crazy during the "boom." Men on other jobs quit wholesale, lured wholesale by the prospect of easy money in real estate or by unheard-of wages in the new "profession" of clearing and staking out subdivisions—wages away beyond the limit of our enterprise, or any other legitimate one.[15]

Those jobs now began drying up. Before, it had been almost impossible to get enough men to fill all the needed positions, especially for skilled labor, such as heavy equipment operators and mechanics, and to keep them for more than one or two rotations. Now they signed up in droves and Otto Neal could report that each crew "consists entirely of picked men of proven worth."[16]

Neal now had 150 men on the job. Once Alexander Ramsey & Kerr had been awarded the state contract to build the Trail from Carnestown to the Dade County line, Graham Copeland called Neal and his other foremen into his office. This was September 1926, and by this time, the Collier crews had already progressed nearly five miles beyond where they had been in April, when Fons Hathaway decided to take over the project. Ten miles remained to the Dade line. Copeland said that Neal's men "had" to make it to Dade by April 1, 1927. Neal said he could do it if Copeland would give him another Bay City walking dredge. "Within a month we had another 'walker' in operation," Neal recalled. "I don't know how long it took him to get the giant down here but we erected it and had it at work within ten days after arrival." A photograph taken about this time also shows a Bay City crawler and two walkers working together.[17]

Neal almost made Copeland's deadline, arriving at the Dade line on April 10. This was far from the completion of work, however. In fact, Copeland's stock of heavy equipment

A Bay City crawler (front) and two Bay City walking dredges at work on the far east end of the Jenkins alignment, near the Collier-Dade line, late 1927. (Photographer unknown. Florida Division of Library and Information Services, No. PR01994.)

continued to increase throughout 1927. Charles Washburn, Graham Copland's assistant supervising engineer, reported that in January 1927, Alexander, Ramsey & Kerr was using $187,000 in heavy equipment. By January 1928 this had increased to $250,000. Most of the new equipment was trucks, scrapers, graders and other surfacing equipment. As the quality and length of the grade increased, Neal was able to replace oxen with White heavy trucks, relieving him of one of his biggest headaches. The average useful life of an ox on the job had been two weeks. They were gone by April 1927.[18]

Similarly, a hundred men and $250,000 in equipment were at work on the 20 miles of the Trail being rebuilt in Dade County. The Winterburn Company of Jacksonville had won the first contract, 669-B, back in 1925, for rebuilding the first ten miles of the Trail. That contract cost $300,000 and was finished in late 1926. The next twelve miles to the west, contract 669-C, had been awarded in October 1926 to the R. C. Huffman Construction Company. They also submitted the winning bid for the next ten miles west of that, awarded in January 1927.[19]

By spring 1927 Huffman Construction had a hundred men, two floating dredges, two dipper dredges, two steam shovels, two dragline steamshovels, a drill barge, and various caterpillar tractors, trucks, earth scrapers and rollers. Road department photographs of the Dade County work show that Huffman essentially ignored the previous McCrary Company work and simply built a new road over the old one. The original bridges and culverts were torn out and replaced with newer, bigger ones. In the places where the old road grade remained somewhat intact, it was used as a service road for dump trucks and caterpillar bulldozers and tractors. In most cases, however, by the time the surfacing crews were finished, nothing remained of the old road grade—it was incorporated into the base of the new one.[20]

It was the application of state-federal money that turned the corner on the Tamiami Trail. For all practical purposes, it is the story of two roads: one built, sort of, during the era of county and local financing, and the final product constructed during the era of federal and state financing.

To qualify for federal funding, a road had to be built to a uniform set of state-federal standards developed by the American Association of State Highway Officials (AASHO).[21] As state officials in Florida discovered, particularly on the Dixie Highway, building to AASHO standards could run as much as $30,000 per mile. In 1916, the total revenue collected by the State of Florida for roadbuilding was $30,246. All of this came from license tag fees, as there was no gasoline tax. Of this, only $13,375 was disbursed. The first year that Florida received any federal funding was 1918, when total revenues, including the federal match, were $475,390.[22]

In 1921, the state initiated a one cent per gallon gas tax to augment the license tag fee. For the first time the money coming from Tallahassee began to rival that spent by the larger urban counties. The state collected $2.2 million in 1921, $3.6 million in 1922 and $4.6 million in 1923. Realizing that a sizeable portion of its gas tax was being paid by wintertime snowbirds, the legislature increased the gas tax to three cents in 1924 and four cents in 1925. In 1925, the first year that the state began to issue contracts on State Road 5, the road department collected $10.4 million, and the following year, when it added State Road 27 to the Miller Bill list of preferential roads, collections ran to $15.9 million, of which the gas tax alone accounted for $11.5 million. Gas tax and tag fees totaled $18.4 million, of which about $5.6 million was transferred directly to the counties and to state agencies other than the road department.

In addition to money raised in-state, the road department received about $5.6 million in federal highway aid. By 1927, after the gas tax had been raised to five cents (with one cent dedicated to the state board of education), gas tax revenues accounted for half of the state's $39.9 million annual income. The road department was the largest agency in the state, both in terms of its budget and number of employees.[23]

The 1921 federal highway act required each state to develop a system of state highways. Georgia, for example, designated a state plan of 5,500 miles of highways. Florida formally adopted its first state road system in 1923.[24] But while Florida's so-called "first system" contained over 1,500 miles, the 1923 Miller Bill restricted the use of state-federal aid to just five roads of about 850 miles. Only one of these, State Road 4, the eastern division of the Dixie Highway, extended south of Lake Okeechobee. The Miller Bill proved to be a lifesaver when the costs of building the Dixie Highway through the sand hills and mangrove estuaries of the east coast escalated beyond anyone's estimate. Nobody dreamed that a highway could cost $30,000 a mile, as the Dixie Highway did in south Palm Beach, Broward and north Dade counties. Had the Miller Bill not restricted expenditures to the five priority highways, it is very likely that the statewide clamor for funds, at a time when revenues were not yet large and the quality standards of Bureau of Public Roads Chief Thomas McDonald not yet universally enforced, would have either scuttled the Dixie Highway or resulted in a substandard, non-federally qualifying road.

By the time the initial Miller Bill roads were substantially finished in 1926, Florida's state highway fund was 530 times larger than it was when the Tamiami Trail commenced in 1916. An engineer could propose spending twenty or thirty thousand dollars a mile for a road without being considered some kind of crank. The state had taken over from the counties as the lead agency for highway development in the state, and it was being run by

Dredge (rear), drill barge (middle) and service boat of the R. C. Huffman Construction Company finishing the Tamiami Trail in Dade, thirty miles west of Miami, 1927. (Photograph by Smiley Nixon. Florida Division of Library and Information Services, No. RC13118.)

a professional administrator, Dr. Fons Hathaway, who was cut from the same mold as Bureau of Public Roads Chief Thomas McDonald. In short, up to 1926 it would have been simply inconceivable to propose building something like State Road 27, a 147-mile highway from Fort Myers to Miami that half a dozen parties had already taken a crack at and failed, let alone admit that finishing the job would require another three years and seven million dollars.

Considering the era, the final figures were nothing short of stupefying. In Collier County, the state road department spent a total of $2,469,145 between 1926 and the completion of work in 1928. Of this, $890,507 was spent on the coastal stretch between the Lee County line and Marco Junction, and $1,578,638 was spent on the east-west portion between Marco Junction and the Dade County line. The Marco-to-Dade stretch was 48.1 miles, an average of $32,820 per mile. The segment from Carnestown to the Dade line ran just under $38,000 per mile. The road department claimed that one twelve-mile segment (probably near Carnestown) cost $55,000 per mile.[25] Keep in mind that this was for a roadbed that Lee and Collier counties and the Collier Company had already been working over for a decade. In Dade, the 10-mile long contract to the Winterburn firm and the two contracts to the Huffman Construction Company, totaling 22 miles, ran to an aggregate of $2,290,983. This, of course, was after Dade County itself had already paid $291,000 to the J. B. McCrary Company. The state and county also spent $160,000 on roadwork in Dade County, to which the cities of Miami and Coral Gables also contributed.[26]

* * * * *

On January 26, 1927, the last contract was awarded for the Dade County part of the trail. Although it was not the low bidder, the R. C. Huffman Company was awarded the contract for the last twelve miles at a price of $2.16 per cubic yard for a state-estimated 153,985 cubic yards, a total price of $332,607. This contract, No. 669-D, was later to become very controversial. Chairman Hathaway explained that he had rejected the lower bid of the T. T. Sweet Dredging Company ($1.90 per cubic yard), not because there was anything wrong with the Sweet firm, but because Huffman was already at work on the next twelve miles to the east (Project 669-C). Awarding the contract to Sweet would have meant either delaying the start of 669-D until after 669-C was finished, or having Sweet move their equipment and supply trucks through the middle of Huffman's construction zone. A second point of controversy was that Huffman had won the contract for the earlier Project 669-C with a low bid of $0.825 per cubic yard, less than half of its bid on 669-D. Hathaway's explanation was that the cost of work at the farther end of the Trail was proportionally more expensive than it was ten or twenty miles closer to Miami. In addition, the J. B. McCrary Company had left the far end of the road grade in much poorer condition than the eastern two-thirds. But the most controversial part of the contract was the cost over-runs that resulted. Instead of 156,000 cubic yards having to be moved, the road work required over 506,000 cubic yards, inflating the contract to $1,093,111. Again, Hathaway explained that McCrary had left the western end of the road grade in such poor shape that it had not been possible for his men to get an accurate estimate on the size of the job. In fact, it appears that at least some of this excess yardage was generated because Hathaway sent the Huffman firm into Monroe County to help the Chevelier Corp. finish on time.[27]

In 1927 Hathaway expected to spend somewhere between 16 and 18 million dollars. He was spending money so fast that not only did he burn through the $4.7 million in reserves the department had built up by the end of 1926, but he told the department's board in October 1927 that the road department was two million dollars short of what it needed to get it through the end of the year and would have to borrow funds, a move the state's supreme court rejected a month later as unconstitutional. Hathaway simply deferred payments due to contractors until after January 1, 1928. But both gas tax and license plate revenues had gone flat; by mid-1928 income from each was almost a million dollars below budget.[28]

Hathaway was no doubt feeling pressure from both the residents and political leaders in Lee, Collier and Dade counties to get the road done as quickly as possible, but he also had his own reasons for putting speed ahead of economy. In the fall of 1927 he decided to run for governor, using his largesse at the state road department in and with the Tamiami Trail counties in particular as a springboard to elected office. The all-important Democratic Party primary was scheduled for the first Tuesday in June. The ribbon-cutting would be his grand parade.

When Otto Neal's men crossed over from Collier to Dade in April 1927, Neal asked Graham Copeland what he should do. Copeland told him to keep going, but to send one of the three dredges and a crew back west eight miles to where the north-south connector was staked out and start working south to link up with the Chevelier road. Neal asked if they had a contract to do road work in Dade. Copeland told him not to worry about it. In fact, Alexander, Ramsey & Kerr had no contract from the state to either do any work in Dade or to build the north-south connector. Apparently they never sought any. The log of state contracts never lists a Dade County contract for the connector, and there is no project inspection and billing forms among the Project 669 records for the four miles of road in Collier County. It appears that Barron Collier paid for both.[29]

Erben Cook and his crew from the Chevelier Corp. reached the place on the Monroe-Collier line where they were supposed to meet Copeland and Neal's crews the previous November, but the road they had built was little more than a trail, so after a brief celebration, they turned their equipment back south and started upgrading the road. Cook and his crew did have a bit of comic relief later that winter when up roared a mechanical creature appearing, for all the world, like a cross between a birdcage and a mud-monster. It was J. W. H. Campbell of Jacksonville on his modified Indian motorcycle, trying to duplicate the Tamiami Trailblazers old route. To avoid getting stuck, he carried several rolls of lightweight wire mesh, which he placed on the ground, taking up the hindmost sheet and putting it down in front as he advanced. He had no trouble following the old 1923 route: the swath cut through the pines by Erben Cook and the Trailblazers still clearly showed. He hoped to make it in a week, but as he pulled up at Cook's Pinecrest work camp he was already into day eleven. One day, he had been able to make only 4,200 feet. Reinforced with food, water, and (probably) a shot or two of courage, he roared off. He made it into Miami on day fourteen—the first to cross the Everglades on a motorcycle.[30]

The 6,000-foot wooden bridge across the Caloosahatchee River at Fort Myers started by the Caloosahatchee River Bridge Company and finished by Lee County was already inadequate, even for a traffic load of only about 1,350 cars per day. Both the population of Fort Myers and the number of households with cars was rapidly increasing. Hathaway promised Governor John Martin that he would finish the Trail "as long as the state treasury held out," and in January 1927 he promised Lee County officials (and, more privately, Barron Collier) that the state road department would pay for a new ferro-concrete bridge at Fort Myers. Even as Hathaway's opponent in the Democratic primary, a bright young Tampa lawyer with a degree from the University of Chicago named Doyle Carlton, kept pounding away on the campaign trail about discrepancies and cost over-runs in road department contracts, the bridge contract was let literally on the eve of the election, a little more

At 30-mile junction, looking west. The Jenkins alignment through Collier County turns to the right, while the Chevelier Road through Monroe County continues straight. Alexander, Ramsey & Kerr's ubiquitous mobile bunkhouses can be seen at the start of the Jenkins alignment. January or February 1928. (Photographer unknown [state road commission]. Collier County Museum, Naples, FL, No. 78.19.23.)

than a month after the Trail's official opening. Despite being touted as the Tamiami Trail's second "million dollar bridge" (the 5,300-foot Manatee River in Bradenton bridge had cost a little over $900,000), the Central Station Equipment Company of Miami submitted a winning bid of $532,015. Work started in August and what was almost immediately named the Edison Memorial Bridge was finished in 1931, three years after the Trail was officially opened.[31]

On December 6, the last gap in the road grade was closed. Although some stretches hadn't received their final surface coating yet, and some bridges were still temporary, the entire Tamiami Trail was passable from Tampa to Miami. In early February, Alexander, Ramsey & Kerr opened the Trail from Naples to the Royal Palm Hammock, about twelve miles past Marco Junction. In January, the Huffman Company completed the Dade County road to the 30-mile junction between the Chevelier road and the Collier route. Huffman's crew continued due west to link up with the Chevelier road; Alexander, Ramsey & Kerr's men continued surfacing the four-and-a-half mile diagonal in Dade County. Both crews reported that they were having to install an average of two bridges per mile. Much of the work over the last three months in the west Dade/east Collier zone involved the removal of temporary wooden bridges and their replacement with concrete spans. The last contracts were all for bridge work.[32]

The opening day was rumored to be May 1. On the afternoon of February 7, Hathaway met with Barron Collier and the representatives of all the contractors at the Rod and Gun Club in Everglades City. It was the consensus that the road would be finished on April 15. Hathaway added ten days for contingencies and announced to the press after the conclusion of the conference that the official opening of the Tamiami Trail would be on April 25. Until that day only official and construction traffic would be permitted, the only exceptions being the Naples-to-Royal Palm Hammock section that Alexander, Ramsey & Kerr had opened so they could use the old grade as a construction road for railroad and bridge work along Allen's river between Everglades City and Carnestown, and those in-town portions of the road in Miami that had been open for months. The last stretch of road to be completed was Chevelier's road in Monroe. It looked for awhile like Erben Cook wouldn't make it, but with much of Huffman's equipment and men assisting them, they finished on April 23, two days before the opening. It hardly mattered—the Chevelier road was completely ignored during the entire three-day motorcade that opened the highway and for much of the next fifty years.[33]

* * * * *

The grand opening was Barron Collier's show, and Collier, paying back his debts, shared the limelight with both the gubernatorial candidate and current Governor Martin. Collier chartered three busses just to carry the 14 newsreel and movietone cameramen and the 22 newspaper correspondents and photographers from around the country. Canned stories were churned out by the mile. Generally, it was a time to bury old grudges. Captain Jaudon was given his due as one of the originators of the Trail, along with Judge Wilkinson of Naples, Francis Perry of Fort Myers and Old Captain Collier of Marco Island. Given Captain Jaudon and John King's original 1915 expedition across the state, this made explaining the uniqueness of the Tamiami Trailblazers' 1923 expedition somewhat awkward, but their trip was artfully re-cast as an effort to stimulate interest in the Caloosahatchee River bridge at a time when Lee and Charlotte could not agree on a division of the costs, which seemed to make everyone happy. Of course, it *was* stretching the truth a bit, in that the bridge was originally a private venture and the question of who was to pay for it did not become an issue until the Bureau of Public Roads said that the state could not give highway funds to a private company, so it would have to take it over. That was six months *after* the 1923 expedition.[34]

Between 150 and 250 cars assembled in Tampa on Wednesday morning, April 25, and started down the Trail. At the "million dollar bridge" across the Manatee River, Barron Collier left the comfort of his yacht, the Baroness, and joined the procession. After a brief stop in Bradenton, the motorcade rolled into Sarasota, where a fish fry was held for lunch. After brief stops in Venice and Punta Gorda (Charlotte Harbor), the motorcade rolled into Fort Myers for the evening at about 5:30. Breakdowns were surprisingly light; despite the pre-staged service vehicles, the only calamities were four flat tires.[35]

Most of the participants pitched tents at the fairgrounds, where the cars were parked. Several new trailblazers joined the next morning for the feature event. Depending on the newspaper, estimates say between 400 and 600 cars left Fort Myers for the cross-Everglades stretch. The main stop, of course, was at Everglades City, where the first annual Collier County fair was underway. "Mr. Collier poured out a stream of gold to create the fair but admitted after the visit of the motorcade that the project paid for itself in one day although there was no admittance change," noted one reporter. "The dividend, Mr. Collier said, came in the form of new laurels for Everglades City and Collier County."[36]

The procession pulled into Miami on Thursday evening, where the final round of speeches, fireworks and food was rolled in Bayfront Park. James Jaudon finally had his turn in the spotlight, opening the evening's program with a talk on "The Early History of the Tamiami Trail." Barron Collier, Fons Hathaway, and the by-now deified Tamiami Trailblazers were, of course, the closers. After an organizational conference the next day to re-orient the Tamiami Trail Association into an advocacy organization for the beautification of the Trail and the elimination of billboards (many of the old-timers participated; neither Collier nor Hathaway did), everyone left for their scattered hometowns around the state.[37]

Once everyone was home, the next order of business was the June 3 Democratic primary election. This was, of course, the *de facto* general election. Fons Hathaway's opponents were Doyle Carlton, the young lawyer from Tampa, and former governor Sidney Catts, the "Cracker Messiah," a lawyer turned fundamentalist preacher who had run the state between

Barron Collier greets Seminole leader Josie Billie and his extended family at the grand opening ceremonies for the Tamiami Trail, Everglades City, April 26, 1928. (Photographer unknown. Florida Division of Library and Information Services, No. RC01673.)

1917 and 1921 like a non-stop tent revival before being term-limited out. A cross between Huey Long, William Jennings Bryan and Sinclair Lewis, he was adored by rural poor whites and feared and hated by the urban middle-class and the chamber of commerce crowd. To this day it is debated whether he was a political genius or crazy.

Unfortunately, Hathaway was more a technocrat than one of the new generation of young, smooth, well groomed Southern urban politicians. Having taken the state road department from a sleepy back-office bureau to one that processed almost half of the state's total budget, there were bound to be individual projects that had gone awry, blown their budgets, or had paperwork gaffs.[38] The truth was, several of the Tamiami Trail contracts had gone over budget because Governor Martin and Hathaway wanted the road finished in time for this election. The fact that the road department wanted to borrow two million dollars in October 1927 after collecting $6.4 million in gas tax revenues in just the six months between January and June 1927 gave several newspaper editors reason to pause, especially after the department had reported a reserve balance of $4.6 million at the end of 1926. The award of the final contract on the west end of the Trail to the Huffman Company instead of the T. T. Sweet company, even though Sweet had significantly underbid Huffman, was brought up several times.[39]

The east coast newspapers were generally against Hathaway. Starting the day after the Tamiami Trail motorcade participants left town, the *Miami Daily News-Metropolis* ran almost daily articles featuring cost over-runs and what it claimed were bidding irregularities.[40] The *Miami Herald*, not really wanting to be on the same side as its competitor, but not enthusiastic about Hathaway either, vacillated back-and-forth between Hathaway and Catts. The Ft. Lauderdale newspapers, angry that the state road department had not acquired the private bridge over the New River and relieved it citizens of what were felt to be onerous and unfair tolls, advocated Carlton. The Gulf coast papers, of course, still looking to get work started on the replacement Fort Myers bridge and bids issued on the Punta Gorda bridge in Charlotte Harbor, were madly for Hathaway. In a tight three-way race in which Catts proved to be the spoiler, Doyle Carleton won by about 10,000 votes.[41]

Despite the flowery speeches in Everglades City and Bayfront Park, the Tamiami Trail was from far from a finished product. In Lee County, south of Fort Myers, the sand road had to be dragged almost daily in the wet season. To the fury of its Chamber of Commerce, auto clubs on the east coast still warned travelers headed to Tampa to take emergency equipment such as a shovel, rope and traction blanket, or to take the established route along Conners Highway from West Palm Beach to the north shore of Lake Okeechobee, then due west to Arcadia and Sarasota. As Doyle Carleton spent the fall at his Tampa law office, passing the interminable delay until the formalities of the November general election were over and the January inauguration rolled around, his whole political world changed.[42]

On September 16, Palm Beach suffered its third hurricane in two years. This one was different from the storm of September 1926, however. It crossed the coastline well north of the city, then swung south, towards Lake Okeechobee. The new levees built after the 1926 hurricane burst, sending a wall of water over Moore Haven, Clewiston, South Bay, and Belle Glade. These were agricultural towns, filled with sugar cane workers, almost all of them of African descent, many from the Caribbean. They had been told by their employers that everything would be fine; they should stay at home with their families, the storm was not a major one. A death count of 1,500 was confirmed within a week. It is believed that about 1,800 to 2,000 ultimately died, mostly by drowning. The most urgent needs were for kerosene and dry wood to burn the bodies; all the destroyed buildings that were still above water had been dismantled for their lumber and there still wasn't enough wood to feed the pyres.[43]

Four weeks later, the stock market tanked, heralding the start of the Great Depression. Carl Fisher, the developer of Miami Beach, later said that he started keeping less than $2,000 in Miami because he believed that every bank in Dade County was on the brink of collapse. In March 1931, the Bank of Bay Biscayne, the late Henry Flagler's own bank, founded to service his Florida East Coast railroad empire, failed. The railroad itself went bankrupt two months later.[44]

After the Lake Okeechobee hurricane, with a month left in office, Hathaway was still promising Gulf Coast residents that he would accelerate the letting of bids for the remaining work needed to finish up the Tamiami Trail. In November 1928 he awarded a $1,200,000 contract to the Central Station and Equipment Company, the same firm building the Caloosahatchee River Bridge in Fort Myers, to erect the Punta Gorda span across the Peace River in Charlotte Harbor. Soon after, he awarded the reconstruction of the Naples-area highway to the W. P. McDonald Construction Company.[45]

Barron Collier added his own dash of color to the Trail in the winter of 1928–29. Two of the problems that had not been foreseen were an unusually a high accident rate along the Trail, and a lack of service stations. The Collier Development Company built six patrol stations at ten to twelve mile intervals, the most easterly a few miles from the Dade County line and the most westerly near Marco Junction. Each was two stories high, about 13 feet by 24 feet, with a covered stairway in back and a large canopy in front. Each was staffed by a couple, who ran a service station on the ground floor and lived upstairs. In addition, the husband served as a motorcycle patrolman in what was called the Southwest Mounted Police, technically a division of the Collier County Sheriff's Office. Each patrolman was to monitor his ten-mile stretch of road, cite those who sped over the Trail's 45 mph speed limit, prevent liquor trafficking with the Seminoles, and provide aid or, if necessary, summon additional assistance as needed.[46]

Lillian Weaver, who, with her husband William, staffed Monroe Station at Monroe Junction, the place where the Jenkins and Chevelier roads split in mid–Collier County, later gave an interview to a National Park Service historian who used it to provide a description of the facility:

> The station had two rooms and two restrooms with a small storage room downstairs. One of the rooms contained a counter and merchandise shelving, and the other acted as a sort of vestibule for the rest rooms, which unlike later in Monroe Station's history, opened on the inside. The apartment on the upper level was also divided into two major spaces—a bedroom and living/dining room with an associated bath and small kitchen. Physical evidence suggests the level was divided in half, with the living/dining/kitchen functions on the western half and the bedroom/bath on the eastern. A Fairbanks-Morse home electric plant pumped the water and as noted by Lillian Weaver, "furnished our lights by direct current." … With indoor plumbing, sewerage and electricity, Monroe Station was an entirely up-to-date building: within the Weavers' period of occupancy (1929–32) they even had the luxury of a telephone.[47]

The Weavers were the second occupants of Monroe Station. The first patrolman, William Irwin, was killed in January 1929 when he ran head-on into a car at night, after either striking or attempting to dodge an animal in the road. Irwin had been on the job

Monroe Station on the Tamiami Trail, 1930. A gas station, store and restrooms downstairs, with a two-room apartment upstairs for the couple hired by the Collier Company to operate the station. The husband patrolled a ten-mile stretch of the Trail on a motorcycle in addition to helping with the gas station. He was deputized to issue tickets and make arrests, but more often acted as a "road ranger," watching for breakdowns or accidents. The injury and fatality rate for patrolmen was extremely high, especially at night. There were six such stations between Marco Junction and the Dade line. Monroe Station was the middle station, located at the west junction of the Jenkins alignment and the Chevelier Road. By the late 1930s, as the county and state took over traffic enforcement duties, the Collier Company sold the stations, most to their operators. Monroe Station still stands, empty but mothballed by the National Park Service. (Photographer unknown. Collier County Museum, Naples, FL, No. 88.42.48.)

less than three months. Incredibly, Irwin was the second patrolman to lose his life. W. B. Richardson died in December 1928 after striking a bridge abutment at night. He had been on patrol 14 days.[48]

The Southwest Mounted Police was disbanded in 1931 when the state took over highway patrol duties. The Collier Company closed the stations and sold them off individually, usually to their proprietors, throughout the 1930s. The Royal Palm Station, the second station as one traveled from west to east, was purchased by Meese Ellis and his wife, who expanded it and operated it as a gas station and restaurant, along with ten tourist cottages, well into the 1990s. Similarly, Fakahatchee Station, the third station as one drove west-to-east, was purchased by S. M. Weaver, and became known as Weaver Station, then Big Cypress Station. Also used as a gas station, restaurant, and convenience store, it was less heavily modified than Royal Palm, primarily with a wraparound porch beneath the second floor windows. It too continued to operate for many years, until the 1970s. Monroe Station, the fifth station from the west, and the least altered from its original configuration, still stands, in its original location, unused but mothballed by the National Park Service.[49]

Organizing the Southwest Mounted Police was D. Graham Copeland's last job for Alexander, Ramsey & Kerr. He retired in May 1929. Asked what he was going to do with himself "he admitted a secret ambition which he believed was in the breast of nearly every naval officer, to become a farmer ... he has leased a place at Deep Lake and will make a section his home and headquarters on a small plantation." Whether he really intended to become a farmer or was simply blowing smoke for the reporters is hard to tell. After taking a European trip with his family for a month or two, he returned to head up all the enterprises loosely affiliated under the name "The Collier Companies"—at one point as many as forty different proprietorships, partnerships and corporations. He was also appointed to the board of the all-powerful Everglades Drainage District, the progenitor of both the South Florida Water Management District and the Southwest Florida Water Management District.[50]

Postscript: On the night of April 11–12, 2016, as this book was going to press, Monroe Station burned to the ground. The cause has not yet been determined. Although the National Park Service had recieved a $450,000 state grant in 2005 to stabilize the building, it was protected only by an improvised chain-link fence and plywood nailed over the doors and windows, (*See:* Jenny Staletovich, "Everglades Fires Scorch Park and Destroy Historic Station," *Miami Herald*, April 12, 2016.)

··13··

A Pullman Car Named "Convict Labor"

Doyle Carlton took office on January 9, 1929. The next day Fons Hathaway tendered his resignation. Carlton named Robert Bentley to replace him. Bentley was a newspaper executive with no prior highway or engineering experience. He was a throwback to the old way of doing business. When the editor of a Tallahassee newspaper ran an editorial decrying the road department's use of $11,000 in federal funds to buy material from an Alabama firm, he walked into the newspaper's office and decked the editor, alleging that he had been libeled. Asked by an Associated Press reporter why he had issued checks to out-of-state firms, Bentley said it was nobody's business but his and Carlton's.[1]

Almost immediately, Bentley cancelled the awards to the Central Station and Equipment Company for the Punta Gorda bridge and to the W. P. McDonald Construction Company for the reconstruction of the Bonita Springs-Naples section of the Tamiami Trail. Bentley explained that while the bid awards had been made, the contracts for the work had not been signed. He was concerned that the projects had not been reviewed by the Bureau of Public Roads and were therefore not eligible for federal matching funds. He complained that the contract for the Edison Bridge in Fort Myers, which the Central Station and Equipment Company was still in the process of erecting, had been processed by the Hathaway administration so quickly that it wasn't eligible for federal funds. This may or may not have been a red herring: former chairman Hathaway likely spent so much money in 1928 that he probably exhausted the state's allocation of federal matching funds, about $2.8 million.[2]

It was clear that Governor Carlton wanted to put the brakes on his predecessor's go-for-broke highway program, for three reasons. First, the roadbuilding binge had left the counties in a very precarious situation. The state comptroller estimated that the counties had an aggregate of $160 million in road and bridge bonds outstanding, most approved before 1926. In many counties, real estate property tax delinquencies for 1929 were approaching thirty percent. In some of the Everglades counties, such as Dade, Broward and Collier, up to half the property taxes on unreclaimed land hadn't been paid since 1927. The giant Empire Land Company began offering land for a dollar or less per acre, just to get out from under the tax obligation. It got no takers, because nobody wanted to be responsible for the back taxes. Under Florida's tax structure, the counties were almost wholly dependent on property taxes, and nobody knew how many were going to be insolvent by the end of 1929 due to tax delinquencies.[3]

Second, Hathaway's go-for-broke highway program had exhausted the state road depart-

The Punta Gorda Bridge over the Peace River at Charlotte Harbor, just after its completion in early 1931. It would soon be renamed the Barron Collier Bridge. (Photographer unknown [State Road Dept.]. Florida Division of Library and Information Services, No. RC15450.)

ment's reserves and left it with a diminished income stream: gas tax income for the first six months of 1927 had been $6.4 million, but projected revenues for the first six months of 1929 were $4.8 million. Also, all those new miles of highway needed maintenance and repair. Those expenditures had to come from out of the highway fund, and they weren't eligible for matching federal money.

Third, there weren't a lot of alternatives to turn to. The legislature, in its regular spring session, rejected two possible solutions: a statewide sales tax and para-mutual betting. That left only one answer: a consumption tax of some sort; one disproportionately paid by visitors and temporary wintertime residents who didn't vote. That pointed to a gas tax. But there already *was* a gas tax: five cents, one of the highest in the nation. It had been three cents up to 1926 when it was raised to four. It was increased again on July 1, 1927, but that one cent was for state and county schools, not roads. Carlton was forced to reallocate the existing gas tax.[4]

His plan was that of the five cents per gallon, only two cents would now go to the state road department. Another two cents would go to the counties to retire their existing road bonds. Of this two cents, one cent would be allocated on a 50/50 matching basis. The more a county contributed to the retirement of its own bonds, the more state funds it would get. The second cent was a straight grant: the amount each county received depended on the amount of its outstanding indebtedness; the deeper the debt, the more it received. The fifth and final cent of the gas tax would go to the counties to build local roads and new schools.

In addition, the motor vehicle license tax, which had been the second-largest source of revenue for the state road department, would be split, with only 75 percent going to the road department and 25 percent to the state's general fund.

Carlton estimated that this revenue plan would allow the road department to spend $6.75 million on new construction in 1929–30 and $2.5 million for maintenance. These figures included an estimated one million dollars in federal matching funds. As a comparison, in 1927 the state road department had spent about $17 million, including contributions from both counties and the federal government and the spend-down of the reserve account.[5]

As has always been the habit of the Florida legislature, both the House and Senate dithered until midnight of the final day of the special session, when the legislators gave Carlton what he asked for, the only amendment of substance being to add on a sixth cent to reinstate the one-cent tax put into place in 1927 for education. In essence, this created a two-cent tax for the counties; one and two-thirds cents for schools, with the remaining one-third cent for new local roads. Legally, the sixth cent dedicated to education was considered a separate tax and the gas tax was always referred to as "the five cent gas tax."[6] The road bond retirement scheme was left virtually unchanged.

Almost immediately, several parties, including Palm Beach County and the City of Jacksonville, sued to prevent the collection of the gas tax under the new structure. Although several provisions were attacked, the most closely watched was the plaintiffs' assertion that distributing a portion of the tax to the counties to retire their old road and bridge bonds violated the state constitution. Carlton had planned to put into place a fairly extensive state board of administration that would take over the bonds, collect payments from the counties that wanted to accelerate their retirement, match those funds with state money collected from the gas tax, and take over the payment of bonds even for those counties unable or unwilling to make a matching contribution. In essence, the bonds would become the responsibility of the state, even for those counties that didn't choose to participate in the state's augmented payback plan. In fact, it appeared that the state would even take over the payment of those bonds upon which a county defaulted and made no payments. In this way, bondholders would have the security that the state was administering the previously local debt, and would thus be less subject to panic selling and litigation.

In early 1930, the Florida Supreme Court held that the gas tax scheme was unconstitutional, but only because it allocated funds back to the counties based on the amount of their outstanding debt. To qualify under the state constitution as a state-collected local tax, the only permissible criteria for distribution was the amount collected. The board of administration was constitutional, but under Carlton's plan, it was now mostly superfluous, because its more far-reaching aspects, such as the state assuming control over the local road bonds and the state-local matching share concept, were now impossible. The larger, more populous counties were the beneficiaries of the decision because they collected more tax. They reaped a windfall if they had been conservative in the 1910s and 1920s and had issued few bonds.

The Supreme Court was unclear if a county with no debt, or one that had paid off all its bonds, could be excluded from the distribution, but the answer appeared to be no: if ten thousand dollars of gas tax was collected in a given county, and the state kept 50 percent of all funds collected statewide, then five thousand dollars had to be returned to that county, regardless of any other criteria, such as its level of bonded indebtedness.[7]

Ironically, probably the biggest loser was Monroe County, which had, for so many years, refused to issue bonds for the Ingraham Highway, then the Tamiami Trail, only to binge on four million dollars in bonds between 1923 and 1928 on the overseas highway. It ended up functioning little better than the ferry from Miami, due to a 40-mile gap south of Lower Matacumbe Key. Engineers estimated that it would cost $10.7 million to fill in that gap. Now dependent only on a portion of its rather minuscule gas tax revenues, Monroe turned to its only other option: it sold the road, and its debt, to a quasi-governmental agency, the Overseas Highway Bridge Corporation, modeled after the organization formed in California to build the Golden Gate Bridge.[8]

But from the point of view of the state road department, the outcome was the same as if Governor Carlton had prevailed. Up to 1929, the road department received four cents a gallon on fuel sales and almost one hundred percent of auto tag revenues. After the Carlton legislation, it had to make due with two cents per gallon and three-quarters of tag sales, along with three-fourths of a new *ad valorem* auto tax. The loss of the gas and auto tag sales was about $5.5 million a year; the *ad valorem* tax made up for about two million of this. However, the value of the average auto would shrink in Florida until 1939 as auto sales dried up and the typical car became older and plainer. Federal aid highway money decreased nationwide, and with less state money now to match to the federal funds that were available, Florida's federal-aid share fell below one million dollars in 1930 for the first time since 1924. Florida's golden age of road building, which had reached its peak with the Tamiami Trail in 1928, was over, and would not recover until after World War II.[9]

Ironically, convicts finished out the Tamiami Trail. After canceling the contract for the reconstruction of the Trail between Estero and Naples, it was reassigned to "state forces," the polite euphemism the road department used to describe convict road gangs. In late October, Captain A. W. Livingston of the state corrections department arrived in Fort Myers in his private rail car "Convict Labor." Accompanying him on the same train, were 60 black prisoners, 6 white guards and an express car of equipment. (Most of the heavy equipment, provided by private contractors, arrived the next day by truck.)[10]

The convicts did not use the Carnestown stockade, as it was too far away. Ed DeGarmo had been hired by the road department as a project engineer for the Miami area in 1929 but,

> I was [soon] taken out of Miami and sent over to the west coast to complete the last leg of the Tamiami Trail from Estero to Naples, and given orders to rush it through. That was the last unfinished gap and we started south from Estero. We were working convicts, but first we had to build a convict camp, and get the convicts in from west Florida, guard them, feed them, nurse them, and take care of them. On top of that we had difficulty of getting supplies. At the time Naples was the tail end of the railroad and it seemed we could never get our limerock in when we wanted it. The grade was already in place [from the county's work] and it was dug from the sides to make the drainage ditches. It was soft sugar sand, and not stabilized at all. This meant an extra job to stabilize the material before the rock was placed. Ocala limerock was shipped in and then placed on the subgrade. Nevertheless, in spite of these headaches, we somehow managed to complete that last ten-mile section in twenty-eight days.[11]

DeGarmo's account provides one major reason why the state road department was able to succeed where the county crews had failed. The counties and their contractors had to rely on balanced cut-and-fill methods: whatever fill was needed had to come from the adjacent borrow canal. One account put it succinctly: "The burning question of the hour with the dredge men was: "Have I got enough material? Grade stakes were set by the engineers, and a large surplus of material was not permitted. Enough must be dredged; but not too much. Payment for the job was canal measurement."

But photographs from state contractor worksites from 1927 and 1928 typically show temporary rail lines in place, and often include rows of hopper cars with finely crushed limestone purchased from quarries upstate waiting to be dumped as top coat. None of this was possible until the Atlantic Coast Line extended one track to Naples and another to Everglades City in 1926 (the latter by absorbing the old Deep Lake shortline), and the

Seaboard Air Line Railroad similarly extended its tracks to Naples a few weeks after the ACL. The state expedited matters after it took over by simply shipping in trainloads of uniform, pre-crushed limestone from as far away as Ocala.[12]

DeGarmo was correct in regards to the completion of the roadgrade: it was finished in 28 days, on December 21, 1929. However, a local contractor was hired to put on an asphalt topcoat in January 1930, and the state road department often referred to February 1930 as the official completion date for the Tamiami Trail.[13] However, even this excludes the two bridges at Fort Myers and Punta Gorda. After canceling the original contract for the Punta Gorda bridge, it was re-bid in December 1929 and awarded to the Raymond Concrete Company for $858,226. At the same, final approval was given for the bridge's name: the Barron Collier Bridge. The Thomas Edison Bridge in Fort Myers was completed in 1930, the Barron Collier Bridge in 1931. The Collier Bridge was replaced with a high span not requiring a drawbridge in 1983. Its name was only slightly changed to the Collier Memorial Bridge. The Edison Bridge was replaced with a high span of almost identical design in 1991. Its name was unchanged. It is the Thomas A. Edison Bridge.[14]

* * * * *

On August 16, 1928, four months after the Trail opened, George Cook and Judge McDougal called a meeting of the Chevelier Corporation directors. President Jaudon opened it by saying that "he had no report and was not in touch with the work of the corporation." In fact, he was weighing whether to sue the corporation to cancel the Spencer Agreement and its subsequent amendment, so he chose to remain silent. (In the end, he decided against it.) Also, as far as he was concerned, his business was now selling the 20,000 acres of Collier County land he had acquired in 1925, not the Chevelier lands, which were controlled by the bondholders.

Cook presented a copy of an audit current as of January 1, 1928. The company was owed $376,000 by others, and in turn owed others $975,000, almost all of it delinquent. Out of the original 207,360 acres, it had left 121,440. According to the audit, the value of the land still held by the corporation did not make up for the negative current account. In short, the corporation was bankrupt.[15]

The next day, after reading it, Jaudon wrote Cook that "I have been trying to reconcile [it] in my mind but the figures are so much at variance with my knowledge of the affairs of this tract of land which I purchased from A. W. Hopkins in 1916 that it is rather difficult."[16] The following April, he would surrender the presidency of the corporation to Judge McDougal.[17] Cook closed with a report that the cost of the Tamiami roadwork could not be precisely estimated yet, but it would be much greater than the $200,000 in bonds allocated to the work. (Cook later estimated $318,000.)

From this point forward, Jaudon played little or no active role in the corporation. The same month he stepped down in favor of Judge McDougal, the Chevelier Corporation's bank, the Southern Bank and Trust Company, failed, taking $14,000 in company funds with it. In 1935, George Cook was successful in recovering 32,000 acres of land that the corporation had sold to Miami land speculator Tom Peters in 1926. Peters had made the down payment but stopped making any mortgage payments after that. Cook foreclosed and Peters surrendered the land rather than fight it out in court. This was one of the last official acts of the Chevelier Corporation. In September 1936 it was dissolved by the State of Florida for failure to pay its corporate taxes, although McDougal and Cook did later resurrect it when the state started condemning land for Everglades National Park.[18]

James Jaudon had a streak of the melodramatic in him. His files contain several vivid

James Jaudon stands beside a billboard advertising one of his last real estate ventures, a small residential subdivision in Bonita Springs, halfway between Naples and Fort Myers, about 1930. By this time he and his wife Maude were living on a farm in Ochopee, about 20 miles away, near Carnestown, where they stayed until shortly before Jaudon's death in early 1938. (Photographer unknown. HistoryMiami, No. 1988-175-13.)

historical accounts of the start of the Tamiami Trail movement, the establishment of the Chevelier Corporation, and his own personal story. In one of the latter, he recollects a tearful scene in October 1930, a year after the Wall Street crash, in which he is forced to admit to his wife Maude that they are bankrupt, that the house is in foreclosure, and that they must move out west and start over as common dirt farmers.[19]

The truth is more prosaic. By May 1929 Jaudon had all but abandoned Miami and was living out on one of the parcels of Collier County farmland he had bought in 1925. He and Bill House were growing watermelons, which Jaudon was selling through the wholesale produce company he and his brother had started in Miami decades earlier. He and House were getting a good price: $1.00 to $1.75 each. Jaudon had a small general store on the Trail as well. Jaudon referred to the spot on the Trail where the store was located as the town of "Jaudon," perhaps in jest, perhaps not. In any event, one of his land customers, Edgar Gaunt, who held 250 acres, started another store a mile west of his, and it soon put him out of business. Gaunt and his neighbors gave their settlement the name "Ochopee," and that's the name that stuck.[20]

Jaudon's long-time secretary, Daisy Aldridge, wrote Jaudon in August 1930 to report that R. A. Coachman, Maude's brother, would be over to the farm by the end of the week to bring the mail. "There is quite a lot of it, and he has it all over at his house," she wrote. If Jaudon's house on Fourth Avenue hadn't actually been sold yet, it was clear from Aldridge's letter that they were no longer living there. Aldridge herself now worked largely from home: "There is no use going [to the office] every day; it's car fare for nothing." Also, the place was a mess: "The last rains flooded the office again. I put everything away from the center the room." Jaudon may have seen, in his mind's eye, the tragedy of the Great Florida Bust exemplified in a teary scene where he admitted to Maude that he was broke, that the house had to go, but with her help he would fight on to make another fortune, but reality outdid fiction. Everything that was the Great Bust could be summed up with Daisy Aldridge, the loyal secretary, in a one-room office in a modest, hurricane-damaged office building by the Miami River docks, moving twenty years of papers, maps and records out of harm's way as the water slowly drips down from the ceiling.[21]

Jaudon's new plan was make his fortune in sugar cane, in spite of the letters he received from the U.S. Department of Agriculture warning him that with the possible exception of the south rim Lake Okeechobee, the Everglades region was not suitable for commercial sugar cane growing. Look at the disaster with Cap Graham's Pennsuco, the government's biologist explained: "you are acquainted with the results of the venture undertaken number of years ago by a sugar company in the area lying a short distance west of Miami," the Department's regional agronomist wrote. "I cite the disastrous outcome as an outstanding example of why any serious proposal to establish a sugar factory should be proceeded by a through investigation.... Random, small-scale plantings of sugar cane may indicate that cane could be successfully produced, but the results of such plantings do not afford dependable information justifying the assumption that it would be commercially feasible to enter into production on a large scale."[22]

The last hope of the remaining Chevelier stock- and bondholders was Ernest Coe's proposed Tropical Everglades National Park. Judge McDougal was all for it, but his daughter and son-in-law, Mary and Ivar Axelson (who had taken over day-to-day management of his interests when they moved to Coral Gables about 1932), were skeptical, because they believed a vast pool of oil lay under the Everglades, untapped, and that the government was really after the oil. The Model Land Company tried to interest the Axelsons in a landowner's coalition, but McDougal cautioned Ivar:

> I think it will be a great mistake if they [the Model Land Company] undertake to boost the price of land too much. The State of Florida is not going to appropriate much money, if any, to buy land. It will donate land that the state already owns, but it will not donate money to buy land from anyone else. And I am convinced that in times like this no one else is going to donate money to buy land down there, if they get an inkling that the land owners are trying to get more than their land is worth.[23]

But oil was discovered in south Florida, and beginning in 1943 an oilfield of modest size was actually developed by Humble Oil at Sunniland, about twenty-five miles north of Deep Lake. In July 1948 the acquisition agents for the state, McKay, Smith and Manley, visited Judge McDougal and his son-in-law and informed them that a 5,600 acre parcel of their land outside the Chevelier Tract would be included in the new national park. "Both stated that the standard price of land, after news that oil had been brought in at Sunniland became public in October 1943, was ten dollars per acre over the bulk of their holdings." Manley told McDougal and Axelson to prepare a bid. They offered $70,200. The state countered with $19,140. They settled for $21,000 by letting the McDougal family retain mineral rights for twenty years.[24]

In 1955, Oklahoma Congressman Victor Wickersham bought out the McDougal-Axelson family's holdings in the Chevelier Tract, paying $176,500 for about 18,000 acres in 37 different parcels, roughly nine percent of Jaudon's original purchase. Violet McDougal (Judge McDougal's widow) and her three daughters retained half of the mineral rights in the land.[25]

In 1954, the Sunniland oil field started to experience salt water intrusion. By 1958, the percentage of salt water was so high that the crude oil had to be separated on-site before it could be piped out. Eventually, the extent of infiltration was so great that separation was no longer economical and the Sunniland operation was shut down by 1962. While the Axelsons and other major landowners received, after a sometimes protracted and bitter fight, mineral rights to their former lands permitting them to sell oil leases through the 1960s, all subsequent test wells (including off-shore bores in Florida Bay) came up dry and the oil companies finally gave up by the mid–1950s. The price most of the large landowners received from the State of Florida for Everglades National Park land was two to five dollars per acre.

Looking back a few years later, Judge McDougal confided to his daughter Mary and her husband Ivar:

> The McCord-Hopkins interests got all the money nearly that was to be realized from Chevelier sales, besides what the Cooks squandered out of road building, etc. The Hopkins estate still have $200,000 of the bonds and McCord had $100,000, but most of them I think were scattered out among his [the bank's] creditors, at a time when they were still supposed to have some value. Several years ago when they thought there was still some hope, McCord indicated that he thought the Hopkins estate would sell me their $200,000 for $40,000 or $50,000. I am satisfied they would sell them now for anything they could get; but of course no one at the present time would agree to pay anything for them.[26]

Out in Ochopee, Jaudon pressed on, building a sugar mill in 1937. It was his last project. That same year, ill and tired, he and Maude moved back to Miami, into a modest home in the southwest part of the city, where he died on February 22, 1938. His gravestone in Miami City Cemetery reads "Father of the Tamiami Trail." His sugar cane mill began operations in 1938, but as the soil chemists from the Department of Agriculture predicted, by World War II, the soil was already giving out. The mill machinery was moved to the Clewiston area and the metal building was then used as a vegetable packing house and warehouse for many years. It was damaged beyond repair by hurricane Donna in 1960.[27]

* * * * *

It is difficult to determine with precision how much was spent overall on the Tamiami Trail. There were so many different jurisdictions involved, using so many different forms of financing, and spending their money through so many different construction firms, that it is hard to avoid double-counting some funds or inadvertently omitting others. In addition, much of the road was built, only to be re-constructed to higher standards by the state road department a couple of years later. It is therefore difficult to determine if a given contract or project should be considered new construction, an upgrade of an existing road, or even maintenance. Even the definition of what the "Tamiami Trail" is varied over the thirteen year life of the project. Originally it was a highway from Tampa to Miami. In the face of criticism from Miami interests over the slow, underfinanced and haphazard pace of work on the west coast, and needing to justify the succession of his new county from Lee County, Barron Collier used the Tamiami Trail Association and the Tamiami Trailblazers to redefine the Tamiami Trail as a predominantly Gulf coast highway stretching from Everglades City to Lake City, the west coast's version of the Atlantic shore's Dixie Highway. After securing his new county and, more importantly, gaining the cooperation of Governor John Martin and road department chairman Hathaway in an aggressive program of highway funding, the Trail shrunk back into a Miami-to-Fort Myers endeavor, the place where, except for the great bridges across the Manatee, Peace (Port Charlotte) and Caloosahatchee Rivers, the money was most needed.

The entire Tampa-to-Miami highway is 284 miles long. (Even this figure varies from one account to another; this measurement is taken from a history prepared by the Florida Highway Department in 1964.) From the City of Miami to Marco Junction is 96 miles.

Marco Junction to Fort Myers is another 51 miles. Fort Myers to Tampa is a further 137 miles. Financial data for the portion of the road from Miami to Fort Myers is good, but for that part from Fort Myers to Tampa it is more speculative. It is known that Charlotte, Sarasota, Manatee and Hillsborough counties all floated bonds, but it not always known how much of those bonds were dedicated to work on the Tamiami Trail. There was no specific earmarking, except in Lee and Dade counties. In other cases improvements were paid for from general revenues without floating bonds. In the Gulf coast counties north of Charlotte Harbor, funds were spent relatively early in the project—before 1923.[28]

The *Miami Daily News-Metropolis* called the road "The Wonder Highway of the Century, the $9,000,000 Tamiami Trail" when it opened in 1928. Their estimate included only the segment from Miami to Fort Myers. An official history of Florida's roads prepared in 1964 by the state, borrowing extensively from figures used in a 1928 book prepared for the Tamiami Trail's grand opening by J. Hugh Reese, estimated seven million dollars, again only for the Miami to Fort Myers portion. Fons Hathaway stated in 1926 that the cost to the state for the entire highway, exclusive of what counties and private interests had contributed, would run between five and seven million dollars, and that the highway would average about $41,000 per mile by the time it was finished.[29]

My own estimate is that the cross-state portion of the road between Miami and Fort Myers (to be precise, by "Fort Myers" I mean the north boundary of Lee County, including the Caloosahatchee River bridge and the nine miles north of the bridge to the Charlotte County line), cost $8,077,394 as of the day the ribbon was cut on April 26, 1928. This includes the first wooden Caloosahatchee River bridge, but not the subsequent Edison Bridge ($532,015) finished in 1930.

This means that the road from Miami to Fort Myers, including the wooden Caloosahatchee River causeway and nine miles north of town, averaged $51,779 per mile for 156 miles. When the J. B. McCrary Company bid on the Dade and Lee County road projects in 1915, they estimated the gross cost of road building at about $6,000 per mile. On the other hand, the estimate of the state highway commission was quite accurate at the time it took over the construction of the road. Commissioner E. P. Green told a meeting of the Tamiami Trail Association in April that the Miami-to-Marco section would require five million dollars in state aid; the final figure appears to be around $4.750 million.[30]

It is clear that except for the huge bridge projects at Punta Gorda (the Barron Collier Bridge) and the Manatee River at Bradenton, there was far less money spent on the coast road. The largest state contract on the Gulf Coast road was 564-B, for $173,000, awarded to the Broadbent Construction Company for ten miles of road in Charlotte County. State contract 614, for 17 miles of road in Sarasota County, cost only $118,086. The state had to spend far less money on them because the costal counties had already been gradually improving them for many years, and except for the need to bridge frequent tidal estuaries, the engineering challenges were relatively minor. As near as can be determined, that portion of the road from Fort Myers (the Lee-Charlotte line) to Tampa cost $2,322,489, which includes the $910,000 spent on the Manatee River bridge, which was completed at the time of the official opening in 1929, but does not include the Barron Collier bridge at Punta Gorda, which was not finished until 1932.

This brings the total for the entire 284 miles at the time of the official grand opening to $10,399,883. In its final configuration, with the ferro-concrete Edison and Barron Collier bridges in place, the total comes to $11,789,898, or $41,513 per mile as of 1932.

* * * * *

Before the Tamiami Trail was completed, getting a transit pass from one of the construction contractors to drive along the finished road grade was considered quite a coup, especially by deer hunters who wanted to save the bother of packing into the middle of the Big Cypress on foot or by horseback. The Hough brothers of Fort Myers had gotten such a pass from Alexander, Ramsey & Kerr in late 1926 and were cruising along before dawn at 35 miles an hour, about 25 miles east of Everglades City, when they were pulled up short, their brakes leaving ruts in the unfinished surface. There, square in the middle of the Tamiami Trail, was an entire village of Seminoles. It had been a wet winter, and the road was the only dry ground from horizon to horizon. Discretion being the better part of valor, they turned around.[31]

In 1939, D. Graham Copeland told Smithsonian Institution field investigator Ethel Cutler Freeman that "one-third of the Indians in Collier County have come out and camped on the Trail and that though some of them commercialized, they were still so crude and simple that he didn't think their ways had changed much."[32]

Since early in the century, extended family groups of Seminoles had been spending the winter tourist season in tourist attractions in Miami, including Coppinger's Gardens, Musa Isle and Osceola's Gardens. Later, they appeared at out-of-state exhibitions, including a Florida promotional show at New York's Madison Square Garden in 1924 and the Canadian National Exhibition in 1931. Generally, they would return to their Big Cypress homes during the off-season, or, after 1926, to the new reservation established for them in Dania (now Hollywood) along the new north-south federal highway (U.S. 441). By 1934, Seminole women had organized a small crafts booth along the highway, and dolls, made of palmetto fiber, sold in large numbers.

The Tamiami Trail construction cut off many of the Seminole's traditional northeast/southwest canoe trails, at the same time it created a major waterborne east-west highway. It was only natural that they would take advantage of the new transport network. In 1936 Stanley Hanson and R. Carl Liddle complied information on the eight roadside Seminole commercial villages they surveyed between Fort Myers and Miami. Most had a population of ten to fifteen; the largest was twenty-five. All were surrounded by a solid eight-foot fence, and all charged a ten- to twenty-cent entry fee. In addition to permitting the visitor a view of village life, most had a modest zoo or botanical garden, mostly palms or orchids. Each offered handmade crafts. None featured alligator wrestling, as was the case with the big commercial attractions in Miami.[33]

Ethel Freeman, who had interviewed D. Graham Copeland, also visited this area and wrote:

> It is only within the last two years that many Indians have made it [the Tamiami Trail] their headquarters. This year [1939] there are thirteen camps. [They] sell what they make to tourists and charge sightseers admission to their villages. These villages are not temporary abodes or show places, but are their real homes during certain seasons. Although the Indians have left their homes in the wilds to gain a living from tourists, these camps along the Trail are not commercialized as one would expect.... In this way they are comparable with the owners of the old houses of Virginia and England who open their homes and gardens for gain—yet they are not seen and their lives are untouched and unaffected by their visitors to whom they are supremely indifferent.[34]

In the mid–1950s, there was a strong sentiment in Congress, especially in the House Indian Affairs Subcommittee, to terminate government assistance to tribes they deemed ready to manage their own affairs. In practice, this meant eliminating reservation lands and treasuries and distributing them to living tribe members. Suspiciously often, this occurred on lands with deposits of oil, hydropower or uranium that powerful corporate

A group of Seminole men, women and children in traditional dress waiting for a bus into Miami, about 1929. (Photographer unknown. Collier County Museum, Naples, FL, No. 78.14.15.)

interests were eager to exploit to an industrial scale, but which the tribes did not wish disturbed or wanted utilized only in sustainable way. In a few cases, such as the Menominee of Wisconsin and the Klamath of Oregon, this actually occurred.[35] Congressman James Haley of Sarasota placed the Seminole Tribe of Florida on this list, not because he believed they were ready for termination (so Haley later asserted), but because he believed his colleagues would so readily see that the Seminoles were *not* ready that they would defeat the entire list of candidates. Two years later the Seminoles were removed from the list and they incorporated in 1957; the legislation proceeded on without them.[36]

During the course of the termination hearings, a separatist movement spread within the Tamiami Trail-based members of the tribe, led largely by Jimmie Billie, based at Musa Isle northwest of downtown Miami on the Miami River. In other times, a compromise might have been worked out, but with the stress and rapidly shifting political winds pressing in on a tribe at a time it still had next to no resources to deal with the crisis—its annual budget was a couple of hundred thousand dollars, not the hundreds of millions, as is the case today—the divisions could not be overcome. A separate tribe, the Miccosukee Tribe of Indians of Florida, was organized on January 11, 1962, comprised of those Seminoles living along the Tamiami Trail. The remaining Seminole Tribe of 1957 maintains its headquarters at the Dania-Hollywood Reservation, across from the Hard Rock Hotel and Casino, which it owns, along with the Hard Rock's parent corporation. The Miccosukees operate a smaller casino at the intersection of the Tamiami Trail and Krome Avenue in west Miami-

Dade County and other investments, including a golf course. However, their headquarters is maintained out on the Trail, at the Thirty-Mile Bend, where the old Chevelier road, now called the Loop Road, splits off from the main highway.[37]

Estimated Costs of Building the Tamiami Trail

Dade
State-Federal Funds	$2,172,295	
County Bond Funds	$566,000	
TOTAL		$2,738,259

Collier
State-Federal Funds	$2,469,146	
County and Collier Co. Funds	$1,100,000	
TOTAL		$3,569,146

Monroe
County Bonds Funds	$210,000	
Chevelier Corp. Funds	$318,000	
TOTAL		$528,000

Lee
State-Federal Funds	$158,000	
Edison Bridge	$532,018	
County Bond Funds	$1,084,000	
TOTAL		$1,774,000

Charlotte
State-Federal Funds	$212,203	
Peace River Bridge	$858,000	
County Bond Funds	$200,000	
TOTAL		$1,270,203

Manatee
State-Federal Funds	$140,000	
Manatee River Bridge	$910,000	
County Bond Funds	$140,000	
TOTAL		$1,190,000

Sarasota
State-Federal Funds	$150,286	
County Bond Funds	$200,000	
TOTAL		$350,286

Hillsborough
State-Federal Funds	$150,000	
County Bond Funds	$220,000	
TOTAL		$370,000
TOTAL*		$11,789,898
TOTAL: MIAMI TO FORT MYERS**		$8,609,409

* Including winter 1928–29 finishing, the Edison Bridge (1930), the Manatee River Bridge (1928) and the Barron Collier Bridge (1931).
** Including winter 1928–29 finishing and the Edison Bridge.

Sources:

J. Hugh Reese, *History of the Tamiami Trail* (Miami: Tamiami Trail Commissioners and the Commissioners of Dade County, 1928).

State Road Department of Florida, Construction Record: Projects 669-V; 669-W; 669-X; 669-Z 0301–104, (Collier County, Florida) ca. December 1928, Collier County Historical Society.

"Status of Road Construction," *Florida Highways* (monthly feature, June 1925–December 1928)

"Speeding up Work on Trail," *Ft. Myers Press* (July 10, 1924).

"Marco-Miami-Road to Cost $50,000 a Mile," *Ft. Myers Press* (April 22, 1926).

"Work on Trail to be Speeded, Hathaway Says," *Miami Metropolis* (November 30, 1926).

"Motorcade to Open $9,000,000 Tamiami Trail This Week," *Miami Metropolis* (April 22, 1928).

"Hathaway Says Roads to Bring Big Population," *Miami Metropolis* (March 31, 1927).

PART III:
CONNERS HIGHWAY

••14••

Don't Call Me Fingy

It would be hard to find a more improbable road developer than William J. "Fingy" Conners. A Buffalo bar owner who leveraged his string of waterfront watering holes into control of that city's docks, he became infamous for shooting at opposing union men while they were trapped, liked rats in a barrel, in the hold of a nearly empty grain freighter. He tried to turn away from this rough trade by becoming a newspaper magnate, following the path blazed by his mentor William Randolph Hearst, only to be shut out of upstate New York society, and eventually, its political machine as well, amidst rumors that he had started his upward climb in life by killing his mother and step-sister for money. Late in life, he retaliated by setting up a foundation to benefit his home town that soon grew to over a million and a half dollars. A Republican turned Tammany Hall Democrat, he crossed the Gotham machine one too many times, and was dumped in 1910, his political career finished.[1]

He did what failed New Yorkers have always done: gone to Florida and started over. And he succeeded. His timing was always good: he died on October 5, 1929, days before the stock market crash heralded the start of the Great Depression. He once told a reporter that "I made most of my money doing damn fool things," and in the case of Conners Highway, he may have been right. He reportedly spent $1.8 million building it, and after he died his estate sold it to Palm Beach County for $660,000. On the other hand, he owned as much as 40,000 acres of land along on the east side of Lake Okeechobee, and over 3,000 platted lots in Okeechobee City, on the north side of the lake. Within eight months of the opening of the highway, he had sold two thousand lots and 340 acres of unplatted land. The highway itself was pulling in almost two thousand dollars a day in tolls during the winter tourist season. Before the Tamiami Trail was finished in 1928, it was the fastest way to get from Miami to Tampa.[2] Had Conners lived longer, who is to say that he might not have turned it into the cross-state turnpike he dreamed of?

William James Conners was born in 1857 to Peter and Mary Collins. Peter was a first-generation immigrant from Ireland; Mary came from Canada. Peter was reportedly a well educated man for his station in life. He had a high school diploma, and some said a year of college as well. Mary had a daughter from a previous marriage, known only as "Mrs. Hayes." Her marriage had failed and she had returned to live with Peter and Mary. After working as a stonecutter and lake sailor, Peter bought a saloon on the Buffalo waterfront, on what was called the "Ohio Basin." Mary either managed or owned a candy store. They owned the cottage they lived in. It is clear that while they lived in Buffalo's rough First Ward, they were not poor.[3]

William Conners quit school early. ("What do I want education for? I can hire all the brains I want for $20 a week. It's as cheap as dirt," he told more than one reporter.) He started as a cook's assistant on a lake steamer, working himself up to chief porter. It was during this time that he lost his left thumb. The most popular story is that he dared another kitchen boy to "chop off 'is fingy," and unfortunately, the other boy had a cleaver at hand when Conners plopped his arm down on the chopping block to make his dare. (Another version of the story is basically the same, only a pistol is involved.) But early in his career, he admitted to a more prosaic (and believable) story: the thumb had been crushed by shifting scrap metal while climbing a junkpile during a dockside game of hide-and-seek when he was six or seven.[4]

One thing is for certain, and that is calling Fingy, well, Fingy was a guaranteed way to lose some teeth or wind up with a permanently bent nose, even after Fingy had become part of New York and Palm Beach society. However, once he was older and established, he would at least wait for you to finish your meal and leave the dining room of the Breakers or the Waldorf, then drop you out front on the sidewalk. A man must keep up appearances, you know.

When he was about sixteen or seventeen, he quit the lake steamers to stack cordwood for the railroad for a short while, then went to work as a longshoreman. In 1879 he opened his own saloon on Louisiana Street. What happened next is a little convoluted and very controversial. Conners's parents and his half-sister, Mrs. Hayes, were living together in the Conners's cottage. The cottage caught fire. Peter and Mary Conners ran out, but Mrs. Hayes rashly ran back into the house, supposedly to rescue her sewing machine. The roof fell in and killed her. Mary Conners died soon thereafter of shock or some illness precipitated by her daughter's death. Some accounts say that Peter Conners then died a few months after Mary. However, most other versions state that Peter Conners died of natural causes a little less than a year *before* the house fire. Regardless of the exact sequence of events, the result was the same: The rest of his family was dead, and Conners inherited both his father's saloon and the insurance settlement from the house fire. Rumors always followed Conners to the effect that he had arranged the death of his mother and half-sister in order to gain the saloon, the insurance on the house, and his father's life insurance policy, made out to his mother. However, William Irwin of *Collier's*, who did the most exhaustive investigatory report on Conners in 1908 (and was unsuccessfully sued for libel for his efforts) does not assert that Conners harmed his family or wanted them hurt, attributing the sequence of events solely to ill fortune.[5]

In 1885 another of the many labor strikes hit the Buffalo docks. The grain boats were not affected, because they did not hire their own longshoremen ("scoopers"); they hired contractors who dealt directly with the men. However the package carriers picked their longshoremen off the dock on when they needed them, and were now paying the price. When the longshoremen were off work they hung out at the bars. Conners took advantage of this and went to the Union Steamboat Company, offering a contract for the loading and unloading of package steamers at a fixed rate. Conners used his bars to recruit, organize and pay longshoring crews, a traditional practice for the grain scoopers but unknown among the package lines, who had always relied on dockside musters and direct hiring. By making sure his men showed up as promised and did the job—sometimes using muscle to guarantee that the contract terms were met—and by judiciously bribing the freight agents of steamship lines and railroads, Conners eventually got contracts with almost all the Buffalo package carriers. In essence, he converted the package lines to the same type of labor hiring system that the gain carriers had been using all along.

He then moved to the grain side of the business. Scooping grain was Buffalo's biggest docking business. It was run by small-scale contractors called "boss shovelers." Most doubled as bar owners. The bar served as meeting hall, bank, post office, and payroll office for the grain longshoremen. The bars, in turn, were subsidized by local breweries or the regional distributors of the big national breweries. They provided mugs, coasters, napkins, decorations, cigars, snack foods, sometimes even furniture. Conners began ingratiating himself with the beer and liquor distributors at the same time he approached the boss shovelers with offers to represent them in their dealings with the steamship lines. In most cases, the boss shovelers/bar owners who started working with Conners's syndicate saw themselves getting better scooping contracts, cheaper brewery prices, and more comps and credit. Ultimately, of course, they wound up losing their scooping crews and their bar. If lucky, they would be allowed to hang on as an employee of the Conners organization.

The grain longshoremen who found themselves now working for "W. J. Conners, Contractor" soon discovered that their paychecks were slowly but steadily diminishing. At first this was due to the crudest of methods, outright padding. Ten men would find themselves on a scooping crew, go do their job, and afterwards stop by the designated saloon to pick up their pay envelopes, only to find eleven envelopes in the pigeonhole for that job, one with a name written on the front they didn't recognize. The saloonkeeper insisted that the eleventh man had been on the job but had just been sent back out again on a rush job and couldn't pick up his pay envelope, which would be forwarded to the Conners Contracting offices for safekeeping.

Later, Conners became more subtle. After he had taken over most of the waterfront bars that had formerly belonged to the boss shovelers, he issued what were called "brass checks" to the men. These were numbered tags, like the ID tags men wore in factories. The grain scoopers were not above taking a break once or twice a shift to walk across the street and hoist a mug. All you had to do was show your brass check in any Conners bar and the drink was put on your tab. There was nothing new in the idea; Conners just perfected it. But the men who avoided the bars, or who only stopped off for a quick one on the way home found themselves being called for fewer and fewer jobs, while those who were putting half or two-thirds of their pay on their brass checks, and thus taking home thin pay envelopes, were always getting the knock on their doors.

Conners had solidified his hold on power in 1893 when he bought the *Buffalo Enquirer*, an evening paper. He established his own newspaper, the *Buffalo Record*, to try to cripple the city's largest paper, the morning *Buffalo Courier*. He succeeded, and in 1897 bought the *Courier*, merging it with the *Record*. He now controlled all the major newspapers in Buffalo.

The men struck in late 1898. The Lake Carrier's Association, the trade group for the ship owners and grain brokers, offered an agreement whereby the saloon–boss system would be abolished, the use of dummies on work crews eliminated, and a contract price fixed at $1.85 per 1,000 bushels. The scoopers rejected this. They had only one demand: that no lake carrier contract with William J. Conners for work. All hiring must be direct.[6]

The strike was long and bloody. Dave Nugent, a nephew of Conners, led a gang of men that fired on a crew of union grain shovelers working in the hold of the *Mather*. Fortunately, they were almost finished and thus far down in the dark, dusty hold of the ship. None were killed, but three were wounded.[7] The new union played just as rough. James Kennedy was a lieutenant of Conners. He had a nephew of the same name, who bore a striking resemblance to his uncle. Roland Mahany, a lawyer who represented many of the union shovelers when they got into trouble, told the younger Kennedy to stay out of the

First Ward—his uncle knew full well that to be caught there would be his last act, and Mahany warned the nephew that things had gotten so bad that if he were spotted, it was possible he may be dead before a proper identification could be sorted out. Young Kennedy entered the First Ward one night and was cut down.

Conners believed that with his control of the bars and the newspapers, it was simply a matter of time and attrition until he prevailed. But with his "brass check" strategy, Conners had made an implacable foe. He may have thought he controlled all the newspapers, but there were two he did not: the *Catholic Union* and the *Catholic Times*, both published by the diocese and edited by Father Cronin. Conners tried to bribe Cronin. Nothing doing. He tried to use his dockers to embargo their newsprint supplies, to no avail. Finally, he brought in protestant strikebreakers. Their clergymen thundered at them from the pulpits: make common cause with the Catholics, brother like brother. Conners was dumbfounded. Cronin was a newspaper editor and a parish priest whose church wasn't even in the First Ward. He wasn't that powerful. Who was pulling the strings?

The union leaders called a meeting at St. Bridget's hall; there were nearly a thousand men inside. It was crowded, stuffy, loud and rowdy; many of the men had just come off the docks. Father Cronin stood at front, made a short speech and announced that he had not called them together, but someone else did, and he had something he wanted to say to them. Starting from the back of the hall, and moving slowly forward, the men stood and fell silent. Bishop Quigley, the bishop of Chicago, in full vestments, walked up the main aisle to the front. He spoke slowly and dispassionately for about ten minutes. He argued that William J. Conners had tried to destroy the livelihood and health of the families of the parishes of Buffalo. This man Conners was anathema in the eyes of God and the church, and would remain so until he made a full repentance and renounced his wickedness. Until then, no one should work for this man until he had fully and completely divested himself of the grain business.

Will Irwin, of *Collier's Weekly* reported:

> That episode, unique I think, in the history of American labor troubles, beat Fingy Conners. Every one in Buffalo knew that, and the grain carrying companies best of all. They had supported him in a half-hearted fashion. Now they withdrew their support and took the business out of his hands. A committee of citizens, headed by the Bishop, met with the carrying companies and arranged a new system—a return to the conditions that prevailed before the advent of Conners, but minus the boss scooper and his saloon.[8]

Other accounts assert that the critical factor was not the meeting at St. Bridget's, but the fact that Bishop Quigley and Father Cronin had the two independent Catholic newspapers at their disposal at a time when Conners had cornered the market on the commercial newspapers in Buffalo. In this way, the bishop was able to communicate and make common cause with the protestant clergy, thereby heading off the ethnic and secular antagonizing that was such a part of east coast labor battles. Both Catholic and protestant clergy were willing to cooperate because Connors had taken an already unpopular system—the saloon-based boss scoopers—and tried to use it to wring more money out of his ownership of bars and breweries through the brass check system. Reportedly, Conners would never again permit Bishop Quigley's name to be printed in any of his newspapers.[9]

* * * * *

Up to 1896, Conners had been a Republican, but he tended to ticket-split when it came to making endorsements with his newspapers: "I plays bot' ends, and I'm in the middle, and I can't lose, see!"[10] He did start out as Republican, running for alderman of his First Ward in 1882. He was defeated. He continued as a Republican through 1896, when his newspapers supported McKinley for president. The man who turned him around was the messianic William Randolph Hearst, newspaper titan, reformer, conspirator, and possibly madman. A California native, the son of a rancher and two-term U.S. Senator, Hearst bought into the *San Francisco Examiner,* taking it over in 1887. He bought the *New York Morning Journal* in 1895, expanding it into both a morning and evening paper. He cut the price to one cent and raided Pulitzer's *New York World* for yellow-journalism expertise. He claimed that he was responsible for starting the Spanish-American war in 1898 by convincing everyone that the explosion of the battleship *Maine* in Havana harbor, almost certainly the result of leaving a coal bunker almost empty without spraying down its coal dust, had been an act of war by Spain.

In 1906, Hearst ran for New York State governor as the Democratic candidate on a reform platform, and narrowly lost to Charles Evans Hughes. Conners was his campaign manager, and worked tirelessly for him.[11] His reward was to be named chairman of the Democratic state committee. The arrangement was a deal brokered between the Hearst reformists and the Tammany Hall forces. The only "no" vote came from the longshoremen's union representative. Bygones were not bygones. Little known, and virtually unreported, a month after the appointment, Conners's 18-year-old son Peter died of an illness while a student at the Oak Lake (Mich.) Military Academy. He never talked about it, and it was never brought up by reporters, no matter how scathing their subsequent reportage.[12]

Conners's support within the New York Democratic committee started to erode after Will Irwin's muckraking article in the July 1908 issue of *Collier's Weekly*. A similar story a month later in the *Sunday New York Times* was probably also written by him. Conners sued *Colliers* for $100,000. The magazine's reply to Conners's complaint was only two pages long, and asserted only one defense: truth. The case never went to trial.[13]

Conners's problems really started in early 1910, a little over three years into his term as chairman, when he returned to New York after wintering in Palm Beach. Hearst had run again in 1909 for mayor, this time relying less on the traditional Democratic machines and more on his own money. His campaign carried a much sharper, anti-corruption, anti-machine message. It sounded almost like the New York mayoral campaign of neo-socialist Henry George in the 1880s. Hearst was starting to exhibit the messianic streak for which he became notorious in his later years. He lost, heavily this time, and those who stuck by him, like Conners, became the targets of party purges. Eventually, Hearst's political career self-destructed in 1924 when he went after Alfred E. Smith for his Catholic background and Tammany connections. Hearst spent the last twenty-five years of his life in self-imposed exile in his castle in San Simeon, California, dying in 1951.

Thus, there was already bad blood by 1910 between Conners and Charles Murphy, the head of Tammany Hall, when, on the gangplank of a steamer coming up from Palm Beach in February, Conners launched into a diatribe before a group of reporters about how Murphy and Tammany Hall "had auctioneered judgeships in New York and that the man who paid the highest price was the man who was nominated."[14]

Hearst still had a lot of clout in the state party, but when Conners went that far, he pulled the rug out from under himself. Hearst may have been an opponent of Murphy and Tammany, but he had no intention of immolating himself and ruining his New York newspapers over an upstate local political boss over an issue he couldn't possibly win. "The fact that Mr. Conners was willing last night to fall back on the charges had made at Palm Beach against 'Murphy, Gaffney & Co.,' was taken as an indication by his friends, as well as his enemies, that he had not succeeded in lining up the forces he had intimated the day before were with him ... last night Mr. Conners was in a state of semi-panic," wrote one reporter the day after Conners arrived in New York City. A day after that, just before Conners was to leave for Albany, it was reported that "while he would not admit he is beaten, his closest friends and supporters had practically given up hope, and when the State Committee meets at Albany tomorrow afternoon, they said Mr. Conners would surely be removed."[15]

But then Hearst stepped in. His representatives asked Conners what his absolute bedrock bottom offer was. Conners replied that he could not be seen as driven from office before the end of term, eight months away. Other representatives, sent to Tammany Hall, asked the same of Murphy. He answered that the accusation of paid judgeships had to be absolutely discredited. Thus followed one of the strangest executive committee meetings in New York Democratic Party history. Conners called the meeting to order. He courteously asked if there was any new business. The Tammany representatives politely said no. Conners pleasantly replied if that was the case, there was a statement he wanted to make. Obviously reading from a prepared text word-for-word, he retracted his Palm Beach accusation and apologized for any concern it may have caused, assuring everyone of the integrity of the judicial selection process in New York, Queens and Kings counties. When he finished he again asked if there were any last minute additions to the agenda. The reply was again no. Conners then calmly announced that the meeting was adjourned, gaveling the meeting to a close. The only outward breach in this kabuki theatre was when Conners inadvertently broke the gavel to end the meeting.[16]

Conners stepped down from the chairmanship of the New York State Democratic Party Executive Committee on schedule in November 1910. The state party had meanwhile moved in a new man, William Fitzpatrick, to replace Conners in Erie, making Fitzpatrick the excise commissioner for Erie County and naming Fitzpatrick's brother-in-law state election commissioner. When the Democratic Party primaries were held in September 1910, all of Conners's men were swept out of office in Erie County and the City of Buffalo. After January 1911 Conners had no political base to work from. His political career was over. In September he resigned from the state Executive Committee, a body he had run less than a year before.[17]

That's not to say Conners himself was finished. He was still a wealthy man—a very wealthy man, whose aspiration was to become a respected and respectable member of Buffalo society. By 1908 he had sold the last of his dockside saloons. His contracting office for longshoremen was still there, although his client list was limited to package carriers—no grain shoveling. He had his newspapers. He held a majority interest in a state-wide electric power and street railway company, the Economic Power and Construction Company, but the state's supreme court ruled in 1909 that its legislative charter, which granted it a right-of-way across any local street in the state, was invalid, and that franchises had to be approved by each municipality or county. That effectively put Conners out of the utility and streetcar business.[18]

His salvation came four years later. In mid-1914 the Interstate Commerce Commission ruled that, under the Panama Canal act, the big northern railroads could not own captive Great Lakes steamship companies. The New York Central had (through subsidiaries) two steamship lines, the Pennsylvania Railroad had one, and the Lehigh Valley, the Erie Railroad and the Lackawanna jointly operated the Mutual Transit Company. About 40 passenger ships and freighters were involved. Except for the Lehigh Valley, the railroads did not contest the ruling. There were two groups of potential buyers for the ships: one wanted them for the transatlantic trade. These buyers were willing to pay quite high prices for top-line equipment. The second group wanted to continue the Great Lakes trade. The prices they were willing to pay was lower and the equipment they sought more modest.

The railroads believed that the Atlantic lines would prevail in the scramble that would occur after any forced divestment, and at the prices they were willing to pay, the marine subsidiaries were worth more broken up than as corporate entities.

The lines were broken up, and most of the high-end equipment went to Charles Morse, owner of the Morse Lines, which operated passenger and mixed passenger/cargo ships between the northeast and Europe and Latin America. Morse bought thirteen ships. The New York Coke and Coal Company, the Pacific-Alaska Steamship Company and the Alaska Steamship Company took six of the largest bulk freighters. Only then did Conners move in, to take the smaller or older or less prestigious ships. But what he did buy, three passenger ships and twenty-one freighters with a combined capacity of 95,150 tons, was enough to make his Great Lakes Transit Corporation the largest common carrier on the Great Lakes for over a decade. He was carrying so much of the New York Central's freight that five years later it leased him their East Buffalo repair shops. He used it to manufacture railroad cars that would travel on his Lakes steamers and for lease to railroads—one of the first examples of the independent boxcar leasing system that is common today. The New York Central paid Great Lakes Transit to service and repair their rolling stock and build new cars.[19]

Conners had been wintering in Palm Beach since about 1907, mostly for the boating. He was crazy about boat racing. Where the elite crowd went in for J-Boats and yachts, Conners was attracted to the raw power of snarling motorboats, and was a participant in closed-course racing, more often than not taking the wheel himself. He even bought a part-interest in a Buffalo firm, the Sterling Engine and Marine Company, just to keep himself supplied with hot boats. Organized winter regattas began to be held in Miami's Biscayne Bay and Palm Beach's Lake Worth about 1910. Other events, especially the Gold Cup in Detroit, came earlier, but the Miami regatta in particular became a professionalized, big-money event starting in December 1913 due to the efforts of Miami Beach developer Carl Fisher. He and James Allison had built the Indianapolis Motor Speedway and founded the Indianapolis 500 auto race in 1911. Fisher donated a trophy to the American Power Boat Association worth $5,000 and provided $1,000 in cash to each class winner for the Miami regatta. Championship racer and boat designer Gar Wood later said that Fisher "did more for the refining and developing of motor boats than anyone in the business."[20]

Conners became famous (infamous, actually) early on, in 1910, just after he had been humiliated at the New York Democratic Party executive committee meeting. He left town immediately, refusing all questions, because he needed to get back to Palm Beach for the Lake Worth regatta. The day before the races, he and C. A. Cragin, the president of Sterling Engine, reportedly a wizard marine motor designer, wanted to break the world's closed-course record with their latest creation, the *Courier II*. For the attempt, Conners hired a professional race crew.

The *Courier II* was running at full-throttle on the southbound straightaway, starting to make the south turn of the oval course, when it was hit by its own reflected wake. The three-man crew was knocked overboard. The boat snap-turned to the north and kept going, the dead-man control apparently failed and the boat stuck at nearly full throttle. The crew had to dive as the boat passed over them. It kept heading north towards the Lake Worth causeway that bisected the lake, everyone waiting with bated breath for the smashup. Incredibly, it passed beautifully under the drawbridge span. Unfortunately, the spectator fleet watching the record attempt was anchored around the north turn, but the *Courier II* made some graceful and daring passes in and out of the assorted launches, sailboats, and yachts— striking none—before breaching itself atop a sandbar, motor screaming, until Conners and

Cragin arrived in Conners's speedboat and Cragin dived in to shut off the engine. The *Courier II* was too banged up to make the races the next day, so it was packed up for the return to Buffalo.[21]

Conners bought his first 4,000 acres of land in Palm Beach County in the winter of 1917–18 near Canal Point, on the east side of Lake Okeechobee. This appears to have been the agricultural research station and test farm for the Southern States Land and Timber Company. As the name suggests, it was the place where the Palm Beach Canal entered Lake Okeechobee. Or, to be more accurate, where it would soon enter the lake. The Palm Beach Canal was not completed until early 1920. That was better than the ill-starred St. Lucie Canal. Started in 1914 as a hydropower project, it wasn't finished until 1926, and ended up as a standard surface canal. The Hillsborough Canal, which ran southeast out of Lake Okeechobee from Belle Glade to the Atlantic just south of Boca Raton, opened in 1918.[22]

Conners was not interested in being a land developer, at least not at first; he wanted to be a commercial farmer. The reason for his purchase was to expand the work of the experimental farm with an eye towards becoming a major supplier of wintertime truck crops to New York state. Some believe this farm was called "Connersville," but according to Gordon Williams, who crewed the Lake Okeechobee mail boats during the summer while attending college, Conners Farm and Connersville were two different places. The mail boat, which ran between 1920 and about 1926, traveled up the Palm Beach Canal from West Palm Beach to Canal Point, then to the various towns lining the shore of Lake Okeechobee, and if needed, to Brown's Farm down the Hillsborough Canal or to Moore Haven on the Caloosahatchee River.

According to Williams, Conners Farm had a dock on the Palm Beach Canal between Loxahatchee and Canal Point, near the Twenty-Mile bend. "The scenery was completely desolate," he recalled, "not a house, bridge, car, road, or any signs of civilization other than the canal, our Mail Boat, and the docks at Loxahatchee and Conners Farm." On the other hand, Williams recalls Connersville as being on the shore of Lake Okeechobee, two or three miles south of Canal Point, near Pahokee. But later on, the dock at Conner's Farm—the one in the canal—also became known as "Connersville," and by the time the road work was underway, if someone referred to Connersville, odds were they were talking about the canal landing near Twenty-Mile bend, not the one in Lake Okeechobee.[23]

By the summer of 1922, Conners had purchased a total of 13,000 acres and the farm was successfully producing a variety of truck crops. "I have only made a small beginning this year," Conners told a reporter, "but for all that I have shipped the first potatoes to four of the big cities—New York, Chicago, Philadelphia and Boston." He had a hundred acres newly planted in onions, peas, lettuce, lima beans, celery, green peppers and tomatoes, and 300 acres of potatoes. It was his goal to have the biggest truck farm in the world, and to supply the majority of the vegetables consumed in the northeast cities during the deep winter months.[24]

Gordon Williams, on the other hand, did not recall the virtues of the east Okeechobee shore in quite such glowing terms:

> Farming, even on that rich soil, was a heart-breaking gamble. With the lake level uncontrolled, in some years the crops would be flooded and in others it would be scorched. Then, after a crop was harvested, it was generally shipped to the rail-head at Okeechobee [City], thence on to some northern city that was selected at random with no knowledge of the prevailing prices in that city at that time. It was not uncommon, after all the work of growing and shipping a crop, to get a bill for part of the freight, the selling price being less than the freight charges. Much of the farm land was too soft for the employment of horses or mules. I once saw a set of four steel mud-shoes to buckle onto a mule's hoofs. They were about eight inches square and one-fourth inch thick but were too clumsy for the mules to learn to walk with.[25]

The Conners residence at Canal Point, with the Conners Highway and Lake Okeechobee in the background. Almost certainly a staged publicity photograph for the Conners Land Company, about 1924. (Photographer unknown. Florida Division of Library and Information Services, No. PR-07727.)

By early 1922, the Palm Beach county commissioners, in reply to criticism from booster organizations in Fort Myers and Lee County, replied that the $400,000 bond issue they had floated to construct the county road along the south shore of Lake Okeechobee to the Lee County line near Clewison (the future State Road 25), would get no farther than Belle Glade, sixteen miles from the county line. While they sympathized with the people of Lee County, who were building their end of their roadway from Fort Myers, through LaBelle, to Clewiston, the tax base in Palm Beach County did not look encouraging, and it was unlikely there would be another bond issue any time in the immediate future. The two counties could agree to nothing more concrete than the appointment of a committee to study the problem. With the Tamiami Trail also bogged down, the Melbourne-Orlando-Tampa route looked like it would continue to be the only reliable four-season cross-state route between Miami and lower Gulf coast for the foreseeable future.[26]

The first inkling that Conners was thinking about building a toll emerged a year later, in January 1923. The first iteration of his plan called for a hard surfaced road between Pahokee, a few miles south of Canal Point, and Okeechobee City. This version only ran along the rim of Lake Okeechobee for about 40 miles, and did not include the segment that jutted out to the southeast from Canal Point towards West Palm Beach. Conners specifically cited the delays the county was experiencing in completing State Road 25. Another factor was the difficulties the Everglades Drainage District was having in getting the St. Lucie Canal to a point where it could be navigated by even small craft. "Unless the citizens of West Palm Beach wake up right away to the seriousness of the situation," Conners told a reporter by phone from New York, "this hard-surfaced road between Pahokee and Okeechobee will undoubtedly be built and business which would come to this city [West Palm Beach] will be diverted to other points."[27]

On February 11, a bill was introduced in the legislature granting Conners a franchise for a toll road. By now, the configuration included the Palm Beach Canal segment. From Canal Point it extended north 35 miles to Okeechobee City and four miles south to Pahokee. (The Pahokee leg was not built.)[28]

On March 10, 1923, Conners acquired an option for the entire holdings of the Okeechobee Model Land Company, between forty and fifty thousand acres, for a million dollars. The Model Land Company, the parent of the Okeechobee Model Land Company, and another Florida land titan, the Consolidated Land Company, had jointly incorporated Okeechobee in 1917 at the preexisting location of a small village of homesteaders called Tantie, after Tantie Huckabee, a popular schoolteacher.[29]

The purchase gave Conners about half of the land along the east rim of Lake Okeechobee in (what is now) Okeechobee, St. Lucie, Martin and Palm Beach counties and close to 3,000 platted building lots in Okeechobee City itself. A week later, Conners appeared before the trustees of the state's Internal Improvement Fund to inform them of his plans to build a toll road from the Twenty-Mile bend in the Palm Beach canal, northeast along the canal to Canal Point on the bank of Lake Okeechobee, then north along the perimeter of the lake to Okeechobee City. He asked the Fund and the Everglades Drainage District to grant him a 66-foot right-of-way along the south bank of the Palm Beach Canal and an easement along the shore of the lake itself. The trustees agreed on the condition that Conners pay half the cost of excavating the canal, and of course, pending approval of the road itself by the legislature.[30]

* * * * *

Many years later, W. G. "Guy" Stovall, a large Okeechobee City area land owner who was, at the time, owner of the *Pahokee News*, claimed that he was responsible for talking Conners into the highway venture. In the winter of 1922–23, Stovall said, he went up to Conners at a party at Conners's winter home in Palm Beach and asked him for a loan of a million dollars. Conners, of course, asked him what he wanted it for. "To build a highway," Stovall replied. "A highway. Let's talk it over," was Conners's reaction. Meeting later, it turned out that Stovall knew what he was talking about. Of course, Conners didn't loan the money to Stovall, and Stovall never expected him to. What Stovall wanted was to interest Conners in making the same kind of investment in land and infrastructure in and around Okeechobee City that, say, Carl Fisher and the Collins family had made in Miami Beach, or that Joseph Young had made at Hollywood. That's not to say that Stovall's interests were entirely altruistic: he did end up being one of the realtors brokering Conners's right-of-way contracts for the road, and he was one of three partners in a sawmill that provided all the timber for the road's bridges and the ties for the temporary railroad used to shuttle crushed rock and other bulk materials.[31]

There is likely some truth to Stovall's story, but overall picture is vastly more complex. As discussed at some length in the history of the Tamiami Trail, Miami Beach developer Carl Fisher proposed the development of the Dixie Highway in 1914. At the American Roads Congress in Atlanta in November 1914 a special conference was scheduled in Chattanooga in April 1915 to designate a route. That meeting degenerated into chaos as hundreds of unofficial representatives, boosters, and politicians vied for the privilege of having the road run through their town or across their land. A second convention was scheduled for May with decision-making limited to two delegates from each state, to be selected by the governors.[32]

From out of the May conference emerged not a single route, but a ladder-like branch of routes. In Florida, the eastern division entered the state at Jacksonville and followed the Atlantic shore to Miami. The western division, after many months of debate and lobbying, was planned to enter the state at Tallahassee, then pass down the center of the state: Gainesville, Ocala, Orlando, Arcada, then east across the state through Okeechobee City to join the eastern division at Jupiter. But after an inspection trip in March 1916, Dixie Highway Association William Gilbreath questioned whether the central Florida route should be included on the Association's first published map, due out in January 1917.

"From Tallahassee to Orlando there are some mighty good stretches of road," Gilbreath wrote to a Miami reporter, "but believe me, that drive across the state from Arcadia to Jupiter is the worst I ever saw. I covered fifteen miles in that trip, sand to my hubs, and in one place I made about twelve miles in two hours." Gilbreath said that the Association was seriously considering the proposal being advanced by the Miami, Tampa and Fort Myers chambers of commerce to re-draw the western division to pass over the Tamiami Trail upon which construction had started the year before.[33]

In 1920, the state road department, in keeping with a mandate handed down from the federal Bureau of Public Roads, designated ten highways as "state aid" roads. Of these, six (1, 2, 3, 4, 5, and 9) were given priority designation. A year later the legislature passed the "Miller Bill," an anti pork-barrel measure, which ordered the road department to spend its federal-aid money *only* on the designated six until they were finished. This selection was somewhat controversial, as the choice appeared to neglect south Florida communities. State Road 4—the eastern division of the Dixie Highway—was the only highway that ran south of Lake Okeechobee.[34]

Conners's big break came in early 1923 when State Road 9, which ran alongside the Apalachicola River in the panhandle east of Tallahassee was struck from the preferential list as impractical. With State Road 9 off the list, State Road 8 was moved up to replace it. State Road 8 ran from Haines City (half-way between Tampa and Orlando) to Fort Pierce on the Atlantic coast (45 miles north of West Palm Beach) via Sebring and Okeechobee City. The road department did adhere to the spirit of the Miller Bill mandate, with only some small technical exceptions, and the last contract for State Road 8 was completed around November 1926.[35] Thus, from the time the Apalachicola Parkway was struck from the priority list, a toll road to Okeechobee City was almost certain to have a state-road connection on its north end that would continue on through Sebring, then split at Haines City and go either west to Tampa or north to Tallahassee.

Therefore, at the time Conners was starting to make a serious investment in Conner's farm in 1922, the situation was this: the western division of the Dixie Highway, connecting Okeechobee City to Arcadia, was in poor shape, and its construction was unfunded, and would probably remain so for another four or five years. Much the same was true for the cross-state highway around the south rim of Lake Okeechobee. The Tamiami Trail wouldn't be finished for another six years. The only reliable way to get from West Palm Beach to Fort Myers was through Melbourne, Orlando (actually, Kissimmee) and Tampa, nine hours in the dry season, as much as two days in the summer. All these factors appeared to make the idea of a toll road an extremely attractive proposition—provided, of course, that one had the million and a half dollars or thereabouts to build the thing.

••15••

"Plenty of grease, gumption and gasoline"

Conners was either supremely confident, or he knew something everyone else didn't. Two weeks before the legislature voted on his road bill, he had already retained a local contractor, Tom Bryan, who then subcontracted to a local ditching specialist, Otis Harden, who owned a Buckeye ditch-maker. By the time Governor Hardee signed the legislation, Conners claimed that Bryan and Harden had already thrown up three miles of roadbed.

Some accounts state that Conners grossly underestimated the scale of work involved, hired Bryan and Harden, then later came to his senses, fired them, and greatly scaled up the size of his operation. This is probably not the case. Although neither the legislative bill nor his agreement with the Internal Improvement Fund specified a completion date, Conners rashly maintained throughout most of 1923 that he would be finished by the end of the year, that is, nine months after hiring Bryan, a patently absurd claim given the magnitude of the job. This was likely the result of a verbal promise he gave to legislators in a moment of excessive zeal.[1]

Bryan was Palm Beach County's regular road builder, and while everyone turned to him for their local farm-to-market roads, he did not have the organization necessary to run a million-and-a-half dollar job. It appears that Bryan and Harden made two important early contributions. First, they built up the roadbase at two vital places, the dock at Conners farm on the Palm Beach Canal and at a location on the St. Lucie Canal near Lake Okeechobee where a rock crushing plant would be built. These would be the two busiest sites, and they needed to be improved first. Second, Bryan and Harden built up these two locations as test sites using the traditional method of dredging up wet marl, letting it dry, then rolling it down. In some Everglades locations the marl had enough calcium carbonate (dolomite) to become brick-like when it was dried and rolled. In other places, it had too much sand and simply became a crumbly, chalky mess. Now was the time to find out. (Marl, unlike limestone—which is a mixture of dolomite and magnesium carbonate with no organic content—will always revert to its claylike form when re-hydrated no matter how hard it sets when dried and compressed. It must be covered with a top coat of crushed rock or waterproofed, usually with oil.)

By mid-summer Conners had brought in his own man, R. Y. Patterson, as construction superintendent. Tom Bryan was back working on the county road between Twenty Mile Bend and Belle Glade in August.[2]

Conners continued to hold to the unrealistic December 1923 completion date in interviews he gave to, for example, *The Highway Magazine*, until almost the end of the year. A clue to this seemingly aberrant behavior comes from testimony Conners's private secretary, John Meegan, gave in a probate hearing after his boss's death. In March 1924, Conners approached a New York bond salesman, George Losey, and asked him to sell a million dollars in bonds on behalf of the Conners-Florida Highway Corporation. As an inducement to purchasers, Conners, who owned all of the stock in the corporation, would sell 25 percent of it at deeply discounted prices to those willing to take on large blocks of the bonds. Losey was told the bonds had to be sold by June 1924. (The road opened a month later.) Losey could not sell the bonds because the prospective buyers, all large institutions such as banks and insurance companies, either wanted Conners to put up part of his newspaper or shipping lines as collateral, or wanted to know the financial details of his overall financial empire, including the newspapers and ships. This he was not prepared to do.[3] It appears the falsely optimistic completion date was based on the need to sell bonds, which in turn was mandated by Conner's financial condition. The bonds were never sold, but in April 1925 Conners did sell $300,000 in building lots and unplatted land in Okeechobee City to a Miami investment group, which eased the cash squeeze.[4]

Within a week after Governor Hardee signed the legislation in April 1923 granting Conners his toll road franchise, he and his men had ordered a massive amount of equipment: five dragline shovels, a rock crusher, two steam shovels, six locomotives, eighty miles of rail, tractors, light and heavy trucks, and canal barges. The railroad was going to be his secret weapon. He intended to take rock not only from the Palm Beach Canal, but the St. Lucie Canal as well, which had a better supply of limestone. He would strip the muck off the underlying rock, the same as J. B. McCrary had done on the Ingraham and the Tamiami roads, and would dig a borrow canal along the road, also as McCrary had done. The difference was that he didn't intend to rely on the rock removed from the canal to provide for the total fill required for the adjacent roadway. In technical terms, he did not plan to depend on a balanced cut-and-fill strategy. In fact, R. Y. Patterson had calculated that a borrow canal adequate for construction boats and roadway drainage wouldn't be nearly big enough to provide all the fill needed to raise the roadway above the level of standing water in summer, and he didn't plan to waste most of his crew's time and effort digging a huge canal simply to make gravel.

Instead, most of the crushed rock would come out of the St. Lucie canal, which did not run beside the road. In fact, the only place the two even came near each other was at Port Mayaca, half-way between Canal Point and Okeechobee City, where the St. Lucie Canal entered Lake Okeechobee. This is where the crushing mill was built. It would be fed from two sources: boulders taken out of the Palm Beach Canal beside the road and excavations made to turn the existing shallow and narrow St. Lucie canal into a deepwater shipping canal.

The material taken from either canal would be dumped into rail gondola cars by steam shovels. Trains of gondola cars would then run over temporary tracks to docks. The location of the docks depended on how far the canals had been excavated sufficiently to accommodate rock barges. At the docks the rock would be tipped into the barges. The barges would be taken down the canal, and in the case of the Palm Beach Canal, across the lake, to the Port Mayaca rock crusher. After being ground into gravel, the process would be reversed: rock crusher to barge, to train, and to the road construction site, where the gondola cars were tipped and the gravel spread by the work crews and compacted by rollers. The temporary tracks were even connected to the Florida East Coast Railroad tracks at West Palm Beach so, if necessary, Conners could simply buy pre-crushed stone from suppliers, although it is not believed he ever did so.[5]

15. "Plenty of grease, gumption and gasoline" 225

The Conners Highway, shortly after it was completed in 1924, near Canal Point. (Photograph by Landis. Florida Division of Library and Information Services, No. N031637.)

There were two major bridges, across the Palm Beach Canal at Canal Point and across the St. Lucie Canal at Port Mayaca, and several smaller bridges, including a third drawbridge across the unfinished Okeechobee Canal (also known as Taylor Creek) just south of Okeechobee City that the landowners and merchants of Okeechobee City were donating.

The highway bill gave the Conners-Florida Highway Company the same powers of eminent domain as a railroad, and prohibited any government from granting a franchise for a competing toll road within five miles. After twenty-five years the county could buy the road whether the Highway Company agreed or not. Pedestrians and cyclists could be charged fifty cents for the entire 51-mile length; cars two dollars plus fifty cents per passenger; a two-ton truck four dollars, plus fifty cents per passenger; a bus five dollars. The tolls from West Palm Beach to Canal Point, or from Okeechobee City to Canal Point, were roughly half of this.[6]

These were fairly steep tolls for the era, and the company reportedly pulled in anywhere between a thousand to two thousand dollars per day after the road was fully operational. In addition, Conners's Okeechobee Land Company had its agricultural land, most of it fronting onto the toll road, and platted subdivisions in Okeechobee City. None of those holdings would start to generate cash until the road was done. Whether he was using his own money, shifted over from other enterprises (Dunn and Bradstreet's valued his Great Lakes shipping lines at seven million dollars) or was borrowing money from other parties, he was undoubtedly under a lot of pressure to get the road open. And he and his men did do a very efficient job, especially when compared to the Ingraham Highway (7 years to open; partially completed only) and the Tamiami Trail (13 years to open; 16 years to fully finish).

But a December 1, 1923, completion date was simply never possible. R. Y. Patterson, Conners's construction superintendent, told *Florida Engineer and Contractor* that the work would take slightly over a year from the time the railroad and rock crushing equipment were up and running, and that proved to be a fairly accurate estimate. There do not appear to have been any major deviations from schedule, although some permanent bridges were not installed until after the highway opened.[7]

One problem with the swiftness of the road's completion is that it left relatively few accounts of the work. Once the winter dry season of 1923–24 arrived, the work force appeared to peak at about 140–150 men. Laborers earned about fifty dollars per week, machine operators around sixty, and foremen, surveyors and field engineers seventy to a hundred dollars. There were 74 trucks, seven power shovels and cranes of various kinds, and 15 launches (some of these appear to be canal boat versions of tugboats, for towing or pushing barges). Most accounts focused on the elevated rock crusher on the St. Lucie Canal and the railroad. Two fourteen ton steam "dinkies" (timber or mining shuttle locomotives) were dedicated to rock and gravel trains, while four eight-ton gas shuttles were used for a variety of tasks. (Judging by their descriptions, these looked much like interurban cars—only shorter—with the back two-thirds turned into flatbeds.) The gas shuttles could pull six rock-filled hopper cars a time, but were often used for lighter, speedier tasks, such as hauling tools, equipment, bridge timber or men. A total of 40 hopper cars were on-site; the dinkies supposedly could haul 25, but nobody ever needed so many at one time.

The roadbed itself was built in the usual manner by dredging a combination of marl (dolomite, sand and organic matter) and limestone out of the adjacent canal, then breaking it up and flattening it when it was still wet and clay-like. This provided the base upon which a smoother, more granulized gravel surface of pure crushed limestone (dolomite, magnesium carbonate and shell fragments, most taken from the St. Lucie canal) was laid.

Superintendent Patterson had originally planned a classic Macadamized surface comprised of two layers of screened gravel, the first six inches thick. This would be allowed to settle with time and moderate rolling, followed by a top layer three inches thick rolled as hard as the material would compress. But based on field tests and on research coming out of the American Association of State Highway Officials, this was dispensed with in favor of a simpler configuration comprised of a single layer seven and a half inches thick rolled twice, then oiled. The road would be allowed to settle for about a year, and a new two-inch coating applied, with another oiling. The road was 16 feet wide with two four-foot unpaved shoulders at the top of the road grade, making a total road grade of 24 feet. The base of the road grade was roughly 36 feet. There were 26 timber bridges and three steel bridges.[8]

The highway to Okeechobee City was completed in the summer of 1924, seven months behind the date Conners had given the legislators, but remarkably quickly given the history of Everglades roadbuilding. On the other hand, the state had made little or no progress towards finishing the north connection to Sebring. Little work had been done on State Road 8 between Okeechobee City and Childs. (State Road 8 ran west out of Okeechobee City and split at Childs. The road north to Sebring, 21 miles farther, was State Road 8. The road west to Arcadia was State Road 18.) The Okeechobee City-Childs segment was now the last unfinished link in the cross state highway between West Palm Beach and Tampa.

Conners believed that the state had promised the completion of the connection between Okeechobee City and Sebring if he would finish the toll road on time. The state road department, on the other hand, believed that the agreement was that if all went well, Conners would build a second phase of his toll road from Okeechobee City to Sebring. The original legislation and agreement with the Internal Improvement Fund makes no reference to any road beyond Okeechobee City, but neither do they prohibit it. (The agreement with the Internal Improvement Fund only granted the Highway Corporation right-of-way to Okeechobee City, but if Conners purchased the land to Sebring privately, nothing in the state agreement blocked this.)[9]

The State Road 8 link was vital. The Seaboard Coast Line had finished an extension into West Palm Beach in January 1924 and were now planning to push on to Hialeah, which they reached in late 1926. But Henry Walters, the chairman of the Atlantic Coast Line Railroad believed that all three of the major trunk lines were on the verge of ruinous overexpansion. The state's best natural seaport, Pensacola, was already locked up by two railroads, the Louisville & Nashville, and the Gulf, Florida & Alabama. Both were major landholders in the panhandle area, the L&N directly and the GF&A indirectly through one of its owners, the giant Southern States Land and Timber Company. (In 1925 that part of the GF&A not owned by Southern States was purchased by the Frisco Railroad.)

As a result, Pensacola and much of the panhandle was invulnerable to expansion by the big downstate railroads. On the other hand, the L&N and the Frisco had no desire to expand much beyond Tallahassee because they were focused on resource extraction, mostly timber. That meant three major railroads (the Florida East Coast, the Atlantic Coast Line, and the Seaboard Coast Line) were competing for the entire down-state trade, especially for shipments to and from the northeast. Moreover, everything that moved between New York/New England and Florida went through a single rail yard at Jacksonville until the ACL finished its Perry Cut-Off in 1927 between Tampa and Birmingham, Alabama.[10]

While the FEC and Seaboard both expanded into Miami and Naples, Walters's ACL went no farther south than Fort Myers (except for a spur line into Everglades City paid for by Barron Collier). Moreover, Walters ran no passenger service past Jacksonville on the east coast and Tampa on the Gulf coast. Instead, to reach Palm Beach, Fort Lauderdale and Miami, he intended to offer luxury over-the road coach service in trailer-type busses built by the Pullman Company. The Conners Highway was to be the vital link in getting these coaches from Tampa to Palm Beach quickly and smoothly. But the Conners Highway couldn't fulfill this role if the state did not build the vital linkage between Sebring and Okeechobee City. It is not known if Walters helped pay for the Conners Highway. Even if he didn't, the tolls alone would go a long ways towards making the road a profitable venture. Walters was planning on running as many as 16 coaches each way from Tampa and Miami during the height of the winter tourist season. The one-way toll for a bus was five dollars; a total of $160 per day—not bad for a project with an initial revenue target of a thousand a day.[11]

Conners and J. W. Young, the developer of Hollywood in Broward County, jointly covered the cost of improving the stretch of State Road 8 west of Okeechobee City to Childs, where the road turned north into Sebring in 1924, building bridges, raising low spots and graveling the right-of-way, but it was not hard surfaced until the state road department brought it up to state standards in 1926.[12]

Why Young helped Conners build the road is something of a mystery. Young, mimicking Carl Fischer's Montauk development on Long Island, had set out to build a resort community, Hollywood-in-the-Hills, in upstate New York, and it is possible that he was trying to woo Conners as a partner by helping with the road. Another possibility is that Young was contemplating a second Hollywood-type development in Florida somewhere around Stuart, where the St. Lucie River opened into the Atlantic. If so, Young never got the chance to start it. His organization was mortally wounded by the hurricane of 1926 and was wiped out by the Great Depression of October 1929. He disappeared into the night, leaving a mansion, a beachfront estate and a million dollars in debt behind.[13]

* * * * *

Conners had promised the 300 or so citizens of Okeechobee City the grandest of grand openings to coincide with their Fourth of July festivities for 1924 and he intended to deliver. Conners's farm dressed 28 head of cattle, 41 hogs and a ton of fish taken from the lake for the barbecue. To everyone's shock, when the Democratic National Convention in New York City deadlocked on June 30 over its presidential nomination and stayed deadlocked, Conners just stood up on the evening of July 2 and nonchalantly walked over to Grand Central Station, where his private car had already been attached to a Florida-bound express. "No candidate will be decided upon for three or four days anyway," he breezily told reporters on his way out of Madison Square Garden, explaining that a token group of trustworthy balloteers would be picked by each side to keep the deadlock going over the holiday until everyone returned and they could get down to business again on Monday. "It will be Oscar Underwood," he added. (John W. Davis defeated Al Smith on the 103rd ballot the week after Conners returned to New York.)[14]

About 15,000 showed up, including those in the motorcades from Palm Beach and Miami. According to the *Miami Daily News*, it was the largest public gathering in the history of the state. It opened in mid-morning, after Conners and his guests arrived from a ribbon-cutting at the West Palm Beach toll gate at Twenty Mile Bend. There was with a parade through downtown Okeechobee City with 90 floats and bands from both coasts, followed by speeches by both incoming governor Martin and outgoing governor Hardee and attorney general Rivers Buford, who was the first state official to meet with Conners in Tallahassee in January 1923 when he came to ask about securing a franchise from the legislature and the Internal Improvement Fund. Then came the barbeque and baseball game between the Stuart and Okeechobee semi-pro teams. The kegs were tapped too, probably to Conners's regret. Three men from the George Merrick's Coral Gables Company had driven up from Miami and spent too much time in front of the beer barrels. When a cheer came up from the baseball game, Jack Davis, the company's transportation manager, asked one of his men for his pistol, saying he wanted to make some noise. He fired off some rounds into the ground, but one shot hit a rock and fragmented. A shard entered the neck of farmer William Cross at the base of his skull, killing him instantly. The three men were arrested on the spot, but the next day only Davis was bound over.[15]

By the spring of 1925, an average of 600 cars each way passed over the highway. Since most were traveling its full length and were carrying passengers, the Conners-Florida Highway Corporation was grossing around $2,200 a day. However, there was still the unfinished gap between Okeechobee City and Sebring and reportedly another near Avon Park north of Sebring where "the sand is deep, but the cars, including the big cross-state busses, get through, but it requires plenty of grease, gumption and gasoline to do the trick." The district supervisor for the state road department assured the reporter that the Avon Park stretch would be completed by fall.[16]

However, John Meegan, Conners's private secretary, wrote a business associate that "the failure of the state to complete the unfinished portion of the State Road has kept the Conners Highway from showing any real earnings."[17] When the highway was originally built, Conners had been allowed to span the St. Lucie Canal at Port Mayaca with a temporary wooden bridge until the Everglades Drainage District completed the job of making the St. Lucie Canal navigable. In May 1924 the chief engineer of the drainage district notified the

Highway Company that the canal would soon be ready and that they needed to install a permanent steel drawbridge. The Highway Company did nothing. In late 1924 the Florida East Coast Railroad began extending their line south from Okeechobee City to West Palm Beach. As part of the construction, they needed to move a derrick barge through the Lake Okeechobee end of the St. Lucie Canal. The temporary bridge did not allow this. The FEC requested that the Highway Company partially dismantle the bridge so their barge could pass. The Highway Company refused. The FEC complained to the state's Internal Improvement Fund. In January 1925 the Fund's trustees told the Highway Company that they had ten days to let the barge pass or the drainage district would take the bridge apart. The Highway Company was also ordered to install the permanent bridge by a deadline to be established by the drainage district. The Highway Company apparently complied, and a steel vertical-lift span was eventually installed. Some parts of the drawbridge remain, although the moveable center span has long since been removed.[18]

The Highway Company was dealt an even bigger setback in August 1925 when the county road southeast of the Twenty Mile Bend—the connection between the toll road and West Palm Beach—was closed for almost six weeks by spoil piled up on the road by a dredging barge. A newspaper described it as "one of the most viscous circles in the history of roads and bridges." The canal bank was washing away, threatening to take the road with it. A state dredge boat was brought in to re-build the bank, but the only place to pile the spoil, dry it and crush it was the county road on top of the embankment. While the Conners Highway was untouched, there was no way to access it from the south. Fortunately, it wasn't the tourist season, but R.Y. Patterson, the Conners Highway superintendent, estimated that on the first day the road was closed his toll booth attendants had to turn back 200 cars from the north end, a loss of about around $900.[19]

But the land in and around Okeechobee City, which was the primary reason for building the road in the first place, continued to do well throughout the Florida land boom of the 1920s. Of the 3,019 lots in Okeechobee City, over 2,000 had been sold by mid–1925 for a total of $1.7 million. The company was selling land near Conners farm and Twenty Mile Bend for $350 an acre.[20]

But it is likely that Conners knew that the days of the toll road were numbered. After 1926, the Florida land boom started to lose its steam. Most blame the October 1926 hurricane, but the damage from the storm was fairly tightly confined to the Miami-Ft. Lauderdale area and the south rim of Lake Okeechobee. There is no reason that it should have collapsed the real estate industry of the entire state. Walter Fuller, a land developer, later published a pamphlet in which he candidly laid the blame for the post–1926 recession on he and his fellow speculators: "We just ran out of suckers. That's all. We got all their money, then started trading with ourselves.... We became the suckers." In fact, the state faced a banking crisis in the summer of 1926 touched off by the collapse of the Mizner Development Corporation, builder of Boca Raton, three months *before* the hurricane. In July 1926 alone, 27 Florida banks folded along with almost 300 in Georgia.[21]

The toll road had other problems as well. By 1926, the road between Fort Myers and Palm Beach around the south rim Lake Okeechobee (State Road 25) was nearing completion. Only a 17-mile gap in Palm Beach County between Clewiston and Belle Glade was yet to be finished. Palm Beach approved a bond issue for this work in 1926 and the Celotex Company, Clewiston's largest employer, submitted the winning bid at cost to guarantee that the project got done.[22] By 1927 motorists headed out of West Palm Beach towards Conners Highway would have a new option: at Twenty Mile Bend they could turn left at the Conners Highway toll booth, leave the canal bank, and head west to Belle Glade, then follow the south shore of Lake Okeechobee to Clewiston, then travel along the south bank of the Caloosahatchee River to LaBelle and Fort Myers. When Conners started his road in 1923, those trying to drive cross-state from Miami had no real options south of Melbourne. By the spring of 1928, they had four: Conners Highway to Sebring and Tampa (1925); Conners Highway to Arcadia and Fort Myers (1927); State Road 25 across the south rim of Lake Okeechobee from Palm Beach to Fort Myers (1927), and the Tamiami Trail (State Road 27) from Miami to Naples (1928).[23] Having served its purpose, Conners realized that it was time to cash in his chips.

The only buyer for something as big as a 51-mile highway was, of course, the state road department. Conners's men descended on Tallahassee during the legislative session over the winter of 1926–27. Rather than propose a set price, they recommended that a committee of engineers be delegated to appraise its value and set the price. The State Comptroller, Ernest Amos, would then issue the necessary time warrants to purchase the highway. The editors of the *Plant City Enterprise* (which lay along the cross-state route created by the Conners Highway) commented that "it is not needed now nearly so much as it was a few years ago, other roads giving good access to the East Coast and back." They concluded that "The Conners highway proposition savors of carpet bagger days."[24]

Conners got his bill, but almost immediately, Y. L.. Watson, a lawyer and former state senator from Quincy, filed suit in Tallahassee seeking an injunction to bar Comptroller Amos from issuing any warrants to pay for the purchase. Watson alleged several breaches of the state constitution, but the most substantial was a claim that the method under which

Makeshift coffins at canal point after the hurricane of 1926, awaiting transport across Lake Okeechobee to Clewiston or Moore Haven, where the dykes had collapsed, killing hundreds. The Seaboard Coast Line lift bridge across the Palm Beach Canal can be clearly seen, with one tower of the roadway draw bridge behind it. (Photographer unknown. Florida Division of Library and Information Services, No. N041598.)

the price of the road was to be determined violated the legislature's appropriation authority. The bill specified that the determination of the purchase price was to be delegated to an appraisal committee of engineers. Comptroller Amos (at this time under indictment for permitting two insolvent banks to remain open) was authorized to issue warrants (a promise to issue bonds at a future date) for whatever amount was necessary to pay the price specified by the committee. According to Watson, the legislature could not, under the state constitution, approve a bonded indebtedness of an indeterminate amount. A fixed price had to be set, that price had to appear in the budget, and approved by both houses.[25]

The circuit court judge upheld Watson, and in February 1928 the State Supreme Court affirmed that decision. "The terms of the act would, in effect," the Supreme Court wrote, "create a binding, continuing interest-bearing contractual obligation of the state to pay money in the future that would violate the intent of the constitution."[26]

As an alternative, Palm Beach, Martin and Okeechobee counties considered leasing the highway. The county governments were responding mostly to their residents in the area around Canal Point and Okeechobee City, who felt themselves unduly burdened by having to pay a toll of between of up to $2.50 for a farm truck every time they wanted to travel to the railhead at Okeechobee City or into West Palm Beach.[27] The Conners-Florida Highway Company was dealt another setback in August 1928 when the short north-south stretch of road connecting Okeechobee City and the north rim of the lake had to be dynamited to let water run across it and into the lake from a flooded area of the city inundated by Taylor's Creek, a tributary of the Kissimmee River. "Shortly after noon," local newspapers reported, "water began spilling over the avenue [Conners Highway] and within a few minutes was flowing over a width of 500 yards. Dynamite was then resorted to in an effort to prevent flood damage to another wide territory."[28]

Almost exactly a month later, the entire area was slammed by the infamous hurricane of September 16, 1928. The hurricane of 1926 had killed about 450 individuals, 300 from the south rim of Lake Okeechobee, mostly poor farm workers in Moore Haven. The 1928 hurricane came ashore just north of Palm Beach, moving south-southwest. It pushed Lake Okeechobee south over the top of the marginal levees that had been erected after the 1926 storm. Everything from Belle Glade to Moore Haven was simply erased. Nobody will know for sure how many died; somewhere around 2,000, almost all poor black farm workers. West Palm Beach was so completely cut off from the south rim that the disaster relief efforts were routed through Fort Myers.[29]

Conners himself never did manage to sell his highway. With rumors of an impending crash in the stock market swirling, and everyone on pins and needles, he died of a heart attack at his home in Buffalo. He woke early in the morning feeling poorly and asked for his personal physician, who arrived within a few minutes, but could do nothing. Conners was dead by 5 a.m. He was survived by his third wife, 35-year-old Grace Hammond Conners. He also had two daughters by his first wife, who died in 1881, and a son and two daughters by his second wife, who died in 1924. His son, William Conners, Jr., already managed his father's newspaper empire, and under the terms of his will, he inherited most of its ownership and all control. The steamship lines were placed into a trust shared between Grace and the daughters. Grace, a Palm Beach native, inherited the Florida properties, including the Highway Company.[30]

John Meegan, Conners's personal secretary, managed the estate, and Walter McGriff, who had been secretary of the Okeechobee Land Co. and auditor for the Conners-Florida Highway Company, took over the management of the Florida properties on behalf of the estate through the W. J. Conners Realty Company.[31]

It appears that there were at least some periods during the summer when the counties agreed to pay the Conners-Florida Highway Corporation a lump sum in return for the company lifting tolls for locals. However, the property owners along the road continued to press their respective commissioners to either buy the road or build a new one parallel to it. In February 1930 the three counties agreed to do this.[32]

However, Meegan asserted that the entire 51.8 miles of the highway from Twenty-Mile Bend almost to Okeechobee City lay within Palm Beach County, because the County's boundary encompassed the entire lake, as measured from a previously established high-water line. Thus, all the highway along the shoreline lay within Palm Beach County. The only part outside Palm Beach County was the short stretch south of Okeechobee City, in Okeechobee County, which the city was preparing to annex. Martin and Okeechobee counties had no objection to this interpretation, especially when Palm Beach County offered to put up all the money to buy the highway.[33]

Meegan and McGriff agreed to sell for a price of $660,000. Of this, $35,000 was due immediately and $625,000 in one year. Alternatively, the $625,000 could be deferred for six more months, but an additional $3,000 would be added to the price for each month's extension. The county planned to borrow the $35,000 from two special road districts and pay it back a few months later. The permanent source of funding would be money already due from the state for work on the road between Belle Glade and Canal Point. After hearing a report from the county engineer that "the entire stretch of road is in satisfactory shape," the Palm Beach County Commissioners voted to suspend tolls at 12:01 am, July 16, 1930, just a few hours after the commission meeting in which they agreed to the sale.[34]

The county was not able to come up with the required $643,000 by the extended deadline of February 16, 1932. However, the state road department stepped in with a proposal to buy the road just ten days after the deadline lapsed. The problem was that there was nothing in the budget to support an immediate $643,000 expenditure.[35] Florida by now had a seven-cent-a-gallon gas tax, of which one cent was allocated for school construction, but since 1929, half of the six cents allocated for roads was reserved for paying off county road and bridge bonds from before 1924, so there was actually less discretionary money in the state road department fund in 1932 than in 1927.[36]

The road department's solution was to buy the Conners Highway in 12-mile long sections and to lease the rest. This was, in essence, a way to buy the road through annual installment payments, something that was not technically permissible because it committed future legislatures to appropriations based on contracts entered into in prior years. The cost of each 12-mile segment was roughly $98,750, with the total price remaining at $620,000, the unpaid balance due by Palm Beach County. The state made a payment in June 1933 leaving a balance due of $133,800. A few weeks later the state paid $19,000 for a lease running through March 1, 1934, but only $4,950 of this was in cash. The remainder was in "other unnamed consideration." Almost certainly this was an offset to pay for the maintenance the state was providing on that portion of the road still owned by the Conners-Florida Highway Corporation. The state had incorporated the entire road into its highway system and was operating it the same as any other state road, and the Highway Corporation owed the state for taking care of its property. There is no record if the state did purchase the remainder of the highway by 1934, but J. J. Meegan, Conners's former private secretary, said in a deposition that the sale had been completed sometime before April 1937. A reporter later described the Conners Highway as "the most important highway link between the coast and the Glades."[37]

Visiting Okeechobee City in 1938, investigators for the Works Progress Administration

15. "Plenty of grease, gumption and gasoline" 233

described it as "a commercial center for the surrounding territories" with a population of 1,795. The primary businesses were vegetable packing houses, boxing up tomatoes, peppers, and cucumbers for shipment at the Seaboard rail station, and bullfrog breeding for frogs' legs for northeastern restaurants. In 1944, Frank J. Pepper, land agent for the Model Land Company, wrote William Kenan, Jr., James Ingraham's successor as president of the MLC, that "all our best lands for farming purposes in Palm Beach, Broward, and Dade counties have been picked over and sold out."[38]

Throughout the 1940s and '50s the highway continued to suffer from high water, particularly the segments alongside the Palm Beach Canal and the stretch between the north shore of the lake and Okeechobee City. The *Palm Beach Post* reported in October 1953 that "a state of emergency existed along Conners Highway in the Glades today, as workmen battled to keep the road open against rising waters." Seven miles of the road starting at Twenty Mile Bend was completely inundated as water overtopped the canal and flowed south. Fortunately, the road had to be closed anyway. The drawbridge at Canal Point had been removed for repairs and replaced with a temporary wooden bridge. A dredge needed to pass from the lake down the canal to West Palm Beach, so the temporary bridge had to be partially dismantled to let it pass. With no traffic on the road, County Engineer Steve Middleton sent his men down to Twenty-Mile Bend to put in sand bags to slow down the flow and put in patches where he could. It appears that the drawbridge was never replaced.[39]

The old Conners Highway, now State Road 90, at Canal Point, 1953. The drawbridge is gone. The only way in or out of Lake Okeechobee for barge traffic on the east side is the St. Lucie Canal, twenty miles north. (Photographer unknown [State Road Dept.]. Florida Division of Library and Information Services, No. DOT1508.

The problem wasn't resolved until the mid–1960s when the eastern perimeter levee was completed. The levee was a part of the giant Central and Southern Florida Flood Control Project, started in 1947 by the Army Corps of Engineers and never fully completed due to massive adverse impacts on Everglades National Park. The West Palm Beach canal runs just inside the north boundary of the C&SF's designated Everglades Agricultural Area. From Twenty Mile Bend to the lake, vegetable fields extended five miles north of the highway before the wetlands began again. South, cane fields wrapped around the entire south side of the lake like a twenty-mile wide donut. But south and east of Twenty Mile Bend start the water conservation areas, essentially freshwater reservoirs to recharge the aquifer upon which the water taps of Broward and Miami-Dade County depend. North of the lake, the Kissimmee River was fed into the C-38 canal, completed in 1971, opening 576,000 acres of new pastureland. The Seminole Tribe, at their Brighton Reservation southwest of Okeechobee City, has become one of the largest producers of beef cattle in the state.[40]

Much of the former Okeechobee Company lands in Palm Beach County ended up in the hands of Alcoa and the Arthur Vining Davis company. Some later became part of Loxahatchee National Wildlife Refuge, and some was purchased for the DuPuis Reserve State Forest. Some is farmland, a little has been urbanized, most is rangeland for cattle. Canal Point and Pahokee are primarily marinas for freshwater sport fishermen plying the waters of Lake Okeechobee. Conners Highway is still there, now known officially as U.S. Highway 98, but everybody along it still uses "Conners Highway" as their address.

Chapter Notes

Introduction

1. John Nordheimer, "I-95 Journal: Road Completed, but Debate Goes On," *New York Times* (December 18, 1987); Gary Enos, "I-95 to Become Whole Today; Missing Link Sets Stage for New Era of Growth," *Ft. Lauderdale Sun Sentinel* (December 19, 1987).

2. Mark Derr, *Some Kind of Paradise: A Chronicle of Man and the Land in Florida* (Gainesville: University Press of Florida, 1998 [1989]): 370. A net of about 250 miles have been added since the original map was issued in 1957, mostly urban bypasses that replaced through-city links.

3. "System Description: Florida's Turnpike": www.floridasturnpike.com/about_system.cfm. Last accessed December 28, 2014.

4. Enos, "I-95 to Become Whole Today; Missing Link Sets Stage for New Era of Growth."

5. Richard Weingroff, "The Man Who Changed America, Part 1," *Public Roads* 66, 5 (March/April 2003); 20-35; _____, "The Man Who Changed America, Part 2," *Public Roads* 66, 5 (May/June 2003); 22-38; Mark H. Rose, *Interstate: Express Highway Politics, 1939-1989* (Knoxville: University of Tennessee Press, 1990 [1979]).

6. Mark S. Foster, *Castles in the Sand: The Life and Times of Carl Graham Fisher* (Gainesville: University Press of Florida, 2000): *Passim*; Tammy Ingram, *Dixie Highway: Road Building and the Making of Modern South, 1900-1930* (Chapel Hill: University of North Carolina Press, 2014): *Passim*.

7. John H. Hahn, *Apalachee: The Land Between the Rivers* (Gainesville: University Press of Florida, 1988): 149-151. See esp. map on page 150.

8. Burke G. Vanderhill, "The Alachua-St. Mary's Road," *Florida Historical Quarterly* 46, 1 (July 1987): 50-67.

9. Joshua C. Chase, "South Florida as I Knew It (Read to the University Ohio of Winter Park), June 27, 1940," MS in James E. Ingraham Papers, Smathers Libraries, University of Florida, http://Ufdc.Ufl.Edu//UF00095317/00001; "Keep Your Head Above the Financial Waters and Bet on the Growth of the Country," *Manufacturers Record* (January 26, 1922): James E. Ingraham Papers, P. K. Yonge Library, University of Florida, http://Ufdc.Ufl.Edu//UF00095313/00001.

10. Erie Canal: Edward L. Throm, *The Popular Mechanics History of American Transport* (New York: Simon and Schuster, 1952): 58-60. Canals in Pennsylvania, Ohio: William Roy, *Socializing Capital: The Rise of the Large Industrial Corporation in America* (Princeton: Princeton University Press, 1997): 50, 56-60.

11. David Howard Bain, *Empire Express: Building the First Transcontinental Railroad* (New York: Viking, 1999); Maury Klein, *Union Pacific: The Birth of a Railroad, 1862-1893* (New York: Doubleday, 1987).

12. Michael Grunwald, *The Swamp: The Everglades, Florida and the Politics of Paradise* (New York: Simon and Schuster: 2008): 67, 73.

13. J. E. [Junius Elmore] Dovell, "The Railroads and the Public Lands of Florida, 1879-1905," *Florida Historical Quarterly* 34, 3 (January, 1956): 236-258; Grunwald, *The Swamp*: 95-97.

14. Edward Akin, *Flagler: Rockefeller Partner and Florida Barron* (Gainesville: University Press of Florida, 1991 [1988]): 141, 177, 182-183, 190.

15. Dovell, "The Railroads and the Public Lands of Florida, 1879-1905": 240-245; Gregg Turner, *A Journey into Florida Railroad History* (Gainesville, University Press of Florida, 2008): 151, 198-200.

16. Turner, *A Journey into Florida Railroad History*: 155. Technically, Margaret Plant sold the Plant System to ACL for stock, then immediately sold the stock back to the ACL. By doing this, the ACL also acquired the Plant System's debt personally guaranteed by Henry Plant, so the sale price was actually higher than $46.6 million.

17. Turner, *A Journey into Florida Railroad History*: 197-198.

18. Foster, *Castles in the Sun*: 100.

19. *Ibid.* at 149. Fisher also loaned Collins $50,000 to finish the bridge.

20. Howard Lawrence Preston, *Dirt Roads to Dixie: Accessibility and Modernization in the South, 1885-1935* (Knoxville: University of Tennessee Press, 1991): 55-57.

21. "Road Department Issues Biennial Financial Report," *Ft. Myers Press* (April 22, 1927); "Gas Tax Charged by Every State in Union but 4," *Ft Myers Press* (October 1, 1925). After January 1, 1925 the Florida gas tax was 4 cents per gallon. Arkansas, N. Carolina and Nevada charged the same; S. Carolina charged 5 cents.

22. Junius Elmore Dovell, "A History of the Everglades of Florida" (Ph.D. dissertation, University of North Carolina-Chapel Hill, 1947); J. E. Dovell, "The Everglades Before Reclamation," *Florida Historical Quarterly* 26, 1 (July 1947): 1-47.

23. In chronological order: Luther J. Carter, *The Florida Experience: Land and Water Policy in a Growth*

State (Baltimore: Johns Hopkins University Press, 1974); Derr, *Some Kind of Paradise: A Chronicle of Man and the Land in Florida* (1989); David McCally, *The Everglades: An Environmental History* (Gainesville: University Press of Florida, 1999); Grunwald, *The Swamp: The Everglades, Florida and the Politics of Paradise* (2006).

24. Railroads: Turner, *A Journey into Florida Railroad History*; Dovell, "The Railroads and the Public Lands of Florida, 1879–1905." Railroads and canals: Edward N. Akin, "The Sly Foxes: Flagler, Miles and Florida's Public Domain," *Florida Historical Quarterly* 58, 1 (July 1979), 22–36. Canals: William G. Crawford, *Florida's Big Dig: The Atlantic Intracoastal Waterway* (Cocoa: Florida Historical Society Press, 2006); Stephen Noll and David Tegeder, *The Ditch of Dreams: The Cross-Florida Barge Canal and the Struggle for Florida's Future* (Gainesville: University Press of Florida, 2009).

25. Preston, *Dirt Roads to Dixie*; Stephen B. Goddard, *Getting There: The Epic Struggle Between Road and Rail in the American Century* (New York: Basic Books, 1994); Tom Lewis, *Divided Highways: Building the Interstate Highways, Transforming the American Life* (New York: Viking, 1997); Michael R. Fein, *Paving the Way: New York Roadbuilding and the American State, 1880–1956* (Lawrence: University Press of Kansas, 2008).

26. See, for example: Sam Bass Warner, *Streetcar Suburbs: The Process of Growth in Boston, 1870–1900* (Cambridge: Harvard University Press, 1962); Mark S. Foster, *From Streetcar to Superhighway: American City Planners and Urban Transportation, 1900–1940* (Philadelphia: Temple University Press, 1981); Paul Barrett, *The Automobile and Urban Transit: The Formation of Public Policy in Chicago, 1900–1930* (Philadelphia: Temple University Press, 1983).

27. Jean C. Taylor, "Scarifying South Dade," *Update* (Historical Association of Southern Florida) 5, 1 (October 1977): 4–5. Also, see the numerous files of correspondence on roadbuilding in the Model Land Co. Collection, Richter Library, University of Miami.

28. Letter from J. E. Ingraham to F. S. Morse, March 26, 1913, Box 4, Folder 125 (MLC File 143), Model Land Co. Collection, Richter Library, University of Miami.

29. "Report on the Lands of the Model Land Company in South Dade and Monroe Counties, Florida [1944]," Box 75, Folder 1441 (MLC File 1871), Model Land Co. Collection, Richter Library, University of Miami. Five dollars an acre: letter from J. W. Hoffman, Model Land Co. to Ivar Axelson, July 3, 1934, Box 75, Folder 1438 (MLC File 1869), Model Land Co. Collection, Richter Library, University of Miami. Sale of Model Land Company holdings: "Superintendent's Narrative Monthly Report for November, 1948": 2, Series 2, subseries B, Everglades National Park Archives, Daniel Beard Center, Homestead; "U.S. Buys Last of Flagler Acreage in Everglades National Park," *Miami Herald* (April 3, 1949). The Model Land Co. sold 134,880 acres in 1948 for $115,000 and 75,177 acres in early 1949 for $180,000.

30. "Waters Threaten Conners Highway," *Palm Beach Post* (October 6, 1953).

Chapter 1

1. Alonzo Church, "A Dash Through the Everglades," *Tequesta* 9 (1949): 15–42. Church's original manuscript is available at the University of Florida's Digital Collections: http://Ufdc.Ufl.Edu/UF00095313/00008. It was only slightly edited for the 1949 article.

2. Gregg Turner, *A Journey into Florida Railroad History* (Gainesville: University Press of Florida, 2008): 120–129; Susan Braden, *The Architecture of Leisure: The Florida Resort Hotels of Henry Flagler and Henry Plant* (Gainesville: University Press of Florida, 2002): 32–39.

3. Joshua C. Chase, "South Florida as I Knew It (Read to the University Ohio of Winter Park), June 27, 1940," James E. Ingraham Papers, Smathers Library, University of Florida, http://Ufdc.Ufl.Edu//UF00095317/00001.

4. The Plant system had 1,196 miles, the Florida Central & Peninsula had 689 and the FEC had 689: Braden, *The Architecture of Leisure*, 37–38.

5. Sidney Walter Martin, "Flagler's Associates in East Florida Developments," *Florida Historical Quarterly* 26, 3 (January 1948): 256–263; Edward Akin, *Flagler, Rockefeller Partner and Florida Baron* (Kent: Kent State University Press, 1988): 182; Junius Elmore Dovell, "A History of Everglades of Florida" (Ph.D. dissertation, University of North Carolina, 1947): 150. The meeting was almost certainly on either February 15 or 16, 1892: Thomas Graham, *Mr. Flagler's St. Augustine* (Gainesville: University Press of Florida, 2014): 267.

6. Allen's Place: Allen Morris, *Florida Place Names* (Coral Gables: University of Miami Press, 1974): S.V. "Immokalee." The location of Fort Shackleford is in Township 48 South, Range 34 East, 32 miles south of Clewiston, near where the county lines of Broward, Palm Beach and Hendry meet.

7. Alonzo Church, "A Dash Through the Everglades": 13–18.

8. John K. Mahon, *History of the Second Seminole War* (Gainesville: University Press of Florida, 1967): 146–151.

9. Wallace R. Moses, "The Ingraham Everglades Exploring Expedition, 1892," ed. Watt P. Marchmann *Tequesta* 7 (1947): 3–43.

10. Church, "A Dash Through the Everglades": 34.

11. Our faces fell: Church, "A Dash Through the Everglades": 38; island about 19 miles out: Moses, "The Ingraham Everglades Exploring Expedition, 1892": 23.

12. We had a fine meal: Church, "A Dash Through the Everglades": 40; Billy Harney shot the rapids: Moses, "The Ingraham Everglades Exploring Expedition, 1892": 27.

13. Church, "A Dash Through the Everglades": 30. Church was still alive in 1949 at age 79.

14. Turner, *A Journey into Florida Railroad History*: 143; 146–152; Braden, *The Architecture of Leisure*, 9.

15. Turner, *A Journey into Florida Railroad History*: 133–134.

16. William G. Crawford, "The Papers of Albert Sawyer and the Development of the Florida East Coast, 1892 to 1912," *Tequesta* 62 (2002): 5–39.

17. Church, "A Dash Through the Everglades," 20–21. Note that Church recalls Newman mocking Ingraham about Flagler's 1880's St. Augustine hotels, not Plant's equally palatial 1890 Tampa hotel. However, Ingraham was still working for Plant at this time, something almost everyone had forgotten by when Church wrote his article several decades later. Also, there was no such highland headwater such as Newman described—just a vast, two-pronged river from Lake O, one prong (Taylor Slough) flowing south to Florida Bay and the other (the Shark River) flowing southwest into Whitewater Bay north of Cape Sable.

18. "Remarks of J. E. Ingraham," in *The Everglades of Florida* (62nd Cong. 1 Sess., Senate Doc. No. 89, 1911): 101–107.

19. *Minutes of the Trustees of the Internal Improvement Fund*, Vol. 4 (May 7, 1892): 197.

20. J. E. Dovell, "A History of the Everglades of Florida" (Ph.D. dissertation, University of North Carolina, 1947): 98–101.

21. J. E. Dovell, "The Railroads and the Public Lands of Florida, 1879–1905," *Florida Historical Quarterly* 34: 3 (January 1956): 236–258; "A Little, Grasping, Weazened-Faced Fellow": *Report of the Joint Commission to Investigate the Trustees of the Internal Improvement Fund Pursuant to Chapter 5632, Session Laws of 1907* (Tallahassee: State of Florida, 1909): 274 (hereinafter "1909 IIF Investigative Report"). For a full explanation of how the railroad bonds worked, see: Turner, *A Journey into Florida Railroad History*: 53–57.

22. Dovell, "A History of the Everglades of Florida": 114; 120; Dovell, "The Railroads and the Public Lands of Florida, 1879–1905," 237–238; Turner, *A Journey into Florida Railroad History*: 92–98.

23. "1909 IIF Investigative Report": 291–293.

24. Michael Grunwald, *The Swamp: The Everglades, Florida, and the Politics of Paradise* (New York: Simon & Schuster, 2008): 96.

25. When Ingraham appeared before the Internal Improvement Fund on May 7 with his offer to drain a million acres, he didn't say who he was representing. However, he did present a petition on behalf of Plant's South Florida Railroad on another, unrelated matter. When the IIF later met on June 10, he was clearly not representing anyone other than himself, as the railroad was represented by its lawyer, E. K. Foster. *Minutes of the Trustees of the Internal Improvement Fund*, Vol. 4 (May 7, 1892): 198; (June 10, 1892): 205–206.

26. *Minutes of the Trustees of the Internal Improvement Fund*, Vol. 4 (May 7, 1892): 196–197; Dovell, "The Railroads and the Public Lands of Florida," 243–245.

27. Technically the lawyer for the South Florida Railroad, E.K. Foster, said that his client had no objection to the drainage scheme, but they asserted that it the lands should not be sold or transferred to the state. That is, half the sections in the checkerboard should go to Ingraham (or whomever) as a grant for drainage, and the other half should go to the railroads to redeem their outstanding certificates for prior railroad construction. *Minutes of the Trustees of the Internal Improvement Fund*, Vol. 4 (June 10, 1892): 206.

28. *Minutes of the Trustees of the Internal Improvement Fund*, Vol. 4 (June 10, 1892): 207.

29. "1909 IIF Investigative Report": 292.

30. Edward Akin, *Flagler: Rockefeller Partner and Florida Baron* (Kent: Kent State University Press, 1988): 181–182.

31. Turner, *A Journey into Florida Railroad History*: 135.

32. Eight thousand acres per mile: *Laws of Florida 1893*, 4260.

33. Edward Akin, "The Sly Foxes: Henry Flagler, George Miles, and Florida's Public Domain," *Florida Historical Quarterly* (July 1979): 22–36; Crawford, "The Papers of Albert Sawyer and the Development of the Florida East Coast": 10–12.

34. Crawford, "The Papers of Albert Sawyer and the Development of the Florida East Coast": 10–12.

35. Transfers of 103K acres and 94K acres from canal co. to FEC: Crawford, "The Papers of Albert Sawyer and the Development of the Florida East Coast": 11; total of 516K acres deeded to the canal co.: Akin, "The Sly Foxes: Henry Flagler, George Miles, and Florida's Public Domain": 28; FEC never received any land grant for Miami extension: Akin, *Flagler: Rockefeller Partner and Florida Baron*: 176.

36. Crawford, "The Papers of Albert Sawyer and the Development of the Florida East Coast": 10, 21; Akin, The Sly Foxes" 31.

37. Completion of canal and railroad to Miami: Crawford, "The Papers of Albert Sawyer and the Development of the Florida East Coast, 1892–1912": 13 (canal); Turner, *A Journey into Florida Railroad History*: 135–136 (railroad). FEC land subsidiaries: William E. Brown, Jr. and Karen Hudson, "Henry Flagler and the Model Land Company," *Tequesta* 56 (1996): 47–78. Okeechobee Model Land Company: "Okeechobee City Land Is Sold for $1,000,000," *Miami Herald* (March 11, 1923).

38. Akin, "The Sly Foxes: Henry Flagler, George Miles, and Florida's Public Domain": 31.

39. Crawford, "The Papers of Albert Sawyer and the Development of the Florida East Coast": 14–17; Akin, "The Sly Foxes: Henry Flagler, George Miles, and Florida's Public Domain": 29–30.

40. Bill McGowan, *Hallandale* (Hallandale: Hallandale Historical Society, 1976): 117–119; Crawford, "The Papers of Albert Sawyer and the Development of the Florida East Coast": 17–18.

41. McGoun, *Hallandale*: 8, 12.

42. Brown and Hudson, "Henry Flagler and the Model Land Company": 55.

43. Akin, *Flagler: Rockefeller Partner and Florida Baron*: 179.

44. Akin, "The Sly Foxes," 33.

45. *Minutes of the Trustees of Internal Improvement Fund*: Vol. 4 (February 16, 1898): 432–434. This works out to a grant of one acre for each four linear *Inches* of canal, assuming a canal thirty feet wide and ten feet deep.

46. Dovell, *The Florida Everglades*: 197, citing Frederick Dau's *Florida Old and New* (1934).

47. Crawford, "The Papers of Albert Sawyer and the Development of the Florida East Coast": 17–18; Akin, *Flagler: Rockefeller Partner and Florida Baron*: 180.

48. Akin, "The Sly Foxes": 27. Ingraham asserted that the short lines were owed 472,473 acres, but had been deeded only 251,000 acres. The FEC had received no land grants at all for the south Florida track extension.

49. *Minutes of the Trustees of the Internal Improvement Fund*, Vol. 5 (July 3, 1902): 118–119; Dovell, "The Railroads and the Public Lands of Florida": 255.

50. Dovell, "The Railroads and the Public Lands of Florida": 257–258.

51. *Minutes of the Trustees of the Internal Improvement Fund*, Vol. 7 ("Annual Report of the General Counsel, December 21, 1908"): 535–536.

52. *Minutes of the Trustees of the Internal Improvement Fund*, Vol. 7 (November 21, 1907): 121–136.

53. *Minutes of the Trustees of the Internal Improvement Fund*, Vol. 8 (June 17, 1910): 415–419; Vol. 9 (December 14, 1912): 598–612. The Cape Sable land totaled 240,000 acres: letter from Frederic Morse to J. E. Ingraham, 25 March 1913, Box 4, File 143, Model Land Co. Collection, Richter Library, Univ. of Miami. Map of the Cape Sable Land: Plat Book 2, Page 94, Public Records of Dade County, Florida (July 20, 1914).

CHAPTER 2

1. The no longer existing village of Longview is the present site of the "Robert Is Here" produce market, a regional landmark at the corner of SW 344 St. and SW 190 Ave. It was named after Camp Longview, two-and-a-half miles farther west at today's SW 344 St. and SW 217 Ave.

2. The location of "Camp Jackson" is uncertain. A plat filed by the railroad in 1904 (Plat Book "B" Page 73) contains a symbol that suggests that it was about half a mile due east of the current main entry to Everglades National Park. However, Krome's descriptions and photographs ("Railway Location in the Everglades," *Engineering Record* (April 2 and 9, 1904)), show the camp in dense pineland, a site more consistent with the

"Pine Island" hammock two miles southwest of this point, in the area now known as the Pine Island Service Area, directly across Taylor Slough from Paradise Key.

3. At the present intersection of SW 217 Avenue and State Road 9336. The 1914 road followed the present SR 9336. The subsequent 1915 road had two routes out of the Homestead/Florida City area: west out of Homestead on SW 320 St. and west out of Florida City on SW 344 St. Both ran approximately three miles to SW 217 Ave., then south along SW 217 Ave. to the 1914 road.

4. Marjory Stoneman Douglas, *Voice of the River* (Englewood, FL: Pineapple Press, 1987): 136. Comments dismissed as "Catty": Michael Grunwald, *The Swamp: The Everglades, Florida, and the Politics of Paradise* (New York: Simon & Schuster, 2006): 401 (nn. 171–2).

5. The other, Taylor Slough, is the river between Camp Jackson and Paradise Key. Long Pine Key is the ridge that separates Shark River and Taylor Slough; the former flowing south and west into Whitewater Bay and the Gulf; Taylor Slough south into Florida Bay.

6. John K. Small, "Exploration in Southern Florida in 1915," *Journal of the New York Botanical Garden* 17 (March 1916): 37–45.

7. John K. Small, "A Cruise to the Cape Sable Region of Florida," *Journal of the New York Botanical Garden* 17 (November 1916): 189–202.

8. Marjory Stoneman Douglas, *The Everglades: River of Grass* (New York: Reinhart & Co., 1947): 223–224; D. LeBaron Perrine, "Cape Sable, Part 1," *The Tropic Magazine* 5, 5–6 (February-March 1917): 81–83; D. LeBaron Perrine, "Cape Sable, Part 2," *The Tropic Magazine* 6, 1 (April 1917): 5–9.

9. "Ever-Verdant Prairies": Grunwald, *The Swamp*: 55. Perrine's death: Douglas, *The Everglades: River of Grass*: 230–234.

10. Grunwald, *The Swamp*: 53, 383 (n.61).

11. Between the early 1960s and 2005 it was a substantial facility, with restaurants, cabins, a motel, a gas station, a full service marina, restaurants, an RV park, and more. The gas station closed in the 1990s, and almost everything else, except for the hardened ranger station, the fresh-water plant and the sewage treatment facility, was wiped out by hurricane Wilma in 2005.

12. Lawrence Will, "Digging the Cape Sable Canal," *Tequesta* 19 (1959): 29–63; Lawrence Will, *A Dredgeman of Cape Sable* (St. Petersburg: Great Outdoors Publishing, 1967): 42–43. Roberts clan: Perrine, "Cape Sable," *The Tropic Magazine* 5:5–6 (February-March 1917): 81–83; Perrine, "Cape Sable (Part 2)": 6–9; 320,000 mosquitoes: Grunwald, *The Swamp*: 151.

13. Will, *A Dredgeman of Cape Sable*: 44; Will, "Digging the Cape Sable Canal": 39–40. Wood could be taken for use if it was down, but felling trees to burn charcoal was a form of poaching.

14. Grunwald, *The Swamp*: 126–127. Smith's house burned: Will, *A Dredgeman of Cape Sable*: 47. Edwin Bradley, Guy's father, had been a "Barefoot Mailman" in Palm Beach and Dade counties, later was Superintendent of Schools in Dade County and land agent for the Model Land Co. He then homesteaded at Flamingo Dock and was, for awhile, postmaster. In short, he was part of the community at Flamingo, and Guy's death was not taken lightly in the village.

15. Will, "Digging the Cape Sable Canal": 37.

16. Perrine, "Cape Sable": 5–9; Letter to F. J. Powers from James Ingraham, July 22, 1913; letter from Frank J. Pepper to James Ingraham, July 10, 1913, both Box 5, Folder 149 (MLC File 165) Model Land Co. Collection, Department of Special Collections, Richter Library, University of Miami, Coral Gables, Florida (hereafter "Model Land Co. Collection, Univ. of Miami").

17. Camp Longwood was located at the present-day intersection of SW 344 Street and SW 217 Avenue, four miles west of Florida City: Plat Book B, Page 73, Public Records of Dade County Florida (Plat of Krome Survey of Cape Sable).

18. Letter from Roy Marsh re: Mrs. Flagler's donation of land for state park, ca. November 1915 (erroneously filed as 1926 correspondence). May Mann Jennings Collection, University of Florida, http://ufdc.ufl.edu//uf00091201/00001.

19. Edward Akin, *Flagler: Rockefeller Partner and Florida Baron* (Kent: Kent State University Press, 1988): 210–214.

20. Thomas Graham, *Mr. Flagler's St. Augustine* (Gainesville: University Press of Florida, 2014): 422–423.

21. Panama Canal treaty: David McCullough, *The Path Between the Seas: The Creation of the Panama Canal* (New York: Simon and Schuster: 1988): 1977): 387–402; Cargo economics: Marc Levinson: *The Box: How the Shipping Container Made the World Smaller and the World Economy Bigger* (Princeton: Princeton University Press, 2006): 6–35.

22. William J. Krome, "Railway Location in the South," ed. Jean C. Taylor, *Tequesta* 39 (1979 [1904]): 5–16. Location of Camp Jackson: Small, "Exploration in Southern Florida in 1915": 38; Letter to Frederick Morse from Frank J. Pepper, 27 April 1912, Box 2, File 58, Model Land Co. Records, Univ. of Miami. See also Plat Book "B", Page 73, Public Records of Dade County, Florida, at Township 58, Range 38, Section 7, northeast quadrant.

23. Krome, "Railway Location in the South": *Passim*; Letter from Frederick Morse to J. E. Ingraham, 25 December 1911, Box 2, File 57–58, Model Land Co. Records, Univ. of Miami.

24. John K. Small, "Exploration in Southern Florida in 1915," *Journal of the New York Botanical Garden* 17 (March 1916): 37–45.

25. Plat Book "B", Page 73.

26. Krome, "Railway Location in the South": *Passim*; Letter from Frederick Morse to J. E. Ingraham December 25, 1911, Box 2, Folder 57–58 (MLC File 64) Model Land Co. Records, Univ. of Miami.

27. Small, "Exploration in Southern Florida in 1915": 38. Federal Writers' Project of the Works Progress Administration, *Florida: Guide to the Southernmost State* [The WPA Guide to Florida] (New York: Oxford University Press, 1939): 326. John K. Small, "Royal Palm Hammock," *Journal of the New York Botanical Garden* 17 (October 1916): 165–172.

28. Letter from F.J. Pepper to Frederick Morse, April 27, 1912, Box 2, Folders 57–58 (MLC File 64) Model Land Co. Records, Univ. of Miami.

29. Letter from Frederick Morse to J. E. Ingraham, August 7, 1913, Letter from Frederick Morse to J. E. Ingraham, August 7, 1913; both Box 5, Folder 143 (MLC File 159), Model Land Co. Records, Univ. of Miami; Roy D. Marsh, "Sectional Map of the Redlands District, 1912," Box 5, Folder 143 (MLC File 159), Model Land Co. Records, Richter Library, Univ. of Miami.

30. Letter from Frederick Morse to J. E. Ingraham, September 22, 1913, Box 5, Folder 143 (MLC File 159), Model Land Co. Records, Univ. of Miami.

31. Frederick Morse to J. E. Ingraham, July 25, 1913, Box 5, File 143 (MLC File 159), Model Land Co. Records, Univ. of Miami.

32. Jean C. Taylor, "Scarifying South Dade," *Historical Association of Southern Florida Update* 5, 1 (October 1977): 4–5.

33. County refuses to provide dynamite: Letter from Frederick Morse to J. E. Ingraham, October 15, 1913, Box 5, Folder 143 (MLC File 159), Model Land Co. Records, Univ. of Miami. Cost $12.50 per 40 acres: letter from Frederick Morse to J. E. Ingraham, August 7, 1913, Box

5, Folder 143 (MLC File 159), Model Land Co. Records, Univ. of Miami. County pays half: letter from Frederick Morse to J. E. Ingraham, September 22, 1913, Box 5, File 143 (MLC File 159), Model Land Co. Records, Univ. of Miami.

34. Letter from Frank J. Pepper to J. E. Ingraham, September 20, 1911, Box 1, Folder 11 (MLC File 12), Model Land Co. Records, Univ. of Miami.

35. Letter from Sidney Harrison to Frederick Morse, May 5, 1911, Box 1, Folder 11 (MLC File 12), Model Land Co. Records, Univ. of Miami.

36. Letter from J. E. Ingraham to F. S. Morse, November 19, 1913, Box 5, Folder 143 (MLC File 159), Model Land Co. Papers, Richter Library, Univ. of Miami.

37. "Railroad Wants Survey to Cape Sable Country, May Build a Road There," *Miami Metropolis* (April 11, 1914).

38. "Cape Sable Highway Is Built for 9 Miles" *Miami Metropolis* (June 22, 1914); Small, "Royal Palm Hammock": 169.

39. Letter from Frederick Morse to J. E. Ingraham, November 19, 1914; letter from unknown (probably Frank Pepper) to J. E. Ingraham, December 11, 1914; letter from F. J. Powers to Fred S. Morse, January 2, 1915, all Box 7, Folder 213 (MLC File 245), Model Land Co. Records, Univ. of Miami. T. A. Feaster's tomatoes: Cape Sable Highway is Built for 9 Miles," Miami *Metropolis* (June 22, 1914).

40. "Cape Sable Highway Built for 9 Miles," *Miami Metropolis* (June 22, 1914). Small, "Royal Palm Hammock": 169–171. William Jennings, "Royal Palm State Park (Data for Use in Writing Articles)" unpublished manuscript, March 1, 1916, May Mann Jennings Collections, Department of Special Collections, University of Florida, Gainesville, URL: http://Ufdc.Ufl.Edu// UF00091150/00001. (hereafter, "May Mann Jennings Collection, UF).

41. Letter from May Mann Jennings to Mrs. John Gifford, March 28, 1916, May Mann Jennings Collection, UF, http://Ufdc.Ufl.Edu/Uf00091148/00001.

42. William Jennings Diary, Entry for April 8, 1914, William S. Jennings Collection, UF, http://Ufdc.Ufl.Edu/ Uf00094873/00093.

43. Small, "Royal Palm Hammock": 166–167. "Royal Palm Visitor Center," 7½ minute topographic map series (Washington: United States Geographic Survey, 1952 [1976 overlay revisions in purple]). Twenty-five percent complete: "Called on Carpet, Contractor Asks Money and Time," *Miami Metropolis* (August 16, 1917).

44. Memo of Roy Marsh re: proposed endowment parcels, ca. January 1916, May Mann Jennings Collection, UF: URL: http://Ufdc.Ufl.Edu//UF00091201/00001. Note that this document is misfiled with papers from September 1926, although the context clearly indicates an early 1916 date. Plank causeway: Small, "Royal Palm Hammock": 166–167. McCrary's estimate: "McCrary People Seem Now to Have Habit of Asking for Favors, Leniency," *Miami Metropolis* (September 7, 1918).

45. Memo to J. E. Ingraham from W. S. Jennings, re: Sub-Drainage District, August 8, 1914, William S. Jennings Collection, UF, http://ufdc.ufl.edu/UF00094874/ 00009.

46. "County Board Making Plans for Highways Thru Glades," *Miami Metropolis* (February 3, 1915); Road District Bonds to Fund County Highway to Cape Sable," *Miami Metropolis* (February 3, 1915). Dewhurst promised Belcher 1000 acres: letter from William Dewhurst to Frank J. Pepper, June 4, 1917, Box 17, Folder 449 (MLC File 538), Model Land Co. papers, University of Miami; 1949 map of land ownership along Old Ingraham Highway and Flamingo area: EVER 303386; 303374; 303382; Department of Archives and Special Collections, Daniel Beard Center, Everglades National Park, Homestead, Florida.

47. "Cape Sable as Part of Dade a Plan of the County Board," *Miami Metropolis* (December 2, 1914); "Sub-Drainage District as Well as Highway District for Cape Sable," *Miami Metropolis* (February 23, 1915); "Dade Ready to Build Road to Cape Sable," *Miami Metropolis* (June 1, 1915); "In Re the Matter of the Application and Petition and Formation of the Homestead Sub-Drainage District," (Fla. 11th Cir., September 1, 1915), William S. Jennings Collection, UF, http://ufdc.ufl.edu/UF00094874/ 00019/.

48. "County Board Making Plans for Highways Thru Glades," *Miami Metropolis* (February 2, 1915); "Road District Bonds to Be Used for Highway to Cape Sable," *Miami Metropolis* (February 19, 1915); Sub-drainage District as Well as Highway District for Cape Sable," *Miami Metropolis* (February 23, 1915).

49. "$100,000 Highway Bonds Voted by an Overwhelming Majority, Early Sale for the Securities," *Miami Metropolis* (April 14, 1915); "Cape Sable Bond Issue Voted by Big Majority of 76 to 12, Last Link in $100,000 Highway," *Miami Metropolis* (April 15, 1915); "Dade Ready to Build Road to Cape Sable," *Miami Metropolis* (June 1, 1915).

50. "Bids for Cape Sable Roads and for Construction Opened," *Miami Metropolis* (November 12, 1915); "Local Men Had No Chance to Bid on Cape Sable Road," *Miami Metropolis* (November 18, 1915); "Called on Contract Contractor Asks Money and Time," *Miami Metropolis* (August 16, 1917).

51. "Begin Work at Once Cape Sable Road," *Miami Metropolis* (November 27, 1915); letter from R. F. Tatum to May Mann Jennings, February 10, 1916, May Mann Jennings Collection, UF, http://ufdc. ufl.edu/UF00091146/ 0000116.

Chapter 3

1. William Jennings, "Royal Palm State Park (Data for Use in Writing Articles)," ca. March 1916, May Mann Jennings Collection, University of Florida, http://ufdc. ufl.edu/UF00091150/00001. To see how it was repeated verbatim, see: Mrs. W. S. Jennings, "Royal Palm State Park," *Tropic Magazine* 4, 1 (April 1916): 11–16, 26.

2. *Minutes of the Trustees of the Internal Improvement Fund*, Vol. 8 (November 13, 1910): 621–628.

3. FEC granted 44 half-sections: *Minutes of the Trustees of the Internal Improvement Fund*, Vol. 8 (June 11, 1910): 415–417. IIF Secretary authorized to approve land swaps for blocking up: *Minutes of the Trustees of the Internal Improvement Fund*, Vol. 8 (April 14, 1910): 365–366.

4. The detailed survey was done by C. H. Zoll of the J. B. McCrary Company in June 1916: letter from C.H. Zoll to George C. Pierce, June 9, 1916, May Mann Jennings Collection, University of Florida: URL: http:// Ufdc.Ufl.Edu//UF00091151/00001; survey maps (2): URL: http://Ufdc.Ufl.Edu//UF0091234/00001; survey map (1) URL: http://Ufdc.Ufl.Edu//UF00091234/00001. Plat Book "B," Page 72, Official records of Dade County Florida. The official baselines for the township and range lines were done in 1911: "Report of J. O. Wright," *Minutes of the Trustees of the Internal Improvement Fund*, Vol. 8 (November 13, 1910): 621–628.

5. "Petition in the Matter of Application and Formation of the Homestead Sub-Drainage District," 9 September 1915, William Jennings Collection, UF: URL: http://ufdc.ufl.edu//UF00094874/00019.

6. Harry A. Kersey, Jr., *The Stranahans of Fort Lauderdale: A Pioneer Family of New River* (Gainesville: University Press of Florida, 2003): *Passim*.

7. Henry E. Johnson III, "The Many Faces of Guy

I. Metcalf," *Broward Legacy* (Summer/Fall 1986): 2–11; "Guy I Metcalf, Head Palm Beach Schools, Takes His Own Life," *Miami Metropolis* (February 7, 1918); "Fear of Losing Mind Cause of Metcalf Suicide," *Miami Metropolis* (February 9, 1918).

8. John K. Small, "Royal Palm Hammock," *Journal of the New York Botanical Garden* 17 (October 1916): 165–172, at 169.

9. Uncertainty known at the time: letter from William Dewhurst to Frederick Morse, January 4, 1918, Box 18, Folders 451–452 (MLC Files 539 and 540), Model Land Co. Collection, Univ. of Miami; Federal survey: *Paradise Prairie Land Co. V. United States*, 212 F. 2d 170 (5th Cir., 1954).

10. Transfer from railroad to Jennings and Dewhurst: letter from J. E. Ingraham to F. S. Morse, March 26, 1913, Box 5, Folder 143 (MLC File 159), Model Land Co. Collection, University of Miami.

11. Purchase of land sought for Seminole use: letter from M. K. Sniffen to Mrs. J. M. [Minnie Mae] Willson, December 21, 1915, letter from to Mrs. J. M. [Minnie Mae] Willson to P. A. Vans Agnew, January 13, 1916, both Box 27, Folder 651 (MLC File 785), Model Land Co. Collection, Univ. of Miami. Gift from Bolles: Junius E. Dovell, "A History of the Everglades of Florida" (Ph.D. dissertation, University of North Carolina, 1947): 232 (n. 39). For discussion of Jennings's role in possible land fraud related to low-balling the estimated costs of Everglades reclamation (the so-called "Wright Report Scandal") see Aaron Purcell, "Plumb Lines, Politics and Projections: The Florida Everglades and the Wright Report Controversy" *Florida Historical Quarterly* 80, 2 (Fall 2001): 161–197. Jennings was Bolles's lawyer during this period.

12. William Jennings, "Royal Palm State Park (Data for Use in Writing Articles)," ca. March 1916, May Mann Jennings Collection, Univ. of Florida, http://ufdc.ufl.edu/UF00091150/00001.

13. Charles T. Simpson, "Paradise Key," *Tropic Magazine* 4, 1 (April 1916): 4–9.

14. Dedication by IIF and appointment of wardens: *Minutes of the Trustees of the Internal Improvement Fund*, Vol. 10 (December 23, 1914): 609–611. Visit to Paradise Key on December 28, 1914: William Jennings, manuscript: "Royal Palm State Park (Data for Use in Writing Articles)," William Jennings Collection, UF, URL: http://ufdc.ufl.edu/UF00091150/00001.

15. Letter from May Mann Jennings to T.S. Palmer, June 4, 1915, May Mann Jennings Collection, UF, URL: http://Ufdc.Ufl.Edu/UF00091134/00001; letter to May Mann Jennings from Sen. Duncan Fletcher, September 25, 1915, May Mann Jennings Collection, UF, URL: http://Ufdc.Ufl.Edu/UF00091138/00001; letter to May Mann Jennings from Gov. Park Trammell, September 29, 1915, May Mann Jennings Collection, UF, URL: http://Ufdc.Ufl.Edu/UF00091138/00001.

16. Letter to May Mann Jennings from F. J. Powers, August 28, 1915, May Mann Jennings Collection, UF, URL: http://Ufdc.Ufl.Edu/UF00091127/00001.

17. Memo of Roy Marsh, re: Proposed Park Endowment Lands, ca. November 1915, May Mann Jennings Collection, UF, URL: http://Ufdc.Ufl.Edu/UF00091201/00001.

18. *Minutes of the Trustees of the Internal Improvement Fund*, Vol. 11 (November 15, 1915): 193–194; letter from May Mann Jennings to Mrs. John Gifford, November 27, 1915, May Mann Jennings Collection, UF, URL: http://Ufdc.Ufl.Edu/UF00091141/00001.

19. Simpson, "Paradise Key": 7–8.

20. Letter from May Mann Jennings to Mrs. John Gifford, March 5, 1915, May Mann Jennings Collection, UF, URL: http://Ufdc.Ufl.Edu/UF00091134/00001; May Mann Jennings to Mrs. John Gifford, March 15, 1916, May Mann Jennings Collection, UF, URL: http://Ufdc.Ufl.Edu/UF00091149/00001; William Jennings, "Royal Palm State Park (Data for Use in Writing Articles)": 3–4.

21. Letter from May Mann Jennings to Mrs. John Gifford, November 27, 1915, May Mann Jennings Collection; UF, URL: http://Ufdc.Ufl.Edu/UF00091141/00001; letter from May Mann Jennings to Mrs. John Gifford, November 16, 1915. May Mann Jennings Collection; UF, URL: http://Ufdc.Ufl.Edu/UF00091143/00001.

22. Letter from May Mann Jennings to Charles H. Mosier, February 25, 1916, May Mann Jennings Collection; UF, URL: http://Ufdc.Ufl.Edu/UF00091147/00001; Linda D. Vance, "May Mann Jennings and Royal Palm State Park," *Florida Historical Quarterly* 60, 1 (July 1976): 1–17.

23. Letter from May Mann Jennings to George Pierce, December 27, 1915, May Mann Jennings Collection; UF, URL: http://Ufdc.Ufl.Edu/UF00091143/00001.

24. Letter from R. F. Tatum to May Mann Jennings, February 10, 1916, May Mann Jennings Collection; UF, URL: http://Ufdc.Ufl.Edu/UF00091146/00001; letter from May Mann Jennings to R.F. Tatum, 23 February 1916, May Mann Jennings Collection; UF, URL: http://Ufdc.Ufl.Edu/UF00091147/00001; letter from May Mann Jennings to Mrs. John Gifford, February 3, 1916, May Mann Jennings Collection; UF, URL: http://Ufdc.Ufl.Edu/UF00091150/00001.

25. Letter from C. F. Zoll to George Pierce, June 9, 1916, May Mann Jennings Collection; UF, URL: http://Ufdc.Ufl.Edu/UF00091151/00001; Letter from George Pierce to May Mann Jennings, June 16, 1916, May Mann Jennings Collection; UF, URL: http://Ufdc.Ufl.Edu/UF00091151/00001.

26. Letter from May Mann Jennings to Mr. Charles A. Mosier, April 3, 1916, May Mann Jennings Collection; UF, URL: http://Ufdc.Ufl.Edu/UF00091150/00001.

27. Shoddy work: letter from May Mann Jennings to Charles A. Moser, April 3, 1916, May Mann Jennings Collection; UF, URL: http://Ufdc.Ufl.Edu/UF00091150/00001. "Tamiami Trail Contract Is Issued," *Miami Metropolis* (4 April 1916). Opening of park: "Beautiful Park but the Road Is Hard to Travel," *Miami Metropolis* (15 May 1916).

28. Letter from May Mann Jennings to Charles A. Mosier, July 5, 1916; letter from B. M. Duncan to May Mann Jennings, July 17, 1916; letter from B. M. Duncan to May Mann Jennings, July 25, 1916, all May Mann Jennings Collection; UF, URL: http://Ufdc.Ufl.Edu/UF00091151/00001.

29. "Superintendent's Monthly Narrative Report for August 1948": 2. Series 2, subseries B, Everglades National Park Archives, Daniel Beard Center, Homestead.

30. In 2007, the author, who was a research fellow at Everglades National Park, was shown photographs of removed pilings by equipment operators of the South Florida Water Management District who had taken out this section of the old road. Unfortunately, the pilings had by this time been destroyed.

31. "Royal Palm State Park Road Be Completed Within a Week," *Miami Metropolis* (November 15, 1916); "Highway to Royal Palm Park Good Repair for Automobiles," *Miami Metropolis* (November 17, 1916); "Florida State Park Committee Complain of Road Conditions," *Miami Metropolis* (January 5, 1917).

32. "Another Request from Contractor for More Time," *Miami Metropolis* (December 28, 1916); Memo from F. S. Morse to Model Land Company, January 25, 1917, Box 17, Folder 449 (MLC File 538) Model Land Co. Collection, Richter Library, Univ. of Miami; letter from C. B. Chinn to Honorable Board of County Commissioners, December 26, 1916, J. B. McCrary Papers, HistoryMiami.

33. Letter from J. E. Ingraham to F. J. Powers, 19 December 19, 1917, Box 17, Folder 449 (MLC File 538), Model Land Co. Collection, Richter Library, Univ. of Miami, letter from Frederick Morse to J. E, Ingraham, December 22, 1917, Box 17, Folder 449 (MLC File 538), Model Land Co. Collection, Richter Library, Univ. of Miami.
34. "Summary Statement of Costs and Losses Sustained by the J. B. McCrary Co. on Dade County Ingraham Highway Contract," ca. April 1921, J. B. McCrary Papers, HistoryMiami.
35. Letter from C. B. Chinn to Honorable Board of County Commissioners, February 19, 1917, J. B. McCrary Papers, HistoryMiami.
36. Only 3.6 percent: compare memorandum from F. S. Morse to Model Land Company, January 25, 1917, Box 17, Folder 450 (MLC File 538), Model Land Co. Collection, Richter Library, Univ. of Miami (41.2% complete) with "Called on Carpet Contractor Asks Money and Time," *Miami Metropolis* (August 16, 1917) (44.8% complete). Second hand outfit: "Called on Carpet Contractor Asks Money and Time," *Miami Metropolis* (August 16, 1917). Slow progress and dredge too big: Letter from Frank J. Pepper to W. W. Dewhurst, June 2, 1917, letter from William Dewhurst to Frank Pepper, both Box 17, Folder 450 (MLC File 538), Model Land Co. Collection, Richter Library, Univ. of Miami.
37. Letter from F. J. Pepper to William Dewhurst, June 2, 1917, Box 17, Folder 450 (MLC File 538), Model Land Co. Collection, Univ. of Miami; "Cape Sable Road Is Already a Year Behind Schedule," *Miami Metropolis* (August 7, 1917).
38. "Called on Carpet Contractor Asks Money and Time," *Miami Metropolis* (August 16, 1917).
39. "McCrary to Tell Why Cape Sable Road Is Delayed," *Miami Metropolis* (August 14, 1917); "Called on Carpet, Contractor Asks for More Time," *Miami Metropolis* (August 16, 1917); "Give McCrary Co. Another Year to Finish Highway, *Miami Metropolis* (September 4, 1917); Letter from J. A. McCrary to Honorable Board of County Commissioners, September 1, 1917, J. B. McCrary Papers, Historymiami.
40. Letter from May Mann Jennings to Mrs. E. C. Loveland, March 20, 1917; Letter from May Mann Jennings to Mrs. Edgar Lewis, April 11, 1919, Both May Mann Jennings Collection; UF, URL: Http://Ufdc.Ufl. Edu//Uf00091155/00001.
41. Letter from J. E. Ingraham to F. J. Powers, December 19, 1917; Letter from F. S. Morse to J. E. Ingraham, December 22, 1917, Both Box 17, Folder 450 (MLC File 538), Model Land Co. Collection, Richter Library, Univ. of Miami.
42. Memorandum from F. S. Morse Dated January 25, 1917; Letter from Frank J. Pepper to W. W. Dewhurst, June 2, 1917; Letter from F. S. Morse to J. E. Ingraham, December 22, 1917, All Box 17, Folder 450 (MLC File 538), Model Land Co. Collection, Richter Library, Univ. of Miami.
43. "Skilled Labor Should Remain at Their Jobs," *Miami Metropolis* (September 4, 1918); "Ban Tightening on Road Work as War Measure," *Miami Metropolis* (September 30, 1918).
44. Memo from F. J. Pepper to A. A. Dooley re: Cape Sable Road, Protection Fresh Water, November 2, 1918, Box 17, Folder 450 (MLC File 538); Model Land Co. Collection, Richter Library, Univ. of Miami; Letter from J. B. McCrary to Dade County Board of County Commissioners, June 1, 1920, J. B. McCrary Company Papers, HistoryMiami, Miami.
45. Letter from May Mann Jennings to Mrs. Edgar Lewis, April 11, 1919, May Mann Jennings Collection, UF, URL: http://ufdc.ufl.edu//UF00091185/00001/102.
46. Lawrence E. Will, "Digging the Cape Sable Canal," *Tequesta* 19 (1959): 29–63.

47. "Ex-Governor Jennings Dead; Funeral to Be Tomorrow," Miami *Metropolis* (February 28, 1920); "Map: Hole in the Donut Agricultural Area, Current Land Uses, from Aerial Photos, 1952," National Park Service, Everglades National Park, http://everglades.fiu.edu/hid/hidmap52.gif; Vance, "May Mann Jennings and Everglades National Park," 15–17.
48. Letter from Frederick Morse to J. E. Ingraham, December 11, 1914; letter from Frederick Morse to J. E. Ingraham, December 28, 1914, both Box 7, Folder 213 (MLC File 245) Model Land Co. Collection, Richter Library, Univ. of Miami. Letter from Sidney Harrison to Frank J. Pepper, June 22, 1920, Box 30, Folder 721 (MLC File 899), Model Land Co. Collection, Richter Library, Univ. of Miami.
49. Contract renewed in January: "Give Contractors One More Year to Finish Trail," *Miami Metropolis* (January 3, 1918). Land owners met with McCrary: letter from J. E. Ingraham to Frederick Morse, January 16, 1918; letter from J. E. Ingraham to Frederick Morse, January 23, 1918, both Box 17, Folder 450 (MLC file 538), Model Land Co. Collection, Richter Library, Univ. of Miami. Ingraham tried to get copy of Dade's proposal: letter from Frederick S. Morse to J. E. Ingraham, April 13, 1918; letter from J. E. Ingraham to Fredrick S. Morse, both Box 17, Folder 450 (MLC file 538), Model Land Co. Collection, Richter Library, Univ. of Miami. Contract executed in mid-May: letter from William Dewhurst to Frederick Morse, May 14, 1918, Box 17, Folder 450 (MLC file 538), Model Land Co. Collection, Richter Library, Univ. of Miami.
50. "Model Land Co. to Extend Road at Cape Sable," *Palm Beach Post* (May 7, 1922); "Another Cape Sable Contract Is Let by Model Land Company," *Miami Metropolis* (May 24, 1922). Amount paid for Dade work: "Summary Statement of Cost and Losses Sustained by the J. B. McCrary Company on Dade County Ingraham Highway Contract," J. B. McCrary Co. Papers, HistoryMiami.
51. Claimed fifty percent: letter from William Dewhurst to Frederick Morse, May 14, 1918; letter from Frederick Morse to W. W. Dewhurst, May 15, 1918; letter from Sidney Harrison to F. S. Morse, May 1, 1919, all Box 17, Folder 450 (MLC File 538), Model Land Co. Collection, Richter Library, Univ. of Miami. Actually retained ten percent: "Summary Statement of Costs and Losses Sustained by the J. B. Mccrary Company on Dade County—Ingraham Highway Contract," undated (ca. April, 1921), J. B. McCrary Papers, HistoryMiami; letter from J. B. McCrary to Model Land Company, July 28 1920, Box 17, Folder 450 (MLC File 538), Model Land Co. Collection, Richter Library, Univ. of Miami. The total retainage was $1,781.
52. "Cape Sable Highway Dredge Now Working Within Six Miles of Monroe Line," *Miami Metropolis* (November 1, 1918); letter from E. W. Russell to Frederick Morse, May 5, 1919, letter from Frederick Morse to Sidney Harrison, June 6, 1919, both Box 28, Folder 673 (MLC file 817), Model Land Co. Collection, Richter Library, Univ. of Miami.
53. "Carlton Bills Likely to Pass in This Week," *Miami Metropolis* (June 10, 1929); "Palm Beach Won't Pay Gasoline Tax," *Ft. Myers Press* (July 16, 1929); "Distribution of Gasoline Tax Invalid," *Ft. Myers Press* (January 24, 1930). The state also collected one cent, later two cents, of the gas tax to pay for schools.
54. Letter from Sidney Harrison to F. S. Morse, June 10, 1919, Box 28, Folder 673 (MLC file 817), Model Land Company Collection, Richter Library, Univ. of Miami. Apparently been dropped: "Cape Sable Highway May Be Traveled Full Distance by Jan. 1," *Miami Metropolis* (November 6, 1919).

Chapter 4

1. Dewhurst sale: Map of Ingraham Highway Right-of-Way Ownership (EVER 303428), Department of Archives and Special Collections, Daniel Beard Center, Everglades National Park, Homestead; letter from Estate of William Dewhurst to Frank Pepper, January 26, 1929, Box 17, Folder 449 (MLC File 538), Model Land Co. Collection, Richter Library, Univ. of Miami. The sale date was March 26, 1919.

2. A photo of the bridge can be found in "Final Location and Construction Report: Flamingo Road (Park Route 1), June 30, 1959," Records of the Superintendent's Office, Series 3, subseries D, file 048, Department of Archives and Special Collections, Daniel Beard Center, Everglades National Park Homestead.

3. "Cape Sable Highway Dredge Now Working Within Six Miles of the Monroe Line," *Miami Metropolis* (November 1, 1918); letter from Frank J. Pepper to A. A. Dooley, November 2, 1918, Box 17, Folder 450 (MLC File 538), Model Land Co. Collection, Richter Library, University of Miami. Dewhurst sold and cement bridge: maps of Ingraham Highway Right-of-Way, EVER 303386, 303374, 303382, Department of Archives and Special Collections, Daniel Beard Center, Everglades National Park, Homestead.

4. Lawrence Will, "Digging the Cape Sable Canal," *Tequesta* 19 (1959): 29–63.

5. Will, "Digging the Cape Sable Canal," 32.

6. Letter from A. A. Dooley to F. J. Pepper, October 26, 1918; letter from F. J. Pepper to A. A. Dooley, October 28, 1918; memo from F. J. Pepper to A. A. Dooley, November 2, 1918, all Box 17, Folder 450 (MLC File 538), Model Land Co. Collection, Univ. of Miami. Letter from Sidney Harrison to F. J. Pepper, re: Proposed Game Preserve, December 11, 1918; letter from F. J. Pepper to Dixie Highway Association, December 13, 1918, both Box 29, Folder 683 (MLC File 828), Model Land Co. Collection, Richter Library, Univ. of Miami.

7. "Road Contractor Asks Release of Money Held Back," *Miami Metropolis* (September 4, 1918); Dade County Board of Commissioners Resolution dated September 4, 1918, J. B McCrary Papers, HistoryMiami.

8. Letter from the Clerk of the Dade County Board of Commissioners to the Third National Bank of Atlanta, December 3, 1918, J. B McCrary Papers, HistoryMiami.

9. Loan contract between J. B. McCrary Co. and Bank of Bay Biscayne, June 28, 1919, J. B McCrary Papers, HistoryMiami. "Tamiami Trail Work to Wait for While Now," Miami *Metropolis*, October 2, 1918.

10. "Cape Sable Highway Within 4 Miles of Monroe County Line," *Miami Metropolis* (March 6, 1919); Frank Pepper, "Memorandum of Observations Made on Trip Over Ingraham Highway or Cape Sable Road, May 7, 1919," Box 17, File 450 (MLC Folder 538), Model Land Company Collection, Richter Library, Univ. of Miami.

11. Dewhurst, Morse and Pepper trip: F. J. Pepper, "Memorandum of Observations Made on Trip Over Ingraham Highway," May 7, 1919, Box 17, Folder 450 (MLC File 538), Model Land Co. Papers, Richter Library, Univ. of Miami. Crabtree and Duncan 1918 survey: letter from F. S. Morse to J. E. Ingraham, February 2, 1918; letter from J. E. Ingraham to F. S. Morse, February 4, 1918, both Box 17, Folder 450 (MLC File 538), Model Land Co. Collection, Richter Library, Univ. of Miami. 1915 survey: letter from F. S. Morse to J. E. Ingraham, September 11, 1915; letter from F. S. Morse to J. E. Ingraham, September 16, 1915; letter from F. S. Morse to J. E. Ingraham, September 25, 1915, all Box 5, Folder 149 (MLC File 165), Model Land Co. Collection, Richter Library, Univ. of Miami.

12. Frank J. Pepper, "Memorandum of Observations Made on Trip Over Ingraham Highway," May 7, 1919; Sidney Harrison to F. S. Morse, May 1, 1919, both Box 17, Folder 450 (MLC File 538), Model Land Co. Collection, Richter Library, Univ. of Miami.

13. Frank J. Pepper, "Memorandum of Observations Made on Trip Over Ingraham Highway," May 7, 1919; Sidney Harrison to F. S. Morse, May 1, 1919, both Box 17, Folder 450 (MLC File 538), Model Land Co. Collection, Richter Library, Univ. of Miami.

14. "To Push Tamiami Trail, Declares J. B. McCrary," *Miami Metropolis* (March 17, 1920); letter from J. B. McCrary to Dade County Board of Commissioners, April 5, 1920, J. B. McCrary Papers, HistoryMiami.

15. "Final Location and Construction Report: Flamingo Road, Narrative Report, June 30, 1959," Records of the Superintendent's Office, Series 2, subseries D, file 084, Department of Archives and Special Collections, Daniel Beard Center, Everglades National Park, Homestead.

16. McCrary had asked for acceptance and been told: letter from J. B. McCrary to Dade County Board of Commissioners, April 5, 1920, J. B. McCrary Papers, HistoryMiami. Pepper could not get all the way: letter from Frank Pepper to Sidney Harrison, June 22, 1920, Box 30, Folder 731 (MLC File 899), Model Land Co. Collection, Richter Library, Univ. of Miami. Commission approved: Letters from J. B. McCrary to Dade County Board of County Commissioners, June 1, 1920 (2 letters this date); letter from J. B. McCrary to Dade County Board of County Commissioners, December 15, 1920; letter from Dade County Board of County Commissioners, December 18, 1920, all J. B. McCrary Papers, HistoryMiami.

17. Letter from J. B. McCrary to Model Land Company, July 28, 1920, Box 17, Folder 450 (MLC File 538), Model Land Co. Collection, Richter Library, University of Miami.

18. Freeman sent to Tamiami Trail: letter from J. B. McCrary to Dade Board of County Commissioners, August 2, 1920, J. B. McCrary Papers, HistoryMiami. The earliest mention of the transfer of Freeman and his men is July 8: "Tamiama [sic] Trail Construction Delays at End," *Miami Metropolis* (July 8, 1920).

19. "Tamiami Trail Work Is Advanced One-Half Mile," *Miami Metropolis* (September 4, 1920).

20. Letter from J. E. Ingraham to J. B. McCrary, March 21, 1921, Box 28, Folder 673 (MLC File 817), Model Land Co. Collection, Richter Library, Univ. of Miami.

21. "Model Land Company to Extend Road at Cape Sable," *Palm Beach Post* (May 7, 1922); "Another Cape Sable Contract Is Let by Model Land Company," *Miami Metropolis* (May 24, 1922).

22. Lawrence Will, *A Dredgeman of Cape Sable* (St. Petersburg: Great Outdoors Publishing Company, 1967): 8–11.

23. Letter from Thomas E. Will to "Marion," January 12, 1922, Thomas E. Will Papers, P. K. Yonge Library, Univ. of Florida, URL: http://ufdc.ufl.edu//AA00000148/00016.

24. "U. S. Buys Last of Flagler Acreage in Everglades National Park," *Miami Herald* (April 3, 1949).

25. Will, "Digging the Cape Sable Canal," 30, 37.

26. Letter from Donald E. Lee, assistant chief counsel, U.S. Dept. of the Interior, to Land Acquisition Project Manager, Everglades National Park, April 8, 1948, Records of the Superintendent's Office, Series 6, subseries A, file 264 (land purchase: McDougal, Violet), Department of Archives and Special Collections, Daniel Beard Center, Everglades National Park, Homestead.

27. Will, "Digging the Cape Sable Canal": 31; Marjorie Stoneman Douglas, *Voice of the River*. (Englewood, FL: Pineapple Press, 1987): 126.

28. "Easy to Reach Cape Sable by Highway," *Miami Metropolis*, (December 26, 1922); "Ingraham Highway to Open Cape Sable Section," *Palm Beach Post* (November 3, 1923); Will, "Digging the Cape Sable Canal," 38.

29. "40,000 Acres!" [advertisement] *Miami Herald* (January 28, 1923); *Annat V. Beard, Et. Al*, 277 F.2d 554 (5th Cir 1960); "Untitled," *St. Petersburg Evening Independent* (September 29, 1925); letter from Pepper & Potter to J. W. Hoffman, Box 75, Folder 1441 (MLC File 1869), Model Land Co. Collection, Richter Library, Univ. of Miami.

30. Death of Morse: "Many Mourn Death Frederick S. Morse, Magic City Pioneer," *Miami Metropolis* (July 3, 1920). Whitewater Bay land requests: Letter from J. W. Hoffman to F. J. Pepper, May 27, 1927 (first letter this date); letter from J. W. Hoffman to F. J. Pepper, May 27, 1927 (second letter this date); letter from J. W. Hoffman to F. J. Pepper, June 1, 1927 (first letter this date); letter from J. W. Hoffman to F. J. Pepper, June 1, 1927 (second letter this date); letter from F. J. Pepper to J. W. Hoffman, June 7 1927, all Box 56, Folder 1196 (MLC File 1634), Model Land Co. Collection, Richter Library, Univ. of Miami.

31. Gregg M. Turner, *A Journey into Florida Railroad History* (Gainesville: University Press of Florida, 2008): 190-198. The ACL and SCL didn't merge until 1967.

32. Letter from J. W. Hoffman to F. J. Pepper, June 1, 1927 (second letter this date); letter from F. J. Pepper to J. W. Hoffman, June 7 1927, both Box 56, Folder 1196 (MLC File 1634), Model Land Co. Collection, Richter Library, Univ. of Miami. Five dollars an acre: letter from J. W. Hoffman to Ivar Axelson, June 3, 1934, Box 75, Folder 1439 (MLC File 1869) Model Land Co. Collection, Richter Library, Univ. of Miami.

33. "Cape Sable Road Is Declared Bad," *Miami Metropolis* (January 20, 1929).

34. Letter from F. J. Pepper to J. W. Hoffman, May 20, 1930, Box 28, Folder 673 (MLC File 817), Model Land Co. Collection, Richter Library, University of Miami; letter from J. W. Hoffman to F. J. Pepper, 24 July 1930, Box 28, Folder 673 (MLC File 817), Model Land Co. Collection, Richter Library, University of Miami.

35. Letter from F. J. Pepper to J. W. Hoffman, August 13, 1930; letter from F. J. Pepper to J. W. Hoffman, August 29, 1930; letter from F. N. Irwin to Monroe County Commissioners, October 20, 1930; letter from F. J. Pepper to J. W. Hoffman, 20 October 1930, all Box 28, Folder 673 (MLC File 817), Model Land Co. Collection, Richter Library, Univ. of Miami.

36. Letter from F. J. Pepper to J. W. Hoffman, October 28, 1930; letter from J. W. Hoffman to Pepper & Potter, December 5, 1930, both Box 28, Folder 673 (MLC File 817), Model Land Co. Collection, Richter Library, Univ. of Miami. Redd quote: "Road Bill to Be Introduced," *Homestead Enterprise* (May 8, 1931).

37. "Cape Sable Road Bill," *Homestead Leader* (February 12, 1931); letter from F. J. Pepper to J. W. Hoffman, December 20, 1934, Box 75, Folder 1438 (MLC File 1896); Model Land Co. Collection, Richter Library, Univ. of Miami.

38. Federal Writers' Project, *Florida: A Guide to the Southernmost State* [WPA Guide to Florida] (New York: Oxford University Press, 1938): 325-327; Douglas, *Voice of the River*: 137; D. Lebarron Perrine, "Cape Sable," *Tropic Magazine* 5, 5 /6 (February-March, 1917) 81-83; 6, 1 (April 1917): 5-9; "$250,000 for 12,000 Acres for New Town on Cape Sable," Miami *Metropolis* (April 18, 1916).

39. Will, *A Bargeman on Cape Sable*: 139-140.

40. Thomas Neil Knowles, *Category 5: The 1935 Labor Day Hurricane* (Gainesville: University Press of Florida, 2009): 271-273; *Florida: A Guide to the Southernmost State*: 326; "11 Skeletons Found in Cape Sable Region," *Miami Metropolis* (May 4, 1936); "Superintendent's Narrative Monthly Report for March 1961," Records of the Superintendent's Office, Series 2, subseries B, Department of Archives and Special Collections, Daniel Beard Center, Everglades National Park, Homestead.

41. "State to Aid Florida's No Man's Land," *Miami Metropolis* (December 3, 1944).

42. For example, see letter from J. W. Hoffman to Ivar Axelson, July 3, 1934, Box 75, Folder 1438 (MLC File 1869), Letter from J. W. Hoffman to Pepper & Coffrin, December 21, 1934, Box 75, File 1438 (MLC File 1869), Model Land Co. Collection, Richter Library, University of Miami; George Cook, "Financial Report of Chevelier Corporation, January 1937," Box 13, File 4, Jaudon Papers, HistoryMiami.

43. Letter from Daniel McDougal to Ivar Axelson, May 5, 1943, Series 7, Folder 308, Mary McDougal Axelson Collection, Richter Library, Univ. of Miami; "Interview with D. A. McDougal and Ivar Axelson by Mackey, Smith and Manley, July 23, 1948, Records of the Superintendent's Office, Series 7, subseries A (Land Acquision Records), File 262, Department of Archives and Special Collections, Daniel Beard Center, Everglades National Park, Homestead.

44. Superintendant's Narrative Monthly Report for November, 1955; Records of the Superintendant's Office, Series 2, subseries B, Department of Archives and Special Collections, Daniel Beard Center, Everglades National Park, Homestead.

45. Letter from J. W. Hoffman to Pepper & Coffrin, December 21, 1934, Box 75, File 1438 (MLC File 1869), Model Land Company Collection, Richter Library, Univ. of Miami; Chris Wilhelm, "Prophet of the Everglades: Ernest Coe and the Fight for Everglades National Park," (Ph.D. dissertation, Florida State University, 2010): 206; "Map of Park Boundaries June 1947 and February 1950," attached to "Superintendent's Monthly Report for February 1950, Records of the Superintendent's Office, Series 2, subseries B, Department of Archives and Special Collections, Daniel Beard Center, Everglades National Park, Homestead.

46. Superintendant's Narrative Monthly Report for November, 1945; Series 2, subseries B; Memorandum from Donald E. Lee, Asst. Chief Counsel to Land Acquisition Project Manager, April 8, 1948, Series 6, subseries A, File 264 (Land Purchase: Mcdougal, Violet), Both Records of the Superintendant's Office, Department of Archives and Special Collections, Daniel Beard Center, Everglades National Park, Homestead.

47. "Park Boundaries of June 20, 1947 and February 22, 1950," appended to Superintendant's Narrative Monthly Report for February 1950: 3, Records of the Superintendant's Office, Series 2, subseries B, Department of Archives and Special Collections, Daniel Beard Center, Everglades National Park, Homestead.

48. *Paradise Prairie Land Co. V. United States*, 212 F.2d 170 (5th Cir. 1954); *Annat V. Beard, Et. Al*, 277 F.2d 554 (5th Cir. 1960).

49. "1,000 Acres Sisal Being Planted on Cape Sable," Miami *Metropolis* (April 3, 1919); "Sisal Plantation of 22,000 Acres to Be Planted at Once," Miami *Metropolis* (May 23, 1919); "Miami Sisal Company in Hands of Receiver," *Miami Herald* (June 19, 1921); *Map: Special Road and Bridge District No. 1, Cape Sable District, 1920*, Mary McDougal Axelson Map Collection, Richter Library, Univ. of Miami.

CHAPTER 5

1. Superintendant's Monthly Narrative Reports for October 1947; September 1949, November 1949 and

August 1950," Records of the Superintendent's Office, Series 2, subseries B, Department of Archives and Special Collections, Daniel Beard Center, Everglades National Park, Homestead.

2. Superintendant's Monthly Narrative Reports for September 1950," Records of the Superintendent's Office, Series 2, subseries B, Department of Archives and Special Collections, Daniel Beard Center, Everglades National Park, Homestead.

3. Superintendant's Monthly Narrative Report for February 1955," Records of the Superintendent's Office, Series 2, subseries B, Department of Archives and Special Collections, Daniel Beard Center, Everglades National Park, Homestead.

4. "Superintendant's Monthly Narrative Report for August 1948," Records of the Superintendent's Office, Series 2, subseries B, Department of Archives and Special Collections, Daniel Beard Center, Everglades National Park, Homestead.

5. "Final Location and Construction Report: Flamingo Road (Park Road 1), Narrative Report, June 30, 1959," Records of the Superintendent's Office, Series 3, subseries D, File 084, Department of Archives and Special Collections, Daniel Beard Center, Everglades National Park, Homestead.

6. "Superintendant's Monthly Narrative Report for January 1950," Records of the Superintendent's Office, Series 2, subseries B, Department of Archives and Special Collections, Daniel Beard Center, Everglades National Park, Homestead.

7. "Vegetation Map of the "Hole in the Donut" Agricultural Area, 1952, Hole in the Donut Restoration Collection, Everglades Digital Library, Florida International Library, Miami, URL: http://everglades.fiu.edu/hid/hidmap52.gif. For many years, park employees could walk or (until the two bridges were removed) take a jeep directly from Pine Island to the Royal Palm Center along the old road grade. However, the embankment was removed about 2003. The stub of the road on the Pine Island side is currently used as boat ramp into Taylor Slough.

8. "Superintendant's Monthly Narrative Report for December 1955," Records of the Superintendent's Office, Series 2, subseries B, Department of Archives and Special Collections, Daniel Beard Center, Everglades National Park, Homestead. It appears that there was a deliberate effort not to leave abandoned structures behind. They were either removed or totally destroyed.

9. Staking completed: "Superintendant's Monthly Narrative Report for November, 1954, Series 2, Subseries B, Everglades National Park Archives, Daniel Beard Center, Homestead. Dredging Fill: "Superintendent's Monthly Narrative Report for December 1955," Series 2, subseries B, Everglades National Park Archives, Daniel Beard Center, Homestead. Eleven feet: "Final Location and Construction Report: Flamingo Road (Park Route 1), Narrative Report, June 30, 1959": 43, Records of the Superintendent's Office, Series 3, subseries D, File 084, Department of Archives and Special Collections, Daniel Beard Center, Everglades National Park, Homestead.

10. Superintendant's Monthly Narrative Report for December 1955," Series 2, subseries B, Department of Archives and Special Collections, Daniel Beard Center, Everglades National Park, Homestead. Borrow pits out of the public eye, such as the one on the driveway to the Pine Island Service area, were not named, nor were they landscaped.

11. Superintendant's Monthly Narrative Report for December 1955," Series 2, subseries B, Everglades National Park Archives, Daniel Beard Center, Homestead. Superintendant's Monthly Narrative Report for January, 1957," Series 2, subseries B, Department of Archives and Special Collections, Daniel Beard Center, Everglades National Park, Homestead. A formal dedication ceremony for the Flamingo Visitor Center was held in the spring.

12. "Final Location and Construction Report: Flamingo Road (Park Route 1), Narrative Report, June 30, 1959": 71.

13. M. A. Stewart, et al., *The Road to Flamingo: An Evaluation of Flow Pattern Alterations and Salinity Intrusion in the Lower Glades, Everglades National Park* (Denver, U.S. Geological Survey, 2002, Report No. Open File 02-59); David Hallac, Sue Perry and Erik Staubenau, *Proposal to Request Fish Passage Funding for FY08: Funding for Culverts on the Old Ingraham Highway in Everglades National Park to Allow for Fish Passage and Enhancement of Marsh Habitat* (Homestead, Everglades National Park, n.d. [2007]).

14. "Superintendant's Monthly Narrative Report for January 1959," Series 2, subseries B, Everglades National Park Archives, Daniel Beard Center, Homestead.

15. "Final Location and Construction Report: Flamingo Road (Park Route 1), Narrative Report, June 30, 1959": [photographic appendix]; James Hammond, *Florida's Vanishing Trail* (n.l.: the author, 2008): 157; author's interview with anonymous ENP staff member, January 28, 2015.

16. "Superintendent's Monthly Narrative Report for June 1963," Series 2, subseries B, Department of Archives and Special Collections, Daniel Beard Center, Everglades National Park, Homestead; "Superintendent's Monthly Narrative Report for August 1963," Series 2, subseries B, Department of Archives and Special Collections, Daniel Beard Center, Everglades National Park, Homestead.; "Superintendent's Monthly Narrative Report for January 1966," Series 2, subseries B, Department of Archives and Special Collections, Daniel Beard Center, Everglades National Park, Homestead.

17. Stewart, et al., *The Road to Flamingo: An Evaluation of Flow Pattern Alterations and Salinity Intrusion in the Lower Glades*; Hallac, Perry and Staubenau, *Proposal to Request Fish Passage Funding for FY08: Funding for Culverts on the Old Ingraham Highway in Everglades National Park*; *Everglades National Park: Bicycle Trail System Study, 2007 Update* (Homestead: Everglades National Park, 2007).

18. William A. Graham, "The Pennsuco Sugar Experiment," *Tequesta* 11 (1959): 27–48.

19. Telegram from F. C. Elliott, State Drainage Engineer, to E. R. Graham, June 23, 1923, "Telegrams and Correspondence Between Ernest Graham and F. C. Elliott," Ernest R. Graham Collection, P. K. Yonge Library, Univ. of Florida, URL: http://Ufdc.Ufl.Edu//AA00007549/00002; letter from E. R. Graham to F. C. Elliott, July 16, 1923, "Telegrams and Correspondence Between Ernest Graham and F. C. Elliott," Ernest R. Graham Collection, P. K. Yonge Library, Univ. of Florida, URL: http://Ufdc.Ufl.Edu/AA00007549/00002.

20. Bought Hopkins tract: letter from C. Torstenson to J. F. Jaudon, April 25, 1917; "Chevelier Corporation Purchase of A. W. Hopkins Tract from J. F. Jaudon and J. F. Jaudon Purchase from A. W. Hopkins," ca. September 1918; both Box 2, File 4, J. F. Jaudon Collection, HistoryMiami. Dredging Chevelier Bay: letter from F. K. Ashworth to J. F. Jaudon, August 20, 1917, Box 2, File 4, J. F. Jaudon Collection, HistoryMiami.

21. Letter from J. F. Jaudon to J. R. Deane, August 22, 1923, Box 2, File 1, J. F. Jaudon Collection, HistoryMiami.

22. Letter from J. R. Deane to J. F. Jaudon, August 24, 1923, Box 2, File 1, J. F. Jaudon Collection, HistoryMiami; letter from William Dewhurst to J. E. Ingraham, June 21 1921, Box 33, Folder 796 (MLC File 1060),

Model Land Co. Collection, Richter Library, Univ. of Miami.

23. Letter from F. J. Pepper to Sidney Harrison, November 8, 1923, Box 39, Folder 922 (MLC File 1274), Model Land Co. Collection, Richter Library, Univ. of Miami.

24. Request to prepare abstract of title: letter from Sidney Harrison to Pepper & Potter, November 17, 1923, Box 39, Folder 922 (MLC File 1274), Model Land Co. Collection, Richter Library, Univ. of Miami. Poorest land: F. S. Morse to J. E. Ingraham, December 25, 1911, Box 2, Folder 58 (MLC File 64), Model Land Co. Collection, Richter Library, Univ. of Miami.

25. Letter from J. F. Jaudon to J. R. Deane, October 20, 1923, Box 2, File 1, J. F. Jaudon Collection, HistoryMiami.

26. Letter from J. E. Ingraham to J. F. Jaudon, 20 June 1924, Box 2, File 1, J. F. Jaudon Collection, HistoryMiami.

27. "An Exceptional Investment with the Best Security on Earth" (brochure published by Royal Palm Sugar Cane Co.), Box 39, Folder 922 (MLC File 1274), Model Land Co. Collection, Richter Library, Univ. of Miami.

28. Letter from F. J. Pepper to J. E. Ingraham, January 14, 1924, Box 39, Folder 922 (MLC File 1274), Model Land Co. Collection, Richter Library, Univ. of Miami.

29. Letter from J. E. Ingraham to Pepper & Potter, January 24, 1924; letter from J. E. Ingraham to Pepper & Potter, January 31, 1924, both Box 39, Folder 922 (MLC File 1274), Model Land Co. Collection, Richter Library, Univ. of Miami.

30. Letter from J. E. Ingraham to Pepper & Potter, January 31, 1924, Box 39, Folder 922 (MLC File 1274), Model Land Co. Collection, Richter Library, Univ. of Miami.

31. Will, "Digging the Cape Sable Canal": 60–61. The Waddell plantation was destroyed in the 1935 hurricane.

32. Mark S. Foster, *Castles in the Sand: The Life and Times of Carl Graham Fisher* (Gainesville: University Press of Florida, 2000): 119–135. Florida Good Roads Assn.: Thomas Graham, *Mr. Flagler's St. Augustine* (Gainesville: University Press of Florida, 2014): 419.

33. Letter from J. R. Deane to J. F. Jaudon, 28 June 1924; letter from J. F. Jaudon to J. R. Deane, 29 July 1924; letter from J. F. Jaudon to J. R. Deane, 7 August 1924, all Box 2, File 1, J. F. Jaudon Collection, South Florida History Museum, Miami, Florida.

34. Chris Wilhelm, "Prophet of the Everglades Ernest Coe and the Fight for Everglades National Park," (Ph.D. dissertation, Florida State University, 2010): Appendix 1.

35. *Ibid.*, 151.

36. *Ibid.*, 137–145.

37. Thomas Neil Knowles, *Category 5: The 1935 Labor Day Hurricane* (Gainesville: University Press of Florida, 2009): 30–36; John A. Stuart, "Constructing Identity: Building and Place in New Deal South Florida." In The *New Deal in South Florida: Design, Policy and Community Building, 1933–1940*, ed. John A. Stuart and John F. Stack (Gainesville: University Press, 2008): 31–70.

38. "Superintendent's Monthly Narrative Report for June 1960," Series 2, subseries B, Department of Archives and Special Collections, Daniel Beard Center, Everglades National Park, Homestead; "Superintendent's Monthly Narrative Report for May 1961," Series 2, subseries B, Department of Archives and Special Collections, Daniel Beard Center, Everglades National Park, Homestead.

CHAPTER 6

1. Dr. John Gifford, "Looking Ahead: Views on Everglades Topics," *Tropic Magazine* 1, 4 (July 1914): 5–10.

2. "Cape Sable People Petition for Road Over Marshy Land," *Miami Weekly Metropolis* (December 13, 1912); "Railroad Wants Survey to Cape Sable Country, May Build a Road There," *Miami Metropolis* (April 11, 1914); "Sable Highway Is Built for 9 Miles," *Miami Metropolis* (June 22, 1914).

3. Linda D. Vance," May Mann Jennings and Royal Palm State Park," *Florida Historical Quarterly* 6, 1 (July 1976) 1–17. Letter from B. M. Duncan to May Mann Jennings, July 17, 1916, May Mann Jennings Collection, University of Florida Libraries, URL: http://Ufdc.Ufl.Edu//UF00091151/00001.

4. Tammy Ingram, *Dixie Highway: Road Building and the Making of the Modern South, 1900-1930* (Chapel Hill: University of North Carolina Press, 2014):47–48.

5. Fisher biography: Mark S. Foster, *Castles in the Sand: The Life and Times of Carl Graham Fisher* (Gainesville: University Press of Florida, 2000): Chapters 1–7. Lincoln Highway technical and political problems: Virginia Rishel, *Wheels to Adventure: Bill Rishel's Western Routes* (Salt Lake City: Howe Brothers, 1983): 105–119.

6. Drake Hoakson, *The Lincoln Highway: Main Street Across America* (Iowa City: University of Iowa Press, 1988): 112.

7. Construction in Utah and Nevada: Rishel, *Wheels to Adventure*: 105–124. Effect on federal authorities: Hoakson, *The Lincoln Highway*: 107–111; Ingram, *Dixie Highway: Road Building and the Making of Modern South*: 48.

8. Howard L. Preston, *Automobile Age Atlanta: The Making of a Southern Metropolis, 1900-1935* (Athens: University of Georgia Press, 1979): 146.

9. Foster, *Castles in the Sand*: 121–122.

10. Ingram, *Dixie Highway*: 76–77. Included among the DHA "Founders" were Fisher (Miami Beach real estate developer); Coleman DuPont (Miami, Boca Raton and north Florida real estate developer); Charles E. James (Chattanooga real estate developer); Claude H. Huston (Chattanooga banker); and Richard Hardy (Chattanooga cement contractor).

11. Reportedly, the multi-route approach was a compromise hammered out behind closed doors between Carl Fisher, who wanted assurance that the route would terminate in Miami, and the conference chairman, Atlanta newspaperman Clark Howell, who wanted flexibility to permit the most deserving states and counties to get the highway: Preston, *Dirt Roads to Dixie: Accessibility and Modernization in the South, 1885-1935*: 55–57.

12. Ingraham, *Dixie Highway*: 56 [map, redrawn from *Atlanta Constitution*, May 20, 1915]; "Dixie Highway Should Not Be Routed Through 'Glades, Says Belcher," *Miami Metropolis* (May 14, 1915); "Highway Bond Issues of State Insure Excellent Travel," *St. Petersburg Daily Times* (October 14, 1915).

13. "Controversy on Route of Dixie Highway Over Western Part of Loop," *Miami Metropolis* (August 17, 1915).

14. "Highway Bond Issues of State Insure Excellent Travel," *St. Petersburg Daily Times* (October 14, 1915).

15. "Trail Argument Continues at County Board Meeting," *Miami Metropolis* (September 5, 1915); Letter from Thomas Will to Palm Beach Board of Commissioners, September 16, 1915, Business Correspondence: Sept. 1, 1915 to Oct. 31, 1915 (1 of 2), Thomas Will Papers, P. K. Yonge Library, Univ. of Florida, URL: http://ufdc.ufl.edu//AA00000147/00027.

16. "Dixie Highway Should Not Be Routed Through 'Glades Says Belcher," *Miami Metropolis* (May 14, 1915).

17. "Tamiami Trail, as Compiled by Workers of the Writers' Program Florida Work Project Administration," *Florida Highways* 10 (December 1941): 8–9; 24.

18. "James Franklin Jaudon," [autobiographical outline] undated manuscript [ca. 1926], Box 6, File 10, James F. Jaudon Collection, HistoryMiami. (hereafter, "Jaudon Collection, Historymiami"). Land ownership and mortgages: "Financial Statement of J. F. Jaudon," August 12, 1923, Box 17, File 1, Jaudon Collection, HistoryMiami. The 1923 statement does not include 20,000 acres in Collier County Jaudon purchased in mid-1925: letter from J. F. Jaudon to Judge H. F. Hancock, March 27, 1935, Box 6, File 1, Jaudon Collection, HistoryMiami.

19. "Mallon & Jaudon's Place," *Miami Metropolis* (February 15, 1901); "Captain James F. Jaudon," [autobiographical sketch] undated manuscript [ca. 1929], Box 6, File 10, Jaudon Collection, HistoryMiami; letter from James F. Jaudon to Francis Reed, Federal Writers Project, April 8, 1936, Box 13, File 3, Jaudon Collection, HistoryMiami.

20. "Central Highway Through State Backed by the New Organization," *St. Petersburg Evening Independent* (June 11, 1915); J. Hugh Reese, *History of the Tamiami Trail* (Miami: Tamiami Trail Commissioners and the County Commission of Dade County, 1928): 6–9; James Lorenzo Walker, "Dedication of the Tamiami Trail Marker," *Tequesta* 19 (1959): 23–28.

21. "Tamiami Trail Name Was Given by D. C. Gillette," *Miami Metropolis* (April 22, 1928).

22. "Lee County Will Build Share of Cross-State Tamiami Trail," *Miami Metropolis* (June 4, 1915).

23. Hill told Jaudon: William Stewart Hill, "Tamiami Trail Turns Dream into Reality," *Miami Herald* (April 26, 1928). Early use of Tamiami Trail name: "Lee County Will Build Share of Cross-State Tamiami Trail," *Miami Metropolis* (June 4, 1915).

24. James Jaudon, "Ochopee, Collier County Florida," manuscript attached to letter from James Jaudon to Francis Reed, Federal Writers Project, April 8, 1936, Box 13, File 3, Jaudon Collection, HistoryMiami.

25. "Belcher Says He Wants New Route in Central and North Florida," *Miami Metropolis* (August 17 1915).

26. "Lee County Will Build Share of Cross-State Tamiami Trail," *Miami Metropolis* (June 4, 1915); "Central Highway Through State Backed by New Organization," *St. Petersburg Independent* (June 11, 1915).

27. "Lee County Will Build Share of Cross State Tamiami Trail," *Miami Metropolis* (June 4, 1915); "Tamiami Trailers Held First Meeting and Plans Were Laid," *Miami Metropolis* (June 19, 1915). Historian Allen Morris claims that the "Map Maker Who Put This Site [Sam Jones Old Town] on the Florida Road Map Was a Practical Joker." The site was the farm and gravesite of Tuscanatofee, a veteran of the Seminole Wars known as Sam Jones, who died in 1861, but no town ever existed. A small monument erected by George Espenlaub of Clewiston in 1951 marks the approximate site of Sam Jones' grave. On the other hand, Brown's Store was a very real place, photographed several times prior to World War I: Allen Norris, *Florida Place Names* (Coral Gables: University of Miami Press, 1974); s.v. "Sam Jones Old Town." The map of "Captain Ker's Route" is on an 1856 military map known as the "Ives Map." See: James Hammond, *Florida's Vanishing Trail* (n.l.: the author, 2008): 32.

28. "County to Select Best Route for Road Across Peninsula," *Miami Metropolis* (June 28, 1915).

29. The land was transferred to Belcher on March 26, 1919. It was located about where the Old Ingraham campground in Everglades National Park is located today. It was returned to Dewhurst when Belcher died. Letter from William Dewhurst to Frank J. Pepper, June 4, 1917, Box 17, Folders 449–450 (MLC File 538), Model Land Co. Collection, Richter Library, Univ. of Miami; Map of Ingraham Highway Right-of-Way, 1949, EVER 303428, Division of Archives and Special Collections, Daniel Beard Center, Everglades National Park, Homestead.

30. North route: "Tamiami Trailers Held First Meeting Friday and Plans Were Laid," *Miami Metropolis* (June 19, 1915). Highleyman's rejection: "Tamiami Trail Now Waits on Some Action by Dade County," *Miami Metropolis* (July 3, 1915); "Controversy on Route of Dixie Highway Over Western Part of Loop," *Miami Metropolis* (August 17 1915).

31. "New Route Along Gulf Coast Is Proposed by Tampa People," *Miami Metropolis* (June 23, 1915).

32. "New Route Along Gulf Coast Is Proposed by Tampa People," *Miami Metropolis* (June 23, 1915); "County to Select Best Route for Road Across Peninsula," *Miami Metropolis* (June 28, 1915).

33. "Tamiami Trail Now Waits on Some Action by Dade County," *Miami Metropolis* (July 3, 1915).

34. "Tamiami Trail Now Waits on Some Action by Dade County," *Miami Metropolis* (July 3, 1915); "Dade to Build Tamiami Trail to Lee's Line," *Miami Metropolis* (July 7, 1915); "County Board Signs Contract with State for Road Work Along Canal Bank," *Miami Metropolis* (July 8, 1915); "Tamiami Trail to Be Built to Miami and Lauderdale," *Miami Metropolis* (July 12, 1915).

35. "Tamiami Trail to Leave City by Twentieth Street," *Miami Metropolis* (August 4, 1915); "Straight Away Tamiami Trail Is Endorsed by County Board; $200,000 State Funds Wanted," *Miami Metropolis* (August 14, 1915).

36. Reese: *History of the Tamiami Trail*: 8–11; "Straight Away Tamiami Trail is Endorsed by County Board; $200,000 State Funds Wanted," *Miami Metropolis* (August 14, 1915); "Captain Jaudon Gives Tamiami Trail's History," Miami Metropolis (May 2, 1928).

37. "Tamiami Trail, Compiled by Workers of the Writers' Program": 8; Patsy West, *The Enduring Seminoles: From Alligator Wrestling to Ecotourism* (Gainesville: University Press of Florida, 1998): 35–36, 76.

38. "County to Select Best Route for Road Across Peninsula," *Miami Metropolis* (June 28, 1915); "Dade to Build Tamiami Trail to Lee's Line," *Miami Metropolis* (July 7, 1915); "County Board Signs Contract with State for Road Along Canal Bank," *Miami Metropolis* (July 8, 1915); "Tamiami Trail to Be Built to Miami and Lauderdale," *Miami Metropolis* (July 12, 1915); "Broward County Trail Bonds Be Voted Before Action Is Taken in Dade County," *Miami Metropolis* (August 3, 1915); letter from Ralph Horton to Thomas Will, October 23, 1915, Business Correspondence Sept. 1, 1915 to Oct. 31, 1915 (Folder 1 of 2), Thomas Will Collection, P. K. Yonge Library, Univ. of Florida, UFL: http://ufdc.ufl.edu//AA00000147/00027.

39. Letter from Thomas Will to Palm Beach County Commissioners, September 14, 1915, letter from Ralph Horton to Thomas Will, October 23, 1915, both Thomas Will Collection, Business Correspondence, Sept. 1, 1915-Oct. 31-1915 (Folder 1 of 2), P. K. Yonge Library, Univ. of Florida, UFL: http://Ufdc.Ufl.Edu//AA00000147/00027.

40. "State Trustees Favor Cross-State Highway, Engineer Says That It Is Feasible," *Miami Metropolis* (August 28, 1915). Letter from Ralph Horton to Thomas Will, October 23, 1915, Thomas Will Collection, Business Correspondence, Sept. 1, 1915-Oct. 31–1915, P. K. Yonge Library, University of Florida, UFL: http://Ufdc.Ufl.Edu//AA00000147/00027.

41. "Tatum Brothers Everglades Lands" [map] *Miami Metropolis* (March 2, 1918).

42. James Lorenzo Walker, "Dedication of the Tamiami Trail Marker": 25–26.

43. "Tamiami Trail Committee Go to Capital to Interview Fund Trustees," *Miami Metropolis* (August 23,

1915); "Meeting of August 25, 1915," *Minutes of the Trustees of the Internal Improvement Fund*, Vol. 11 (August 25, 1915): 157–159. "Our Idea": letter from James F. Jaudon to E. G. Wilkinson, 29 September 29, 1915, Box 12, File 7, Jaudon Collection, HistoryMiami. August 25 meeting: *Minutes of the Trustees of the Internal Improvement Fund*, Vol. 11 (August 25, 1915): 157–159.

44. "Trail Argument Continues at County Board Meeting," *Miami Metropolis* (September 5, 1915).

45. "Trail Argument Continues at County Board Meeting," *Miami Metropolis* (September 5, 1915); "Tatum Replies to Stahl," *Miami Metropolis* (September 21, 1915).

46. "Belcher Decides on Dixie Highway Route," *Miami Weekly Metropolis* (September 17, 1915); "Highway Bond Issues of State Insure Excellent Travel," *St. Petersburg Times* (October 14, 1915).

47. "20,000 Acres State Lands for Tamiami Trail, Trail Designated as Part of Dixie Highway," *Miami Metropolis* (October 13, 1915); Ingraham, *Dixie Highway*: 114 [map].

48. "Trail Argument Continues at County Board Meeting," *Miami Metropolis* (September 5, 1915); "Tatum Replies to Stahl," *Miami Metropolis* (September 21, 1915).

49. *Minutes of the Trustees of the Internal Improvement Fund*, Vol. 11 (October 9, 1915): 176–177; "20,000 Acres State Lands for Tamiami Trail, Trail Designated as Part of Dixie Highway," *Miami Metropolis* (October 13, 1915); "Enough Land for Road and Canal Across South Florida Peninsula Be Set Aside by State Trustees," *Miami Metropolis* (October 14, 1915).

50. "Bond Issue in Lee County Is Successful," *Miami Metropolis* (October 11, 1915); "$275,000 is Voted Tamiami Trail to the Gulf," *Miami Metropolis* (October 20, 1915); "Bonds for the North Route Tamiami Trail Failed to Carry at Election," *Miami Metropolis* (November 23, 1915).

51. Walker, "Dedication of Tamiami Trail Marker": 24; "West-East Road First Advocated at Orlando in '15," *Ft. Myers Press* (April 25, 1928). James Lorenzo Walker, in 1959, recalled that the $177K in funds for District No. 1 was mainly for right-of-way, and was intended for construction only from Naples to Marco. However, road contractor K. H. Harvey told a reporter in 1916 that he had received a contract to build 55 miles of road from Fort Myers to Marco at $44 an acre: "Building a Rock-Paved Highway Through the Everglades," *Miami Daily Metropolis* (November 21, 1916).

52. "Specifications Tamiami Trail on File with the Board," *Miami Metropolis* (January 5, 1916).

53. "Work Will Begin in March on Tamiami Trail Across State," *Miami Metropolis* (December 28, 1915); "Specifications Tamiami Trail on File with the Board," *Miami Metropolis* (January 6 1916); "Premium on Bonds for Tamiami Trail," *Miami Metropolis* (February 7, 1916); "Tamiami Trail Contract Been Delayed Weeks," *Miami Metropolis* (February 11, 1916); Reese, *History of the Tamiami Trail*: 15.

54. Reese, *History of the Tamiami Trail*: 16; "Surveyors for Tamiami Trail Will Meet at the County Line," *Miami Metropolis* (March 11, 1916); "Building of Tamiami Trail Feasible and Construction Costs Will Be Low, Belief of County Surveyor Crabtree," *Miami Metropolis* (March 15, 1916); "More Land for Tamiami Trail May Be Given by I. I. Board," *Miami Metropolis* (January 12, 1916). The precise zero point is where the Tamiami Canal branches off to the northeast from the Tamiami Trail, very near the present-day intersection of SW 8th Street and the Palmetto Expressway.

55. "Tamiami Trail Contract Is Issued," *Miami Metropolis* (April 4, 1916). McGill quote: "Tamiami Trail Contract Is Let by Commissioners to the M'creary [*sic*] Company," *Miami Metropolis* (May 3, 1916).

56. "Tamiami Trail Contract Is Let by Commissioners to the M'creary [*sic*] Company," *Miami Metropolis* (May 3, 1916).

57. Lee County contract: "Contract Is Let for Building Tamiami Trail Through Lee Co.," *Miami Metropolis* (December 11, 1916). McCrary's plan to transport dredge overland: "Take Two More Years to Build the Tamiami Trail, Engineer Estimates Fourteen Miles Done," *Miami Metropolis* (August 9, 1917); ultimate failure: "Dredge Marks Ending Point of Old Trail," *Miami Metropolis* (April 22, 1928); "Derelict Dredge at Carnestown Relic of Lee County's Effort at Trail Building Ten Years Ago," *Ft. Myers Press* (April 25, 1928).

58. "Begin Work Monday on Tamiami Trail Across Peninsula of Florida," *Miami Metropolis* (June 24, 1916); "Work began Today on Two Everglade Roads Leading From Miami," *Miami Metropolis* (June 26, 1916).

59. No deaths from blasting: "Trail Building Used $500,000 in Machinery," *Miami Metropolis* (April 22, 1928). However, two men died in 1926 in a garage at a work camp when an explosives shed was struck by lightening: "Two Die in Dynamite Blast When Lighting Demolishes Iron Shed," *Ft. Myers Press* (August 24, 1926).

60. "The Tamiami Trail," *Florida Trails to Turnpikes* (Tallahassee: Florida Department of Highways, 1964): 71–73. Average life of a bucket: "Trail Building Used $500,000 in Machinery," *Miami Metropolis* (April 22, 1928).

61. "Excavators on the Jobs," *Miami Metropolis* (August 15, 1916); "Use Powerful Excavator Building Tamiami Trail," *Miami Metropolis* (September 13, 1916); "Build Mile Every Week on Tamiami Trail Soon," *Miami Metropolis* (November 7, 1916). The burning question: "Trail Building Used $500,000 in Machinery," *Miami Metropolis* (April 22, 1928).

62. "Building a Rock-Paved Highway Through the Everglades," *Miami Metropolis* (November 21, 1916).

63. "Building a Rock-Paved Highway Through the Everglades," *Miami Metropolis* (November 2, 1916).

64. Telegram from James Jaudon to George Cook, Box 3, File 3, Jaudon Collection, HistoryMiami.

65. John W. King, "Report of Exploration, Examination and Reconnaissance of the Tamiami Trail in Dade County," MS dated March 23, 1917, Box 18, Files 1–3, Jaudon Collection, HistoryMiami. Tiger Tail expedition: West, *The Enduring Seminoles*: 14. Jaudon quote: "Lost Men Spied from Airship, May Reach King Party in Time," *Miami Metropolitan* (March 9, 1917). The report was erroneous: "No Trace Found of the Lost Men in the Everglades," *Miami Metropolis* (March 12, 1917).

66. "Effort Now Is to Recall Men Out in Glades Hunting King," *Miami Metropolis* (March 15, 1917); "Lost in Everglades for Several Weeks," *Key West Citizen* (March 14, 1917); Letter from John King to Richard Talbot, ca. April 1, 1917, Box 18, Files 2, James Jaudon Collection, HistoryMiami. Reese, *History of the Tamiami Trail*: 16.

67. "Jack Tigertail, Seminole Chief, Shot to Death," *Miami Metropolis* (March 8, 1922); "Coroner's Jury Holds Veber as Slayer of Chief," *Miami Metropolis* (March 10, 1922).

68. "Counsel for Veber Attempts to Break Story of Seminole," *Miami Herald* (November 25, 1922); "Veber Freed in Second Trial for Murder of Chief Jack Tigertail," *Miami Herald* (November 29, 1922).

69. West, *The Enduring Seminoles*: 35–36.

70. "His Injuries Prove Fatal," *Ft. Myers Press* (August 23, 1923).

CHAPTER 7

1. "Supreme Court Turns Down F. J. Jaudon's Petition to Take Shepard's Name from the Ballot," *Miami*

Metropolis (October 24, 1916); "Jaudon Explains His Actions in Regard to Race," *Miami Metropolis* (October 24, 1916).
  2. Minutes of December 18, 1916," *Minutes of the Trustees of the Internal Improvement District* 11 (December 18, 1916): 369-370. Map of Tamiami Trail lands accompanying advertisement for J. F. Jaudon Land Company, *Miami Metropolis* (February 25, 1917); "Status of Payments on Mortgage for Lands Embraced in Deed No. 16,550," Box 3, File 3, Jaudon Collection, HistoryMiami.
  3. King, "Report of Exploration, Examination and Reconnaissance of the Tamiami Trail in Dade County": photos, 502-509; conclusions, 518-519.
  4. James Jaudon, "Tam-Iami; Tampa, Miami—Trail" undated manuscript (ca. March 1923), Box 12, File 5, James Jaudon Collection, HistoryMiami.
  5. "Abstract of Title [For A. W. Hopkins Tract], June 12, 1917," Box 17, File 3, James Jaudon Collection, History Miami. "Chevelier," manuscript ca. September, 1917, probably written by James Jaudon, Box 2, File 1, Jaudon Collection, HistoryMiami.
  6. An old man: Letter to J. F. Jaudon from Carl Torstenson, April 25, 1917, Box 3, File 4, Jaudon Collection, HistoryMiami; Floete and McCord: letter from Citizens Nat'l. Bank of Spencer to J. F. Jaudon, 21 May 1917, Box 2-1, File 3, Jaudon Collection, HistoryMiami.
  7. "Nansen Torstenson Visits," *Milford Mail* (July 3, 1924). Nansen Torstenson died January 12, 1939: *Milford Mail* (January 13, 1939).
  8. Telegram from J. H. McCord to J. F. Jaudon, September 30, 1916, Box 2-1, File 3, Jaudon Collection, HistoryMiami.
  9. John King, "Report of Examination and Reconnaissance of the Eastern Portion of the Property of A. W. Hopkins, March 23, 1917," Box 18, Files 2-4, James Jaudon Collection, HistoryMiami.
  10. "Option Contract," March 3, 1917, Box 17, File 3, James Jaudon Collection, HistoryMiami. Will not wire ten thousand dollars: telegram from J. F. Jaudon to George Cook, March 1, 1917, Box 3, File 3, Jaudon Collection, HistoryMiami. $7,900 paid: Letter from Bank of Bay Biscayne to J. F. Jaudon, April 12, 1917, Box 3, File 4, Jaudon Collection, HistoryMiami. Payment of $10,000: letter from J. F. Jaudon to Carl Torstensten, May 1, 1917, Box 3, File 6, Jaudon Collection, HistoryMiami.
  11. Jaudon quote: telegram from James Jaudon to George Cook, March 1, 1917, Box 3, File 3, Jaudon Collection, HistoryMiami. Scraped together June payment: letter from S. C. Littlefield to J. F. Jaudon, May 19, 1917, Box 3, File 6, Jaudon Collection, HistoryMiami; "Chevelier Corporation Purchase of A. W. Hopkins Tract from J. F. Jaudon and J. F. Jaudon Purchase from A. W. Hopkins," ca. March 1917, Box 2-2, File 5, Jaudon Collection, HistoryMiami.
  12. "George F. Cook, Adventurer, Found Heart's Desire Here," *Miami Herald* (July 27, 1924).
  13. Letter from C. Torstenson to J. F. Jaudon, April 25, 1917; letter from S. C. Littlefield to J. F. Jaudon, May 3, 1917, both Box 2, File 4, Jaudon Collection, HistoryMiami.
  14. Letter from J. F. Jaudon to S. C. Littlefield, May 4, 1917, Box 3, File 6, Jaudon Collection, HistoryMiami.
  15. Torstensen quote: letter from C. Torstensen to J. F. Jaudon, April 25, 1917, Box 2, File 4, Jaudon Collection, HistoryMiami. Price of Tamiami Trail Lands: *Minutes of the Internal Improvement Fund*, Vol. 14 (December 18, 1916): 369-370. Price of land: "Abstract of Title," June 12, 1917, Box 12, File 3; "Abstract of Title, May 19, 1917—July, 1920," both Box 17, File 3, Jaudon Collection, HistoryMiami.

  16. "Option Contract," March 3, 1917, Box 17, File 3, Jaudon Collection, HistoryMiami.
  17. Letter from J. F. Jaudon to S. C. Littlefield, May 4, 1917; letter from J. F. Jaudon to S. C. Littlefield, May 8, 1917, both Box 3, File 6, Jaudon Collection, HistoryMiami.
  18. Today, this problem would be dealt with through title insurance.
  19. "Abstract of Title, May 19, 1917—July, 1920"; "Draft Bill of Complaint [For Declaratory Judgment] of James F. and Maude Jaudon v. the Chevelier Corporation," August 1, 1928, Box 2-1, File 5, Jaudon Collection, HistoryMiami. It appears this legal action was never filed. Hopkins and Floete were both dead and the Citizens National Bank of Spencer was in receivership by this time.
  20. Letter from J. R. Kenly, Atlantic Coast Line R.R. to J. R. Jaudon, April 16, 1917, Box 2, File 4, Jaudon Collection, HistoryMiami "A Railroad Across the State Will Be a Reality in 3 Years," *Miami Metropolis* (April 4, 1917).
  21. Letter from J. F. Jaudon to J. H. McCord, August 15, 1917, Box 6, File 6, Jaudon Collection, HistoryMiami.
  22. "No Railroad on Tamiami Trail Across State," *Miami Metropolis* (May 2, 1917). The road grade was 26 feet wide at the top, 38 at the base. The canal was 30 feet wide. There was six feet between the two. That amounted to 74 feet, with 12 feet at either side for landscaping and future needs. The Everglades Drainage District started widening the canal in 1919, well before the road was finished.
  23. "Start Work Next Monday on the Construction of Tamiami Trail Railway," *Miami Metropolis* (January 4, 1918); "Tamiami Railway Franchise Now Up to Citizens," *Miami Metropolis* (January 29, 1918).
  24. "Tamiami Railway Franchise Given by Big Majority," *Miami Metropolis* (April 10, 1918). Comprehensive plan: letter from F. K. Ashworth to J. F. Jaudon, August 28, 1917, Box 2-1, File 6, Jaudon Collection, HistoryMiami.
  25. Letter from J. F. Jaudon to D. R. House, July 24, 1917, Box 3, File 8; "Report of J. F. Jaudon Trip to Hopkins Tract: September 14th to 25th Inclusive, 1917, Box 2-1, File 1, both Jaudon Collection, History Miami; "Westward the Path of Miami's Farm Empire Wends Its Way," *Miami Metropolis* (May 5, 1929).
  26. D. Graham Copeland, "Research Notes and Papers," Microform copy of complied notes, transcribed interviews, and correspondence, department of history and genealogy, Regional Library Site, Collier County Library System (1115-1116; 1133-1137); Charlton W. Tebeau, *The Story of the Chokoloskee Bay County* (Miami: University of Miami Press, 1966).
  27. "Draft Complaint of James and Maude Jaudon [For Declaratory Judgment and Equitable Relief]," August 1, 1928, Box 2-1, File 5, James Jaudon Collection, History Miami.
  28. W. F. Brown leasing Watson Place: "Report of J. F. Jaudon Trip to Hopkins Tract: September 14th to 25th Inclusive, 1917," Box 2-1, File 1, Jaudon Collection, History Miami. Four thousand to buy Brown's lease: "Draft Complaint of James and Maude Jaudon [For Declaratory Judgment and Equitable Relief]," August 1, 1928, Box 2-1, File 5; "Itemized Statement of Liabilities, Chevelier Corporation, Showing Total Liabilities, Amounts and Dates When Payments Are Due," Box 17, File 3, both Jaudon Collection, History Miami. Used by Chevelier Corp.: "New Equipment Ordered to Rush Tamiami Railway," *Miami Metropolis* (March 23, 1918). Brown allowed to farm through 1920: "To the Owners in Equity in the A. W. Hopkins Tract, December 22, 1919 [1919 Annual Report]," Box 2-1, File 5, Jaudon Collection, HistoryMiami. See also the photo album

and diary of Mary McDougal's [later Mary McDougal Axelson] trip with her father, D. A. McDougal in mid-June 1922 to visit the Tamiami Trail and Chevelier including the Watson "Murder Farm": Mary McDougal Axelson Collection, Richter Library, University of Miami.

29. "Sale of Tamiami Trail Lands Made Subject of Criticism by Improvement Association," *Miami Metropolis* (June 13, 1917).

30. "Nothing Wrong in the Sale of Tamiami Lands Says Head of the Syndicate," *Miami Metropolis* (June 14, 1917); "Expenses of Sale of Tamiami Land Were to Be Paid," *Miami Metropolis* (June 15, 1917).

31. "Supervisor Fight Mixed in Tamiami Trail Land Row," *Miami Metropolis* (June 18, 1917).

32. "No Profit for Anybody in Tamiami Trail Land Deal, Says J. F. Jaudon," *Miami Metropolis* (June 15, 1917); Letter from Paul Taylor to J. F. Jaudon, September 27, 1918, Box 3, File 3, Jaudon Collection, HistoryMiami.

33. Land was mortgaged: "Status of Payments on Mortgage for Lands Embraced in Deed No. 16,550," ca. March 29, 1918, Box 3, File 3, Jaudon Collection, HistoryMiami. Payments to state made on schedule: "Let Contract for Snapper Canal on 15th of February," *Miami Metropolis* (January 4, 1918).

34. "Expenses of Sale of Tamiami Lands Were to Be Paid," *Miami Metropolis* (June 15, 1917); "Status of Payments on Mortgage for Lands Embraced in Deed No. 16,550," ca. March 29, 1918, Box 3, File 3, Jaudon Collection, HistoryMiami.

35. "Take Two Years More to Build the Tamiami Trail, Engineer Estimates—Fourteen Miles Done," *Miami Metropolis* (August 9, 1917); "Work on Trail in Dade County Now About Half Done," *Miami Metropolis* (September 27, 1917); "Tamiami Trail Is to Be Completed by Next Fall," *Miami Metropolis* (November 17, 1917).

36. "Working Hard on the Tamiami Trail," *Miami Metropolis* (August 16, 1917); "Derelict Dredge at Carnestown Relic of Lee County's Effort at Trail Building Ten Years Ago," *Ft. Myers Press* (April 25, 1928); "Dredge Marks Ending Point of Old Trail," *Miami Metropolis* (April 22, 1928). It is more likely that McCrary's subcontractor, James & Green, quit after one of the partners died of influenza: Letter from P. F. Jenkins, Office of Chief Road Engineer, Lee County, to J. F. Jaudon, May 31, 1918, Box 12, File 6, Jaudon Collection, HistoryMiami; "Jaudon Would Aid in Building Rest of Tamiami Trail," *Miami Metropolis* (January 22, 1919).

37. "Ask for More Time to Finish Up the Tamiami Trail," *Miami Metropolis* (January 2, 1918); "Give Contractors One More Year to Finish Up Trail," *Miami Metropolis* (January 3, 1918).

38. "Tamiami Trail Is Assured Through to Fort Myers," *Miami Metropolis* (March 6, 1918); Letter from P. F. Jenkins, Office of Chief Road Engineer, Lee County, to J. F. Jaudon, May 31, 1918, Box 12, File 6, Jaudon Collection, HistoryMiami; Letter from J. F. Jaudon to P. F. Jenkins, Office of Chief Road Engineer, Lee County, May 31, 1918, Box 12, File 6; letter from J. F. Jaudon to F. E. Harrison, June 1, 1918, Box 12, File 6, Jaudon Collection, HistoryMiami; letter from F. E. Harrison to J. F. Jaudon, June 5, 1918, Box 12, File 6, Jaudon Collection, HistoryMiami; letter from J. F. Jaudon to Lee County Board of County Commissioners, January 2, 1922, Box 12, File 8, Jaudon Collection, HistoryMiami.

39. Mary S. Lundstrom, "Marco Florida in 1925," *Tequesta* 31 (1971): 29–40, quote at 30.

40. Letter from J. F. Jaudon to J. H. McCord, September 7, 1918, Box 12, File 6, Jaudon Collection, HistoryMiami.

41. "Try to Negotiate Everglades in Two Ford Cars," *Miami Metropolis* (April 9, 1918). Cape Sable Sisal Plantation: "1,000 Acres Sisal Being Planted on Sable Plantation," *Miami Metropolis* (April 3, 1919); "Sisal Plantation of 22,000 Acres to Be Cultivated at Once," *Miami Metropolis* (May 23, 1919); "Miami Sisal Company in Hands of Receiver," *Miami Herald* (June 19, 1921). Jaudon apparently tried to interest U.S. Sisal in buying part of the Hopkins Tract, without success: letter from J. H. McCord to J. F. Jaudon, Box 2–1, File 4, July 19, 1918, Jaudon Collection, HistoryMiami.

42. "Try to Negotiate Everglades in Two Ford Cars," *Miami Metropolis* (April 9, 1918); "Motor Trip Through Glades," *Miami Metropolis* (April 19, 1918); "West Coasters Use Old Trail," *Miami Metropolis* (June 20, 1918); letters from F. E. Harrison to J. F. Jaudon, May 30, 1918, June 3, 1918 and June 5, 1918, all Box 6, File 7, Jaudon Collection, HistoryMiami.

43. Clark quote: letter from Ross Clark to J. F. Jaudon, May 22, 1918, Box 2, File 4, Jaudon Collection, HistoryMiami; McCord quotes: letter from J. H. McCord to J. F. Jaudon, July 9, 1918, Box 2–1, File 5, Jaudon Collection, HistoryMiami; letter from J. H. McCord to J. F. Jaudon, July 19, 1918, Box 2–1, File 5, Jaudon Collection, HistoryMiami. Jaudon quote: letter from J. F. Jaudon to Ross L. Clark, July 30, 1918, Box 2–1, File 4, Jaudon Collection, HistoryMiami.

44. Draft of editorial for *Ft. Myers Press* by F. Harrison, ca. May 30, 1918, Box 12, File 8, Jaudon Collection, HistoryMiami.

45. Taxes were $8,500 a year: "Itemized Statement of Liabilities of Chevelier Corporation," Box 17, File 3 Jaudon Collection, History Miami. Other documents imply that the property taxes may have been as high as $11,000. The taxes may have varied from year to year. The $8,500 was for 1916.

46. Letter from J. H. McCord to J. F. Jaudon, July 19 1918, Box 2 File 4; Jaudon Collection, HistoryMiami; letter from J. F. Jaudon to J. H. McCord, 7 September 1918, Box 2, File 5, Jaudon Collection, HistoryMiami.

47. Letter from J. F. Jaudon to Ross L. Clark, July 30, 1918, Box 2, File 4, "Itemized Statement of Liabilities of Chevelier Corporation Showing Total Liabilities," Box 17, File 3, both Jaudon Collection, HistoryMiami.

48. "Skilled Labor Should Remain at Their Jobs," *Miami Metropolis* (September 4, 1918); "Road Contractor Asks Release of Money Held Back," *Miami Metropolis* (September 4, 1918); "Ban Tightening on Road Work as War Measure," *Miami Metropolis* (September 30, 1918); "Resolution of Board of County Commissioners, Dade County Florida, September 4, 1918," J. B. McCrary Company Papers, HistoryMiami.

49. "Tamiami Trail Work to Wait for Now," *Miami Metropolis* (October 2, 1918).

CHAPTER 8

1. Jaudon ill and brother died: letter from J. F. Jaudon to J. H. McCord, October 9, 1918, Box 12, File 3, Jaudon Collection, HistoryMiami. DuPont payments: "Road Builders Sued by Dupont," *Miami Metropolis* (December 14, 1918). James & Green: "Jaudon Would Aid in Building Rest of Tamiami Trail," *Miami Metropolis* (January 22, 1919); letter from P. F. Jenkins, Office of the Chief Road Engineer, Lee County, to J. F. Jaudon, May 16, 1918, Box 12, File 6, letter from J. F. Jaudon to P. F. Jenkins, Office of Chief Road Engineer, Lee County, May 31, 1918, Box 12, File 6, Jaudon Collection, HistoryMiami. Letter from J. F. Jaudon to J. H. McCord and Franklin Floete, September 7, 1918, Box 12, File 3, Jaudon Collection, HistoryMiami.

2. Otto Neal, "Early Stages of Trail Building Reviewed by Neal, Dredge Master," MS ca. March 1928, Box 12, File 9, Jaudon Collection, HistoryMiami.

3. Letter from J. F. Jaudon to P. F. Jenkins, Office of Chief Road Engineer, Lee County, May 31, 1918, Box 12, File 6, Jaudon Collection, HistoryMiami.

4. "Jaudon Would Aid in Building Rest of Tamiami Trail," *Miami Metropolis* (January 22, 1919).

5. The name "Jenkins Route" does not appear to have been widely used until adopted by the Collier companies about 1925. Apparently, the alignment follows the approximate route of a proposed cross-state railroad laid out about 1915 by a surveyor of that name. See: "The Tamiami Trail," *Florida Highways* 3, 4 (April 1926): 4–6; "Complete Tamiami Trail Is Shown in New Map," *Miami Metropolis* (April 25, 1926). However, the route being used in 1918–1919 was that laid out by Hobart Crabtree and the Lee County engineering office in 1915.

6. "Tamiami Trail Open Next Year Safe Prediction," *Ft. Myers Press* (February 2, 1919). James and Green went 18 miles: "Open Tamiami Trail by January, 1920 Is Outlook by New Plan," *Miami Metropolis* (February 13, 1919). Still 2.5 miles to Carnestown: "Early Stages of Building Reviewed by Neal, Dredge Master," undated MS (ca. March 1928) File 12, Box 9, Jaudon Collection, History Miami.

7. Resolution of Special Road and Bridge Tax District No. 3 Awarding Contract to Chevelier Corp., February 3, 1919, Box 2, File 4, Jaudon Collection, HistoryMiami.

8. "Work on Rock Road Tampa to Miami to Be Resumed Soon," *Miami Metropolis* (January 31, 1919); "Tamiami Trail Open Next Year Safe Prediction," *Ft. Myers Press* (February 2, 1919); "Open Tamiami Trail by January 1920 Is Outlook by New Plan," *Miami Metropolis* (February 13, 1919); "Leave on Trip of Inspection Tamiami Trail," *Ft. Myers Press* (February 13, 1919); "Tamiami Trail Be Finished Within a Year at Least," *Miami Metropolis* (February 20, 1919).

9. Letter from George Cook to J. F. Jaudon, August 9, 1919, Box 2, File 9, Jaudon Collection, HistoryMiami; "Partial List of Expenses, A. W. Hopkins Tract," ca. September 1, 1919, Box 2-1 File 3, Jaudon Collection, HistoryMiami.

10. Letter from George Cook to J. F. Jaudon, August 29, 1919, Box 2-1, File 4, Jaudon Collection, HistoryMiami.

11. "Work Is Under Way Again on Highway Across the State," *Miami Metropolis* (August 13, 1919); "Work on Chevelier Corporation Still Jogging Along," *Miami Metropolis* (January 9, 1920);

12. Development costs: "Partial List of Expenses A.W. Hopkins Tract," ca. September 1919, Box 2-1, File 3, Jaudon Collection, HistoryMiami. Jaudon told he had two options: "Draft Complaint of James and Maude Jaudon [For Declaratory Judgment and Equitable Relief]," August 1, 1928, Box 2, File 5, Jaudon Collection, HistoryMiami.

13. "Draft Complaint of James and Maude Jaudon [For Declaratory Judgment and Equitable Relief]," August 1, 1928, Box 2, File 5; letter from J. F. Jaudon to officers, directors and stockholders of Chevelier Corporation, Miami, February 8, 1923, [Spencer Agreement Amendment], Box 2, File 5; "Chevelier Corporation Bonds," [Draft Bond Prospectus], ca. December 1918, Box 2, File 3, "Chevelier Corporation" [Bond Prospectus], ca. January-April, 1919, Box 2, File 5, all Jaudon Collection, HistoryMiami.

14. Control reverted to trustees: "Draft Complaint of James and Maude Jaudon [For Declaratory Judgment and Equitable Relief]," August 1, 1928, Box 2, File 5; Judge McDougal thought it would raise money: letter from J. F. Jaudon to J. H. McCord, April 21, 1924, Box 2, File 5, both Jaudon Collection, HistoryMiami.

15. After Roland Oil lease: letter from J. F. Jaudon to officers, directors and stockholders of Chevelier Corporation, Miami, February 8, 1923, [Spencer Agreement Amendment], Box 2, File 5; in 1937: George Cook, "Chevelier Corporation: Report, January, 1937," Box 2, File 5, Jaudon Collection, HistoryMiami.

16. "Chevelier Corporation" [Bond Prospectus], n.d. [January-April, 1919], Box 6, File 5, Jaudon Collection, HistoryMiami.

17. Letter from J. B. McCrary to Dade County Board of County Commissioners, April 21, 1919; letter from G. E. McCaskill, County Attorney, to Board of County Commissioners, re: J. B. McCrary Co., August 1, 1921; letter from G. E. McCaskill, County Attorney, to Bank of Atlanta, December 13, 1918, all J. B. McCrary Company Papers, HistoryMiami; "Action by Board Means Resumption of Work on Trail," *Miami Metropolis* (June 24, 1919); "Tamiami Trail Construction Delays at End," *Miami Metropolis* (July 8, 1920).

18. "Action by Board Means Resumption of Work on Trail," *Miami Metropolis* (June 24, 1919); "Work on Tamiami Trail Still Jogging Along," *Miami Metropolis* (January 9, 1920); Letter from J. B. McCrary [J. F. Morgan & Co. letterhead] to Hobart Crabtree and Dade County Commissioners, November 29, 1919 (first letter this date); letter from J. B. McCrary [J. F. Morgan & Co. letterhead] to Hobart Crabtree and Dade County Commissioners, November 29, 1919 (second letter this date); letter from J. B. McCrary Co. [J. F. Morgan & Co. letterhead] to Boad of County Commissioners, November 29, 1919, J. B. McCrary Company Papers, HistoryMiami.

19. Letter from Frank J. Pepper to Sidney Harrison, June 10, 1921; letter from W. W. Dewhurst to J. E. Ingraham, June 13, 1921; letter from Sidney Harrison to Frank J. Pepper, June 13, 1921, all Box 33, Folder 796 (MLC File 1060), Model Land Co. Collection, Richter Library, Univ. of Miami.

20. "Deeper and Wider Tamiami Canal Is Land Owners' Plea," *Miami Metropolis* (July 15, 1919); "Connecting Ditch Between Tamiami and Miami Canals," *Miami Metropolis* (August 5, 1919); "Alleged Hold-Up by J. B. Mccrary Halting Drainage," *Miami Metropolis* (August 15, 1919).

21. "Airplane Is Searching Everglades for M'crary," *Miami Metropolis* (March 15, 1920); "Mccrary Party Is Back Home Safe, Days Overdue," *Miami Metropolis* (March 16, 1920).

22. "Drainage Canals Be Connected and Larger Acreage Be Made Tillable," *Miami Metropolis* (October 22, 1919); "Tamiami Trail Water Is Lowered and Adjacent Land Dries," *Miami Metropolis* (November 5, 1919); "New Empire Is Opened by Huge Dredge," *Miami Herald* (April 10, 1921); two letters from J. B. McCrary to Hobart Crabtree, both dated November 29, 1919, J. B. McCrary Company Papers, HistoryMiami; "Give Contract to Widen Canal," *Miami Herald* (March 30, 1921).

23. New Dredge Is Launched in Tamiami Trail Canal," *Miami Metropolis* (April 26, 1920); "Tamiami Trail Work Is Advanced One-Half Mile," *Miami Metropolis* (September 4, 1920).

24. "To Get Estimate of Cost Finishing Tamiami Trail," *Miami Metropolis* (September 10, 1920); "Contractor Declares That War Took All Profits," *Miami Metropolis* (September 11, 1920); "County Should Meet Payrolls of M'crary Co. to Speed Trail," *Miami Metropolis* (October 13, 1920); "Tamiami Trail Fund Available," *Miami Herald* (January 25, 1921); "Tamiami Trail Reaches Point 14 Miles from Lee County Boundary," *Miami Herald* (January 27, 1921).

25. "Progress of Tamiami Trail in Lee County," *Miami Metropolis* (July 28 1920). Otto Neal, "Early Stages of Trail Building Revised by Neal, Dredge Master," MS in Box 12, File 9, Jaudon Collection, History Miami.

26. Twelve miles from Marco Junction: "Tamiami Trail Inspected by Dade Commissioners," *Miami Herald* (April 3, 1921). Earlier reports put progress as far as 22 miles: "Progress of the Tamiami Trail in Lee County," *Miami Metropolis* (July 28, 1920).

27. McCaskell quote: "Lee Men Impressed with Tamiami Trail," *Miami Metropolis* (May 18, 1921); "Dade's Work on Tamiami Trail Spurs Lee on to New Efforts," *Miami Herald* (May 18 1921).

28. Bruce Seeley, *Building the American Highway System: Engineers as Policy Makers* (Philadelphia: Temple University Press, 1987); *Passim*; Tammy Ingraham, *Dixie Highway: Road Building and the Making of the Modern South, 1900–1930* (Chapel Hill: University of North Carolina Press, 2014): 87–89; Michael R. Fein, *Paving the Way: New York Road Building and the American State, 1880–1956* (Lawrence: University Press of Kansas, 2008): 70–75.

29. Tom Lewis, *Divided Highways: Building the Interstate Highways, Transforming American Life* (New York: Viking, 1997): 10–17.

30. *The State Road System of 1937* (Tallahassee: Florida State Road Department, 1937): 2–6; "State Is to Give Aid to the Tamiami Trail," *Miami Metropolis* (July 23, 1920); "Road Across River to Be Number 5," *Ft. Myers Press* (February 9, 1922); "Lee County Busy These Days in Road Building," *Ft. Myers Press* (June 13, 1922).

31. "Dade County Commission Now in Lee County in Consultation with the County Commission," MS prepared by James Jaudon for newspapers ca. March 30, 1921, Box 6, File 3, Jaudon Collection, HistoryMiami. (for published extracts see: "Tamiami Trail Inspected by Dade Commissioners," *Miami Herald* (April 3, 1921).

32. Seeley, *Building the American Highway System: Engineers as Policy Makers*: 90–110; Lewis, *Divided Highways: Building the Interstate Highways, Transforming American Life*: 17–21.

33. Chapter 9311, Acts of 1923, State of Florida.

34. "Gas Tax Now Goes in Every State in Union but 4," *Ft. Myers Press* (October 1, 1925); "Road Department Issues Biennial Report," *Ft. Myers Press* (April 22, 1927); "Gasoline Users Pay Users Near Half State's Revenue," *Ft. Myers Press* (June 3, 1927).

35. James Hammond, *Florida's Vanishing Trail* (n.l.: Lulu Press, 2008): 42–48; "The Truth About Collier County," MS prepared by James Jaudon, ca. April 26, 1923, Box 12, File 6, Jaudon Collection, HistoryMiami; Letter from Basil Scott to James Jaudon, July 11, 1922, Box 11, File 6, Jaudon Collection, HistoryMiami.

36. "Barron Gift Collier" *Marco News* (April 20, 2008).

37. "Barron Collier: Man of Action," *Ft. Myers Press* (March 12, 1924).

38. Storter family and Lucas survey: "Chevelier" [MS prepared by James Jaudon ca. October 1917]. Box 2, File 1, Jaudon Collection, History Miami; letter from J. F. Jaudon to Francis Reed, Federal Writer's Project, April 8, 1936, Box 13, File 3, Jaudon Collection, History Miami.

39. The story of Jaudon and Storter's June 1921 expedition is taken from three sources: Capt. G. W. Storter, "Footing It Across the Everglades," (MS ca. April 1928), Box 6, File 6, Jaudon Collection, HistoryMiami; "See Tamiami Trail on 70-Mile Trudge," *Miami Herald* (August 6, 1921); "Walks Over Proposed Tamiami Trail Route from Gulf to Ocean," *Miami Metropolis* (August 6, 1921). Jaudon's relationship to Deep lake Company: Letter from J. F. Jaudon to Barron Collier, February 15, 1922, Box 3, File 3; letter from J. F. Jaudon to Deep Lake Company, March 18, 1922, Box 12, File 10, both Jaudon Collection, HistoryMiami; "Captain James F. Jaudon," Advance Press Service Biography No. J-2276, November 2, 1926, Box 12, File 2, Jaudon Collection, HistoryMiami.

CHAPTER 9

1. "County Officials Offer $50,000 for Trail Completion," *Miami Herald* (September 15, 1921); "Reach No Agreement as to Work on Trail," *Miami Metropolis* (September 28, 1921).

2. Letter from G.E. McGaskill to Dade County Commissioners, August 1, 1921, J. B. McCrary Papers, HistoryMiami; letter from J. B. McCrary Company to Dade County Board of County Commisioners, April 21, 1919, J. B. McCrary Papers, History Miami; "Action by Board Means Resumption of Work on Trail," *Miami Metropolis* (June 24, 1919); "County Board Fails to Agree on Trail Construction Work," *Miami Herald* (September 28, 1921).

3. Glademoor is at the present southwest corner of the Tamiami Trail (U.S. Hwy. 41) and The Palmetto Expressway (State Road 826). It was never extensively developed as planned.

4. "Girl's Body Taken from Tamiami Canal by Divers; Companion in Auto Trip Held for Coroner's Hearing," *Miami Herald* (August 12, 1921); "Thinks Girl Had Engagement with White Night of Tragedy," *Miami Herald* (August 13, 1921), "White Says He Swam About Trying to Find Girl After Car Leaped Water of Canal," *Miami Herald* (August 13, 1921).

5. "Trail Deaths Mount: State Aroused," *Ft. Myers Press* (April 17, 1937).

6. "County Officials Offer $50,000 for Trail Completion," *Miami Herald* (September 15, 1921); "Reach No Agreement as to Work on Trail," *Miami Metropolis* (September 28, 1921); "Trail Contractor Turns Down Offer on Last 11 Miles," *Miami Herald* (October 4, 1921); "Tamiami Trail Difficult Engineering Feat, to Be Finished by July, Commissioner Says," *Miami Herald* (November 13, 1921).

7. Letter from J. F. Jaudon to Judge E. G. Wilkinson, January 2, 1922, Box 12, File 9, Jaudon Collection, HistoryMiami; "Bulletin" [Lee Commissioners Indefinitely Postpone Bond Issue], *Ft. Myers Press* (February 8, 1922); "Road Across River to Be Number 5," *Ft. Myers Press* (February 9, 1922).

8. "Palm Beach and Lee Counties Are Pledged to Push Highway," *Ft. Myers Press* (January 16, 1922); "Road Meeting Will Be Held Here Tonight," *Ft. Myers Press* (January 23, 1922).

9. "To the Stockholders of the Chevelier Corporation [1921–22 Annual Report], Appendix: Disbursements and Revenues, 1921 and 1922," Box 2, File 5, Jaudon Collection, HistoryMiami; letter from J. F. Jaudon to the officers and stockholders of the Chevelier Corporation [Spencer Agreement Amendment], February 8, 1923, Box 2, File 5, Jaudon Collection, HistoryMiami.

10. Jaudon February 1922 contract: "Tamiami Trail Contract," Box 12, File 9, Jaudon Collection, HistoryMiami; "Contract with Capt. Jaudon Signed," *Ft. Myers Press* (February 8, 1922). February 1919 agreement signed: "Tamiami Trail Open Next Year Prediction," *Ft. Myers Press* (February 2, 1919): "Leave on Trip of Inspection Tamiami Trail," *Ft Myers Press* (February 13, 1919); Chevelier claims Dade road must be finished first: "Lee Men Impressed with Tamiami Trail," *Miami Metropolis* (May 18, 1921).

11. Letter from James Jaudon to Barron G. Collier, February 25, 1922, Box 3, File 3, Jaudon Collection, HistoryMiami; "Lee County Will Push Trail Work," *Miami Herald* (February 9, 1922).
12. Memo from J. F. Jaudon to The Deep Lake Company, March 18, 1922, Box 12, File 10, Jaudon Collection, HistoryMiami.
13. "Tamiami Trail Contract," ca. February 8, 1922, Box 12, File 9; letter from J. F. Jaudon to R. P. Ranson, Box 12, File 9, both Jaudon Collection, HistoryMiami.
14. "Tamiami Trail Contract," ca. February 8, 1922, Box 12, File 9; letter from D. A. McDougal to J. F. Jaudon, May 16, 1922, Box 6, File 7, both Jaudon Collection, HistoryMiami.
15. "Tamiami Trail to Cross into Monroe," *Miami Herald* (February 14, 1922).
16. Holdings of large land companies: Junius E. Dovell, "History of the Everglades of Florida," (Ph.D. dissertation, University of North Carolina-Chapel Hill, 1947): 234–236; Collier's purchase: "Million Dollar Land Sale Is Recorded Here," *Ft. Myers Press* (March 1, 1922).
17. Letter from D. A. McDougal for J. F. Jaudon, May 20, 1922, Box 6, File 7, Jaudon Collection, HistoryMiami.
18. *Paradise Prairie Land Co. v United States*, 212 F. 2d 170 (5th Cir. 1954).
19. George Cook, "Annual Report to Stockholders of Chevelier Corporation," ca. December, 1922, Box 6, File 7, Jaudon Collection, History Miami.
20. Memorandum from J. F. Jaudon to Mr. Collier, re: Tamiami Trail, May 5, 1922, Box 6, File 5, Jaudon Collection, HistoryMiami. Crabtree survey: "Work Goes on Constructing Tamiami Trail," *Ft. Myers Press* (February 2, 1922); "Lost County Line Search Approved," *Miami Herald* (June 16, 1922); "Counties Reach Agreement About Boundary, Road," *Miami Metropolis* (June 20, 1922).
21. "First Tamiami Trail Crossing Made by 'Gadget' 6 Years Ago," *Miami Metropolis* (April 22, 1928).
22. George Cook, "Annual Report to Stockholders of Chevelier Corporation," ca. December, 1922, Box 6, File 7, Jaudon Collection, History Miami.
23. "Partial List of Expenses: A. W. Hopkins Tract," ca 1919, Box 6 File 4, Jaudon Collection, HistoryMiami. McDougal biggest contributor under amended Spencer Agreement: letter from J. F. Jaudon to officers, and directors and stockholders of Chevelier Corporation, February 8, 1923 [Spencer Agreement Amendment]. McDougal out of cash: letter from D. A. McDougal to J. F. Jaudon, June 7, 1922, Box 2–1, File 6, Jaudon Collection. Sale to Willingham: "Draft Complaint for Declaration of Rights of James and Maude Jaudon," ca. August 1, 1928, Box 2, File 5, Jaudon Collection, HistoryMiami.
24. Letter from J.F. Jaudon to Alexander, Ramsey and Kerr, July 5, 1922, Box 7, File 7; memo from J. F. Jaudon to AR&K, July 5, 1922, re: Expenses by J. F. Jaudon on Tamiami Trail, Box 7, File 7, both Jaudon Collection, HistoryMiami; "Barron Collier Will Build Part of Tamiami Trail," *Ft. Myers Press* (July 6, 1922).
25. Letter from Basil Scott to J. F. Jaudon, July 11, 1922, Box 12, File 9, letter from Basil Scott to J. F. Jaudon, January 11, 1923; letter from J. F. Jaudon to Basil Scott, January 14, 1923 (2 letters this date); letter from J. F. Jaudon to AR&K, January 18, 1923; letter from O. C. Bozeman to J. F. Jaudon, January 21, 1923, Box 12, File 9, letter from O. C. Bozeman to J. F. Jaudon, January 25, 1923, Box 12, File 9, all Jaudon Collection, History Miami; "Lee County Is Pushing Work on the Trail," *Ft. Myers Press* (August 11, 1922).
26. Letter from J. F. Jaudon to Bozeman, Bookhart & Co, January 27, 1923, Box 6, File 7, Jaudon Collection, HistoryMiami.

27. Letter from Walter O. Sheppard to J. F. Jaudon, July 26, 1923; letter from Walter O. Sheppard to J. F. Jaudon, August 17, 1923, both Box 12, File 9, Jaudon Collection, HistoryMiami.
28. Letter from O. Z. Bozeman to J. F. Jaudon, January 21, 1923, Box 12, File 9, Jaudon Collection, HistoryMiami.
29. Letter from James Jaudon to Judge E. C. Wilkinson, February 21, 1923, Box 12, File 9, Jaudon Collection, HistoryMiami.
30. Letter from J. F. Jaudon to Walter O. Sheppard, July 27, 1923; letter from Walter O. Sheppard to J. F. Jaudon, July 30, 1923; letter from J. F. Jaudon to Walter O. Sheppard, August 3, 1923; letter from Walter O. Sheppard to J. F. Jaudon, August 17, 1923; letter from J. F. Jaudon to Walter O. Sheppard, September 6, 1923, all Box 12, File 7, Jaudon Collection, HistoryMiami.
31. Letter from J. F. Jaudon to D. A. McDougal, July 10, 1922 Box 6, File 6, Jaudon Collection, HistoryMiami.
32. "May Switch Trail to Original Route," *Miami Herald* (October 25, 1922); "County to Proceed on Tamiami Trail," *Miami Herald* (October 26, 1922).
33. "Route of Tamiami Trail Now Defined," *Ft. Meyers Press* (December 20 1922). Dredge location: "Report to the Stockholders of the Chevelier Corporation, Jan. 1, 1923," manuscript in Box 10, File 3, Jaudon Collection, HistoryMiami.
34. "Sugar Company Will Ditch Tamiami Canal," *Miami Herald* (December 10, 1922).
35. "How Man Transformed the Everglades into a Venerable Eden Is an Alluring Story, *Miami Herald* (March 19, 1922).
36. "Sugar Company Will Ditch Tamiami Canal," *Miami Herald* (December 10, 1922): "Cutting of Outlets in Tamiami Trail Is Favored by Board, *Miami Metropolis* (December 29, 1922). Apparently, the Contract Specifications Called for Few If Any Culverts Across the Road. the Southern Drainage District, and Later the State Road Department, Ended Up Installing Them at Their Cost.
37. Telegram from F. C. Elliott to E. R. Graham, June 23, 1923, Letter from E. R. Graham to F. C. Elliott, July 16, 1923, Both in "Telegrams and Correspondence Between Ernest Graham and F. C. Elliott," E. R. Graham Collection, P. K. Yonge Library, Univ. of Florida, URL: http://Ufdc.Ufl.Edu//AA00007549/00002; letter from M. B. Garris, Watson & Garris, to Miami Rotary Club, August 16, 1924, Correspondence File, E. R. Graham Collection, P. K. Yonge Library, Univ. of Florida, URL: http://Ufdc.Ufl.Edu//AA00007549/00004; "This Is Our Answer," manuscript for newspaper editorial, ca. August 17, 1924, Box 12, File 10, Jaudon Collection, HistoryMiami.
38. "Work on Road No. 5 Will Start Tomorrow," *Ft. Myers Press* (January 25, 1923); "At the Birth of the Tamiami Trail Association," *Miami Herald* (January 30, 1923).
39. "The Tamiami Trail Is the Name of Organization Headed by Mr. Collier," *Ft. Myers Press* (January 26, 1923); "Elect Officers to Supervise Tamiami Trail," *Ft. Myers Press* (January 27, 1923).
40. Otto Neal, "Early Stages of Trail Building Reviewed by Neal, Dredge Master," ms. dated ca. 1928, Box 12, File 9, Jaudon Collection, HistoryMiami.
41. Neal, "Early Stages of Trail Building Reviewed by Neal, Dredge Master": 2.
42. George Hosmer, "Take Trip Over Tamiami Trail to Near End of Grade," *Ft. Myers Press* (February 3, 1923). See also: "Says Tamiami Trail in Lee County Has 65 Miles Good Road," *Miami Metropolis* (February 8, 1923).

43. "That Tamiami Trail," *Miami Metropolis* (March 26, 1923). The Metropolis was reprinting an article featured in the *Estero Eagle* of March 23, 1923 and widely reprinted around the state.
44. "Barron G. Collier Is Here Is Boost Work on the Tamiami Trail," *Ft. Myers Daily Press* (March 22, 1923); letter from J. F. Jaudon to Judge D. A. McDougal, March 29, 1923, Box 2, File 5, Jaudon Collection, HistoryMiami.
45. "Frank Jaudon at Capitol Working for Tamiami Trail Plan," *Miami Metropolis* (April 10, 1923); "Creation of Two New Counties Considered," *Miami Metropolis* (April 10, 1923).
46. "The Truth About Collier County" MS written by J. F. Jaudon, ca. April 26, 1923, Box 10, File 4, Jaudon Collection, HistoryMiami.
47. Letter from J. F. Jaudon to Judge D. A. McDougal, March 20, 1923, Box 2, File 5, Jaudon Collection, HistoryMiami.
48. Letter from J. F. Jaudon to Judge D. A. McDougal, March 20, 1923, Box 2, File 5, Jaudon Collection, HistoryMiami.
49. Letter from J. F. Jaudon to George Cook, April 5, 1923, Box 2, File 5, letter from Maude Jaudon to Jimmie Jaudon, Box 4, File 5, both Jaudon Collection, HistoryMiami.

CHAPTER 10

1. "Tam-Iami—Tampa—Miami—Trail," MS written by J. F. Jaudon, ca. April 22, 1923, Box 10, File 5, Jaudon Collection, HistoryMiami; "West Coasters Use Old Trail," *Miami Metropolis* (June 20, 1918); "Airplane Is Searching Everglades for Mccrary," *Miami Metropolis* (March 15, 1920); "Walks Over Proposed Tamiami Trail Route from Gulf to Ocean," *Miami Metropolis* (August 6, 1921); letter from Ralph Ranson to James Jaudon, April 6, 1928, Box 2-1, File 6, James Jaudon Collection, HistoryMiami.
2. "First Tamiami Trail Crossing Made by Gadget 6 Years Ago," *Miami Metropolis* (April 22, 1928); Letter from D. A. McDougal to R. D. Deford, June 14, 1922, Box 34, File 306, Mary McDougal Axleson Collection, Richter Library, Univ. of Miami.
3. Letter from J. F. Jaudon to Judge D. A. McDougal, March 20, 1923, Box 2, File 5, HistoryMiami, "Annual Report of J. F. Jaudon to the Shareholders and Directors of the Chevelier Corporation," January 22, 1924, Box 2, File 5, James Jaudon Collection, HistoryMiami.
4. Russell Kay, "Tamiami Trail Blazers: A Personal Memoir," *Florida Historical Quarterly* (January 1971): 278–287.
5. Frank Lewis, "Complete Story of the Pioneer Trip Across the Everglades as Told by Mr. Frank S. Lewis of Everglades, Who Was a Member of the Original Tamiami Trail Blazers," *Miami Herald* (April 22, 1923) (hereafter "Frank Lewis Story"); A. H. Andrews, "Blazing the Tamiami Trail Across Florida," *Dearborn Independent*, Part 1 (February 2, 1924): 10–11; Part 2 (February 9, 1924): 10–11; Steve Glassman, "Blazing the Tamiami Trail," *South Florida History Magazine* 1 (Winter 1989): 3–5; 12–13; letter from J. F. Jaudon to George Cook, April 5, 1923, Box 2, File 5, Jaudon Collection, HistoryMiami.
6. "Fort Myers Motorcade Finds It Impossible to Cross Muck Flats of 'Glades; Turns Back," *Miami Metropolis* (April 10, 1923).
7. MS prepared probably ca. 1979 by Frank Lewis to accompany photo album and other memorabilia relating to Tamiami Trailblazers trip of April 4–20, 1923, Fla./R/975.944/LEWI/ Florida Collection, Miami Public Library.
8. "Frank Lewis Story," *Miami Herald* (April 22, 1923); A. H. Andrews, "Blazing the Tamiami Trail Across Florida," *Dearborn Independent*, Part 1 (February 2, 1924): 10–11; Part 2 (February 9, 1924): 11. Andrews misidentifies Erben Cook as his father, George Cook.
9. "Ft. Myers Motorcade Firm in Determination to Complete Crossing of Everglades," *Miami Metropolis* (April 13, 1923); "Frank Lewis Story," *Miami Herald* (April 22, 1923); "Diary of Everglades Traveler Tells of Seminole Legend, of Hardships, and of Most Dogged Determination," *Miami Metropolis* (April 16, 1923).
10. "1924 Annual Report of J. F. Jaudon to the Shareholders and Directors of the Chevelier Corporation," January 22, 1924, Box 2, File 5, Jaudon Collection, HistoryMiami.
11. Cut in Tamiami Trail bank: "Frank Lewis Story," *Miami Herald* (April 22, 1923). Only ten left: "Last Motorists Reach City and Are Welcomed at Park," *Miami Metropolis* (April 23, 1923).
12. "Frank Lewis Story," *Miami Herald* (April 22, 1923); "Motorcade Now Hopelessly Stuck in the Everglades Muck," *Miami Metropolis* (April 19, 1923); "Enthusiastic Trail Blazers Home Again," *Ft. Myers Press* (April 19, 1923); "Trail Blazer Keeps Diary of His Trip," *Ft. Myers Press* (April 19, 1923); "Motorcade Bills of $1,118 Turned Down by the C. of C. Board," *Miami Metropolis* (April 24, 1923); "1924 Annual Report of J. F. Jaudon to the Shareholders and Directors of the Chevelier Corporation," January 22, 1924, Box 2, File 5, Jaudon Collection, HistoryMiami.
13. "Important Highway Conference Will Be Held Here Saturday," *Miami Metropolis* (April 17, 1923).
14. "Motorcade Members Urge National Park for the Everglades," *Miami Metropolis* (April 16, 1923); "The Tamiami Trail Blazers Say Route Should Be Changed," *Ft. Myers Press* (April 19, 1923); "Dade Will Not Take Part in Contest on Tamiami Road Route," *Miami Metropolis* (April 20, 1923).
15. Kay, "Tamiami Trail Blazers: A Personal Memoir": 287.
16. Copy of letter from W. O. Sheppard to W. H. Malone, March 28, 1923 [attachment to letter from J. Otto Kirchheimer to G. F. Cook, March 31, 1923], Box 2, File 5, Jaudon Collection, HistoryMiami.
17. Letter from J. Otto Kirchheimer to G. F. Cook, March 31, 1923, Box 2, File 5; letter from G. F. Cook to J. F. Jaudon, April 3, 1923, Box 2, File 5, Jaudon Collection, HistoryMiami.
18. "Route of Tamiami Trail Now Defined," *Ft. Myers Press* (December 20, 1922); "Commissioners Vote to Retain Tamiami Trail as Outlined," *Miami Metropolis* (December 30, 1922).
19. "Chevelier Company Is Bonded to Build Part of Tamiami Trail," *Miami Metropolis* (March 30, 1922).
20. "May Switch Trail to Original Route," *Miami Herald* (October 25, 1922); "County to Proceed on Tamiami Trail," *Miami Herald* (October 26, 1922); "Dade Will Not Take Part in Contest on Tamiami Road Route," *Miami Metropolis* (April 20, 1923). "Text of Laws of Florida, Chapter 8730," appended to form letter prepared by J. F. Jaudon, June 23, 1924, Box 12, File 10, Jaudon Collection, HistoryMiami.
21. "Looks Like Collier May Be Defeated," *Ft. Myers Press* (April 19, 1923); "House Committee Gives Barron Collier Rehearing on His Bill," *Ft. Myers Press* (April 26, 1923); "Collier County to Be a Fact on July 8," *Ft. Myers Press* (May 17, 1923).
22. Letter from Walter O. Sheppard to J. F. Jaudon, August 17, 1923, Box 12, File 9; letter from J. F. Jaudon to Walter O. Sheppard, September 6, 1923, Box 12, File 9, both Jaudon Collection, HistoryMiami.
23. "Lee County Takes Over New Bridge," *Ft. Myers Press* (November 1, 1923); "Eight Mile Stretch of Tamiami Trail Is Being Constructed in Lee County," *Miami Herald* (January 30, 1923).
24. "State Road Department Favors Road No. 5," *Ft.

Myers Press (December 8, 1922); "Tamiami Trail to Be Rushed," *Ft. Myers Press* (February 21, 1923); "Road No. 5 Will Open Up Much New Land," *Ft. Myers Press* (August 23, 1923); "Gas Tax Collected by Every State in Union but 4," *Ft. Myers Press* (October 1, 1925). Florida collected $2,731,387 for the five months ending June 1, 1925.

25. "Lee County Takes Over New Bridge," *Ft. Myers Press* (November 1, 1923); "Tamiami Trail Day Planned at Fair at Tampa," *Ft. Myers Press* (January 11, 1924).

26. "Completion of Tamiami Trail Waits of Collier County," *Miami Metropolis* (October 10, 1923); "To View Trail in Absence of Mccrary Friday," *Miami Metropolis* (October 11, 1923); "Pushes Trail Building with Modern Outfit," *Ft. Myers Press* (January 14, 1974); "To Name Board to Dispose of Trail Dispute," *Miami Metropolis* (January 15, 1924); "E. B. Douglas to Head Tamiami Trail Board," *Miami Herald* (March 14, 1924). McCrary's bonding company, the Hartford Insurance Co., agreed to the arbitration contingent upon a maximum adverse award of $50,000. Dade County agreed to this.

27. A Bay City walking dredge is preserved (without its wooden cab or deck) at the Collier Seminole State Park near Everglades City.

28. Otto Neal, "Early Stages of Trail Building Reviewed by Neal, Dredge Master," MS ca. March 1928, Box 12, File 9, Jaudon Collection, HistoryMiami; "Trail Building Used $500,000 in Machinery," *Miami Metropolis* (April 22, 1928); "Map Showing Location of the 207,000 Chevelier Tract, by Robert Ranson," *Miami Post* (August 8, 1924).

29. Culverts in Tamiami Trail: "J. F. Jaudon Thinks State Road Department Should Help Tamiami Trail Now," *Ft. Myers Press* (March 17, 1924); "Advertisement of E. R. Graham," *Miami Herald* (August 19, 1924).

30. Starts work: "Pushes Trail Building with Modern Outfit," *Miami Metropolis* (January 10, 1924); "Map Showing Location of the 207,000 Chevelier Tract, by Robert Ranson," *Miami Post* (August 8, 1924).

31. "West Coast Asks Data on Tamiami Trail," *Miami Metropolis* (February 15, 1924).

32. "All Roads Lead to Fort Myers as Celebration Begins," *Ft. Myers Press* (March 12, 1924): "Barron Collier Man of Action," *Ft. Myers Press* (March 12, 1924); "President of the Tamiami Trail Association," *Ft. Myers Press* (March 13, 1924).

33. "All Roads Lead to Fort Myers Today as Celebration Begins," *Ft. Myers Press* (March 12, 1924).

34. "Says Trail Is Being Hurried from the West," *Ft. Myers Press* (April 15, 1924).

35. "Facts Concerning the Trail," *Miami Metropolis* (July 1, 1924).

36. "Says Trail Is Being Hurried from the West," *Ft. Myers Press* (April 15, 1924).

37. "Tamiami Trail Condition in Every County Is Discussed in Detail in Story by Chapin," *Ft. Myers Press* (August 19, 1924).

38. "The Eagle Screams for the Tamiami Trail Association," *Ft. Myers Press* (September 18, 1924).

39. "Lake City Greets Tamiami Blazers with Big Ovation," *Ft. Myers Press* (November 12, 1924); "Unity of Purpose Marks All Tamiami Trail Activities," *Ft. Myers Press* (March 30, 1925); "Tamiami Trail Gains in Friends in Miles," *Ft. Myers Press* (July 28, 1925); Miami organization: "Tamiami Trail Group Forming to Urge Work," *Miami Metropolis* (August 15, 1925).

40. "State Will Finish the Tamiami Trail," *Miami Herald* (March 11, 1925); "Fort Myers-Miami Road to Be Rushed to Early Completion by State," *Ft. Myers Press* (March 14, 1925).

41. "Opposition Gone," *Ft. Myers Press* (August 18, 1924); "Tamiami Trail Condition in Every County Is Discussed in Detail in Story by Chapin," *Ft. Myers Press* (August 19, 1924).

42. "Trail to Be Most Popular, Says Hosmer," *Miami Metropolis* (April 15, 1924); "Says Trail Is Being Hurried," *Ft. Myers Press* (April 15, 1924).

43. "Facts Regarding the Trail," *Miami Metropolis* (July 1, 1924).

44. "State Road Department of Florida: Construction Record: S.R. 27, Section and Job No. 0304-101 and 102, December 1928, Collier County Historical Society, Naples, FL.

45. Form Letter by J. F. Jaudon, with Attachments, June 23, 1924, Box 12, File 3, Jaudon Collection, History Miami; "Speeding Up Work on Tamiami Trail," *Ft. Myers Press*, July 10, 1924.

46. "Advertisement by Everglades Development Association," *Miami Herald* (August 18, 1924). One eighth mile: letter from E. R. Graham to F. C. Elliott, July 16, 1923, Telegrams and Correspondence between Ernest Graham and F. C. Elliott; P. K. Yonge Library, Univ. of Florida, URL: http: ufdc.ufl.edu//AA00007549/00002.

47. Letter from M. B. Garris to Miami Rotary Club, August 16, 1924, Correspondence File, Ernest R. Graham Papers, P. K. Yonge Library, Univ. of Florida, URL: http: ufdc.ufl.edu//AA00007549/00004; letter from Charles H. Ruggles, C. E. to R. E. [sic] Graham, November 28, 1924, Correspondence File, Ernest R. Graham Papers, P.K. Yonge Library, Univ. of Florida, URL: http: ufdc.ufl.edu//AA00007549/00004.

48. "Graham Tells Drainage Plan," *Miami Metropolis* (July 24, 1924); William A. Graham, "The Pennsuco Sugar Experiment," *Tequesta* 11 (1951): 27–49; "Drainage Plans Being Amicably Adjusted Is Claim," *Miami Metropolis* (July 26, 1924).

49. Guy S. Cunliffe, "New View in Words and Pictures: Automobile Traverses Trail to Beyond Dade County Line," *Miami Herald* (March 22, 1925).

50. "Collier Inspects the Tamiami Trail," *Miami Tribune* (July 2, 1924); "Chokoloskee Visitor Is Trail Booster," *Ft. Myers Press* (August 13, 1924).

51. "Seven Items in the County's Bond Issue Approved," *Miami Metropolis* (August 20, 1924); Graham, "The Pennsuco Sugar Experiment": 35–38.

52. "Miami Public Opinion Favors Work of Trail," *Ft. Myers Press* (July 23, 1924).

Chapter 11

1. Otto Neal, "Early Stages of Trail Building Reviewed by Neal, Dredge Master," manuscript ca. March 1928, Box 12, File 9, Jaudon Collection, HistoryMiami; "C. G. Washburn Gives Striking Picture of Magnitude of Work," in "Tamiami Trail History Notes," URL: http://Digitool.Fcla.Edu. An abridged version was printed under the same title in the *Miami Metropolis* (April 22, 1928).

2. Neal, "Early Stages of Trail Building Reviewed by Neal, Dredge Master": n.p.; "Trail Building Used $500,000 in Machinery," *Miami Metropolis* (April 22, 1928).

3. "Tamiami Tail Is Booming," *Ft. Myers Press* (March 13, 1924); "Tamiami Trail to Be Opened in November 1925 Is Prediction," *Miami Herald* (July 11, 1924); "Complete Tamiami Trail Is Shown in New Map," *Miami Metropolis* (April 25, 1926).

4. "Collier County Bond Issue Sells at Near Par Value," *Ft. Myers Press* (September 8, 1924).

5. Form letter from J. F. Jaudon dated June 23, 1924, Box 12, File 9, Jaudon Collection, HistoryMiami; "Speeding Up Work on Tamiami Trail," Ft. Myers Press (July 10, 1924); "Road Bonds Approved; Work Will Prob-

ably Be Started Within Month," *Ft. Myers Press* (September 4, 1924).

6. "State Will Finish the Tamiami Trail," *Miami Herald* (March 11, 1925); "Road Department Resources Placed at $8,180,480.03," *Ft. Myers Press* (January 31, 1925); "For the State Highway System," Ft. Myers Press (January 27, 1925); "State to Finish Trail in Dade County," Miami Metropolis (March 11, 1925).

7. Guy S. Cunliffe, "New View in Words and Pictures: Automobile Traverses Trail to Beyond Dade County Line," *Miami Herald* (March 22, 1925).

8. Tax revenues: "Gas Tax Collected by Every State in Union but 4," *Ft. Myers Press* (October 1, 1925). Bill passes legislature: "Fort Myers-Miami Highway May Be on Preferential List," *Ft. Myers Press* (May 15, 1925); "Cross State Trail Aid Is Voted by House," *Ft. Myers Press* (May 28, 1925).

9. "Unanimously Elected to Succeed Phillips; Secretaryship Open," *Ft. Myers Press* (July 25, 1925).

10. "Tamiami Trail Contracts Let for Dade Work," *Miami Metropolis* (August 11, 1925); "Tamiami Trail Group Forming to Urge Work," *Miami Metropolis* (August 15, 1925); "Status of Road Construction Through October 31st, 1926," *Florida Highways* 3, 11 (November 1926): 15. Project 669-A: "Coral Gables to Pave Trail," *Miami Metropolis* (November 20, 1925).

11. Letter from J. H. McCord to J. F. Jaudon, Box 2, File 5, Jaudon Collection, HistoryMiami.

12. Spencer agreement and amendment: "Draft Complaint of James and Maude Jaudon for Equitable Relief by Declaratory Judgment, August 1, 1928," Box 2, File 5; letter from James Jaudon to the Officers, Directors and Stockholders of the Chevelier Corporation, February 28, 1923 [text of Spencer Agreement amendment], Box 2, File 5, Jaudon Collection, History Miami.

13. Roland Company pulled out: letter from J. H. McCord to J. F. Jaudon, August 7, 1924, Box 8 File 7, Jaudon Collection, HistoryMiami. Freeland did not pull out: Minutes of special meeting of Directors of Chevelier Corporation, August 16, 1928, Box 2-1, File 6, Jaudon Collection, HistoryMiami.

14. D. A. McDougal to C. S. Walker, October 19, 1925, Series 7, File 305, Mary McDougal Axelson Collection, Richter Library, Univ. of Miami.

15. George F. Cook Co.-Collins Causeway Papers (21 items), HistoryMiami.

16. D. A. McDougal to Mary McDougal Axelson, January 11, 1934, Series 8, File 344, Mary McDougal Axelson Collection, Richter Library, Univ. of Miami.

17. Otto Neal, "Early Stages of Trail Building Reviewed by Neal, Dredge Master," Box 12, File 9, Jaudon Collection, History Miami. "C. G. Watson Gives Striking Picture of Magnitude of Work," in "Tamiami Trail History Notes," URL: http://Digitool.Fcla.Edu. An truncated version of this article also appeared in the *Miami Metropolis* (April 22, 1928).

18. "Complete Tamiami Trail Is Shown in New Map," *Miami Metropolis* (April 25, 1926). Meeting point agreed to: "Speeding Up Work on Tamiami Trail," *Miami Herald* (July 6, 1924); "Tamiami Trail Junction Point Agreed To," *Miami Metropolis* (July 16, 1924).

19. "Monroe Wants State to Take Up Trail Work," *Miami Metropolis* (January 27, 1926). Eventual costs to the Chevelier Corporation officially came to between $200,000 and $400,000 and appear to be between $318,000 and $333,000. See: "Minutes of Special Meeting of the Directors of the Chevelier Corporation, August 16, 1926," Box 3, File 12, Jaudon Collection, HistoryMiami; "The Tamiami Trail" in *Florida Trails to Turnpikes* (Tallahassee: Florida Department of Highways, 1964): 68–87, at 83. Position of Dade Commission and state surveyors: "Dade County to Ask State to Speed Trail," *Miami Metropolis* (January 26, 1926).

20. "The Tamiami Trail," *Florida Highways* 3, 3 (March 1926): 7–8; "The Tamiami Trail," *Florida Highways* 3, 4 (April 1926): 9";Chairman to Inspect Miami End of Trail," *Miami Metropolis* (January 28, 1926); "State Highway Heads to View Tamiami Trail," *Miami Metropolis* (January 30, 1926); "Highway Heads to Fix Trail Route on Trip," *Miami Metropolis* (January 31, 1926).

21. "Tamiami Trail Routed Direct, Dade-Collier," *Miami Metropolis* (April 20, 1926); "Complete Tamiami Trail Is Shown in New Map," *Miami Metropolis* (April 25, 1926); "Hathaway Explains Detailed Plan for Trail's Completion," *Ft. Myers Press* (April 29, 1926).

22. "Tamiami Trail Routed Direct, Dade-Collier," *Miami Metropolis* (April 20, 1926). "Trail to Dade Line by Jan. 1, Collier Says," *Miami Metropolis* (April 23, 1926). Chevelier's claim: "C. of C. Party Inspects Trail Route on Foot," *Miami Metropolis* (May 3, 1926); "Tamiami Link Near Complete," *Miami Metropolis* (October 21, 1926); "The Tamiami Trail," *Florida Highway* 3, 4 (April 1926): 9–10.

23. Actual completion in 1928: "Trail's South Fork Complete," *Miami Metropolis* (April 23, 1928). Work required another 18 months: "The Tamiami Trail." In *Florida Trails to Turnpikes* (Tallahassee: Florida Department of Highways, 1964): 68–87, at 87.

24. "An Evil Day": "When Do We Cross?" *Miami Metropolis* (April 20, 1926). "Declared Useless": "Route of the Trail Shown by This Map," *Miami Metropolis* (April 20, 1926). Later position: "Tamiami Trail Truths," *Miami Metropolis* (May 6, 1926). Watson quote: "Legal Battle Is Threatened on Trail Route," *Miami Metropolis* (April 21, 1926).

25. Leffler quote: "Legal Battle Is Threatened on Trail Route," *Miami Metropolis* (April 21, 1926). Schilling quote: "Mass Meeting Here to Talk Tamiami Trail," *Miami Metropolis* (April 22, 1926); Letter from C. H. Hartley to J. F. Jaudon, Box 12, File 6, Jaudon Collection, HistoryMiami.

26. "Blazers Discuss Trail Situation," *Ft. Myers Press* (April 21, 1926); "County Heads Demand State Agree on Trail," *Miami Metropolis* (May 6, 1926).

27. Letter from J. F. Jaudon to James M. Carson, April 22, 1926, Box 12, File 6, Jaudon Collection, HistoryMiami; "Mass Meeting Here to Talk Tamiami Trail," *Miami Metropolis* (April 22, 1926); "Gessler Will Protest Trail Route Change," *Miami Metropolis* (April 24, 1926); "Transcript of Open Meeting of Chamber of Commerce at Central High School, Miami Fla. on Night of April 26, 1926," Box 12, File 6, Jaudon Collection, HistoryMiami; "Trail Route Discussed," *Miami Herald* (April 27, 1926); "C. of C. Meet Bitter Against Changing Trail," *Miami Metropolis* (April 27, 1926).

28. "Trail Routing Is Defended by R. A. Henderson," *Ft. Myers Press* (June 4, 1926).

29. "Mass Meeting Here to Talk Tamiami Trail," *Miami Metropolis* (April 22, 1926); "Short Route Favored," *Miami Herald* (May 4, 1926).

30. C. of C. Party Inspects Trail Route on Foot," *Miami Metropolis* (May 3, 1926). Trail in Dade impassible: letter from G. H. Hartley to J. F. Jaudon, May 3, 1926, Box 12, File 6, James Jaudon Collection, HistoryMiami; "New Views in Words and Pictures of the Tamiami Trail," *Miami Herald* (March 22, 1925); "The Tamiami Trail," *Florida Highways* 3, 4 (April 1924): 9.

31. "Chamber Group Upon Trail Trip Near Shipwreck," *Miami Metropolis* (May 5, 1926). Dismissed by highway department: "The Tamiami Trail," *Florida Highways* 3, 4 (April 1924): 9.

32. Jaudon had purchased 20,000 acres: Letter from J. F. Jaudon to Judge H. F. Hancock, March 27, 1935, Box 6, File 1, Jaudon Collection, HistoryMiami; Map: "Approximate Locations, Numbered Sections, 20,000

Acres, Collier County, [Ca. 1927], Drawer M105aa, Folder 3, Jaudon Collection, Historymiami. Pinecrest Optioned to Willingham: Draft Bill of Complaint for Declaratory Judgment, *James and Maude Jaudon v. Chevelier Corp. Et. Al.*, Ca. August 1, 1928, Box 2, File 5, Jaudon Collection, HistoryMiami.

33. Stoneman Douglas Biography: Michael Grunwald, the *Swamp: The Everglades, Florida, and the Politics of Paradise* (New York: Simon and Schuster, 2006): 178–180. Stoneman Douglas Purchase of Land and Subsequent Foreclosure: Letters from Jaudon Realty Co. to Marjorie Stoneman Douglas, December 19, 1925 and September 1, 1926. Letter from Daisy Aldridge to Marjorie Stoneman Douglas, September 16, 1930, All Box 5, File 1, Jaudon Collection, Historymiami.

34. Letter from Daniel Mcdougal to Mary Mcdougal Axelson, January 11, 1934, Series 8, Folder 344, Mary Mcdougal Axelson Collection, Richter Library, Univ. of Miami.

35. "Dade to Confer with Martin on Tamiami Trail," *Miami Tribune* (May 5, 1926); "Joint Session on Trail Route Will Be Held," *Miami Metropolis* (May 5, 1926); "County Heads Demand State Agree on Trail," *Miami Metropolis* (May 6, 1926); "Hathaway Makes Final Statement Regarding Trail," *Ft. Myers Press* (May 10, 1926).

36. "State to Take Over Trail in Collier County," *Ft. Myers Press* (July 7, 1926); $11,326,987 in '26 for State Roads," *Ft. Myers Press* (December 31, 1926).

37. "Board Awaits New Contract for Trail Job," *Miami Metropolis* (June 16, 1926); "Contract Ready for Rebuilding of Trail Link," *Miami Metropolis* (June 17, 1926).

38. "State to Open Bids on More Jobs on Trail," *Ft. Myers Press* (July 30, 1926); "Transactions of the State Road Department, October 15, 1926," *Florida Highways* 3, 11 (November 1926): 14; "C. G. Watson Gives Striking Picture of Magnitude of Work," in "Tamiami Trail History Notes," URL: http://Digitool.Fcla.Edu. An truncated version of this article also appeared in the *Miami Metropolis* (April 22, 1928).

39. "Hathway Explains Detailed Plan for Trail's Completion," *Ft. Myers Press* (April 29, 1925).

40. Tammy Ingraham, *Dixie Highway: Road Building and the Making of the Modern South: 1900–1930* (Chapel Hill: University of North Carolina Press, 2014): 130–138.

41. "Ex-Convict Says Tabert Got 119 Lashes at Camp," *Palm Beach Post* (April 22, 1923); "Whip Convicts at Turpentine Camp Is Report," *Palm Beach Post* (April 23, 1923).

42. "Senate Passes Bill Abolishing Convict Leasing," *Ft. Myers Press* (April 26, 1923); Stetson Kennedy, *Southern Exposure: Making the South for Democracy* (Tuscaloosa: University of Alabama Press, 2011): 61.

43. "Road Camps Lead in Escapes Says Report to State," *Ft. Myers Press* (August 26, 1926).

44. "Stockade Will House Convict Road Workers," *Tampa Times-Tribune* (May 27, 1926); "Collier County, Construction Job No. 00304–101, Completed December, 1928" and "Collier County, Construction Job No. 00301–103, Completed December, 1928," both Form RR-20 (Construction Records), State Road Department of Florida, Division of Research and Records. Copies of these records, a series apparently dedicated to the 1926–28 state work on the Tamiami Trail, are located at the Collier County Historical Society, Naples, FL.

45. "Trail Workers Back on Job," *Ft. Myers Press* (May 27, 1927).

46. The story of the Tamiami Trail breakouts is taken from three sources: "13 Negro Convicts Escape Trail Camps," *Ft. Myers Press* (October 25, 1927); "8 Fleeing Convicts Captured: Hunt Resumed Across River for 5 Others," *Ft. Myers Press* (October 26, 1927); "3 Convicts Killed in Gun Battle: The Tampa Kid and Two Pals Slain by Posse," *Ft. Myers Press* (October 27, 1927).

47. James Hammond, *Florida's Vanishing Trail* (n.l.: the author, 2005): 215.

Chapter 12

1. Mark S. Foster, *Castles in the Sand: The Life and Times of Carl Graham Fisher* (Gainesville: University Press of Florida, 2000): 230–234.

2. Raymond B. Vickers, *Panic in Paradise: Florida's Banking Crash of 1926* (Tuscaloosa: University of Alabama Press, 2004): 32–74.

3. "No New Banks Added to List Closing Doors," *Ft. Myers Press* (July 18, 1926).Technically, the stock of the bank was purchased by William White, a director of the Mizner Development Company, and the bank purchased its headquarters building, previously rented, at a below-market rate.

4. Virginia Elliott TenEick, *History of Hollywood (1920 to 1950)* (Hollywood: City of Hollywood, 1966): 240–260; Bill McGoun *Hallandale* (Hallandale: Hallandale Historical Society): 19. Technically, Dania never was a city; it sought incorporation from the legislature in late 1925 solely for the purpose of being annexed into Hollywood at the latter's inaugural city commission meeting.

5. "Palm Beach Smashed by Hurricane," *Ft. Myers Press* (July 28, 1926).

6. "Truck Driver and Assistant Are Mangled," *Ft. Myers Press* (August 24, 1926).

7. L. F. Reardon, *The Florida Hurricane and Disaster* (Coral Gables: Arva Parks & Co., 1986 [1926]); *passim*; Thomas Neil Knowles, *Category 5: The 1935 Labor Day Hurricane* (Gainesville: University Press of Florida, 2009): Chapter 1.

8. "Everglades Is Badly Buffeted," *Ft. Myers Press* (September 20, 1926); "Trail to South Is Not Damaged," *Ft. Myers Press* (September 27, 1926).

9. Letter from Charles S. Krom to Carl Fisher, January 14, 1927, Box 7, File 2, Carl Fisher Papers, HistoryMiami.

10. *Scharnberg v. Citizens Nat'l. Bank of Spencer*, 33 F.2d 673 (8th Cir. 1929).

11. Daniel McDougal to Mary McDougal Axelson, January 11, 1934, Series 8, Folder 344, Mary McDougal Axelson Collection, Richter Library, University of Miami.

12. Telegram from L. K. Meek, Security State Bank to J. E. Lummus, Southern State Bank, December 22, 1926; letter from J. E. Lummus to J. K. Meek, December 23, 1926; letter from J. F. Jaudon to L. K. Meek, December 28, 1926, Box 2–1, File 7, Jaudon Collection, HistoryMiami. No meeting in six months: minutes of special meeting of directors of Chevelier Corp., August 16, 1928 (supplemental notes), Box 12, File 7, Jaudon Collection, HistoryMiami.

13. Letter from J. F. Jaudon to George F. Cook, October 14, 1927; letter from J. F. Jaudon to Chevelier Corp., August 17, 1928, both Box 2–2, File 8, Jaudon Collection, HistoryMiami.

14. Foster, *Castles in the Sand: The Life and Times of Carl Graham Fisher*: 234–238; TenEick, *History of Hollywood*: 265–75.

15. "Early Travel on Trail Told by F. J. Holmes," *Miami Metropolis* (April 22, 1928).

16. Irving Holmes, "Early Travel on Trail Told by F. J. Holmes," *Ft. Myers Press* (April 22, 1928).

17. Otto Neal, "Early Stages of Trail Building Reviewed by Neal, Dredge Master," MS in Box 12, File 9, Jaudon Collection, HistoryMiami.

18. "C G. Washburn Gives Striking Picture of Magnitude of Work," MS in "Tamiami Trail History Notes" folder, http://Digitool.Fcla.Edu. A condensed version can be found in "Trail Building Used

$500,000 in Machinery," *Miami Metropolis* (April 22, 1928).

19. Thomas L. Stephens, "State Engineer Draws Vivid Picture of Trail Work," MS in "Tamiami Trail History Notes" folder, http://Digitool.Fcla.Edu.

20. "State to Push Tamiami Trail Work in Dade," *Miami Metropolis* (August 18, 1925); "State Aid for Bridge Promised by Dr. Hathaway," *Ft. Myers Press* (January 24, 1927); "Status of Road Construction," *Florida Highways* 3, 11 (November, 1926): 32; "Hathaway Sees Trail Opened in 1928," *Miami Metropolis* (March 29, 1927); Horace Dunn, "The Tamiami Trail," *Florida Highways* 5, 3 (March, 1928): 1–12.

21. Early development of federal aid: Michael R. Fein, *Paving the Way: New York Road Building and the American State, 1880–1956* (Lawrence: University Press of Kansas): Chapter 2; Tom Lewis, *Divided Highways: Building the Interstate Highways, Transforming American Life* (New York: Viking, 1997): 16–20.

22. "$2,872,867 to State by Gasoline Tax," *Ft. Myers Press* (April 4, 1927).

23. "Road Department Issues Biennial Financial Report," *Ft. Myers Press* (April 22, 1927); "Road Department Resources Placed at $8,180,480," *Ft. Myers Press* (January 3, 1925); "Gas Tax Collected by Every State in Union but 4," *Ft. Myers Press* (October 1, 1925); $11,326,987 in '26 For State Roads," *Ft. Myers Press* (December 31, 1926); "Gasoline Users Pay Near Half State's Revenue," *Ft. Myers Press* (June 3, 1927); $30,980,815 Paid in State Tax by Florida Motorists Since 1921," *Ft. Myers Press* (September 5, 1921).

24. Chapter 9311, Acts 1923. See also: *The State Road System of 1937* (Tallahassee: Florida State Road Dept., 1937).

25. These figures are taken from seven State Road Department of Florida Construction Records for Job Nos. 301 and 304 (each broken down into several subparts), comprising the cost record for the state construction of the Tamiami Trail in Collier County. These Construction Record sheets are in the collection of the Collier County Historical Society, Naples. The claim of $55,000 per mile is written on the back of a Department of Roads photo from 1928: Collier County Museums Photo No. 88.42.15.

26. "Coral Gables to Pave Trail," *Miami Metropolis* (November 20, 1925); "Glaring Irregularities in Hathaway's Trail Contracts in Dade County," *Miami Metropolitan* (May 16, 1928).

27. "Fons Hathaway Still Evading Waste Charges," *Miami Metropolis* (April 29, 1928);); "The Huffman Contracts and the Desoto County Maintenance Charges—Two More of Carlton's Unsupported Allegations," *Miami Metropolis* (May 8, 1916); "Glaring Irregularities in Hathaway's Trail Contracts in Dade County Revealed," *Miami Metropolis* (May 16, 1928).

28. $2,872,867 to State by Gasoline Tax," *Ft. Myers Press* (April 4, 1927); "Road Department Issues Biennial Financial Report," *Ft, Myers Press* (April 22, 1927); "Road Department to Borrow 2 Million," (October 4, 1927); "Court Rules Against State Highway Loan," *Ft. Myers Press* (November 24, 1927), "Thanks for Dr. Hathaway," *Ft. Myers Press* (July 26, 1928).

29. Otto Neal, "Early Stages of Trail Building Reviewed by Neal, Dredge Master," MS in File 12, Box 9, James Jaudon Collection, HistoryMiami; "Status of Road Construction," *Florida Highways* 3, 11 (November 1926): 32; State Road Department of Florida, Construction Record, Projects 669-V, 669-W, 669-X (Job Nos. 0301 and 0304), June to December, 1928, Collier County Historical Society, Naples.

30. "Tamiami Trail Progress Suits Fons Hathaway," *Miami Metropolis* (November 6, 1926); "Motorcyclist Covers Trail," *Ft. Myers Press* (March 15, 1927).

31. "State Aid for Bridge Promised by Dr. Hathaway," *Ft. Myers Press* (January 24, 1927). 1,350 cars per day: "4,036 Cars Pass Over River Span During 3 Days," *Ft. Myers Press* (February 27, 1928). As long as the budget holds out: "Trail Opening Date Definitely Set for May 1," *Ft. Myers Press* (January 9, 1928). "Bridge Work to Be Under Way by Aug. 1," *Ft. Myers Press* (June 16, 1928).

32. "Trail Builders Rush Section from Palm Hammock to Naples," *Ft. Myers Press* (November 1, 1927); "Grade Is Completed on Tamiami Trail," *Ft. Myers Press* (December 18, 1927); "Trail Section Opened for Use of Promoters," *Ft. Myers Press* (February 6, 1928).

33. "Trail's South Fork Complete," *Miami Metropolis* (April 23, 1928); "Trail Opening Dade Definitely Set for May 1," *Ft. Myers Press* (January 9, 1928); "Definite Opening Day Will Be Set by Road Chairman," *Ft. Myers Press* (February 6, 1928); "Trail Date Advanced by Hathaway," *Ft. Myers Press* (February 8, 1928).

34. "Barron Collier Here to Direct Big Trail Show," *Ft. Myers Press* (April 21, 1928); "East-West Road First Advocated at Orlando in '15," *Ft. Myers Press* (April 25, 1928); "Lee County Takes Over New Bridge," *Ft. Myers Press* (November 1, 1923).

35. "Motorcade to Open $9,000,000 Tamiami Trail This Week," *Miami Metropolis* (April 22, 1928); "Tamiami Trail Dedicated to Nation's Use," *Tampa Tribune* (April 25, 1928); 2000 Journey Over Trail in Celebration," *Tampa Tribune* (April 26, 1928); "Tamiami Caravan to Miami," *Miami Metropolis* (April 26, 1928).

36. "Miami Greets Motorists at End of Trail," *Tampa Tribune* (April 27, 1928).

37. "Miami Greets Motorists at End of Trail," *Tampa Tribune* (April 27, 1928); "Tamiami Trail Beautification Plan Set Afoot," *Miami Metropolis* (April 27, 1928).

38. Funding in 1919 was $724,540: "Road Department Issues Biennial Report," *Ft. Myers Press* (April 22, 1927). Half of budget: "Gasoline Users Pay Near Half State's Revenue," *Ft. Myers Press* (June 3, 1927).

39. First six months of 1927: $30,980,815 Paid in State Tax by Florida Motorists Since 1921," *Ft. Myers Press* (September 5, 1927). Reserve balance at end of 1926: "Road Department Issues Biennial Financial Report," *Ft. Myers Press* (April 22, 1927).

40. "Questions the People Are Asking That Dr. Hathaway Has Failed to Answer," *Miami Metropolis* (April 28, 1928); "Fons Hathaway Still Evading Waste Charges," *Miami Metropolis* (April 29, 1928); "Glaring Irregularities in Hathaway's Trail Contracts in Dade County Revealed," *Miami Metropolis* (May 16, 1928).

41. "State Canvassing Board Meets Monday," *Ft. Myers Press* (June 16, 1928).

42. "Chamber Denies Trail Is 'Bad' South of the City," *Ft. Myers Press* (July 12, 1928); "Speeding Up of Highway Work Sought," Ft, Myers Press (July 23, 1928).

43. Death Toll Now Stands 1,500 in Okeechobee Area," *Ft. Myers Press* (September 22, 1928).

44. Foster, *Castles in the Sand*: 238.

45. "Hathaway Promises Early Completion of Entire Trail," *Ft. Myers Press* (November 10, 1928); "Caloosahatchee Span Builders May Receive Punta Gorda Contract," *Ft. Myers Press* (November 26, 1928).

46. "Southwest Mounted Police Mark New Progress," *Ft. Myers Press* (November 26, 1928).

47. National Park Service, *Historic American Building Survey: Monroe Station* (Washington: National Park Service, Historic Preservation Training Center, June 2007, HABS No. FL-544).

48. "Tamiami Trail Rider Killed," *Miami Metropolis* (January 20, 1929): James Hammond, *Florida's Vanishing Trail* (n.l.: the author, 2008): 156.

49. National Park Service, *Historic American Building Survey: Monroe Station*: 4–5, 13–16.

50. "D. G. Copeland Resigns Position as Chief Engi-

neer," *Ft. Myers Press* (May 4. 1929); "Gov. Carlton Names Men on Drain Board, D. Graham Copeland Member of Glades Group," *Ft. Myers Press* (August 2, 1929).

CHAPTER 13

1. "Road Chairman and Editor in Fistic Battle," *Ft. Myers Press* (September 5, 1929).
2. "Hathaway Quits Highway Dept., Changes Loom," *Ft. Myers Press* (January 10, 1929); "Bentley Gives Facts on Road Work," *Ft. Myers Press* (February 14, 1929); "Road Chairman Here to Rush River Span Job," *Ft. Myers Press* (April 29, 1929).
3. County indebtedness: "Carlton Law Defended," *Ft. Myers Press* (July 16, 1929). Property taxes: letter from J. F. Jaudon to H. F. Hancock, March 27, 1935, Box 6, File 1, Jaudon Collection, HistoryMiami; letter from Daniel McDougal to Mary McDougal Axelson, June 10, 1934, Series 8, Folder 344, Mary McDougal Axelson Collection, Richter Library, University of Miami.
4. $11,326,987 in '26 for State Roads," *Ft. Myers Press* (December 31, 1926); "Road Department Issues Biennial Report," *Ft. Myers Press* (April 22, 1927); $30,980,815 Paid in State Tax by Florida Motorists Since 1921," *Ft. Myers Press* (September 5, 1927); "Redistribution of Motor, Gas Revenue Urged," *Ft. Myers Press* (May 22, 1929). Sales tax and para-mutual proposals: "State Solons Close Special 20-Day Session," *Miami Metropolis* (June 21, 1929).
5. "Redistribution of Motor, Gas Revenue Urged," *Ft. Myers Press* (May 22, 1929). Seventeen million dollars in 1927: "Road Building Speed Is Told," *Ft. Myers Press* (March 5, 1927).
6. "Carlton Plan Held Up by Opposition," *Ft. Myers Press* (June 7, 1929); "Carlton Bills Likely to Pass This Week," *Ft. Myers Press* (June 10, 1929); "Legislature Session Ends in Wee Hours," *Ft. Myers Press* (June 21, 1929). The sixth cent wasn't considered part of the five cent gas tax because it was to be returned to each county based on the amount collected in that county, thereby making it a "Local" tax.
7. "Palm Beach Won't Pay Gasoline Tax," *Ft. Myers Press* (July 16, 1929); "Tax Decision Appealed to High Court," *Ft. Myers Press* (July 26, 1929); "Distribution of Gasoline Tax Invalid," *Ft. Myers Press* (January 24, 1930); "Supreme Court Halts Gas Tax Distributions," *Miami Metropolis* (January 24, 1930).
8. Thomas Neil Knowles, *Category 5: The 1935 Labor Day Hurricane* (Gainesville: University Press of Florida, 2009): 30-33.
9. "Distribution of Gasoline Tax Invalid," *Ft. Myers Press* (January 24, 1930); "Davis Warns Against Too Quick Action," *Ft. Myers Press* (January 24, 1930); "Redistribution of Motor, Gas Revenue Urged," *Ft. Myers Press* (May 22, 1929); $65,349,033 Spent on Roads, *Miami Metropolis* (April 18, 1928); "$30,980,815 Paid in State Tax by Florida Motorists Since 1921," *Ft. Myers Press* (September 5, 1927); "Gasoline Users Pay Near Half State's Revenue," *Ft. Myers Press* (June 3, 1927); "Road Department Issues Biennial Report," *Ft. Myers Press* (April 22, 1927); "Road Building Speed Is Told," *Ft. Myers Press* (March 5, 1927); "$11,326,987 in '26 For State Roads," *Ft. Myers Press* (December 31, 1926).
10. "Convict Labor to Top Naples Trail Stretch," *Ft. Myers Press* (October 10, 1929); "Convicts Arrive to Do Work on Tamiami Trail," *Ft. Myers Press* (October 22, 1929).
11. Florida Department of Transportation, *Florida Trails to Turnpikes* (Tallahassee: FDOT, 1964): 86-87. The work was finished on December 21, 1929.
12. "Trail Building Used $500,000 in Machinery," *Miami Metropolis* (April 22, 1928). For ubiquitousness of hopper cars: "Projects on Trail in Various Stages of Shaping," *Miami Metropolis* (April 22, 1928). Rail extensions: Greg M. Turner, *A Journey into Florida Railroad History* (Gainesville: University Press of Florida, 2008): 194-198.
13. "Last Section of Tamiami Trail to Be Opened Sunday," *Ft. Myers Press* (December 21, 1929).
14. "J. L. Lofton Co. Gets Fill Work on Collier Span," *Ft. Myers Press* (December 5, 1929); "Grading of Bridge Road Starts Soon," *Ft. Myers Press* (January 8, 1930).
15. George Cook, "Chevelier Corporation: January 1937," (history and financial report), Box 7, File 3; "Minutes of Special Meeting of Chevelier Corp., August 16, 1928," Box 2-2, File 7, both Jaudon Collection, HistoryMiami.
16. Letter from J. F. Jaudon to Chevelier Corporation, August 17, 1928, Box 2-1, File 8, Jaudon Collection, HistoryMiami.
17. "Special Meeting Called Informally of the Directors of the Chevelier Corporation," August 16, 1928, Box 12, File 6, Jaudon Collection, HistoryMiami; Draft Bill of Complaint, James and Maude Jaudon v. Chevelier Corporation, August 1, 1928, Box 2, File 5, Jaudon Collection, HistoryMiami; "Chevelier Corporation: Memo of George F. Cook, Secretary Treasurer, January 1937," January 5, 1937, Box 12, File 6, Jaudon Collection, History Miami.
18. George Cook, "Chevelier Corporation: January 1937," (history and financial report), Box 7, File 3; "Minutes of Special Meeting of Chevelier Corp., August 16, 1928," Box 2-2, File 7, "Notice of Special Meeting: Chevelier Corporation, May 31, 1937" (May 10, 1937), Box 8, File 3, both Jaudon Collection, HistoryMiami.
19. "Untitled" [Begins: "Is It as Bad as That?"], dated June 21, 1933, Box 13, File 3, Jaudon Collection, History Miami.
20. "Westward the Path of Miami's Farm Empire Wends Its Way," *Miami Metropolis* (May 5, 1929).
21. Letter from Daisy Aldridge to James Jaudon, August 20, 1930, Box 2-1, File 6, Jaudon Collection, History Miami.
22. Letter from S. F. Sherwood to J. F. Jaudon, Box 7, File 5, Jaudon Collection, HistoryMiami.
23. Letter from Daniel McDougal to Mary McDougal Axelson, June 10, 1934, Series 8, Folder 344, Mary McDougal Axelson Collection, Richter Library, Univ. of Miami.
24. "Interview with D. A. Mcdougal and Ivar Axelson by Mckay, Smith and Manley, July 23, 1948"; Memo from Manley to Violet McDougal, June 14, 1951; letter from Hillary Tolson, Dept. of the Interior to Office of the U.S. Attorney General, November 16, 1951, all Records of the Superintendant's Office, Series VII (acquisition records), subseries A, File 262, Everglades National Park.
25. "Oklahoma Congresman Purchases Oil Land," *Miami Herald* (June 14, 1955).
26. Letter from Daniel McDougal to Mary McDougal Axelson, January 11, 1934, Series 8, Folder 344, Mary McDougal Axelson Collection, Richter Library, University of Miami.
27. "Captain Jaudon, Miami Pioneer, Taken by Death," *Miami Metropolis* (February 23, 1938); Federal Writers Project, *Florida: A Guide to the Southernmost State* [The WPA Guide to Florida] (New York: Oxford University Press, 1939): 408.
28. 284 miles: *Florida Trails to Turnpikes* (Tallahassee: Florida Department of Highways, 1964): 83. Other mileages are taken from *Florida: A Guide to the Southernmost State [The WPA Guide to Florida]* (New York: Oxford University Press, 1939): 400-402; 406-412.

Other version of "Official" distances: Tampa-Miami: 274; Ft. Myers-Miami: 143. Source: Horace A. Dunn, "The Tamiami Trail," *Florida Highways* 5, 3 (March 1928): 1–12.

29. "Motorcade to Open $9,000,000 Tamiami Trail This Week," *Miami Metropolis* (April 22, 1928); "Work on Trail to Be Speeded, Hathaway Says," *Miami Metropolis* (November 30, 1926). The best summary of total costs is provided in J. Hugh Reese, *History of the Tamiami Trail* (Miami: Tamiami Trail Commissioners and the Commissioners of Dade County, 1928): 23–26. While I have found Reese's figures generally accurate, they only cover the Ft. Myers-to-Miami portion of the highway.

30. "Motorcade to Open $9,000,000 Tamiami Trail This Week," *Miami Metropolis* (April 22, 1928). "Hathaway Says Roads to Bring Big Population," *Miami Metropolis* (March 31, 1927) (Dixie Highway costs); "Marco-Miami-Road to Cost $50,000 a Mile," *Ft. Myers Press* (April 22, 1926); "Speeding Up Work on Trail," *Ft. Myers Press* (July 10, 1924).

31. "Trail Good for 40 Miles an Hour," Ft. Myers Press (December 2, 1926).

32. Patsy West, *The Enduring Seminoles: From Alligator Wrestling to Ecotourism* (Gainesville: University Press of Florida, 1998): 84.

33. W. Stanley Hanson and R. Carl Liddle, "Seminole (Commercial) Camps on Tamiami Trail Going from Fort Myers to Miami," September 28, 1936, Box 42B, Ethyl Cutler Freeman Papers, National Anthropological Archives, Smithsonian Institution.

34. Ethel Cutler Freeman, "Field Notes, Florida, 1939," Box 40, Ethel Cutler Freeman Papers, National Anthropological Archives, Smithsonian Institution, Washington, DC.

35. One subplot in Ken Kesey's novel *One Flew Over the Cuckoo's Nest* (1965) is the psychological destruction of the Klamath people caused by this act of government-facilitated conversion.

36. Harry A. Kersey, *The Stranahans of Fort Lauderdale* (Gainesville: University Press of Florida, 2003): 138–142.

37. West, *The Enduring Seminoles*: 112–114; Kersey, *The Stranahans of Fort Lauderdale*: 114–145.

CHAPTER 14

1. "Conners Libel Suit Asks for $100,000," *New York Times* (August 9, 1909); "W.J. Conners Gives $1,000,000 for Poor," New York Times (July 31, 1925).

2. "W.J. Conners Dies in Buffalo," *New York Times* (October 6, 1929); "Conners Road Booming Real Estate Values," *Miami Metropolis* (April 12, 1925); "Conners Road Lease Sought," *Miami Metropolis* (November 12, 1927).

3. The biography of Conners is taken from four sources, in order of importance: Will Irwin, "The Rise of 'Fingy' Conners," *Colliers Weekly* 41, 16 (July 11, 1908): 10–11; 23–26; "The Variegated Story of Mr. Conners, of Buffalo," *New York Times* (August 16, 1908); "'Fingy' Conners's Career," *New York Times* (October 2, 1906); "William J. Conners Dies in Buffalo," *New York Times* (October 6, 1929).

4. All of the above stories contain some version of the "Dare" story. The hide-and-seek story: "New York's Big Noise Is Unique Character," *Pittsburg Press* (July 2, 1908).

5. Irwin, "The Rise of 'Fingy' Conners": 10–11 (Peter died last); "The Variegated Story of Mr. Conners, of Buffalo" (*N.Y. Times*) (Peter died first). The *Times* story likewise does not assert foul play in the death of the Conners family.

6. "Buffalo Shovelers' Strike," *New York Times* (May 7, 1899).

7. It's also a miracle they didn't blow up the *Mather*: grain dust is extremely explosive; that's why the scoopers of the era used wooden shovels, and today they use aluminum—no sparks.

8. Irwin, "The Rise of Fingy Conners," 23.

9. "The Variegated Story of Mr. Conners of Buffalo," *New York Times* (August 16, 1908).

10. Irwin, "The Rise of Fingy Conners," 23.

11. "Conners of Buffalo Democratic Chairman," *New York Times* (October 2, 1906). Hearst served two undistinguished terms as U.S. Representative from New York State (1903–07) and ran for, and lost, the election for New York City mayor (1905).

12. "Chairman Conners's Son Dead," *New York Times* (November 11, 1906).

13. Irwin, "The Rise of Fingy Conners," 23; "The Variegated Story of Mr. Conners of Buffalo"; "Conners Libel Suit; Asks for $100,000," *New York Times* (August 9, 1909).

14. "Conners Arrives Ready for a Fight," *New York Times* (February 21, 1910).

15. "Conners Prompts Judgeship Inquiry," *New York Times* (February 22, 1910); Conners Friends Admit He's Beaten," *New York Times* (February 23, 1910).

16. "Conners Apology Keeps Place a While," *New York Times* (February 25, 1910).

17. "Conners Quits State Committee," *New York Times* (September 22, 1911).

18. "Statewide Charter Invalid," *New York Times* (May 5, 1909).

19. "Railway Lake Ships in New Combination," *New York Times* (January 12, 1916): "William J. Conners Dies in Buffalo," *New York Times* (October 6, 1929).

20. Mark S. Foster, *Castles in the Sand: The Life and Times of Carl Graham Fisher* (Gainesville: University Press of Florida, 2000): 184–186.

21. "Conners's Boat Runs Away," *New York Times* (March 14, 1910).

22. James R. Knott, "Fingy Conners and the Conners Highway," *Palm Beach Post* (July 20, 1980); David McCally, *The Everglades: An Environmental History* (Gainesville: University Press of Florida: 1999): 112–114; 131–132.

23. Gordon L. Williams, "I Remember the Everglades Mail Boats," *Tequesta* 36 (1976): 78–88. Canal dock known as Connersville: "Conners Goes to New York on Road Business," *Palm Beach Post* (April 29, 1923).

24. "Conners Discusses Farm," *New York Times* (May 18, 1922).

25. Williams, "I Remember the Everglades Mail Boat": 86. A levee all the way around the lake—beyond the south rim—was not built until the Herbert Hoover dyke project was completed by the Corps of Engineers in the 1950s.

26. "Cross State Rail Route Urged," *Ft. Myers Daily Press* (January 16, 1922); "Road Meeting Will Be Held Here Tonight," *Ft. Myers Press* (January 23, 1922).

27. "East Beach Pike to Okeechobee Contemplated," *Palm Beach Post* (January 22, 1923).

28. "Plan to Build Toll Road from West Palm Beach," *Miami Herald* (February 12, 1923).

29. Allen Morris, *Florida Place Names* (Coral Gables: University of Miami Press, 1974): s.v. "Okeechobee."

30. "Okeechobee City Land Is Sold for $1,000,000," *Miami Herald* (March 11, 1923); *Minutes of the Trustees of the Internal Improvement Fund*, Vol. 21 (March 17, 1923): 23–24.

31. "Stovall Tells of Road's Beginnings," *Palm Beach Post* (June 6, 1925); "Conners Plans Work Railroad to Aid Highway," *Palm Beach Post* (April 12, 1923).

32. Tammy Ingram, Dixie Highway: Road *Building and the Making of the Modern South, 1900-1930* (Chapel

Hill: University of North Carolina Press, 2014): 43–87; Howard Preston, *Automobile Age Atlanta: The Making of a Southern Metropolis* (Athens: University of Georgia Press, 1979): 146–149; Howard Lawrence Preston, *Dirt Roads to Dixie: Accessibility and Modernization in the South, 1885–1935* (Knoxville: University of Tennessee Press, 1991): 53–61.
 33. "Possible That Dixie Highway Travel Be Over Tamiami Trail," *Miami Metropolis* (March 4, 1916).
 34. "State Is to Give Aid to the Tamiami Trail," *Miami Metropolis* (July 23, 1920); "Road Across River to Be Number 5," *Ft. Myers Press* (February 9, 1922); "Lee County Busy These Days in Road Building," *Ft. Myers Press* (June 13, 1922).
 35. "Climax in Highway History of Florida Reached Says Chapin," *Ft. Myers Press* (March 21, 1925); "Fort Myers-Miami Highway May Be Placed on Preferential List," *Ft. Myers Press* (May 15, 1925); "Status of Road Construction Through October 31, 1926," *Florida Highways* 3, 11 (November 1926): 32; *The State Road System of Florida, 1937* (Tallahassee: Florida Road Department, 1937): 5.

CHAPTER 15

 1. "Text of Conners Highway Bill," *Palm Beach Post* (April 21, 1923); "Memorandum of Agreement" in *Minutes of the The Trustees of the Internal Improvement Fund*, Vol. 23 (April 28, 1923): 123. Promise of December 1923: "Conners Goes to New York on Road Business," *Palm Beach Post* (April 29, 1923). "Building a Private Road Through the Everglades," *The Highway Magazine* 14, 11 (December 1923): 11–12.
 2. Conners Goes to New York on Road Business," *Palm Beach Post* (April 29, 1923); letter from Thomas Will to C. W. Bell, August 30, 1923, Thomas Will Collection (General Correspondence, Aug. 1, 1923 to Aug. 23, 1923), P. K. Yonge Library, University of Florida, Gainesville.
 3. Judicial Settlement of Grace I. Conners, et al., *In Re: Estate of William J. Conners*, Record on Appeal, Claim of George Losey, Filed April 27, 1937 (Sup. Ct. New York, 4th Dept.): 14–24.
 4. "Miami Men Buy in Okeechobee," *Palm Beach Post* (April 5, 1925).
 5. "Conners Highway Is Opened," *Florida Highways* 1, 9 (August 1924): 21–24; "Building a Private Road Through the Everglades," *The Highway Magazine* 14, 11 (December 1923): 11–12; "Great Celebration at Okeechobee City July 4 Will Open Conners Highway," *Miami Metropolis* (July 4, 1924).
 6. "Conners Highway Bill Passed," *Palm Beach Post* (April 21, 1923); "Text of Conners Highway Bill," *Palm Beach Post* (April 21, 1923).
 7. "Conners Highway Is Opened," *Florida Highways* 1, 9 (August 1924): 21–24. Disagreement over St. Lucie Canal bridge: *Minutes of the Trustees of the Internal Improvement Fund*, Vol. 24 (January 7, 1925): 3–6. A vertical-lift drawbridge was eventually installed at the St. Lucie Canal.
 8. "Conners Highway Is Opened," *Florida Highway* 1, 9 (August 1924) 21, 24.
 9. Road opening: "Conners Highway Is to Be Opened Today," *Miami Herald* (July 4, 1924). Conners believed state would finish road to Sebring: "Great Celebration at Okeechobee City July 4 Will Open Conners Highway," *Miami Metropolis* (July 4, 1924). State believed Conners would finish: "Conners Highway Is Opened," *Florida Highways* 1, 9 (August 1924): 21–24. The article is ambiguous as to whether Connors was planning to build the Okeechobee City—Sebring link or assist the state in building it. Text of agreement: "Text of Conners' Highway Bill," *Palm Beach Post* (April 21, 1923). "Text of Conners Highway Bill," *Palm Beach Post* (April 21 1923).
 10. Turner, *A Journey into Florida Railroad History*: 203; 205–206.
 11. Train service: Turner, *A Journey into Florida Railroad History*: 195–198. Pullman coaches: "Conners Road Booming Real Estate Values," *Miami Metropolis* (April 12, 1925).
 12. "New Highway Opened Connecting South and North Florida," *Ft. Myers Press* (December 17, 1924); "Status of Road Construction Through October 31, 1926," *Florida Highways* 3, 11 (November 1926).
 13. Virginia Elliott TenEick, *History of Hollywood, 1920 to 1950* (Hollywood: City of Hollywood, 1966): 260.
 14. "Conners Party Is Here for Road Opening," *Miami Metropolis* (July 2, 1924).
 15. "Conners July 4 Festivities Set Florida Record," *Miami Metropolis* (July 5, 1924); Okeechobee is Scene of Dual Celebration," *Miami Herald* (July 5, 1924); "State Officials Praise Conners for Highway," *Miami Herald* (July 6, 1924); Man is Fatally Shot at Okeechobee Fete," *Miami Herald* (July 6, 1924).
 16. Ferman A. Wilson, "Conners Road Booming Real Estate Values," *Miami Metropolis* (April 12, 1925).
 17. Letter from John T. Meegan to George H. Losey, April 10, 1925, Judicial Settlement of Grace I. Conners, et al., *In Re: Estate of William J. Conners*, Record on Appeal, Claim of George Losey, Filed April 27, 1937 (Sup. Ct. New York, 4th Dept.): 14–24. Not finished until 1926: "Status of Road Construction Through October 31, 1926," *Florida Highways*, 3, 11 (November 1926): 32.
 18. *Minutes of the Trustees of the Internal Improvement Fund*, Vol. 25 (January 7, 1925): 3–6.
 19. "Conners Highway Is Closed to All Autos," *Palm Beach Post* (August 19, 1925); Letter from John T. Meegan to George H. Losey, October 19, 1925, Judicial Settlement of Grace I. Conners, et al., *In Re: Estate of William J. Conners*, Record on Appeal, Claim of George Losey, Filed April 27, 1937 (Sup. Ct. New York, 4th Dept.): 14–24.
 20. "Conners Road Booming Real Estate Values," *Miami Metropolis* (April 12, 1925).
 21. Fuller quote: William W. Rogers, "Fortune and Misfortune: The Paradoxical 1920's" in *The History of Florida*, ed. Michael Gannon (Gainesville, University Press of Florida, 2013): 296–312. Bank failures: "No New Banks Added to List Closing Doors," *Ft. Myers Press* (July 18, 1926).
 22. "The Cross-State Highway," *Miami Metropolis* (May 6, 1926).
 23. See map "Early History of the Trail," *Ft. Myers Press* (April 25, 1928). Much like the Tamiami Trail, State Road 25 would continue to be upgraded for several years after it was finished, mostly by acquiring right-of-way to straighten the road by eliminating 'square corners': "Bentley Gives Press Facts on Road Work," *Ft. Myers Press* (February 14, 1929).
 24. "The Highway Deal," *Ft. Myers Press* (June 16, 1927) (reprinted from the *Plant City Enterprise*, June 14, 1927).
 25. "Road Injunction Action Postponed," *Ft. Myers Press* (September 19, 1927).
 26. "Conner Highway Purchase Ruled Illegal by Court," *Ft. Myers Press* (February 8, 1928).
 27. "Conners Road Lease Sought," *Miami Metropolis* (November 12, 1927).
 28. "Conners Highway Dynamited to Let Loose Flood Water," *Ft. Myers Press* (August 21 1928).
 29. "Death Toll Now Stands 1,500 in Okeechobee Area," *Ft. Myers Press* (September 22, 1928).
 30. "Conners Highway Builder Dies at N.Y. Home,"

Ft. Myers Press (October 5, 1929); "William J. Conners Dies in Buffalo," *New York Times* (October 6, 1929).
  31. "Conners Road Sale Deal Near Finish; Action Is Due Today," *Palm Beach Post* (July 15, 1930).
  32. "May Buy Conners Highway," *Sarasota Herald* (February 5, 1930).
  33. "Conners Road Is Open Today Free of Toll," *Palm Beach Post* (July 16, 1930).
  34. "Conners Road Sale Deal Nears Finish, Action Is Due Today," *Palm Beach Post* (July 15, 1930); "Conners Road Is Open Today Free of Toll," *Palm Beach Post* (July 16, 1930).
  35. "State Will Purchase Conners Highway," *Palm Beach Post* (February 26, 1932).
  36. "Carlton Bills Likely to Pass This Week," *Miami Metropolis* (June 10, 1929); "Palm Beach Won't Pay Gasoline Tax," *Ft. Myers Press* (July 16, 1929). The tax was originally five cents, with two cents to local bonds, three cents to the state and one cent to schools, but was raised in 1933: *Florida: A Guide to the Southernmost State* [The WPA Guide to Florida] (New York: Oxford University Press, 1939): 74–75.
  37. "State Buys Portion of Conners Highway," *Palm Beach Post* (June 25, 1933); "Conners Highway Leased by State," *St. Petersburg Times* (July 18, 1933); "Testimony of J. J. Meegan," Judicial Settlement of Grace I. Conners, et al., *In Re: Estate of William J. Conners,* Record on Appeal, Claim of George Losey, Filed April 27, 1937 (Sup. Ct. New York, 4th Dept.): 14–24. Most important link: "Waters Threaten Conners Highway," *Palm Beach Post* (October 6, 1953).
  38. *Florida: A Guide to the Southernmost State*: 463; Letter from Frank J. Pepper to William Kenan, Jr., January 21, 1944, Box 96, Folder 1703 (MLC File 2155), Model Land Company Collection, Richter Library, University of Miami.
  39. "Waters Threaten Conners Highway," *Palm Beach Post* (October 6, 1953).
  40. Michael Gunwald, *The Swamp: The Everglades, Florida and the Politics of Paradise* (New York: Simon & Schuster, 2006): 228, 266–267. The Corps and the State of Florida are now trying to undo the C-38 by converting the canal back into a meandering watercourse, but only a small portion of the originally inundated land will be re-flooded.

Resources and Bibliography

Archival Sources

Collier County Museums and Collier County Library

The Collier County Museum in Naples was the source of the original construction logs of the Florida Road Department for the Tamiami Trail in 1927–28 (Project 669-). The Naples main library of the Collier County Library System indicates on their on-line catalog that they hold a microform copy of D. Graham Copeland's 1,200-page "Research Notes on the History of Collier County," the basis for Charlton Tebeau's *The Story of the Chokoloskee Bay Country* and *Man in the Everglades: 2000 Years of Human History in Everglades National Park*, the raw material for Peter Matthieson's *Killing Mister Watson*. Several private websites contain excerpts from this microform, some quite extensive. However, the staff told me after I asked to make an appointment in 2014 to use the material that the reel was missing. (The hardcopy original is held by the Florida Division of Historical Resources in Tallahassee.)

The Collier Company is still an active builder and land developer. However, a telephone inquiry indicated that the firm prefers to make its historical material available to researchers through donations to the Collier County Museums, and that its corporate archives are not open to the public or historians.

Everglades National Park; Archives, Manuscripts and Special Collections Division

The Park's archives and manuscripts division is located at the Daniel Beard Center on Research Road, near the Royal Palm Visitor Center.

The finding aid to "Records of the Superintendent's Office 1934–2011" is not available online, but can be sent digitally to anyone requesting a copy by email. Contact the Park's archives office and ask for the finding aid for record series EVER-22965 (Records of the Superintendant's Office, 1934–2011). Several documents were used in the preparation of this book. The first were the *Superintendent's Monthly Narrative Reports*, which have been digitized from Daniel Beard's first two-page report in 1944 to the year 1967. They are in Adobe Acrobat (PDF) format. (EVER-22965; series II; subseries B (Superintendent's Monthly Reports); (nos. 1 [1947–52] and 2 [1947–67]). These documents are too big to send via email, but if a researcher sends a USB drive to the Archives Center with a stamped-self-addressed padded envelope, the staff will load them on the USB drive and mail it.

The second report that proved valuable was the "Final Location and Construction Report: Flamingo Road (Park Route 1), June 30, 1959," in EVER-2265; series III; subseries D (Subject Files 1949-1987), File 084. This report established conclusively that the Cement Bridge had been destroyed in early 1959, and that the "three mile" gap in the Ingraham Highway at Sweet Bay Pond was not created for reasons related to water flow, but to end the Ingraham's viability as a through highway.

I also used several files in series VI, subseries A (Landowner Records, 1944–1962) and subseries B (Albert B. Manley Records, 1947–1968). These records all pertain to land acquisition for the park, sometimes on an involuntary basis. (Manley was the State of Florida's land agent. It was the state that actually acquired the land, transferring it to the NPS.) The series A records are alphabetical by landowner, the series B records are topical. The final document consulted was a detailed right-of-way ownership map of the old Ingraham Highway prepared in 1949. The Model Land Company neglected to sell most of the plots along (i.e. under) the road with easements or rights-of-way reservations in place. They maintained that the 1912 conveyance contained a 100-foot roadway corridor. The state was unwilling to rely on such an indeterminate grant of rights. Hence, parcels with roadway rights had to be mapped and purchased separately. This oversize map, in three sheets, has a separate catalog number, EVER 303428.

Note that as of this writing (fall 2015), the park has announced that its library will be moved to Florida International Library in Miami. This appears to be the library holdings in the headquarters building at the Ernest Coe Center and Museum at the Homestead entrance, not the archives and manuscript material at the Daniel Beard Center, but researchers should call or email to clarify the current situation.

HistoryMiami (The South Florida History Museum)

HistoryMiami's Archives and Research Center is located in downtown Miami at 101C W. Flagler Street, on the same plaza as the main branch of the Miami-Dade County Public Library. HistoryMiami's list of finding aids is available on-line at www.historymiami.org. They are arranged in alphabetical order.

HistoryMiami holds two important manuscript collections, the James Franklin Jaudon Collection and the J. B. McCrary Company Papers. The Jaudon Collection is comprised of 20 boxes and 2 map drawers, about 8 linear feet in total. There are about 1,200 documents, 200 photographs and 50 maps. About half relate to Jaudon's investment in the Hopkins/Chevelier Tract and the Tamiami Trail.

The McCrary Papers are comprised of one box and one file, with about sixty papers, all relating to the firm's work on the Ingraham Highway and Tamiami Trail. Most are communications to and from the County Commission and County Attorney. There are no maps or photographs.

Many, but not all, of the Jaudon Collection is available through Florida International University's "Reclaiming the Everglades" website. However, its "DigiTool" user interface is very awkward. A search will return groups of documents or images, some from HistoryMiami, some from the half-dozen or so other contributing institutions. Clicking on an individual document will return a good-quality image, but the metadata only indicates the source institution and collection, not the box and file number of the document. Thus, a researcher using a document retrieved through the DigiTool can discern only that a given institution contributed a document, but not the collection, box or file number in which it is located in. It can only be cited by the ascension number in which it was digitized into DigiTool. (Most photographs, however, do carry a serial number unique to the contributing institution and it appears that DigiTool was designed mainly to handle photographs.) Therefore, a researcher cannot cite to either a box/file or a URL location, at least until he or she is quite familiar with the organization of the (paper) collection.

In addition to the above, HistoryMiami has hardbound copies of its history magazine *Tequesta*. *Tequesta* is available on-line through HistoryMiami's website, so researchers may find its hardcopy collection of regional and local history magazines more valuable. HistoryMiami also has an extensive and well-indexed photograph collection.

Miami-Dade Public Library

The library's Florida Collection is located in the main downtown library, on the second floor. The Florida Collection has one manuscript collection that was used for this book, a box of writings, photographs and other memorabilia relating to the Tamiami Trailblazers trip of April 4–20, 1923 that was collected by Trailblazer Frank Lewis, a Miami resident. This material has call number Fla./R/975.944/LEWI/.

The most frequently used material in the Florida Collection was its significant collection of Miami and South Florida newspapers on spooled microform. The best and most readable newspaper prior to the mid-1920s was the *Miami Metropolis*. This newspaper actually went through many name changes during the period 1914–1935, including the *Miami Metropolis*, *Miami Metropolis and News*, *Miami News-Metropolis*, the *Miami Daily News and Metropolis*, and finally the *Miami Daily News*, its name for many decades until its demise in the early 1990s. The Florida Collection, unlike the University of Miami's Richter Library, has maintained the *Metropolis* as a single series under that name and has not broken it down by its literal name for any given time period. This practice has been maintained in the endnotes of this book. Regardless of the actual masthead name, it is referred to in the endnotes as the *Miami Metropolis*.

The Florida Collection also has a complete run of the *Miami Herald*, although the *Herald* is suffering from heavy wear, and has developed contagious acetate disintegration ("vinegar rot"). Its typeface prior to 1930 is small, and some reels are difficult to read. (The University of Miami's Richter Library has both the *Herald* and the *Metropolis* in spooled microform but it files the *Metropolis* under its literal name, so it is in at least four different locations.) The Florida Collection also has a nearly complete run of the *Ft. Myers Press*, several Tampa Bay-area newspapers, and most of the various (and usually short-lived) newspapers published in Homestead.

Smithsonian Institution, Washington, D.C.

The Ethel Cutler Freeman Collection contains her own 1939 field notes of Seminole life along the Tamiami Trail (Box 40), and an unpublished survey paper by W. Stanley Hanson and R. Carl Liddle entitled "Seminole (Commercial) Camps on Tamiami Trail Going from Fort Myers to Miami," September 28, 1936 (Box 42B). The Ethyl Cutler Freeman Papers have been stored in the National Anthropological Archives of the Smithsonian Institution but likely will be, or have already been, transferred to the new National Museum of the American Indian, so researchers wanting to consult this collection should consult the new museum or the Smithsonian's division of libraries and archives.

University of Florida Library System

The University's P.K. Yonge Library electronic library and Smathers Library are linked to the "Reclaiming the Everglades" website at Florida international University, but unlike most of the other contributors, the University of Florida maintains its own in-house search engine and electronic filing system, which is collection-based. Thus, one can make a Boolian search of all collections, or can, for example, search through the May Mann Jennings collection in chronological order from start to finish, just as one would with a paper collection. Also, each document has its own URL, so every document can be individually addressed in an endnote.

The P. K. Yonge library and Smathers Library have digitized the entire collection of F. C. Elliott (state drainage engineer); Ernest Graham, James E. Ingraham (although the holdings are small and of a personal nature, from late in life); Governor William Jennings and his wife, May Mann Jennings (two separate collections); and Thomas Will (father of Lawrence Will). The finding aids are on-line, but largely redundant, as each collection is arranged on-line in chronological order. However, they can be searched by content, with various degrees of accuracy. (Holographic letters, for example, may or may not return a hit depending on the quality of the handwriting.)

University of Miami, Richter Library, Department of Special Collections

The Richter Library is not open to the public. However, the Richter Library's Special Collections Department is open to non-university researchers, so one must call ahead and arrange for a pass into the library so that one can access the special collections room.

The finding aids for most manuscript collections are available on-line and are extensive.

The special collections department holds two important collections, the Model Land Company Records and the Mary McDougal Axelson Papers. Despite the name, The Model Land Company (MLC) records are not the records of that firm, which was the real estate arm of the Florida East Coast Railroad. The Model Land Co. was headquartered in St. Augustine and its records were destroyed about 1965. These records are actually those of the Model Land Company's local real estate agent Frederick Morse and his successors, Pepper & Potter. The records are very extensive: 113 boxes, 1,953 files.

Confusing matters, especially for those using the digital "Reclaiming the Everglades" site and its DigiTool search engine (see the comments for HistoryMiami above) is that each document was originally filed by the Morse real estate firm using a three-digit filing number written on the upper right-hand corner of each document. However, this number is not used by the University of Miami, which has adopted its own box and file number system. Fortunately, the finding aid for the collection cross-reference the University of Miami and Model Land Co. numbering systems, and both numbers are used in the endnotes of this book.

The second relevant collection is the Mary McDougal Axelson Collection. Mrs. Axelson was the daughter of Judge Daniel McDougal, and she and her husband Ivar Axelson managed Judge McDougal's Everglades land holdings after he retired in the 1930s. Judge McDougal was active in many enterprises in Oklahoma and Florida and served in the early Franklin Roosevelt administration. Mrs. Axelson herself was a noted novelist and playright whose death was rather sensational. With two such notable individuals, only a relatively small portion of the collection relates to the family's Monroe County land holdings. In all, the collection comprises 48 boxes and 432 files, of which about ten percent relate to Chevelier.

NEWSPAPERS

Estero Eagle	*Miami Daily Metropolis*	*Miami Tribune*
Fort Myers Press	*Miami Daily News*	*New York Times*
Homestead Enterprise	*Miami Daily News and Metropolis*	*Palm Beach Post*
Homestead Leader	*Miami Metropolis*	*St. Petersburg Evening Independent*
Miami Herald	*Miami News*	

BOOKS, ARTICLES, DISSERTATIONS

Akin, Edward N. *Flagler: Rockefeller Partner and Florida Barron*. Gainesville: University Press of Florida, 1991 [1988].

———. "The Sly Foxes: Flagler, Miles and Florida's Public Domain," *Florida Historical Quarterly* 58, no. 1 (July 1979): 22–36.

Andrews, A. H. "Blazing the Tamiami Trail Across Florida, Part 1." *Dearborn Independent* (February 2, 1924): 10–11.

———. "Blazing the Tamiami Trail Across Florida, Part 2." *Dearborn Independent* (February 9, 1924): 10–11.

Bain, David Howard. *Empire Express: Building the First Transcontinental Railroad*. New York: Viking, 1999.

Barrett, Paul. *The Automobile and Urban Transit: The Formation of Public Policy in Chicago, 1900–1930*. Philadelphia: Temple University Press, 1983.

Braden, Susan. *The Architecture of Leisure: The Florida Resort Hotels of Henry Flagler and Henry Plant.* Gainesville: University Press of Florida, 2002.
Brown, William E., Jr., and Karen Hudson. "Henry Flagler and the Model Land Company." *Tequesta* 56 (1996): 47–78.
"Building a Private Road Through the Everglades." *The Highway Magazine* 14, no. 11 (December 1923): 11–12.
Carter, Luther J. *The Florida Experience: Land and Water Policy in a Growth State.* Baltimore: Johns Hopkins University Press, 1974.
Church, Alonzo. "A Dash Through the Everglades." *Tequesta* 9 (1949): 15–42.
"Conners Highway Is Opened." *Florida Highways.* 1, no. 9 (August 1924): 21–24.
Crawford, William G. *Florida's Big Dig: The Atlantic Intracoastal Waterway.* Cocoa: Florida Historical Society Press, 2006.
_____. "The Papers of Albert Sawyer and the Development of the Florida East Coast, 1892 to 1912." *Tequesta* 62 (2002): 5–39.
Derr, Mark. *Some Kind of Paradise: A Chronicle of Man and the Land in Florida.* Gainesville: University Press of Florida, 1998 [1989].
Douglas, Marjory Stoneman. *The Everglades: River of Grass.* New York: Reinhart & Co., 1947.
_____. *Voice of the River.* Englewood, FL: Pineapple Press, 1987.
Dovell, J. E. [Junius Elmore]. "The Everglades Before Reclamation." *Florida Historical Quarterly* 26, no. 1 (July 1947): 1–47.
_____. "A History of the Everglades of Florida." Ph.D dissertation, University of North Carolina–Chapel Hill, 1947.
_____. "The Railroads and the Public Lands of Florida, 1879–1905." *Florida Historical Quarterly* 34, no. 3 (January 1956): 236–258.
Dunn, Horace A. "The Tamiami Trail." *Florida Highways* 5, no. 3 (March 1928): 1–12.
Edgerton, David. *The Shock of the Old: Technology and Global History Since 1900.* New York: Oxford University Press, 2007.
Everglades National Park: Bicycle Trail System Study, 2007 Update. Homestead: Everglades National Park, 2007.
Federal Writers' Project of the Works Progress Administration. *Florida: Guide to the Southernmost State* [The WPA Guide to Florida] (New York: Oxford University Press, 1939): 326.
Fein, Michael R. *Paving the Way: New York Roadbuilding and the American State, 1880–1956.* Lawrence: University Press of Kansas, 2008.
"'Fingy' Conners's Career," *New York Times* (October 2, 1906).
Flink, James J. *America Adopts the Automobile, 1895–1910.* Cambridge, MA: MIT Press, 1970.
_____. *The Automobile Age.* Cambridge, MA: MIT Press, 1988.
Foster, Mark S. *Castles in the Sand: The Life and Times of Carl Graham Fisher.* Gainesville: University Press of Florida, 2000.
_____. *From Streetcar to Superhighway: American City Planners and Urban Transportation, 1900–1940.* Philadelphia: Temple University Press, 1981.
Gannon, Michael, ed. *The History of Florida.* Gainesville: University Press of Florida, 2nd ed., 2013.
Gantz, Charlotte Orr. *A Naturalist in Southern Florida.* Coral Gables: University of Miami Press, 1971.
Gifford, John. "Looking Ahead: Views on Everglades Topics." *Tropic Magazine* 1, no. 4 (July 1914): 5–10.
Glassman, Steve. "Blazing the Tamiami Trail." *South Florida History Magazine* 1 (Winter 1989): 3–5; 12–13;
Goddard, Stephen B. *Getting There: The Epic Struggle Between Road and Rail in the American Century.* New York: Basic Books, 1994.
Graham, Thomas. *Mr. Flagler's St. Augustine.* Gainesville: University Press of Florida, 2014.
Graham, William A. "The Pennsuco Sugar Experiment." *Tequesta* 19 (1959): 11–23.
Greene, Ann Norton. *Horses at Work: Harnessing Power in Industrial America.* Cambridge, MA: Harvard University Press, 2008.
Grunwald, Michael. *The Swamp: The Everglades, Florida and the Politics of Paradise.* New York: Simon & Schuster: 2008.
Hahn, John H. *Apalachee: The Land Between the Rivers.* Gainesville: University Press of Florida: 1988).
Hallac, David, Sue Perry and Erik Staubenau. *Proposal to Request Fish Passage Funding for FY08: Funding for Culverts on the Old Ingraham Highway in Everglades National Park to Allow for Fish Passage and Enhancement of Marsh Habitat.* Homestead, Everglades National Park, n.d. [2007].
Hammond, James. *Florida's Vanishing Trail.* n.l.: the author, 2008.
Hoakson, Drake. *The Lincoln Highway: Main Street Across America.* Iowa City: University of Iowa Press, 1988.
Hugill, Peter J. "Good Roads and the Automobile in the United States, 1880–1929." *Geographical Review* 72 (July 1982): 329–337.
Ingraham, James E. "Keep Your Head Above the Financial Waters and Bet on the Growth of the Country." *Manufacturers Record* (January 26, 1922): 60–62.

_____. "Remarks of J. E. Ingraham." In *The Everglades of Florida* (Senate Document No. 89, 62nd Cong., 1st Sess., 1911): 101–107.
Ingram, Tammy. *Dixie Highway: Road Building and the Making of Modern South, 1900–1930*. Chapel Hill: University of North Carolina Press, 2014.
Irwin, Will. "The Rise of 'Fingy' Conners." *Colliers Weekly* 41, no. 16 (July 11, 1908): 10–11; 23–26.
Jennings, Mrs. W. S. [May Mann]. "Royal Palm State Park." *Tropic Magazine* 4, 1 (April 1916): 11–16, 26.
Jackle, John A., and Keith A. Sculle. *Motoring: The Highway Experience in America*. Athens: University of Georgia Press, 2008.
Jahoda, Gloria. *The Other Florida*. New York: Charles Scribners Sons, 1967.
Johnson, Henry E., III. "The Many Faces of Guy I. Metcalf." *Broward Legacy* (Summer/Fall 1986): 2–11.
Kay, Russell. "Tamiami Trail Blazers: A Personal Memoir." *Florida Historical Quarterly* (January 1971): 278–287.
Kennedy, Stetson. *Southern Exposure: Making the South for Democracy*. Tuscaloosa: University of Alabama Press, 2011.
Kersey, Harry A., Jr. *The Stranahans of Fort Lauderdale: A Pioneer Family of New River*. Gainesville: University Press of Florida, 2003.
Klein, Maury. *Union Pacific: The Birth of a Railroad, 1862–1893*. New York: Doubleday, 1987.
Knowles, Thomas Neil. *Category 5: The 1935 Labor Day Hurricane*. Gainesville: University Press of Florida, 2009.
_____. *Long Key: Flagler's Island Getaway for the Rich and Famous*. Gainesville: University Press of Florida, 2014.
Krome, William J. (ed. Jean C. Taylor). "Railway Location in the South." *Tequesta* 39 (1979 [1904]): 5–16.
Levinson, Marc. *The Box: How the Shipping Container Made the World Smaller and the World Economy Bigger*. Princeton: Princeton University Press, 2006.
Lewis, Tom. *Divided Highways: Building the Interstate Highways, Transforming the American Life*. New York: Viking, 1997.
Lundstrom, Mary S. "Marco Florida in 1925." *Tequesta* 31 (1971): 29–40.
McCally, David. *The Everglades: An Environmental History*. Gainesville: University Press of Florida, 1999.
McGowan, Bill. *Hallandale*. Hallandale: Hallandale Historical Society, 1976.
McShane, Clay. *Down the Asphalt Path: The Automobile and the American City*. New York: Columbia University Press, 1994.
McShane, Clay, and Joel A. Tarr. *The Horse in the City: Living Machines in the Nineteenth Century*. Baltimore: Johns Hopkins University Press, 2007.
Mahon, John K. *History of the Second Seminole War*. Gainesville: University Press of Florida, 1967.
Martin, Sidney Walter. "Flagler's Associates in East Florida Developments." *Florida Historical Quarterly* 26, no. 3 (January 1948): 256–263.
Matthiessen, Peter. *Killing Mister Watson*. New York: Random House, 1990.
Minutes of the Trustees of the Internal Improvement Fund, Vol. 4 (1889-Nov. 1899); Vol. 5 (Dec. 1899–1904); Vol. 6 (1905–1906); Vol. 7 (1907–1908); Vol. 8 (1909–1910); Vol. 9 (1911–1912); Vol. 10 (1913–1914); Vol. 11 (1915–1916); Vol. 12 (1917–1918). Tallahassee: State of Florida.
Minutes of the Trustees of the Internal Improvement Fund for the Year 1923. Tallahassee: State of Florida, 1924.
Minutes of the Trustees of the Internal Improvement Fund for the Year 1925. Tallahassee: State of Florida, 1926.
Monroe, Ralph Middleton, and Vincent Gilpin. *The Commodore's Story: The Early Days on Biscayne Bay*. Miami: Historical Association of South Florida, 1985 [1930].
Morris, Allen. *Florida Place Names*. Coral Gables: University of Miami Press, 1974.
Moses, Wallace (ed. Watt P. Marchmann). "The Ingraham Everglades Exploring Expedition, 1892." *Tequesta* 7 (1947): 3–43.
Muir, Helen. *Miami, U.S.A.* New York: Henry Holt, 1953.
National Park Service. *Historic American Building Survey: Monroe Station*. Washington: National Park Service, Historic Preservation Training Center, June 2007. HABS No. FL-544.
Noll, Stephen, and David Tegeder. *The Ditch of Dreams: The Cross-Florida Barge Canal and the Struggle for Florida's Future*. Gainesville: University Press of Florida, 2009.
Perrine, D. LeBaron. "Cape Sable." *The Tropic Magazine* 5, no. 5–6 (February-March 1917): 81–83.
Preston, Howard L. *Automobile Age Atlanta: The Making of a Southern Metropolis, 1900–1935*. Athens: University of Georgia Press, 1979.
_____. *Dirt Roads to Dixie: Accessibility and Modernization in the South, 1885–1935*. Knoxville: University of Tennessee Press, 1991.
Purcell, Aaron. "Plumb Lines, Politics and Projections: The Florida Everglades and the Wright Report Controversy." *Florida Historical Quarterly* 80, no. 2 (Fall 2001): 161–197.
Reardon, L. F. *The Florida Hurricane and Disaster*. Coral Gables: Arva Parks & Co.,1986 [1926].
Reese, J. Hugh. *History of the Tamiami Trail*. Miami: Tamiami Trail Commissioners and the County Commission of Dade County, 1928.

Report of the Joint Commission to Investigate the Trustees of the Internal Improvement Fund Pursuant to Chapter 5632, Session Laws of 1907. Tallahassee: State of Florida, 1909.
Rishel, Virginia. *Wheels to Adventure: Bill Rishel's Western Routes.* Salt Lake City: Howe Brothers, 1983.
Rogers, William W. "Fortune and Misfortune: The Paradoxical 1920's." In *The History of Florida*, ed. Michael Gannon. Gainesville, University Press of Florida, 2013, 296–312.
Rose, Mark H. *Interstate: Express Highway Politics, 1939–1989.* Knoxville: University of Tennessee Press, 1990 [1979].
Roy, William. *Socializing Capital: The Rise of the Large Industrial Corporation in America.* Princeton: Princeton University Press, 1997.
Scupholm, Carrie. "Connecting the East and West Coasts: The Tamiami Trail of the Sunshine State." In *Looking Beyond the Highway: Dixie Roads and Culture*, ed. Claudette Stager and Martha Carver. Knoxville: University of Tennessee Press, 2006, 73–86.
"Seaboard Air Line R. R. Builds Florida Extension." *Railway Review Magazine* (August 1925): 16–21.
Seeley, Bruce. *Building the American Highway System: Engineers as Policy Makers.* Philadelphia: Temple University Press, 1987.
Shaler, Nathan. *American Highways.* New York: Century Publishing, 1896.
Simpson, Charles T. "Paradise Key." *Tropic Magazine* 4, no. 1 (April 1916): 4–9.
Small, John K. "A Cruise to the Cape Sable Region of Florida." *Journal of the New York Botanical Garden* 17 (November 1916): 189–202.
_____. "Exploration in Southern Florida in 1915." *Journal of the New York Botanical Garden* 17 (March 1916): 37–45.
_____. "Royal Palm Hammock," *Journal of the New York Botanical Garden* 17 (October 1916): 165–172.
The State Road System (Edition of 1937). Tallahassee: Florida State Road Department, 1937.
"Status of Road Construction Through October 31, 1926." *Florida Highways* 3, no. 11 (November 1926): 32.
Stewart, M. A., et al. *The Road to Flamingo: An Evaluation of Flow Pattern Alterations and Salinity Intrusion in the Lower Glades, Everglades National Park.* Denver: U.S. Geological Survey, 2002. Report No. Open File 02-59.
Stuart, John A. "Constructing Identity: Building and Place in New Deal South Florida." In The *New Deal in South Florida: Design, Policy and Community Building, 1933–1940*, John A. Stuart and John F. Stack, eds. Gainesville: University Press, 2008, 31–70.
Tebeau, Charlton W. *Man in the Everglades: 2000 Years of Human History in Everglades National Park.* Coral Gables: University of Miami Press, 1968.
_____. *The Story of the Chokoloskee Bay Country.* Coral Gables: University of Miami Press, 1966.
"The Tamiami Trail," *Florida Highways* 3, no. 4 (April 1926): 4–6.
"The Tamiami Trail." In *Florida Trails to Turnpikes.* Tallahassee: Florida Department of Highways, 1964: 68–87.
"Tamiami Trail, as Compiled by Workers of the Writers' Program Florida Work Project Administration." *Florida Highways* 10 (December 1941): 8–9; 24.
Turner, Gregg. *A Journey into Florida Railroad History.* Gainesville, University Press of Florida, 2008.
Taylor, Jean C. "Scarifying South Dade." *Update* [of the Historical Association of Southern Florida] 5, no. 1 (October 1977): 4–5.
TenEick, Virginia Elliott. *History of Hollywood (1920 to 1950).* Hollywood: City of Hollywood, 1966.
Throm, Edward L.. *The Popular Mechanics History of American Transport.* New York: Simon & Schuster, 1952.
Vance, Linda D. "May Mann Jennings and Royal Palm State Park." *Florida Historical Quarterly* 60, no. 1 (July 1976): 1–17.
Vanderhill, Burke G. "The Alachua-St. Mary's Road." *Florida Historical Quarterly* 46, no. 1 (July 1987): 50–67.
"The Variegated Story Mr. Conners, of Buffalo." *New York Times* (August 16, 1908).
Vickers, Raymond B. *Panic in Paradise: Florida's Banking Crash of 1926.* Tuscaloosa: University of Alabama Press, 2004.
Walker, James Lorenzo. "Dedication of the Tamiami Trail Marker." *Tequesta* 19 (1959): 23–28.
Warner, Sam Bass. *Streetcar Suburbs: The Process of Growth in Boston, 1870–1900.* Cambridge: Harvard University Press, 1962.
Weeks, David C. *Ringling: The Florida Years, 1911–1936.* Gainesville: University Press of Florida, 1993.
Weingroff, Richard. "The Man Who Changed America, Part 1," *Public Roads* 66, no. 5 (March/April 2003): 20–35.
_____. "The Man Who Changed America, Part 2," *Public Roads* 66, no. 6 (May/June 2003): 22–37.
West, Patsy. *The Enduring Seminoles: From Alligator Wrestling to Ecotourism.* Gainesville: University Press of Florida, 1998.
Wilhelm, Chris. "Prophet of the Everglades: Ernest Coe and the Fight for Everglades National Park." Ph.D. dissertation, Florida State University, 2010.
Will, Lawrence. "Digging the Cape Sable Canal," *Tequesta* 19 (1959): 29–63.

_____. *A Dredgeman of Cape Sable*. St. Petersburg: Great Outdoors Publishing Company, 1967.
Williams, Gordon L. "I Remember the Everglades Mail Boats." *Tequesta* 36 (1976): 78–88.
WPA Guide to Florida. See Federal Writers Project.
Ziewitz, Katheryn, and June Wiaz. *Green Empire: The St. Joe Company and the Remaking of Florida's Panhandle*. Gainesville: University Press of Florida, 2004.

LEGAL CASES

Annat v. Beard, et al, 277 F.2d 554 (5th Cir 1960).
In re: Estate of William J. Conners (Sup. Ct. New York, 4th Dept., April 27, 1937).
J. B. McCrary Engineering Co. v. Dade County, 86 So. 612 (Fla. 1920).
Paradise Prairie Land Co. v. United States, 212 F. 2d 170 (5th Cir., 1954).
Scharnberg v. Citizens Nat'l. Bank of Spencer, 33 F.2d 673 (8th Cir. 1929).

Index

Numbers in ***bold italics*** refer to pages with photographs.

Akin, Edward 34
Alachua–St. Mary's Road 3
Aldridge, Daisy 202–3
Alexander, Ramsey and Kerr 141–42, 152, 155, 164, 166, 170–71, 176, 178, 186–87, 190, 191
Allen's Place (FL) 14; *see also* Immokalee
Allen's River ***135***, 157
Alligator Bay (Thousand Islands) 122, 136, 140
Alligator Bight (Florida Bay) 68
Allison, James 217
American Association of State Highway Officials (AASHO) 129–30, 161, 163, 187, 226
American Road Congress 6, 87–89, 221
American Steel (dredge) 60
Amos, Ernest 230–31
Annat, Elizabeth D. 67, 72, 138
Annat, Hugh 67, 72
Anthony, J.R. 182
Arcadia (FL) 90, 994, 98, 113, 156, 181, 221
Army Corps of Engineers 22, 234
Ashworth, F.K. 111
Atlantic and Gulf Coast Canal and Okeechobee Land Co. 20
Atlantic Coast Line Railroad 4, 5, 17, 67, 136, 180–81, 200, 227
Audubon Society 32; *see also* Bradley, Guy
Avon Park (FL) 228
Axelson, Ivar 71, 176–77, 203–4
Axelson, Mary McDougal 148, 177, 203–4

Baker, Francis 69
Baker, Frank 114
Bank of Bay Biscayne 62, 99, 194
Bank of Fort Myers 141
Bank of Little River 182
Bankford-Shackelford Highway Act (U.S.) *see* Highway Act of 1916
Barbette, F.A. & Co. 43
Barfield, R.M. 113, 154

Bay City dredges ***126***, ***157***, 158, ***159***, 166, 171, 183, ***186***, 254n27
Bayfront Park 192
Beard, Daniel 71, 72, 74–77; Research Center (Everglades National Park) 78
Belcher, Samuel A. 42, 43, 88–90, 92–94, 97, 98, 103
Belle Glade (FL) 6, 136, 194, 218, 219, 223, 231, 232
Benedict, C.L. 50
Benson, Thomas 60, 67
Bentley, Robert 197
Big Cypress National Preserve (National Park Service) 6, 10, 32
Big Cypress Swamp 6, 14, 32, 150, 206; *see also* Corkscrew Swamp
Billie, Charlie 103
Billie, Jimmie 207–8
Billy Robert's Camp 151–52
Biscayne (Miami Shores) (FL) 25, 49
Biscayne Bay 15
Bloxam, William 20
Boca Grande (FL) 130
Boca Raton (FL) 25, 182–83, 218, 229; *see also* Mizner, Addison and Wilson
Bolles, R.J. 46, 80, 81
Bonita Springs (FL) 94, 167, 197, ***202***
Boston and Florida Atlantic Coast Land Co. 22–27
Bowen, William 69
Bowlegs, Billy 14
Boy Scout Camp (Long Pine Key) 72, 77
Boyd and Bradshaw Construction Co. 53, 55
Boynton (Boynton Beach)(FL) 23–27
Bozeman, O.Z. 141
Bradenton (FL) 92, 94, 144, 155, 156, 161, 171, 191, 192, 205
Bradley, George 23
Bradley, Guy 32, 238n14
Brady, C.S., Construction Co. 53
Brandon, Dr. E.W. 81
Brickell, William 15, 16, 17

Broward, Napoleon B. 26–27
Broward County (FL) 22, 23, 24, 25, 26, 117, ***162***, 164, 165, 183, 188, 197, 227; created (1915) 45; decides not to participate in Trail 98–99; proposed for Tamiami Trail route 93–97
Brown, W.F. 114
Browne, Jefferson B. 34
Brownell, Leverett 32
Brown's Landing (Brown's Store) 93
Bryan, C. Farris 1, 2
Bryan, Tom 223
Bryan, William Jennings 193
Buffalo (NY): Conners replaced as political boss (1910) 215–16; dock strike (1898) 213–14; home of Conners family 211
Buffalo Courier 213
Buffalo Enquirer 213
Buford, Rivers 228
Bureau of Public Roads (U.S.) 8, 128, 129, 155, 168, 192, 197
Burr, E.V.D. 56, 119
Burwell, A.W. 175
Buttonwood Canal 66, 75

Caloosahatchee River 14, 20, 93–94, 98, 118, 144, 218, 230; bridge at Fort Myers 94, 116, 144, 155–56, 159, 167, 180, 190, 192, 204, 205; Edison cement bridges (1931 and 1980s) 190–91, 194, 204, 205
Camp Jackson 28, 29, 33, 36, 39, 41, 47
Camp Longview 31, 33, 36
Campbell, Neil 64–66
Campbell, W.H. 190
Canal Point 6, 218, ***219***, 220, ***225***, 225, 231, 232, 233, 234
Cape Canaveral (FL) 1, 2, 18, 22
Cape Sabal Canal 64–66
Cape Sable 9, 27, 28, 57, 40, 42, 44, 45, 80–82, 87, 216; geography and history 31–34; graves from 1935 hurricane 70; Krome survey (1902–3) 34–36

Index

Cape Sable Railroad Plat (1903), 28–31, *29*
Cape Sable Road *see* Ingraham Highway
Cape Sable Road and Bridge District 9, 29, 83
Captain Ker's Route 14–15
Captiva Island 130
Card Sound Road and Bridge 80, 85
Carlton, Doyle 190, 192–93, 197–201; elected governor (1928) 194
Carnestown (FL) 120, 121, 127, **128**, 131, 132, 136, 144–45, 149–52, 156–57, 166, 167–68, 181, 186, 189
Carr, L.B. 151
Carter, W.T. 92, 95
Catholic Union and Times (Buffalo) 214–15
Catlow, W.R. 102
Catts, Sidney 192–94
Cement Bridge 29, 49, 61, 64, 67, 72–73, 74–77, 79, 94; built 60; destroyed (1959) 77
Central & Southern Florida Flood Control Project 234
Central Florida Highway Assn. 91–92, 98
Central Station and Equipment Co. 191, 197
Chapin, Ora 148, 152, 160–163; *see also* Tamiami Trailblazers
Charlotte Harbor and Charlotte Harbor Bridge *see* Punta Gorda
Chatham Bend Corp. 123, 169
Chatham River 107, 111–14, 165
Chevelier, Guy 32, 112
Chevelier Bay 118, 122
Chevelier City 110, 147–48
Chevelier Corp. 9, 10, 71, 117, 118, 150; assists Tamiami Trailblazers 148–53; collapse 176–77, 185; created by Jaudon (1916) 107–8; dissolved by state 201; first proposes Loop Road 121; restructured through Spencer Agreement 123–24, 169; second attempt to build Loop Road 136–37; surveys Hopkins Tract 111–12
Chevelier Road (Loop Road) **122**, 135, 171–78, 208; adopted by Miccosukee Tribe (1960s) 10, 207–8; construction starts from Dade end 158; cost estimate from Geo. Cook 140; fail of first effort 122–24; final cost 201; financing plan 123–24, 169–70; first proposed by Jaudon 121–22; Huffman firm takes over work 189–90; ignored at grand opening 194–96; second contract from Lee County 136–37
Chevelier Tract: bought by Jaudon 106–110; map 96; site of Watson "murder farm" 111–14; timber harvesting 108–9; title lien problems 109–110
Chicago Street Railway Co. 130
Chinn, C.B. 53
Chokoloskee Island 84, 87, 113–14, 117, 122, 147, 164
Christensen, Alfred 150
Chuluota Land Co. 23
Church, Alonzo 13, 35

Citizens National Bank of Spencer (Iowa) 106–9, 118, 123; bankruptcy 169, 184–85
Clark, Ross 117–18, 148
Clewiston (Sand Point) (FL) 14, 93, 98, 136, 143, 153, 194, 219
Coachman, R.A. 143, 154, 202
Coachman, Walter 153
Coconut Grove (Cocaonut Grove)(FL) 30, 31, 37, 87, 100
Coe, Ernest 67–68, 69, 83–84, 203; *see also* Ernest Coe Visitor Center
Coffrin, Milo 68, 71
Coker, George 180–81
Collier, Barron G. 9, 67, 141–42, 153, 159–61, 164, 170–71, 172, 175, 190–91, 227; buys one million dollars in Lee County Land 137–38; early biography 130–31; forms Collier County 146–48; hires D. Graham Copeland 170; returns Trail to Jenkins alignment 142, 146, 153–54, 158–63; sponsors Tamiami Trailblazers 144, 148–51; takes over work on Gulf side of Trail 140–41, 144–45, 153–54; and Tamiami Trail opening 191–93
Collier, C.M. 131, 141–42, 153
Collier, R.M. ("Capt. Bill") 131, 192
Collier County: approves $350,000 bond issue for Trail 166–67; split off from Lee 146–48, 153–56
Collier County Canning Co. 181
Collier Development Co. 127, 194
Collier Memorial Bridge *see* Punta Gorda Bridge
Colliers Magazine 212, 214
Collins, E.E., Paving and Const. Co. 53
Collins, John 6
Collins Causeway 2, 6, 170
Commercial Bank and Trust Co. (of Palm Beach) 183
Conners, Grace Hammond 231
Conners, Mary 211, 212
Conners, Peter (father of William J.) 211, 212
Conners, Peter (son of William J.) 215
Conners, William J. 8, 9, 10; builds Conners Highway 220–34; buys Okeechobee lands 217–18, 220; death 231; early biography 211–13; is defeated in longshoring by Bishop Quigley 214; ostracized from N.Y. Republican committee 216–17, 224; powerboat racing 217–18; takes over Buffalo longshoremen 212–14
Conners, William J., Jr. 231
Conners Farm 218, 223
Conners-Florida Highway Corp. 224, 225, 227, 228–29, 231, 232
Conners Highway: bond financing attempted 224; construction 224, 226–227; described 6, 8–9, 10; grand opening 228; legislative approval for 221, 226–27; origins 219–21; problems with flooding 229, 231, 234; sale to government 230–32; start of work 223; toll schedule 225
Conners Land Co. **219**

Connersville 218
Consolidated Land Co. 138, 153, 220
Consolidated Street Railway Advertising Co. 130–31
convict labor: escapes 179–81; history in Florida 178–81; used on Ingraham Highway 74; used on Trail 179–81, 200–1; *see also* Copeland Road Prison
Cook, Erban 108, 149, 158, 160, 164, 166, 167, 170, 190, 191–92; crosses Everglades in "Gadget" 139–40, 148; and Tamiami Trailblazers 148–53
Cook, George F. 118, 122, 123, 153, 160, 164, 169, 170, 177, 201, 204; agrees state completion of Trail will take 3 years 175–76; becomes Chevelier Corp. stockholder 107–8; crosses Everglades in "Gadget" 139–40, 148; early biography 107–8; estimates cost of building Chevelier Road (Loop Road) 140; runs Chevelier Corp. after 1926, 170, 185, 201
Coot Bay (water body) 31
Coot Bay (village and ranger station) *see* Flamingo (Coot Bay)
Copeland, D. Graham 145, 170–71, 180, 186–187, 190; as historian of Southwest Florida 111, 206; retires 196
Copeland Road Prison 179–81
Coppinger's Gardens 95, 103, 143, 206; and death of Jack Tiger Tail 103
Coral Gables (FL) 49, 169, 177, 189, 228
Corbett, A.W. 160
Corkscrew Swamp 6, 96; *see also* Big Cypress National Preserve; Big Cypress Swamp
Cotton Belt Route 6
Courier II (boat) 217–18
Cox, Leslie 111–14
Crabtree, Hobart 55, 56, 61, 63, 64, 95, 98, 99–100, 121, 137, 139, 142–43, 148, 145
Cragin, C.A. 217–18
Cronin, Father 214
Cross, James 67–68
Cross, William 228
Crow, Worth 176
Cuban Missile Crisis 78
Cunliffe, Guy 167–68
Curtiss, Glenn 103
Curtiss Flying School 102, 134
Cuthbert Lake 63
Cutler (Cutler Bay) (FL) 31, 34

Dade County Commission 9, 40, 54, 56, 57, 58, 95–98, 110–111, 119, 159–61; accepts state routing decision of Trail 177–78; approves Chevelier Road project 121–22; awards bid on Trail to McCrary firm 99–100; creates special road district for Ingraham 42; extends McCrary contract for Ingraham to Jan. 1918 54–55, 61–62; extends McCrary contract for Ingraham to mid-1917 53; makes Tamiami Trail routing decision 95–98;

Index

refuses to return to Jenkins alignment 154; rejects McCrary's finished work on Trail 156; turns over $125,000 to state to finish Trail 162, 167, 172-73
Dade Drainage District 164
Dania (Modelo; Dania Beach) (FL) 23, 184-85
Dania Beach Blvd. 24
Davis, Jack 228
Davis, John W. 228
Daytona (FL) 18, 22, 26
Deane, J.R. 81-83
Deep Lake (FL) 130, 136-37, 150-52, 170, 184; bought by Barron Collier 131
Deep Lake Railroad 67, 120, 127, 131-32, 149, 200; see also Atlantic Coast Line Railroad
Deering, Charles 49
DeGarmo, Ed 200-1
Detroit (Florida City) (FL) 28, 37
Dewhurst, William W. 53, 54, 57, 58, 60, 61, 72, 81, 124, 138; helps pay for first Cape Sable Road 40-43; is given 24,000 acres by Model Land Co. 9
Dewhurst Tract 46, 48-49, 57, 63, 77, 81, 138; portion sold to Paradise Prairie Land Co. 60
Dickie, L.P. 92
Dill, J.B. 67
Disney World 2
Disston, Hamilton 4, 20, 25
Dixie Highway 2, 5-6, 37, 83, 85, 87, 88, 187, 188; first organizing conference (April 1915) 88-89; precursor to Tamiami Trail 93-97; second organizing conference (May 1915) 90, 92; western division routing dispute in Florida 88-95
Dixie Highway Association 92, 98, 160, 221
Domestic Electrical Mfg. Co. 22
Douglas, Marjory Stoneman 30, 66, 69, 177
Douthit, Joe 69-70
Douthit family 32, 69
Dovell, J.E. 6-7, 26
Duncan, A.O. 52, 63, 139
DuPont, Coleman 159, 182, 245n10
Dupont Explosives Co. 120
DuPuis State Reserve 234
dynamite: accidental explosion 1926 183; used in roadmaking 37-38; used on Trail 101-166

Economic Power and Construction Co. 216
Edison Memorial Bridge see Caloosahatchee River Bridge
Elliott, Fred 143-44, 164
Erie Canal 3
Ernest Coe Visitor Center 40, 78, 84
Estero (FL) 167, 200
Estero Eagle 146, 161
Everglade (FL) see Everglades City
Everglades City (FL) 67, 80, 85, 111, 113, 116, 125, 130, **135**, 136-37, 144-45, 154, 156-57, 166, 170-71, 176, 176, 184, 192, 200, 227; becomes county seat of new Collier County 147-48; hosts Tamiami Trailblazers 149-53; renamed from Everglade (1918) 131
Everglades Drainage and Development League 95-96
Everglades Drainage District 80, 97, 124, 144, **162**, 196, 220, 228
Everglades National Park 6, 8, 10, 11, 28, 30, 32, 35, 39, 40, 44, 46, 49, 57, 64, 67-69, 71, 75, **76**, 77-79, 83, 108, 201, 203, 204, 234; construction of new main road 74-78; effect on Old Ingraham Highway 72-73; as land purchaser of last resort 71, 201-4; proposed by Ernest Coe 83-84
Everglades Park Road Number One (new Everglades National Park main road) 26, 39, 49; construction 74-78; objections of Daniel Beard 77; and removal of parts of Ingraham 77-78
Everglades Rod and Gun Club 15, 146, 150, 184, 191

Fairchild, David 49, 82
Fakahatchee Station 196
Feaster, T.A. 39
Fernandina Beach (FL) 3
Fisher, Carl 2, 5, 6, 80, 93, 184, 194, 217, 220-21, 227-28; promotes Dixie Highway 87-89; promotes Lincoln Highway 5, 87-88
Fitzpatrick, William 216
Flagler, Henry 4, 13, 17, 18, 21, 25-26, 44, 45, 83, 84, 183, 194; builds Key West extension 34-35; develops Dade and Broward towns 22-27; suggests 1892 Ingraham expedition 14-15
Flagler, Mary Kenan 44, 45, 48
Flamingo (general area) (FL) 8, 28, 29, 30, 41, 49, 56, 58, 69, 77, 84
Flamingo Dock (Flamingo Post Office) (FL) 32, 66, 68, 69, 70, 72, 74
Flamingo Village and ranger station (Coot Bay) (FL) 32, 63, 64, 65-66, 69, 72, 74, 77
Flamingo Visitor Center (National Park Service 1957-58), 32, 76-77, 84
Floete, Franklin 106, 121, 123, 149; death 169; sells Hopkins Tract to Jaudon 106
Florida Bay 31, 35, 61, 63, 68, 69, 71, 76, 84-85, 176, 204; causeway across (unbuilt) 83-85
Florida Coast and Gulf Railroad 18
Florida Coast Line Canal and Transportation Co. 22-27
Florida Department of Transportation see State road department
Florida East Coast Drainage and Sugar Co. 25
Florida East Coast Railroad 4, 13, 18, 21, 22-26, 28, 89, 182, 224, 227, 229; blocks Seaboard RR line into Cape Sable 67-68; builds company towns 22-27; builds Key West line 34-35; forms Model Land Company subsidiary 23; given Cape Sable lands by state 27, 44-46; gives tracts to Jennings and Dewhurst 9, 46; Key West route destroyed 84; receivership 84, 194; see also Model Land Co.
Florida Engineer and Contractor 226
Florida Federation of Women's Clubs 30, 50; and formation of Royal Palm State Park 46-53
Florida Highway Funding 129-30, 168-69, 187-89; amounts collected for highway fund 178, 187-88, 193, 198; gas tax in general 6, 167, 178, 187-89; Gov. Carlton reorganizes gas tax (1928) 58, 190, 197-201; revenue decline after 1926 hurricane 58, 190; state imposes gas tax (1923) 129; see also Highway Trust Fund (federal)
Florida Highways 172
Florida State University 169
Florida City (Detroit) (FL) 25, 42, 29, 39, 57, 72, 80, 82
Florida Road Commission see state road department
Florida Highway Department see state road department
Florida's Turnpike 1-2
Fort Brooke (FL) 3
Fort Dallas (Miami) (FL) 15, 17, 21-22
Fort Dallas Land Co. 23; see also Model Land Co.
Fort Lauderdale (FL) 23, 45, 65, 93, 96, 183
Fort Mellon 3
Fort Myers 5, 9, 13, 14, 20, 67, 92, 93, 94, 100, 101, 113, 114, 117, 122, 130, 144, 145, 146, 153, 155, 156, 161, 168, 180, 181, 190, 200, 219
Fort Myers Chamber of Commerce 93-94, 144, 175
Fort Myers Press 145-46, 160, 161, 162, 164, 165
Fort Pierce (FL) 1, 2, 22
Fort Shackelford 14, 15, 16, 93
Frederick, Audley 95
Freeland, C.L. 169-70
Freeman, Ethel Cutler 206-7
Freeman, Harry 53, 63, 64, 126, 131, 135, 142-43, 154, 156; rescues Tamiami Trailblazers 151-53
Freeman, Louis 107
Fuller, Walter 131, 229

"Gadget," 139-40, 148
Gainesville (FL) 2, 3, 90, 92, 98, 156, 221
gas tax, Florida see Florida highway funding
Gaunt, Edgar 202
George, Henry 215
Gifford, John T. 47, 87
Gifford, Mrs. John 49, 50
Gilbert, Maude 134
Gilbreath, William 88, 90, 98, 221
Gillette, Collins 92, 94
Glademoor 134
Gomes, Jose, General 80
Graham, Ernest R. ("Cap") 80, 143-44, 152, 203; opposes Trail bond election 164-65

Index

Grain Longshoremen ('scoopers') 212–14
Great Coastal Highway (Cape Sable, unbuilt) 80–85
Great Labor Day Hurricane of 1935 *see* Hurricanes, 1935
Great Lakes Transit Corp. 217, 225
Green, E.P. 155, 171, 205
Green Construction Co. 121, 127; *see also* James and Green Co.
Groom, W.W. 169
Gulf Oil Co. 71
Guy, S.F. 66

Halland, Luther 24
Halland (Hallandale) (FL) 23–27, 72, 117, 183–85
Halland Land Co. 25
Hammond, James 78
Hansford, Capt. J.H. 181
Hanson, Stanley 206
Harden, Antonette **105**
Harden, Otis 223
Hare, Claude 183
Harney, Billie 15
Harney, William 31
Harney's Boat Landing 143
Harrison, F.E. 117–18
Harrison, Sidney 38, 57, 58–59, 63, 64, 81
Harvey, K.H. 101–2
Hathaway, Fons 169, 171–78, 186, 189, 190; accused of mismanagement on Trail work 189–90; negotiates state takeover of Trail 172–75; predicts Trail needs three years to finish after takeover 175–76; runs for governor 189–90, 192–94
Hawkins, Carl 66
Hays, Mrs. 211; death 212
Hearst, William Randolph 211, 215, 216
Helm, Vance 92
Henderson, R.A. 175
Hendry County 153
Hialeah (FL) 67, 80, 103, 143
High Springs (FL) 144, 156, 160–64
Highleyman, Locke 92, 94–95, 96, 97, 98, 104–6, 114–15, 125, 148
Highway Act of 1916 (federal) 128
Highway Act of 1921 (federal) 129, 155, 161, 188; and use of convict labor 179
Highway Funding, state *see* Florida highway funding
Highway Research Board 129
Highway Magazine 224
Highway Trust Fund (federal) 2, 6, 168
Hill, William Stewart 92
Hillsborough Canal 218
Hillsborough County 155
HM-69 Missile Unit *see* Nike Missile Unit HM-69
Hoffman, J.W. 67–68, 71
Hole-in-the-Donut (agricultural area) 56, 72, 74, 77–80
Holloway, Hampton 65–66
Holloway, Scott 65–66
Hollywood (FL) 183–85, 220; (NY), 227–28
Hollywood Hills (FL) 183–85

Holmes, Irving 184, 185–86
Homberg, J.L. 115
Homestead (FL) 1, 9, 28, 29, 35, 37, 38, 39, 42, 50, 56, 57, 67, 69, 78, 80, 81, 117
Homestead Leader 68–69
Homesteaders, in Flamingo 32–33
Hopkins, A.W. 9, 106, 114, 123, 149, 169, 204; buys Hopkins Tract 105; sells Hopkins Tract to Jaudon 106–9
Hopkins Tract 10, 113, 114, 118, 121 123, 125, 127, 131, 170, 185, 201; acquired by A.W. Hopkins 105–6; boundaries in dispute 138–135; sold to Jaudon 106–110; title clouded by tax lien 109
Horton, Ralph 95–96
Hosmer, George 145–46, 161
Houlton (ME) 1
House, D.D. 114
House, D.R. ("Dan") 110, 111–14
House, W.W. ("Bill") 111, 114, 164, 202–3
House Fish Co. 71, 72
Howe, Charles 31
Huffman, R.C., Construction Co. 178, 181, 187, 189, 191, 193
Hughes, Charles Evans 215
Humble Oil Co. 71, 203
Humpback Bridge 63, 64, 65, 68, 69, 74
Hurd, Addy **105**
hurricanes: 1910 113; 1926 69, 183–84, 229, **230**; 1928 194, 231; 1935 (Great Labor Day) 35, 69–70, 84; 1960 (Donna) 70, 204; 1992 (Andrew) 57; 2005 (Wilma) 78

Immokalee (FL) 14, 71, 93, 117, 170; *see also* Sunniland oil field
Indianapolis (IN) 5, 87
Indianapolis 500 5, 87, 217
Ingraham Highway 6, 9, 28–29, 87, 100, 124, 126, 225; bond financing approved 41–42; built as private scarified road 40; built through Royal Palm State Park 48–52; named 49; parts preserved as trail 80–81; removal planned by Everglades National Park 79–80; replaced by National Park Road 75–78; subsidized by Model Land Co. 60–65
Ingraham, James 3, 44, 56, 57, 59, 83, 87, 125, 233; concerns about Deane's Penn Sugar Co. 82–83; early biography 14; hired by Flagler and starts Model Land Co. 21; leads 1892 expedition across Everglades 13–15, 21; proposes to drain Everglades (1893) 18–21; "sugar company" reclamation plan (1898) 25–26
Internal Improvement Act of 1855 (FL), 19, 21, 27
Internal Improvement Fund (FL) 21, 25, 40, 44, 45, 48, 72, 115, 220, 226–27; bankrupted by railroad bonds 4, 20; origins and creation 4, 18–20; rescued by Disston purchase 20; sale of Hopkins Tract to Scott (1901) 105–106; "Tamiami

Trail Lands" sale to Jaudon 95, 98, 102–3, 104–6, 115
Interstate Highway System 2
Interstate 95 1–2
Intracoastal Waterway 22–23
Iori Farms 78–79
Irwin, Frank 68–69
Irwin, William 195–96, 212, 214
Irwin family 32, 49, 69, 77
Ivey, Captain and Mrs. 122

Jack's Hotel 57
Jackson, John 33, 48
Jacksonville (FL) 1, 2, 3, 5, 7, 17, 18, 25, 83, 110, 122, 169, 190, 198–201; and Dixie Highway 89, 90, 221
Jacksonville, St. Augustine and Indianville Railroad 18
James, John 120
James and Green Construction Co. 120, 121, 127
Jaudon, James F. 9, 10, 11, 93, 42, 71, 72, 83, 89, 93, 105, 106, 107, 108, 109, 110, 111, 112, 116, 120, 121, 122, 123, 124, 125, 129, 131, 132, 135, 136, 137, 138, 139, 140, 141, 142, 143, 144, 157, 158, 159, 160, 164, 170, 185; buys Tamiami Trail Lands 97, 98, 114–15; buys 20,000 acres near Carnestown 176; creation of Collier County 146–47; death 204; Dixie Highway routing 90; early biography 90–92; ends involvement with Chevelier Corp. 201–4; fights state takeover of Trail 172–76; and Ingraham Highway 9, 42; joins Deane's Penn Sugar scam 81–82; lobbies for initial bond issue 97, 98; moves to Ochopee 202; participates in Trail grand opening 192–94; pays for King survey 102–3, 104; promotes Seminole Trail 117–18; proposes "straight ahead" Trail alignment 94–95; and Spencer Agreement 169; and Tamiami Trailblazers 148–55
Jaudon, Maude 132, 147, 153, 202
Jaudon, Paul 91, 120
Jaudon Brothers Mercantile Co. **91**
Jaudon Reality Co. 115, 176
Jenkins Route 121, 135, 150, 152–54, 158–59, 160, 171; Jenkins-Chevelier connector 170, 175, 176, 190; state designates as primary route 27, 171–78
Jennings, Bryan 72
Jennings Grove 56–57, 60, 79
Jennings, May Mann 9, 30, 40, 43, 44, 48, 49, 50, 53, 55, 67, 72, 74, 87, 117; creates Royal Palm State Park 44–53; death 72
Jennings, William 26–27, 30, 40, 41, 42, 44, 50, 56, 57, 58, 80, 130; is given 48,000 acres by Florida East Coast Railroad 9, 30
Jennings Tract 46, 56, 60, 72, 77, 138; sold to Hugh Annat 67
Joe Kemp Key 32
Junkin, Thomas 140
Juno (FL) 45
Jupiter (FL) 93, 98, 221

Keene, Arthur 156
Kenan, William 233
Kennedy, James 213–14
Key Largo 35, 80, 84
Key West 13, 32, 58, 64, 69, 70, 84, 102, 110, 113, 122, 176, 182
King, John 102–3, 104, 107, 139, 148, 192; on environmental hazards of Everglades drainage 105–6
Kings Highway (FL) 3
Kirchheimer, Otto 153
Kissimmee (FL) 2, 13, 94, 222
Kissimmee River 20, 231
Klamath Indian Nation 207
Krom, Charles 184
Krome, William 28, 30, 33, 39, 45, 46, 47, 49, 87; leads Cape Sable survey (1902-3) 34–36, 63
Krome Avenue (Dade County) 15, 115, 167, 207

LaBelle 118, 136, 153, 219
Labor Day Hurricane of 1935 see hurricanes, 1935
Lake Carriers' Assn. 213–14
Lake City (FL) 89, 93, 161
Lake Ingraham (Ninemile Lake) 66, 82, 83
Lake Monroe (FL) 3
Lake Okeechobee 6, 8, 10, 20, 23, 81, 93–94, 95, 98, 118, 136, 184, 188, 194, 203, 211, 218, 220, 221, 224, 229, 230, 231, 234
Lake Worth (FL) 18, 21, 23; power-boat racing 217–18
Langford, Walter 113
Lanier, W.D. 158
Lantana (FL) 45
Lee County Board of Commissioners 9, 94, 98, 100, 116, 120, 121, 135; approves $534,000 bond issue (1924) 167; approves special district 1 (Ft. Myers to Marco) 94, 135; approves special district 3 (Marco to Dade) 98, 135; awards work to J.B. McCrary 116; changes back to Jenkins alignment 142, 153, 154–55; fails to unify special districts 136; fires McCrary 116; transfers Chevelier road contract to AR&K 141–43
Leffler, C.D. 173
Lemon City (FL) 45
Lincoln Highway 5, 83, 87–89, 160
Lewis, Frank 150–55; see also Tamiami Trailblazers
Liddle, R. Carl 206
Lindgren A.W. ("Al") 37
Lindstrom, Mary 116
Linton (Delray Beach) (FL) 23, 27
Livingston, Capt. A.W. 200–1
Livingston, Guy 144
Livingstone, A.R. 66
Long, Huey 193
Long Key see Long Pine Key
Long Lake 63, 66
Long Pine Key 30, 35, 39, 49, 56, 57, 72–73, 117
Long Pine Key Road 49, 72–73; becomes Research Road (Everglades National Park) 78–79; origins 74–75; used for Nike missile base 78

Longview (FL) 28; see also Camp Longview; Florida City (FL)
Loop Road (Tamiami Trail) see Chevelier Road
Losey, George 224
Lott, E.P. 170
Loudon, L.W. 68
Louisville and Nashville Railroad 5, 227
Loxahatchee (FL) 218
Lucas, E.J. 106, 131

Macushla (boat) 118, 122
Mahaney, Roland 213–14
Main Road, Everglades National Park (1956-57) see Everglades Park Road Number 1
Mallon, Darrah 91, 111
Mallon, Emma 91
Mallon and Jaudon Co. 91
Malone, William H. 153
Manatee (FL) see Bradenton (FL)
Manatee River Bridge 155, 161, 191, 192; estimated costs 205, 209
Manetto Co. 102
Manley, Marion 177
Manley-Anthony System (of banks) 182–84
Marathon (FL) 176
Marathon Oil Co. 71
Marco (and Marco Junction)(FL) 6, 90, 92, 94, 97, 98, 99, 100, 101, 113, 116, 118, 120, 121, 127, 131, 135, 136, 144–146, 149, 150, 152, 153, 154, 155, 161, 167, 171, 178, 179, 189, 191, 192, 194, **195**, 204, 205
Marion Steam Shovel Co. 135, **139**, 144, 156, 157, 161, 171
Marl (dolomite): defined 223; difference from limestone 224
Marsh, Roy 37, 41, 42, 48
Martin, John 168–69, 175, 178, 190, 192–94, 228
Mather (ship) 213–14
Matthieson, Peter 111
Mattox, Sam 22
McBride, Matthew 60
McCaskell, G.E. 57, 124, 127, 133, 142, 154
McCord, J.H. 117–18, 121, 149, 177, 204; and Citizens National Bank 106, 169, 184; sells Hopkins Tract to Jaudon 107–9
McCrary, J.A. 54, 55
McCrary, J.B. (John Boyd) 57, 61, 148
McCrary, J.B., Construction Co. 41, 49–50, 55, 56, 57, 58, 80, 100–2, 167, 169, 170, 172, 176, 177, 178, 187, 189, 205, 224; Ingraham work 41, 43, 49, 50, 52, 53, 54, 60, 61, 62, 63, 64, 65, 66, 74, 78, 80, 99; Trail work 99, 100, 101, 115–16, 118–19, 120, 121, 124, 125, 126, 127, 131, 132, 133, 134, 135, 136, 137, 139, 140, 142, 143, 148, 150, 151, 152, 154, 156, 158, 159, 160, 162, 163, 164
McDonald, R.E. 95, 104–6
McDonald, Thomas 128, 129, 188
McDonald, W.P., Construction Co. 197
McDougal, Daniel A. 71, 123, 138,

148, 169, 185, 201; becomes Chevelier partner 107–8; dissatisfaction with Chevelier partners 170–177; sells Chevelier land for national park 203–4; and Spencer Agreement 136–37, 140
McDougal, Mary see Axelson, Mary McDougal
McDougal, Violet (Mrs. Daniel) 71, 203–4
McGriff, Walter 231–32
Meegan, John 224, 228, 231, 232
Megathlin and Clark Co. 126, 131
Melbourne (FL) 45, 93, 117
Melville, Dutchy 111–14
Merrick, George 177, 228
Metcalf, Guy 45–46, 48
Metcalf, Will 45–46
Miami (FL) 1, 2, 4, 6, 9, 13, 14, 15, 18, 21, 22, 23, 25, 27, 33, 34, 35, 36, 50, 53, 55, 60, 62, 67, 69, 70, 75, 81, 82, 83, 87, 88, **89**, 90, **91**, 92, 93, 94, 95, 97, 98, 99, 100, 102, 103, 104, 107, 108, 109, 111, 114, 115, 117, 118, 122, 123, 124, 125, 127, 129, 131, 132, 133, 135, 141, 142, 143, 145, 148, 150, 152, 153, 154, 156, 160, 161, 162, 163, 165, 166, 168, 169, 170, 171, 172, 173, 175, 176, 177, 178, 181, 182, 183, 184, 185, **188**, 189, 190, 191, 192, 194, 199, 200, 201, 202, 203, 204, 205, 206, 207, 211, 217, 219, 221, 224, 227, 228, 229, 230, 234; see also Fort Dallas
Miami Beach (FL) 2, 6, 89, 183, 220
Miami Canal (Miami River Canal) 80, 115, 117, 143; as proposed route for Trail 90, 96–97
Miami Chamber of Commerce 92, 144, 160, 175–76
Miami Falls (Miami Rapids) 15, **16**, **19**
Miami Herald 92, 145–46, 150, 164, 167–68, 177, 193
Miami Metropolis 50, 55, 95, 150, 162, 172–73 174–75, 193
Miami Post 161
Miami River 15, 21
Micanopy (FL) 3
Miccosukee Tribe of Indians of Florida, Inc. 10, 207–8
Middleton, Steve 233
Miles, George 23–27
Miller Act (Miller Bill) (1923), 161, 167, 187, 188, 189, 221; Trail added to (State Road 27, 1925), 168–69
Missing Link (I-95) 1–2
Mizner, Addison and Wilson 182–83
Model Land Co. 8, 9, 10, 23, 56, 57, 80, 94, 126, 138, 203, 233; develops Dade and Broward company towns 23–27; donates land for Royal Palm State Park 48–49; fires McCrary firm, hires Holloway Bros. 64–68; gives large tracts to Jennings and Dewhurst 46; helps build south Dade farm roads 37–38; helps pay for road to Paradise Key 28–29, 39–42, 46; pays McCrary firm to finish Ingraham Hwy. 57–59; sells Cape Sable land to homesteaders 33; sells land for

Index

J.R. Deane's Penn Sugar land scam 81–83; sells 210,000 acres for national park 71
Modelo (Dania; Dania Beach) (FL) 23–27
Monahan, E.J. 60
Monroe County: accepts state highway dept. routing decision 177–78; asks state to take over Chevelier road work 176; cancels Chevelier road building contract (1923) 153; considers and refuses bonds for Ingraham 57–59, 64, 126; general reluctance to build mainland roads 56, 68, 70; Hopkins/Chevelier history and taxes 106–110; refuses maintenance for Ingraham 68, 70; refuses to transfer mainland area to Dade 42; turns over $200,000 bond money to state for Chevelier road 175–77
Monroe County Toll Bridge Commission 84
Monroe Junction 195
Monroe Station 78, 194–97
Moore Haven 194, 218, 231
Morgan, J.F., and Co. 100, 119, 120, 125, 126
Morse, Frederick 25, 37, 38, 39, 53, 56, 57, 58, 81; death (1920) 67
Morse Lines 217
Moses, Wallace 15–16
Mosier, Charles 47, 49, 50, 55
Murphy, Charles 215–16
Munroe, Kirk 44, 87
Munroe, Mary Barr 44, 45, 48, 87; proposes name "Ingraham Highway" 49
Munroe, Ralph Middleton 16, 17
Musa Isle 206-7
Mutual Transit Co. 216

Naples (FL) 6, 67, 70, 92, 94, 118, 127, 154, 158, 183, 191, 197
National Indian Rights Assn. 46
National Park Service 28, 39, 64, 69, 71, 75, 79, 83, 114, 195, 196; see also Everglades National Park
National Timber Co. 105–106, 131, 139
Neil, Otto 121, 144–45, 152, 156, 158, 160, 166, 170–71, 186–87, 190
New River 23, 96
New York Botanical Garden 35, 39, 45
New York Central Railroad 216–17
New York Times 215
New York World 215
Newman, John 15–16, 18
Nike Missile Unit HM-69 79
Ninemile Bend (Ingraham) 63, 64, 76–77
North Miami (FL) 80
North Miami Beach (FL) 80
North Miami Improvement Assn. 114–15
Norton, I.G. 104
Nugent, Dave 213

Ocala (FL) 1, 89, 161, 221
Ochopee (FL) 111, 202–4
Okeechobee City (FL) 6, 8–9, 10, 220, 221, 224–29, 232–34; and Dixie Highway 90, 93, 98; see also Lake Okeechobee
Okeechobee Model Land Co. 23, 220, 225
Okeechobee Road (Dade) 15
Old Cutler Road (Dade) 37
Old Spanish Trail 2, 3, 7, 161; and Dixie Highway 89
Olga (FL) 94, 116, 118, 156
Orange Glade Highway 87
Orlando (FL) 2, 3, 7, 90, 91; and Dixie Highway 90, 93, 98, 221
Overseas Highway 84, 85, 199–200
Overseas Railway 34–35
Oxen (as used on Trail) 187
Oyster Bay 31

Pahokee (FL) 218–219
Palatka and Indian River Railway 27
Palm Beach Canal 6, 144, 218, 220, 221, 224, 225, 233, 234
Palm Beach County 9, 198–201, 218; Broward split off from (1915) 45; Conners buys 30,000 acres of land 218–20; County buys Conners Highway 211, 232; Guy Metcalf embezzles from school fund 44–46, 48; split off from Dade (1907) 45
Palm Beach National Bank 182–83
Paradise Key 9, 28, 29, 30, 33, 39, 40, 45, 49, 87; Ingraham Highway built through 43–53; Ingraham Highway partially removed to reduce traffic in 78–79; kept hidden by Bill Krome 35–36; Long Pine Key Road built in 72–73; state park established 44–50
Paradise Prairie Land Co. 60, 67, 72; see also Dewhurst Tract
Parker, Dorothy Dewhurst 72
Parrott, Joseph 17, 25
Patterson, R.Y. 223, 224, 226, 229
Paurotis Pond (Everglades National Park) 77
Peace River Bridge see Punta Gorda Bridge
Pennsylvania Sugar Co. 80, 142–44, 152, 164, 165
Pennsylvania Sugar Lands Co. 81–83
Pensacola (FL) 2, 89, 227
Pensuco (Pennsuco) (FL) 80, 143, 203
Pepper, Frank J. 38, 53, 57, 60, 62–63, 64, 67–68, 81, 82, 124, 233
Pepper and Potter Real Estate Co. 68, 71, 81
Perrine, Ann 38
Perrine, Henry 23, 31, 38
Perrine Grant 23, 31, 38
Perrine Land Co. 23, 38
Perry, Francis 192
Peters, Thomas J. 170, 201
Phillips, Hendry 168
Pierce, George 43, 50, 52, 53, 55, 55, 99–100
Pine Island Service Area (Everglades National Park) 75, 79
Pinecrest (FL) 10, 136, 140, 147, 150, 165, 171, 176–77, 190
Piper, George 22

Plant, Henry 4, 5, 17; early biography 13–14; Ingraham gives credit for 1893 drainage plan 18; sends Ingraham on cross-state expedition (1892) 14
Plant, Margaret 4, 5
Plant System (railroads, hotels, ships) 4, 5, 13–14, 17, 20; see also Atlantic Coast Line Railroad
Port Charlotte (FL) 6, 13, 17, 192; see also Punta Gorda
Port Dupont (FL) 131, 136–37, 144–45, 157, 170–71, 184
Port Mayaca (FL) 224, 225, 228
Powers, Frank 39, 40, 48, 56, 57, 61
Prest-O-Lite 87
Prichard Hauling Co. 183
Prince Valdemar (ship) 182
Project 669 (Tamiami Trail, 669-B through 669-X) 169, 178, 187; alleged cost over-runs 189–90; convict labor (669-X) 179–80; see also State Road
Public Works Administration 84
Pulsifer, Royal M. 13
Punta Gorda 5, 12
Punta Gorda Bridge (Barron Collier Bridge) 161, 191, 197, **198**, 201, 205, 209

Quigley, Bishop 214

Rader, Phil 102
Raiford Prison 179–80
Ranson, R.P. 137, 148, 158
Redd, J.D. 68
Reed, Anna Speyer **52**
Reed, Lewis **52**
Reed, Ollie (Olivia) **52**
Reese, J. Hugh 205, 209
Rensselaer Polytechnic Institute 170
Research Road 49, 78–80; see also Long Pine Key Road
Richardson, W.B. 196
Riddell, C.E. 175
Riffle, Edward 66
Ringling, Charles 144
Roach, Charles 130
Roberts, Billy see Billy Robert's Camp
Roberts, Frank 70
Roberts, Steve ("uncle Steve") 32, 33
Roberts family 32, 49, 69
Roberts Lake 150
Rockefeller, John D. 13
Rockledge (FL) 18, 22, 26
Roland Oil Co. 123, 136, 140, 169
Roosevelt, Franklin 2
Rose, Rufus 25
Roses Bluff (FL) 3
Rowdy Bend Trailhead (Everglades National Park) 75
Royal Palm Hammock State Park (Collier County) 149–52, 180, 190
Royal Palm State Park (Dade County) 8, 28, 36, 40, 87, 94, 100, 117; becomes part of national park 71, 75; creation 44–53; grand opening (1916) 50–52; lodge as temporary headquarters 56; lodge built 55–56; lodge moved to Homestead 78; new entry road 74–77; traffic problems before

Index

new road 74–78; *see also* Paradise Key, Everglades National Park
Royal Palm Sugar Cane and Planting Co. 81–83
Russell, E.W. 58

St. Augustine (FL) 2, 3, 17, 22, 25, 40, 63, 67, 89
St. Johns River 3, 25
St. Lucie Canal 218, 220, 221, 224, 225, 226, 228
Sam Jones Old Town 93, 94–95, 97, 117
San Francisco Examiner 215
Sand Point (FL) *see* Clewiston (FL)
Sanford, Henry 3, 13, 14
Sanford (FL) 3
Sarasota (FL) 144, 156, 192
Saunders, A.B., and Co. 43
Sawyer, Albert P. 22–26
Saxon, G.W. 88–90, 93, 98
Scarified Roads 37
Schilling, I.E. 108, 129, 144, 171, 173, 175
Scott, Basil 170
Scott, Charles 105–6
Seaboard Air Line Railroad 4, 67, 201, 227
Sebring (FL) 221, 226–27, 228
Seminole Trail 93, 117–18
Seminole Tribe [of Florida, Inc.] 14, 16, 23, 26, 31–32, 46, 103, 113, 142–43, 206–9, 234
Seminole Wars 14, 15, 23, 31, 38; compared to Vietnam War 16
Senghaas, Claus ("Snooky") 145
Senghaas, Stephanie **145**
Sewell, E.G. 160
Shark River (slough) 61, 102, 105; Jack Tiger Tail demands bridge 142–43
Shaver, Robert 183
Shepard, Ben 104
Sheppard, Walter O. 141–42, 153, 154, 155
Short, Henry 113–14
Simpson, Charles 30, 47, 49
Small, John K. 30, **33**, 35, 36, 39, 40, 46, 47, **47**, 49, **51**, **62**, 87
Smith, Alfred E. 215, 228
Smith, Hanna
Smith, Walter 32
Smithsonian Institution 30, 31
Snake Bight Road 64
Snapper Creek Canal 104, 114
South Florida Fruit and Vegetable Co. 72
South Florida Historical Museum 111
South Florida Railroad 13
Southern Bank and Trust Co. 201
Southern Drainage District 115, 124–25, 131, 158, 164
Southern Express Co. 13
Southern States Land and Timber Co. 96, 227; sells experimental farm to W.J. Conners 218; sells 603,000 acres to Barron Collier 137–38
Southern Sugar Co. 80–81
Southwest Mounted Police 194–96
Spencer Agreement 123, 136, 140, 169–70, 176–77

Stahl, Eugene 92, 95
Standard Oil Co. 13
Star Lumber Co. 55, 143
Starr, Belle 113
State Road Department: created (1915) 7, 128; state road system 129, 167; takes over Tamiami Trail 171–78; *see also* highway funding in Florida; Miller Act
State Road 5 (High Springs—Ft. Myers) 129, 144, 155, 156, 161–65, 187; incorporated into Trail 163
State Road 8 (Haines City—Ft. Pierce) 129, 230; and Conners Highway 221, 226–27, 228
State Road 25 (Ft. Myers—Palm Beach) 136, 153, 219, 220, 229–30
State Road 27 (Tamiami Trail, Ft. Myers—Miami) 168, 171, 187–89
State Road 205 (Homestead—Royal Palm) 28, 39
State Road 9336 (Homestead—Flamingo) 28, 39
Sterling Engine and Marine Co. 217–18
Stoneman, Frank 156, 177
Storter, Claude 113
Storter, George W., Jr. 131, 148, 157; hikes across state with Jaudon 131–33
Storter, George W., Sr. 113–14; sells store to Barron Collier 131
Storter, R.B. 113–14
Stout, Harley 111
Stovall, W.G. ("Guy") 220–221
Stranahan, Frank 23, 45
Stuart (FL) 2
Sunniland Oil Field 10, 71, 203–4
Sunny Isles (FL) 80
Sunshine Parkway *see* Florida's Turnpike
Surfside (FL) 80
Sweet, T.T., Dredging Co. 189–90, 193
Sweet Bay Pond (Everglades National Park) 77

Tabert, Martin 179
Talbot, Richmond 102
Tallahassee (FL) 2, 7, 114; and Dixie Highway 89, 90, 93, 98, 221
Tamiami Canal 114, 124–25
Tamiami Railway 109–11, 122
Tamiami Trail 6, 9, 78, 225, 230; Chevelier route first proposed 121–24; Chevelier second effort to build road 136–40; Collier Co. starts building 144–147; cost estimates 189–93, 204–9; current route first proposed 94; Dade County bonds approved 99; derived from Dixie Highway 93–99; drainage district cuts culverts across 142–44; dredging described 100; grand opening 191; Lee County bonds approved 94, 98, 99; maps 173–74; origin of concept 87, 91–93; origin of name "Tamiami Trail" 91–93; route determined 98–99; route options debated 94–98; work taken over by state 169–78, 189–92; *see also*

Chevelier Route; highway funding in Florida; State Road 27
Tamiami Trail Association 144, 148, 160–65, 175, 192–93; attempts to redefine Trail as "Gulf Coast Dixie Highway" 161–65; as propaganda organization for Collier 152–53, 160–63
Tamiami Trail Builders' Committee 144
Tamiami Trail Businessmen's Association 175–76
Tamiami Trail Corporation *see* Tamiami Railroad
Tamiami Trail Lands 98, 102–3, 104–6, 115; King "lost expedition" 102–3
Tamiami Trailblazers 144, 148–55, 175, 190, 192; benefits to Barron Collier 152–55; origins 144; trip across state 148–55
Tammany Hall 211, 215, 216
Tampa (FL) 3, 5, 6, 13, 90, 93, 94, 117, 144, 155, 156, 167, 190, 192, 221, 226
Tampa Board of Trade 92, 160
Tampa Kid (Will Brown) 180–81
Tampa Trail 3, 5
Tantie (FL) 220
Tatum, B.B. 80
Tatum, J.H. 97
Tatum, R.F. 43, 50, 80
Tatum Land Co. 96, 114, 124
Taylor, Paul 109, 118
Taylor Creek (Okeechobee County) 225, 231
Taylor Slough (Dade County) 28, 29, 39, 40–41, 47, 49, **52**, 74–75, 78–78, 87; first causeway 41, 52; second causeway 52–53, 74, 79
Tebeau, Charleton 111
Thirty-Mile Junction (Trail) 10, 191, 208
Tiger Tail, Jack 102, 117; demands Shark River bridge 142; killing 102–3
Tippins, Frank 113, 117
Tommy, Charlie 125
Tony, Captain 132
Torstenson, Carl 107, 109, 149
Torstenson, Nansen 149, 176–77; and Tamiami Trailblazers 150–55
Tropic Magazine 87
Tropical Everglades Park Assn. 67–68, 83
Tucker's Corner 181
Turner's River 116, 117–18, 120, 127, 131, 136, 158, 150–52, 157
turpentine camps 179
Tuttle, Julia 15, 16, 17, 21–22, 23
Twenty Mile bend 6, 218, 223, 227, 229, 233, 234

United States Department of Agriculture 81, 203; *see also* Bureau of Public Roads
United States Department of Transportation *see* Bureau of Public Roads
United States Sisal Trust 72, 74, 81, 117
University of Florida 169
Untermyer, Samuel 69
Useppa Island 130–31

Vailima (boat) 176
Veber, Charles 103
Viscaya Estate 49
Vose, Francis 20

Waco (TX) 90
Waddell Plantation 82–83
Walker, Clifford 156
Walker, Josiah 156
walking dredges 116, 158, *158*, 159, *159*, 171, *186*, 254n27
Waller, Green 111–14
Walters, Henry 4, 5, 227; *see also* Atlantic Coast Line Railroad
Walters, William 4, 5, 227; *see also* Atlantic Coast Line Railroad
Ward, Henry 83
Warfield, S. Davies *see* Seaboard Air Line railroad
Washburn, Charles 187
Watson, Edgar J. 111–14, 130, 165
Watson, W. Cecil 173
Watson, Y.L. 230
Watson Place 111–14, 125, 148; as used by Chevelier Corp. 114, 140
Weaver, Lillian 194–96; *see also* Monroe Junction
Weaver, William 194–96; *see also* Monroe Junction
Weaver Station 196
Webb, James 31
West, Patsy 103
West Lake 56, 61, 63, 64, 68, 69
West Palm Beach (FL) 1, 18, 22, 45, 95, 153, 183, 218, 220, 224–29, 231
Westcott, John 22
White, Edward 134
Whitewater Bay 31, 32, 35, 39, 49, 61, 67
Whittle, Capt. A.N. 102
Wickersham, Victor 203
Widden, G.D. 181
Wild Cotton Eradication (Cape Sable) 69, *76*
Wildwood (FL) 1
Wilhelm, Chris 83–84
Wilkinson, Judge E.G. 92–93, 97, 136, 136, 141, 159, 192
Will, Lawrence 56–57, 60–61, 65, 69, 83, 95–96
Will, Marion 65
Will, Thomas
Williams, Gordon 218
Williams, M.A. 33–34, 48
Willingham, W.J. 136–37, 147, 176
Winter Haven (FL) 20
Winterburn, M.C., Construction Co. 169, 178, 187, 189
Wolfe, T.L. 99
Works Progress Administration 69, 232–33
World War I *38*, 40, 71; impedes roadbuilding in Florida 56, 99, 118–19

Young, Joseph 183, 220, 227–28
Yulee, David Levy 32

Zetterland, Olog 24, 25
Zoll, C.H. 39, 40, 43, 48, 50, 53, 55

www.ingramcontent.com/pod-product-compliance
Lightning Source LLC
Chambersburg PA
CBHW081545300426
44116CB00015B/2755